RITUALS OF POWER

THE TRANSFORMATION OF THE ROMAN WORLD

A SCIENTIFIC PROGRAMME OF THE EUROPEAN SCIENCE FOUNDATION

Coordinators

JAVIER ARCE · EVANGELOS CHRYSOS · IAN WOOD

Series Editor

IAN WOOD

VOLUME 8

RITUALS OF POWER

RITUALS OF POWER

From Late Antiquity to the Early Middle Ages

EDITED BY

FRANS THEUWS

AND

JANET L. NELSON

BRILL
LEIDEN · BOSTON · KÖLN
2000

This book is printed on acid-free paper.

Library of Congress Cataloging-in-Publication Data

The Library of Congress Cataloging-in-Publication Data is also available.

Die Deutsche Bibliothek - CIP-Einheitsaufnahme

Rituals of power : from Late Antiquity to the Early Middle Ages /
ed. by Frans Theuws and Janet L. Nelson. – Leiden ; Boston ; Köln :
Brill, 2000
   (The transformation of the Roman world ; Vol. 8)
   ISBN 90–04–10902–1

ISSN 1386–4165
ISBN 90 04 10902 1

PRINTED IN THE NETHERLANDS

CONTENTS

PREFACE

This book is one in a series produced in the context of the European Science Foundation programme *The Transformation of the Roman World*. It is the product of the sub-group of scholars working under the title 'Power and Society'. The meetings during which the papers were presented and at times fiercely debated in an admirably open-minded way, took place between 1993 and 1996. It has taken some time to prepare the volume for the press, since some papers were submitted only after a fairly extended process of further revision. The patience of other contributors can be considered a sign of the friendship that grew among the members of the group. It is they, the contributors to this volume, to whom we are grateful for the productive and congenial atmosphere they created.

Originally, it was envisaged that this volume would be edited by the first editor alone, but his request to Jinty Nelson to do some translating and 'englishing' led to such a large involvement that he asked her to co-operate in the editing. Her acceptance of this extra work is highly valued by the first editor and he is very grateful.

We would like to thank Professor H.H. van Regteren Altena for his support in the first years of the programme. Our thanks also go to the ESF and the members of its staff who have been involved in the Transformation of the Roman World programme, especially Max Sparreboom, Vuokko Lepistö and Genevieve Schauinger. We have greatly appreciated the support of the co-ordinators of the programme, Evangelos Chrysos, Javier Arce and Ian Wood. Javier Arce, who supervised our group though we always considered him a member of it too, was always ready to help in organising our meetings ('he must know everyone in the Mediterranean world . . .'; 'this letter will open that door . . .'!) Ian Wood gave invaluable encouragement in the editing of the papers. We also want to thank our publishers Brill, in the person of Julian Deahl: his patience is especially appreciated. The first editor would like to thank the members of the Pionier-Project 'Power and Elites' at the University of Amsterdam, which provided an inspiring home-context during the first years of our ESF programme, as well as the National Science Foundation in the Netherlands which financed it and provided the opportunity to participate in both the Pionier and ESF programmes. The second editor would like to thank the Earlier Medieval Seminar at the Institute of Historical Research, University of London, for constant stimulus to rethink the early medieval centuries.

Frans Theuws
Janet L. Nelson

ABBREVIATIONS

AB	*Annales Bertiniani*
AF	*Annales Fuldenses*
BAR	British Archaeological Reports
CCSL	Corpus christianorum Series Latina (Turnhout, 1954–)
CCSL 148	*Concilia Galliae A. 314-A. 506*, ed. C. Munier (Corpus christianorum Series Latina 148) (Turnhout, 1963)
CCSL 148A	*Concilia Galliae A. 511-A. 695*, ed. C. de Clercq (Corpus christianorum Series Latina 148A) (Turnhout, 1963)
CESL	Corpus scriptorum ecclesiasticorum latinorum (Vienna 1866–)
ed.	edited, editor
MGH	Monumenta Germaniae Historica
MGH AA	Monumenta Germaniae Historica Auctores Antiquissimi
MGH Capit.	Monumenta Germaniae Historica Capitularia
MGH Conc.(II)	Monumenta Germaniae Historica Concilia aevi Karolini, (II: ed. A. Werminghoff (Hannover 1871–1920)
MGH DD	Monumenta Germaniae Historica Diplomata
MGH Epp.	Monumenta Germaniae Historica Eppistolae
MGH Epp. KA	Monumenta Germaniae Historica Eppistolae Karolini Aevi
MGH LL	Monumenta Germaniae Historica Leges
MGH SS	Monumenta Germaniae Historica Scriptores
MGH SSRL	Monumenta Germaniae Historica Scriptores Rerum Langobardicarum
MGH SSRG	Monumenta Germaniae Historica Scriptores Rerum Germanicarum
MGH SSRM	Monumenta Germaniae Historica Scriptores Rerum Merovingicarum
MS	Manuscript
NF	Neue Folge
NS	New Series
PG	Patrologiae Cursus Completus, Series Graeca, ed. J.-P. Migne
PL	Patrologiae Cursus Completus, Series Latina, ed. J.-P. Migne
transl.	translated, translator, translation

INTRODUCTION:
RITUALS IN TRANSFORMING SOCIETIES[1]

Frans Theuws

Since the days of Gibbon's *History of the Decline and Fall of the Roman Empire*, the historiography of the Transformation of the Roman world has been characterised by a grand narrative well into the twentieth century. The core element of the narrative was the disappearance of civilisation and the rise of barbarism or a society in contra-evolution. A range of developments were thought to be responsible: the Christian religion was one of them, the barbarians another. The histories were often unilineal and one-dimensional.

The grand narrative had a number of characteristics, that have been analysed before. In an attempt to name a few of these I can only be very sketchy, at some risk of oversimplification. It is not necessary to analyse the narrative in detail for our purpose here, which is demonstrating why the study of ritual may be important for our understanding of the transformations (in the plural) of the Roman world.

What we now call the transformation (in the singular) of the Roman world, was viewed from the perspective of the dominant culture, from the perspective of the powerful, be it Romans or men. From this perspective non-Romans (or those defined as such), the powerless and women most of the time only had bad effects or did not contribute at all to the continuation of civilisation. Their interpretations and representations of change and their consequent actions, were not considered to be of importance neither to the general historical development nor to the historical debate.

The grand narrative also was mainly of a socio-political nature and often an *histoire evenementielle*. Although 'civilisation' was central in the analysis, to what extent its decline was in the minds of contemporary elite and non-elite Roman men, let alone barbarians or women was seldom considered.

---

[1] I would like to thank Jinty Nelson and Mayke de Jong for their comments on an earlier version of this paper and Jinty for correcting the English.

Finally, cultures whether Roman, Barbarian and/or other, were seen as fairly homogeneous. There was a barbarian or Germanic culture opposing Roman culture, there were Christians opposing heathens, the literate vs the illiterate, etc.

In the last decades each of these aspects has been criticized extensively, in historiography in general and for late Roman and medieval history in particular. In scholarly debates the programme of the Transformation of the Roman world has its specific place and contributed and still contributes significantly to the development of Late Antique and Early Medieval studies.[2] Of course, scholarly debate on Late Antiquity and on the evaluation of the sources was already underway when the programme started and many scholars of Late Antiquity did not participate in it, so that the transformation of Late Antique studies itself cannot be linked exclusively to this programme. Still, the very fact that the programme existed was the result of the need felt in different fields that, now that so much was changing, an interdisciplinary dialogue was vital. Those who did not work with texts on a regular basis learned that many texts on which the grand narrative rests are not necessarily accurate accounts of sociopolitical practice, but are literary works, textual representations of more or less subjective, more or less compelling constructions of perceived realities[3] Future approaches will have to be multi-dimensional in character including the observable (social) practices as well as systems of ideas and representations. Late-Roman and medieval archaeology seems to have gone through this revisionist phase only recently, and if so mainly in anglophone countries. In German and French archaeology far more than in the anglophone traditions, many conceptions of the traditional grand narrative still linger on and determine the outcome of research.[4]

---

[2] I. Wood, "Report: The European Science Foundation's Programme on the Transformation of the Roman World and Emergence of Early Medieval Europe", *Early Medieval Europe* 6, 1997, pp. 217–227.

[3] An important incentive of this debate was: W. Goffart, *The narrators of barbarian History (AD 550–800). Jordanes, Gregory of Tours, Bede and Paul the Deacon* (Princeton 1988). Wood suggested that we see the transformation of the Roman world as a history of representations: Wood, "Report: The European Science Foundation's Programme on the Transformation of the Roman World and Emergence of Early Medieval Europe", pp. 217–227.

[4] A recent example is the discussion on the possibilities of distinguishing between Romanic and Germanic people on the basis of burial ritual in the 4th to the 6th centuries: H. Ament, "Franken und Romanen im Merowingerreich als archäolo-

Criticism of the old grand narrative has focussed on the concept of culture. The development of this critique may have been an important incentive for the growing interest in the study of ritual in late Antique and medieval times. In this introduction therefore I shall both amplify the critique, offer an alternative concept of culture which I think will prove helpful in understanding the role and meaning of ritual in societies under transformation. My observations are naturally of an archaeologist, but they are relevant too to debates on historiography.

Traditionally the grand narrative was dominated by a concept of culture in which cultures or rather societies were represented as homogeneous totalities in which (all) actors shared the same ideas, norms and values irrespective of their social and intellectual horizons. Cultures as totalities acted upon one another and acculturation took place as a result of this contact. Culture was thus seen as a blueprint for acts.[5] It was a set of preconceived conditions and ideas, historically given, to which individual members of that society had to adhere and which gave them their identity.[6] In this conceptualisation it was difficult to include the capacity of individuals and groups to reflect upon their own situation. This concept of culture gained popularity in historiography in the context of the nineteenth

---

gisches Forschungsproblem", *Bonner Jahrbücher* 178, 1978, pp. 377ff; P. Périn, "A propos de publications recentes concernant le peuplement en Gaule à l'époque mérovingienne: la question franque", *Archéologie Médiévale* 11, 1981 pp. 125–145; P. Périn, "L'assimilation ethnique vue par l'archéologie", *Dossiers de l'archeologie* 56, 1981, pp. 38–47; A. Koch, *Bügelfibeln der Merowingerzeit im westlichen Frankenreich* (Mainz 1998), pp. 535–580.

[5] F. Barth, "Towards greater naturalism in conceptualizing societies", *Conceptualizing Society*, ed. A. Kuper (London and New York 1992), p. 23.

[6] In archaeology this led for instance to the supposition (still in vogue among certain scolars in the German speaking scholarly world) that women especially are bound to specific clothing rules that they have to follow throughout their lives using for instance only one particular type of fibula as defined on the basis of modern formalistic criteria (Koch, *Bügelfibeln der Merowingerzeit im westlichen Frankenreich*, pp. 537–538). Women are not thought to have possessed another 'non-ethnic' pair. Looking at the burial ritual as also representing aspects of the system of a society's ideas, norms and values, rather than just simply mirroring specific rules, social statuses and situations, would bring us much further in analysing the early medieval burial ritual (see below). See also: R. Samson, "Social structures from Reihengräber: mirror or mirage", *Scottisch Archaeological Review* 4 (1987), pp. 116–126. D.M. Hadley and J.M. Moore, "'Death makes the man'? Burial rite and the construction of masculinities in the Early Middle Ages", *Masculinity in Medieval Europe*, ed. D.M. Hadley (London and New York, 1999), pp. 21–38. See also the references to the work of Härke and Halsall in the contribution of Theuws and Alkemade to this volume.

century: as Barth and many others explained it was in fact the nation-
state that served as a model for all organised human sociability.[7] In
the twentieth century this line of reasoning has been criticized by
those who stressed the cultural variety within a society. Dualistic concepts were formulated, like Le Goff's distinction between a *culture
savante* and a *culture populaire* or a *culture cléricale* and *traditions folkloriques*.[8] Others distinguished between a popular culture and an aristocratic culture, or between a profane culture and a religious culture.
At the same time since the 1960's theory-formulating archaeologists
took another route. In the 'new archaeology' (later termed processual archaeology, which barely affected archaeologists specialising in
Early Medieval Europe[9]) culture was defined as man's extrasomatic
means of adaptation and became equivalent to socio-economic behaviour. This modern notion had little attraction for classical and medieval
archaeologists because of its inadequacy both in dealing with non-
economic aspects of human culture and in grasping individuals particular experiences. The result was a prolonged lingering-on of
traditional ideas.

The new dualistic concepts were unsatisfactory too.[10] A much larger
constellation of groups in society (however defined) than those concepts envisaged had their own cultures, norms and values, and own
ideas and cosmologies. As an alternative concept to the homogeneous society, Frederic Barth formulated that of the 'disordered society': 'not only interests [in society], but also values and realities are
contested between persons in stable social interaction with each other.
The perfection of mutual comprehension and communication which
is generally enshrined in our definition of society is not paradigmatic
of social life. All social behaviour is interpreted, construed and there
is nothing to indicate that two persons ever place the same interpre-

---

[7] Barth, "Towards greater naturalism in conceptualizing societies", p. 21.

[8] J. Le Goff, "Culture cléricale et traditions folkloriques dans la civilisation
mérovingienne", J. Le Goff, *Pour une autre Moyen Age. Temps, travail et culture en occident: 18 essais* (Paris, 1977 [1967]), pp. 223–235. R. Künzel, "Enige benaderingen
van de middeleeuwse cultuur van West-Europa", *Middeleeuwse cultuur. Verscheidenheid,
spanning en verandering*, eds. M. Mostert, R.E. Künzl and A. Demyttenaere (Hilversum, 1994), pp. 7–18.

[9] D. Austin, "The 'proper study' of medieval archaeology", *From the Baltic to the
Black Sea. Studies in Medieval Archaeology*, eds. D. Austin and L. Alcock (London and
New York, 1990), pp. 9–42.

[10] Künzl, "Enige benaderingen van de middeleeuwse cultuur van West-Europa",
pp. 13–16.

tation on an event.'[11] The constant process of negotiating interests, norms, values etc. contrasts with the consensus central to the concept of homogeneous societies. For that reason 'disorder' is central to Barth's conceptualisation. This disorder brings about 'inconsistencies, contradictions, ambiguities, lacunae and loose interconnections to be socially distributed and problematically shared and to be personally construed and constituted'.[12] Ideas and norms are constantly reflected upon: hence occurs an ongoing process of interpretation. In Hannerz' words, meanings and their externalized forms are socially distributed.[13] The process of reflection, interpretation and negotiation is essential in bringing about change and transformations. Such a conceptualisation would therefore be a better tool for analysing the transformation of the Roman world than the traditional postulate of opposing homogeneous cultures which leaves little room for individuals so many of whom we know as authors of texts or as important characters. Some might say that using the dichotomy Romans-Barbarians etc. is not always regrettable as an heuristic device, but then, such a device can only be used in relation to specific questions.[14]

Barth's, Poole's and Hannerz's theses also have their problems when applied to non-modern societies. Are the concepts of the individual and of individualism relevant? To what extent did persons (literate ones and illiterate, powerful and powerless) in late Antiquity and the Early Middle Ages negotiate norms, values and interests as individuals, or did they operate, instead, as members of larger entities?

What about shared values, norms and interests? In each society shared values and norms will have existed in order to prevent a total fragmentation of society. The 'disordered' society cannot develop into a totally disintegrated one. For archaeologists and historians, however, concepts on the distribution of culture have their attraction in

---

[11] Barth, "Towards greater naturalism in conceptualizing societies", p. 20.

[12] F.J.P. Poole, "Socialization, enculturation and the development of personal identity", *Companion encyclopedia of anthropology*, ed. T. Ingold (London and New York, 1994).

[13] U. Hannerz, *Cultural complexity. Studies in the social organisation of Meaning* (New York, 1992), pp. 3–22.

[14] Most of the time these questions are not specified. It is often accepted that 'history' in general can be written on the basis of material thus ordered. Moreover, material ordered on the basis of this dichotomy cannot be used to analyse more complex processes of transformation. The ordering of material is not neutral in relation to other research questions.

analysing processes in the past because they provide a means of
analysing change throught the constant process of reflection and
interpretation by persons and groups.

Both the problems just mentioned are discussed by Barth. Part of
his response was the concept of 'discursive reflection': 'Interpretations and reinterpretations may be performed jointly, in interaction,
conversation and reminiscence with third parties. Discursive reflection will promote a convergence of understanding, knowledge and
values among those who engage in them and an enhanced focus on
reality orientation in the actor'.[15] Discursive reflection counteracts
individual divergence and will have taken place within specific cultural contexts in Late Antiquity and the Early Middle Ages, for
instance among peasants, women, peasant women, aristocrats of different kinds, bishops, local priests, etc. Late Antique and early medieval
culture will have consisted of many discourses, fragments of which
we know from texts or patterns of material culture. Some of them
are quite individual, others more discursive.

This process of reflection and interpretation does not mean that
everything changes all the time. You cannot live in a situation where
tomorrow will be quite different from today. Many things are stable and immutable, or represented as such. Many actions are of an
habitual character, hence repetitive, but not for that reason without
meaning, nor performed unreflectingly? Keeping things as they are
may be as concious a choice as the choice to change them. Meanings are socially distributed and here power is crucially involved.
Actors may have reflected upon matters and interpreted them, but
they were not necessarily able to negotiate on them succesfully in
their own interests either to bring about change or to keep things
unaltered. On the other hand some groups or actors may change
discourses in accordance with many different situations. The various
discourses in society are registors of power relations. A major problem thus arises from the relationship between the capacity of the
actors to reflect upon and interpret an infinite number of subjects
and the significance of shared norms and values that are not supposed to change all the time.

To complete a model of the conceptualisation of culture and the
role of rituals therein, we may add to Barth's 'disordered society'

---

[15] Barth, "Towards greater naturalism in conceptualizing societies", p. 22.

Braudel's distinction between *histoire evenementielle, histoire de conjunctures* and *histoire de longe durée*. Long term history is made up of elements whose transformations are hardly observable: the physical environment, and some parts of the systems of ideas, mentalities and cosmologies.[16]

Schematically presented our model is as follows: actors have different cultural sources that are the subject of reflection, interpretation and cultural appropriation. For an aristocrat in northern Gaul in the fifth century a number of cultural sources may be identified: the norms and values of the Roman aristocracy (he/she might even distinguish between those of the republic and those of the empire), the norms and values of aristocrats from outside the empire, the concepts of christianity in its different forms, etc. A person might integrate these concepts through a process of reflection and did not necessarily have to choose between them, that is s/he did not have to become exclusively a barbarian aristocrat, or a Roman, a heathen or a christian, as models of homogeneous culture concepts would predict they would. S/he might become a person with a new complicated set of ideas, norms and values. Where in the old model persons copy cultural elements of the Other, in this model persons appropriate elements of the Other. In practice this means that two fibulae that are identical according to the archaeologist's list of formal characteristics are different objects for two women in different societal contexts, while even one and the same fibula belonging to a single woman may mean different things in different contexts.[17] An important element of the model is that actors, either individually or in groups are actively engaged in discursive reflection, interpretation and cultural appropriation. This process takes place within the setting of more stable elements such as the enduring values or the landscape. The term landscape is used here, instead of physical

---

[16] Barth did include the 'material context', in his analysis for he thought it could not be seen as a system separate from the social. Hannerz too points in this context to the importance of considering 'nature' and control over material items although the remark seems to be a bit casual (Hannerz, *Cultural complexity. Studies in the social organisation of Meaning*, p. 18). F. Braudel, *The Mediterranean and the Mediterranean World in the Age of Philip II* (London/New Tork, 19783 [1972] [English translation of second revised edition *of La Méditerranée et le Monde Méditerranéen à l'époque de Philippe II* from 1969, original publication 1949]), I.J. Bintliff, "The contribution of an Annaliste/structural history approach to archaeology", *The Annales school and Archaeology*, ed. J. Bintliff (Leicester, 1991), pp. 1–33.

[17] See also K. Green, "Gothic material Culture", *Archaeology as long-term history*, ed. I. Hodder (Cambridge, 1987), pp. 117–131.

environment or nature, to indicate that even this is subject to reflection and interpretation too. The result of this proces is the development of cultural forms that are, or are perceived as, new.

Now, at last, ritual comes in. It is important to our subject that we understand that rituals, as one form of externalisation[18] of ideas, play a crucial role in creating and representing new cultural forms. The results of the process of reflection, interpretation and cultural appropriation will also have been externalized (represented) through the creation of texts and material culture. While modern historiography puts increasing stress on this aspect of texts,[19] in late Antique and early medieval archaeology material culture remains insufficiently analysed from this point of view.

Thus, rituals are not to be considered meaningless habitual acts repeated time and again, although many may look like that. In understanding and interpreting these rituals we, like anthropologists, are confronted with the problem of intercultural communication between us and the people we study, on our case actors and writers in the past. As for antrhopologists, two or more hermeneutic circles exist.[20] Asked for the reason why 'they' perform the ritual like this actors might answer in terms of traditional behaviour: 'it has always been like this'. However, even when actors cannot explain the meaning of their ritual acts in terms satisfactory to the anthropologist, the repeated performances may have some meaning and significance for the participants, because they may have the idea that

---

[18] That is: made available to the senses and thus to interpretation and appropriation by others. Other forms of externalisation are writing, speaking, making objects and pictures, making gestures, creating landscapes.

[19] One example out of many: L. Coon, *Sacred fictions. Holy women and Hagiography in Late Antiquity* (Philadelphia, 1997). Her treatment of 'the rhetorical use of clothing' is an important source of inspiration for archaeologists studying late antique and early medieval burial ritual.

[20] S. Bekaert, "Multiple levels of meaning and the tension of conciousness, *Archaeological Dialogues* 5 (1998), pp. 6–29. In this contribution Bekaert draws attention to the central problem of intercultural communication in anthropology and in general. This is a central problem for historians and archaeologists as well. See also: H. Moore, "Paul Ricoeur: Action, meaning and text, *Reading material culture. Structuralism, hermeneutics and Post-structuralism*, ed. Chr. Tilley (Oxford, 1990), pp. 85–120. M. Shanks and Chr. Tilley, ed., *Re-constructing archaeology: theory and Practice* (Cambridge, 1987). For a discussion of this in relation to early medieval burial rite: G. Halsall, "Burial, Ritual and Merovingian Society", *The community, the family and the Saint. Patterns of Power in Early Medieval Europe. Selected proceedings of the International Medieval Congress University of Leeds 4–7 july 1994, 10–13 july 1995*, eds. J. Hill and M. Swan (Turnhout, 1998), pp. 325–338.

without these rituals the encompassing order would be disturbed. Rituals, however, that are not explained by the actors themselves, may be interpreted by anthropologists in a way the actors would not recognize or might reject althogether.

Godelier explains that rituals as acts are '<faits sociaux totaux> en ce sens qu'ils résument et expriment—donc totalisent en un moment exceptionnel, en une configuration particulière de la vie sociale—les principes de l'organisation qui sous-tend ce mode de vie'.[21] Rituals are actions and statements at the same time.[22] They represent ideas and concepts but also play a role in transforming these. Hence rituals not only represent things, they also do things.[23] As Bazelmans has observed: ideology and ritual encompass the way in which people know, name, experience and shape their natural, super-natural and social environment and their place within it.[24] Rituals can be related to many aspects of a whole body of ideas, norms and values, of social organisation and nature, not just to power alone, as the title of this book might seem to suggest. Rituals, especially 'rites of passage' can be related to the constitution of the person and the creation of identities, they may relate to the organisation of the agricultural cycle, or of the ancestral and supernatural world. In many rituals the exchange of objects between persons, and between persons and the super-natural world, is important.

The material culture involved thus provides archaeologists with an *entrée* to the analysis of rituals, although an indirect one. Our group discussions focused on the material aspects of rituals in order to develop an interdisciplinary debate. Although historians have already dealt extensively with particular rituals in the fourth to ninth centuries, their concern with material aspects has remained limited. It is clear that the texts of this period contain a wealth of references to the objects and specific places used in ritual acts. In this volume with its emphasis on rituals and objects, we try to explore the meaning and significance of Late Antique rituals in the process of transformation.

---

[21] M. Godelier, *L'idéel et le matériel. Pensée, économies, sociétés* (Paris, 1992 [1984] Fayard), p. 66.

[22] D. de Coppet, "Introduction", *Understanding Rituals*, ed. D. de Coppet (London and New York, 1992), p. 9.

[23] D. Parkin, "Ritual as spatial direction and bodily division", *Understanding Rituals*, ed. D. de Coppet (London and New York, 1992), p. 14.

[24] J. Bazelmans, "Grand narratives and early Germanic societies. A review of Hedeager's *Iron Age Societies*", *Helinium* 34 (1994), pp. 165–175.

One field of research that presented itself from the very beginning of our work was that concerning the burial ritual and its significance in creating (new) identities. That it presented itself as such
is partly due to the enormous importance of cemetery evidence for
the archaeology of Late Antiquity in the West (which was the main
geographical area of interest in the discussions of our group). I would
like to comment below on this field, for several contributions deal
with burial rituals and related life-cycle rituals or with the circulation in society of objects used in burial rituals. One source of inspiration for interpreting archaeological data on burial rituals is the
new attentiveness of historians towards saints' lives from the same
period.[25] Modern studies of late antique and early medieval *vitae*
stress the importance of the contextualisation of those texts in a system of representations adapted to a specific group of producers of
the texts and (a) specific group(s) that form(s) the audience.[26] A similar attentiveness is now being developed towards the material culture of late antique burials. The same should be the case for acts
(which we unfortunately only know through texts, material culture
and images) that also need to be contextualised in relation to a system of representations. We need to study the 'rhetorics of rituals'
including in the analysis the authors of the rituals, the audience and
the main characters as is done in the analysis of *vitae*. The application of this methodology to burial rituals would permit the analysis
of a rhetoric involving ideas on the cultural construction of the person (a king, a warrior, a queen, a peasant woman, a nun, a bishop
etc.), the cultural construction of the body (an important element in
the burial ritual), and the cultural construction of ancestors. The
analysis could concentrate on the authors of the burial ritual, the
main character (the deceased person) and the present and future
audience. As is the case in saints' *vitae*, we may even question the
possibility of reconstructing the deceased person as an historical person.[27] To put it simply on the basis of a well-known example: can

---

[25] L. Coon, *Sacred fictions. Holy women and hagiography in Late Antiquity* (Philadelphia,
1997).
[26] Contextualisation of archaeological evidence was propagated already some time
ago by Hodder (I. Hodder, ed., *The Archaeology of contextual meanings* (Cambridge,
1987); I. Hodder, *Symbols in action. Ethnoarchaeological studies of material culture* (Cambridge, 1982) but his approach has not had much impact on archaeologists of Late
Antiquity and the Early Middle Ages up till now. On the other hand his approach
needs further elaboration in relation to the study of historical processes.
[27] Coon, *Sacred fictions. Holy women and hagiography in Late Antiuity*, p. xv.

Funerals about departed or those performing it??

we reconstruct Childeric I († c. 480) as an historical person on the basis of the material remains deposited in his grave at the funeral, as is usually done, or is the rhetoric of the burial ritual (and Childeric's clothing) related to other aspects (the construction of kingship in this context by the author(s) of the ritual [Clovis?] and the audience [aristocrats from different parts of the late Roman world, including bishops?]) directed at the future?[28]

The rhetorics of the burial ritual may be directed towards creating identities rather than mirroring them.[29] New burial rituals, as they emerge in late antique Gaul and especially in northern Gaul, may be directed at creating new identities, but identities of a different sort from those that archaeologists have mostly considered hitherto. Here I refer to the debate on ethnic identities that was central on several occasions to the programme on the Transformation of the Roman World. Changing burial rituals in Gaul have been interpreted mainly in terms of ethnic identities, although one of the major developments is the gender differentiation of burials in the late third and fourth centuries. Why was it considered necessary to represent gender differences more clearly than before? Why was it considered necessary to bury the dead instead of cremating them? Both developments point to changing ideas on the body and the person rather than to ethnic differences. One can ask why a woman in a village in northern Gaul should have been buried according to the ethnic concepts of the Franks as represented in literary form by Gregory of Tours and others? It is time that we start analysing the rhetorics of rituals and the rhetorics of material constructions of identities and ideas. Grasping at the same time the character of texts and the representations present in them and their rhetorical nature, we will be better able to understand the reflective discourses taking place in various niches of the societies under consideration and the rituals related to them. Our task is to confront these discourses and understand the forms in which they come down to us.

This volume contains contributions that aim to break new ground for this type of analysis or to be critical of present interpretations of rituals and their material correlates. As already noted, a number of papers deal with rituals relating to death, life cycles or the circulation

---

[28] I will elaborate on this at another place where I will go into the interpretation of the late Roman burial ritual in Northern Gaul in more detail.

[29] Samson, "Social structures from Reihengräber: mirror or mirage".

in other contexts of objects otherwise used in the burial ritual. Other papers are concerned with the symbolism and ideology of royal power, the formation of a political ideology east of the Rhine from the mid-fifth century onwards or penance rituals in relation to a Carolingian episcopal discourse on ecclesiastical power and morale. In the end all the contributions deal with the creation of new identities. I will not try to pull together the themes discussed in the papers, for Jinty Nelson in her conclusion will do that. The reader will discover interesting differences between this introduction and the conclusion. The introduction is written by an archaeologist looking forward from the fourth century and trying desperately to grasp some new concepts in order to bring to life mute material culture, so important in most contributors' papers, and to avoid mere admiration on the basis of modern aesthetics, of all those marvellous objects and buildings as the key to analysing past peoples' thoughts. He tries to make room for alternative interpretations. The conclusion is written by a historian looking backwards from the Carolingian period and concentrating on the elements of the title: transformation, ritual and power, as well as the Church so important in Carolingian life.

Our groups' intellectual quest took place between these poles of time, disciplines, regions and cultures (past and modern). Let the reader make up his/her own mind as to its usefulness.

BIBLIOGRAPHY

Ament, H., "Franken und Romanen im Merowingerreich als archäologisches Forschungsproblem", *Bonner Jahrbücher* 178, 1978, pp. 377ff.
Austin, D., "The 'proper study' of medieval archaeology", *From the Baltic to the Black Sea. Studies in Medieval Archaeology*, eds. D. Austin and L. Alcock (London and New York, 1990), pp. 9–42.
Barth, F., "Towards greater naturalism in conceptualizing societies", *Conceptualizing Society*, ed. A. Kuper (London and New York 1992), pp. 17–33.
Bazelmans, J., "Grand narratives and early Germanic societies. A review of Hedeager's *Iron Age Societies*", *Helinium* 34 (1994) pp. 165–175.
Bekaert, S., "Multiple levels of meaning and the tension of conciousness, *Archaeological Dialogues* 5 (1998), pp. 6–29
Bintliff, J., "The contribution of an Annaliste/structural history approach to archaeology", *The Annales school and Archaeology*, ed. J. Bintliff (Leicester, 1991), pp. 1–33.
Braudel, F., *The Mediterranean and the Mediterranean World in the Age of Philip II* (London/New York, 1978³ [1972] [English translation of second revised edition *of La Méditerranée et le Monde Méditerranéen à l'époque de Philippe II* from 1969, original publication 1949]).

Coon, L., *Sacred fictions. Holy women and Hagiography in Late Antiquity* (Philadelphia, 1997).

Coppet, D, de, "Introduction", *Understanding Rituals*, ed. D. de Coppet (London and New York, 1992),

Godelier, M., *L'idéel et le matériel. Pensée, économies, sociétés* (Paris, 1992 [1984] Fayard).

Goffart, W., *The narrators of barbarian History (AD 550–800). Jordanes, Gregory of Tours, Bede and Paul the Deacon* (Princeton, 1988).

Green, K., "Gothic material Culture", *Archaeology as long-term history*, ed. I. Hodder (Cambridge, 1987), pp. 117–131.

Hadley D. M. and J.M. Moore, "'Death makes the man'? Burial rite and the construction of masculinities in the Early Middle Ages", *Masculinity in Medieval Europe*, ed. D.M. Hadley (London and New York, 1999), pp. 21–38.

Halsall, G., "Burial, Ritual and Merovingian Society", *The community, the family and the Saint. Patterns of Power in Early Medieval Europe. Selected proceedings of the International Medieval Congress University of Leeds 4–7 july 1994, 10–13 july 1995*, eds. J. Hill and M Swan (Turnhout, 1998), pp. 325–338.

Hannerz, U., *Cultural complexity. Studies in the social organisation of Meaning* (New York, 1992).

Hodder, I., ed., *The Archaeology of contextual meanings* (Cambridge, 1987).

———, *Symbols in action. Ethnoarchaeological studies of material culture* (Cambridge, 1982).

Koch, A., *Bügelfibeln der Merowingerzeit im westlichen Frankenreich* (Mainz 1998).

Künzel, R., "Enige benaderingen van de middeleeuwse cultuur van West-Europa", *Middeleeuwse cultuur. Verscheidenheid, spanning en verandering*, eds. M. Mostert, R.E. Künzl and A. Demyttenaere (Hilversum, 1994), pp. 7–18.

Le Goff, J., "Culture cléricale et traditions folkloriques dans la civilisation mérovingienne", J. Le Goff, *Pour une autre Moyen Age. Temps, travail et culture en occident: 18 essais* (Paris, 1977 [1967]), pp. 223–235.

Moore, H., "Paul Ricoeur: Action, meaning and text, *Reading material culture. Structuralism, hermeneutics and Post-structuralism*, ed. Chr. Tilley (Oxford, 1990), pp. 85–120.

Périn, P., "A propos de publications recentes concernant le peuplement en Gaule à l'époque mérovingienne: la question franque", *Archéologie Médiévale* 11, 1981 pp. 125–145.

———, "L'assimilation ethnique vue par l'archéologie", *Dossiers de l'archeologie* 56 (1981), pp. 38–47.

Poole, F.J.P., "Socialization, enculturation and the development of personal identity", *Companion encyclopedia of anthropology*, ed. T. Ingold (London and New York, 1994).

Samson, R., "Social structures from Reihengräber: mirror or mirage", *Scottisch Archaeological Review* 4 (1987), pp. 116–126.

Shanks, M. and Chr. Tilley, ed., *Re-constructing archaeology: theory and Practice* (Cambridge, 1987).

Wood, I., "Report: The European Science Foundation's Programme on the Transformation of the Roman World and Emergence of Early Medieval Europe", *Early Medieval Europe* 6, 1997, pp. 217–227.

MIGRATION PERIOD EUROPE:
THE FORMATION OF A POLITICAL MENTALITY

Lotte Hedeager

Introduction[1]

The study of the European peoples' early histories is complex and difficult to synthesize. Part of the explanation lies in the tendency for researchers to rely upon terminology and concepts stemming from the early twentieth century.[2] Research in the field of prehistory, both then and now, has served to establish and legitimise the authenticity of national or ethnic identities[3] and the dominant historical-ethnographical questions have been where did these peoples come from, where did they migrate to, and what became of them? From an early stage it has been assumed that these peoples belonged to well defined, ethnically homogeneous groups, biological entities that have somehow remained intact, untouched by other kinds of historical change.

This idea of ethnic homogeneity was initially called into question through the pioneering work of Reinhard Wenskus in *Stammesbildung und Verfassung*, published in 1961. Since that time it has no longer been possible to take for granted the complexities of migration, or

[1] I am indebted to the Carlsberg Foundation, Copenhagen, for the four-year grant that financed my work on the Migration Period. This article was originally completed in 1996. I am especially grateful to all the members of the 'Power and Society'—group for inspiring discussions and provocative questions. I am special thankful to Janet Nelson who has acted as a 'superviser' in the field of history. Thanks to Tim Earle, Peter Heather, Frands Herschend, Richard North and Elisabeth Vestergaard for the use of still unpublished articles and to Peter Heather, Janet Nelson, Frans Theuws, Walter Pohl, Herwig Wolfram and Ian Wood for extremely useful and inspiring comments. I have to stress that whatever deficiencies remain are the fault of no one but myself.

Fiona Campbell and Janet Nelson translated this paper.

[2] W. Pohl, Tradition, Ethnogenese und literarische Gestaltung eine Zwischenbilanz. *Ethnogenese und Überlieferung*, eds. K. Brunner and B. Merta (Wien and München, 1994), p. 10.

[3] S. Shennan, "Introduction. Archaeological approaches to cultural identity", *Archaeological Approaches to Cultural Identity*, ed. S. Shennan (One World Archaeology 10) (London, 1989), p. 9.

the term 'ethnicity' itself.[4] That term should be taken to mean simply the manifestation of a (sizeable) group's self-consciousness, deriv-
ing from that group's own perception of a set of distinguishing
characteristics, whether real or imagined.[5] Archaeologists too have
had to review the concepts previously used quite unselfconsciously
by their predecessors in the discipline. Gustav Kossina's concept of
Kulturkreislehre (theory of culture-zones) which assumed a direct relationship between material culture and ethnic identity, has effectively
been abandoned.[6]

---

[4] See for example H. Wolfram, "The shaping of the early Medieval Kingdom"
Viator 1 (1970), pp. 1–20; H. Wolfram, *History of the Goths* (Berkeley, 1990); W. Pohl,
"Die Gepiden und die gentes an der mittleren Donau nach dem Zerfall des Attilareiches", *Die Völker an der mittleren und unteren Donau im fünften und sechsten Jahrhundert*, ed. H. Wolfram and F. Daim (Österreichische Akademie der Wissenschaften
145) (Wien, 1980), pp. 240–305; Pohl, "Tradition, Ethnogenese und literarische
Gestaltung eine Zwischenbilanz"; P. Geary, "Ethnic identity as a situational construct in the Early Middle Ages", *Mitteilungen der Anthropologischen Gesellschaft in Wien*
113 (1983), pp. 15–26; P. Geary, *Before France and Germany. The creation and transformation of the Merovingian world.* (Oxford, 1988); F. Daim, "Gedanken zum Ethnosbe-
griff", *Mitteilungen der anthropologischen Gesellschaft in Wien* 112 (1982), pp. 58–71;
J.H.W.G. Liebeschuetz, *Barbarians and Bishops* (Oxford, 1992); P. Heather, *Goths and
Romans 332–489* (Oxford, 19942); P. Heather, "Theoderic, king of the Goths", *Early
Medieval Europe* 4 (1995), pp. 145–173; P. Heather, *The Huns and the end of the Roman
Empire in Western Europe*, (forthcoming a); D. Harrison, "Dark Age Migrations and
Subjective Ethnicity the Example of the Lombards", *Scandia* 57:1 (1991), pp. 19–36;
I. Wood, "Ethnicity and the ethnogenesis of the Burgundians", *Typen der Ethnogenese
unter besonderer Berücksichtigung der Bayern* I, eds. H. Wolfram and W. Pohl (Vienna,
1990), pp. 53–69; I. Wood, *The Merovingian Kingdoms, 450–751* (London and New
York, 1994).
[5] P. Amory, "The meaning and purpose of ethnic terminology in the Burgundian laws", *Early Medieval Europe* 2 (1993), p. 3.
[6] U. Veit, "Ethnic concepts in german prehistory, a case study on the relationship between cultural identity and archaeological objectivity", *Archaeological Approaches
to Cultural Identity*, ed. S.J. Shennan (One World Archaeology 10) (London, 1989),
pp. 35–56; S. Shennan, "Introduction. Archaeological approaches to cultural identity", *Archaeological Approaches to Cultural Identity*, ed. S. Shennan (One World Archaeology 10) (London, 1989), pp. 1–32; further examples can be found in S. Shennan,
ed., *Archaeological Approaches to Cultural Identity* (One World Archaeology 10) (London,
1989); F. Daim, *Awarenforschungen I–II* (Wien, 1992); H. Härke, "Changing symbols
in a changing society. The Anglo-Saxon weapon burial rite in the seventh century",
The Age of Sutton Hoo, ed. M. Carver (Woodbridge, 1992), pp. 149–166; T. Dickinson and H. Härke, *Early Anglo-Saxon Shields* (London, 1992); J. Hines, *The Scandinavian Character of Anglian England in the pre-Viking Period* (British Archaeological Reports,
British series 124) (Oxford, 1984); J. Hines, "The Scandinavian Character of Anglian
England An update", *The Age of Sutton Hoo*, ed. M. Carver (Woodbridge, 1992), pp.
315–330; J. Hines, *Clasps, Hektespenner, Agraffen. Anglo-Scandinavian claps of classes A–C
of the 3rd to the 6th centuries AD. Typology, diffusion and function* (Stockholm, 1993);
J. Hines, "The becoming of English Identity, material culture and language in Early
Anglo-Saxon England" *Anglo-Saxon Studies in Archaeology and History* 7 (Oxford, 1994);

This change has in practice led to an interpretative vacuum between, on the one hand, the steadily rising number of refined typological studies of local variations across a wide range of archaeological material and, on the other hand, historical sources which correspond at best to only a small part of that range. The development of theories and methods capable of accommodating archaeological variation in material culture is badly needed. In attempting to identify a specific people or particular clan, people or group in the archaeological record, researchers have too easily overlooked similarities in the cultural codes they encounter.

However, codes expressed in a given material culture can also be found in rituals, myths and legends in many parts of Europe. In what follows I suggest that origin myths and epic poetry may have actively served to create identities for warrior elites during the Migration Period. Furthermore, I shall argue that texts and material culture represent two only apparently unrelated, but in fact ideologically linked elements in the creation and articulation of a new socio-cosmological order.

My point of departure is that ideology must be understood as a central element in every cultural system.[7] If ideology is looked upon as a source of social power, control over ideas, beliefs and values is assumed to be a precondition for the consolidation of social and thus political legitimacy.[8] The materialisation of these ideas and vasues occurs through the performance of ritual or cemermonial acts, the deployment of objects with symbolic meanings, the construction and shared use of public monuments, the formation of oral traditions, the telling of tales and the production of the written word. Together they mould individual beliefs for collective social action.[9] Sharing

---

and L. Hedeager, "Kingdoms, ethnicity and material culture, Denmark in a European perspective" *The Age of Sutton Hoo*, ed. M. Carver (Woodbridge, 1992), pp. 279–300; L. Hedeager, "The creation of Germanic identity", *A European origin myth. Frontiéres D'Empire. Nature et signification des frontiéres romaines*, eds. P. Brun, S. van der Leeuw, C. Whittaker (Mémoires du Musée de Préhistoire d'lle-de-France 5) (Nemours, 1993), pp. 121–132.

[7] Cf. Bazelmans in this volume.

[8] I follow here Michael Mann's identification of the four elements of power: economic, political, military, and ideological (M., Mann, *The sources of social Power. A history of power from the beginning to AD 1760* (Cambridge, 1986).
    E. De Marrais, L.J. Castillo and T. Earle, "Ideology, materialization and power strategies", *Current Anthropology*, forthcoming.

[9] De Marrais, Castillo and Earle, "Ideology, materialization and power strategies", p. 16.

common cultural codes promotes a feeling of unity and shared belief about the concept of the world which could be especially accentuated—or mobilized—in periods of social stress. However, it also served to veil or accentuate social differences and—in the case of groups we shall be looking at here—common or different origins.

Migration Period cosmology and symbolism created internal similarities and differences within the society of the Germanic warriors and, at the same time, also accentuated the differences between their world and the Roman world that many warriors would eventually become part of. It was in this turbulent political landscape of the fifth and early sixth centuries, that material culture became a symbolic materialization of new social and political identities,[10] and it was in the hybrid Romano-Germanic culture, that the oral Germanic tradition including origin myths, tribal histories and royal genealogies, vitally important for political legitimation within the cosmological world of the Germanic peoples, became transformed and written down as part of the Germans' integration into the Classical Roman imperial tradition. Despite their mythical character, these stories ought to be seen as of prime relevance in this historical process and therefore worth discussion in the present volume.

Origin myths of the Early Middle Ages

In early medieval ethnic histories, three origin myths recur, and in all of these, migration is a central theme first, there is the Greco-Roman story of the escape of the Trojans westwards after the fall of Troy; second, there is the Biblical story of the emigré people of Israel; third, there is the story of the Goths' migration from "Scandza", that is, Scandinavia. The first and the second stories are understandable in light of the Greco-Roman and Christian influences of the Late Antique Period, and the barbarians' interest in demonstrating connections with the civilised Mediterranean world. But the story that is less comprehensible from this perspective is the third one. It can be traced to Ablabius,[11] who in the mid-fifth century

---

[10] Hedeager, "Kingdoms, ethnicity and material culture, Denmark in a European perspective"; Hedeager, "The creation of Germanic identity".

[11] *Getica*: Jordanes, *The Gothic History*, transl. C.C. Mierow (Princeton, 1915), 28, 82.

wrote a (now lost) history of the Goths.[12] This myth of migration is, however, also found in the majority of early ethnic-national origin myths, for instance, those of the Lombards, the Burgundians, the Anglo-Saxons and the Herules. Cassiodorus, probably drawing on Ablabius, wrote his *Historia Gothorum* in twelve volumes (c. 525) and dedicated it to Theoderic, king of the Goths.[13] Cassiodorus' objective was to make the Ostrogoths, and Theoderic's family the Amals, equal in birth to the Romans, whose ancestors had come (as every reader of the *Aeneid* well knew) from Troy. Cassiodorus' work is now lost; but he may well have included the story of the Goths' migration from the lands north of the Black Sea.

In creating a royal Gothic genealogy comprising seventeen generations between the first king, Gaut/Odin, and Theoderic's grandson Athalaric, Cassiodorus obviously used the Roman royal genealogy (with seventeen generations between Aeneas and Romulus) as a model. Yet, in the Old Norse *Grimnismal*, Odin says that Gautr is his name among the gods.[14] Thus, although Cassiodorus' account incorporates a classical-literary feature, it perhaps represents his adaptation (and expansion?) of a Gothic genealogy which had been orally transmitted. Cassiodorus may at the same time have excluded a number of kings and lineages in order to present the Amals as the royal family of the Goths.[15] While it remains possible that he constructed the Amal genealogy himself, without any basis in tradition, let alone historical reality,[16] it is likely that the Amals were the central actors throughout Cassiodorus's presentation of Gothic history, and it is

[12] R. Hachmann, *Die Goten und Skandinavien* (Berlin, 1970), pp. 109ff; P. Heather, "The historical culture of Ostrogothic Italy", *Theoderico il Grande e i Goti D'Italia.* (Atti del XIII Congresso internazionale di studi sull'Alto Medioevo) (Spoleto, 1993), p. 318; Heather, *Goths and Romans 332–489*, p. 64.

[13] Cf. a discussion in Wolfram *History of the Goths*, p. 4; W. Goffart, *The Narrators of Barbarian History* (Princeton, 1988), p. 36. My view differs from that of Goffart, who understands early medieval 'barbarian history' as that of fictitious literary texts, and their authors not only as reporters of the past but as inventors of the past they transmit (Goffart *The Narrators of Barbarian History*, p. 15, cf. also P. Heather, "Cassiodorus and the rise of the Amals Genealogy and the Goths under Hun domination", *Journal of Roman Studies* 79 (1989), p. 114).

[14] *Grimnismal* (54). Part if not all was probably composed in Norway in the late ninth or tenth century. The Old Norse form cognate with Gapt is Gautr (R. North, *Heathen Gods in Old English Literature* (Cambridge, 1997).

[15] Wolfram, *History of the Goths*, pp. 29ff; H. Wolfram, "*Origo et religio*. Ethnic traditions and literature in early medieval texts", *Early Medieval Europe* 3 (1994), p. 31.

[16] Heather "Cassiodorus and the rise of the Amals Genealogy and the Goths under Hun domination".

clear from his own testimony that he wanted the credit for having 'drawn forth from the hiding-place of antiquity long-forgotten kings of the Goths'.[17] A closer look at the written sources implies, however, that the 'Amal dynasty' first developed into a family of standing only as late as the middle of the fifth centrury during the reign of Valamer, Theoderic's uncle. Victory over a number of rival leaders may have been the reason. The Goths in Valamer's reign were only a conglomerate of several groups that had previously been under Hunnic domination.[18]

Athalaric, in a letter to the Roman senate explaining why he had promoted Cassiodorus to the rank of praetorian prefect, praised among his other merits the writing of the *Historia Gothorum*

> From Gothic origins he made a Roman history . . . Think how much he loved you in praising me, when he showed the nation of your prince to be a wonder from ancient days. In consequence, as you have ever been thought noble because of your ancestors, so you shall be ruled by an ancient line of kings.[19]

Jordanes in his *Getica*, c. 550, adopted Cassiodorus' Amal genealogy despite the fact that by the time he wrote the Amals really had no further role to play in Italy. Thus Jordanes, like Cassiodorus, depicted the Amals as descended from the warrior king Gapt.[20] Moreover, Jordanes recounted the story that the Goths had come originally from Scandinavia. Cassiodorus and Jordanes were writing almost two hundred years after the Goths and their kings had adopted Chris-

---

[17] Cassiodorus, *Variae* IX.25.4.

[18] P. Heather, "Disappearing and reappearing tribes", *Strategies of Distinction. The construction of ethnic communities, 300–800*, eds. W. Pohl with H. Reimitz (Leiden, 1998), pp. 92–111.

[19] Cassiodorus, *Variae* IX.25.6. This letter in Athalaric's name was actually written by Cassiodorus himself.

[20] Cf. above n. 14, and J. De Vries, *Altgermansiche Religionsgeschichte* (Berlin, 1956), § 372. North, *Heathen Gods in Old English Literature*, on the other hand, argues that the Amal 'Gapt' and the Lombard 'Gausus' were names derived from Gothic *gáut*, and that *gáut* was an epithet denoting a ritual aspect of Enguz, a god whose name identifies him not only with Ingvi-freyr but also with Ingui or Ing. Before Gautr became a byname of Odin in Scandinavia, *gautr* may have been an epithet for the sacrificed Ingvi-freyr (North, *Heathen Gods in Old English Literature*, chapter 6). Although discussion about Gautr's identification is ongoing, his connection to the pagan Scandinavian pantheon seems clear. Discussing the direction of influence through Europe from the etymological and literary evidence deals with the fundamental problem that written evidence does not appear in Scandinavia until the thirteenth century, by which time any contact seems to go from south to north. So far, the archaeological evidence is needed as an important—and independent—source of information.

tianity. Yet these learned historians credited the Goths with a pagan prehistory. The Ostrogoths were in this respect not so different from other Germanic groups, such as the Lombards who from the 560s settled in Italy or the Anglo-Saxons who from the fifth century were settling England. For Lombards and Anglo-Saxons alike, once they had become christianised, ecclesiastical writers incorporated something of a pagan past into "gentile" histories.

The production in Italy of the first documented Lombard royal genealogy seems to have been associated with the issue by King Rothari in 643 of the Lombard law code known as the *Edictus Rothari*. Genealogy and code are transmitted in the same manuscripts. The basic elements of this code are Germanic, and there are unmistakable similarities to, for instance, Scandinavian law.[21] Like the Gothic and the Roman royal genealogies, that of the Lombards consisted of seventeen generations back to Scandinavia and Gausus, Old Norse Gautr/Odin.[22]

The edict and the royal genealogy were later prefaced with a brief historical work, the *Origo Gentis Langobardorum*, probably written during the reign of King Grimoald (662–671), in which the Lombards' origins and their name are traced back to Odin and Scandinavia. The *Origo* was taken over and much expanded by Paul the Deacon in his *Historia Langobardorum* (ca. 790) to supply his own account of the Lombards' Scandinavian origins:

> . . . If anyone may think that this is a lie and not the truth of the matter, let him read over the prologue of the edict which King Rothari composed of the laws of the Lombards and he will find this written in almost all the manuscripts as we have inserted in this little history.[23]

In spite of the similarities between the royal genealogies and the origin myths found in the *Origo* and Jordanes' *Getica*, there are also many details that do not coincide. For this reason we must surely dismiss the notion that the Lombard origin myth is nothing more than a copy of the Gothic one. These dissimilarities also argue against the possibility that the authors of the texts were mere compilers.

---

[21] L. Boje Mortensen, *Civiliserede Barbarer. Historikeren Paulus Diaconus og hans forgæn-gere*, (Studier fra Sprog og Oldtidsforskning) (Copenhagen, 1991), p. 68. *The Laws of the Salian Franks*, ed. K. Fischer Drew (Philadelphia, 1993), p. 26.

[22] Cf. the discussion by de Vries, *Altgermansiche Religionsgeschichte*, § 369.

[23] Paul the Deacon, *The History of the Lombards*, transl. W.D. Foulke. (1917/1974), I, 21.

These authors had aims and intentions in producing their works
and were certainly aware of the meaning and importance of what
they wrote.[24]

The next question, then, is to ask whether these early histories
should be taken as expressions of independent Gothic or Lombard
oral traditions, still being maintained up to the time that they were
documented in written form,[25] or alternatively as the authors' original literary compositions.[26] The former hypothesis is supported by,
for example, the Lombard royal genealogy described in the *Origo*
and repeated by Paul the Deacon, to the effect that King Agilmund,
the son of Agio and the first historical chief of the Lombards, belonged
to the race or stock of the Gugingus.[27] The expression *ex genere Gugingus* has been related to the name of Odin's great spear Gungnir.
Together with the Lombard royal inauguration ritual with the transfer of the royal symbol, the spear or lance, as described by Paul the
Deacon,[28] it has been argued that the Lombard kings were descen-

---

[24] Further reading from this perspective can be found in S. Teillet, *Des Goths á
la nation gothique. Les origines de l'idée de nation en Occident du Ve au VIIe siécle* (Paris,
1984); B. Croke, "Cassiodorus and the Getica of Jordanes", *Classical Philology* 82
(1987), pp. 117–134; Goffart, *The Narrators of Barbarian History*, pp. 15–18.

[25] Wolfram, "*Origo et religio*. Ethnic traditions and literature in early medieval
texts", p. 32. As pointed out by Tonkin (among others), orality is the basic human
mode of communication. Although peoples all over the world now use literate means
to represent pastness, and written records have existed for many hundreds of years,
the business of relating past and present for social ends has for most of the time
been done orally. Even in so-called traditional societies, there can still be skilled
historians (E. Tonkin, *Narrating our Pasts. The social construction of oral history* (Cambridge, 1995), p. 3). People remember what they need to remember, and in some
societies, genealogical knowledge for example is an important resource, used to support the legitimacy of a claim to political office or land. In some cases it is possible to remember thirty generations. This implies some memorising, which most
people are not required to do. But the fact that it *can* be done implies special interest or incentives, not some special memory IQ (Tonkin, *Narrating our Pasts. The social
construction of oral history*, p. 11). I shall leave aside the question of whether or not
they remember the 'truth'. (Cf. P. Veyne, *Did the Greeks believe in their Myths? An essay
on the Constitutive Imagination* (Chicago and London, 1988), who discusses 'truth' as
'the constitutive imagination'.) Foley has argued that word-power derives from the
enabling event of performance and the enabling referent of tradition. All verbal art
projects meaning from coded signals, and a text with roots in oral tradition is
reduced from performed event to textual cenotaph (J.M. Foley, *The Singer of Tales
in Performance* (Bloomington, 1995).

[26] The latter point of view is maintained by Goffart and by Heather, especially
as regards the Amals' genealogy.

[27] Origo Gentis Langobardorum c. 3, and Paul the Deacon, *The History of the
Lombards*, transl. W.D. Foulke (1917/1974), I, 14.

[28] Paul the Deacon, *The History of the Lombards*, I, 15.

dants from Odin and whoever possessed the holy spear was assumed to be king.[29]

An earlier oral tradition is expressed in Jordanes' *Getica* in written form:

> Of course if anyone in our city [i.e. Constantinople] says that the Goths had an origin different from that which I have related, let him object. For myself, I prefer to believe what I have read, rather than put my trust in old wives' tales (*fabulae aniles*).[30]

Other authors too commented on their own times and referred to their own particular sources. In Book I, c. 8 of the *Historia Langobardorum*, Paul the Deacon went so far as to apologise for what he had to write about the way in which the Lombards got their name from Odin "At this point, the men of old tell a silly story of the Vandals coming to Godan (Wotan) . . ." and the chapter finishes "These things are worthy of laughter and are to be held of no account".[31] Both Jordanes and Paul the Deacon claimed familiarity with oral traditions which they affected to despise yet felt obliged to mention.

Tribal legends or national histories are not attested for all early medieval Germanic peoples, but only for those who perceived their ancestors as having come from Scandinavia. The royal families claimed divine origin and relationship to the pagan Nordic pantheon. Another feature common to the Goths and the Lombards, and also the Angles, the Saxons, the Vandals, the Svear and the Herules, was that they were all mentioned, at an earlier date, by Tacitus, as bearing 'true and old names'.[32] These traditions seem to have played an important part in the formation of peoples (*gentes*) in early medieval Europe.

The Franks' origin myths, on the other hand, form a remarkable exception to the pattern. According to the *Chronicle of Fredegar*, written in the 660s, probably in Burgundy, the Franks came from Troy,

---

[29] S. Gasparri, *La Cultura Tradizionale Dei Longobardi* (Spoleto, 1983), p. 24, and in the present volume.

[30] *Getica* V:38. According to Jordanes several different Gothic origin myths existed, relating to regions named as Scandza, Thule or Brittania (*Getica* IV.25, V.38). The common factor here was some mystical island, which according to Heather is only identifiable through Greco-Roman geography (Heather, *Goths and Romans 332–489*), p. 66 which includes a discussion on the views of Goffart.

[31] Paul the Deacon, *The History of the Lombards*, I, 8; Origo Gentis Langobardorum c. 1.

[32] Wolfram, *History of the Goths*, p. 324; Wolfram, "*Origo et religio*. Ethnic traditions and literature in early medieval texts", pp. 34ff.

where their first king was Priam. Thence they migrated to Macedonia, moving on to the regions of the Danube and then, under the leadership of Francio, to the Lower Rhine, where they then settled and remained undefeated. The Trojan origin myth was also related in the *Liber Historiae Francorum*, written up in or soon after 727, but it seems not to have been known to Gregory of Tours.[33] In his *Historiae*, completed 593–94, Gregory recorded a story that the Fraks had come from Pannonia, and had migrated via the Rhine.[34] The origin myth of the Franks may have been consciously constructed in opposition to the Gothic histories related by Cassiodorus and Jordanes,[35] or it may be that the Franks adopted their myth from the Romans, and thus distanced themselves from the more generally accepted Nordic origin myth.[36] Such an explanation would also accord with the fact that the Franks, in contrast to other Germanic-Christian peoples, moved directly from paganism to Catholicism without going through an Arian phase in this way the Franks distanced themselves from other "barbarian" forms of Christian belief, perhaps because Clovis saw himself as the successor of the Roman Emperor in the West.

The historical meaning of the Scandinavian origin myth

If we accept that early medieval historical writers referred to myths and legends which, in one form or another, had a previous existence as oral traditions,[37] it does not automatically follow that we

---

[33] R.A. Gerberding, *The Rise of the Carolingians and the Liber Historiae Francorum* (Oxford, 1987) and Wood, *The Merovingian Kingdoms, 450–751*, pp. 33ff, discuss the origin legends of the Franks and the Merovingians.

[34] Gregory of Tours, *The History of the Franks*, transl. L. Thorpe (Harmondsworth, 1974/1988), II, 9.

[35] Wood, *The Merovingian Kingdoms, 450–751*, p. 35.

[36] James argues that this myth was concocted by some erudite Frank, or Gallo-Roman, around the year 600, to give the Franks a dignified ancestry by making them the equals of the Romans. The Frankish origin myth continued to develop and was well established by the tenth and eleventh centuries. As late as the eighteenth century genealogies of the French kings began with Priam (E. James, *The Franks* (Oxford, 1991), pp. 235ff).

[37] The main question is of course whether these myths really were told among the elite in the various groups—Goths, Lombards, Heruli or whatever. Heather is convinced that what we have in Cassiodorus and Jordanes are echoes of tales transmitted via a court literature which also loved things classical, and can be shown to have worked classical elements into other material (pers.comment). My point of

accept these stories as accurate accounts of genuine historical events.[38] These writers, nevertheless, depicted their own past in a way, that had meaning for them, using their own criteria of accuracy and correct presentation. If some credibility was to be retained, there were limits, at any given time, to how far it was possible to alter a people's oral traditions or change its sacred tales and legends.[39] The legitimacy and the political dominance which family histories and origin myths effect would have disappeared if manipulated too obviously.[40] These stories, in other words, cannot have been invented on the spur of the moment, but were most probably constructed, developed and altered over many generations thus the stories' power derived from their being retold and performed as embodiments of tradition.[41]

This might help to explain why some of the Germanic peoples have a longer and more varied historical tradition than others. At the same time, this allows for the possibility that the royal genealogies of, for instance, the Amals, were constructed on the basis partly of fiction, and partly of actual events. By adapting an oral tradition and circulating written explanations, Cassiodorus was able to construct a historical "truth" that legitimised the power of Theoderic and his family. In any case, as Cassiodorus explained in the letter

---

departure is more anthropological and I therefore hesitate to see the core of the Gothic origin myth as fundamentally different from for instance the Heruli who had no classical court literature.

[38] Meulengracht Sørensen, P., "Håkon den Gode og guderne. Nogle bemærkninger om religion og centralmagt i det tiende århundrede—og om religion og kildekritik", *Høvdingesamfund og Kongemagt*, eds. P. Mortensen and B. Rasmussen (Jysk Arkæologisk Selskabs Skrifter XXII:2) (Århus, 1991), pp. 235–244. As pointed out by Finnegan, interest in 'oral tradition', particularly 'myths' collected from overseas peoples or European 'folklore', also led historians to shift their focus away from current forms or meanings towards the search for the 'pure', 'original' or 'traditional' stages (R. Finnegan, *Oral Traditions and the Verbal Arts* (London and New York, 1992), p. 277).

[39] Vansina argues in his pioneering work on African material that oral history could be used as a historical source in a way parallel to written history. He claims that there is a kind of historical testimony, an 'original tradition' undergoing distortion through time until it is finally recorded by the historian as a historical testimony (J. Vansina, *Oral Tradition A Study in Historical Methodology* (London, 1965); J. Vansina, *Oral Tradition as History* (London, 1985)). For a discussion see e.g. Tonkin, *Narrating our Pasts. The social construction of oral history*, pp. 83ff. with further references.

[40] A. Weiner, *Inalienable Possessions. The Paradox of Keeping While Giving.* (Berkeley and Los Angeles, 1992), p. 11.

[41] The relationship between word-power, performance and tradition has been analysed by Foley, *The Singer of Tales in Performance*.

ghost-written by him to the senate of Rome on behalf of Athalaric, Theoderic's grandson and successor

> He [Cassiodorus] extended his labours even to the ancient cradle of our house, learning from his reading what the hoary recollections of our elders scarcely preserved (*lectione discens, quod vix maiorum notitia cana retinebat*). From the lurking-place of antiquity he led out the king of the Goths, long hidden in oblivion. He resoted the Amals, along with the honour of their family, clearly proving me [Athalaric] to be of royal stock to the seventeenth generation. From Gothic origins he made a Roman history, gathering, as it were, into one garland, flowerbuds that had previously been scattered throughout the fields of literature.[42]

The question of historicity is thus impossible to answer. Some kings may have been mythical, others perhaps were genuinely historical characters, but their connections with the Amals merely a construction.[43] What is important in this context is that which unites the long lines of histories of the early medieval period, namely, the myth of pagan Nordic origin. In the specific case of the Amals, it was not only their founding father Gaut who had close links with Scandinavia but also his son Humli/Hulmul, whom later written tradition depicted as the divine ancestor of the Danes.[44] If the Scandinavian origin myth of the Germanic peoples represented some ancient collective memory of tribal history, which was subsequently transformed

---

[42] Cassiodorus, *Variae* IX. 25. 4–5. Cf. above and n. 19. Discussions of this passage can be found in Heather, "Cassiodorus and the rise of the Amals Genealogy and the Goths under Hun domination"; P. Heather and J. Matthews, *The Goths in the Fourth Century* (Liverpool, 1991); Heather, "The historical culture of Ostrogothic Italy". Heather argues that the Amals' genealogy is more or less the fictitious work of Cassiodorus himself ("The historical culture of Ostrogothic Italy", p. 344). On the role of rhetorical hyperbole in delineating the past and in staking claims to its heritage, see D. Lowenthal, "'Trojan forebears', 'peerless relics'. The rhetoric of heritage claims", *Interpreting Archaeology*, eds. I. Hodder *et al.* (London, 1995), pp. 125–130.

[43] The Amals themselves could equally well be a late construction of the fifth century: cf. the ongoing debate about whether the Amal tradition was 'real', in the sense that such a dynasty had provided kings in the fourth century for the Gothic Greuthungi (Wolfram, *History of the Goths*; Wolfram, "*Origo et religio*. Ethnic traditions and literature in early medieval texts") or a late invention (e.g. Heather, "Theoderic, king of the Goths").

[44] As pointed out by Wolfram (Wolfram, *History of the Goths*, p. 31, p. 37; Wolfram, "*Origo et religio*. Ethnic traditions and literature in early medieval texts", p. 28). Humli/Humbli, mentioned c. 1200 by Saxo Grammaticus, *Gesta Danorum* I, 10, as the Danes' founding father, could thus have been part of Scandinavian myth already in the sixth century. According to Heather *Goths and Romans 332–489*, p. 21, however, 'Hulmul was a figure common to Germanic folklore'.

into the language of myth and the sacred identity of the people, then what does this Scandinavian origin actually imply?

Jordanes himself put forward the classical authors' explanation, namely, that population explosion in Scandinavia was the reason for emigration *en masse*. This, however, is something of a literary topos, and there is little reason to take it seriously. The same can be said of Jordanes' notion of the Nordic peoples' powerful and long-lasting fertility, thought to be due to climatic conditions, such as the long, dark winter nights. Nevertheless, that these explanations cannot be used to confirm the historicity of the origin myth does not mean that the Goths and many others did not originate from Scandinavia. Several independent, unrelated, pieces of evidence, both philological and archaeological,[45] indicate that there might be a grain of historical truth in these stories. If Scandza is a literary motif, it might also reflect some long-gone historical reality,[46] at least for the Goths, the Lombards and the Anglo-Saxons, and perhaps even for groups like the Heruli, the Vandals and the Burgundians too. Several of the tribal groups that settled within the boundaries of the Roman Empire are said to have spoken a Germanic language and for that reason must have come from 'the North'.

What matters is not whether these people emigrated in small groups from Scandinavia, but that their identity and self-perception

---

[45] Hachmann, *Die Goten und Skandinavien*; J. Svennung, Jordanes und die gotische Stammsage. *Studia Gothica*, ed. U.E. Hagberg (Antikvariske Serien 25, Kungl. Vitterhets Historie och Antikkvitets Akademien) (Stockholm, 1972), pp. 20–56; Hines *The Scandinavian Character of Anglian England in the pre-Viking Period*; Hines, "The Scandinavian Character of Anglian England An update"; Hines, *Clasps, Hektespenner, Agraffen. Anglo-Scandinavian claps of classes A–C of the 3rd to the 6th centuries AD Typology, diffusion and function*; Hines, "The becoming of English Identity, material culture and language in Early Anglo-Saxon England"; J. Hines, "Cultural change and social organisation in Early Anglo-Saxon England", *After Empire. Towards an Ethnology of Europe's Barbarians*, ed. G. Ausenda (Woodbridge, 1995), pp. 75–87; W. Menghin, *Die Langobarden. Archäologie und Geschichte* (Stuttgart, 1985); U. Näsman, "Analogislutning i nordisk jernalderarkæologi. Et bidrag til udviklingen af an nordisk historisk etnografi", *Jernalderens Stammesamfund*, eds. P. Mortensen and B. Rasmussen (Jysk Arkæologisk Selskabs Skrifter XXII:1) (Århus, 1988), pp. 123–140; P. Heather and J. Matthews, *The Goths in the Fourth Century* (Liverpool, 1991) with further references; M. Kazanski, *Les Goths* (Paris, 1991); Härke "Changing symbols in a changing society. The Anglo-Saxon weapon burial rite in the seventh century", p. 164; Dickinson and Härke, *Early Anglo-Saxon Shields*; V. Bierbrauer, "Archäologie und Geschichte der Goten vom 1.-7. Jahrhundert", *Frühmittelalterliche Studien* 28 (1994), pp. 51–171; N. Christie, *The Lombards* (Oxford, 1995).

[46] Wolfram, "*Origo et religio*. Ethnic traditions and literature in early medieval texts", pp. 27f.

were tied up with the Nordic regions.[47] Over generations, the origin myths would have been handed down and recreated in a multitude of ritual contexts, associated with the social reproduction of the people and the warrior-kings' sacred position.

When Theoderic became a Roman citizen, in 484 at the latest, he and his family, the Amals, also became *Flavii*. They became, in other words, relatives of the great Roman emperors of the first century, such as Vespasian, Titus and Domitian[48] in much the same way as eminent 'Goths' were allowed to become related to the Amals. As the Ostrogothic king of Italy, however, Theoderic continued to uphold his pagan Nordic ancestry. The question remains what was it that made Theoderic, whose connections with the Roman environment and with Christianity can hardly be denied, link the Amals' nobility and the Goths' ancestry to a pagan Nordic origin? A similar question arises even if it was Cassiodorus who constructed the story.

One explanation might be that that this origin myth was already so firmly rooted among the Ostrogoths that it could easily become the foundation of the king's authority and legitimacy among the Ostrogoths themselves. Even if this was presented in a Roman literary style by Cassiodorus in order to explain the king's divine and ancient ancestry, it was hardly something invented by Cassiodorus, or, for that matter, by Theoderic. Had this been the case, it would surely have been completely worthless as a persuasive argument in legitimising the Ostrogoths' royal genealogy.

Genealogies and heroic legends had long been active agents and instruments of legitimation. What Cassiodorus or Paul the Deacon

---

[47] Cf. the ongoing discussion about the factual basis of the origin myth: C. Weibull, *Die Auswanderung der Goten aus Schweden* (Götenborg, 1958); J. Svennung, *Jordanes und Scandia* (Stockholm, 1967); Svennung, "Jordanes und die gotische Stammsage"; N. Wagner, *Getica. Untersuchungen zum Leben des Jordanes und zur frühen Geschichte der Goten* (Quellen und Forschungen zur Sprach- und Kulturgeschichte der germanischen Völker, N.F.22) (Berlin, 1967); Hachmann, *Die Goten und Skandinavien*; W. Goffart, *Barbarians and Romans* (Princeton, 1980), pp. 22ff; Goffart, *The Narrators of Barbarian History*, p. 85; Wolfram, *History of the Goths*; Wolfram, "*Origo et religio*. Ethnic traditions and literature in early medieval texts"; Heather, "Cassiodorus and the rise of the Amals Genealogy and the Goths under Hun domination"; Heather, "The historical culture of Ostrogothic Italy"; Heather, *Goths and Romans 332–489*; Pohl, "Tradition, Ethnogenese und literarische Gestaltung eine Zwischenbilanz"; V. Bierbrauer, "Archäologie und Geschichte der Goten vom 1.-7. Jahrhundert", *Frühmittelalterliche Studien* 28 (1994), pp. 51–171.

[48] Wolfram, "*Origo et religio*. Ethnic traditions and literature in early medieval texts", p. 33.

did for the Ostrogoths and the Lombards—that is, present a royal
genealogy with sufficient time-depth, together with a detailed history
of the migration—could not be done for the Franks by Gregory of
Tours. In the *Historiae*[49] Gregory wrote "Many people do not even
know the name of the first king of the Franks. The *Historia* of
Sulpicius Alexander gives many details about them, while Valenti-
nus does not name their first king but says that they were ruled by
war-leaders". Then followed an account of what Sulpicius Alexander had written about the early battles of the Franks. Here Gregory
vented a certain irritation "A few pages further on, having given up
all talk of 'duces' and 'regales', [Sulpicius Alexander] clearly states
that the Franks had a king, but he forgets to tell us what his name
was". Having cited yet another authority, Renatus Profuturus Frigeridus,
Gregory was finally forced to conclude "The historians whose works
we still have give us all this information about the Franks, but they
never record the names of the kings". He continued with the origin myth "It is commonly said that the Fraaanks came originally
from Pannonia and first colonised the banks of the Rhine. Then
they crossed the river, marched through Thuringia, and set up in
each country district and city, long-haired kings chosen from the
foremost and most noble family of their race."

Gregory was unable to give the Merovingian family an ancient
genealogy,[50] nor could he provide the Salian Franks with an origin
myth, because he had neither the sources to turn to, nor a common body of knowledge to manipulate. He could not create a story
for the occasion, so he had to make do with naming Clovis as the
fourth king of the Merovingian line, and all this in spite of the fact
that, as Goffart once wrote, ". . . everyone agrees in recognising Gregory's outstanding talent for anecdote . . ."[51] It is clear that Gregory
knew little about the origin of the Franks, and that his ignorance
reduced him to recording an origin-story that was inferior to the

---

[49] Gregory of Tours, *The History of the Franks*, II. 9.
[50] Heather sees striking parallels between the rise of the Amals over at least two
generations between c. 450 and c. 485, and the emergence of the Merovingians as
the dominant Frankish dynasty at roughly the same time. Representatives of both
families managed to defeat a series of rivals to incorporate ever larger numbers of
followers under their control (Heather, "Theoderic, king of the Goths", p. 149).
There are remarkable differences, however, between the Amal and the Merovingian genealogies.
[51] Goffart, *The Narrators of Barbarian History*, p. 113.

traditions which assigned other peoples a glorious and noble past.[52] This reticence was hardly due to the fact that Gregory's main objective was to document the history of the Church and the histories of the nobility at a local level, rather than explicitly to document the history of the Frankish people.[53] Even if he knew, but was reluctant to repeat, the story (known only from Fredegar, writing c. 660) of Merovech's conception after his mother coupled with a sea-beast, what Gregory does tell of early Frankish and Merovingian history is hardly very impressive. It is also clear that the Franks had no place in Tacitus's reckoning of the old names of the *gentes*.[54] Both archaeological and historical sources indicate that they started as a confederation in the regions immediately east of the Rhine[55] and as such they differ from other Germanic tribes in that they are a creation within the Roman empire. In the written sources from the mid-third century onwards, a number of small groups, Chamavi, Usipii, Bructeri, Salii, amongst others, appear loosely associated under the name of Franks, 'the free'. The name Frank designates a variety of tribes so loosely connected that some scholars have denied that they formed a confederation.[56]

Some scholars have inferred from Gregory's personal notes in his *Histories* that the absence of myths in some sense denied the Franks' historical legitimacy. For the warrior tribes of the Migration Period, the power of origin myths to create historical and ideological identity was so great that these could hardly have appeared out of thin air. Through the works of Cassiodorus, Jordanes and (later) Paul the Deacon, it is evident that neither Christianity nor new political/geographical realities made the origin myths superfluous perhaps they had quite the opposite effect. We must now, therefore, delve more deeply into the myths' nature and meaning.

---

[52] Geary, *Before France and Germany. The creation and transformation of the Merovingian world*, p. 77.

[53] Boje Mortensen, *Civiliserede Barbarer. Historikeren Paulus Diaconus og hans forgængere*, p. 39. Gregory's main purpose in writing the *Histories* is discussed by I. Wood, *Gregory of Tours* (Gwynedd, 1994).

[54] Wolfram, "*Origo et religio*. Ethnic traditions and literature in early medieval texts", p. 34.

[55] James, *The Franks*, pp. 35ff.

[56] Geary, *Before France and Germany. The creation and transformation of the Merovingian world*, p. 78.

Epic poetry and historical reality 'collective memory'
among the Germanic peoples

Myths, legends and poetry exist as 'remembered history', the collective memory; they are significant as reality and as symbol.[57] Myths and histories survive as long as they can be adapted to incorporate any unforeseeable events and new developments. Prominent myths in a culture therefore take on different forms at different moments in time. Despite these variations the myths or legends retain a core of substance, of 'hard facts'—perhaps a name, a time, a place—probably transformed into an archetypical situation. Without this accepted echo of historical "truth", the myth or legend loses its capacity to unite the past and the present, and to organise the present.[58] Time is a necessary component if historical events are to develop into indispensable myths of cultural identity,[59] while, on the other hand, myths are disposed of when it is no longer possible for them to be absorbed into changes of a social and political nature. Thus origin myths and legends can be perceived as being one and the same, in that they were both of particular importance in the formation of the new Germanic kingdoms. The Migration Period was a period of rapid change with needs for the creation of a new socio-cosmological order. In this case, the invention of tradition could use specific ancient stories for new purposes.[60] The origin myths and the legends thus convey a feeling that allows them to be perceived

---

[57] B. Lewis, *History Remembered, Recovered, Invented* (Princeton, 1975), pp. 11–12. For a summary discussion of the role of oral tradition and verbal art from different theoretical viewpoints, see Finnegan, *Oral Traditions and the Verbal Arts*, pp. 25ff.

[58] N. Howe, *Migration and Mythmaking in Anglo-Saxon England.* (New Haven, 1989), p. 4. Cf. the continuing debate over the processes through which 'traditions' are created, transformed or maintained in specific historical conditions to fit particular interests or values (Vansina, *Oral Tradition A Study in Historical Methodology*; Vansina, *Oral Tradition as History*; Finnegan, *Oral Traditions and the Verbal Arts*; E. Hobsbawm and T. Ranger, eds., *The Invention of Traditions* (Cambridge, 1983); Tonkin, *Narrating our Pasts. The social construction of oral history* and others). The time-span considered by the contributors to Hobsbawn and Ranger (eds) *The Invention of Traditions* is the last two hundred years a period of rapid, global, transformations which weakened or destroyed the social patterns for which 'old' traditions had been created. These studies nevertheless demonstrate how ancient materials can be used to construct 'new' traditions.

[59] Cf. Weiner, *Inalienable Possessions. The Paradox of Keeping While Giving.*

[60] As Hobsbawm describes in E. Hobsbawm, "Introduction Inventing traditions", *The Invention of Traditions*, eds. E. Hobsbawm and T. Ranger (Cambridge, 1995[2]), p. 6.

as an inheritance for people with a wide variety of backgrounds and identities and as such serving as the backbone in the creation of a new socio-cosmological order.

The turning-point for Europe and the catalyst in the political turbulence of the Migration Period was the emergence of Hunnic power in the late fourth century.[61] From the beginning of the fifth century, until 453–69, when the Huns eventually disappeared from Europe, the Germanic peoples were steadily taking over the West-Roman Empire.[62] The Huns' presence forced the Goths, the Vandals, the Alamans, the Swabians, the Burgundians, the Anglo-Saxons and others over and into the frontiers of the Empire, where, as independent political/military entities, they took—or were given—large portions of land in Gaul, Italy, Spain, Africa and Britain.[63] Large numbers of people did, however, remain in the Germanic regions, where willingly or otherwise they became a part of the Hunnic confederation, only to "re-emerge" at a later stage, as independent political entities.[64] The historical events are uncertain, and it is not known how far north the power of Attila stretched. Questions about the effects of those political and military developments in Germanic Europe have hardly begun to be asked. It has always been taken for granted that the Huns came and went in some brief episode in European history, leaving no lasting impression on areas to the north and east of the Roman Empire.[65] This, I believe, is an underestimate of their historical importance.

---

[61] P. Heather, "Disappearing and reappearing tribes", *Strategies of Distinction. The construction of ethnic communities, 300–800*, eds. W. Pohl with H. Reimitz (Leiden, 1998), pp. 92–111. L. Hedeager, "Cosmological endurance: Pagan identities in Early Christian Europe", *Journal of European Archaeology* 3 (1998), pp. 383–397.

[62] Debate over the Huns' and the Germanic peoples' influence on the West-Roman Empire's eventual disintegration is never-ending, but in this particular instance, not so relevant.

[63] Goffart stresses that hardly any movement of the invasion period fits into the pattern of one people being pressed onward by another because of the Huns (Goffart, *Barbarians and Romans*, p. 17). My point of departure, like Heather's, is to see the Huns' role in the Western collapse in a more indirect way, as the effect of the insecurity they generated in Central- and Eastern Europe by coming and vanishing.

[64] Heather, "Disappearing and reappearing tribes".

[65] Cf. Heather, "Theoderic, king of the Goths". Archaeological traces of the Huns in Europe are almost non-existent (cf. J. Werner, *Beiträge zur Archäologie des Attila-Reiches* (München, 1956); I. Bóna, *Das Hunnenreich* (Stuttgart, 1991) and without the written sources we should never have been able to recognise the Huns as a distinctive group. This further implies that archaeologists and historians have never considered the Hunnic impact on the northern part of Europe.

It is now beyond dispute that a common denominator in Europe, during the period c. 375 to 455–69, was the Huns, till then a relatively unkown military power, whose centre was neither Roman nor Germanic, but Asiatic. The importance of these Hunnic encounters both outside and inside the Roman borders needs to be emphasised all the more strongly in that the contemporary written sources tend to favour the "imperial" Germanic peoples who survived to write their histories, while the Huns disappeared. A fraction of the Migration Period's dramatic history is intimated, however, through a number of shared themes in early-medieval epic poetry and the Nordic sagas, which I will now briefly discuss.[66]

The great epic cycle of the Volsunga and the Nibelungen is probably the best known of the Germanic legends. It consists of several stories which are either interwoven with each other, or composed of separate parts but deeply embedded in these is the story of the fall of the Burgundians after the Hunnic attack. The Volsunga Saga, which tells of Odin's grandchild Volsunga and his descendants, is known from a number of Old Norse sources such as the *Poetic Edda*, written down in Iceland in c. 1100, supposedly by Saemundur Frodhi. This story is also known as *Sjurdarkvadene* in the Faroe Islands, where it was recited in conjunction with the chain dance, a custom still in practice as late as the ninteenth century. The German *Nibelungenlied* was written down around 1200 in the Bohemian-Austrian region by an unknown author, supposedly attached to the royal court,[67] and one of the more recent branches on the tree is Richard Wagner's interpretation in *The Ring of the Nibelungen*.

As mentioned earlier, the historical basis of this story is the fate of the Burgundian kingdom which had been founded on the left bank of the Rhine, south of and around Worms, in 413. In 437 King Gundicar fell, along with a great majority of his people, in an

---

[66] For a more in-depth discussion see E. Wamers, "Die Völkervanderungszeit im Spiegel der germanischen Heldensagen", *Germanen, Hunnen und Avaren* (Nürnberg, 1987), pp. 69–94.

[67] Various forms of cultural transformation from a pagan to a Christian universe are suggested in early Christian artwork, and in written form through examples such as the *Nibelungenlied*. The story is not exactly the same, even though various components including the main characters were kept. Changes are found, however, in the the story's social context, i.e. in terms such as honour, guilt, generosity, and in the depiction of certain relationships (E. Vestergaard, *Völsunge-Nibelungen Traditionen. Antropologiske studier i en episk traditions transformation i forhold til dens sociale sammenhæng* (Århus University, Unpublished Phd thesis 1992). The myth has been reproduced throughout the centuries in many different parts of Europe.

attempt to halt the Huns. Attila is not recorded as having been personally involved in the attack, but he is linked, in a natural, conving-
ing way, with the Burgundian kingdom's downfall. Attila, of course,
was not solely responsible for its demise, and he himself would not
long outlive it. According to fifth- and sixth-century sources, Attila
died suddenly in 453, on the night of his wedding to Hildico, daughter of a Germanic king.[68] Although these sources attribute his death
to an apoplectic stroke, rumour may have suggested that Attila had
been murdered by Hildico. In legend, with little respect for the
chronological order of things, Hildico became a Burgundian princess,
the sister of Gundicar, and thus the status of her brother, and that
of the Burgundian people, were enhanced. The core of the legend
is the story of the king's son Sigfred (Nordic Sigurd); his widow, the
Burgundian Princess Kriemhild (Nordic Gudrun), the historic Hildico;
her marriage to Etzel (Nordic Atle), the historic Attila; and the final
demise of King Gundicar (Nordic Gunnar) and the other Burgundians (here called Gjukungs).[69]

Over the course of time other stories were incorporated, including that of the Gothic King Ermanrik (Nordic Jörmunrek), attested
in fourth-century historical sources as lining on the northern shores
of the Black Sea. He died, according to the Roman historian Ammianus Marcellinus, writing in 392–393, by committing suicide, whilst
involved in meeting the Hunnic attack in 375. A complete legend
was composed about him, in which his wife Wunilda became Svanhild and was then transformed, in the so-called Svanhild Saga, into
Gudrun's daughter through marriage to Sigurd.[70] Later on other historical characters appeared, for instance, the Visigothic princess Brunhild and her sister Galswinth, wedded to two Merovingian brothers,
King Sigibert of Austrasia and King Chilperic of Neustria, in the
560s. Legend transformed their dramatic and violent lives and deaths
into a tale of conflict between Burgundians and Franks.

Another fragment of dramatic early medieval European history is
The Battle of the Huns. The historical roots of this cycle, the fourth-

---

[68] *Priscus, fragm.*, C.D. Gordon, *The Age of Attila* (Ann Arbour, 1960), c. 23;
Jordanes, *Getica*, XLIX.
[69] C.D. Gordon, *The Age of Attila*. (Ann Arbour, 1960), p. 111, cf. N. Lukman,
Skjoldunge und Skilfinger. Hunnen- und Herulerkönige in Ostnordischer Überlieferung (København, 1943).
[70] Cf. N. Lukman, *Ermanaric hos Jordanes og Saxo* (Studier fra Sprog- og Oldtidsforskning, Det Filologisk-Historiske Samfund 208) (København, 1949).

century struggles of the Goths against the Huns, have several echoes in epic poetry prior to the year 1000, and also in the Anglo-Saxon legend of Widsith, the old Icelandic saga of Hervarar and Heidrik's crowning, and the *Gesta Danorum* of Saxo Grammaticus.[71] Of three distinct versions, that recorded in *Widsith* seems to be by far the oldest. The Old English poem was transcribed in the single extant manuscript c. 970 but, according to the evidence of the language, had already been put into written form considerably earlier,[72] and clearly draws on much earlier traditions. *Widsith* describes several times how the Goths of the Vistula had to defend their ancestral seats against Hunnic attacks. The historical basis of the story is evidently the destruction of Ermanaric's kingdom and the subsequent driving of many Goths south across the Danube in and after 376.[73] In the version of Saxo's *Gesta Danorum*,[74] the war is turned into a struggle between Danes and Huns, but the Ostrogoths survive under another name.[75] The Icelandic version, in prose and verse alike, keeps the Goths but replaces the king.[76] In the *Hervara Saga*, the historical basis for the account of battles against the Huns is believed to be older than that of the other episodes, and the verses include a number of place-names that point in the direction of Central and Eastern Europe, exactly where the Huns and the Goths met in the decades around 400.[77] The three versions, of the *Hervara Saga*, Saxo's *Gesta Danorum*, and *Widsith*, all agree in certain fundamental traits (1) they tell a tale of warfare between the Huns and a Baltic nation (2) they make the

---

[71] The two oldest Danish chronicles, Svend Aggesen (ca. 1180) and Lejrekrøniken (ca. 1170) tell their own versions of Adils (= Attila) and his battle. Both in the Nordic countries and in England a great battle is described, in which Adils played a major role, as ever involved in great fights (Lukman, *Skjoldunge und Skilfinger. Hunnen- und Herulerkönige in Ostnordischer Überlieferung*, p. 41).

[72] *Widsith*, ed. K. Malone (Copenhagen, 1962), p. 116. For more recent discussion of the tenth-century context of the poem as we have it, as distinct from the early date of the poem's historical references, see J. Hill, "Widsið and the tenth century" Neuphilologische Mitteilungen 85 (1984), pp. 305–315.

[73] *Widsith*, p. 103; Heather, *Goths and Romans 332–489*, pp. 13–4. Precisely how *Widsith* combines literary and oral traditions must of course remain a matter for debate. I have discussed a similar question in reference to Cassiodorus and the *Getica*. It must be stressed that I have never argued that any of these texts must represent simply a written form of an oral tradition.

[74] *The History of the Danes. Saxo Grammaticus, Books I–IX*, transl. Peter Fischer, edited and commented by Hilda E. Davidson (Cambridge, 1998) [first ed. 1979–80].

[75] *Widsith*, p. 103.

[76] *Widsith*, p. 103.

[77] L. Lönnroth, *Isländska Mytsagor. Översättning och kommentarer av Lars Lönnroth* (Stockholm, 1995), p. 219.

Huns the aggressors (3) they put the struggle in the Vistula vallley and thereabouts (4) they tell the tale from the point of view of the Huns' foes.[78]

Not much more than the names are left of what was once historical reality, that is, the battles between the Huns, the Burgundians, the Goths, the Gepids and the Lombards. The stories that survived are the closest we are likely to come to the actual events that gave rise to the Germanic legends.[79] They show how loosely the legends were linked to their roots in historical events and thus how impossible it is to deduce any exact historical knowledge from them. What is important, however, is that the characters and events belong to the history of Europe during the period 375 to 568 that is, to the period between the Huns' first attack and the Lombards' Italian migration. These shared Germanic legends go back to the formative centuries in which the Germanic kingdoms built themselves up from the foundations of the Roman Empire, even if only to collapse at a later stage. Strangely enough, though, there are practically no traces of the Late Antique period to be found in them.

As in a patchwork quilt, pieces of different legends, and the various characters, are attached to each other in patterns that have nothing whatsoever to do with their original contexts. In legendary space, the time and place of historical elements cease to exist. These are the legends of heroes, where the themes focus upon tragic destinies, on the murders of brothers and sons, on the duties of revenge and the consequences thereof, on the universal, and on the ethics fundamental to the people of the past. A myth cannot be understood as some continuous sequence, it cannot be read as if it were a novel or a story, but ought to be understood as a meaningful whole. And even though actual historical events form the basis for the Germanic legend tradition, we must "read" the stories in a quite different way from that in which we understand the historical writings of Cassiodorus, Jordanes, Gregory or Paul the Deacon. The conventions of discourse structure the myth on many levels, as pointed out by Elizabeth Tonkin in her book *Narrating our Pasts*:

---

[78] *Widsith*, p. 104.

[79] The similarities between the names of the kings of the Huns and those in the Nordic royal genealogies of the Skjoldunger and Skilfinger are quite remarkable. In the Nordic tradition the kings of the Huns become Danish and Swedish kings (Lukman, *Skjoldunge und Skilfinger. Hunnen- und Herulerkönige in Ostnordischer Überlieferung*, p. 108).

Historians have labelled as 'myth' what seem unrealistic ways of representing the past, but it can sometimes be shown that mythic structures encode history, that is, they register actual happenings or significant changes. 'Realism', on the other hand, is an equally culture-bound judgment of likelihood. An audience always has expectations about the nature of reality, and judges whether the linguistic and genre patterns, as well as the content of the discourse, are appropriate for its representation . . . . . 'Realism' includes criteria of intelligibility and rationality which are open to dispute.[80]

Germanic origin myths and legends thus arose out of turbulent events and changes rooted in military encounters. In the transformation of events into myths and legends, order was brought to chaos. How, then, are these changes reflected in the material culture?

Germanic styles in a historical perspective

Narrative, telling stories, is a basic human way of making sense of the world as particular details are given meaning through their incorporation into story forms.[81] Ornamentation and decoration of the material world is a meaningful human action in all cultures, even if it is not articulated, and it will serve here as a concrete illustration.[82] This decoration, these styles, are used by archaeologists as a mirror, or perhaps a key, to the interpretation of prehistoric cultures in much the same way as art-historians use their objects of study. The categorisation of style by means of style-types and style-definitions is used in the study of prehistory and of archaeological cultures to create operational time-space divisions this is how prehistory is constructed. Reduced to patterns and distributions, styles are, however, necessarily distanced from their original significance and function.[83] Archaeologists

---

[80] Tonkin, *Narrating our Pasts. The social construction of oral history*, p. 8.

[81] M. Shanks, M. and I. Hodder, "Processual, postprocessual and interpretive archaeologies", *Interpreting Archaeology. Finding meaning in the past*, ed. I. Hodder *et al.* (London, 1995), p. 25. P. Ricoeur, *Time and Narrative*, vol. 3, trans. K. McLaughlin & D. Pellauer (Chicago, 1989). S. Cohan and L.S. Shires, *Telling Stories: Theoretical Analysis of Narrative Fiction* (London, 1988).

[82] See for example M. Bloch, "Questions not to ask of Malagasy carvings", *Interpreting Archaeology*, eds. I. Hodder et al. (London, 1995), pp. 212–215 on the decoration of wooden pillars in the houses of Madagascar. At first glance these pillars might seem insignificant, but in fact they are central symbols, indicating the family's identity and survival.

[83] M. Conkey and C. Hastorf, eds,. *The Use of Style in Archaeology* (Cambridge, 1990), p. 2.

have often tended to treat style as a passive, neutral, tradition, that is, one without content. While stylistic differences have proved useful in defining 'archaeological cultures', more often than not any discussion of style in relation to social and historical change is omitted. In other words, style is perceived as being essentially meaningless.[84]

The adoption of a theoretical/anthropological approach, by contrast, entails a perception of style as an active medium for communication, for both individuals and/or groups in a given cultural system. On this premise, elements of style, not least iconographic ones, are presumed to have been selected with a great deal of care, just as objects are very carefully selected for use in ceremonies because they are the bearers of important messages, communicating, for example, social relationships, group membership and ethnic identity.[85] Style, then, must also be seen as involved in the creation and maintenance of the socio-cosmological order and as such participates in the legitimisation of power. Upholding style can be regarded as a part of the elite's strategy in the same way as the maintenance of ritual functions, myths, legends and symbolic objects—in short, all that embodies the group's identity. Seen in this light, Germanic animal styles acquire a new, more significant function.

It is not my intention here to discuss the mythological content of animal ornament, if such a thing existed, even if neither clearly expressed nor articulated.[86] Instead, with the ideological function of animal ornament as my starting point, I will briefly summarise the ways in which its typology can be linked, not only to the Nordic peoples, but also to the "continental" warrior peoples, the Lombards, the Goths, the Alemanni, the Anglo-Saxons etc., whose myths assign them a Scandinavian origin. Günther Hasseloff has analysed the earliest developments of animal-styles in Scandinavia, on the Continent and in England, using typological, chronological and geographical criteria.[87] Haseloff has shown how the development of Nydam Style/

---

[84] M. Shanks, "Style and the design of a perfume jar from an archaic Greek city state" *Journal of European Archaeology* 1 (1993), p. 86, see also Shanks and Hodder, "Processual, postprocessual and interpretive archaeologies", p. 33.

[85] T. Earle, "Style and iconography as legitimation in complex chiefdoms", *The Use of Style in Archaeology*, eds. M. Conkey and C. Hastorf (Cambridge, 1990), p. 73.

[86] M. Bloch, "People into Places: Zafimaniry Concepts of Clarity", *The Anthropology of Landscape*, eds. E. Hirsch and M. OiHanlon (London, 1997 [1995]), pp. 63–77.

[87] G. Haseloff, *Die germanische Tierornamentik der Völkervanderungszeit* (Berlin and New York, 1981).

Style I was closely connected with southern Scandinavia, i.e. Jutland, the Danish islands, southern Sweden and the southernmost parts of Norway. A remarkably rich variety of forms and figures, often with human features (masks), developed in this area during the first half of the fifth century (fig. 1). It has not been possible to trace immediate predecessors, either in Scandinavia or elsewhere, and as Nydam Style/Style I contains a wide variety of elements, including some drawn from Late Roman carved bronzes, and from Asiatic ornamental and polychrome work,[88] the only plausible conclusion to draw is that this style, characterised by its unique artistic skills and craftsmanship, must have originated from the Scandinavian region. Finds on the Continent and in England are well represented from the latter half of the fifth century up to the end of the sixth, when a new style, Style II, emerges, homogenous from Italy to the Nordic countries.[89]

Style I artefacts from the Continental and Anglo-Saxon regions, usually relief brooches, can be divided into two categories. The first includes the Nordic brooches, imported or copied (fig. 2), the second the Continental/Anglo-Saxon brooches with their own independent development of the Nordic Style I (fig. 3). The Nordic brooches (whether "originals" or "replicas") have been found distributed along the Rhine, as well as in areas like Alemannia and Thüringia, and even southern England, once it had been settled by the Anglo-Saxons.[90] The Continental Style I is prevalent in Pannonia, where it can be linked to the Lombards' presence, and also in the Alemannic regions of south-west Germany, but it is also widespread over many other parts of the Continent and southern England.[91] On the Continent these Style I brooches were in circulation

---

[88] A fuller study of the styles can be found in G. Haseloff, "Stand der Forschung Stilgeschichte Völkervanderungs- und Merowingerzeit", *Festskrift til Thorleif Sjøvold på 70-årsdagen*, Eds. M. Høgestøl, J.H. Larsen, E. Straume and B. Weber (Universitetets Oldsaksamlings Skrifter 5) (Oslo, 1984).

[89] B. Salin, *Die altgermanische Thierornamentik* (Stockholm and Berlin, 1904), see also U. Lund Hansen, "Die Hortproblematik im Licht der neuen Diskussion zur Chronologie und zur Deutung der Goldschätze in der Völkerwanderungszeit", *Der historische Horizont der Götterbild-Amulette aus der Übergangsepoche von der Spätantike zum Frühmittelalter*, ed. K. Hauck (Göttingen, 1992), p. 187 with literature.

[90] Hines, *The Scandinavian Character of Anglian England in the pre-Viking Period*, U. Näsman, *Glas och Handel i Senromersk tid och Folkvandringstid* (Uppsala, 1984), map 10; U. Näsman, "Sea trade during the Scandinavian Iron Age. Its character, commodities and routes", *Aspects of Maritime Scandinavia AD 200–1200*, ed. O. Crumlin-Pedersen (Roskilde, 1991), fig. 8.

[91] Haseloff, *Die germanische Tierornamentik der Völkervanderungszeit*, Abb. 359. It is worth

Fig. 1. Fibula from Zealand, Denmark (after Salin 1935, Abb. 134).
Fig. 2. Fibula from Bifrons, grave 41, Kent (after Haseloff 1981, Abb. 25).
Fig. 3. Fibula from Tamasi, grave 7, Hungary (after Haseloff 1981, Abb. 492).

Fig. 4. Gold bracteate from Maglemose/Gummersmark, Denmark (after Hauck et al. 1985-89, Abb. 300).

Fig. 5. Gold bracteate from Gunheim, Norway (after Hauck et al. 1985-89, Abb. 263).

Fig. 6. Fibula from Frederikshald, Norway (Style I/II) (after Salin 1935, Abb. 131).

much longer than in Scandinavia, and developed into Style II,[92] a slow-curving, interlaced animal design of ribbon-like form, executed in carved bronze.[93] The completeness of detail, the delicate execution of the work, and the precision in the shaping indicate some correspondence to a given idea, as is found for example, in Classical Greek pottery.[94]

Besides the brooches, Nordic gold bracteates are also to be found dispersed over much of the Continent, from England to Hungary and the Ukraine.[95] The iconography of the bracteates, in contrast to that of the brooches, can be interpreted in terms of scenes from Nordic mythology, revolving around the war-god and the prince of the gods, Odin (fig. 4),[96] which suggests that the Nordic pantheon and mythology documented in the Early Scandinavian Middle Ages were already present in the Migration Period. The bracteates have been interpreted as a political medium, used in situations where political relations were made manifest, namely, on the occasion of great feasts held in association with religious cerimonies and demonstrations of loyalty.[97] Although their motifs and designs are unmistak-

---

mentioning the gilded silver brooch in Scandinavian or Anglo-Saxon style from grave 10, Saint-Brice, Tournai, the site of Childeric's grave (R. Brulet, et al., "Das merowingische Gräberfeld von Saint-Brice", *Tournai, die Stadt des Frankenkönigs Childerich. Ergebnisse neue Ausgrabungen. Katalog*, ed. R. Pirling (Krefeld, 1990), Abb. 28; depicted in James, *The Franks*, p. 102).

[92] The first typological and chronological distinction between the animal styles in Styles I and II was made by Salin, *Die altgermanische Thierornamentik*.

[93] Lund Hansen. "Die Hortproblematik im Licht der neuen Diskussion zur Chronologie und zur Deutung der Goldschätze in der Völkerwanderungszeit", p. 187.

[94] For references, see Shanks, "Style and the design of a perfume jar from an archaic Greek city state".

[95] Haseloff, *Die germanische Tierornamentik der Völkervanderungszeit*, Abb. 92.

[96] K. Hauck, "Götterglaube im Spiegel der goldenen Brakteaten", *Sachsen und Angelsachsen* (Veröffentlichungen des Helms-Museums 32) (Hamburg, 1978), pp. 189–218; K. Hauck, "Die Wiedergabe von Göttersymbolen und Sinnzeichen der A-, B- und C-Brakteaten auf D- und F-Brakteaten exemplarisch erhellt mit Speer und Kreuz", *Frühmittelalterliche Studien* 20 (1986), pp. 476–512; K. Hauck, "Gudme in der Sichte der Brakteaten-Forschung", *Frühmittelalterliche Studien* 21 (1987), pp. 147–181; M. Axboe, "Goldbrakteaten und Dänenkönige", *Iconologia Sacra, Festschrift für Karl Hauck zum 75. Geburtstag*, eds. H. Keller and N. Staubach (Berlin and New York, 1994), pp. 144–155; M. Axboe and A. Kromann, "DN ODINN PF AUC? Germanic, Imperial Portraits on Scandinavian Gold Bracteates", *Acta Hyperborea. Danish Studies in Classical Archaeology* 4 *Ancient Portraiture Image and message* (Copenhagen, 1992), pp. 271–305; L. Hedeager, *Skygger af en anden virkelighed. Studie i oldnordiske og tidligeuropæiske myter* (Copenhagen, 1997).

[97] A. Andrén, "Guld och makt—en tolkning av de skandinaviska guldbrakteaaternas funktion", *Samfundsorganisation og Regional Variation. Norden i Romersk Jernalder og Folkevandringstid*, eds. C. Fabech and J. Ringtved (Århus, 1991), pp. 245–256.

ably Nordic, the bracteates have their origin in Late Antique art and Byzantine emperor-medallions (fig. 5).[98]

Many of the Germanic peoples on the Continent and in England will have had an understanding of the depictions on the bracteates and the brooches. From about the beginning of the fifth century up until the seventh, the Nordic figurative world was used as a symbolically significant, style amongst the migrating Germanic peoples. It was imitated and elaborated becoming an impressive elite style. Surprisingly, "new" peoples, with no connection to the Scandinavian origin myth—for instance, the Franks—did not adopt animal ornament in their symbolic language, but instead used a bird the Roman or Gothic eagle.

Once animal style is accepted as an important aspect of social praxis and the ideology, then the more conventional art-historical analyses of animal ornament can be seen as inadequate, because they fail to take social contexts into consideration. They refer in a descriptive way to the background of the animal style simply in terms of "social contacts" or "trading contacts", and their prevailing assumption is of a diffusion of cultural attributes.[99] If we accept that style is meaningful, the same must apply to changes in style such changes then become central to our understanding of social and political changes. If, however, style is perceived instead as mere decoration, devoid of meaning, then explanations such as diffusion, "change in taste" or "trade" have to be found. The break in style thus loses its analytical significance, and continuous style development remains the focus of research centred on making up chronologies.[100] This has been the fate of Germanic animal style.[101] Research has over-

---

[98] K. Hauck, *Die Goldbrakteaten der Völkerwanderungszeit* (München, 1985–86).

[99] Shanks, "Style and the design of a perfume jar from an archaic Greek city state", p. 101.

[100] Chronologies are a necessary part of archaeological research, but stylistic studies become unfruitful when the cultural-historical aspects are not taken into consideration.

[101] E.g. Salin, *Die altgermanische Thierornamentik*; M. Ørsnes, Südskandinavische Ornamentik in der jüngeren Germanischen Eisenzeit. *Acta Archaeologica* 40 (1969), pp. 1–121; Haseloff, *Die germanische Tierornamentik der Völkerwanderungszeit*; W. Menghin, *Das Schwert im Frühen Mittelalter. Chronologisch-typologische Untersuchungen zu Langschwertern aus germanischen Gräbern des 5. bis 7. Jahrhunderts n.Chr.* (Wissenschaftliche Beibänder zum Anzeiger des Germanischs Nationalmuseums 1) (Stuttgart, 1983) and many others; for exceptions see e.g. K. Høilund Nielsen, "Centrum og periferi i 6.-8.årh. territoriale studier af dyrestil og kvindesmykker i yngre germansk jernalder i Syd- og Østskandinavien", *Høvdingesamfund og Kongemagt*, eds. P. Mortensen and B. Rasmussen (Fra Stamme til Stat i Danmark 2; Jysk Arkæologisk Selskab Skrifter XXII:2) (Århus, 1991) pp. 127–154.

looked the significance of the two most striking changes in the style's
development, which coincide with the beginning and the end of the
'Migration Period', and are represented by Nydam Style/Style I and
Style II.

The beginning of the Migration Period, during the first half of
the fifth century, is marked by the introduction of animal ornament,
in the form of a contorted multi-faceted single animal (Nydam Style/
Style I), whilst at the end of the Migration Period, the animal depiction, produced with remarkable uniformity throughout Europe, is
distorted almost beyond recognition into a twisted pattern where the
four-legged animal as the main element in the composition has disappeared (Style II) (fig. 6). The phasing-out of animal depiction represents the conclusion of a long developmental sequence. The main
difference between the two stylistic traditions is that the animal is
the central motif in Style I, while in Style II the animals are eclipsed
by complex ornamental patterns.

The origins of Style II (= Vendel Style A–C) have been much
debated some experts have ascribed them to Scandinavia,[102] some to
Late-Roman art[103] or to Italy (the Lombards),[104] others to the south-
west Alemannic regions.[105] On the whole, this debate reveals that
the new style was so homogenous that it is impossible to isolate a
distinct "region of innovation" in Europe, even if most scholars agree
in dating its appearance to the latter half of the sixth century
(560/70).[106] But once linked to their broad historical context, the rise
and decline of Style I and Style II become meaningful. The arrival
and the departure of early Germanic animal ornament (Nydam Style/
Style I) covers the influential period between the Huns' intervention

---

[102] G. Arwidsson, *Vendelstile, Email und Glas* (Valsgärdestudien I) (Uppsala, 1942).

[103] S. Lindqvist, *Vendelkulturens Ålder och Ursprung*, (Kungl. Vitterhets Historie och
Antikvitets Akademien:s Handl. 36:I) (Stockholm, 1926).

[104] N. Åberg, *The Occident and the Origin in the Art of the Seventh century, II. Lombard
Italy* (Uppsala, 1946); J. Werner, *Münzdatierte austrasische Grabfunde* (Germanische
Denkmäler der Völkerwanderungszeit 3) (Berlin/Leipzig, 1935); G. Haseloff, "Die
langobardischen Goldblattkreuze. Ein Beitrag zur Frage nach dem Ursprung von
Stil II", *Jahrbuch des Römisch-germanischen Zentralmuseums Mainz* 3 (1956), pp. 143–163.

[105] Haseloff, *Die germanische Tierornamentik der Völkervanderungszeit*, pp. 597ff; Haseloff,
"Stand der Forschung Stilgeschichte Völkervanderungs- und Merowingerzeit",
p. 117; Lund Hansen, "Die Hortproblematik im Licht der neuen Diskussion zur
Chronologie und zur Deutung der Goldschätze in der Völkerwanderungszeit",
p. 187.

[106] A summary can be found in Lund Hansen, "Die Hortproblematik im Licht
der neuen Diskussion zur Chronologie und zur Deutung der Goldschätze in der
Völkerwanderungszeit"; this author, however, dates the transitional period to 520/30.

in Europe and the period of the last great migrations, namely the Lombards' conquest of Italy (568). The development of animal style is therefore closely linked to historically turbulent periods of great social change and the establishment of new kingdoms. The style, on the one hand, demonstrated similarities between the migrating warrior elite, and, on the other, marked distinctions between different groups.

Nydam Style/Style I is, like Style II, remarkably uniform, and both styles are found on jewellery and weapons from most parts of Europe. Animal style must have represented a common elite ideology combining the many conflicting and competing groups in the Migration Period and the early Middle Ages. These various elite groups must have been connected by political alliances and marriage ties which were strengthened by being anchored in a common symbolic language and—presumably—common rituals.[107]

Style II continued into the late seventh century, and from then on, it is no longer possible to define a common Germanic animal style. Once Catholic Christianity had put down firm roots, the pagan Nordic origin myth was bound to lose its official political-ideological significance. With the Frankish realm's consolidation as the main heir to the Western Roman Empire, there came to an end the political processes in which Nordic myths and symbols played an organising role in establishing political legitimacy for most Germanic groups in Central and Western Europe. From now on, it was to be Christian myths, stories and symbolic language which served to legitimate the socio-political order. A new iconographic style developed accordingly one that blended insular with Frankish elements, and was closely connected to the Irish/Anglo-Saxon mission which began in Frisia in 678/79 and reached Central and South Germany during the first half of the eighth century.

While this style was so indisputably linked with missionary activity, and can be found on a lengthy series of different ecclesiastical objects, it is not restricted to "church art" alone. A wide variety of secular objects of precisely the same kind as earlier were now decorated with this new Christian style dress accessories, riding equipment, stirrups, spurs, bracelets and so on, thus signalled a new form of ideological legitimisation for their owners. Southern Scandinavia,

---

[107] Earle "Style and iconography as legitimation in complex chiefdoms", p. 78.

in particular, was not uninfluenced by the ideological attachment to Latin Christendom of the European warrior elite and their powerful rulers. Though Nordic animal style continued independently, with the disintegrated animal figures being to some extent recreated to recover their zoomorphic character, the new style from the eighth century onwards absorbed some insular elements, such as decorative plant motifs. In Scandinavia a pagan warrior elite and a fragmented state structure persisted during the Viking Age and pagan myths and iconographic symbols—the animal style—therefore continued to play an organizing role in the cosmology of this warrior society, up to the end of the Viking Period. Although still in use, the Nordic animal style ceased to develop from around 1100 and ended with the consolidation of both Christianity and medieval kingdoms in Scandinavia around 1200, as reflected in the new "official" history written by Saxo and Snorre and the adoption of the Romanesque art style with its unambiguous Christian symbols.[108] In what follows we shall examine how myths and material culture both played their part in the shaping of new political ideologies of cultural identity and ethnic homogeneity.

Migration Period Europe the formation of a political mentality

Political realities amongst the Germanic peoples seem to have been even more complex than those presented at the beginning of this article in the discussion of "ethnic homogeneity" in Migration Period Europe. This complexity is perhaps best illustrated through the difficulties incurred by late Roman authors when they attempted to depict an extremely variegated scene.[109] On two separate occasions Claudian gave an account of the different tribes that congregated round Alaric at the beginning of his career in the Danube regions. In one of these accounts he mentioned Sarmatians, Dacians, Massagetae, Alani, Geloni and Getae, and in the other, Visi, Bastarnae, Alani, Chuni, Sarmatians, Geloni and Getae. In much the same way Sidonius Apollinaris named the tribes along the Danube as being

---

[108] L. Karlsson, *Nordisk Form* (Statens Historiska Museum, studies 3) (Stockholm, 1983), p. 81.
[109] Heather, *The Huns and the end of the Roman Empire in Western Europe*. The following is mainly based on this study.

the Bastarnae, Sueves, Pannonii, Neuri, Chuni, Getae, Daci, Halani, Bellonoti, Rugi, Burgundi, Vesi, Aliti, Bisalti, Ostrogothi, Procrusti, Sarmatae and Moschi. Even if some of this can be credited to a literary tradition,[110] it indicates that these and other authors' general understanding of the Germanic peoples, an understanding we have inherited from them, as large, ethnic, well-defined and homogenous *gentes* or nations, does not accord with fourth- and early fifth-century historical realities in Central Europe. From this multitude, during the course of the fifth century, some of these tribes grew into historically well attested kingdoms, for instance, those of the Ostrogoths, the Visigoths, the Burgundians, the Vandals and, last but not least, the Franks.

All this was not, however, the result of successive concentrations of power or the expansion of some groups at the expense of others. It was a long and discontinuous process, in which the various groups and kingdoms, torn by internal conflict and liable to fragment, frequently replaced one another. Some disappeared completely, others for a short time, to reappear in the literary texts at a later date as having survived after all, or as resuming their old tribal names or political identities. Peter Heather has shown how such groups, willingly or by force, could give up their political autonomy for a while, as happened with the Heruli, the Goths and the Rugi. In the case of the Rugi, a group that followed Theoderic from the Balkans to Italy in 489, Procopius wrote (c. 540):

> These Rogi . . . in ancient times used to live as an independent people. But Theoderic had early persuaded them, along with certain other nations, to form an alliance with him, and they were absorbed into the Gothic nation and acted in common with them in all things against their enemies. But since they had absolutely no intercourse with women other than their own, each successive generation of children was of unmixed blood, and thus they had preserved the name of their nation among themselves.[111]

During a period of approximately 60 years it seems that the Rugi succeeded through sheer will-power in holding on to an independent identity separate from both the Ostrogoths and the Romans in

---

[110] Heather, *The Huns and the end of the Roman Empire in Western Europe.*
[111] Procopius, *Wars* 7.2.1–3, cited and translated in Heather, *The Huns and the end of the Roman Empire in Western Europe.* Cf. Heather, "Theoderic, king of the Goths, p. 155.

Italy. Nor is this case unique some other tribes managed to do the same, giving up their political autonomy yet retaining their identity, as for instance, the Goths and several other peoples did when they came under the control of the Huns. Priscus' account confirms that the Huns' political and economic dominance was established by force, yet most of the existing social hierarchy of the many Gothic groups remained unchanged, thus maintaining their internal structure, and, through that, their sense of identity.[112]

Heather's research into the ethnic identity of tribes and peoples which, according to the literary texts, disappeared only to re-emerge many decades later, has led him to distance himself from the interpretation of ethnicity as something for the most part individually chosen.[113] Sometimes, it is manipulable by individuals (or groups), but sometimes not. Furthmore, it is capable of operating at greatly differing strengths. Distinctive ethnic character is sometimes thought of by modern analysts as a socially inherited factor, on the whole unchanging, hence outside the individual's capacity to alter at will. Heather underlines, as does Pohl,[114] that it is through military action that the (male) individual demonstrates his identity.

If this interpretation is accepted, origin myths suddenly become more intelligible. They represented a sort of cultural inheritance which could preserve a collective identity through periods of social and political stress. While such an identity may have been related originally to a specific "ethnic" elite, new political groups could take shape during the Migration Period around a core of ethnic tradition, which would now bind together tribes with separate backgrounds in a new political partnership. Myths, by connecting the past with the present, provided the political-ideological element needed to erect and maintain these kaleidoscopic groups of peoples as political units. This again implies that origin myths cannot have been conjured out of thin air, were not pure fiction or mere literary compilations. Rather, they represented an ancient wisdom for at least a minority of the new "peoples", and must have contained a kernel of historical truth and recognisability/familiarity if they were to serve as sources

---

[112] Heather, *The Huns and the end of the Roman Empire in Western Europe.*

[113] E.g. F. Barth, "Introduction", *Ethnic Groups and Boundaries*, ed. F. Barth (Oslo and London, 1969), pp. 9–38; R. Wenskus, *Stammesbildung und Verfassung* (Köln, 1961); Geary, "Ethnic identity as a situational construct in the Early Middle Ages".

[114] Pohl, "Tradition, Ethnogenese und literarische Gestaltung eine Zwischenbilanz", p. 24.

of legitimisation. This relationship of myth to group-identity is high-lighted from another angle by the Nordic contents and development of the Migration Period's Germanic style. Early Nordic, pagan, iconog-raphy, must have had, like myth, an organisational role in the build-ing of the new Germanic kingdoms from around the year 400, and must have functioned as an active element in the political legitimi-sation of a Continental elite, whose official religious universe was Christian.

The creation of, or re-emphasis on, the Germanic royal genealo-gies with their divine pagan origins was a further link in this strate-gic legitimisation, a necessary condition for the emergence of royal power and its power strategies, even for Christian kings. Even if, for example, the Amals' genealogy was extensively manipulated, and even if there is nothing to indicate that the dynasty was more than a few generations old when Cassiodorus wrote about it,[115] this does not necessarily entail that all the kings listed there were merely fictional.[116] As Heather argues, even Jordanes' propaganda in the *Getica* could not completely obscure the fact that there was an inter-val of forty years in the Amal family's tenure of power, and this coincided with the time during which the Goths had actually lost their political independence, and therefore also their kings, through being under Hunnic rule. The Migration Period's Nordic Germanic myths were however not based purely on ancient stories. They were recreated in light of the violent historical events that shook Europe, and in that way were manipulated to take on a new, more con-temporary perspective.

The encounter with the Huns was of vital importance in the cre-ation of the early medieval Germanic kingdoms and their traditions, whether within or far beyond the boundaries of the Roman Empire. The first half of the fifth century, when the then independent Ger-manic peoples met a military power which was neither Germanic nor Roman, and which was stronger than themselves, was on the one hand extremely traumatic, and on the other hand represented an experience shared by a large proportion of the Germanic peo-ples in Europe. It is these violent events, and responses to Attila,

---

[115] Heather, "Cassiodorus and the rise of the Amals Genealogy and the Goths under Hun domination"; Heather, "Theoderic, king of the Goths".

[116] Wolfram, "*Origo et religio.* Ethnic traditions and literature in early medieval texts".

that make up the first layer of historical reality in the shared traditions of Germanic epic poetry. Other layers and new events emerged over the course of the two following centuries. This means that the many Germanic legends with traces of the history of Europe from the fifth and sixth century can hardly have come to the Nordic regions as literary borrowings to be written down, but surely must be much older than the twelfth or thirteenth centuries.[117] They have their roots in the common historical experiences of northern and central Europe.

A selection of the violent and macabre historical events, and some of the great figures, of the Migration Period were transformed into the language of myth, as an expression for the self-perception, ethics and morals, shared by the warrior elite among the Germanic peoples. The myths were not mere entertainment in the halls of kings, they were the language of the gods, a core for the new socio-cosmological order, building a leading group amidst the turbulence of the later fourth and fifth centuries.[118] But when the migrations ceased with the Lombards' move into Italy, and as the Germanic kingdoms came to be reasonably clearly defined geographically, the production and renewal of the legends also ceased. Thereafter, the stories lived on in unchanging form, to be integrated later into the European literary tradition.

Concluding remarks

Origin myths, royal genealogies, mythical tales and legends, together with the symbolic language of animal style, ought to be perceived as the ideological articulation of a new Germanic warrior-elite and

---

[117] Analysis of the medieval legend cycles has largely focused on explaining their Continental origin in terms of later diffusion to the North, whether as a result of the Viking Age trading routes of the ninth century linking the Frankish Empire and Denmark, or of earlier contacts through Eastern Europe to Sweden in the sixth century (Wamers, "Die Völkervanderungszeit im Spiegel der germanischen Heldensagen", p. 86; Lukman, *Skjoldunge und Skilfinger. Hunnen- und Herulerkönige in Ostnordischer Überlieferung*). According to Andrén's analysis, the rune stones (from c. 800), and the rituals associated with the great Swedish boat burials from Vendel and Valdgärde (from ca. 600), reflected the heroic myth in the Sigurd Legend. Cf. also Hedeager, "The creation of Germanic identity", where a common mythological basis in the Nordic regions and on the Continent during the sixth, seventh and eighth centuries, is argued for.

[118] Frands Herschend (*The Idea of the Good in Late Iron Age Society*, (Occasional

the prerequisite for the emergence of Germanic royalty. In their own way, they played an organisational role in the establishment of the new Germanic kingdoms and served to demonstrate common cultural codes.[119]

Whilst the myths were the warrior-elites' political ideology and a type of legitimisation performed on special occasions, the iconography of animal style functioned in an overt context, depicting a Nordic symbolic universe and a shared Germanic identity among the elite. In this way myths and iconography complemented each other. The fifth and sixth centuries were to a great extent characterised by contact between the various parts of Europe, from Italy in the south to Norway in the north. A universe of shared experience was created, in sharp contrast to the segmented and divided Europe that some researchers have wanted to identify from the historical sources. In today's research on material culture, Nordic iconography sheds new light on the interpretation of the historical sources.[120]

The close connection between the creation of myths and the creation of symbols/iconography was emphasised by the separate social and political developments in the Nordic regions and in Central Europe in the centuries that followed. In Central Europe the creation of myth and the development of Nordic iconography gradually ceased

---

Papers in Archaeology 15) (Uppsala, 1998)) discusses the creation of kingship among the North European peoples in the Late Iron Age. He explains the role of poetry as part of aristocratic hall-life, and the hall as a royal symbol developing in the Migration Period.

[119] Theoderic's mausoleum in Ravenna is decorated with a frieze around the dome depicting stylised 'birdheads' like those on some of the Nydam Style/Style I brooches from Scandinavia, to which Guy Halsall kindly drew my attention during an ESF-meeting in Ravenna. Later on, I realised that Johannes Brøndsted, in his fundamental book on Danish prehistory, mentions this (Brøndsted, J., *Danmarks Oldtid III: Jernalderen* (Copenhagen, 1960). The explanation of this similarity can, of course, be further discussed.

[120] If the context described above, linking the appearance of a new "international" iconography in the material culture, historical-political changes, and myth-construction, is transposed into other historical and prehistoric epochs, it will allow for new possibilites and new interpretations for numerous archaeological phenomena, for instance, the development and distribution of La Tène culture, Scythian animal ornament, Mycenaean culture, Urnemark culture and the Tumulus cultures. The model could apply for all of these, in that during a relatively short period of time a new ritual universe and a new cosmology were established which covered most parts of Europe and similarly left behind traces in the early heroic and historic literature. These periods, like the Migration Period, have suffered from archaeologists' tendency to focus on single-factor explanations trade, diffusion, migration etc. There are undoubtedly great opportunities for research here, and an untouched potential for interpretations from a more historical/contextual perspective.

as the new Germanic kingdoms consolidated and later integrated Christianity, whereas in the Nordic regions they persisted. Viking Age style continued to develop in a pagan universe, and in the same way, the legends and royal myths continued to be renewed. They ceased only with the consolidation (and written documentation) of the early medieval Christian Nordic kingdoms around the year 1200. A characteristic feature of "ancient" Nordic myths is that they are preserved in fossilised form on the Nordic periphery (the history of the Goths in Byzantium; *Beowulf* in England, the sagas of Iceland), whilst the more recent royal families and their genealogies dominate the later writing-up of Nordic mythology, by Saxo Grammaticus, for instance. Here the main characters from the "ancient" layers are reduced to minor roles or given new mythical functions. Thus in the Nordic regions, the myths and the symbolic production associated with them continued to play a central role in political ideology until the end of the Viking Age, or, more precisely, until the new Christian iconography (the Romanesque art style with its clear Christian symbolism) and Christian myths succeeded in gaining a foothold amongst the Germanic peoples on the Continent and in England.

BIBLIOGRAPHY

Primary sources

Cassiodorus, *Variae*, transl. S.J.B. Barnish (Liverpool, 1992).
Gregory of Tours, *The History of the Franks*, transl. L. Thorpe (Harmondsworth, 1974/1988).
Getica:: Jordanes, *The Gothic History*, transl. C.C. Mierow (Princeton, 1915).
The Laws of the Salian Franks, ed. K. Fischer Drew (Philadelphia, 1993).
Paul the Deacon, *The History of the Lombards*, transl. W.D. Foulke. (1917/1974).
Priscus, fragm., C.D. Gordon, *The Age of Attila* (Ann Arbour, 1960).
The History of the Danes. Saxo Grammaticus, Books I–IX, transl. Peter Fischer, edited and commented by Hilda E. Davidson (Cambridge, 1998) [first ed. 1979–80].
Widsith, ed. K. Malone (Copenhagen, 1962).

Secondary sources

Åberg, N., *Die Goten und Langobarden in Italien* (Uppsala, 1923).
——, *Førhistorisk Nordisk Ornamentik* (Uppsala, 1925).
——, *The Occident and the Origin in the Art of the Seventh century, II. Lombard Italy* (Uppsala, 1946).
Amory, P., "The meaning and purpose of ethnic terminology in the Burgundian laws", *Early Medieval Europe* 2 (1993), pp. 1–28.
Andrén, A., "Guld och makt—en tolkning av de skandinaviska guldbrakteaaternas funktion", *Samfundsorganisation og Regional Variation. Norden i Romersk Jernalder og Folkevandringstid*, eds. C. Fabech and J. Ringtved (Århus, 1991), pp. 245–256.

Arwidsson, G., *Vendelstile, Email und Glas* (Valsgärdestudien I) (Uppsala, 1942).

Axboe, M., "Goldbrakteaten und Dänenkönige", *Iconologia Sacra, Festschrift für Karl Hauck zum 75. Geburtstag*, eds. H. Keller and N. Staubach (Berlin and New York, 1994), pp. 144–155.

———, and A. Kromann, "DN ODINN PF AUC? Germanic, Imperial Portraits on Scandinavian Gold Bracteates", *Acta Hyperborea. Danish Studies in Classical Archaeology* 4 *Ancient Portraiture Image and message* (Copenhagen, 1992), pp. 271–305.

Barth, F., "Introduction", *Ethnic Groups and Boundaries*, ed. F. Barth (Oslo and London, 1969), pp. 9–38.

Bierbrauer, V., "Archäologie und Geschichte der Goten vom 1.–7. Jahrhundert", *Frühmittelalterliche Studien* 28 (1994), pp. 51–171.

Bloch, M. "Questions not to ask of Malagasy carvings", *Interpreting Archaeology*, eds. I. Hodder et al. (London, 1995), pp. 212–215.

———, "People into Places: Zafimaniry Concepts of Clarity", *The Anthropology of Landscape*, eds. E. Hirsch and M. OiHanlon (London, 1997 [1995]), pp. 63–77.

Boje Mortensen, L., *Civiliserede Barbarer. Historikeren Paulus Diaconus og hans forgængere.* (Studier fra Sprog og Oldtidsforskning) (Copenhagen, 1991).

Bóna, I., *Das Hunnenreich* (Stuttgart, 1991).

Brulet, R. et al., "Das merowingische Gräberfeld von Saint-Brice", *Tournai, die Stadt des Frankenkönigs Childerich. Ergebnisse neue Ausgrabungen. Katalog*, ed. R. Pirling (Krefeld, 1990), pp. 17–34.

Brøndsted, J., *Danmarks Oldtid III: Jernalderen* (Copenhagen, 1960).

Christie, N., *The Lombards* (Oxford, 1995).

Cohan, S. and L.S. Shires, *Telling Stories: Theoretical Analysis of Narrative Fiction* (London, 1988).

Conkey, M. and C. Hastorf, eds,. *The Use of Style in Archaeology* (Cambridge, 1990).

Croke, B., "Cassiodorus and the Getica of Jordanes", *Classical Philology* 82 (1987), pp. 117–134.

Daim, F., "Gedanken zum Ethnosbegriff", *Mitteilungen der anthropologischen Gesellschaft in Wien* 112 (1982), pp. 58–71.

———, ed., *Awarenforschungen I–II* (Wien, 1992).

DeMarrais, E., L.J. Castillo and T. Earle, "Ideology, materialization and power strategies", *Current Anthropology*, forthcoming.

Dickinson, T. and H. Härke, *Early Anglo-Saxon Shields* (London, 1992b).

Earle, T., "Style and iconography as legitimation in complex chiefdoms", *The Use of Style in Archaeology*, eds. M. Conkey and C. Hastorf (Cambridge, 1990), pp. 61–72.

Finnegan, R., *Oral Traditions and the Verbal Arts* (London and New York, 1992).

Foley, J.M., *The Singer of Tales in Performance* (Bloomington, 1995).

Gasparri, S., *La Cultura Tradizionale Dei Longobardi* (Spoleto, 1983).

———, *Lombard Inaguration Rituals*, Paper presented at the European Science Foundation meeting in Merida, 1994.

Geary, P., "Ethnic identity as a situational construct in the Early Middle Ages", *Mitteilungen der Anthropologischen Gesellschaft in Wien* 113 (1983), pp. 15–26.

———, *Before France and Germany. The creation and transformation of the Merovingian world* (Oxford, 1988).

Gerberding, R.A., *The Rise of the Carolingians and the Liber Historiae Francorum* (Oxford, 1987).

Goffart, W., *Barbarians and Romans* (Princeton, 1980).

———, *The Narrators of Barbarian History* (Princeton, 1988).

Gordon, C.D., *The Age of Attila* (Ann Arbour, 1960).

Hachmann, R., *Die Goten und Skandinavien* (Berlin, 1970).

Halsall, G., "The origins of the 'Reihengräberzivilisation' forty years on", *Fifth-Century gaul. A Crisis of Identity?*, eds. J. Drinkwater and H. Elton (Cambridge, 1992), pp. 196–207.

Härke, H., "Changing symbols in a changing society. The Anglo-Saxon weapon burial rite in the seventh century", *The Age of Sutton Hoo*, ed. M. Carver (Woodbridge, 1992a), pp. 149–166.

Harrison, D., "Dark Age Migrations and Subjective Ethnicity the Example of the Lombards", *Scandia* 57:1 (1991), pp. 19–36.

Haseloff, G., "Die langobardischen Goldblattkreuze. Ein Beitrag zur Frage nach dem Ursprung von Stil II", *Jahrbuch des Römisch-germanischen Zentralmuseums Mainz* 3 (1956), pp. 143–163.

——, *Die germanische Tierornamentik der Völkervanderungszeit* (Berlin and New York, 1981).

——, "Stand der Forschung Stilgeschichte Völkervanderungs- und Merowingerzeit", *Festskrift til Thorleif Sjøvold på 70-årsdagen*, Eds. M. Høgestøl, J.H. Larsen, E. Straume and B. Weber (Universitetets Oldsaksamlings Skrifter 5) (Oslo, 1984).

Hauck, K., "Götterglaube im Spiegel der goldenen Brakteaten", *Sachsen und Angelsachsen* (Veröffentlichungen des Helms-Museums 32) (Hamburg, 1978), pp. 189–218.

——, *Die Goldbrakteaten der Völkervanderungszeit* (München, 1985–86).

——, "Die Wiedergabe von Göttersymbolen und Sinnzeichen der A-, B- und C-Brakteaten auf D- und F-Brakteaten exemplarisch erhellt mit Speer und Kreuz", *Frühmittelalterliche Studien* 20 (1986), pp. 476–512.

——, "Gudme in der Sichte der Brakteaten-Forschung", *Frühmittelalterliche Studien* 21 (1987), pp. 147–181.

Heather, P., "Cassiodorus and the rise of the Amals Genealogy and the Goths under Hun domination", *Journal of Roman Studies* 79 (1989), pp. 103–128.

——, "The historical culture of Ostrogothic Italy", *Theoderico il Grande e i Goti D'Italia*. (Atti del XIII Congresso internazionale di studi sull'Alto Medioevo) (Spoleto, 1993), pp. 317–353.

——, *Goths and Romans 332–489* (Oxford, 1994[2]).

——, "Theoderic, king of the Goths", *Early Medieval Europe* 4 (1995), pp. 145–173.

——, "Disappearing and reappearing tribes", *Strategies of Distinction. The construction of ethnic communities, 300–800*, eds. W. Pohl with H. Reimitz (Leiden, 1998), pp. 92–111.

——, *The Huns and the end of the Roman Empire in Western Europe*, (forthcoming).

——, and J. Matthews, *The Goths in the Fourth Century* (Liverpool, 1991).

Hedeager, L., "Kingdoms, ethnicity and material culture, Denmark in a European perspective" *The Age of Sutton Hoo*, ed. M. Carver (Woodbridge, 1992), pp. 279–300.

——, "The creation of Germanic identity. A European origin myth", *Frontiéres D'Empire. Nature et signification des frontiéres romaines*, eds. P. Brun, S. van der Leeuw, C. Whittaker (Mémoires du Musée de Préhistoire d'lle-de-France 5) (Nemours, 1993), pp. 121–132.

——, *Skygger af en anden virkelighed. Studie i oldnordiske og tidligeuropæiske myter* (Copenhagen, 1997).

——, "Odins offer. Skygger af en shamanistisk tradition i nordisk folkevandringstid", *TOR* 29 (1997), pp. 275–278.

——, "Cosmological endurance: Pagan identities in Early Christian Europe", *Journal of European Archaeology* 3 (1998), pp. 383–397.

——, "Scandinavia (c. 500–700 AD)", *New Cambridge Medieval History* I, ed. P. Fouracre (Cambridge, forthcoming).

Herschend, F.: The Idea of the Good in Late Iron Age Society, (Occasional Papers in Archaeology 15) (Uppsala, 1998).

Hill, J., "Widsið and the tenth century", *Neuphilologische Mitteilungen* 85 (1984), pp. 305–315.

Hines, J., *The Scandinavian Character of Anglian England in the pre-Viking Period* (British Archaeological Reports, British series 124) (Oxford, 1984).

——, "The Scandinavian Character of Anglian England An update", *The Age of Sutton Hoo*, ed. M. Carver (Woodbridge, 1992), pp. 315–330.

——, *Clasps, Hektespenner, Agraffen. Anglo-Scandinavian claps of classes A–C of the 3rd to the 6th centuries AD. Typology, diffusion and function* (Stockholm, 1993).

——, "The becoming of English Identity, material culture and language in Early Anglo-Saxon England" *Anglo-Saxon Studies in Archaeology and History* 7 (Oxford, 1994).

——, "Cultural change and social organisation in Early Anglo-Saxon England", *After Empire. Towards an Ethnology of Europe's Barbarians*, ed. G. Ausenda (Woodbridge, 1995), pp. 75–87.

Hobsbawm, E., "Introduction Inventing traditions", *The Invention of Traditions*, eds. E. Hobsbawm and T. Ranger (Cambridge, 19952), pp. 1–14.

——, and T. Ranger, eds., *The Invention of Traditions* (Cambridge, 1983)

Hodder, I., "Style as historical quality", *The Use of Style in Archaeology*, eds. M. Conkey and C. Hastorf (Cambridge, 1990), pp. 44–51.

Howe, N., *Migration and Mythmaking in Anglo-Saxon England*. (New Haven, 1989).

Høilund Nielsen, K., "Centrum og periferi i 6.-8.årh . . . territoriale studier af dyrestil og kvindesmykker i yngre germansk jernalder i Syd- og Østskandinavien", *Høvdinge-samfund og Kongemagt*, eds. P. Mortensen and B. Rasmussen (Fra Stamme til Stat i Danmark 2; Jysk Arkæologisk Selskab Skrifter XXII:2) (Århus, 1991) pp. 127–154.

James, E., *The Franks* (Oxford, 1991).

Karlsson, L., *Nordisk Form* (Statens Historiska Museum, studies 3) (Stockholm, 1983).

Kazanski, M., *Les Goths* (Paris, 1991).

Lewis, B., *History Remembered, Recovered, Invented* (Princeton, 1975).

Liebeschuetz, J.H.W.G., *Barbarians and Bishops* (Oxford, 1992).

——, "Alaric's Goths, nation or army?", *Fifth-Century Gaul A Crisis of Identity?*, eds. J. Drinkwater & H. Elton (Cambridge, 1992), pp. 75–83.

Lindqvist, S., *Vendelkulturens Ålder och Ursprung*, (Kungl. Vitterhets Historie och Antikvitets Akademien:s Handl. 36:I) (Stockholm, 1926).

Lowenthal, D., "'Trojan forebears', 'peerless relics'. The rhetoric of heritage claims", *Interpreting Archaeology*, eds. I. Hodder *et al.* (London, 1995), pp. 125–130.

Lukman, N., *Skjoldunge und Skilfinger. Hunnen- und Herulerkönige in Ostnordischer Überlieferung* (København, 1943).

——, *Ermanaric hos Jordanes og Saxo* (Studier fra Sprog- og Oldtidsforskning, Det Filologisk-Historiske Samfund 208) (København, 1949).

Lund Hansen, U., "Die Hortproblematik im Licht der neuen Diskussion zur Chronologie und zur Deutung der Goldschätze in der Völkerwanderungszeit", *Der historische Horizont der Götterbild-Amulette aus der Übergangsepoche von der Spätantike zum Frühmittelalter*, ed. K. Hauck (Göttingen, 1992), pp. 183–194.

Lundström, A., *Gravgåvorna i Vendel. Vendeltid* (Stockholm, 1980a).

——, *Gravgåvorna i Valdgärde* (Stockholm, 1980b).

Lönnroth, L., *Isländska Mytsagor. Översättning och kommentarer av Lars Lönnroth* (Stockholm, 1995).

Mann, M., *The sources of social Power. A history of power from the beginning to AD 1760* (Cambridge, 1986).

Menghin, W., *Das Schwert im Frühen Mittelalter. Chronologisch-typologische Untersuchungen zu Langschwertern aus germanischen Gräbern des 5. bis 7. Jahrhunderts n.Chr.* (Wissenschaftliche Beibänder zum Anzeiger des Germanischs Nationalmuseums 1) (Stuttgart, 1983).

——, *Die Langobarden. Archäologie und Geschichte* (Stuttegart, 1985).

Meulengracht Sørensen, P., "Moderen forløst af datterens skød", *Medeltidens Födelse*, ed. A. Andrén (Lund, 1989), pp. 263–275.

——, "Håkon den Gode og guderne. Nogle bemærkninger om religion og centralmagt i det tiende århundrede—og om religion og kildekritik", *Høvdingesamfund og Kongemagt*, eds. P. Mortensen and B. Rasmussen (Jysk Arkæologisk Selskabs Skrifter XXII:2) (Århus, 1991), pp. 235–244.

North, R., *Heathen Gods in Old English Literature* (Cambridge, 1997).

Näsman, U., *Glas och Handel i Senromersk tid och Folkvandringstid* (Uppsala, 1984).
——, "Analogislutning i nordisk jernalderarkæologi. Et bidrag til udviklingen af an nordisk historisk etnografi", *Jernalderens Stammesamfund*, eds. P. Mortensen and B. Rasmussen (Jysk Arkæologisk Selskabs Skrifter XXII:1) (Århus, 1988), pp. 123–140.
——, "Sea trade during the Scandinavian Iron Age. Its character, commodities and routes", *Aspects of Maritime Scandinavia AD 200–1200*, ed. O. Crumlin-Pedersen (Roskilde, 1991), pp. 23–40.
Ørsnes, M., *Südskandinavische Ornamentik in der jüngeren Germanischen Eisenzeit*. *Acta Archaeologica* 40 (1969), pp. 1–121.
Pohl, W., "Die Gepiden und die gentes an der mittleren Donau nach dem Zerfall des Attilareiches", *Die Völker an der mittleren und unteren Donau im fünften und sechsten Jahrhundert*, ed. H. Wolfram and F. Daim (Österreichische Akademie der Wissenschaften 145) (Wien, 1980), pp. 240–305.
——, "Tradition, Ethnogenese und literarische Gestaltung eine Zwischenbilanz", *Ethnogenese und Überlieferung*, eds. K. Brunner and B. Merta (Wien and München, 1994), pp. 9–26.
Ricoeur, P., *Time and Narrative*, vol. 3, trans. K. McLaughlin & D. Pellauer (Chicago, 1989).
Salin, B., *Die altgermanische Thierornamentik* (Stockholm and Berlin, 1935).
Shanks, M., "Style and the design of a perfume jar from an archaic Greek city state" *Journal of European Archaeology* 1 (1993), pp. 77–106.
——, and I. Hodder, "Processual, postprocessual and interpretive archaeologies", *Interpreting Archaeology. Finding meaning in the past*, ed. I. Hodder *et al.* (London, 1995), pp. 3–33.
Shennan, S., "Introduction. Archaeological approaches to cultural identity", *Archaeological Approaches to Cultural Identity*, ed. S. Shennan (One World Archaeology 10) (London, 1989), pp. 1–32.
——, ed., *Archaeological Approaches to Cultural Identity* (One World Archaeology 10) (London, 1989).
Svennung, J., *Jordanes und Scandia* (Stockholm, 1967).
——, "Jordanes und die gotische Stammsag", *Studia Gothica*, ed. U.E. Hagberg (Antikvariske Serien 25, Kungl. Vitterhets Historie och Antikkvitets Akademien) (Stockholm, 1972), pp. 20–56.
Teillet, S., *Des Goths á la nation gothique. Les origines de l'idée de nation en Occident du Ve au VIIe siécle* (Paris, 1984).
Tonkin, E., *Narrating our Pasts. The social construction of oral history* (Cambridge, 1995).
Vansina, J., *Oral Tradition A Study in Historical Methodology* (London, 1965).
——, *Oral Tradition as History* (London, 1985).
Veit, U., "Ethnic concepts in german prehistory a case study on the relationship between cultural identity and archaeological objectivity", *Archaeological Approaches to Cultural Identity*, ed. S.J. Shennan (One World Archaeology 10) (London, 1989), pp. 35–56.
Vestergaard, E., *Völsunge-Nibelungen Traditionen. Antropologiske studier i en episk traditions transformation i forhold til dens sociale sammenhæng* (Århus University, Unpublished Phd thesis 1992).
Veyne, P., *Did the Greeks believe in their Myths? An essay on the Constitutive Imagination* (Chicago and London, 1988).
Vries, J. de, *Altgermansiche Religionsgeschichte* (Berlin, 1956).
Wagner, N., *Getica. Untersuchungen zum Leben des Jordanes und zur frühen Geschichte der Goten* (Quellen und Forschungen zur Sprach- und Kulturgeschichte der germanischen Völker, N.F. 22) (Berlin, 1967).
Wamers, E., "Die Völkervanderungszeit im Spiegel der germanischen Heldensagen", *Germanen, Hunnen und Avaren* (Nürnberg, 1987), pp. 69–94.

Weibull, C., *Die Auswanderung der Goten aus Schweden* (Götenborg, 1958).

Weiner, A., *Inalienable Possessions. The Paradox of Keeping While Giving* (Berkeley and Los Angeles, 1992).

Wenskus, R., *Stammesbildung und Verfassung* (Köln, 1961).

Werner, J., *Münzdatierte austrasische Grabfunde* (Germanische Denkmäler der Völkerwanderungszeit 3) (Berlin/Leipzig, 1935).

——, *Beiträge zur Archäologie des Attila-Reiches* (München, 1956).

Wolfram, H., "The shaping of the early Medieval Kingdom" *Viator* 1 (1970), pp. 1–20.

——, *History of the Goths* (Berkeley, 1990).

——, "*Origo et religio*. Ethnic traditions and literature in early medieval texts", *Early Medieval Europe* 3 (1994), pp. 19–38

Wood, I., "Ethnicity and the ethnogenesis of the Burgundians", *Typen der Ethnogenese unter besonderer Berücksichtigung der Bayern* I, eds. H. Wolfram and W. Pohl (Vienna, 1990), pp. 53–69.

——, *The Merovingian Kingdoms, 450–751* (London and New York, 1994).

——, *Gregory of Tours* (Gwynedd, 1994a).

THE THEORETICAL STRENGTH AND PRACTICAL WEAKNESS OF THE VISIGOTHIC MONARCHY OF TOLEDO

Pablo C. Diaz and Mª.R. Valverde

The development of a royal propaganda programme in seventh-century Visigothic Hispania is in itself clear proof of the Visigothic monarchy's possession of a strong ideology in that period. It is obvious that only when a clearly defined concept of power exists can this be formulated for propaganda purposes, and, further, that in order to make the concept clearly visible, the existence of an independent and sovereign power structure with distinct government institutions is required. These preconditions, in the case of Visigothic Spain, appeared only when the kingdom of Toledo had taken shape. They reflected Visigothic political conceptions which, while they had undergone marked development, had not lost touch with the ideology and ruling practices of the Late Empire. Thus, even though from an early date the Visigoths were committed to kingship as their form of government, it was only from the late sixth century on that a monarchy now bent on consolidating an autonomous power structure began to create a political symbology of its own.

The transformation process undergone by this monarchy was a slow and gradual one.[1] When in 376 the Goths crossed the Danube and were admitted within the borders of the Empire by the emperor Valens, whatever form of monarchy may have been incipient among them was not yet a permanent institution, and had an elective character. The first testimonies we possess for the Goths, and the reliability of these is limited for they contain a mixture of history, myth and legendary traditions,[2] attribute a sacred character to royalty. This character was allegedly lost, and thereafter kings were elected when the state of war required a central authority whose concentrated

---

[1] Cf. E.A. Thompson, *The Early Germans* (Oxford, 1965); E.A. Thompson, *The Visigoths at the times of Ulfilas* (Oxford, 1966); H. Wolfram, *A History of the Goths* (Berkeley, 1988).

[2] Cf. T.S. Burns, *The Ostrogoths. Kingship and society* (Wiesbaden, 1980), p. 10.

command enabled it to face military necessities more effectively. The king's mission was none other than to lead his people in arms and, consequently, his right to power ceased when the war was over.[3] According to legend, the survival of kingship had until then been a consequence of historical circumstances: the long migration from the Baltic to the Black Sea, and subsequently down to the Danubian territories, brought about a situation of permanent conflict which made most Gothic tribes normally subordinate to kings. The irruption of the Huns had a strong impact on the process of Gothic ethnogenesis in 376,[4] causing the division of the Goths into two main branches from which the historical Visigoths and Ostrogoths would derive. Once the Goths were settled within the frontiers of the Roman Empire, monarchy was re-established among the Visigoths with Alaric. According to a view still widely current in the historiography, from this moment on and up to the year 418, when the Visigoths were settled by the Romans in the territory of Gaul with their centre at Toulouse, they were led in their journeyings by leaders who already gave enduring form to their status as kings, finding in the imperial government both a Roman magistracy which would help to mantain their pre-eminent position, and a territory in which to settle their followers for good. Against this view, T.S. Burns[5] has recently suggested that the fundamental aim of Alaric and of his immediate successors was to become Roman generals and that it was only the Imperial refusal to grant them such commanding offices within the Roman army that forced the Gothic leaders to base their government on kingship. Whatever interpretation we accept, the undeniable fact is that, throughout this period, the monarchy, profiting from military successes as well as from constant contact with the Roman world, had turned into the central and permanent institution of government: it had inaugurated the formation of a royal patrimony, the material basis indispensable for the strengthening of kingship; it had been able to attract the loyalty of an increasing number of followers, among which, in a parallel process, a sense of ethnic-political identity was emerging; and the Balth clan, claiming

---

[3] On the theory of "military rulership", see W. Schlesinger, *Beiträge zur deustchen Verfassungsgeschichte des Mittelalters* (Göttingen, 1963).

[4] *Cf.* P. Heather, *Goths and Romans. 332–489* (Oxford, 1991), pp. 10–17 and pp. 310–316.

[5] T.S. Burns, *Barbarians within the Gates of Rome. A Study of Roman Military Policy and the Barbarians, ca. 375–425 AD* (Bloomington and Indianapolis, 1994), pp. 247–279.

a divine or heroic descent, had monopolised the development of royal functions.[6] We could conclude from all this that "above all kingship was an office which responded to political change".[7]

The settlement of the Visigoths in Gaul by virtue of the treaty of alliance (*foedus*) of 418[8] established the profound and stable relationship between the Visigothic kings and a specific territory. The treaty implied the acknowledgement by the Visigoths of the emperor's political supremacy. In practice, however, the effective power which the Visigoths' military capacity conferred on them, together with the empire's abject weakness, allowed the Visigothic kings to put an end to the relationship of political dependence which attached them to Rome and progressively to assert a full sovereignty over the territories on which the Visigoths were settled. Processes of both territorial expansion and extending royal involvement in all aspects of life were simultaneously under way, while at the same time the exercise of royal authority was gradually being extended over Roman provincials. The demise of the Western Roman Empire in 476 brought with it the disappearance of the original duality of political formations, based on the *foedus*, and the kingdom of Toulouse obtained the recognition *de iure* of an independence which it already enjoyed *de facto*.[9] But although the Visigothic king already had a clear monopoly of power, there were no clear legal rules to regulate his relationship with his subjects. Inspired by imperial models, signs of prestige associated with the monarch began to appear, such as the adoption of the dating system based on regnal years used in the *Breviarium Alaricianum*, or the inclusion in this code of clearly imperial ways of addressing the Visigothic monarch, such as *gloriosissimus Dominus noster* (*Subscriptio*) or the king's reference to himself as *nostra clementia*. But as yet, and following logically from the lack of any political

---

[6] The process which allowed this degree of political evolution has been recently analyzed by Mª.R. Valverde, "De Atanarico a Valia, aproximación a los orígenes de la monarquía visigoda", *Studia Historica. Historia Antigua* 12 (1994), pp. 143–158.

[7] I. Wood, "Kings, kingdoms and consent", *Early Medieval Kingship*, eds. P.H. Sawyer and I. Wood (Leeds, 1977), p. 26.

[8] Burns, *Barbarians within the Gates of Rome. A Study of Roman Military Policy and the Barbarians, ca. 375–425 AD*, pp. 270–283.

[9] As was pointed out long since by M. Torres Lopez, "El estado visigótico. Algunos datos sobre su formación y principios fundamentales de su organización política", *Anuario de Historia del Derecho Español* 3 (1926), pp. 395–398, the disappearance of political duality was the result of a process which started almost at the same time as the arrangement of the *foedus*, and not of any granting of sovereignty by the Empire.

theory legitimising the sovereign, there was no systematic policy of royal propaganda promoted by the supreme power to reinforce its authority.

With the defeat of Alaric II by Clovis in the battle of Vouillé (507) the kingdom of Toulouse collapsed, and only after an initial stage, usually termed the Ostrogothic Interlude, which concluded when Athanagild managed to free himself from the Ostrogoths' protection, can we rightly speak of the Visigothic kingdom of Toledo. Leovigild's final securing of his position in 572 and the official conversion to Catholicism of his son Reccared in 589 were key moments in the process whereby the Visigothic kingdom of Toledo was consolidated as an independent, sovereign power in what had once been Roman imperial territory. The conversion of the Arian Visigothic monarchy to Catholicism only served to strengthen the policy of reinforcing royal power undertaken by Leovigild with the intention of establishing a stable, centralised monarchy in the Peninsula. One measure Leovigild adopted for this purpose was the surrounding of the monarchy with lavish external pomp: thus emerged a policy of royal display and propaganda which, always imitating imperial models, would be kept in force up to the disappearance of the Visigothic kingdom itself.

First and foremost, Leovigild appropriated Roman insignia of sovereignty to exalt the institution of monarchy. According to the testimony of Isidore of Seville, Leovigild was the first Visigothic monarch to imitate Roman-Byzantine court customs in this way: "among his men, he took his seat on a throne, dressed in royal clothing; for before him, style of dress and type of seat were common to the people and the kings".[10] If we relied on this reference alone, we might categorically affirm that the kingship of Leovigild involved a radical change as regards the externalisation of the sovereign power in visible signs. But a problem is posed when we read Sidonius Apollinaris' description of Leovigild's predecessor, Theodoric II (453–66). In his account, this monarch is not only presented to us in a lavish royal environment (the Audience Hall of the palace at Toulouse) but he is described as seated on a special seat or throne (*sella, solium*).[11]

---

[10] Isidorus, *Historia Gothorum, Wandalorum, Sueborum*, 51.

[11] Sidonius Apollinaris, *Epistolae* I, 2, 4: '*Reliquum mane regni administrandi cura sibi deputat. Circumsistit sellam conus armiger . . . Hora est secunda: surgit e solio aut thesauris inspiciendis uacaturus aut stabulis*'.

How can the discrepancy between the two bits of evidence be resolved? Since Sidonius did not mention the term *thronus*, P.S. Barnwell[12] maintains that before the end of the sixth century there is no evidence for any Visigothic king sitting on a throne. *Sella*, Barnwell points out, refers to a magistrate's chair and therefore the radical difference between Theodoric II and Leovigild is that the former saw himself as a Roman magistrate, while the latter put himself on the same level as the Emperor. An alternative (but not incompatible) solution focuses on Isidore's use of the phrase *inter suos*, which seems to suggest that what Leovigild did was to take his seat for the first time on a throne among his own people,[13] thereby introducing the Visigoths to the kind of ceremonial used by the Romans in similar circumstances. Such a reconstruction would perfectly fit Leovigild's attempt to reinforce his dominant position vis-à-vis the Visigothic nobility, whom he pretended to put on the same level as the Hispano-Roman one.[14] From our point of view, the two interpretations are not contradictory: rather, they emphasise the strong impulse given by Leovigild to the transformation of the Visigoths' ideology of monarchy. Only when the phase in which the federative relationship with the Empire was kept in force had been superseded, and only when the Visigothic monarchy had come to be associated with a territory, would the monarch become fully aware of the reach of his already independent sovereignty. Only then would he be able to manifest that sovereignty externally through lavish ceremonial which at the same time placed him above the rest of the nobility, so detaching him in an absolute way from ancient Germanic tradition in which the king was conceived as *primus inter pares*.

We must ask ourselves now which were the royal vestments (*regali ueste*) alluded to by Isidore and the use of which would identify the

---

[12] P.S. Barnwell, *Emperor, Prefects and Kings. The Roman West. 395–565* (London, 1992), pp. 73–74.

[13] *Cf.* M. McCormick, *Eternal Victory. Triumphal rulership in late antiquity, Byzantium and the early medieval West* (Cambridge, 1986), p. 299. This idea would be reinforced by the fact that in the account of Sidonius Apollinaris (*Epistolae* I, 2, 4) Theodoric II appears sitting in an elevated place to receive foreign ambassadors.

[14] See K.F. Stroheker, *Germanentum und Spätantike* (Zürich-Stuttgart, 1965), pp. 142–161, for whom Leovigild's establishment or reinforcement of royal ritual was directly aimed against the Gothic aristocracy. See also D. Claude, *Adel, Kirche und Königtum im Westgotenreich* (Sigmaringen, 1971), pp. 80–84; P.D. King, *Law and Society in the Visigothic Kingdom* (Cambridge, 1972), pp. 12–14; M. Reydellet, *La royauté dans la littérature latine de Sidoine Apollinaire à Isidore de Séville* (Roma, 1981), pp. 243–247.

figure of the king. To reconstruct them, and so understand their symbolic character, we must turn to various sources, on the assumption that this royal clothing probably didn't vary very much with Leovigild's succesors.[15] Seventh-century texts allude to the purple and the diadem as the essential elements. Both are mentioned in Visigothic legislation[16] and are probably behind expressions such as *uestem fulgentem*[17] and even *vestis fulgens regalia indumenta* or *regalis uestis*.[18] Isidore refers to the diadem, possibly with precious stones, by the expression *lumina lapillorum*,[19] luminosity that, again following imperial traditions, would give its bearer an almost divine significance.[20] The ruler thus offered a dazzling visual image of himself which constituted the best way to impress his subjects, arousing the admiration of the whole of the population for the institution of monarchy. It is revealing in this context that, as a sign of humiliation, the usurper Paulus, after his defeat by Wamba, had his head crowned with a diadem made of black leather.[21] The diadem similarly formed an important part of the monetary iconography of the Visigothic kings.[22] It can be argued that the die-makers simply imitated earlier coin moulds, but the coin-images may well have served as a model for the insignia kings actually used. The diadem also recurs in the representations of kings in early mediaeval manuscripts. Here two different kind of diadem appear: a two-horned one and another of a disk shape, beautifully decorated with motifs resembling precious

---

[15] The information supplied by Isidore of Seville in his *Etymologiae* about the purple toga and the chlamys (XVIII, 2, 5 and XIX, 24, 2), the sceptre (XVIII, 2, 5), the *paludamentum* (XIX, 24, 9), the *regillum* (XIX, 25, 19) and the crown (XIX, 30, 1), when referring to imperial insignia, cannot be alleged as a proof of such elements being kept in force throughout the Visigothic period.

[16] *Lex Visigothorum* I, 2, 6: . . . '*post diadema et purpuram gloriam et coronam*'.

[17] Isidorus, *Sententiarum libri tres* III, 48, 6.

[18] *Iulianus Toletanus, HistoriaWambae regis*, 20.

[19] Isidorus, *Sententiarum libri tres* III, 48, 6.

[20] As R. Teja, "Il ceremoniale imperiale", *Storia di Roma. L'età tardoantica. I. Crisi e trasformazioni* 3 (Torino, 1993), pp. 635–636 has pointed out, from Constantine onwards the golden diadem covered with pearls and precious stones, as well as the chlamys fastened by a round fibula (both elements are well documented in Visigothic monetary iconography) were unmistakable symbols of royal power, whose glittering (a reflection of the divine light) endowed the emperor with a supernatural character.

[21] Iulianus Toletanus, *Historia Wambae regis*, 30: . . . '*picea ex coreis laurea coronatus*'.

[22] G.C. Miles, *The coinage of the Visigoths of Spain. Leovigild to Achila II* (New York, 1952), pp. 51–53; F. Mateu y Llopis, "Los atributos de la realeza en los trémises godos y las categorías diplomáticas coetáneas", *Anales Toledanos. Estudios sobre la España visigoda* 3 (Toledo, 1971), pp. 150–158.

stones, for instance, in the portraits of Recceswinth appearing in the Codex Vigilianus illustrating the Ninth and Tenth Councils of Toledo.[23] The diadem and the purple seem, then, the indispensable elements to be borne by anyone who wished 'to get hold of the royal dignity', as the Spaniard Orosius put it when writing about imperial usurpers in the early fifth century.[24]

A problem is posed by the existence of golden crowns. The famous crowns of the Guarrazar treasure seem to have had an evidently votive character: it is necessary to stress here the Byzantine origin of the royal practice of placing crowns and votive crosses in churches. We are, therefore, confronted by another manifestation of *imitatio imperii* on the part of the Visigothic monarchy.[25] This may be true of other Visigothic crowns as well, as seems implied, for instance, by Julian of Toledo's reference[26] to the golden crown offered by Wamba to the body of S. Felix at Gerona and which the tyrant Paulus dared to put on his own head. Some scholars, relying only on this report of the behaviour of the rebel Paulus, as well as on the iconography of crowned busts on Visigothic coins,[27] prefer to think that the verb *coronare* in Isidore's reference to Reccared's succession,[28] clearly alludes to the imposition of a crown.[29] However, *corona* is curiously contrasted with *diadema* in the *Lex Visigothorum* (I,

---

[23] S. de Silva, "La más antigua iconografía medieval de los reyes visigodos", *Los visigodos. Historia y civilización. Antigüedad y Cristianismo* 3 (Murcia, 1986), pp. 537–544.

[24] Orosius, *Historia adversum paganos* VII, 40, 6.

[25] See P. Palol de Salellas, "Esencia del arte hispánico de época visigoda: romanismo y germanismo", *Settimane di Studi sull'Alto Medioevo* 3 (Spoleto, 1956), p. 122 and H. Schlunk, "Relaciones entre la Península Ibérica y Bizancio durante la época visigoda", *Archivo Español de Arqueología* 18 (1945), p. 202.

[26] Iulianus Toletanus, *Historia Wambae regis*, 26.

[27] Leovigild would be the first Visigothic king to appear on coins with a crown (see, G.C. Miles, *The coinage of the Visigoths of Spain. Leovigild to Achila*, p. 48 and p. 82), but, as P.D. King, *Law and Society in the Visigothic Kingdom*, p. 12, n. 7, has pointed out, 'the dependence of this upon Byzantine models renders it of doubtful value', provided that, of course, this value is not corroborated by other evidence.

[28] Isidorus, *Historia Gothorum, Wandalorum, Sueborum*, 52 (in both redactions): . . . '*Leuuigildo defuncto filius eius Recaredus regno est coronatus*'.

[29] E.A. Thompson, *The Goths in Spain* (Oxford, 1969), p. 220; C. Sanchez Albornoz, "La *ordinatio principis* en la España goda y postvisigoda", *Cuadernos de Historia de España* 35 (1962), pp. 6–9; G. Garcia Herrero, "Julián de Toledo y la realeza visigoda", *Arte, sociedad, economía y religión durante el Bajo Imperio y la Antigüedad tardía. Antigüedad y Cristianismo* 8 (Murcia, 1991), pp. 250–51; L.A. Garcia Moreno, "El estado protofeudal visigodo: precedente y modelo para la Europa carolingia", *L'Europe Héritière de l'Espagne wisigothique*, eds. J. Fontaine and Ch. Pellistrandi (Madrid, 1992), p. 28.

2, 6) to symbolise the opposition between divine glory and earthly glory. *Corona* is used in the same sense in the councils of Toledo,[30] where it is always associated with the idea of celestial reward. Besides, although, as we shall see, the rite of royal unction was certainly practised, the only reference in the Visigothic period to a coronation ritual is that made by Isidore in his *Etymologies*,[31] and this can hardly be used as evidence since it refers to the Roman imperial rite.

The place occupied by the sceptre among royal symbols is much better documented. The references of John of Biclar,[32] Isidore of Seville,[33] Julian of Toledo,[34] the *Lex Visigothorum*,[35] and the *Chronica regum visigothorum*,[36] show us a physical object, probably the one which among the royal insignia could be defined most accurately as an "inalienable possession",[37] but always in the symbolic sense, and not necessarily legitimating the monarchical authority in itself. The characteristics of this sceptre are not described in the texts, but from the kingship of Wamba onwards the cruciform sceptre is included in Visigothic monetary types[38] and this same element appears in miniatures representing kings Chintila, Chindaswinth, Recceswinth and Egica in early medieval manuscripts,[39] which might resolve any doubt

---

[30] *Concilium Toletanum* III (a. 589) *praefacio*, p. 110, *subscribtio*, p. 116 and *homelia sancti Leandri*, p. 139; *Concilium Toletanum* IV (a. 633), c. 41, p. 206; *Concilium Toletanum* VIII (a. 653), c. 12, p. 286; *Concilium Toletanum* X (a. 656), c. 7, p. 315 and *decreto pro Potamio episcopo*, p. 320; *Concilium Toletanum* XI (a. 675), *de relatione gratiarum*, p. 367; *Concilium Toletanum* XVI (a. 693), *praefacio*, pp. 495 and 496. All references to the Toletan councils come from the edition by J. Vives, *Concilios visigóticos e hispano-romanos* (Barcelona-Madrid, 1963).

[31] Isidorus, *Etymologiae* XIX, 30, 1–3.

[32] Iohannis abbatis biclarensis, *Chronica* 586, 2: . . . *'Reccaredus cum tranquillitate regni eius sumit sceptra'*.

[33] Isidorus, *Historia Gothorum, Wandalorum, Sueborum*, 57 (brief red.): . . . *'post Recaredum . . . Liuua regni suscepit sceptra*; 62 (long red.): . . . *Suinthila . . . regni suscepit sceptra'*; 70 (*recapitulatio*): . . . *'Sisebutus princeps regni sumpsit sceptra'*.

[34] Iulianus Toletanus *Insultatio vilis provincia Galliae* 3: *'subornas sceptrum'* . . . .

[35] *Lex Visigothorum* II, 1, 7: . . . *'cum divine voluntatis imperio principale caput regnandi sumat sceptrum'*.

[36] *Chronica Regum Visigothorum* 47: . . . *'gloriosus dominus noster Ervigius regni sceptra, quod fuit idus Octobris, luna XVI, era DCCXV[III] dilata unctiones sollemnitate usque in superviniente die dominico'*, where the physical appropriation of the sceptre means the first act defining his position as king, even before being officially anointed as such.

[37] A.B. Weiner, *Inalienable possessions. The paradox of keeping-while-giving* (Berkeley, 1992).

[38] See Miles, *The coinage of the Visigoths of Spain. Leovigild to Achila*, pp. 51–52 and E. Ewig, *Spätantikes und Fränkisches Gallien* (München, 1976), pp. 21–22.

[39] See S. de Silva, "La más antigua iconografía medieval de los reyes visigodos",

about the metaphorical nature of previous references. Besides, the texts when talking about the sceptre clearly differentiate between the acceptance of the kingdom or royal government,[40] and the acceptance of the royal dignity.[41]

If those were the usual symbols of royal dignity, this does not alter the fact that certain others existed which were temporarily used by the king. Royal insignia of a military kind referred by Julian of Toledo[42] and mentioned too in the *Liber Ordinum* come into this category. We find banners (*bandos suos*), among them those directly identifying the king, and the golden cross: *sed mox accedit diaconus ad altare, et leuat crucem auream, in qua lignum beate crucis inclusum est, que cum rege semper in exercitu properat.*[43] This is a reliquary with a piece of the True Cross, with which divine help was demanded, and which according to the liturgical text, in the late Visigothic period at least, "always goes forward swiftly with the king on campaign". From the letter sent by Gregory the Great to Reccared after his conversion to Catholicism we learn that the Pope sent the Visigothic king, together with some other relics, a fragment of the True Cross,[44] in all probability the same fragment we have just mentioned. Through this letter we also know about the series of gifts Reccared had previously sent to the bishop of Rome,[45] one of the rare examples preserved in Visigothic sources of the importance of gift exchange as a

---

pp. 537–558. Those illustrations show a long sceptre with a pommel of nail-head shape, except for one codex which represents Recceswinth holding a sceptre with a flaming hilt.

[40] Iulianus Toletanus, *Historia Wambae regis* 3: . . . '*regnumque suscipiens*' . . .; *Chronica Regum Visigothorum* 44: '*Suscepit autem dominus Wamba regni gubernacula*'. We do not exclude the possibility that there was another sceptre, but the texts do not reveal it.

[41] Iulianus Toletanus, *Historia Wambae regis* 4: . . . '*ad regni meruerit peruenisse fastigium . . . regale absumpsisse fastigium*' . . .

[42] Iulianus Toletanus, *Historia Wambae regis* 16: . . . '*regem sine signis non posse procedere. Ad quod ille commentabat, ideo illum cum bandorum signis absconditis accessisse*' . . .

[43] *Liber Ordinum* 48.

[44] Gregorius I Papa, *Epistolae* IX, 228, '*Crucem quoque latori praesentium dedimus vobis offerendam, in qua lignum dominicae crucis inest*' . . .

[45] Gregorius I Papa, *Epistolae* IX, 228, '*Beatus vero Petrus . . . quam libenter munera excellentiae vestrae susceperit . . . Vestra itaque oblatio quam sit grata ostenditis qui daturi aurum prius ex conversione gentis subditae animarum munera dedistis . . . Praeterea dona vestrae excellentiae, quae pauperibus beati Petri apostoli sunt transmissa, trecentas cucullas accepimus*' . . . Through the *Epistola Reccaredi Regis Visigothorum* included between the epistles of Gregorius Magnus (*Epistolae* IX, 227a) we know that he had sent also a '*calicem auream desuper gemmis ornatum*'.

prestige symbol. The greatness of monarchy was also expressed through the sumptuousness of the gifts the ruler had to offer[46] and, therefore, we must include generosity among the means used by the different Visigothic kings to exalt their royal power. These symbolic objects were of great importance: they made the king stand out above the rest of the aristocracy and set him apart from the rest of his subjects. They called to mind the transmission of royal power, the heritage of the Empire and even, after 589, the king's status as God's chosen one. Nevertheless, in the seventh century those objects were not enough to assure success or stability, nor were they a sufficient guarantee of tenure for the one who held them. In the words of Isidore of Seville: *Non statim utile est omne potestatis insigne, sed tunc vere est utile, si bene geratur.*[47]

Other mechanisms were developed to display the Visigothic monarchy and its theoretical strength. These must now be considered. Following once more the imperial model, Leovigild definitively consolidated the condition of Toledo as the kingdom's capital.[48] This fact in itself, however practical it might seem, also possessed symbolic importance and expressed the distinctive evolution of the Visigothic monarchy, already clearly territorialised, moving away from the Germanic model of a barbarian kingdom with a peripatetic court. Thus, the royal treasury was largely supplanted by the capital as the defining element of the sovereign authority: its holder had supreme power as well. The sources show this clearly. Gregory of Tours tells how Cloderic, after murdering his father Sigibert, sent an embassy to Clovis announcing his death with these words: "*Pater meus mortuus est, et ergo thesauros cum regno ejus penes me habeo*".[49] Shortly after, Gregory tells

---

[46] See M. Mauss, *The gift. Forms and functions of exchange in Archaic Societies* (London, 1954), pp. 3–4 and p. 59; G. Duby, *Guerreros y campesinos. Desarrollo inicial de la economía europea (500–1200)*, (Madrid, 1983), pp. 64–71. (English translation: *The Early Growth of the European Economy* (London, 1975).

[47] Isidorus, *Sententiarum libri tres* III, 48, 5: 'every symbol of power is not useful immediately, but [only] then is it truly useful if it is wielded well'.

[48] In 546 Theudis had already enacted at Toledo his law on legal costs, which leads C. Codoñer Merino, *El "De Viris Illustribus" de Ildefonso de Toledo. Estudio y edición crítica* (Salamanca, 1972), p. 58 to think that already at that time Toledo had become the capital of the Visigothic kingdom. It is usually mantained that it was Athanagild who first clearly took up residence in the city of Toledo. See J.F. Rivera Recio, "Encumbramiento de la sede toledana durante la dominación visigótica", *Hispania Sacra* VIII (1955), p. 13; J. Sanchez-Arcilla Bernal, *Temas de Historia de la Administración. I. Hispania romana y visigoda* (Madrid, 1983), p. 249.

[49] Gregorius Turonensis, *Historiarum libri X* 40: 'My father is dead, and I therefore have the treasure in my possession along with the realm'.

us that Clovis brought Sigibert's people under his dominion, after having obtained his treasury and kingdom.[50] John of Biclar, when recounting the conquest of Gallaecia by Leovigild, says that he *"suevorum gentem, thesaurum et patriam in suam redigit potestatem et Gothorum provinciam facit"*.[51] After the disaster of the battle of Vouillé (507) the so-called Ostrogothic Interval began with the appropriation of the royal Visigothic treasury by Theodoric the Great and its later removal to Ravenna,[52] and only when Athanaric recognised the independent sovereignty of Amalaric over the Peninsula was the treasure returned.[53] Conversely, the end of the Visigothic kingdom is linked, in the Rota Chronicle, to the falling of the city of Toledo into Muslim hands.[54] The suggestion of the anthropologist Annette Weiner[55] that certain precious possessions—such as gold, jewelry, furs or silk robes..., in short, objects always present in royal treasuries—constitute the material symbols which legitimate rank, may thus be valid for the Germanic monarchies in an early stage of their political evolution, but not for the period when they found themselves in a very advanced stage of territorialisation and had a complex political organisation already at their disposal, as is the case with the monarchy of Toledo. In that kingdom, the treasury continued to be a prestigious power symbol, but ceased to be the material element which legitimated sovereignty. Relevant here was the fact that the *thesaurus regalis* (the *res privata* of the Balt family during the period when the Visigothic kingdom was based in Toulouse) came to be regarded, in the kingdom of Toledo, as state property, being integrated, together with the royal estates, within the public *patrimonium*. This change was accomplished after the extinction of the Balt dynasty with the death of Amalaric.[56]

---

[50] Gregorius Turonensis, *Historiarum libri X* 40: *'Regnumque Sigiberti acceptum cum thesauris, ipsos quoque suae ditioni asciuit'*.

[51] Iohannus abbatis biclarensis, *Chronica* 585, 2: 'He brought the people of the Sueves, the treasure and the fatherland under his power made [their land] the province of the Goths'. This same association between treasury and monarchic power is stressed by John in regard to the Lombards (*Chronica* 573, 1) and Sueves (*Chronica* 576, 2), but never when talking about Visigoths.

[52] See R. D'Abadal, *Del reino de Tolosa al reino de Toledo* (Madrid, 1960), pp. 54–63 and L. Garcia Iglesias, "El intermedio ostrogodo en Hispania (507–549 d. C.)", *Hispania Antiqua* 5 (1975), pp. 93–95.

[53] Procopius, *Bellum Gothicum* I, 13.

[54] *Adefonsi tertii chronica (edit. Rotensis)* 8: *'Urbs quoque Toletana, cunctarum gentium uictris, Ismaeliticis triumfis uicta subcuberit et eis subiugata deseruit'*.

[55] Weiner, *Inalienable possessions. The paradox of keeping-while-giving*, p. 37.

[56] *Cf.* Sanchez-Arcilla Bernal, *Temas de Historia de la Administración. I. Hispania romana y visigoda*, pp. 315–317.

While the Visigoths were in Gaul, the holding of Toulouse, the city in which the court had chosen to settle, already played an important role in the transmission of royal power, at least from the accession of Turismund onwards. The facts surrounding this event are very revealing. According to Jordanes, after Theodoric I's death in the Battle of the Catalaunian Fields, his eldest son Turismund was acclaimed as king by the army, following traditional custom. But from Jordanes' account we can deduce that this act of acclamation, which in principle established the new king's legitimacy, was no longer enough to guarantee the kingship. The historian of the Goths tells us that the patrician Aetius persuaded Turismund of the necessity of coming back to his own "seat" (*sedes propias*) to assume the kingship so as to forestall his brothers' appropriation of the royal treasure and usurpation of power.[57] By the expression *sedes propias*, Jordanes was probably alluding to Toulouse, as he later affirms that Turismund began to reign after coming into this city and obtaining the consent of his brothers and of the rest of the nobility.[58] Both elements, possession of the treasury and of the city, seem to have been determinative in the assumption of power. Other documentary references confirm this point. The *Chronica Gallica* states clearly that it was in this city that Euric killed his brother Theodoric II and therefore here that he became king.[59] In the same text, the news of the Frankish conquest of Gaul is related to the burning of Toulouse.[60] And what is still more revealing is that although Theodoric II died in Arles, Alaric II assumed the royal power in Toulouse.[61] However,

---

[57] Iordanes, *De origine actibusque Getarum (Getica)* XLI: (Aetius) ... '*praebet hac suasione consilium, ut ad sedes propias remearet, regnumque quod pater reliquerat, arriperet; ne germani ejus, oplibus sumptis paternis, Vesegotharum pervaderet, graviterque dehinc cum suis, et quod pejus est, miserabiliter pugnaret*'.

[58] Iordanes, *De origine actibusque Getarum (Getica)* XLI: '*Thorismund ergo patre mortuo, in campis statim Catalaunicis, ubi et pugnaverat, regia majestate subvectus, Tolosam ingreditur. Hic licet fratrum et fortium turba gauderet, ipse tamen sic sua initia moderatus est, ut nullius reperiret de regni successione certamen*'. As Wolfram, *A History of the Goths*, p. 358 affirms, we do not know if it would be enough to obtain the possession of both treasure and *sedes* or if it was necessary that these be confirmed by some institutional act which would take place in Toulouse. The consent alluded to by Jordanes leads us to consider the second possibility, but the lack of further references prevents certainty on this matter.

[59] *Chronica Gallica* 643: '*Theudericus rex Gothorum ab Eurico fratre suo Tolosa occiditur*'.

[60] *Chronica Gallica* 688: '*cisus Alaricus rex Gothorum a Francis. Tolosa a Francis et Burgundionibus incesa*' ...

[61] This fact is highlighted by both *Chronica Gallica* 666: '*Mortuus est Euricus Arelate*

the importance acquired by the chief city of the kingdom did not yet supplant the transcendental role of the holding of the royal treasure in the legitimation of power. This is proved by the fact that after the disaster of the battle of Vouillé (507) the so-called Ostrogothic Interval began with the appropriation of the Visigothic royal treasury by Theodoric the Great and its later removal to Ravenna,[62] and only when Athanaric recognised the independent sovereignty of Amalaric over the Peninsula was the treasury returned.[63] Hence, it seems beyond doubt that already in the Visigothic kingdom of Toulouse the city which stood out as the royal seat acquired the same political relevance that the treasury had as a basis of royal power. But, given that the process of territorialisation in that kingdom had begun relatively recently, both elements existed on the same level; only with the marked political evolution produced by Leovigild's strengthening of the monarchy would the holding of the royal treasury be relegated to second place beneath the importance that control of the chief city of the kingdom now began to acquire as an indispensable element in the gaining and keeping of royal power.

In the light of the foregoing, we should not be surprised to find an inspection of the treasury and stables among the daily activities of Theodoric II,[64] whereas Leovigild saw to beautifying the city which served as the king's court and residence. It becomes understandable, then, that from Leovigild onwards the Visigothic monarchs developed a building policy in the city of Toledo in order to raise its status and prestige, turning it into a real *urbs regia*,[65] the seat of the kingdom,[66] which included an important set of palace outbuildings (*praetorium*), with a court chapel dedicated to the Apostles Peter and

---

et ordinatur filius suus Alaricus Tolosa', and Isidorus, *Historia Gothorum, Wandalorum, Sueborum* 35–6 (long red.): '*Obiit Arelato Euricus . . . Alaricus filius eius apud Tolosensem urbem princeps Gothorum constituitur'* . . .

[62] See D'Abadal, *Del reino de Tolosa al reino de Toledo*, pp. 54–63 and Garcia Iglesias, "El intermedio ostrogodo en Hispania (507–549 d. C.)", pp. 93–95.

[63] Procopius, *Bellum Gothicum*. I, 13.

[64] Sidonius Appolinaris, *Epistolae* I, 6. In the Visigothic kingdom of Toledo this function of watching over the royal treasury was assumed by the *comes thesaurorum*, who, according to P.D. King, *Law and Society in the Visigothic Kingdom*, p. 53, held the office of royal treasurer.

[65] Toledo is thus called, for example, in the dating of the Eighth Council of Toledo: '*In urbem regia celebrata'* . . ., and this description is precisely the same as that given to the capital of the Byzantine Empire, Constantinople.

[66] *Chronica Regum Visigothorum* 49: . . . '*domino Egicane ad sedem regni in Toleto accederent'*.

Paul—with a clear Constantinopolitan resonance—as well as a major basilica dedicated to the Virgin Mary.[67] Seventh-century kings continued this building activity. We know that Sisebut ordered the building of a church dedicated to St Leocadia,[68] a Toledan martyr: here were held the first councils summoned after the church's foundation.[69] The anonymous author of the Mozarabic Chronicle of 754 transmits the account of Wamba, in the third year of his reign, commissioning important works of restoration and renewal in Toledo. For this purpose, Wamba used precious materials (the chronicler mentions marble) and he had an epigraph engraved on the city gates in which he called himself "illustrious, through God's work", manifesting his link with the divinity as well,[70] and thus reinforcing the propagandistic value which this building activity purveyed.

A similar value must be imputed to the city foundations carried out by the Visigothic kings. Two were the newly-built cities erected by Leovigild: *Reccopolis*, in 578, thus named after his son Reccared[71] and *Victoriacum*,[72] in 581, with the purpose of strengthening his authority over the Basque country.[73] Some years later, and with the same purpose, Suinthila built the stronghold of *Ologicus*, the present Olite, 40 km. from Pamplona, after repressing the Basque revolt of 621. With these actions the Visigothic kings once more assumed a prerogative which until then had belonged only to emperors. *Imitatio imperii* appeared even in the names given to the new cities, the onomastics of which, in the case of the Leovigild's foundations, referred

---

[67] L.A. Garcia Moreno, *Historia de España visigoda* (Madrid, 1989), p. 120.

[68] *Chronica Albendensia* XIV, 24.

[69] These were the Fourth, Fifth and Sixth councils of Toledo. See H. Schwöbel, *Synode und Könige in Westgotenreich. Grundlagen un Formen ihner Beziehung* (Kölh-Wien, 1982), p. 33.

[70] Chronica Muzarabica, 29: '*Qui iam in supra fatam eram anni tertii sceptra regia meditans ciuitatem Toleti mire et eleganti labore renobat, quem et opere sculptorio uersiuicando pertitulans hoc in portarum epigrammata stilo ferreo in nitida lucidaque marmora patrat: Exerit factore Deo rex inclitus urbem Uuamba sue celebrem protendens gentis honorem*'.

[71] Isidorus, *Historia Gothorum, Wandalorum, Sueborum*, 51 (in both redactions): '*Condidit etiam civitatem in Celtiberia, quam ex nomine filii sui Recopolim nominauit*'; Iohannis abbatis biclarensis, *Chronica* 578, 4: . . . '*civitatem in Celtiberia ex nomine filii condidit, quae Recopolis nuncupatur*'.

[72] Its actual location is disputed; it was either near the present Vitoria or else on the site of ancient Veleia, some kilometres to the west of Vitoria. See G. Nieto, *El oppidum de Iruña (Alava)* (Vitoria, 1958); A. Azkarate, *Arqueología cristiana de la Antigüedad tardía en Alava, Guipúzcoa y Vizcaya* (Vitoria, 1988), p. 496.

[73] Iohannis Abbatis biclarensis, *Chronica* 581, 3: '*Leovegildus rex partem Vasconiae occupat et civitatem, quae Victoriacum nuncupatur, condidit*'.

to dynastic continuity or to feats of arms, hence offering a striking parallel to the city foundations of Justinian.[74] The propagandistic value of these foundations is nowhere more evident than in the case of Reccopolis. According to John of Biclar, Leovigild saw to beautifying the city with buildings worthy of admiration[75] and, fully conscious of his work as a symbol of the new reinforcement of the monarchy, commemorated it in a series of medals with the legend *"Leovigildus rex Reccopoli fecit".*[76] As recently pointed out by Cristina la Rocca,[77] Reccopolis was born out of pure self-congratulation, not to satisfy any royal policy of population redistribution; a good indication of this was the city's undistinguished future as a populated settlement.

Leovigild also introduced an independent royal coinage, which, as shown by G. Miles,[78] opened a new age in Western European minting. His predecessors on the throne, and Leovigild himself in the first years of his reign, limited themselves to issuing anonymous imitations of imperial coins, on which appeared not only the images and names of the emperors, but sometimes even the names of imperial mints.[79] In the last years of his reign, however, Leovigild broke definitively with this tradition and arrogated to himself such imperial prerogatives as the minting of coins by issuing trientes which, while keeping the emperor's portrait and name on the obverse, had the king's own name in the genitive on the reverse, thus making evident that it was a royal issue.[80] At a later point, which can be dated about 575,[81] Leovigild introduced fully autonomous trientes on which

---

[74] As demonstrated by Garcia Moreno, *Historia de España visigoda*, p. 323.

[75] Iohannis abbatis biclarensis, *Chronica* 578, 4: . . . *'quam miro opere in moenibus et suburbanis adornans privilegia populo novae urbis instituit'.*

[76] See J. Orlandis, *Historia de España. La España visigoda* (Madrid, 1977), p. 98.

[77] C. La Rocca, "Una prudente maschera antiqua. La politica edilizia di Teoderic", *Teoderico il Grande e i Goti d'Italia. Atti del XIII Congresso internazionale di studi sull'Alto Medioevo* (Spoleto, 1993), pp. 477–478.

[78] Miles, *The coinage of the Visigoths of Spain. Leovigild to Achila*, p. 14.

[79] Systematically, W.J. Tomasini, *The Barbaric Tremissis in Spain and Southern France: Anastasius to Leovigild* (New York, 1964). Also: X. Barral i Altet, *La circulation des monnaies suèves et visigotiques* (München, 1976), pp. 53–58; L. Garcia de Valdeavellano, "La moneda y la economía de cambio en la Península Ibérica desde el s. VI hasta mediados del s. XI", *Settimane di Studi sull'Alto Medioevo* 8 (Spoleto, 1961), pp. 207–209; W.M. Reinhart, "Nuevas aportaciones a la numismática visigoda", *Archivo Español de Arqueología* 18 (1945), pp. 215–222.

[80] See E. Spaulding, "El epíteto *pius* en las monedas visigodas", *Numisma* 192–203 (1985–86), p. 35.

[81] It is not possible to determine the exact moment at which this fundamental

no reference to the Byzantine emperor appeared[82] but instead Leovigild himself appropriated imperial titles and appellations such as *Dominus noster* and *pius, inclitus, valens, iustus* and *victor*.[83] From then on, the royal effigy, represented with the royal attributes, would always appear on the Visigothic tremissis, legalising the issues. At the same time, monetary legends contained, on the obverse, the latinised name of the sovereign with his title of *rex*, frequently shortened to RE or R, sometimes introduced by the abbreviation of the expression *Dominus Noster* (D.N.) and, from the days of Wamba on, usually preceded by abbreviations of the formula *in Dei Nomine* (I.D.N.M.N.); and on the reverse, the mint name, accompanied very often by one or more royal epithets, *pius* and *iustus* being the most common,[84] referring to precisely those virtues Isidore considered essential traits of monarchy.[85] We can say, then, that the kings saw to it that their coinage synthetized essential aspects of Visigothic political theory: first, through the inclusion of their names and titles and their appearing with the insignia of majesty which at the same time placed them above the nobility, their own sovereignty over an independent territory; second, through the expression *Dominus noster*, the king's position as lord of all his subjects, bound to him by the oath of loyalty; and third, with the formula *in Dei nomine*, the idea that power comes from God.

Through this series of symbolic manifestations, Leovigild and his succesors, as we have seen, tried to strengthen their authority and express, on the one hand, their position as removed from and above their people and especially their superiority to the nobility, and on

---

change in Visigothic minting took place. A. Heiss, *Descripción general de las monedas de los reyes visigodos de España* (Paris, 1872), p. 28, is inclined to think that it was in 584 that Leovigild issued the first coins in his name. Reinhart, "Nuevas aportaciones a la numismática visigoda", p. 231 places it around 585 and Garcia de Valdeavellano, "La moneda y la economía de cambio en la Península Ibérica desde el s. VI hasta mediados del s. XI", p. 209, is even more imprecise, indicating the decade from 575 to 585 as the period in which Leovigild's independent minting emerged.

[82] Descriptions of Leovigild's coins are found in Heiss, *Descripción general de las monedas de los reyes visigodos de España*, pp. 79–85 and in Miles, *The coinage of the Visigoths of Spain. Leovigild to Achila*, pp. 175–198.

[83] See Ewig, *Spätantikes und Fränkisches Gallien*, pp. 21–22; F. Mateu y Llopis, "Las fórmulas y los símbolos cristianos en los tipos monetares visigodos", *Analecta Sacra Tarraconensia* 14 (1941), pp. 75–81; F. Mateu y Llopis, "Notas sobre el latín de las inscripciones monetarias godas", *Revista de Archivos, Bibliotecas y Museos* 61 (1955), p. 296 and pp. 312–313.

[84] In Miles, *The coinage of the Visigoths of Spain. Leovigild to Achila*, pp. 23–68, we find a detailed study of the monetary legends appearing on Visigothic issues.

[85] Isidorus, *Etymologiae* IX, 3, 5: '*Regiae virtutes praecipuae duae: iustitia et pietas*'.

the other hand, the absolute independence of their sovereignty over Hispanic territory, comparing their position with that of the Byzantine emperor. With the official conversion of Reccared at the Third Council of Toledo (589), the prestige policy begun by Leovigild received a new impulse. From that moment onwards, the Church was to supply the monarchy with a solid conceptual basis on which it could found its authority, whose central point, the idea of power coming from God, we have seen joining the elements which stand out in the symbology of power so far analysed. In a parallel direction, new symbolic manifestations were developed aiming at the exemplification and popularisation of the main axioms of the descending power theory then in force. We note the appearance, in the documentation of this period, of a series of royal metaphors which, proceeding from the late Roman and imperial tradition, function in ways that at once represent and exalt the king. The most elaborate is the so-called anthropomorphic metaphor which held that just as God created the head at the top of the body so that it could lead the *subdita membra*, so and for the same purpose did He place the king at top of society,[86] a simile that perfectly expressed the basic socio-political ideas of theocratic theory: the notion of the divine origin of power, the necessity of protecting the king[87] and the submission owed by all the subjects to the monarch. The Isidorian concept of government established by God in order to prevent and correct the consequences of the sin that overwhelms mankind[88] is perfectly expressed when the king is described as the healer of sin, whose duty it is to diagnose the body's diseases and administer the proper medicines to neutralise them,[89] which in turn makes it necessary for the king to possess ultimate power in the whole kingdom. And the royal epithets, Apostle of Christ,[90] Servant of God,[91] or shepherd of

---

[86] No doubt the clearest and most complete formulation of the anthropomorphic metaphor appears in the law of Recceswinth II, 1, 4.

[87] The words of Recceswinth, '*regendorum membrorum causa salus est capitatis*', included in the *Tomus* presented to the Eighth Council of Toledo could not be clearer on the matter.

[88] Isidorus, *Sententiarum libri tres* III, LI, 4 and 5.

[89] This is how the laws *Lex Visigothorum* II, 1, 29 express it: '*Tranquilitatis nostre uno medicamine concedimus duo mala sacrare*'; and *Lex Visigothorum* XII, 2, 1: '*Propriis membris confecto medicamine salutem*'.

[90] *Concilium Toletanum* III (a. 589), *Praef.*: '*Ipse mereatur veraciter apostolicum meritum qui apostolicum implevit officcium*' . . .

[91] *Concilium Toletanum* IV (a. 653), *Praef.*: . . . '*primum gratias Salvatori nostro Deo omnipotenti egimus, post haec antefato ministro eius excellentissimo glorioso regi*' . . .

his people,[92] highlight the special relationship which linked God with the monarch and justified all the "interferences" of the temporal power in the internal affairs of the Church.

Together with these metaphorical constructions, monarchy was exalted through the use of the royal titulature which, though very succinct, since it only consisted of the epithet Flavius, combined with the first name of the monarch and the appellation *rex*,[93] was a clear expression of the Visigothic kings' view of themselves as the successors to imperial power in the Peninsula. They compared themselves to the Roman Empire: this was clear from 589 onward, when, at the Third Council of Toledo, Reccared was not only acclaimed with *laudes*, as happened under similar circumstances in the case of the Roman-Byzantine emperors, but in addition he was openly identified as a new Constantine and a new Marcian.[94] If the former convoked the Council of Nicaea and the latter the Council of Chalcedon, Reccared behaved now in an identical way by summoning the Third Council of Toledo. He assumed, correspondingly, the characteristics of the imperial Constantinean dynasty,[95] which, like him, had created strong links between the Catholic Church and the State.

The same thing happened with the system of dating by the kings' regnal years. The earliest evidence for a Spanish Visigothic king using this dating system when talking about himself is supplied by the minutes of the 589 Council, in which Reccared ordered all his subjects to observe what was established *"in hoc sancto concilio habito in urbem Toletanam anno regni nostri feliciter quarto"*.[96] We find here both elements, the relevant ordinal number and the adverb *feliciter*, which, starting at this moment and until the end of the Visigothic kingdom of Toledo, would characterise the dating-formulae used in diplomatic.[97]

---

[92] *Concilium Toletanum* III (a. 589), *Tomus*: *Me quoque . . . Dominus excitavit, ut depulsa obstinatione infidelitatis et discordiae submoto furore populum . . . ad agnitionem fidei et ecclesias catholicae consortium revocarem'*.

[93] M.C. Diaz y Diaz, "Titulaciones regias en la monarquía visigoda", *Revista portuguesa de Historia* 16 (1976), pp. 134 and pp. 139–140 asserts that these were the constitutive elements of the royal titulature during the whole history of the Toledan kingdom. To these only the epithet *gloriosus*, with which the titulature was extended in the days of Erwig, would need to be added.

[94] *Cf.* A. Isla Frez, "Las relaciones entre el reino visigodo y los reyes merovingios a finales del s. VI", *España Medieval* 13 (1990), p. 32.

[95] *Concilium Toletanum* III (a. 589), *Subscriptio*: *'Flavius Recaredus rex hanc deliberationem quam cum sancta definivimus synodo confirmans subscribsi'*.

[96] *Concilium Toletanum* III (a. 589), *Edictum regis*.

[97] There are plenty of royal dating-clauses in the collections of Visigothic laws.

The ordinal of the monarch's reign in dating-clauses had an important political symbolism: it conferred on the king a kind of consecration by turning his power into a means and measure for determining his subjects' activity.[98] It is not strange to find the formula *in Dei nomine* or the expression *nostre glorie*[99] (this one a characteristic invocation of deity) in royal dating-clauses, with which the monarch showed the almost sacred nature his own person had received through his being the agent of God on earth. In this same sense we note the application to the Visigothic kings of epithets characteristic of Byzantine emperors. The conciliar minutes provide the best evidence, since in them titles such as *gloriosissimus, piissimus, sanctissimus, christianissimus, clementissimus, severissimus, excellentissimus, inclytus*..., are invariably associated with any mention of royalty. The greatness of monarchy was also shown in a solemn way through a kind of ritual protocol by which the king's role in particularly important governmental acts was highlighted. At general councils especially, the most important figures of the kingdom assembled, laymen as well as ecclesiastics, and it was only natural that the king's presence was accompanied with a ceremonial displaying his eminent position at the head of the society.[100]

But it was, undoubtedly, royal unction which was the most important royal ritual in the Visigothic kingdom. The bishops, by anointing the sovereigns with sacred oil, symbolically granted them the halo of sacrality and sanctity which corresponded to their being the

---

For instance: *Lex Visigothorum* III, 1, 5: '*Data et confirmata lez pridie idus Ianuarias, anno feliciter tertio regni nostri*'; *Lex Visigothorum* IX, 1, 21: '*Data et confirmata lex in Cordoba anno feliciter sextodecimo regni nostri*'; *Lex Visigothorum* IX, 2, 8: '*Data et confirmata lex die kalendarum Novembrium anno feliciter secundo regni nostri*'. We observe that the adverb *feliciter* is always interposed between the ordinal and the word *anno* and this is due to the fact that, again, models from the Later Empire were being adopted. See Diaz y Diaz, "Titulaciones regias en la monarquía visigoda", pp. 140–141.

[98] Diaz y Diaz, "Titulaciones regias en la monarquía visigoda", p. 140.

[99] Both expressions appear, for example, in the following: *Lex Visigothorum* XII, 1, 3: '*Edita lex in confirmatione concilii Toleto sub die idus Nov. era DCCXXI, ano quoque feliciter quarto regni glorie nostre in Dei nomine, Toleto*'; *Concilium Toletanum* XIII (a. 683), '*Tomus: Datum sub die pridie nonas novembres anno feliciter quarto regni gloriae nostrae in Dei nomine*'.

[100] Royal opening of the Councils was carried out with a solemn ceremonial in which four crucial moments could be distinguished: the entrance of the being, the royal speech and handing over of the *tomus* from the Eighth Council of Toledo onwards, prayers praising the king, and the ritual farewell by the monarch. *Cf.* H. Schwöbel, *Synode und Könige in Westgotenreich. Grundlagen un Formen ihner Beziehung,* C. Munier, "L'*Ordo de celebrando concilio* wisigothique. Ses remaniements jusqu'du Xe siècle", *Revue des Sciences Religieuses* 37 (1963), pp. 250–271.

chosen of God. According to Walter Ullmann,[101] though in this case
with reference to the Carolingian world, unction replaces a sovereign protected by blood and kinship bonds with another one deriv-
ing his power from Grace and divine intervention; it is the definitive
step from Germanic to Christian king. We do not know the exact
date at which this ritual act was introduced in Visigothic Spain. The
only thing we know for sure is that unction was already performed
in the times of Wamba[102] and that all his successors in the throne,
Erwig,[103] Egica,[104] Roderic[105] and Witiza,[106] were solemnly anointed
by the hands of the bishops. However, we find nowhere any statement that Wamba's unction was the first one to be performed and,
according to Jean de Pange,[107] texts referring to such unction indicate that the rite was not new. Different dates have thus been proposed for the origin of royal unction.[108] This ritual is possible in
different contexts, but among them the Fourth Council of Toledo
of 633 marked a weak point for the monarch and a strong point
for the bishops, which would have justified the appearance of this
ritual. Sisenand had overthrown Suinthila, and his position was so
weak that he presented himself to the Council and, prostrating himself on the ground—*cum lacrimis et genitibus pro se interveniendum Deo
postulavit*—, implored the bishops to sanction his rule. The bishops

---

[101] W. Ullmann *The Carolingian Renaissance and the Idea of Kingship* (London, 1969),
pp. 53f.
[102] Iulianus Toletanus, *Historia Wambae regis* 2: 'Wambae . . . quem digne principare
Deus voluit, quem sacerdotalis unctio declaravit'.
[103] *Concilium Toletanum* XII (a. 681), 'tomus: . . . quibus clara divinorum iudiciorum dis-
positione praeventus et regnandi conscenderim sedem ad sacro sanctam regni perceperim unctionem'.
[104] *Chronica Regum Visigothorum* 50: 'Unctus es autem dominus noster Egica in regno in
eclesia sanctorum Petri et Pauli praetoriensis sub die VIII real Dec., die dominico' . . .
[105] *Chronica Albendensia* XIX, 1a: (Ruderico) 'unctus est in regno Vitiza die XVIII Kalen-
das Decembris, s die dominico' . . .
[106] *Chronica Regum Visigothorum* 51: 'Unctus est autem Vitiza in regno' . . .
[107] J. de Pange, *Le roi très chrètien* (París, 1949), pp. 121–122.
[108] J. M. Wallace – Hadrill, *Early Germanic kingship in England and on the Continent*
(Oxford, 1971), p. 55, defends the view that it was Wamba who was the first
monarch to be anointed, whereas Sanchez Albornoz, "La *ordinatio principis* en la
España goda y postvisigoda", pp. 14–15, maintains that it was in the reign of Reccared (586–601) that this practice was begun. As for King, *Law and Society in the
Visigothic Kingdom* p. 48, n. 5 and A. Barbero, "El pensamiento político visigodo y
las primeras unciones regias en la Europa medieval", *Hispania* 30 (1970), p. 73, they
are inclined to think it was in the reign of Sisenand (631–639). These references
suffice to show the extent of discussion of this question among historians. For more
information, we refer to the works of the last two authors mentioned, where the
main opinions on the subject are set out.

agreed and his power was legitimated. No text refers to a legitimating ritual; unction would not have been improvised in the Council, but the bishops would have started to reflect on the best formula for making it clear that the king was pleasing in their eyes and therefore in the eyes of God. It is no coincidence that Isidore of Seville, who chaired the sessions of the Council, in commenting on the references in the Old Testament to unction, considered that when applied to the ruler, this was a *sacramentum mysticae unctionis*.[109] He was perhaps, despite Ullmann's opinion to the contrary,[110] influenced by the thinking of Gregory the Great,[111] for whom unction, again in relation to the kings of Israel, was inseparably attached to the concept of divine Grace. The transition to the ritual anointing of early medieval kings, taking the remote precedents of the Old Testament as a model, was just a question of time. Whatever the date in which this ritual was introduced, it seems unquestionable that it was in the Visigothic kingdom of Toledo that the rite of royal anointing was first performed. Since anointings were unknown both in Rome and in the contemporary Byzantine Empire, we can affirm that the Visigothic clergy, inspired by models from the Old Testament and in particular by the figure of Saul, the first anointed king of the Bible,[112] were able to create[113] a specific ceremonial symbolism through which to underline the almost divine position reached by the monarch, based on theocratic postulates legitimating temporal power. Prodigies described in the sources when relating the unction ceremony[114] showed that this, as a sacramental act, effectively communicated grace to the Visigothic sovereign, turning him into

[109] *Isidorus, Questiones in vetus Testamentum: in Genesia* 29,8: *nec ei sacramento ielo mysticae unctionis . . .*

[110] Ullmann, *The Carolingian Renaissance and the Idea of Kingship*, p. 74.

[111] Gregorius I Papa, *In librum primum Regum expositionum libri VI*, IV, 5,2: '*cum rex super haereditate Domini unctus asseritur. Unctionis ergo fructus est, cultus divinae haereditatis . . .* Cf. Ullmann, *The Carolingian Renaissance and the Idea of Kingship*, p. 73.

[112] Garcia Herrero, "Julián de Toledo y la realeza visigoda", pp. 228–251, has carried out an exhaustive analysis of all the links that appear in the *Historia Wambae regiae* between Wamba and Jewish royalty, concluding that, in such a work, the influence of Byzantine imperial ideology had been in great part replaced by a standardization of the ideal monarch inspired by the Old Testament.

[113] As Barbero, "El pensamiento político visigodo y las primeras unciones regias en la Europa medieval", p. 75 affirms, we confront here "the original creation of an institution".

[114] Iulianus Toletanus, *Historia Wambae regis*. Cf. R. Collins, "Julian of Toledo and the Royal Succession in Late Seventh-Century Spain", *Early Medieval Kingship*, eds. P.H. Sawyer and I. Wood (Leeds, 1977), p. 46, who recalls here, in relation

the chosen of God, to whom, because of this, submission and respect were owed. One can understand, therefore, why this ceremonial act, replacing previous elements, became the most important rite for marking the beginning of the Visigothic king's reign. This is shown by the fact that the unction was postponed in relation to the date on which government was assumed, searching for both a day of great solemnity (Sunday) and a suitably sumptuous place—the High Mass was celebrated in the pretorian church of Toledo—for the performance of this ritual.[115] R. Collins[116] has insisted upon the significance of the place of unction, Toledo. Unction in itself would not have been any guarantee of legitimacy—the rebel Paulus too was anointed, after all—but unction became precisely that when it was the culmination of a process of accession to power and when it was applied in the *urbs regia*. We should add that it was such a guarantee for the further reason that the metropolitan of Toledo applied it.

It seems clear that sacred unction was the main legitimating act of the accession to the throne, regardless of the way this accession occurred.[117] It signified, therefore, the ecclesiastical authority's approval, validating a previous decision taken either by the nobility or by the preceding king, or even a usurpation. It is not surprising, then, that some authors have seen in this religious act a ritual expression of the supremacy of the priesthood over the king,[118] the submission of monarchy to the Church, a proof of the weakness of the monarch before the Catholic hierarchy; we must not forget that "the anoint-

---

to the see of Toledo, the close association between the royal office and military function.

[115] Wamba (Iulianus Toletanus, *Historia Wambae regis* 44) as well as Ervig (*Chronica Regum Visigothorum* 47), postponed the unction date so that it could be performed on Sunday and in the pretorian church of Toledo.

[116] Collins, "Julian of Toledo and the Royal Succession in Late Seventh-Century Spain", p. 45.

[117] As we will see later, three of those kings on whose unctions we have clear evidence, got hold of power through totally different means: Wamba assumed the royal dignity through election, Erwig through usurpation and Egica through the designation of the previous monarch. Curiously enough, Paulus, as usurper, declared himself the anointed king of the east, i.e. *Narbonnensis* (*Epistola Pauli: 'Flauius Paulus unctus rex orientalis Wambani regi austro'*) as an irrefutable proof of his position as a king; in this period, and in the view of Archbishop Julian, it was the unction that made a king.

[118] This point of view is maintained, among others, by Barbero, "El pensamiento político visigodo y las primeras unciones regias en la Europa medieval", p. 61 and Garcia Moreno, *Historia de España visigoda*, p. 324.

ing was by its very nature a clerical monopoly".[119] But we must always keep in mind that the monarch, thanks to the unction, ceased to be a simply secular personage, but became capable of interference in ecclesiastical matters, and this, to a certain extent, placed him above the Church itself. Therefore the putting into practice of this ceremony served "to raise the king even higher above his people and thus to protect him even more securely against any lingering populist notions".[120] The contradiction between those positions was nothing but the reflection of the paradoxical attitude of the Church with regard to the monarchy. As an institution, the ecclesiastical hierarchy provided the political-religious theory on which secular power supported itself, contributing to the strengthening of royalty and endowing it with enough powers in the religious field to submit conciliar meetings to its control. In the socio-economic field, however, the Church became the main property-holder of the kingdom, cutting down the economic resources of the monarchy and opposing it, as the lay nobility often did, in defence of their own interests.[121] The royal unction, a reflection of this ambiguous situation, was undoubtedly the ritual of majesty which best expressed all the political-religious theory and practice in force in seventh-century Hispania.

Everything discussed so far clearly shows the continuous literary and symbolic exaltation of monarchy in the Visigothic kingdom of Toledo and the existence in it of doctrinal principles which legitimated the eminent position of the monarch as well as the extensive powers acquired when he became the supreme authority in the state organisation. This has given rise to the labelling of the Visigothic monarchy by some modern authors as an absolutist one.[122] The label is totally unacceptable, however, not only because it has to do with a term which implies an anachronistic transposition of political ideas

---

[119] J.L. Nelson, "Inauguration rituals", *Early Medieval Kingship*, eds. P.H. Sawyer and I. Wood (Leeds, 1977), p. 62, who, although dealing with the Carolingian world, mentions parallel phenomena which can prove useful in comparison. J.L. Nelson, "The Lord's anointed and the people's choice: Carolingian royal ritual", *Rituals of Royalty. Power and Ceremonis in Tradicional Societies*, eds. D. Cannadine – S. Price (Cambridge, 1987), pp. 137–180.

[120] King, *Law and Society in the Visigothic Kingdom*, p. 48.

[121] The paradoxical attitude of the Church with regard to the monarchy has been analysed by Mª.R. Valverde Castro, "La Iglesia hispano-visigoda: ¿fortalecedora o limitadora de la soberanía real?", *Hispania Antiqua* 16 (1992), pp. 381–392.

[122] See T. Gonzalez, *La política en los concilios de Toledo* (Roma, 1977), pp. 46ff.

which would only appear much later, but also because socio-economic realities prevented the Visigothic monarchs from applying in practice the wide powers with which political-religious theory provided them. We must bear in mind that the ideological framework in force in the Visigothic kingdom was one of recent formation, and was still undergoing definition and consolidation as new material conditions appeared in society. This is why political theory and reality did not always correspond. R. D'Abadal i de Vinyals[123] pointed this out when talking about the permanent contradiction between legal theory and actual practice in Visigothic Hispania. The Visigothic monarch had turned into the highest representative in the military, financial, administrative and judicial organisation in the kingdom and, with the conversion to Catholicism, acquired enormous powers in the religious field. We must now examine how far royalty possessed the necessary means to exercise the wide powers attributed to it.

In the seventh-century Visigothic kingdom, the king still had control of the army in his hands. The oath taken to the monarch at his accession to the throne defined the king's duty to safeguard the security of the kingdom and to consecrate himself to the spreading of peace.[124] Consequently, and in order to fulfil this duty, the ruler had to hold supreme authority in the military field. Calling up and dismissing troops, leading them into battle, and determining the composition of armies, were royal functions. However, the public nature of the army had nearly disappeared in seventh-century Hispania and the royal military household was not able to meet from its own resources the military requirements of the kingdom. The monarch was forced to appeal to private retinues.[125] The oath of loyalty was meant to make the subjects observe their military duties,[126] but fre-

---

[123] R. D'Abadal i de Vinyals, "La Monarquía en el regne de Toledo", *Dels visigots al catalans* 1 (Barcelona, 1969), p. 59.

[124] Reccared stated this clearly at the Third Council of Toledo, *Praef.*: . . . '*si quieti et paci propagandae opem debemus inpendere*'.

[125] These warbands were first officially recognised in the law issued by Euric, which begins: '*si quis buccellario arma dederit vel aliquid donaverit, si in patroni sui manserit obsequio, paut ipsum quae sunt donata permaneant*' (*Codex Euricianus, 305*) and goes on to regulate the rights and duties into which patron and follower entered; legislation incorporated into the *Lex Visigothorum* V, 3,1 with few modifications (see A. D'Ors, *El codigo di Eurico. Edicion, Palingenesia, Indices. Estudios visigóticos* 2 (Roma-Madrid, 1966), pp. 32–35).

[126] The comments on this matter by D. Perez Sanchez, *El ejército en la socidad visigoda* (Salamanca, 1989), p. 137 are significant: military duties were an active aspect of the loyalty owed to the sovereign. The oath of loyalty implied, among

quent rebellions in the course of the seventh century revealed the futility of this measure as these troops were used by the nobility for their own profit instead of for the *publica utilitas*. The military laws of Wamba and Erwig[127] showed this clearly. One can note in both laws that the public army was composed by the monarch's private army, with which the private armies of the main ecclesiastical and lay landholders were to combine. The harsh punishments imposed by Wamba (exile, loss of dignity and the confiscation of properties) on all those not fulfilling their military duties are explained, according to Wamba's own words, because "from previous times to the present, the bad habit of neither coming to the defence of the provinces nor contributing to maintaining their unity has become deeply rooted".[128] It is thus implicitly assumed that private armies had turned into the main prop of the kingdom's defence on an internal as well as an external level and, therefore, although in theory the sovereign had full powers with regard to the army, in practice he lacked the means to exercise them.

We have a similar situation in the case of administration. Although in theory the power of the king was purely personal, he had to delegate part of his powers, to make them practically effective, to a series of people or institutions who had to collaborate with him in the carrying-out of his government tasks. In the words of P.D. King, "his own control of, and participation in, all aspects of government always remained as a necessary consequence of his supreme accountability to God, but he had no choice but to rely upon others to carry out the bulk of the work".[129] In principle, this did not need to limit the monarch's supreme authority, especially if we consider that the appointment as well as the removal of royal officers was an exclusively royal function. The only source of power is God, who delegates it to the king, who in turn, practising the royal grace, redistributes it among his subjects. This principle was regularly supported by the conciliar canons[130] and such an insistence was a consequence

---

other things, answering the king's call when he demanded the presence of his loyal subjects. Not answering this call was considered by law an act of disloyalty.

[127] We refer to the work of Perez Sanchez, *El ejército en la sociedad visigoda*, pp. 155–70, where both laws are exhaustively analysed.

[128] *Lex Visigothorum* IX, 2, 8.

[129] King, *Law and Society in the Visigothic Kingdom*, p. 52.

[130] For example *Concilium Toletanum* VI (a. 638), c. 14 or *Concilium Toletanum* XIII (a. 683), c. 2.

of the weakness actually suffered by royal power in face of the members of the nobility who held high office.[131] These conciliar provisions would therefore be nothing other than a royal attempt to affirm the king's authority and to take into account the trend towards hereditary office-holding. Clearly the existence of institutions and offices with governmental power limited in practice the theoretical supremacy of the monarch. Even though theocratic postulates denied the possibility of any power not the king's, in fact the needs of government made possible—even inevitable—the existence of autonomous aristocratic power. Those with administrative offices were a curb on the king's sovereignty and the provincial noble's actual power waxed and waned at every point according to the changing rhythms of authority at Toledo.

The king was also at the top of the financial system and no doubt the possession and administration of the substantial patrimony represented by the royal fisc was one of the major bases of effective royal power. The king replaced the emperor in exercising the sovereign right to order taxation and it was his further duty to moderate, increase or exempt from taxes.[132] The king had to prevent the officers of the fisc from abusing their powers as well as the taxpayers from avoiding their fiscal duties. The extensive legislation on this subject[133] is a clear proof that problems of both kinds were rife. Tax remissions decreed by Erwig and Egica[134] can be understood if we take into account that both kings reached the throne in difficult circumstances and both needed the support of the grandees of the kingdom to keep power. Again, socio-economic reality limited in fact the wide powers which the king held by right. The potent segmentation process undergone by Visigothic society meant that the great lay and ecclesiastical landowners gradually attained a greater power and autonomy with regard to the state machinery: if not by right at least in fact, great properties were free from tax-paying. This led

---

[131] *Cf.* A. Barbero – M. Vigil, *La formación del feudalismo en la Península Ibérica* (Barcelona, 1978), pp. 124–25.

[132] *Cf.* E. Perez Pujol, *Instituciones sociales de la España goda*, t. 2 (Valencia, 1892), p. 182.

[133] We can find examples in conciliar legislation (*Concilium Toletanum* III (a. 589), c. 18; *Concilium Toletanum* XIII (a. 683), *Edictum*) as well as in civil laws (*Lex Visigothorum* V, 4, 19; X, 1, 15 and 16).

[134] Evidence of such tax remissions is provided by the conciliar minutes: *Concilium Toletanum* XIII (a. 683), *tomus* on the remission ordained by Erwig, and *Concilium Caesaraugustanum* III (a. 691), c. 5 on that by Egica.

inevitably to the diminishing of the fisc and the Visigothic kings were more and more forced, on the one hand, to turn to their own resources in order to meet the state expenses and, on the other, to resort to confiscations, more than to tax payments, to increase the patrimony at the monarchy's disposal.[135] In practice, neither the kings (who tried to add the fiscal patrimony to their private one) nor the nobility (who avoided paying tax whenever they could) respected the fiscal system. All this was due to the structural changes which affected late Visigothic society as a whole.

It was maybe in the judicial field that the king could better put into effect his sovereign functions as the only law-giver and supreme judge of the kingdom, to whom all subjects could and should appeal as the last resort.[136] Law was the essential instrument which the ruler counted on to fulfil his task, this task being no other than, according to theocratic principles, to lead a Christian society to reach the goals ordained by God. The definition of norms to rule society therefore fell exclusively within the royal competence. All this was reflected in the dating-clauses of laws, in which the king spoke not only in his own name, but also in the name of the deity. However, in this field too the magnates of the kingdom tried to control the use of royal power in those cases in which its exercise could damage their own interests. The second canon of the Thirteenth Council of Toledo offers forceful evidence on this point. The magnates of the kingdom thereby obtained the right to be publicly judged before courts constituted by bishops and members of the high nobility. This brought them judicial and procedural guarantees against possible royal condemnation.[137] Basically, the aim was to reduce the king's freedom in political processes, through which he was empowered to pass judgement and carry out confiscations of property. This canon shows the antagonism between the monarchy's power on the one hand, and the Church and nobility, united in the defence of their common interests, on the other.

In conclusion, despite both the wide range of sovereign powers and the constant exaltation of the monarchy, socio-economic reality

---

[135] See A. Barbero – M. Vigil, "Algunos aspectos de la feudalización del reino visigodo en relación con su organización financiera y militar", *Sobre los orígenes sociales de la Reconquista* (Barcelona, 1974), pp. 131–35.

[136] Chindaswinth's law II, 1, 24 and Erwig's II, 1 30 B regulated the appeal process.

[137] *Concilium Toletanum* XIII (a. 683), c. 2.

prevented the Visigothic kings from developing the almost unlimited power provided by theocratic theory. The needs of government forced them to delegate some of their powers, so that the nobility, lay as much as ecclesiastical, came to take part in important spheres of the state organisation. But what really determined the political relevance of the nobility was its economic and social strength. The possession of great domains and of the people living in them provided the grandees of the kingdom with enough power to be in a position to face the monarchy in order to increase and defend their own interests. Only through a constant policy of giving out wealth could the sovereign assure for himself the nobility's loyalty and co-operation, but this reduced the real bases of monarchic power and disabled the sovereign in future efforts to mantain the organisation of the state. Therefore, although in theory there was no authority but the king's, in practice the lay and ecclesiastical nobility turned into a real force, which actually limited royal sovereignty.

The consequence of this antagonism between monarchy and aristocracy was the lack of a clearly defined system of succession to the throne. The attempts to regulate the royal succession carried out by the Fourth Council of Toledo, establishing election as the method for succession to the throne,[138] were not effective. It was only natural that nobility and Church opted for election: they sought a solution to the succession problem which facilitated the state's and their own survival as the dominant social class.[139] They thus averted the successor's appointment turning into a royal prerogative and preserved for themselves an important political power through their interference with the king's election. But the history of the Visigothic kingdom shows that the repeated conciliar provisions on royal succession[140] were not observed. In the period between the Fourth Council in 633 and the end of the Visigothic kingdom of Toledo in 711, only two monarchs gained power through the electoral procedure, Chintila and Wamba. As for the rest, three of them owed their

---

[138] *Concilium Toletanum* IV (a. 633), c. 75. *Cf.* J. Orlandis, "La iglesia visigoda y los problemas de la sucesión al trono en el s. VII", *Settimane di studi sull'Alto Medioevo* 7 (Spoleto, 1960), pp. 333–51.

[139] M. Vigil – A. Barbero, "La sucesión al trono y evolución social en el reino visigodo", *Hispania Antiqua* IV (1974), p. 392.

[140] The elective nature of the Visigothic monarchy is confirmed by *Concilium Toletanum* V (a. 636), c. 3; *Concilium Toletanum* VI (a. 638), c. 17 and *Concilium Toletanum* VIII (a. 653), c. 10.

thrones to revolts and depositions (Chindaswinth, Erwig and Roderic) and four (Tulga, Recceswinth, Egica and Witiza) were appointed by their predecessors. The existence of a noble class of great landowners with private armies and, therefore, enough power and wealth to wish to get hold of the throne, gave rise to endemic struggles; election, appointment and usurpation alternated depending on the strength of the monarchy or the noble factions at a given moment. Consequently, the transmission of power would be determined not by the existence of clear and respected institutional principles, but rather by the relative strength of kings and nobles. Theocratic principles and the centralisation policy attempted by the monarchs led to the establishing of a hereditary succession system. Feudalisation, and the existence of a strong nobility with enough wealth and power to force its rights to be recognised and respected, kept in force the elective procedure, but the nobility itself did not respect this when it had the chance forcibly to impose its own candidates. The problem of royal succession remained unresolved during the Visigothic period. It was the essential point of the monarchy's weakness and revealed the incapacity of the monarchy to impose itself definitively over the nobility.

Parallel to the attempt to establish a clearly defined succession system, an important set of laws were issued during the seventh century, laws which, while protecting the king and the royal family, were aimed at putting an end to the existing chronic political instability. The first ecclesiastical intervention against rebellions can be found in the Fourth Council of Toledo, whose canon 75, which as we have seen established the elective principle, also anathematised all those who conspired against the king and hence violated their oaths of fidelity. Such oaths obliged men to respect the monarch's person, not to harbour resentments against him, not to offend him, not to put him to death, not to remove him from the throne tyrannically.[141] The fathers of the Fifth Council of Toledo (636) laid down that this canon should be read in all councils subsequently celebrated, "in order that, when this has been many times inculcated, the hearts of the iniquitous ones may be corrected, terrified by insistence, which leads to prevarication through forgetfulness and guile".[142] But, conscious that the cause of internal discords was the struggle

[141] *Concilium Toletanum* IV (a. 633), c. 75.
[142] *Concilium Toletanum* V (a. 636), c. 7.

between the various nobles and the king to improve and assure their respective positions, the fathers assembled in Council tried to solve the problem. This led them, on the one hand, to protect the king's descendants, decreeing that these should enjoy the properties justly acquired or received as inheritance from their fathers, and to anathematise anyone who tried to transgress these decrees;[143] and, on the other, to protect the *fideles* against royal rapacity, establishing the inviolability of their estates.[144] Only eighteen months later, these decisions were reiterated in the Sixth Council of Toledo, which ratified what was established in the previous council about the stability of the properties of the king's descendants,[145] while with regard to the *fideles*, the council wanted them to keep, after the king's death, not only the full property of their estates, but also their offices.[146] Chindaswinth, in the second year of his reign (644), issued a new and harsh law against fugitives, those accused of high treason and conspirators. This law had retrospective force back to the days of Chintila for all those rebels who had demanded help from outside the kingdom. Capital punishment and confiscation of property would be applied for all these crimes. The mere intention of acting against the king was to be punished with the same penalties.[147]

Despite the extensive legislation that already existed in favour of the king and his family,[148] Erwig felt the necessity of further protecting his descendants, and again the Thirteenth Council of Toledo approved a canon which safeguarded the lives and estates of the royal family.[149] The last two councils held in the Visigothic kingdom of Toledo also included canons insisting on the protection which had to be offered to the king's relatives.[150] The necessity of continuously

---

[143] *Concilium Toletanum* V (a. 636), c. 2.

[144] *Concilium Toletanum* V (a. 636), c. 6: '*Ut quisquis supprestis principum extiterit iuste in rebus profligatis aut largitate principis adquisitis nullam debeat habere iacturam*'. . .

[145] It does so through c. 16, whose title is *De incolomitate te adhibenda dilectione regiae prolis.*

[146] *Concilium Toletanum* VI (a. 638), c. 14: *De remuneratione conlata fidelibus regum.*

[147] *Lex Visigothorum* II, 1, 8: '*De his, qui contra principem vel gentem aut patriam refugi sive insulentes existunt*'.

[148] The defence of the person of the king reached such a point that insults against him were punished by law (*Lex Visigothorum* II, 1, 9; *Concilium Toletanum* V (a. 636), c. 5), as was the consulting of fortune-tellers concerning for his health (*LV* VI, 2, 1).

[149] *Concilium Toletanum* XIII (a. 683), c. 14: *De munitione prolis regiae.*

[150] *Concilium Toletanum* XVI (a. 693), c. 8: *[De munime prolis regiae]* and *Concilium Toletanum* XVII (a. 694), c. 7: *De munitione coniugis atque prolis regiae.*

reiterating laws of this kind is in itself a clear proof that they did not obtain the desired result and explicitly shows that the king's enemies were internal and not external ones. Hence, as Michael McCormick[151] has pointed out, triumphs were celebrated by Visigothic kings to reaffirm their own position against the nobility. This was consistent with the rest of the symbolic manifestations of monarchy in seventh-century Hispania.

The contradiction between political theory and real practice that we have seen in operation right through the Visigothic period is better understood if we take into account that, despite repeated attacks against individual Visigothic sovereigns, the grandees of the kingdom never disputed monarchy itself. "Their purpose was to replace the existing monarch by another of their own choice",[152] but they never intended to replace the system of monarchical government by a different one, probably because this was the only one known and accepted in that historical period and because, as A. Barbero and M. Vigil have shown,[153] if the king needed the support of the *optimates* to reach the throne and retain it, the *optimates* required the existence of the monarchy, which shaped the state organisation essential to the consolidation of their privileged and dominant position above the rest of the Gothic people. It is not strange, therefore, that the Church, always united with the nobility in the defence of their particular interests, provided the monarchy with a solid conceptual basis on which to found its authority. It was precisely this concept of power, in the abstract, not personalised in a particular monarch, which was exteriorised through the elaboration of royal pomp and ceremonial.[154]

The royal propaganda policy inaugurated by Leovigild in the Visigothic kingdom of Toledo was able to accomplish its task in foreign politics. With the acquisition of pomp and ceremonial largely taken from Byzantium[155] the Visigothic monarchs stressed their own

---

[151] McCormick, *Eternal Victory. Triumphal rulership in late antiquity, Byzantium and the early medieval West*, pp. 302–323.

[152] This is the opinion of Thompson, *The Goths in Spain*, p. 188.

[153] Barbero and Vigil, *La formación del feudalismo en la Península Ibérica*, pp. 39–40.

[154] Very revealing in this context are the words of P. Delogu, "Germani e Carolingi", *Storia delle idee politiche, economiche e sociale. Ebraismo e Cristianesimo. Il Medioevo* 2, ed. L. Firpo (Torino, 1983), p. 16: 'Gli attributi regi, i simboli del potere e i luoghi del suo esercizio furono intesi, nella seconda metà del VII secolo, come rappresentazioni simboliche dell'essenza giuridica della regalità... una dimensione transpersonale della regalità'.

[155] Despite the objections made by Claude, *Adel, Kirche und Königtum im Westgotenreich*, p. 63, we think a Byzantine origin must be accepted.

sovereignty over an independent territory, put their power on the same footing as that of the Byzantine emperors and exteriorised their *civilitas*, thus increasing their prestige in the eyes of the world around them. At home, on the contrary, the monarchy, though made stronger through the introduction of a whole series of symbolic manifestations which exalted the sovereign's position at the head of society, was not strong enough to crush the nobility. Ideologically, the king, through these manifestations, defended and demonstrated his supremacy over the rest of the nobles, but in practice he lacked the necessary resources to impose his authority in a stable way. The Visigothic kingdom of Toledo lived therefore in a permanent contradiction between the strength of its monarchy and the fragility of its king.

BIBLIOGRAPHY

Primary Sources

Adefonsi tertii chronica. ed. J. Gil – J.L. Moralejo – J.I. Ruíz de la Peña, *Crónicas asturianas* (Oviedo, 1985), pp. 113–149.
Chronica Albendensia. ed. J. Gil – J.L. Moralejo – J.I. Ruíz de la Peña, *Crónicas asturianas* (Oviedo, 1985), pp. 151–188.
Chronica Gallica, a. CCCCLII et DXI. ed. Th. Mommsem, *Monumenta Germania Historica. Auctores antiquissimi* 9 (Chronicorum minorum saec. IV, V, VI, VII. vol. 1) (Berlin, 1892), pp. 615–666.
Chronica Muzarabica. ed. L. Gil, *Corpus scriptorum muzarabicorum*, 1 (Madrid, 1973), pp. 15–54.
Chronica Regum Visigothorum. ed. K. Zeumer, *Monumenta Germania Historica. Legum nationum Germanicarum* 1 (Hannover-Leipzig, 1902), pp. 457–461.
Codex Euricianus. ed. A. D'Ors, *El código de Eurico. Edición, Palingenesia, Índices. Estudios visigóticos* 2 (Roma, 1960), pp. 20–43.
Concilia Hispaniae. ed. J. Vives, *Concilios visigóticos e hispano-romanos* (Barcelona-Madrid, 1963).
Gregorius Turonensis, *Historiarum libri X.* ed. B. Krush – W. Lewison, *Monumenta Germania Historica. Scriptores rerum Merovingicarum* 1, 1 (Hannover, 1951).
Gregorius I Papa, *Epistolae.* ed. D. Ewald – L.M. Hartmann, *Monumenta Germania Historica. Epistolae* 1–2 (Berlin, 1891–1897).
Gregorius I Papa, *In librum primum Regum expositionum libri VI.* ed. J.P. Migne, *Patrologia Latina* 79 (Paris, 1849) cols. 17–468.
Iohannis abbatis biclarensis, *Chronica.* ed. Th. Mommsem, *Monumenta Germania Historica. Auctores antiquissimi* 11 (Chronicorum minorum saec. IV, V, VI, VII. vol. 2) (Berlin, 1894), pp. 207–220.
Iordanes, *De origine actibusque Getarum (Getica).* ed. Th. Mommsem, *Monumenta Germania Historica. Auctores antiquissimi* 5, 1 (Berlin, 1882), pp. 53–138.
Isidorus, *Etymologiae.* eds. J. Oroz Reta, M.A. Marcos Casquero, *Isidoro de Sevilla. Etimologías*, 1–2 (Madrid, 1982–83).
——, *Historia Gothorum, Wandalorum, Sueborum.* ed. C. Rodríguez Alonso, *Las historias de los godos, vándalos y suevos de Isidoro de Sevilla. Estudio, edición crítica y traducción* (León, 1975), pp. 167–321.

——, *Quaestiones in vetus Testamentum*. ed. J.P. Migne, *Patrologia Latina* 83 (Paris, 1850), col. 207–444.

——, *Sententiarum libri tres*. eds. J. Campos – I. Roca, *Santos padres españoles*. 2. *San Leandro, San Isidoro, San Fructuoso. Reglas monásticas de la España visigoda. Los tres libros de las "Sentencias"* (Madrid, 1971), pp. 213–525.

Iulianus Toletanus, *Epistola Pauli. Historia Wambae regis. Insultatio uilis prouinciae Galliae*. ed. W. Lewison, *Monumenta Germania Historica. Scriptores rerum Merovingicarum* 5 (Hannover-Leipzig, 1910), pp. 486–535.

Lex Visigothorum. ed. K. Zeumer, *Monumenta Germania Historica. Legum nationum Germanicarum* 1 (Hannover-Leipzig, 1902), pp. 34–456.

Liber Ordinum. ed. M. Ferotin, *Le 'Liber Ordinum' en usage dans l'Eglise wisigothique et mozarabe d'Espagne du V au XI siècles*. Monumenta Ecclesiae Liturgica (Paris, 1904).

Orosius, *Historia adversum paganos*. ed. C. Zangemeister, *Pauli Orosii Historiarum adversum paganos libri VII*. Corpus Scriptorum Ecclesiasticorum Latinorum, 5 (Viena, 1882).

Procopius, *Bellum Gothicum*. ed. H.B. Dewing, *Procopius with an English translation. III. History of the wars, books V and VI* (London, 1919).

Sidonius Apollinaris, *Epistolae*. ed. A. Loyen, *Sidoine Apollinaire. II. Lettres (livres I–V)* (Paris, 1970).

Secondary sources

Azkarate, A., *Arqueología cristiana de la Antigüedad tardía en Alava, Guipúzcoa y Vizcaya* (Vitoria, 1988).

Barbero, A., "El pensamiento político visigodo y las primeras unciones regias en la Europa medieval", *Hispania* 30 (1970), pp. 245–326.

—— and M. Vigil, "Algunos aspectos de la feudalización del reino visigodo en relación con su organización financiera y militar", *Sobre los orígenes sociales de la Reconquista* (Barcelona, 1974), pp. 107–137.

—— and M. Vigil, *La formación del feudalismo en la Península Ibérica* (Barcelona, 1978).

Barnwell, P.S., *Emperor, Prefects and Kings. The Roman West. 395–565* (London, 1992).

Barral i Altet, X., *La circulation des monnaies suèves et visigotiques* (München, 1976).

Burns, T.S., *The Ostrogoths. Kingship and society* (Wiesbaden, 1980).

——, *Barbarians within the Gates of Rome. A Study of Roman Military Policy and the Barbarians, ca. 375–425 AD* (Bloomington and Indianapolis, 1994).

Claude, D., *Adel, Kirche und Königtum im Westgotenreich* (Sigmaringen, 1971).

Codoñer Merino, C., *El "De Viris Illustribus" de Ildefonso de Toledo. Estudio y edición crítica* (Salamanca, 1972).

Collins, R., "Julian of Toledo and the Royal Succession in Late Seventh-Century Spain", *Early Medieval Kingship*, eds. P.H. Sawyer and I. Wood (Leeds, 1977), pp. 30–49.

D'Abadal i de Vinyals, R., "La Monarquía en el regne de Toledo", *Dels visigots al catalans* 1 (Barcelona, 1969), pp. 57–67.

D'Abadal, R., *Del reino de Tolosa al reino de Toledo* (Madrid, 1960).

D'Ors, A., *El Código de Eurico. Edicion, Palingenesia, Indices. Estudios visigóticos* 2 (Roma-Madrid, 1966).

Delogu, P., "Germani e Carolingi", *Storia delle idee politiche, economiche e sociale. Ebraismo e Cristianesimo. Il Medioevo* 2, ed. L. Firpo (Torino, 1983), pp. 3–54.

Diaz y Diaz, M.C., "Titulaciones regias en la monarquía visigoda", *Revista portuguesa de Historia* 16 (1976), pp. 133–141.

Duby, G., *Guerreros y campesinos. Desarrollo inicial de la economía europea (500–1200)*, (Madrid, 1983) (English translation: *The Early Growth of the European Economy* (London, 1975).

Ewig, E., *Spätantikes und Fränkisches Gallien* (München, 1976).

Garcia de Valdeavellano, L., "La moneda y la economía de cambio en la Península Ibérica desde el s. VI hasta mediados del s. XI", *Settimane di Studi sull'Alto Medioevo* 8 (Spoleto, 1961), pp. 203–230.

Garcia Herrero, G., "Julián de Toledo y la realeza visigoda", *Arte, sociedad, economía y religión durante el Bajo Imperio y la Antigüedad tardía. Antigüedad y Cristianismo* 8 (Murcia, 1991), pp. 201–255.

Garcia Iglesias, L., "El intermedio ostrogodo en Hispania (507–549 d. C.)", *Hispania Antiqua* 5 (1975), pp. 89–120.

Garcia Moreno, L.A., *Historia de España visigoda* (Madrid, 1989).

———, "El estado protofeudal visigodo: precedente y modelo para la Europa carolingia", *L'Europe Héritière de l'Espagne wisigothique*, eds. J. Fontaine and Ch. Pellistrandi (Madrid, 1992), pp. 17–43.

Gonzalez, T., *La política en los concilios de Toledo* (Roma, 1977).

Heather, P., *Goths and Romans. 332–489* (Oxford, 1991).

Heiss, A., *Descripción general de las monedas de los reyes visigodos de España* (Paris, 1872).

Isla Frez, A., "Las relaciones entre el reino visigodo y los reyes merovingios a finales del s. VI", *España Medieval* 13 (1990), pp. 11–32.

King, P.D., *Law and Society in the Visigothic Kingdom* (Cambridge, 1972).

Mateu y Llopis, F., "Las fórmulas y los símbolos cristianos en los tipos monetares visigodos", *Analecta Sacra Tarraconensia* 14 (1941), pp. 75–96.

———, "Notas sobre el latín de las inscripciones monetarias godas", *Revista de Archivos, Bibliotecas y Museos* 61 (1955), pp. 293–315.

———, "Los atributos de la realeza en los trémises godos y las categorías diplomáticas coetáneas", *Anales Toledanos. Estudios sobre la España visigoda* 3 (Toledo, 1971), pp. 139–158.

Mauss, M., *The gift. Forms and functions of exchange in Archaic Societies* (London, 1954).

McCormick, M., *Eternal Victory. Triumphal rulership in late antiquity, Byzantium and the early medieval West* (Cambridge, 1986).

Miles, G.C., *The coinage of the Visigoths of Spain. Leovigild to Achila II* (New York, 1952).

Munier, C., "L'*Ordo de celebrando concilio* wisigothique. Ses remaniements jusqu'au Xè siècle", *Revue des Sciences Religieuses* 37 (1963), pp. 250–271.

Nelson, J.L., "Inauguration rituals", *Early Medieval Kingship*, eds. P.H. Sawyer and I. Wood (Leeds, 1977), pp. 123–153.

———, "The Lord's anointed and the people's choice: Carolingian royal ritual", *Rituals of Royalty. Power and Ceremonis in Traditional Societies*, eds. D. Cannadine and S. Price (Cambridge, 1987), pp. 137–180.

Nieto, G., *El oppidum de Iruña (Alava)* (Vitoria, 1958).

Orlandis, J., "La iglesia visigoda y los problemas de la sucesión al trono en el s. VII", *Settimane di studi sull'Alto Medioevo* 7 (Spoleto, 1960), pp. 333–351.

———, *Historia de España. La España visigoda* (Madrid, 1977).

Palol de Salellas, P., "Esencia del arte hispánico de época visigoda: romanismo y germanismo", *Settimane di Studi sull'Alto Medioevo* 3 (Spoleto, 1956), pp. 65–126.

Pange, J. de, *Le roi très chrètien* (Paris, 1949).

Perez Pujol, E., *Instituciones sociales de la España goda* 2 (Valencia, 1892).

Perez Sanchez, D., *El ejército en la sociedad visigoda* (Salamanca, 1989).

Reinhart, W.M., "Nuevas aportaciones a la numismática visigoda", *Archivo Español de Arqueología* 18 (1945), pp. 212–235.

Reydellet, M., *La royauté dans la littérature latine de Sidoine Apollinaire à Isidore de Séville* (Roma, 1981).

Rivera Recio, J., "Encumbramiento de la sede toledana durante la dominación visigótica", *Hispania Sacra* 8 (1955), pp. 3–34.

Rocca, Chr. La, "Una prudente maschera antiqua. La politica edilizia di Teoderic", *Teoderico il Grande e i Goti d'Italia. Atti del XIII Congresso internazionale di studi sull'Alto Medioevo* (Spoleto, 1993), pp. 451–515.

Sanchez Albornoz, C., "La *ordinatio principis* en la España goda y postvisigoda", *Cuadernos de Historia de España* 35–36 (1962), pp. 5–36.

Sanchez-Arcilla Bernal, J., *Temas de Historia de la Administración. I. Hispania romana y visigoda* (Madrid, 1983).

Schlesinger, W., *Beiträge zur deustchen Verfassungsgeschichte des Mittelalters* (Göttingen, 1963).

Schlunk, H., "Relaciones entre la Península Ibérica y Bizancio durante la época visigoda", *Archivo Español de Arqueología* 18 (1945), pp. 177–204.

Schwöbel, H., *Synode und Könige in Westgotenreich. Grundlagen und Formen ihrer Beziehung* (Köln-Wien, 1982).

Silva, S. de, "La más antigua iconografia medieval de los reyes visigodos", *Los visigodos. Historia y civilización. Antigüedad y Cristianismo* 3 (Murcia, 1986), pp. 537–558.

Spaulding, E., "El epíteto *pius* en las monedas visigodas", *Numisma* 192–203 (1985–86), pp. 33–38.

Stroheker, K.F., *Germanentum und Spätantike* (Zürich-Stuttgart, 1965).

Teja, R., "Il ceremoniale imperiale", *Storia di Roma. L'età tardoantica. I. Crisi e trasformazioni* 3 (Torino, 1993) pp. 613–642.

Thompson, E.A., *The Early Germans* (Oxford, 1965).

——, *The Visigoths at the times of Ulfilas* (Oxford, 1966).

——, *The Goths in Spain* (Oxford, 1969).

Tomasini, W., *The Barbaric Tremissis in Spain and Southern France: Anastasius to Leovigild* (New York, 1964).

Torres Lopez, M., "El estado visigótico. Algunos datos sobre su formación y principios fundamentales de su organización política", *Anuario de Historia del Derecho Español* 3 (1926), pp. 307–475.

Ullmann, W., *The Carolingian Renaissance and the Idea of Kingship* (London, 1969).

Valverde Castro, Mª.R., "La Iglesia hispano-visigoda: ¿fortalecedora o limitadora de la soberanía real?", *Hispania Antiqua* 16 (1992), pp. 381–392.

Valverde, Mª.R., "De Atanarico a Valia, aproximación a los orígenes de la monarquía visigoda", *Studia Historica. Historia Antigua* 12 (1994), pp. 143–158.

Vigil, M. and A. Barbero, "Sucesión al trono y evolución social en el reino visigodo", *Hispania Antiqua* 4 (1974), pp. 379–393.

Wallace – Hadrill, J.M., *Early Germanic kingship in England and on the Continent* (Oxford, 1971).

Weiner, A.B., *Inalienable possessions. The paradox of keeping-while-giving* (Berkeley, 1992).

Wolfram, H., *A History of the Goths* (Berkeley, 1988).

Wood, I., "Kings, kingdoms and consent", *Early Medieval Kingship*, eds. P.H. Sawyer and I. Wood (Leeds, 1977), pp. 6–29.

KINGSHIP RITUALS AND IDEOLOGY IN LOMBARD ITALY

Stefano Gasparri

Any study of rituals of royal power in the barbarian societies of the early medieval West involves considerable methodological problems which mainly arise from features of these rituals which have no consistent connection with the written evidence. To surmount these difficulties, we need to make use of a particular type of source: stories that may be taken to reflect the pre-invasion history of the Germanic peoples. That there is a kernel of historical reliability in these myths has sometimes been denied; but, in my view, they did transmit a living core of ancient tradition, however much this was distorted by the process of transmission and by the literary culture of the writers who recorded them.[1]

This kind of evidence suggests that very difference kinds of inauguration were used for early Germanic kings. Visigoths and Ostrogoths raised on a shield the chief who had been elected king by his warriors. Such ceremonies may have taken place, sometimes, on the battlefield: thus, following the Battle of the Catalaunian Fields in 451 when Attila and the Huns were defeated, the Visigoths elected Torismund, son of their king Theoderic who had fallen in the battle, 'among the clash of arms ... among the warriors on the battlefield'. The likelihood that Torismund was raised on his warriors' shield is strengthened by analogy with the case of the last Ostrogothic king in Italy, Witigis, who was inaugurated in a military ceremony: 'a shield was put under him (*scudo subposito*)', according to 'ancestral custom (*mos maiorum*)'.[2] Witigis's election took place in the camp near

---

[1] Cf. S. Gasparri, *La cultura tradizionale dei Longobardi. Struttura tribale e resistenze pagane* (Spoleto, 1983); and, for a very different view, W. Goffart, *The Narrators of Barbarian History. Jordanes, Gregory of Tours, Bede and Paul the Deacon* (Princeton, 1988), pp. 382–388, for Paul the Deacon, and *idem, Barbarians and Romans AD 419–584: The Techniques of Accommodation* (Princeton, 1980), p. 8, for Jordanes and the origins of the Goths, with Goffart's observation that these old stories about the origins of Germanic peoples "have nothing in common with our standard of credible history".

[2] Jordanes, *Getica* XLI, 215, ed. F. Giunta and F. Grillone, *Fonti per la storia d'Italia*, 117 (Rome, 1991).

Rieti (Lazio) on the eve of the Ostrogoths' final defeat, in the mid-sixth century.[3]

The Goths were not the only people who practised this ritual: it is in fact widely documented in the Germanic world. The earliest evidence is found in Tacitus' *Annales*, where Brinnius, a famous warrior of the Cannanefates who lived in the reign of Vespasian (69–79 AD), is said to have been elected war-leader (*dux*) 'by being raised on a shield and on men's shoulders, according to the custom of his people (*mos gentis*)'.[4] Brinnius was made, not king, but commander-in-chief of his people's army for the duration of the Cannanifates' rebellion against the Romans. In Germanic antiquity, kingship and military leadership were very close and, during the invasions of the late-fourth and fifth centuries, they merged.[5]

Another case quoted by Ammianus raises further issues. For now, the protagonist was not a barbarian chief but a Roman emperor, Julian the Apostate, proclaimed emperor (*augustus*) in Paris in 360 by the soldiers of the Gallic legions 'by being raised on a shield', in the same way as Brinnius or Witigis.[6] Reciprocal influences between the Roman and Germanic worlds also appear in other aspects of inauguration rituals. Germanic customs probably lay behind the raising of Julian, and it is also very likely that the troops who took part were Frankish or Alamannic federates—warriors belonging to peoples whom the Romans knew well, whether as enemies or as allies. Julian's inauguration really combined two cultures, and underlines the point that it is difficult to impute a particular origin to a given ritual. Adoption by arms is a ritual very close to the investiture of a new king with weapons, and I shall return to it below. Written sources attest the existence of this rite of adoption among the Germans and the Iranians (of the Sassanid period). There is also evidence for the Byzantine emperor Justin's adoption of the Persian king Chosroes 'by arms and armour, as is proper for a barbarian', and also for the same emperor's planned adoption of Eutharic, son-

---

[3] Cassiodorus, *Variae* X, 31, ed. T. Mommsen, *MGH Auctores Antiquissimi* XII (Berlin, 1894).

[4] Tacitus, *Historiae*, IV, 15.

[5] W. Schlesinger, "Über germanischen Heerkönigtum", *Das Königtum. Seine geistige und rechtliche Grundlagen*, ed. E. Ewig (Lindau-Konstanx, 1956), pp. 105–141. On the pre-invasion Germanic world and its links with the Roman Empire, see E.A. Thompson, *The Early Germans* (Oxford, 1965).

[6] Ammianus Marcellinus, *Res gestae* XX, 4: 13–18.

in-law of the Ostrogothic king Theoderic. Justin's former colleague Zeno had adopted Theoderic, who in his turn had adopted several other western Germanic rulers.[7] These examples indicate a structural core of customs common to many peoples and cultures in Late Antiquity, including the Roman (Byzantine) and Persian Empires.

The rituals of the ancient Germans merged with those of the Romans, and modern scholars have suggested that the inauguration rituals of the early medieval kingdoms were the result. In the case of ritual, moreover, Roman roots very often meant Christian roots, because of the profound christianisation of late imperial power. Even in this case, the sacral character of the rituals was not new, but had been equally prominent in pagan Germanic antiquity. In this context, we can recall not only the famous (and controversial) case of the long-haired Merovingian kings,[8] but also more ancient evidence. Tacitus, for example, in a passage very close to that describing Brinnius' elevation, tells of an atistocrat named Julius Civilis, who was elected chief of the Batavians 'in a barbarian rite (*barbaro ritu*): Civilis gathered the Batavians in a sacredwood where they all feasted together: we know that the banquet was a central feature in the system of beliefs and values held by Germanic aristocrats.[9]

During the early Middle Ages, there is evidence of other types of royal ritual, like enthronement and, most famous of all, anointing (*unctio; consecratio*), derived from the Old Testament. In 672, the Visigoth Wamba, already elected by the people, was consecrated king with holy oil by Archbishop Julian of Toledo.[10] Later, the same ceremony was introduced among the Franks, when Pippin, father of Charlemagne, was anointed king in 751, and a generation later among the Anglo-Saxons, with the consecration of Ecgferth son of Offa in 787.[11]

---

[7] Procopius, *History of the Wars. The Persian War* I, 11, for Chosroes' adoption; Jordanes, *Getica* LVII, 289, for Zeno's adoption of Theoderic; Cassiodorus, *Variae* IV, 2, for Theoderic's adoption of Rodulf, king of the Herules, and VIII, 1, for Justin's adoption of Eutharic; Isidore, *Historia Svevorum*, ed. T. Mommsen, *MGH Auctores Antiquissimi* XI, i, 302, for Theoderic's adoption of Remismund, king of the Sueves.

[8] See J.M. Wallace-Hadrill, *The Long-Haired Kings and Other Studies in Frankish History* (London, 1962), pp. 148–163.

[9] Tacitus, *Historiae* IV, 14.

[10] See below the contribution by P. Diaz and M.R. Valverde.

[11] See J.L. Nelson, "Inauguration rituals", *Early Medieval Kingship*, ed. P. Sawyer and I.N. Wood (Leeds, 1977), pp. 50–71.

All the above is well known. By contrast, Lombard royal inauguration rituals, like many other features of the history of this people,
have not been analysed with the attention they deserve.[12] Lombard
inaugrations belong to a different class of rituals, based on the bestowal
of arms on the new king. The main purpose of the following discussion is to reconstruct the royal rituals of the Lombard monarchy,
and to set them in the historical context of the transition from a
tribal and heathen kingship in the age of invasions, that is, in the
first half of the seventh century, to a christian one in the second
half of the seventh and eighth centuries. This christian Lombard
kingship lasted until it was displaced by Charlemagne in 774.

Lombard Rituals: the King, the People, the Lance

We do not know exactly how Lombard kings were elected or consecrated (whether in the heathen or christian sense). We can, though,
be certain of two things: the king, who was commander-in-chief of
the *exercitus Langobardorum*, was elected in a military assembly whose
Lombard name was *gairthinx*, "assembly of the lances",[13] in the presence of his people in arms: it may well be that in the age of the
migrations, the whole Lombard people of free men had been expected
to gather, but once they were settled in Italy, this was out of the
question. Nevertheless, many warriors evidently participated in this
ceremony, which therefore took place in the open air, in a large
space, probably ourside a town. One of the ceremonies is described
in the Edict of Rothari, issued in 643: according to c. 386, the Edict
was approved by the *exerctus Langobardorum* gathered in Pavia, and by
a typical act: *per gairethinx*, meaning 'in the assembly of the lances',
or, more precisely, 'by striking shields with lances'.[14]

Clearly, there were some links between this ceremony and those
involved in the elections of OIstrogothic and Visigothic kings.[15] But

---

[12] Contrast the views of M. McCormick, *Eternal Victory. Triumphal Rulership in Late
Antiquity, Byzantium and the Early Medieval West* (Cambridge, 1986), p. 288: "... Lombard accessions have been thoroughly studied..." Yet "the scarcity of evidence
bars forever a full understanding of these rites." See also R. Schneider, *Königswahl
und Königserhebung im Frühmittelalter. Untersuchungen zur Herrschaftsnachfolge bei den Langobarden und Merowinger* (Stuttgart, 1972), pp. 5–63, and *passim*.
[13] J. Jarnut, *Geschichte der Langobarden* (Stuttgart, 1982), p. 50.
[14] Edict of Rothari c. 386, ed. C. Azzara and S. Gasparri, *Le leggi dei Langobardi.
Storia, memoria e diritto di un popolo germanico* (Milan, 1992), p. 102.
[15] See above, nn. 2 and 3.

a second feature was evidently typical of Lombard inaugurations. Lombard kings, on their election, received a lance (contus, or hasta) as symbol of their new power. Paul the Deacon, the historian of the Lombards, writing during the reign of Charlemagne (768–814), tells how Hildeprand became king at Pavia in 735. The inauguration was performed near the church and cemetery of Sta Maria *ad Perticas*. Here, 'the Lombards raised up Hildeprand as king, and gave to him a lance, according to custom'.[16] Paul reports that a cuckoo alighted on the tip of Hildeprand's lance, and that this was onterpreted by some wise men (*prudentes*) as an evil omen. In fact, the election was not entirely valid, since Liutprand, Hildeprand's uncle, who at that moment was dangerously ill, subsequently recovered. Furthermore, nine years later when Liutprand died and Hildeprand succeeded him as legitimate king, his reign lasted only a few months. Interestingly, in the nearby cemetery of Sta Maria, the monuments (cenotaphs) to the Lombard warriors who had died far away from their country were indeed marked with a design showing a lance surmounted by a bird (a dove), symbolising the soul of the dead man.[17]

Everything I have just said means that the royal inauguration ritual and the burial ritual were linked with each other. Other evidence that the meaning of the combination of lance and bird was not exclusively connected with burial, can be found in an ornamental shield-plaque of the eighth century, now in the National Museum of Lucca, which shows a Lombard warrior, the so-called Daniel figure, holding a lance in his right hand: the lance is surmounted by a cross, and the cross by a bird.[18] It is possible, therefore, that the *hasta regia*, the king's ceremonial lance, also had a bird on its top, since the king was, first and foremost, a warrior, the commander-in-chief of the *populus-exercitus* (as Giovanni Tabacco has termed it), that is, the people who were also the army.[19]

The lance seems to have been the principal symbol of kingship among Lombards. Further evidence is supplied by the *lamina* of the Val di Nievole, which is the front part of a bronze helmet dating

---

[16] Paul the Deacon, *Historia Langobardorum* VI, 55, ed. G. Waitz, *MGH Scriptores rerum Langobardicarum et Italicarum saec. VI–IX* (Hanover, 1878): "*Langobardi . . . Hildeprandum . . . regem levaverunt. Cui dum contum, sicut moris est, traderent.*"

[17] Paul the Deacon, *Historia Langobardorum* V, 34.

[18] P.E. Schramm, "Die heilige Lanze", P.E. Schramm, *Herrschaftszeichen und Staatssymbolik*, 3 vols. (Stuttgart, 1955), ii, pp. 492–537; and S. Gasparri, *La cultura*, p. 64.

[19] G. Tabacco, "La storia politica e sociale", *Storia d'Italia*, ed. G. Galasso II, i (Turin, 1974), pp. 39–72.

from the late sixth or early seventh century, and now in the Bargello Museum in Florence. On this plaque, a king, Agilulf, is depicted sitting on a throne, with two warriors armed with lances on wither side of him. I shall have more to say later about this plaque—the earliest portrait of a Germanic king enthroned.[20] For the moment, it is worth noting that there were Lombard warriors with the specific duty of carrying the kin's lance. At the battle of Forino (Campania) between the Lombards of Benevento and the Byzantine army of Constans II in 663, King Grimoald was not present, but the warrior Amalongus "who was accustomed to carry the royal lance" decided the battle's outcome by an amazing blow delivered with none other than the king's lance.[21] Dukes too, at any rate the more important ones, had their lance-bearers: according to Paul the Deacon, Duke Ratchis of Friuli (later king, 744–749) had a lance-bearer who accompanied him into battle.[22]

The lance was the symbol of power (*Herrschaftszeichen*) characteristic of a people of horsemen, for it is a typical rider's weapon; and it is virtually certain that the Lombards developed this royal symbol as a result of the contacts they had in the migration-period with the nomadic peoples in the Danube region and the Balkans, for instance, with the Avars who are known to have used the lance surmounted by a bird as a military standard.[23] But we must stress again the complex roots of early medieval rituals of power: in fact, the lance as a symbol was also important among the most western Germanic peoples, for whom contacts with nomads are a less plausible explanation. For instance, Tacitus says that when the young men of the Germanic tribes became warriors, they received shield and *framea*, perhaps a kind of lance.[24] Later, in the Merovingian period, according to Gregory of Tours, King Guntramn in 585 gave a lance (*hasta*) to his nephew Childebert with the words, "this is the proof that I grant you all my kingdom".[25] It is true that this is the only evidence, apart from some images on coins, that the lance was part of ancient Frankish inauguration rituals, but it is significant because, unlike

---

[20] See n. 18, and McCormick, *Eternal Victory*, pp. 289–293.

[21] Paul the Deacon, *Historia Langobardorum* V, 10: "*Qui regium contum ferre erat solitus...*"

[22] Paul the Deacon, *Historia Langobardorum* VI, 52.

[23] See above, n. 18.

[24] Tacitus, *Germania* 13. Whether the *framea* was a kind of lance is uncertain.

[25] Gregory of Tours, *Libri Historiarum* VII, 33, ed. B. Krusch, *MGH Scriptores rerum Merovingicarum* I (Hanover, 1951): "*Hoc est iudicium quod tibi omne regnum meum tradedi*".

Tacitus's story about the young warriors of Germania,[26] it also relates to kingship. To return to the Lombards: a story told by Paul the Deacon provides further evidence for my topic. Paul describes King Authari's arrival, late in the sixth century, at Reggio Calabria, in the deep South of Italy. Authari did not cross the sea to Sicily. Instead, seated on a horse, he advanced no further than a pillar which rose up our of the waves: touching this with his lance, he declared: "The Lombards' borders will extend up to this point!"[27] This tale was probably told in the royal palace at Pavia in the eighth century, long after the date to which it purported to refer: the Lombards had never got so far south in Authari's time. Nevertheless the gesture imputed to Authari is interesting: here, touching the pillar with the lance meant subjecting territory to the king's rule, and the king himself is depicted as a horseman. [He would have got his socks wet otherwise . . .]

To complete the picture, we should note the importance of the lance or spear in the iconography of later Roman emperorship. Not only is the emperor commonly depicted with a lance, but he is often flanked by two lance-bearing warriors. It therefore seems likely that here again, we find a merging of Germanic and Roman symbolic representations of power and authority.

Lombard Kingship, the Worship of Odin, and the Nomads

The Lombard inauguration ritual was characterised by a warrior ideology of non-christian origin. Forty years ago, Karl Hauck defined Lombard kingship as "wodanic" (*ein wodanistisches Königtum*), referring precisely to the royal lance.[28] I think he was right. In Old Norse literature, the name of Odin's lance is gungnir: thrown at the enemy, this divine lance terrified the opposing warriors and put them to flight.[29] Some Lombard kings mentioned in the sagas and in the

---

[26] Schramm, "Die heilige Lanze", pp. 493–497.
[27] Paul the Deacon, *Historia Langobardorum* III, 32: "*Usque hic erunt Langobardorum fines*".
[28] K. Hauck, "Herrschaftszeichen eines wodanistisches Königtums", *Jahrbuch für fränkische Landesforschung* 14 (1966), pp. 9–66.
[29] O. Höfler, "Abstammungstradition", *Reallexicon der germanischen Altertumskunde*, ed. J. Hoops, 2nd edn. (Berlin-New York, 1973), pp. 18–29.

prologue to Rothari's Code, were said to be 'from the lineage of the
Gungingi', that is, descended from a lineage whose name derived
from that of Odin's lance, hence, surely, that these men were considered Odin's descendants.[30] There seems to be a clear link between
Odin's lance and Lombard kingship: whoever possessed Odin's royal
lance was king. At this point, I must quote again from Paul the Deacon: one day, King Agelmund, the first Lombard king, saw seven
children in a pond abandoned by their mother and in danger of
drowning. Thinking they were indeed dead, the king prodded them
with his royal lance, whereupon one of the boys reached out and
seized it. The king was astonished: he ordered the boy to be res-
cued and "foretold his great future".[31] Why did Agelmund speak
thus? Clearly, because the boy, whose name was Lamissio (from the
Lombard word *lama*, "marsh") had made the very same gesture as
that made by the newly-chosen king of the Lombards, who had to
grasp the royal lance as a symbol of his new power. And indeed,
after Agelmund had been killed by the Bulgars, Lamissio succeeded
him as king.[32]

Paul, writing in the 790s, gives no further explanation. The story
was, I suggest, intended to say something more: it presented the
Lombards with a model of royal election and indicated the religious
content of the election itself. Agelmund is "from the lineage of the
Gungingi". Lamissio, by grasping the royal lance, becomes his adoptive son and one of his family, and will reign after him. In Lombard ritual practice, by grasping the royal lance, a newly-elected man
became one of Gungingi's divine descendants and, hence, became
king; and it was probably at this very moment that the warriors
struck their shields with their lances. Finally, the story shows the
"Bulgars", that is, the Huns, as Agelmund's and Lamissio's enemies.
This tallies with the suggestion that the origins of Lombard warrior
kingship (*Heerkönigtum*) lay in eastern-central Europe: precisely where,
in the fifth and early sixth centuries, the Lombards came under the
influence of the westernmost nomadic tribes.[33] Mounted combat, and
rituals involving lances, were fundamental elements of the new traditions the Lombards assimilated.

---

[30] Gasparri, *La cultura*, pp. 23–7.
[31] Paul the Deacon, *Historia Langobardorum* I, 14: "*Rex misericordia motus factumque
altius ammiratus, eum magnum futurum pronuntiat*". The strory of the *cyncephali* is included
in I, 15–7 as well.
[32] Paulus Diaconus, *Historia Langobardorum* I, 16.
[33] For battles against the Huns, see Jarnut, *Geschichte*, p. 18.

Other Warrior Rituals

A very interesting ritual was performed in southern Italy in 663, during the Byzantine invasion of the Lombard duchy of Benevento, led by Constans II. The episode is recorded in the *Vita Barbati*, a hagiographic text written at the beginning of the ninth century. Outside the town of Benevento, a skin was hung on a tree, called *sacra arbor* by the hagiographer, by a group of Lombard horsemen, who first rode away, then raced headlong back to it, spurring their horses until blood flowed, then tore the skin into pieces, and ate it.[34]

This was probably a totemic rite, dedicated to the heathen god Odin (or Thor-Donar). But in relation to the present topic, its principal interest is that the Lombards practised this ritual on horseback. In fact, this is the only known case of such a rite among the Germanic peoples, and this in itself could strengthen the hypothesis of nomadic influence on the Lombards.[35]

It is not clear wheteher the Lombards of Benevento broke the animal-skin with their hands or with their lances: in light of what I have said above, it might be expected that lances were part of the rite, becuase the ceremony discussed by the author of the *Vita Barbati*, even though it was not a royal ritual, was in any case a ritual linked with the exercise of power, and perhaps the duke of benevento himself participated in it. The Lombards of Benevento, according to the hagiographer, used this performance to show their strength, their internal unity, their lordship over the duchy at a very dangerous time, when the region was invaded by the Byzantines led by the emperor himself—the first Roman emperor to come westwards for two centuries.[36] It is therefore reasonable to suppose that Duke Romoald was also present at the ceremony of the *arbor sacra* as well.

Other Lombard warrior-rites are documented, some of them unconnected with kingship. According to Paul the Deacon, on the eve of an important battle against the Assipitti who wanted to stop them entering Mauringa (that is, probably, the region of Mecklenburg[37]),

---

[34] *Vita Barbati episcopi Beneventani*, ed. G. Waitz, *MGH Scriptores rerum Langobardorum*, p. 557.

[35] But see the Anglo-Saxon Synod of Clovesho (747), c. 16, which prohibits horse races (*cursus equorum*) and other heathen practices during the three days before Ascension Day: *Councils and Ecclesiastical Documents Relating to Great Britain and Ireland*, eds. A. Haddan and W. Stubbs, 3 vols. (Oxford, 1881), ii, p. 365.

[36] Gasparri, *La cultura*, pp. 69–91.

[37] J. Jarnut, "I Longobardi nell'epoca precedente all'occupazione dell'Italia", *Langobardia*, ed. S. Gasparri and P. Cammarosano (Udine, 1990), p. 12.

some Lombard warriors put on dog masks, and it was said that
they drank human blood. This is an exceptional story, worth quot-
ing in full:

> [The Lombards] pretended to have some *cynocephali* (that is, men with
> dogs' heads) in their camp, and they circulated among their enemies
> a rumour that these warrior never tired of fighting, that they drank
> human blood, and if they could not lay hands on an enemy, sucked
> their own blood. In order to make this story more credible, the Lom-
> bards increased the number of tents and lit many fires in their camp.[38]

Paul in recounting this story says that it was merely a trick on the
part of the men of old to defeat the Assipitti. But it is very likely
that the story has a further significance: namely, it suggests that the
rits was part of the warrior-worship of Odin, because the Lombard
cynocephali—half-men, half-beasts—seem to resemble the *berserkr*
among the Vikings. The mention of camp-fires could hint at a ceremony in which warrior-devotees of Odin took hallucinogenic drugs
through which the god's "sacred possession" took place: a transformation which made them, like the berserkr, into wild beasts and
invincible warriors.[39] All these are well-known shamanistic practices
typical of the peoples of the steppe: already in the fifth century BC,
Herodotus told a story that could recall similar practices among the
Scythians.[40] Nor should we forget that the Lombards' most ancient
name, *Winnili*, could mean precisely "winning dogs".[41]

Another interesting ritual is described by Paul the Deacon shortly
after the cynocephali episode: when they entered Mauringa, the Lombards freed many slaves by touching them with an arrow "in order

---

[38] Paul the Deacon, *Historia Langobardorum* I, 11.

[39] See F. Cardini, *Alle radici della cavalleria medievale* (Florence, 1981), pp. 71–86.
Herodotus, *Histories* IV, 64, writes that the Scythian warrior drank the blood of the
first enemy he had slain. See also nn. 40 and 45.

[40] Herodotus, *Histories* IV, 73: "After the burial, the Scythians cleanse themselves
as I will describe: they anoint and wash their heads; as for their bodies, they set
up three poles leaning together to a point and cover these over with woolen mats;
then, in the place so enclosed to the best of their power, they make a pit in the
centre beneath the poles and the mats and throw red-hot stones into it"; IV, 75:
"The Scythians then take the seed of their hemp and, creeping under the mats,
they throw it on the red-hot stones; and, being so thrown, it smoulders and sends
forth so much steam that no Greek vapour-bath could surpass it. The Scythians
howl in their joy at the vapour-bath" (English translation by A.D. Godley, The
Loeb Classical Library (Cambridge, Mass., 1957)).

[41] Gasparri, *La cultura*, p. 14.

to increase the number of warriors".[42] In this case, the ceremony had mainly military features. It is possible, however, to find in other warrior-rites a link with kingship. Two such stories are recounted by Paul. Prince Alboin, when young, after demonstrating his courage in a bloody battle with the Gepids in 551, was obliged by his father King Audoin to go and receive arms from the defeated king of the Gepids, Turisind, whose son Turismod had been slain by Alboin. Should Alboin succeed, he could become his father's table-companion (*in convivio comes*), because, according to Lombard custom (*ritus gentis*), a king's son could eat with his father only after having received arms from a foreign king. Obeying Audoin's orders, Alboin took forty young warriors, went to Turisind's court; and at risk of losing his own life, obtained the arms of Turismod.[43] The second rite also concerns Alboin. Many years after his visit to Turisind, and not long after after invading Italy in 569, Alboin forced his wife Rosamund to drink from the skull of his enemy the Gepid king Cunimund, Rosamund's father, whom he had just slain. This act provoked Rosamund to bring about the death of the great Lombard hero-king himself.[44] In this case, it is Herodotus who helps explain the meaning of Alboin's strange behaviour:

> [A Scythian warrior] will carry to his king the skulls of all the men he has slain in battle. He receives a share of the booty if he brings a skull, but not otherwise. . . . If the warrior is rich, he covers the skull with a piece of rawhide, gilds the inside of it, and uses it for a drinking-cup. If honoured guests visit him, he serves them with these skulls . . .: this they call manly valour.[45]

From the eighth century, we have evidence of a very different ritual. Charles Martel, mayor of the Frankish palace, sent his son Pippin, who was later to become the first Carolingian king, to the Lombard king Liutprand, "so that, according to custom, Liutprand would cut his hair".[46] Liutprand thus became Pippin's adoptive father, and the Franks and Lombards made an alliance with each other. Here as in other cases, it is impossible to know whether the original

---

[42] Paul the Deacon, *Historia Langobardorum* I, 13: ". . . *ut bellatorum possint ampliare numerum.*"
[43] Paul the Deacon, *Historia Langobardorum* I, 23–4.
[44] Paul the Deacon, *Historia Langobardorum* I, 27 and II, 28.
[45] Herodotus, *Histories* IV, 64–5.
[46] Paul the Deacon, *Historia Langobardorum* VI, 53: ". . . *ut eius iuxta morem capillum incideret.*"

ritual was Frankish or Lombard: it may indeed have belonged to a structured code of rituals that developed in the migration period among the early medieval north-western European tribes. Another possibility is that this, or a similar, ritual was of Roman origin, for we know that at the beginning of the seventh century, the Byzantine patrician of Oderzo, Gregory, caught Duke Taso of Friuli in a trap after promising to adopt him as his son by shaving his beard.[47]

Roman Influence: 'the Summer of the Dead' and the Bavarian Dynasty

The nomadic tribes were not the only source of influence on Lombard ritual. Roman elements can also be identified. This is something we too often underrate, for we tend to assume that the Lombards had minimal contacts with the empire before 569, yet this was clearly not so. In spite of their alien character, so strongly emphasised by Roman writers,[48] the Lombards had contacts with the Roman-barbarian civilization of the Merovingians and, during the period of their stay in Pannonia and the North Balkans, they were Byzantine federates. Moreover, once they settled in Italy, the Lombards fell under the spell of classical civilization. Roman (both Italic and Byzantine) influences on the Lombards in Italy were very strong.[49] They appear, for instance, in the use of co-regency practised by many Lombard kings who associated their sons (or other kinsmen) with them on the throne. Thus, in the eighth century, Ansprand shared the throne with his son Liutprand, who in turn shared it with his nephew Hildeprand.[50] But this custom long predated the eighth century: in 604, Adaloald, Agilulf's son, was made king by his father in the circus at Milan. The circumstances were very unusual: not because Agilulf's decision was confirmed by the Lombard warriors—for that was normal—but because the ceremony was performed in the circus, just as Byzantine imperial elections were confirmed in Constantinople by the crowd who acclaimed new emperors in the

---

[47] Paul the Deacon, *Historia Langobardorum* IV, 38. Cf. also below the contribution by R. Le Jan.

[48] For example, Velleius Paterculus, *Historia romana* II, 106: "*Langobardi, gens etiam Germana feritate ferocior.*"

[49] McCormick, *Eternal Victory*, pp. 284–7.

[50] Paul the Deacon, *Historia Langobardorum* VI, 35 and 55.

Hippodrome. Thus the inauguration ritual of 604 shows a blend of Roman and Germanic elements; and even in the absence of explicit evidence, it is likely that Romans were present alongside Lombard warriors in the circus at Milan Lombard royal elections. It is harder to be sure, though, that they joined in the acclamations typically associated with these rituals.[51] In any event, the 604 ceremony betrays the Lombard kings' desire to imitate imperial rituals in order to exalt royal power further than Germanic tradition would allow.[52]

The reigns of Agilulf, with his wife Theodelinda, and their son Adaloald (590–626), have been termed by Giamperto Bognetti 'the summer of the dead', meaning a short period in which Roman influence on the Lombard court was very strong. This was so, firstly, because of Queen Theodelinda, who was a Catholic and very close to Pope Gregory the great. She dedicated herself, in concert with Agilulf, to her people's conversions from paganism or arianism to catholicism: she built churches and backed the mission of the Irish monk Columbanus, founder of the monastery of Bobbio in the Appenines near Piacenza. Secondly, some members of the old Italo-Roman bureaucracy, and also some bishops such as Secundus of Nona, collaborated with the Lombard court.[53] In this period, the Lombard rulers tried to treat the defeated Italians by methods that were not just crudely repressive. From Authari's reign (584 = 590) onwards, each Lombard king bore the title Flavius, further proof of a desire to present himself as the successor of the Roman emperor and legitimate ruler of Italy.[54] On the basis of what has been said so far, it cannot be regarded a coincidence that a crown (now lost) offered by Agilulf to the church of Monza bore the inscription: 'Agilulf gratia Dei vir gloriosissimus rex totius Italiae'. Thus Agilulf is described as king not just of the Lombards but of the whole of Italy.

Today, in the light of Reinhard Elze's recent studies, it is a near-certainty that this crown should be dated to the age of Agilulf.[55] It

---

[51] Paul the Deacon, *Historia Langobardorum* IV, 30.

[52] P. Delogu, "Il regno longobardo", *Storia d'Italia*, I, *Longobardi e Bizantini*, ed. G. Galasso (Turin, 1980), pp. 39–44.

[53] G.P. Bognetti, "S. Maria foris Portas di Castelseprio", *L'età longobarda* II (Milan, 1966), pp. 179–302; *idem*, "I ministri romani dei re longobardi e un'opinione di Alessandro Manzoni", *L'età longobarda* III, (Milan, 1967), pp. 49–74.

[54] See n. 52.

[55] R. Elze, "Die Agilulfkrone des Schatzes von Monza", *Historische Forschungen für W. Schlesinger*, ed. H. Beumann (Cologne-Vienna, 1974), pp. 348–357.

is not clear that Agilulf ever wore this crown, however; and similar doubts surround the crown of Theodelinda, the only Lombard crown still extant, at Monza. Were these made as votive crowns, to be offered to a church? Or were they actually used as royal headgear, as crowns certainly were in later periods, and later given to churches? I return to this problem below, noting for the moment only that it does not relate exclusively to the Lombard crowns but concerns the votive crowns of the Visigothic kings as well.[56]

For a short period following Adaloald's death, during the reigns of Arioald and Rothari (626–652), the Germanic character of royal rituals seems to have become more pronounced. But in the last century of the independent Lombard regime, Roman influences became increasingly dominant/pervasive. From the second half of the seventh century, the so-called Bavarian dynasty, that is, the catholic dynasty of Lombard kings descended from Theodolinda's brother, began to change the ideology of royal power. As in the period of Agilulf and Theodolinda, Roman influence assumed a strongly catholic and quasi-Byzantine form. Kings and queens founded churches and monasteries; the image of St Michael was impressed on the coinage;[57] perhaps (but this is not certain) the kings also celebrated triumphal entries into the capital, Pavia.[58] Moreover, St Michael, from the reign of Cunicpert (678–700), and St John the Baptist, from as early as Theodolinda's time, became the patrons of the Lombard kingdom. The increasing importance of the cults of saints is indicated by Paul the Deacon, who wrote that no-one could conquer the Lombards because Queen Theodolinda founded a church in Monza dedicated to St John, "but one day this temple will no longer be respected and this people will be destroyed"—a reference, rare in Paul's work, to the Frankish conquest of 774.[59] The cult of the saints had become enmeshed in the Lombards' warrior traditions and rites of victory.[60]

---

[56] See note 10.

[57] P. Delogu, *Mito di una città meridionale. Salerno, secoli VIII–X* (Naples, 1977), pp. 17–18; *idem*, "Il regno longobardo", p. 113.

[58] As suggested by McCormick, *Eternal Victory*, p. 294.

[59] Paul the Deacon, *Historia Langobardorum* V, 6.

[60] McCormick, *Eternal Victory*, pp. 294–5, referring precisely to Cunicpert's building of the church of St. George at Coronate.

Roman Influences: the Age of Liutprand

We return now to the problem of the royal crown. Apart from the two extant crowns dating from the reign of Agilulf and Theodolinda, one other crown is known from the written records of Lombard history. In Rome, in 728, King Liutprand, after making peace with Pope Gregory II, laid before the altar of St Peter "his mantle, corslet, sword-belt, broad-sword and pointed sword, all gilded, and a golden crown and a silver cross".[61] In this case too, it is unclear whether Liutprand's crown was only a votive one, or one that could actually be worn. The evidence of Isidore of Seville does not help resolve the question: his assertion that "Roman emperors and *some barbarian kings (reges quidam gentium)* wear golden crowns" clearly implies that *not all* such kings did. Whether or not the crown was among the insignia of Visigothic kings is equally unclear.[62] We must therefore reconcile ourselves to uncertainty on this point. We might even agree with C.-R. Brühl that crowns formed part of the insignia of *most* barbarian kings, including those of the Lombards.[63] What needs to be stressed is that Liutprand's golden crown, whether votive offering or headgear, was evidently a Herrschaftszeichen.

There is only one further piece of evidence to add: according to the *Chronicon Salernitanum*, the Lombard prince Arichis II, at the beginning of the Carolingian period, provoked Charlemagne's wrath by wearing a precious crown, interpreted by the Frankish king as indicating a claim to independence.[64] This source is, however, of tenth-century date, and so provides no good grounds for accepting the story as evidence for the late eighth century.

Seven years after Liutprand's spectacular offering of regalia to St Peter's shrine, Hildeprand was invested as king by being given a lance, not a crown. But Hildebrand was an enemy of the Byzantines, and commanded the Lombard amy that conquered Ravenna for a time: his inauguration ritual accordingly shows non-Roman features.

---

[61] *Liber Pontificalis*, Vita Gregorii II, c. 22, ed. L. Duchesne, 2 vols. (Rome, 1886–1892). The translation is that of R. Davis, *The Lives of the Eighth-Century Popes (Liber Pontificalis)* (Liverpool 1992), p. 15.

[62] Isidore, *Etymologiae* XIX, 30, 3: "*imperatoes Romani et reges quidam gentium aureas coronas utuntur.*" See also n. 10.

[63] C.-R. Brühl, "Kronen- und Krönungsbrauch im frühen und hohen Mittelalter", *Historische Zeitschrift* 234 (1980), pp. 155–163.

[64] *Chronicon Salernitanum*, ed. U. Westerbergh (Stockholm, 1956), p. 17.

Liutprand, by contrast, though he too fought against the Byzantines, was above all a Catholic king who decided in the end to make his peace with both the empire and the Roman Church.[65] The clearest evidence for this stance is provided by the prologues of Liutprand's Laws: these deploy the ideology of a Catholic king whose authority is said to derive directly from God and whose power can thus be claimed as stronger than that of the kings of old. In this context, the prologue of Liutprand's Laws of 713, which declares them 'inspired, we think, by God himself',[66] marks a significant departure from Rothari's professed need to 'find' the laws in the memory of old men.[67]

Liutprand's building activities are also noteworthy. He built many churches and monasteries, most important of them in ideological terms the church of St Anastasius founded in Cortelona near Pavia sometime after 729, together with a monastery and a palace. The church's dedicatory inscriptions express the king's intentions: "I pray you, O Son of God, that the Catholic order may grow with me, to the benefit of your faithful people; and grant to this temple the same function you assigned to the Temple of Solomon".[68] The Liutprand wanted to forge an alliance between Christ and the Lombard people, here called "the faithful people". The church of St Anastasius was to be the sign of this covenant, as Solomon's Temple had been the sign of God's covenant with the Jews. Furthermore, because of the iconoclast heresy of the emperor Leo III, Liutprand thought it possible for himself to take the emperor's place as leader of the Catholic community of which the Lombards, together with "the Italic people", formed part. Liutprand thus showed himself as a Catholic king of the whole of Italy, a realm whose patron was to be Christ Himself.[69] Clearly this Lombard king used ritual means—the building of churches and the offering of gifts to God and the saints—which he could load heavily with a political message.

---

[65] Delogu, "Il regno longobardo", pp. 155–163.

[66] Liut. prol. a. 713, in Azzara and Gasparri edd., *Le legge dei Longobardi*, p. 128: "*divinitus ut credimus inspirati.*"

[67] See n. 14.

[68] Ed. E. Dümmler, *MGH Poetae latini Aevi Karolini* I, pp. 105–106: "*Dei fili, pro plebe fideli . . . fac, precor, ut crescat mecum catholicus ordo, et templo concede isti ut Salomoni locutus.*"

[69] See n. 65.

From the lance to the anointing: the end of Odin's kingship

In what were to prove the last decades of the Lombard kingdom's existence, old barbarian rituals had not been wholly replaced by Roman and Catholic ones, nor had nobles and warriors wholly abandoned customs rooted in pre-Christian times.[70] Lombard kingship itself was not yet completely Catholic. The difference between Liutprand and Hildeprand was not an isolated case. Ratchis' replacement by Aistulf has also been interpreted as the reaction of a traditionalist Lombard party against a Catholic and pro-Roman one.[71]

Returning to the different royal symbols used by Liutprand and Hildeprand, the crown and the lance, we may be able to support the hypothesis hinted at above,[72] namely, that Liutprand and Hildeprand deliberately selected distinct royal symbols in order to highlight their differing political attitudes. It is my contention that those kings who were most influenced by Roman (that is, also ecclesiastical) culture used crowns among their Herrschaftszeichen, at least when addressing the Church hierarchy and the native population of Italy. By the eighth century, the king's power was no longer based exclusively on leadership of the people, the gens, but now contained a strong element of territoriality. A king now had to mention Italy in his official acts and had to use a Roman title (the appellative Flavius), Roman rituals, like circus ceremonial, and Roman symbols. In the eighth century, the king also had to imitate the piously philanthropic activities of Byzantine emperors by building churches and monasteries.[73]

Among Lombard inauguration procedures, the circus ritual of 604 remained an isolated case, understandable only in the particular circumstances of the Lombard court during the so-called "summer of the dead".[74] The crown was of more durable importance because of its clear association with the spreading of Christianity among the Lombard kings. Yet it is still worth stressing that there was never a Lombard inauguration ritual involving a crown or coronation.[75] Only

---

[70] Cf. Gasparri, *La cultura*, pp. 135–151.
[71] Jarnut, *Geschichte*, pp. 106–109.
[72] See above and n. 65.
[73] See nn. 57 and 65, and McCormick, *Eternal Victory, passim*.
[74] See n. 53.
[75] The use of the iron crown for crowning the rulers of the medieval kingdom of Italy, as is well known, is only a late legend. As Brühl, "Kronen- und Krönungsbrauch",

with the Carolingians did coronation, together with anointing, become
part of king-making (and emperor-making) rituals in Italy. And it
was in fact the anointing that constituted the most important element in the ritual process, because it imprinted a fully ecclesiastical
seal on the king's accession to the throne.[76]

The lance, although a pagan symbol (in terms of both classical
and barbarian traditions), always remained the true symbol of Lombard kingship: witness the fact that when the Franks conquered Italy,
they immediately abandoned the Lombard ritual and introduced their
own, centred on the anointing. We have no evidence of the ceremonies by which Charlemagne assumed the Lombard kingship in
774, but we know that his son Pippin was consecrated and crowned
king of the Lombards in 781 by a papal rite in Rome.[77] The Lombard kingdom had only recently been conquered and the conquerors
were respectful of almost all the political institutions of their new
kingdom: only the royal inauguration ritual was changed. If we can
believe the sole source for this, namely the Royal Frankish Annals,
the procedures of young Pippin's inauguration in 781 contained a
clear political message: they were performed inside a church; the
Lombard warriors played no part in any symbolic election and indeed
by implication had no role at all; and, last but not least, the anointing replaced the handing over of the lance. All this meant the definitive end of the Lombards' *wodanistisches Königtum* (Wodanic kingship).
As an alternative, the new rulers of Italy based their power on the
ideological support of the Roman Church which had always tended
to oppose the Lombards.[78]

Finally, there is just one more detailed account of a royal inauguration ritual performed in Italy some sixty years after the young Pippin's consecration. In June 844, Pope Sergius II made Louis II (later

---

pp. 20–21, points out, in the early Middle Ages, and not only in Lombard Italy,
there was only a *Kronenbrauch*, that is, a simple crown-wearing by the king, and not
a *Krönungsbrauch*, that is, a royal inauguration in which the crown was one of the
main elements.

[76] Nelson, "Inauguration rituals', *passim*, for discussion of the Carolingians' use
of anointing.

[77] *Annales regni Francorum* s.a. 781, ed. F. Kurze, *MGH Scriptores rerum Germanicarum
in usum scholarum* 6 (Hanover, 1895), p. 57: "*Et cum ibi sanctum pascha celebraret, bap-
tizavit idem pontifex filium eius Pippinum unxitque eum in regem. Unxit etiam et Hludowicum
fratrem eius; quibus et coronam imposuit.*" Louis was crowned king of Aquitaine.

[78] See Tabacco, "La storia politica", pp. 39–72.

emperor) king of the Lombards: "with his own hands [the pope] anointed him with holy oil and crowned him with a most preious crown".[79] The papal biographer adds: "handing over the royal sword, [the pope] told [Louis] to gird it on".[80] Once and for all, the Carolingian idea of a royal *militia*, symbolised by the sword and the *cingulum militiae*, and representing the ruler's main duty as the protection of the christian people and the Church, had imposed itself in the ancient Lombard kingdom.[81]

BIBLIOGRAPHY

Primary sources

Ammianus Marcellinus, *Res gestae*, ed. W. Seyfarth, 2 vols. (Leipzig, 1978).
Cassiodorus, *Variae*, ed. T. Mommsen, *MGH Auctores Antiquissimi* XII (Berlin, 1894).
Councils and Ecclesiastical Documents Relating to Great Britain and Ireland, eds. A. Haddan and W. Stubbs, 3 vols. (Oxford, 1881).
Edict of Rothari c. 386, ed. C. Azzara and S. Gasparri, *Le leggi dei Langobardi. Storia, memoria e diritto di un popolo germanico* (Milan, 1992).
Gregory of Tours, *Libri Historiarum*, eds. B. Krusch and W. Levison, *MGH Scriptores rerum Merovingicarum* I,1 (Hannover, 1951).
Herodotus, *Histories*, translation by A.D. Godley, The Loeb Classical Library (Cambridge, Mass., 1957).
Isidore, *Historia Svevorum*, ed. T. Mommsen, *MGH Auctores Antiquissimi* XI (Berlin, 1894).
Jordanes, *Getica*, ed. F. Giunta and F. Grillone, *Fonti per la storia d'Italia*, 117 (Rome, 1991).
Paul the Deacon, *Historia Langobardorum*, ed. L. Bethmann and G. Waitz, *MGH Scriptores rerum Langobardicarum et Italicarum saec. VI–IX* (Hannover, 1878).
Procopius, *History of the Wars. The Persian War* I, transl. H.B. Dewing (London and Cambridge Mass., 1953–1954).
Tacitus, *Historiae*, transl. C.H. Moore (London and Cambridge Mass., 1979–1980).
Vita Barbati episcopi Beneventani, ed. G. Waitz, *MGH Scriptores rerum Langobardorum* (Hannover, 1878).

Secondary sources

Gasparri, S., *La cultura tradizionale dei Longobardi. Struttura tribale e resistenze pagane* (Spoleto, 1983).
Goffart, W., *Barbarians and Romans AD 419–584: The Techniques of Accommodation* (Princeton, 1980).

---

[79] *Liber Pontificalis* II, 89: *"Tunc almificus pontifex manibus suis . . . oleo sancto perungens, regali ac pretiosissima coronavit corona."*
[80] *Ibid.*: *". . . cui regalem tribuens gladium illique subiungere iussit."*
[81] H. Keller, *"Militia.* Vasallität und frühes Rittertum im Spiegel oberitalienischer *Miles*-Belege des 10. und 11. Jahrhunderts", *Quellen und Forschungen aus italienischen Archiven und Bibliotheken* 62 (1982), pp. 59–117.

Goffart, W., *The Narrators of Barbarian History. Jordanes, Gregory of Tours, Bede and Paul the Deacon* (Princeton, 1988).

Hauck, K., "Herrschaftszeichen eines wodanistisches Königtums", *Jahrbuch für fränkische Landesforschung* 14 (1966), pp. 9–66.

Höfler, O., "Abstammungstradition", *Reallexicon der germanischen Altertumskunde*, ed. J. Hoops, 2nd edn (Berlin-New York, 1973), pp. 18–29.

Jarnut, J., *Geschichte der Langobarden* (Stuttgart, 1982).

McCormick, M., *Eternal Victory. Triumphal Rulership in Late Antiquity, Byzantium and the Early Medieval West* (Cambridge, 1986).

Nelson, J.L., "Inauguration rituals", *Early Medieval Kingship*, ed. P. Sawyer and I.N. Wood (Leeds, 1977), pp. 50–71.

Schlesinger, W., "Über germanischen Heerkönigtum", *Das Königtum. Seine geistige und rechtliche Grundlagen*, ed. E. Ewig (Lindau-Konstanx, 1956), pp. 105–141.

Schneider, R., *Königswahl und Königserhebung im Frühmittelalter. Untersuchungen zur Herrschaftsnachfolge bei den Langobarden und Merowinger* (Stuttgart, 1972).

Schramm, P.E., "Die heilige Lanze", P.E. Schramm, *Herrschaftszeichen und Staatssymbolik*, 3 vols. (Stuttgart, 1955), ii, pp. 492–537.

Tabacco, G., "La storia politica e sociale", *Storia d'Ialia*, ed. G. Galasso II, i (Turin, 1974), pp. 39–72.

Thompson, E.A., *The Early Germans* (Oxford, 1965).

Wallace-Hadrill, J.M., *The Long-Haired Kings and Other Studies in Frankish History* (London, 1962).

IMPERIAL FUNERALS IN THE LATER ROMAN EMPIRE: CHANGE AND CONTINUITY

Javier Arce

Introduction

Not long ago, in September 1997, the whole world had the opportunity to attend, via television, the funeral of Lady Diana Spencer, Princess of Wales, in London. The ceremony, meticulously organised by the protocol-specialists of the British monarchy, involved the expenditure of every possible resource so as to convey all the symbolic details in a political situation that was rather delicate for the British monarchy itself. The cortège and the *translatio* of the body along a route where every point was very carefully chosen—Kensington Palace, St James' Park, Buckingham Palace, Westminster Abbey—represented an affecting demonstration of grief and public mourning on the part of thousands of people. The Queen of England herself appeared, and came down to the gates of her palace to watch and offer respects to the coffin. Prince Charles, former husband of the dead woman, and his sons and heirs, joined the cortège at a precisely-detemined moment (the heirs ought, always, to preside at the funeral cortège in order to be identified as such). In the Abbey, the duty of giving the *laudatio funebris* fell to the princess's brother (among the Romans of the Republican period, Polybius says the *laudatio* had to be given by the son or by a very close member of the family of the deceased). This funeral oration was nothing other than an *elogium* (eulogy), and also a statement and public proclamation of the rights of the heirs. Then there followed the *nenia* (among the Romans, it was a funeral chant), which on this occasion was performed by a famous popular singer, Elton John.

Double funerals

The funeral of Diana was not that of a chief of state or a king or an emperor. Yet Diana's role as consort of the heir to the throne,

together with her fame and popularity, endowed the ceremony with
a remarkable political and symbolic content. It was, indeed, precisely
the dead woman's fame and popularity that made genuine mourn-
ers of those who watched the event, whether on the spot or far
away, and evoked a profound collective sadness and emotion. Confronted by this recent experience, this contemporary ceremony honouring a famous woman, the historian or anthropologist can hardly
fail to be aware of an observable, and hence indisputable, reality: a
continuity, in a sense a universal phenomenon, in the series of common elements in the funerals of princes, kings, rulers, emperors and
political leaders in every period of European history, whose origin,
in this case, certainly goes back to the Roman period.[1]

A consideration of the funerals of rulers (kings and emperors) shows
that society reacts in similar ways, unless the dead man was a dic-
tator (in which case it may well react in a similar way, but in a
contrary sense). The fact of the death of the emperor or the king,
in political regimes that are monarchic or dynastic, poses a real test:
for here there emerges starkly the problem of the succession to
power—the problem of continuity. The funeral is the social expression of an acute political crisis, and highlights this through its ceremonial dimension. The rituals of a ruler's funeral thus have special
features 'through the very fact that they form part of a political
drama in which large numbers of people are involved'.[2] The drama
is invested sometimes, perhaps always, with symbolic and cosmological—hence political—traits of enormous importance which are
bound to be expressed in one form or another in the funeral ceremony.

In the Roman imperial period, within a tradition that began in
Hellenistic times and left its earliest traces in the funerals of Sulla
and, later, Julius Caesar,[3] imperial funerals followed a precise, fixed

---

[1] Funeral ceremonies were included in the excellent study of D. Cannadine, "The
context, performance and meaning of ritual: the British monarchy and the 'Invention of Tradition' (1820–1977)", *The Invention of Tradition*, eds. E. Hobsbawm and
T. Ranger (Cambridge, 1983, repr. 1997), pp. 101–64. For Roman imperial funerals,
see S. Price, "From noble funerals to divine cult: the consecration of Roman Emperors", *Rituals of Royalty. Power and Ceremonial in Traditional Societies*, eds. D. Cannadine
and S. Price (Cambridge, 1987, repr. 1992), pp. 56–105, and J. Arce, *Funus imperatorum* (Madrid, 1988), with full bibliography.

[2] R. Huntingdon and P. Metcalf, *Celebrations of Death. The Anthropology of Mortuary
Ritual* (Cambridge, 1979), p. 122.

[3] Both these men showed in their political careers features that verged on dic-
tatorship and monarchy, or at least an aspiration to monarchy of the Hellenistic
type. That is why their funerals, though occurring in the republican period, are

ritual, consisting of a spectacular ceremony (the *funus imperatorum*) which culminated in the *crematio* on the *rogus*, or funeral-pyre. This episode, the *crematio*, was the prerequisite to the declaration by the Senate of the *consecratio*, that is, the decree which officially proclaimed that the dead emperor was now considered another of the *divi*.[4] The effect of this declaration was the immediate organisation of the emperor's cult, which was then carried on through the length and breadth of all the provinces of the empire, with the consequent building of temples, recruiting of priests responsible for the cult, the celebration of annual *ludi* in his honour, etc. . . .[5] *Funus, consecratio* and imperial cult thus appeared inseparably linked.

The ceremony of the imperial *funus*, with its ostentatious trappings, as the historians show very clearly for certain cases (Augustus, Pertinax, Septimius Severus),[6] was nothing other than a preliminary: it prepared the way both sociologically and psychologically, through public exaltation and ceremonial symbolism, for a whole society to join in the great act of divinization. The Roman emperor once made a *divus*, and publicly declared as such, was not a god in the full sense of the word: he was not like Jupiter or Mars. The divinized emperor did not form part of what was termed the *coetus divum*, he was only considered to be a *coelicola*, a dweller in heaven who, while living with the gods, remained in a position inferior to theirs.[7] In reality, what was venerated in him, and what was sacrificed to, was not the emperor Augustus or Trajan or whoever, but his *numen*. Moreover, not all emperors were *divi*: for divinization depended on a declaration by the Senate, and that in turn depended on political circumstances, namely the relationship that the dead emperor had had with

---

particularly significant and full of symbolic meaning. For the funeral of Sulla, see Arce, *Funus Imperatorum*, pp. 17–34; for the funeral of Julius Caesar, the best study is that of S. Weinstock, *Divus Iulius* (Oxford, 1970), pp. 346–355.

[4] On the *crematio* as necessary preliminary to divinization, see Plutarch, *Quaestiones Romanae* 14. On the consecratio, cf. Tertullian, *Apologia* 5.1., and amongst modern scholarly studies, E. Bickermann, "Die römische Kaiserapotheose", *Archiv für Religionswissenschaft* 27 (1929), pp. 1–34.

[5] On the imperial cult, see S. Price, *Rituals and Power. The Roman Imperial Cult in Asia Minor* (Cambridge, 1984), and idem, "From noble funerals to divine cult". On the imperial cult in the West, cf. D. Fishwick, *The Imperial Cult in the Latin West* (Etudes préliminaires sur les religions orientales dans l'empire Romain 108) (Leiden, 1987).

[6] For Augustus: Suetonius, *Augustus*, 100; Tacitus, *Annales*, 1, 8, 4–5; for Pertinax: Dio Cassius, 75, 4, 2; Herodian, 4, 2, 3–4; for Severus: Herodian, 4, 2.

[7] Arce, *Funus Imperatorum*, pp. 153–4. See further M. Beard, J. North and S. Price, *Religions of Rome*, vol. I (Cambridge, 1998), pp. 142–149, 206–210.

the Senate and with its various groups, whether detractors or supporters. Divinization, in other words, was a political act.

Among the many ceremonies and rites that made up the Roman imperial funeral, some, at any rate, had a feature that was not only spectacular but ideologically very important: the *crematio in effigie*, that is, the public burning, as the finale of the funeral ceremony, of an *imago* of the emperor in a case where he had died and been cremated far from Rome. This kind of funeral was termed *funus imaginarium*. The *crematio*, as noted above, was an indispensible prerequisite for proclaiming a divinization. Therefore, when there was no corpse, a body was simulated in an *imago*. The *crematio in effigie* was a rite of substitution, or at least it belonged in a similar category.[8] Its forerunners can be found in Ancient Greece. Herodotus recounts that if a Spartan king died on a military campaign, 'it was their custom to make an image (*eidolon*) and carry it on a richly-decorated bier'.[9] Pausanias reports that to avoid the evil consequences that were being caused by an *eidolon* at Orchomenos, the oracle of Delphi ordered Acteon's corpse to be looked for; and only if it could not be found did the oracle recommend that a bronze image of the 'fantasma' should be made. The *eidolon* was the *psyche* of the dead man, and once attached to his tomb, it substituted for him. In this way, they could prevent the psyche wandering in the air, and by confining it in the image, enabled it to pass over into the other world.[10]

This double cremation did not mean that the Romans believed in the existence of the emperor's two bodies, one material and perishable, the other symbolic, represented in the wax image. Nor did they think that the life of the one passed into the other. We have no evidence that any such idea was entertained in Roman popular belief or in Roman philosophy. That idea was to appear much later, however, although initially without any direct Roman influence, in fourteenth- and fifteenth-century royal funerals in England and France. Such a double funeral is attested for the first time in England for Edward II in 1327, and in France for Charles VI in 1422.[11] In these cases, it was a matter of placing over the coffin an *imago ad similitudinem regis* which rendered visible what from then on was to be

---

[8] See J.-P. Vernant, *Figures, idoles, masques* (Paris, 1990), pp. 60ff, 71ff.
[9] Herodotus, VI, 58.
[10] Vernant, *Figures, idoles, masques*, pp. 39–40.
[11] For what follows, see G. Ricci, *Il principe e la morte* (Bologna, 1998), pp. 25ff.

invisible, namely, the body enclosed in the coffin. This gave rise to the idea that the king's mortal body was one thing, while his political, immortal one remained, represented by a *persona ficta*. On this basis, Ernst Kantorowicz built his theory of the king's two bodies.[12] Here Kantorowicz posed the question of whether this theory, or rather doctrine, had pagan origins in the classical world. Briefly, the doctrine held that in addition to his material, natural and mortal body, the king had another body that did not die but which continued to represent the royal *dignitas*, the abtract idea of the Crown, or the State, and which, in the Beyond, as the body politic, the embodiment of the constitution, outlasted any earthly manifestation. The abstractions could remain alive even if the material body was dead.[13] This concept drew its origins from the Pauline doctrine of the mystical body of the Church. With it were combined the speculations of English jurists of the Tudor period. Kantorowicz found precedents and parallels for this theory in the classical world, in Aristotle, and in Neopythagorian writers of 'treatises on kingship', such as Ecphantus, fragments of whose work had been published by Delatte.[14] Kantorowicz was keen to pursue his enquiries in order to pin down just how far classical parallels and long-term influences contributed to the elaboration of a full political theology which, he nevertheless maintained, was part of "Christian political theology", but had not been part of pagan political thought. As we shall see, however, elements of the theory, and indeed a clear formulation of it, can be found in Eusebius of Caesarea's biography of Constantine.

Constantines funeral

Descriptions of imperial funerals are not plentiful in classical historiography: far from it, they are meagre and fragmentary. Only in a

---

[12] E.H. Kantorowicz, *The Kings' Two Bodies* (Princeton, 1957). See further R. Giesey, *The Royal Funeral Ceremony in Renaissance France* (Geneva, 1960).

[13] By contrast, the pope, who from the thirteenth century onwards did not think he had two bodies, like the king, but only one natural body, whose disappearance did not affect the eternal character of the Church of Christ: see A. Paravicini Bagliani, *Il corpo del Papa* (Turin, 1994), pp. xv–xvii, and 223; and Ricci, *Il principe et la morte*, p. 26.

[14] L. Delatte, *Les traités de la royauté d'Ecfante, Dioctogène et Sthénidos*, (Bibliothèque de la Faculté de Philosophie et des Lettres de l'Université de Liège, XCVII) (Liège, 1942).

few cases do we have details carefully specified by the historians.
The case of Augustus's funeral, quite fully described in Suetonius,
Dio, and Tacitus, is rare.[15] We have to look to the historians of the
third century to find some really detailed accounts of the funeral of
Pertinax, by Dio, and that of Septimius Severus, by Herodian.[16] In
the intervening period, what we find on funerals in the imperial
biographies, or in fourth-century epitomes, is no more than a few
bits and pieces. Yet, judging even from these brief references, it looks
as if the funeral ceremonies, when it was possible to celebrate them,
did not change fundamentally, nor did they undergo significant modi-
fication throughout the entire imperial period from Augustus to Constantine. It is worth stressing two points. On the one hand, the
appearance of detailed accounts of funerals in Dio and Herodian
show continuity in the ceremonial and symbolism of the *funus* at least
through two centuries, and though we find some expansion of the
material in these two authors, that is because both wrote for Greek,
and Greek-speaking, audiences mainly in the eastern part of the
empire, unfamiliar with the ceremonials practised in Rome. For the
imperial funeral, real or simulated, was a ritual that had to be performed in Rome, and received all its symbolic value through being
enacted in the *Urbs*. On the other hand, the much-disturbed impeiral
history of the third century, which produced a large number of
emperors in a variety of different geographical parts of the empire,
who were elected, or simply seized power, through very varied routes
(conspiracies, assassinations, acclamations by the army), had the result
that the imperial funeral ceremony either could not be celebrated
at all or lost its specific feature because of taking place in Rome
itself. Even so, evidence for continuity in most of the basic elements
is what we in fact find in the accounts we have of the funerals of
Constantine and some of his successors. With Constantine, it seems
that the ceremony returned to being a sharply-defined performance,
and it was the object of attention, once more, from contemporary
historians. The explanation lies in one great political and institutional fact: the moment a 'strong monarchy' established itself anew,
with such a clear dynastic thrust as Constantine's regime had, and
which deliberately remade the links with Roman rulers before the
third century, the funeral ceremonies in turn had to be re-estab-

---

[15] Suetonius, *Augustus*, 100.
[16] Pertinax: Dio, 75, 4, 2, and also Herodian, 4, 2, 3–4; Severus: Herodian 4. 2.

lished with all their potency, in so far as it was through them that the idea of the dynasty and its continuity could be strongly reinforced.[17] Constantine's funeral itself, while clearly showing traits of continuity, also showed innovative elements which probably served as a model, in the longer run, for later ceremonies in the Byzantine world and in the *regna* of the West. Georges Dagron recently put this point clearly: 'Having got to the end of his *Vita Constantini* . . . Eusebius knew that his account of the emperor's last days would assure for Constantine a reputation for sanctity, and that the description of his funeral—the first of a Christian emperor—would impose the idea of a new ceremonial, of a new relationship between the emperors and death, and, further, of the institution of empire itself with Christianity.'[18]

Eusebius's *Vita Constantini* was a veritable treatise on political theology, a panegyric produced, of course, after the 'heros' death. It is hard to draw a clear distinction between what was Eusebius's own creation and what was not.[19] Constantine's funeral was described in the *Vita* in a way adapted to a narrative context which persistently stressed the exceptional and paradigmatic traits of the Christian emperor chosen by God. The *Vita* obviously laid more emphasis on Christian features than on possibly pagan aspects which appear so often in the biography and which constitute one of the most striking paradoxes of the reign.

Certain rites and traditions persisted in Constantine's funeral because the fact that the emperor was a Christian was not in itself enough to change them. The army, the people and various elements of society lived out a nostalgia for paganism, and for the stability of religious custom, including whatever was purely formal and external. When Constantine realised that his death was approaching, after Easter 337, he left Constantinople and went to take the waters at Helenopolis, where he could have recourse to prayer at the tombs of the martyrs. Thence he moved to Anchyrona, a country estate near Nicomedia. Eusebius describes the scene preparatory to the funeral: after getting the bishops assembled, the emperor told them of his wish to go and be baptised in the River Jordan. But this was

---

[17] On Constantinian monarchy, see for example T. Barnes, *Constantine and Eusebius* (Harvard, 1981); but now above all G. Dagron, *Empereur et prêtre* (Paris, 1996).
[18] Dagron, *Empereur et prêtre*, p. 148.
[19] See among others, Barnes, *Constantine and Eusebius*, pp. 267ff.

simply not possible. Putting off the purple, he vested himself in white, ready for baptism. On Whitsunday, Constantine died, and, as Dagron aptly stresses,[20] Eusebius hastens to record that 'the emperor left his body to mortals and joined his soul to God'.[21] Constantine's death did not only cause a political problem of the succession, a power-vacuum. Nor did it only mean the departure of the victorious ruler and reformer, the founder of New Rome, or Second Rome. It was, at the same time, the disappearance of the first Christian ruler. The funeral, more than any other ritual, could signify a break, indeed a total rupture. But the quintessential Constantinean ambiguity was also there in his funeral: its novelty lies in Eusebius's interpretation.

Then came the next stage of the ceremony and the transfer of the body to Constantinople to be buried in the mausoleum that Constantine had prepared for himself and his family.[22] Eusebius's description of the ceremony clearly distinguishes, or allows us to do so, pagan from Christian elements, the latter consisting of ceremonies in the church of the Holy Apostles and the religious service at which the emperor's son, Constantius II, could not be present because he was only a catechumen.[23] The truth is that we know very little about the details of these ceremonies. Yet Eusebius's account reveals that there were still many pagan features: the *iustitium* was proclaimed, that is, all baths and markets were closed, as were the games,[24] while statues were erected in honour of the dead emperor, and the corpse was on show for a considerable time so that the people and the high officials could pay their respects to and 'adore' it. The *pompa funebris*, the procession, headed by the army and the imperial heir, was in no way different from those described by imperial biographers in earlier cases.[25]

---

[20] Dagron, *Empereur et prêtre*, p. 149.

[21] Eusebius, *Vita Constantini* IV, 24.

[22] C. Mango, "Constantine's mausoleum and the translation of relics", *Byzantinische Zeitschrift* 83 (1990), pp. 56–62.

[23] On Constantine's funeral, see the classic work of P. Franchi de Cavalieri, "I funerali ed il sepolcro di Constantino Magno". *Mélanges de l'École française de Rome* 26 (1916–17), pp. 205ff. Cf. Eusebius, *Vita Constantini* IV, 60ff.

[24] The *iustitium* following the murder of Germanicus in 19 AD. is mentioned on the cenotaph of Pisa in honour of Lucius and Gaius, and also on the *Tabula Hebana following the murder of Germanicus in 19 AD*. On the *iustitium*, see now the fine pages of A. Fraschetti, *Roma e il Principe* (Laterza, 1990), pp. 94ff.

[25] Franchi de Cavalieri, "I funerali et il sepolchro di constantino Magno"; S.G. MacCormack, *Art and Ceremony in Late Antiquity. The Transformation of the Classical Heritage* (Berkeley, 1981), pp. 117ff.

Eusebius theory and the future of imperial and royal burials

Beyond the description of the ceremonial, what acquires real importance, and what is really new, is the theory expounded by Eusebius on the basis of his 'hero's' death. For, according to Eusebius, Constantine was not bodily carried towards to gods, but received in heaven by God. Calderone[26] has rightly observed that with Constantine, it was not a matter of an *apotheosis* but of an *anabiosis*. Constantine was not a *divus*: rather, in Eusebius's view he was a *redevivus*, in other words, a saint.[27] Eusebius, furthermore, expounded the theory that Constantine remained in the *basileia*, the imperial government itself, as if it were a *basileia meta thanatou*, a government after death. This conception, elaborated by the theologian and panegyrist Eusebius, was the embryo of the theory of 'the king's two bodies', discussed above. At the same time, it represented a quite new idea in the theory of Roman imperial power. Once again, it is Calderone who has fully explored this question:[28] Constantine was to remain the *omnium maximus imperator*, and his sons would be his reflection in the future, although after his death, for the moment, there would be no new Augustus. The explanation for this lies in the actual situation after Constantine's death in May 337: while his three sons were all proclaimed Augusti, there was an interregnum lasting three-and-a-half months. During this period, the 'live' body of the emperor continued to rule by virtue of its charisma. In this context, Barnes has asked what was (or may have been) the hidden significance of Eusebius's insistence that Constantine went on ruling even after his death. Barnes points to a document, the Oxyrhynchus papyrus 3244, dated 13 August 337, still by Constantine's reign years, which contains an echo of the situation at that moment.[29] Precedents for 'the king's two bodies' seem clear,[30] although the treatises on kingship of Ecphantus and others already provided a basis for the theory's development.[31] MacCormack has her own interpretation of the evidence.[32]

---

[26] S. Calderone, "Teologia politica, successione dinastica e consecratio in età constantiniana", *Le culte du souverain dans l'empire romain*, ed. W. den Boer (Entretiens Fondation Hardt 19) (Geneva, 1982), pp. 215–261, at 237ff.

[27] Ibid.

[28] Ibid.

[29] Barnes, *Constantine and Eusebius*, p. 267. See also Dagron, *Empereur et prêtre*, 148–149.

[30] Kantorowicz, *The King's Two Bodies*, p. 400, n. 374.

[31] Ibid., pp. 264ff.

[32] MacCormack, *Art and Ceremony in Late Antiquity*, pp. 117–119.

She thinks that the lapse of time necessitated a sort of simulation until a new successor was named: a phenomenon that can be detected on previous similar occasions at the deaths of certain emperors.[33] My view is that in Eusebius's theory of Constantine's *post mortem* reign there is much more than the simple idea of covering up the emperor's death until the naming of the successor.

Nevertheless, and in clear contradiction to Eusebius, Constantine was declared *divus*, and in the West coins of *consecratio* were issued in his honour.[34] The series of *consecratio* coins minted for Constantine by his sons has engendered a great deal of discussion.[35] For some scholars, the fact itself is seen as implausible, given that Constantine had been the first Christian emperor; and some have even gone so far as to deny the existence of these coins, or at least refused to regard them as a *consecratio*, on the grounds that the legend CONSECRATIO does not appear on them.[36] Such conclusions simply cannot be maintained. Constantine's coins bore the legend DIVUS or DIVO, which clearly demonstrates the meaning they carried. There was a divinization of Constantine, probably in Rome. A coin-issue with the title DIVUS implies that the Senate had declared Constantine to be just that.[37]

Can we say that with Constantine's funeral, the history of Roman imperial funerals came to an end? Or was Constantine's funeral destined to serve as a model for Byzantine emperors in later centuries? How far did the kings of the barbarian kingdoms follow or imitate the ceremonial of Roman imperial funerals? Did a ceremony that was of such transcendental importance in a social and political sense preserve its essential Roman traits?

As far as the ceremonial itself is concerned, it is clear that some pagan features survived right through the fourth century, but these diminished steadily until they were turned into Christian, or at least christianised, rites. Many elements in the ritual did not change, but

---

[33] Eusebius, *Vita Constantini* IV, 68; cf. Suetonius, Tiberius, 22–3; Suetonius, Claudius, 45.

[34] Arce, *Funus Imperatorum*, pp. 164ff.

[35] P. Bruun, "The consacration coins of Constantine the Great", *Arctos*, 1 (1954), pp. 19–31. L. Koep, "Die Konsekrationsmünzen Kaiser Konstantins und ihre religions-politische Bedeutung", *Jahrbuch für Antike und Christentum* 1 (1958), pp. 94–104.

[36] Calderone, "Teologia politica, successione dinastica e consecratio in età constantiniana", pp. 242ff.

[37] Arce, *Funus Imperatorum*, pp. 167–168.

rather were christianised. The *laudatio funebris* turned into a homily packed with biblical citations. And so it went on. At the funeral of Constantius II, a fervent Arian emperor who died in Cilicia in 361, many pagan features can still be seen. The historian Ammianus describes them in detail. The funeral consisted of two clearly distinct parts: one, derived from pagan tradition, appeared in the exequies performed at the place the emperor died, while the other was strictly Christian and consisted of his burial and *funus* at Constantinople, presided over by his successor, the pagan Julian, right up to the church itself. Constantius's military funeral took place in accordance with the traditional sequence of *conclamatio*, that is, the official mourning, the *decurio equitum* around the corpse, the embalming, followed by the *translatio cum regia pompa*, accompanied by *duces* and *comites*. The details of the service in the church of the Holy Apostles are unknown. But all the same, and yet again, Constantius *inter divos relatus est.*[38] Corippus, the court-poet of the emperor Justin II in the sixth century, extolled the virtues of his patron, praising his *pietas* towards his predecessor Justinian, a *pietas* expressed in the splendid funeral accorded him.[39] Justinian was the *imperator christianissimus*, yet in his funeral ritual proper, things had hardly changed. Justinian's corpse lay in the palace on a golden bier raised on a pedestal. He was crowned with a diadem and wearing the purple robe, just like Constantine in Eusebius's description: *diademate comptus purpureaque in veste iacens*. Justin, the successor to the empire, bent over the bier and addressed Justinian's body, just as the successor had done at Pertinax's funeral. The senators waited in the porticoes: 'they poured fragrant honey ... and exotic unguents to preserve the holy body for all time', just as they had done with the body of Nero's wife Poppaea or that of King Herod, preserved in honey, 'in the oriental manner',[40] and just as they did with the body of Theodosius I (*aromatus sepultus est*). But at the carrying of Justinian to his tomb, there were no wax images, nor did the army take part: instead there was 'a venerable line of singing deacons, and ... a choir of virgins'. The people accompanied them with flaming torches: these too had been

---

[38] Ibid., pp. 160–1. For the term *divus*, see Eutropius, *Breviarium*, 10, 15, 2.

[39] Corippus, *In laudem Iustini Augusti minoris libri IV*, ed. A. Cameron (London, 1976), III, 1–61, pp. 60–2, trans. pp. 102–3, with commentary, pp. 179–82, on Justinian's funeral.

[40] Tacitus, *Annales* 16, 2.

part of the pagan ceremonies in the nocturnal funeral procession, but now, with Justinian, their significance had changed to represent the eternal light of the resurrection.

The Constantinian model was to have only a peripheral influence on Byzantine funerals.[41] Byzantine emperors did not continue with the declaration of the emperor's sanctification, nor with the sort of beatification Eusebius ascribed to Constantine. As Dagron observes, 'Byzantine emperors were not saints, but they were just Christians like the rest. . . . Constantine's Christian "sanctity", problematic and equivocal as it was, would remain the exception'.[42] Many western kings in the Early Middle Ages and later, however, were called 'new Constantines', and in some cases kings attained sanctity.[43]

As for the funerals of the kings of the Franks, Visigoths, Lombards, and so on, this is not the place to pursue that theme. Yet, in conclusion, Jordanes' account of Attila's funeral seems worth citing.[44] When the Hunnic leader died, says Jordanes, his people 'cut off part of their hair and hacked their flesh with deep cuts'. This is a custom which we also find among the Romans, especially their women.[45] Jordanes goes on to describe how the corpse was laid out in the open air beneath a silk awning, so that all could see it, while *electissimi equites in eo loco, quo erat positus, in modo circensium cursibus ambientes*: in other words, they celebrated what at Roman funerals was called the *decursio equitum*.[46] These warriors chanted a funeral dirge enumerating the deeds and victories of the dead man.[47] After the chanting and the cavalry ride, *ingenti commessatione concelebrant*, which they called in their language *strava*: in other words, this was the funeral banquet richly attested for Roman funerals. Finally, during the night, the body was laid in the ground, placed in three sarcophagi, one of gold, one of silver, and the third of iron. Over the grave, they set up 'the trophies of weapons captured from slaughtered enemies, collars gleaming with gems, and various insignia by which the glory of a palace is celebrated' (*addunt arma hostium caed-*

[41] Dagron, *Empereur et prêtre*, p. 168.
[42] Ibid., pp. 167–8: 'Il y a peu de saints reconnus parmi les *basileis* de Constantinople'.
[43] Ibid., p. 160.
[44] Jordanes, *Getica*, 49.
[45] Arce, *Funus Imperatorum*, p. 47, fig. 7.
[46] Ibid., p. 53.
[47] Ibid., p. 54.

ibus acquisita, phaleras vario gemmarum fulgore pretiosas, et diversi generis insignia, quibus colitur aulicum decus). Last of all, all those who had contributed to making the grave were put to death.

All these features are characteristic of Roman funerals, especially in military contexts. The rites and ceremonies are identical (the noctural interment, the offering of collars, torques and rings on the tomb or the pyre): we find these described for the funerals of Sulla, Julius Caesar, Augustus, Otho, Pertinax, and Constantius II.[48] Was Jordanes describing the funeral rites of a romanised barbarian king? Or did he transpose the Roman ceremonial to Attila's funeral? If the first hypothesis is right, that would be truly significant for the history of the transformation of the Roman world.

BIBLIOGRAPHY

Primary sources

Corippus, *In laudem Iustini Augusti minoris libri IV.*, ed. and trans. A. Cameron (London, 1976).
Dio Cassius, *Dios Roman History*, with an English Translation by E. Cary, (Loeb Classical Library) (London, 1914ff.) V.P. Boisserain, *Casii Dionis Cocceiani Historiarum Romanarum quae supersunt*, Vol. 1–3 (text) (Berlin, 1898–1931).
Eusebius, *Vita Constantini*, ed. F. Winkelmann, *Eusebius Werke.*
Erster Bd. Erster Teil. Die Griechischen Christlichen Schriftsteller (Berlin, 1975).
Eutropius, *Breviarium ab urbe condita*, (ed. C. Santini) (Bibliotheca Teubneriana) (Leipzig, 1992).
Herodianus, *History* (ed. and trans. C.R. Whittaker), (Loeb Classical Library) (London and Cambridge, Mass., 1976).
Herodotus, *Hérodote. Histoires.* Texte établi et traduit par Ph.E. Legrand, 1–10 (Paris, 1931–1954).
Jordanes, *Gethica*, ed. Th. Mommsen, MGH AA, 5, (Berlin, 1982).
Plutarcus, *Quaestiones Romanae*, ed. H.J. Rose, *The Roman Questions of Plutarch* (Oxford, 1924).
Suetonius, *De vita Caesarum libri VIII*, ed. M. Ihm, (Bibliotheca Teubneriana) (Leipzig, 1907).
Tacitus, E. Koestermann, *Cornelii Taciti Libri qui supersunt, t. I: Ab Excessu Divi Augusti* (Bibliotheca Teubneriana, 3 th. ed.) (Leipzig, 1971).
Tertulianus, *Apologia*, ed. and trans. T.R. Glover, *Tertulian, Apology, De Spectaculis* (Loeb Classical Library) (London and Cambridge, Mass., 1931).

Secondary sources

Alföldi, A., *Die monarchische Repräsentation im römischen Kaiserreiche* (Darmstadt, 1970).
Arce, J., *Funus Imperatorum. Los funerales de los Emperadores romanos* (Madrid, 1988).

---

[48] *Ibid.*, p. 55.

Barnes, Th., *Constantine and Eusebius* (Harvard, 1981).

Beard, M., North, J. and S. Price, *Religions of Rome*, I–II (Cambridge, 1998).

Bickermann, E., "Die römische Kaiserapotheose", *Archiv für Religionswissenschaft* 27 (1929), pp. 1–34.

——, "Consecratio", *Le culte des souverains dans l'Empire Romain*, (Entretiens Fondation Hardt 19) (Geneve, 1973), pp. 3–25.

Bonamente, G., "Apoteosi e imperatori cristiani", *I cristiani e l'Impero nel IV secolo, Atti Coll. 1987* (Macerata, 1988), pp. 107–142.

Bruun, P., "The Consecration Coins of Constantine the Great", *Arctos* 1 (1954), pp. 19–31.

Calderone, S., "Teologia politica, succesione dinastica e consecratio in etá constantiniana", *Le culte des souverains dans l'Empire Romain*, (Entretiens Fondation Hardt 19) (Geneve, 1973), pp. 215–261.

Cannadine, D., "The context, performance and meaning of ritual: the British Monarchy and "the Invention of Tradition" (1820–1977)", *The Invention of Tradition*, eds. E. Hobsbawn and T. Ranger (Cambridge, 1983, repr. 1997), pp. 101–164.

Dagron, G., *Empereur et prêtre* (Paris, 1996).

Engels, J., *Funerum sepulchrorumque magnificentia* (Hermes Einzelschriften 78) (Stuttgart, 1998).

Fishwick, D., *The Imperial Cult in the Latin West*, Etudes préliminaires sur les religions orientales dans l'empire Romain 108 (Leiden, 1987).

Flower, H.I., *Ancestors Masks and Aristocratic Power in Roman Culture* (Oxford, 1996).

Franchi de Cavalieri, P., I funerali e il sepolcro di Constantino Magno, *MEFR* 26 (1916–7), pp. 205ff.

Fraschetti, A., *Roma e il Principe* (Roma-Bari, 1990).

Giesey, R., *The Royal Funeral Ceremony in Renaissence France* (Geneve, 1960).

Huntingdon, R. and P. Metcalf, *Celebrations of Death. The Anthropolgy of Mortuary Ritual* (Cambridge, 1979).

Kantorowicz, E.H., *The King's Two Bodies* (Princeton, 1957) (spanish transl.: *Los dos cuerpos del Rey* (Madrid, 1985)).

Koep, L., "Die Konsekrationsmünzen Kaiser Konstantins un ihre religions-politische Bedeutung", *Jahrbuch für Antike und Christentum* 1 (1958), pp. 94–104.

MacCormack, S., *Art and Ceremony in Late Antiquity* (Berkeley, 1981).

Mango, C., "Constantine's Mausoleum and the Translation of Relics", *Byzantinische Zeitschrift* 83 (1990), pp. 51–62.

Morris, I., *Death-Ritual and Social Structure in Classical Antiquity* (Cambridge, 1992).

Nelson, J., "The Lord's anointed and the people's choice: Carolingian royal ritual", *Ritual of Royalty. Power and Ceremonial in Traditional Societies*, eds. D. Cannadine and S. Price (Cambridge, 1987), pp. 137–180.

Paravicini Bagliani, A., *Il corpo del Papa* (Torino, 1994).

Price, S., From noble funerals to divine cult: the consecration of Roman Emperors, *Ritual of Royalty. Power and Ceremonial in Traditional Societies*, eds. D. Cannadine and S. Price (Cambridge, 1987), pp. 56–105.

Ricci, G., *Il principe e la morte* (Bologna, 1998).

Richard, J.Cl., "Recherches sur certains aspects du culte imperial: les funérailles des Empereurs Romains aux deux premiers siècles de notre ére", *Aufstieg und Niedergang der Römischen Welt* II, 16,2 (Berlin-New-York, 1978), pp. 1121–1134.

Scheid, J., "Contraria facere. Renversements et déplacements dans les rites funéraires", *Archaeologia e Storia Antica* 4 (Fapoli, 1984), pp. 117ff.

Toynbee, J.M.C., *Death and Burial in the Roman World* (London, 1971).

Vernant, J.P., *Figures, idoles, masques* (Paris, 1990).

Vollmer, Fr., "De funere publico romanorum", *Jahrbuch für Klassische Philologie*, Supp. 18 (1891), pp. 319–364.

Waurick, G., "Untersuchungen zur Lage der Römischen Kaisergräber in der Zeit von Augustus bis Constantin", *Jahrbuch des Römish-Germanischen Zentralmuseum Mainz* 20 (1973), pp. 107–146.

Weinstock, St., *Divus Iulius* (Oxford, 1971).

Wesch-Klein, G., *Funus Publicum* (Stuttgart, 1993).

CAROLINGIAN ROYAL FUNERALS*

Janet L. Nelson

1. *Monarchic deaths and burials*

The tombs of rulers, built to resist the ravages of time, often constitute the most imposing remains of historic cultures. Tombs conceived as statements of monarchic and dynastic legitimacy may survive as potent symbols of the continuity of states: official guides show visitors to modern China the magnificently refurbished tombs of the Ming emperors, and modern Egyptians take pride in the tombs of the pharoahs. While European state-builders have exploited similar resources, the tombs of monarchs are ambivalent symbols for republicans acting in the name of equality and fraternity. Successive decommissionings and recommissionings of monarchic tombs at St-Denis reflected the oscillations of French politics: in 1793, the royal bones were taken from their funerary monuments and thrown into a ditch, whence they were retrieved some years later at Napoleon's behest.[1] The modern visitor to the crypt encounters a series of huge, black marble catafalques with elaborate inscriptions to the effect that the royal bones of each dynasty are within, en masse. In 1859, Viollet-le-Duc constructed, not far from the Bourbons' bones, a special new vault in which Napoleon III planned that his and his successors' remains would lie alongside those of his predecessors, the kings of France. After the Second Empire's collapse, the vault was discreetly dismantled. While Napoleon III's tomb is cared for, by Catholic monks, in exiled obscurity at Farnborough, Hampshire, that of his great-uncle is maintained by the French state not at St-Denis but at

* I should like to thank all my fellow-members of Group 5 for their helpful comments. I am especially grateful to Frans Theuws and Mayke de Jong, to Julia Smith (who joined the Group only when the preparation of the present volume was at a fairly advanced stage), and to Stuart Airlie, for additional advice and criticism.

[1] E.A.R. Brown, "Burying and Unburying the Kings of France", *Persons in Groups: Social Bewhavioour as Identity Formation in Medieval and Renaissance Europe*, ed. R.C. Trexler (Binghampton NY, 1985), pp. 241–266, repr. Brown, *The Monarchy of Capetian France and Royal Ceremonial* (London, 1991), ch. IX. In this chapter, I use St-Denis (etc) to denote a religious institution, St Denis (etc) for the saint.

Les Invalides, an aptly military as well as metropolitan locale. The
ruler's tomb remains a potent symbol of national identity, just as in
the Middle Ages, the graves of kings often became focal sites of
dynastic and monarchic cult.

In the late twentieth century, despite the secularisation of the state,
a ruler's funeral may constitute a key ritual of national consensus
legitimising the onward transmission of power and symbolising the
sempiternity of the state.[2] Nowadays such rituals are played before
a large public, expanded through television to include the mass of
the population. In the central and later Middle Ages, royal funerals
came to be relatively fully recorded, and, notably in France, were
'grandiose spectacles', whose symbolic importance in demonstrating that 'the king never dies' was all the greater because the coronation in a legal sense 'no longer made the king', once the new
monarch was deemed to succeed from the moment of his predecessor's death.[3] Though automatic generalising from France is a
temptation to be resisted, it is clear that later medieval royal funerals tended to become more elaborate and highly public affairs, in
line with wider cultural trends.[4]

For the period before the thirteenth century, comparable evidence
is patchy and thin. Royal tombs in later Anglo-Saxon England clearly
were numinous places. The West Saxon *aetheling* (king's son) bidding

---

[2] This was vividly demonstrated in Belgium in 1993 at the funeral of King Bau-
douin. Nominal republics, even today, may adopt quasi-monarchic rituals, likewise
respresenting the ruler's two bodies: *vide* the elaborate arrangements for the funeral
of Deng Hsiao-ping in Beijing in 1997.
[3] B. Guenée, *States and Rulers in Later Medieval Europe* (London, 1985), pp. 26–27.
R. Giesey, *The Royal Funeral Ceremony in Renaissance France* (Geneva, 1960), pp. 41–50,
105–144, and *idem*, "Inaugural aspects of French royal ceremonials", *Coronations.
Medieval and Modern Monarchioc Ritual*, ed. J.M. Bak (Berkeley CA and London, 1990),
pp. 35–45; E.H. Kantorowicz, *The King's Two Bodies* (Princeton, 1957), pp. 409–419,
and *passim*; J. Le Goff, "Le roi dans l'Occident médiéval", *Kings and Kingship in
Medieval Europe*, ed. A. Duggan (London, 1993), pp. 1–40, esp. p. 19. Note, however, that the heralds' famous shout of *le roi est mort—vive le roi* became a regular
feature of royal funerals only from the very end of the fifteenth century. For the
rather different history of monarchic ritual in Spain, see T.F. Ruiz, 'Une royauté
sans sacre: la monarchie castillane du bas moyen âge', *Annales ESC* 39 (1984), pp.
429–453 (trans. in *Rites of Power: Symbolism, Ritual and Politics since the Middle Ages*,
ed. S. Wilentz (Philadelphia, 1983)); also R. McCluskey, "The early history of San
Isidoro de León (X–XIIc)", *Nottingham Medieval Studies* 38 (1994), pp. 35–59, and
M. Shadis, "Piety, politics and power: the patronage of Leonor of England and her
daughters Berenguela and Blanche of Castile', *The Cultural Patronage of Medieval Women*,
ed. J.H. McCash (Athens GA, 1996), pp. 202–227.
[4] P. Binski, *Medieval Death: Ritual and Representation* (London, 1996).

for the throne against his cousin Edward the Elder in 899 made for his own father's tomb at Wimborne.[5] The outlawed Helmstan, appealing against that same Edward, made a solemn protestation 'over your father's [i.e. King Alfred's] body'.[6] Probably both Harold, and then William, in 1066 asserted the legitimacy of their claims by having themselves consecrated in the church where Edward the Confessor was buried.[7] Conversely in Old (Continental) Saxony in 1074 peasant rebels challenged the royalty of the German king Henry IV in a particularly shocking way by desecrating the royal tombs of Henry's kin on the Harzburg.[8] From the earliest medieval centuries, archaeologists have identified pagan royal burials from their locations and from the particularities and richness of their contents.[9] Conversion to Christianity, though its effects on funerary practices at large were gradual and by no means always easy to detect in the archeological record,[10] seems to have brought immediate change in royal burial in the kingdom of the Franks: while the funeral of Clovis's father Childeric, presumably supervised by Clovis himself, was conducted at Tournai with pagan pomp including horse-burials,

---

[5] *The Anglo-Saxon Chronicle. MS. 'A'*, ed. J.M. Bately (Cambridge, 1986), 901, *recte* 899, p. 61, and cf. 871, p. 48. Note, however, that the author of the 899 annal does not make explicit the connexion with the royal tomb.

[6] S. Keynes, 'The Fonthill Letter', *Words, Texts and Manuscripts: Studies in Anglo-Saxon Culture presented to Helmut Gneuss*, eds. M. Korhammer, K. Reichl and H. Sauer (Woodbridge, 1992), pp. 53–97, at 88: '*Da gesahte he ðines fæder lic 7 brohte insigle to me . . .*'.

[7] J.L. Nelson, "The rites of the Conqueror", *Proceedings of the Battle Conference on Anglo-Norman Studies* 4 (1982), pp. 117–132, repr. Nelson, *Politics and Ritual in Early Medieval Europe* (London, 1986), p. 389.

[8] Lampert of Hersfeld, *Annales*, s.a. 1074, *Lamperti Opera*, ed. O. Holder-Egger, *MGH SSRG* (Leipzig, 1894), p. 184.

[9] M.O.H. Carver, "Kingship and material culture in early Anglo-Saxon East Anglia", *The Origins of Anglo-Saxon Kingdoms*, ed. S. Bassett (Leicester, 1989), pp. 141–158; *idem*, "The Anglo-Saxon cemetery at Sutton Hoo: an interim report", *The Age of Sutton Hoo: the Seventh Century in Northern Europe*, ed. M. Carver (Woodbridge, 1992), pp. 343–371; M. Müller-Wille, "Königsgrab und Königsgrabkirchen: Funde und Befunde im Frühmittelalterlichen und Mittelalterlichen Nordeuopa", *Bericht der Römisch-Germanischen Kommission* 63 (1982), pp. 350–411. Still valuable is the wide-ranging review-article of J.M. Wallace-Hadrill, "The graves of kings", *Studi Medievali* 3rd ser. 1 (1960), pp. 177–194, reprinted in his collected papers, *Early Medieval History* (Oxford 1975), pp. 39–59.

[10] D. Bullough, "Burial, community and belief in the early medieval west", *Ideal and Reality in Frankish and Anglo-Saxon Society*, eds. P. Wormald *et al.* (Oxford, 1983), pp. 177–201; Halsall, *Settlement*, pp. 246–7, with further references, and idem, *Early Medieval Cemeteries* (London, 1995), pp. 61–3; B. Effros, "Beyond cemetery walls: early medieval funerary topography and Christian salvation", *Early Medieval Europe* 6 (1997), pp. 1–23, at 8–10, esp. n. 33.

all known Merovingian kings from Clovis onwards were buried in churches.[11] Similar documentation survives for the Anglo-Saxon kingdoms: in East Anglia, the burial in Mound 1 Sutton Hoo may have been a forthright statement of a dynasty's pagan identity in face of political rivals, but later seventh-century kings were buried in monasteries. By the eighth century, inhumation *ad sanctos*, despite clerical efforts to restrict it to clergy, became throughout western Christendom the mark of the socially privileged.[12] Yet written evidence for royal funerals is strikingly hard to find.

The dawning of light on the subject has been hailed by specialists on Ottonian Germany: here at last, is relatively full information which has been taken to reflect the alleged hallmarks of a new kind of strongly ritualised and sacralised kingship.[13] The argument is a shade circular. Further it assumes, rather than demonstrates, a contrast with earlier monarchic self-representation. Recent re-excavations at Tournai and Sutton Hoo leave no doubt that those pagan royal burials were attended by rituals of a fairly elaborate and relatively public kind. Those particular rituals might have been modified, if not abandoned, when kings converted. But are we to imagine that the burials of christian kings lacked ritual accompaniment, became private affairs? Is this a plausible scenario when the learned advisers of christian kings had before them the models of later imperial Rome and Byzantium? These questions need to be set in a wider context. Recent work on mortuary liturgy has revealed a notable

---

[11] Childeric's burial: M. Kazanski and P. Périn, "Le mobilier funéraire de la tombe de Childéric", *Revue Archéologique de Picardie* 3–4 (1988), pp. 13–38, and R. Brulet *et al.*, *Les fouilles du quartier Saint-Brice à Tournai. L'environnement funéraire de la sépulture de Childéric*, 2 vols. (Louvain-la-Neuve, 1990, 1991); burials of christian Merovingians: Périn, "Saint-Germain-des-Prés, première nécropole des rois de France", *Médiévales* 31 (1996), pp. 29–36.

[12] Y. Duval and J.-C. Picard eds., *L'Inhumation privilegiée du IVe au VIIIe siècle* (Paris, 1986); K.H. Krüger, *Königsgrabkirchen der Franken, Angelsachsen und Langobarden bis zur Mitte des 8.Jhdts*, (Munich, 1971); Périn, "Saint-Germain-des-Prés"; R. Le Jan, *Famille et pouvoir dans le monde franc (VIIe-Xe siècle). Essai d'anthropologie sociale* (Paris, 1995), pp. 45–52; M. Richter, "Neues zu den Anfängen des Klosters Reichenau", *Zeitschrift für die Geschichte des Oberrheins* 144 (1996), pp. 1–18, esp. 9–10.

[13] L. Bornscheuer, *Miseriae regum. Untersuchungen zum Krisen- und Totesgedanken in der herrschaftstheologischen Vorstellungen der ottonisch-salischen Zeit* (Berlin, 1968). More recently, the work of the late Karl Leyser and of Gerd Althoff has been especially important. See, with further references, Leyser, *Communications and Power in Medieval Europe*. vol. 1, *The Carolingian and Ottonian Centuries*, ed. T. Reuter (London, 1994); Althoff, *Verwandte, Freunde und Getreue* (Darmstadt, 1990), and idem, *Spielregeln der Politik im Mittelalter. Kommunikation in Frieden und Fehde* (Sigmaringen, 1997).

dearth of documentation before the mid-eighth century anywhere in the christian West with the partial exceptions of Spain and Ireland.[14] It is not only royal funerals, not only case material, for which evidence fails us, but funerals in general, and prescription as well as practice. How should this be explained? One possibility is that funerary rites long remained the purview of layfolk including, conspicuously, women and that clergy therefore preferred to draw a discreet veil over them. Royal funerals went unrecorded not because they were regarded as unimportant, still less because they actually were low-key affairs, but because they were problematic for ecclesiastical recorders. Even after churchmen had come to terms with royal burial *ad sanctos*, clerical liturgification of was only part of the story. Like royal inaugurations, the burials of kings may have been barely noticed in the written sources until clergy gained a directive hand in their design and performance; and even then, accounts were highly selective.

In my view, royal exequies are likely always to have been invested in as important symbolic events. The deaths of early medieval kings were exceptionally sensitive political and social events, given systems of indeterminate succession, elective and hereditary, which precluded any automatically-qualified single heir. In principle a king's death created an interregnum: the heir had to be found and then made.[15] The royal funeral could remain a critical moment in the transfer of power from one ruler to his successor. Against the claim that the alleged deficiences of early medieval political ideas, the alleged lack of any concept of the state in this period, would have precluded any public significance for royal exequies, it can be argued that the dating of private documents by royal reign-years presupposes the fairly rapid diffusion of news of a king's death as well as a widespread acknowledgement of the significance of a change of regime. Further, royal rituals had their public, their primary audience, in the shape of the court, that is, the royal entourage, enlarged on occasion by the elite of the realm. The auditorium at the Northumbrian royal

---

[14] F.S. Paxton, *Christianizing Death. The Creation of a Ritual Process in Early Medieval Europe* (Ithaca NY and London, 1990), pp. 61–91, stresses the evidence for deathbed penance; see further Y. Hen, *Culture and Religion in Merovingian Gaul, AD 481–751* (Leiden, 1995), pp. 143–149.

[15] J. Goody, *Succession to High Office* (Cambridge, 1966), Introduction, pp. 1–56, offers a stimulating cross-cultural analysis. For change in France in the central medieval period, see A.W. Lewis, *Royal Succession in Capetian France: Studies on Familial Order and the State* (Cambridge MA, 1981).

residence of Yeavering could seat 300.[16] True, there was no urban
crowd in the early medieval West to follow a lengthy processional
route through an extensive built-up area. Nevertheless, the early
medieval king did not possess only one body, a private and personal
one.[17] The distinction between mortal tenant and enduring office
was appreciated, and royal burial rites were likely media for its
expression.

For royal funerals in the period before the eighth century, the
excavated tomb itself often constitutes all our evidence. Tombs can
be, and in the case of rulers often are, prepared by their future
incumbents themselves;[18] but a royal burial by definition, even if
planned by this or that ruler, is always staged by others, normally
including the heir.[19] A complete chronology of any royal funeral
would take into account the very beginning of the planning stage,
but also allow for possible divergences between original plan and

---

[16] B. Hope-Taylor, *Yeavering: an Anglo-British Centre of Early Northumbria* (London,
1977), p. 121.

[17] Two fine forthcoming papers use gender to explore this issue: J. Smith, "Gender and ideology in the earlier Middle Ages", *Studies in Church History* 34 (1997),
and S. Airlie, "'The virgin secrets of women': private bodies and the body politic
in the divorce case of Lothar II", *Past and Present* 158 (1998). For earlier medieval
ideas of the public body, see S. Reynolds, "The Historiography of the Medieval
State", *Companion to Historiography*, ed. M. Bentley (London, 1997), pp. 117–138, at
121–127.

[18] A good early medieval example is the mausoleum of Theoderic at Ravenna,
with the reused classical prophyry sarcophagus: see B. Ward-Perkins, *From Classical
Atiquity to the Middle Ages. Urban Public Building in Northern and Central Italy AD 300–850*
(Oxford, 1984), pp. 215–216, noting that whereas Theoderic otherwise preferred
new work to *spolia*, in this case 'a large enough block of new porphyry was almost
certainly unobtainable' from Egypt by the early sixth century. Cf. below and
n. 133.

[19] E. James, "Burial and Status in the Early Medieval West", *Transactions of the
Royal Historical Society* 5th series, 39 (1989), pp. 23–40 makes this point for burials
in general. Cf the comments of G. Halsall, *Settlement and Social Organization. The
Merovingian region of Metz* (Cambridge, 1995), pp. 247–248, writing of the deposition
of grave-goods in the sixth century: 'Rather than being a passive mirror of social
organization, it is an active strategy in the creation of social reality, and act of
"social theatre"'. A Carolingian royal burial clearly was 'a passive mirror' of social
hierarchy, but at the same time it was both active strategy and "theatre". For
wider comparative contexts, see R. Huntingdon and P. Metcalf, *Celebrations of Death*
(Cambridge, 1979), esp. pp. 121–183. Further fruitful perspectives can be found in
S.C. Humphreys and H. King eds., *Mortality and Immortality: the Anthropology and Archaeology of Death* (London, 1981); M. Bloch and J. Parry, Introduction to their co-edited
volume, *Death and the Regeneration of Life* (Cambridge, 1982), pp. 1–44; M. Bloch,
"Death, Women and Power", *ibid.*, pp. 211–230; *Rites of Power*, ed. S. Wilentz; and
D. Cannadine, Introduction to Cannadine and S. Price eds., *Rituals of Royalty. Power
and Ceremonial in Traditional Societies* (Cambridge, 1987), pp. 1–19.

actual execution, hence for differences between participating individuals and groups. For no case in the early Middle Ages do we have anything approaching full evidence of this kind. Nevertheless, for the Carolingian period, thanks to the proliferation of the written word and rulers' preoccupation with correct liturgical practice, there is a good deal more evidence than earlier for rites of all kinds.[20] Rituals of royalty were only slowly and partially affected by these general changes. But the evidence for the Carolingians is very much better than for other and earlier dynasties.[21] Carolingian royal funerals

---

[20] Excellent general discussions with plentiful bibliographical suggestions can be found in A. Angenendt, *Das Frühmittelalter, Die abendländische Christenheit von 100 bis 900* (Stuttgart, 1990), pp. 245–251, 327–348, R. Reynolds, "The organization, law and liturgy of the western Church, 700–900', *The New Cambridge Medieval History*, vol. II, ed. R. McKitterick (Cambridge, 1995), pp. 587–621 and 991–3 (bibliography), and especially J.M. Smith, "Religion and lay society", *ibid.*, pp. 654–678, 1002–6 (bibliography); see also C. Vogel, "La réforme liturgique sous Charlemagne", *Das geistige Leben*, ed. B. Bischoff, vol. 2 of *Karl der Grosse*, general ed. W. Braunfels, 5 vols. (Düsseldorf, 1965), pp. 95–155. For the sources, see C. Vogel, *Medieval Liturgy. An Introduction to the Sources*, revised and trans. W.G. Story and N. Rasmussen (Washington, 1986); E. Palazzo, *Le moyen âge des origines au XIIIᵉ siècle (Histoire des livres liturgiques)* (Paris, 1993). See further, for the pre-Carolingian context, Hen, *Culture and Religion*, pp. 121–153; and, for the Carolingian period, on funeral rites: Paxton, *Christianizing Death*, pp. 92–192; on episcopal consecration: A. Santantoni, *L'ordinazione episcopale* (Rome, 1976), pp. 163–176; on baptism and confirmation: Angenendt, "Bonifatius und das *Sacramentum initiationis*. Zugleich ein Beitrag zur Geschichte der Firmung", *Römische Quartalschrift für christliche Altertumskunde und Kirchengeschichte* 72 (1977), pp. 133–183. S.A. Keefe, "Carolingian baptismal expositions: a handlist of tracts and manuscripts", *Carolingian Essays*, ed. U. Blümenthal, (Washington, 1983), pp. 169–237, J. Lynch, *Godparents and Kinship in Early Medieval Europe* (Princeton, 1986), esp. pp. 210–213, Nelson, "Parents, children and the Church in the earlier Middle Ages", *Studies in Church History* 31 (1994), pp. 81–114, and, still useful, J.D.C. Fisher, *Christian Initiation in the Medieval West* (London, 1965), pp. 52–77; on child oblation, M. De Jong, *In Samuel's Image. Child Oblation in the Early Medieval West* (Leiden, 1996); on marriage: Vogel, "Les rites de la célébration du mariage: leur signification dans la formation du lien durant le haut Moyen age", *Settimane Spoleto* 24 (1976), pp. 397–465; on rites surrounding warfare: M. McCormick, *Eternal Victory. Triumphal Rulership in Late Antiquity, Byzantium and the Early Medieval West* (Cambridge, 1986), pp. 342–384, *idem*, "The liturgy of war in the early Middle Ages", *Viator* 15 (1984), pp. 1–23, and Nelson, "Violence in the Carolingian world and the ritualization of ninth-century warfare", *Violence and Society in the Early Medieval West: Private, Public and Ritual* (Woodbridge, 1997), ed. G. Halsall, pp. 90–107; on ordeals: J. Gaudemet, 'Les ordalies au moyen âge', *Receuils Jean Bodin* 17 (1965), pp. 99–135; D. Barthélemy, "Diversité des ordalies médiévales", *Revue Historique* 280 (1988), pp. 3–25 at 7–8.

[21] For acclamations, invocations and *adventus*, see E.H. Kantorowicz, *Laudes regiae. A Study in Liturgical Acclamations and Medieval Ruler Worship* (Berkeley CA, 1946), esp. pp. 41–76, and McCormick, *Eternal Victory*, pp. 347–84; for these and other forms of royal ritual, see Nelson, 'Royal inaugurations', *Early Medieval Kingship*, eds. P. Sawyer and I. Wood (Leeds, 1977), pp. 50–71, repr. in her collected papers,

have scarcely been studied until very recently[22] and more evidence
may in fact be available for them than has yet been realised. At
least by comparison with historians of earlier periods, Carolingianists are fortunate to have, often, both the tomb, however much
altered over time, and some, however little, contemporary written
information on such tantalisingly elusive yet crucial matters as the
intentions and ideas of those involved, gaps between plans and out-
comes, and the effects of particular choices. On this modestly opti-
mistic note—which deserves to be sounded more loudly than lament
for the thinness of eighth- and ninth-century material compared with
the fuller tenth-century accounts—I shall examine a series of case-
studies in detail,[23] but I begin with brief consideration of the general context of Carolingian royal funerary practice.

2. *The background to Carolingian royal funerals*

Recent research has highlighted two important shifts in the way in
which Roman imperial funerals were conducted.[24] The first occurred

---

Politics and Ritual in Early Medieval Europe (London, 1986), pp. 283–308, and *idem*,
"Symbols in context: rulers' inauguration rituals in Byzantium and the West in the
earlier Middle Ages", *Studies in Church History* 13 (1976), pp. 97–119, repr. in *Politics and Ritual*, pp. 259–282; also *idem*, 'Carolingian royal ritual', *Rituals of Royalty*,
eds. Cannadine and Price, pp. 137–180, repr. *idem*, *The Frankish World* (London,
1996), pp. 99–132, with further references; for royal marriage and queenly consecration, see Nelson, "Early medieval rites of queen-making and the shaping of
medieval queenship', *Queens and Queenship in Medieval Europe*, ed. A. Duggan (Woodbridge, 1997), pp. 301–315.

[22] Exceptionally important are the path-breaking studies of A. Dierkens, "Le
tombeau de Charlemagne", *Byzantion* 61 (1991), pp. 156–180; *idem*, "La mort, les
funérailles et la tombe du roi Pépin le Bref (768)", *Médiévales* 31 (1996), pp. 37–52.
See further, especially for later periods, A. Erlande-Brandenburg, *Le roi est mort:
Étude sur les funérailles, les sépultures et les tombeaux des rois de France jusqu'à la fin du
XIIIe siècle* (Geneva, 1975); Bornscheuer, *Miseriae regum*; Brown, *The Monarchy of
Capetian France*, chs. VI–IX; E. Hallam, "Royal burial and the cult of kingship in
France and England, 1060–1330", *Journal of Medieval History* 8 (1982), pp. 359–80;
D. Carpenter, "The Burial of King Henry III, the Regalia and Royal Ideology",
in his collected papers, *The Reign of Henry III* (London, 1996), pp. 427–461; and
J. Parsons, "'Never was a body buried in England with such solemnity and honour':
the Burials and Posthumous Commemorations of English Queens to 1500", *Queens
and Queenship*, ed. Duggan, pp. 317–337.

[23] I should make clear that I have examined by no means all Carolingian royal
funerals, and that even the selected cases are not treated below in equal depth.
What follows is a preliminary foray: I hope others will tackle the subject as com-
prehensively as it deserves.

[24] See S. Price, "From noble funerals to divine cult: the consecration of Roman

in the first and second centuries AD: republican, noble practice was changed into divine cult, with imperial apotheosis through the ritual of the pyre. Then, as inhumation became increasingly common for everyone else, the emperor's corpse was cremated to signal his uniqueness. The second shift came with Christianity. Emperors could no longer become gods. On the one hand, funeral rites still emphasised sacrality: Constantine became the thirteenth apostle. Embalming skills made possible protracted post-mortem 'survival', and that gave time and space for elaborate rituals, and complex politicking, without the instability of a formal interregnum. On the other hand, the abandonment of the practice of cremation emphasised what the emperor shared with other men: his mortality. That was one kind of ambiguity. Another kind was evident in a coin showing Constantine in a four-horse chariot 'with a hand stretched downwards to receive him up':[25] both pagan and Christian interpretations of this were possible.

The christian Clovis and his wife Clotild planned their own mausoleum dedicated to the Holy Apostles, near to the tomb of St Genevieve in Paris: they were clearly imitating Constantine.[26] Their successors, however, were buried in other churches. Clothar I was interred at St-Médard, Soissons, several Austrasian kings at Metz, and a number of the Neustrians at Ste-Croix-and-St Vincent, later known as St- Germain-des-Prés, in Paris.[27] Sarcophagi believed to have been used for the royal burials at St-Germain were unearthed in the seventeenth century. In one of these, in 1645, Childeric II's alleged remains were discovered, with, still visible, his heavy, decorated belt (which could be in keeping with a later seventh-century date), and spurs on his feet (which seem less so).[28] Multiple Merovingian royal burial sites directly reflect succession practices, that is, the series of divisions of the realm, and lineage segmentation; but they probably also reflects a wider range of ideological factors—cults of local saint-protectors, devotion to monastic communities—which themselves affected succession practices. In the seventh century, the

---

Emperors", *Rituals of Royalty*, eds. Cannadine and Price, pp. 56–105; also J. Arce, *Funus Imperatorum: Los funerales de los emperadores romanos* (Madrid, 1988), esp. pp. 159–163, and *idem*, above in the present volume.

[25] Eusebius, *Vita Constantini* iv, 73. Such coins were not minted in Rome, however.
[26] Périn, "Saint-Germain-des-Prés", p. 30.
[27] Périn, "Saint-Germain-des-Prés", p. 32, evokes 'des innombrables inhumations *ad sanctos* qui s'accumulèrent autour du sanctuaire ou à l'intérieur' of St-Germain.
[28] Périn, "Saint-Germain-des-Prés", p. 33.

burials of Dagobert and his wife Nanthild at St-Denis,[29] and of Balthild at Chelles,[30] may indicate nothing more than personal choices. While there are hints of a fixed custom, *mos*, for royal inaugurations,[31] there is no comparable evidence for royal burials. Perhaps aristocratic form was followed.

After Dagobert, few of the burial-places of Merovingian rulers are recorded. Childebert III (d. 711) is an exception: his burial-place was the monastery of Choisy-au-Bac (dép. Oise), near the palace of Compiègne.[32] By the early eighth century, too, the burial of aristocrats *ad sanctos* was the corollary of aristocratic church-foundation. The mayor of the palace Pippin of Herstal was buried in 714 in the church of the Virgin at his *castellum* of Chèvremont.[33] His son Drogo, who predeceased him, had been buried at St-Arnulf Metz. There was no sign of a single family burial-church for the Pippinids. The convent of Nivelles was the resting-place of three women of Pippinid family in the seventh century, and of Charlemagne's first wife, Himiltrude, in the eighth, but no Pippinid menfolk seem to have been buried there.

---

[29] Fredegar, *Chronicon* IV, 79, ed. Wallace-Hadrill, *The Fourth Book of the Chronicle of Fredegar with its Continuations* (London, 1960), p. 67.

[30] *Vita Domnae Balthildis*, c. 15, ed. B. Krusch, *MGH SSRM* II (Hanover, 1888), p. 502. For Balthild's recently-rediscovered burial-attire, see J. Laporte, *Le trésor des saints de Chelles* (Chelles, 1988), pp. 92–101, with colour-plates III, IV and VI–VIII.

[31] Nelson, "Royal inaugurations", Nelson, *Politics and Ritual*, pp. 286, 290–291.

[32] *Liber Historiae Francorum*, c. 50, ed. B. Krusch, *MGH, SSRM* II, p. 321. The same source records the deaths of Clovis II (657), Clothar III (673), Theuderic III (691), Clovis III (695), Dagobert III (715), but nothing about their burials. Chilperic II is said to have been buried (720) 'in the *civitas* of Noyon', *Liber Historiae Francorum*, c. 53, p. 324.

[33] The *Genealogia Dagoberti*, extant in a twelfth-century manuscript, contains brief extracts from the so-called *Annales Mettenses Priores*, and adds at 714: '[Pippinus] was buried by his wife Plectrude and a large crowd of Franks in the church of Mary holy mother of God at Chèvremont where when living he had built a great fortified residence [*Capremontis in ecclesia sancte Dei genetricis Marie, ubi castellum magnum vivens construxerat*]', cited by B. von Simson in the notes to his edition of the *Annales Mettenses Priores*, *MGH SSRG* (Hanover-Leipzig, 1905), p. 19, n. 4, and for the manuscript, *idem*, preface, p. ix. For the date and likely authorship of these annals, see Nelson, "Gender and genre in women historians of the earlier Middle Ages", *L'historiographie médiévale en Europe*, ed. J.-P. Genet (Paris, 1991), pp. 149–163, repr. Nelson, *The Frankish World*, pp. 183–98, at 191–4. Interestingly, Chèvremont was still cherished by the Emperor Lothar in the mid-ninth century, when the church's privileges were confirmed, *MGH DD Karol., Lothar I*, ed. T. Schieffer (Berlin-Zürich, 1966), no. 86, pp. 209–210, for 'Abbot Lothar to whom we have committed it to rule'. The abbot's name suggests that he belonged to the wider Carolingian family. Was he identical with the Hlotharius who was priest and custos at St-Amand in the years around 800? See H. Löwe, "Eine Kölner Notiz zum Kaisertum Karls des Grossen", *Rheinische Vierteljahrsblätter* 14 (1949), pp. 7–34, at 22.

Something new and significant occurred when Charles Martel was buried in 741 at St-Denis. This was a prime Frankish and Merovingian cult-site (though infrequently used as a royal mausoleum), and the Carolingians' muscling-in on it thus marked a key moment in their advance. The reign of Dagobert had marked the dynastic hayday of the Merovingians, beyond the limits of living recall but still very much alive in social memory. In death Martel joined this mightiest of kings. The choice of burial-place, evidently Martel's own, can be interpreted in more than one way. The quitting of ancestral ground in favour of Neustria underlined a longer-term westward shift of Martel's interests, and the supersession of the old dynasty's power at its geographical heart. Martel had appointed his (half)-nephew Hugh as abbot of St-Denis, and sent his younger son Pippin to St-Denis to be brought up.[34] He had granted St-Denis important favours, not least in his last charter issued within days of his death. Yet this very document was attested by Martel's second wife, the *illustris matrona* Swanahild, and her son Grifo, who thus evidently attended— as Pippin did not—Martel's deathbed, and the grant, convincingly read as an attempt to secure the future of these two by enlisting St-Denis's (and St Denis's) protection, thus reveals rifts and tensions in the new dynasty's familial heart.[35] Swanahild may well have accompanied her late husband's corpse on its last journey, and participated in the funeral arrangements.[36] At the same time, Martel's burial may have been an occasion for displaying familial rapprochement, and Pippin, St Denis's *alumnus*, who had emerged, perhaps surprisingly, as co-heir alongside his elder brother, and in whose kingdom St-Denis lay, may have played a leading role alongside his stepmother and half-brother.[37] St-Denis was also to be Pippin's choice for his own burial.

---

[34] Pippin's own assertion: *MGH DD Karol. I, Pippin I*, ed. A. Dopsch *et al.*, revd. E. Mühlbacher (Hanover, 1906), no. 8, p. 13: '*ad monasterium beati domini Dionisii ubi enotriti* [sic] *fuimus*'. Cf. the later Merovingian Theuderic IV *enutritus* at Chelles: *Liber Historiae Francorum*, c. 53, p. 328.

[35] I. Heidrich, "Titulatur und Urkunden der arnulfischen Hausmeier", *Archiv für Diplomatik* 11/12 (1965/66), no. 12, p. 242; see further *idem*, "Die Urkunden Pippins der Mittler und Karls Martells. Beobachtungen zu ihrer zeitlichen und räumlichen Streuung", *Karl Martell in seiner Zeit*, eds. J. Jarnut, U. Nonn and M. Richter (Sigmaringen, 1994), pp. 23–33, at 31–32.

[36] For the role of women in the care and commemoration of the dead in the tenth century, see P. Geary, *Phantoms of Remembrance. Memory and Oblivion at the End of the First Millenium* (Princeton, 1994), pp. 51–73. See further, below.

[37] Martel died at Quierzy on 22 October, and was taken (by boat down the Oise?) to St-Denis for burial: Continuator of Fredegar, c. 24; *Annales Mettenses Priores*,

3. *Pippin I*

Pippin, having fallen ill in Aquitaine in late summer 768, went north via St-Martin, Tours, where he prayed for the saint's help in seeking God's forgiveness for his sins, to St-Denis, where he felt the approach of death. He summoned a large gathering of lay and ecclesiastical magnates, and after gaining their approval for the division of the realm between his sons, Pippin died on 24 September.[38] Whereas the father had been buried in the choir of St-Denis, Pippin had left orders that he should be interred under the entranceway or narthex (porch) of the church.[39] His sons, who saw to the burial, evidently carried out these instructions. If Suger of St-Denis, writing in the twelfth century, can be believed, Pippin was found, when his tomb was opened, to have been interred 'face-downwards, not on his back (*prostratum non supinum*)': thus the significance of the porch as a location of penitential humility was reinforced by the positioning of the corpse.[40] Two points about Pippin's funeral mentioned by the Continuator of Fredegar are worth mentioning: one is the large-scale participation of the Frankish elite, which (though is there no clear evidence) may well have accorded with Merovingian tradition; the other is the presence with the dying Pippin of his wife Bertrada as well as their two sons.[41] Her role, if any, in the funeral, is unmentioned, however.

---

s.a. 741, p. 32, which also reveal that Pippin's half-brother Grifo was given a share of their father's *principatus*.

[38] Most of these details come from the Continuator of Fredegar, c. 53, ed. Wallace-Hadrill, pp. 120–121, a virtually contemporary source, written up for the years between 751 and 768 by Pippin's cousin Count Nibelung: R. Collins, "Deception and misrepresentation in early eighth century Frankish historiography," *Karl Martell*, eds. J. Jarnut *et al.*, pp. 227–247. The date of Pippin's death is supplied by the *Annales regni Francorum*, ed. F. Kurze, *MGH SSRG* (Hanover, 1895), p. 26.

[39] Letter of Louis the Pious to Abbot Hilduin of St-Denis, *MGH Epp. KA* III, ed. E. Dümmler (Berlin, 1899), no. 19, pp. 182–183: '*ante limina basilicae sanctorum martyrum*'. Note, however, that there is no reference in the sources to any *mandata* from the ruler, following Roman custom, about his own funeral.

[40] Suger, *Liber de rebus in administratione sua gestis*, ed. A. Lecoy de la Marche, (Paris, 1867), c. 25, p. 187. See A. Angenendt, "*In porticu ecclesiae sepultus*. Ein Beispiel von himmlisch-irdischer Spiegelung", *Iconologia Sacra. Mythos, Bildkunst und Dichtungin der Religions- und Sozialgeschichte Alteuropas. Festschrift für Karl Hauck*, eds. H. Keller and N. Staubach (Berlin and New York, 1994), pp. 68–80. For face-down inhumation, Dierkens, "La mort et les funérailles", p. 44. Dierkens, rightly I think, infers that this was in accord with Pippin's own wishes.

[41] Continuator of Fredegar, c. 53, pp. 120–121: '*omnes proceres suos, ducibus vel comitibus Francorum, tam episcopis quam sacerdotibus, ad se venire precepit. Ibique una cum con-*

4. *Carloman*

While Pippin, following his father and some of their Merovingian predecessors, sought to associate himself, in death, with St-Denis, his son Carloman made a deliberate break with that double tradition, and planned for his own burial at St-Remi, Rheims.[42] If he was ailing for some time before his death, on December 771, he would have had plenty of time to plan.[43] It was not that Carloman lacked devotion to St Denis: among a dozen charters extant from his short reign, four were for St-Denis's benefit, and the last of these, issued on his deathbed, mentioned that Pippin *cum sociis suis* was buried at St-Denis.[44] As striking, however, and forming a notable contrast with Pippin's neglect, is Carloman's generosity to St-Remi. Though none of the relevant charters survives, they were inspected in the mid-tenth century by Flodoard who preserved their substance in his *History of the Church of Rheims*. Four confirmed the monastery's immunity and freedom from tolls, one and perhaps two released St-Rémi's beneficed men in the environs of Rheims from the military service their owed the king, while a further grant, most valuable of all, of the estate of Neuilly, was made 'for the place of his [Carloman's] burial . . . at the church and monastery of St-Rémi, where he is indeed known to have his burial-place.[45] That Carloman's wishes

---

sensu Francorum et procerum suorum seu et episcoporum, regnum Francorum . . . inter [filios] divisit'; he died 'a few days later', and his sons buried him *cum magno honore.*

[42] M. Sot, *Un historien et son Église. Flodoard de Reims* (Paris, 1993), pp. 378–459; cf. also P. Depreux, "Saint Remi et la royauté carolingienne", *Revue Historique* 285 (1991), pp. 235–260, and *idem*, "La dévotion à saint Rémi de Reims aux IXe et Xe siècles", *Cahiers de civilisation médiévale* 35 (1992), pp. 111–129.

[43] J. Jarnut, "Ein Bruderkampf und seine Folgen: die Krise des Frankenreiches (768–771)," *Herrschaft, Kirche, Kultur. Beiträge zur Geschichte des Mittelalters. Festschrift für Friedrich Prinz zu seinem 65. Geburtstag*, eds. G. Jenal and S. Haarländer (Stuttgart, 1993), pp. 165–176.

[44] *MGH DD Karol.* I, *Pippin I*, no. 53, p. 74.

[45] Flodoard, *Historia Remensis Ecclesiae*, II, 17, eds. I. Heller and G. Waitz, MGH SS XIII (Hanover, 1881), 17, p. 464. For this and Carloman's other grants, see M. Stratmann, "Die Königs- und Privaturkunden für die Reimser Kirche bis gegen 900", *Deutsches Archiv* 52 (1996), pp. 1–56, at 13–14, 33–36. In his account of the Neuilly estate, *de villa Noviliaco*, ed. H. Mordek, "Ein exemplarischer Rechtsstreit: Hinkmar von Reims und das Landgut Neuilly-Saint-Front", *Zeitschrift für Rechtsgeschichte*, kan. abt. 114 (1997), pp. 86–112, at 104, Hincmar says he has ('quod habemus') Charlemagne's confirmation of Carloman's grant of Neuilly, and he repeats this in a letter to count Odalric, Flodoard, *Historia Remensis Ecclesiae*, III, c. 26, p. 544. There can be no doubt that Charlemagne did confirm his dead brother's grant, but this could reflect something other than favour to Rheims: see below.

were carried out is confirmed by the nearest thing to a Carolingian house-history that this period produced: the so-called *Annales Mettenses Priores*, written up, I think, at the behest of Carloman's (and Charlemagne's) sister Gisela, abbess of Chelles. These same Annals also reveal, uniquely, that Carloman had two sons at this point, and it was their claims that Charlemagne would overrule in imposing his *monarchia*.[46] Samoussy, where Carloman died, is some 43 km. from Rheims as the crow flies. The royal funeral procession probably took at least three days to reach St-Rémi.[47] Carloman's widow and her sons presumably were part of the cortège: the sources imply that their flight to Italy did not follow Carloman's death immediately but only after substantial numbers of the aristocracy of his kingdom had abandoned his sons and declared for Charlemagne, perhaps expressing this decision by absenting themselves from Carloman's exequies.

Various reasons can be suggested for Carloman's choice of burial-place: first, given Charlemagne's already publicly-expressed intention to follow their father's choice of St-Denis,[48] a strong desire on Carloman's part to differentiate his own descent-line from that of his older brother, and so to strengthen Rheims' support for the succession of his own sons; second, the strategic location of Rheims in Carloman's own kingdom and in the centre of Francia; third, St-Rémi's special association with Clovis and the Frankish past, and, continuing into the present, with the Franks' military success.[49] That evocations of Frankish identity and military success played some part in Carloman's thinking is further indicated by his choice—if indeed it was his personal choice, and not that of archbishop Tilpin and/or Carloman's wife Gerberga—of burial not, humbly, *in porticu ecclesiae*, but in the basilica of St-Rémi itself, and in a fine fourth-century Roman sarcophagus still extant at Rheims. Thanks in part to the work of the seventeenth-century Rheims historian Marlot, we can

---

[46] *Annales Mettenses Priores*, s.a. 771, pp. 57–58. Cf. above, n. 31.

[47] The map of the Rheims area at the back of vol. III of J. Devisse, *Hincmar, archevêque de Reims, 845–882*, 3 vols. (Geneva 1976) indicates a Roman road running most of the way. Samoussy is slightly nearer Soissons, but there was no road-link.

[48] Charlemagne, charter for St-Denis (13 January 769), *MGH DD Karol.* I, no. 55, pp. 81–82.

[49] In *Laudes regiae* preserved in MS Montpellier 409, ed. O. Holder Egger, appendix to his edition of Einhard's *Vita Karoli*, MGH SSRG (Hanover-Leipzig, 1911) p. 47, and dating from 784x792, St Remi is invoked to protect the *iudices et cunctus exercitus Francorum*. It is worth noting that Charles Martel had named one of his bastard sons Remigius, and made him bishop of Rouen.

be fairly sure that the sarcophagus of the consul Jovinus was reused for Carloman. This particular receptacle, with its vivid depiction of a lion-hunt, and of the consul himself as both general and huntsman, may well have been chosen because of its perceived appropriateness for a Frankish king who, had he lived, might well have continued his father's military exploits and also his renewal of things Roman.[50] As for the *chi-rho* monogram in a roundel on one face of the sarcophagus, some observers, at least, might have registered the reference to the victorious Constantine. Burial in a reused Roman sarcophagus was an innovation, as far as we know, for Frankish royalty. Subsequent Carolingians were to imitate it, but they were to choose other sites than Rheims.

5. *Charlemagne*

For anyone researching Carolingian funerals, Alain Dierkens's recent paper on Charlemagne's tomb is the essential starting-point.[51] On the basis of his study of Charlemagne's tomb, Dierkens lists the following traits as distinguishing the royal burials of the 'monde occidental' from those of Byzantium during the eighth and ninth centuries:

1. no developed ritual
2. no dynastic burial-church
3. relatively low-profile tombs which were not objects of careful commemorations ('des tombeaux relativement discrets qui ne sont pas l'objet de commemorations attentives')
4. no elaborate preparation of the corpse; no embalmment
5. burial without insignia[52]

There is a problem in generalising from one possibly exceptional occasion. The features identified by Dierkens *à propos* Charlemagne's funeral may not have been staples of Carolingian practice; and some features might indeed be considered distinctly curious. The most

---

[50] R. Hamann-MacLean, "Die Reimser Denkmale des französischen Königtums im 12. Jhdt. Saint-Remi als Grabkirche im frühen und hohen Mittelalter", *Beiträge zur Bildung der französischen Nation im Früh- und Hochmittelalter*, ed. H. Beumann (Sigmaringen, 1983), pp. 93–259, at 126–138, with plates 21–23, illustrating the various relocations of the Jovinus-sarcophagus at Rheims.

[51] "Autour de la tombe de Charlemagne", pp. 156–180.

[52] *Ibid.*, pp. 179–80.

obvious near-contemporary source, namely Einhard, is economical with the truth. He describes a series of procedures: 'The body was washed and prepared in the solemn customary way . . ., carried to the church and buried . . . There was doubt as to where he ought to be buried because while alive he had given no instructions about this.'[53] The identity of the 'doubters', which is to say, those in charge of the burial, is clumsily concealed by use of the passive rather than the active voice. Einhard surely misleads. Although at the beginning of his reign Charlemagne had envisaged burial at St-Denis,[54] he had since then based himself firmly at Aachen, and, as Einhard says, founded the church there.[55] Einhard's wording at first seems to imply quite prolonged uncertainty (*Tandem omnium animis sedit . . .*); yet the delay was clearly minimal: Charlemagne was buried on the same day as he died.[56] Who were the *omnes* who made up their minds on the suitability of Charlemagne's burial at Aachen? Did Einhard neglect to identify them because he found their identity, and the whole situation, a source of embarrassment—or worse? The speed with which the burial was conducted is important. Preparations had evidently been made in advance, probably long in advance, and Charlemagne must surely have been party to them. Did he in fact, *pace* Einhard, plan the details of the burial, as well as its location, himself? The Astronomer says that the funeral was organised by 'the children and the leading men of Charlemagne at the palace'.[57] Since his only surviving adult son Louis the Pious was meanwhile far away in Aquitaine, and since Charlemagne's other living sons were still quite young, the children who saw to the funeral must, I suggest, have been his daughters.[58]

---

[53] *Corpus more sollemni lotum et curatum . . . ecclesiae inlatum atque inhumatum est. . . . Dubitatum est primo ubi reponi deberet eo quod ipse vivus de hoc nihil praecepisset'*, Einhard, *Vita Karoli*, c. 31, p. 35. See now also the perceptive comments of M. Innes, "Charlemagne's Will: Piety, Politics and the Imperial Succession", *English Historical Review* 112 (1997), pp. 833–55, at 840 and n. 3.

[54] See above, n. 46.

[55] *Ibid.*, '. . . *nusquam eum honestius tumulari posse quam in ea basilica quam ipse . . . proprio sumptu in eodem vico construxit'*.

[56] *Ibid.*, '. . . *sepultus est eadem die, qua defunctus est'*. Einhard's statement is born out by Thegan, *Gesta Hludowici* Imperatoris, c. 7, ed. E. Tremp, MGH SSRG (Hannover, 1995), p. 186, and, *pace* Innes, p. 839, not really contradicted by the Astronomer, *Vita Hludowici*, c. 22, ed. E. Tremp, *MGH SSRG* (Hanover, 1995), p. 350. See below.

[57] Astronomer, *Vita Hludowici*, c. 21, p. 346: a messenger was sent *'ab eis qui sepulturam eius [sc. Karoli] curarunt, liberis scilicet et proceribus palatinis'*.

[58] Cf Nelson, "Women at the court of Charlemagne: a case of monstrous regiment?", *Medieval Queenship*, ed. J.C. Parsons (New York, 1993), pp. 43–61, reprinted (with a few revisions) in Nelson, *The Frankish World*, pp. 223–242, at 240–242.

Why did Charlemagne, and/or those daughters, reversing earlier plans involving St-Denis, decide on the church at Aachen as the emperor's burial-place, and a potential dynastic mausoleum? Perhaps it needs to be stressed that this church was an exceptional choice in that it was neither monastic shrine nor cathedral.[59] Aachen was a Carolingian new town, which had become a veritable *sedes regni* during Charlemagne's imperial years, with his daughters and other close kin at the core of the palace personnel.[60] Here at Aachen, then, was a new church for a new empire: a parish church, hence a baptismal church, open to all the inhabitants of the royal demesne of Aachen, it was also open to all, women as well as men, who might come to the *sedes regni*. Significantly, the very earliest reference to the church in the making is Alcuin's recalling of a conversation at Aachen with a *filia* of his who was also a *famula fidelissima* of Charlemagne, about the newly set-up columns in 'the wonderful church'.[61] Staffed by twelve canons with a titular abbot to head them, this church had an empire-wide 'parish' as well as a local one. Its main altar, on the ground-floor, was dedicated to the Virgin, together with another to St Peter, its gallery altar to the Saviour. These heavenly patrons had power and responsibility for the whole world. Whereas Pippin was buried *in porticu ecclesiae* at St-Denis, Charlemagne was buried beneath the west entrance to the Aachen church.[62] What united the forms of these two burials was the symbolism of personal humility and dependence on very special heavenly protectors. What distinguished them was the replacement of an old, explicitly franco-centric, and traditionally monastic location, by a new, avowedly universal, pastorally-orientated one. We might think of this (even if Charlemagne's contemporaries seldom used such terms) as a shift of register from private to public.

To control Aachen was to run the empire: to be the custodians of Charlemagne's tomb was to claim a key role in ordering the succession. The daughters of course were ineligible themselves, like

---

[59] Thanks to the work of L. Falkenstein, esp. his *Karl der Grosse und die Entstehung des Aachener Marienstiftes* (Paderborn and Munich, 1981), and "Charlemagne et Aix-la-Chapelle", *Byzantion* 61 (1991), pp. at 252–264, it is clear that the Aachen church, often mistakenly called 'the palace chapel', was a parish church. My remarks take Falkenstein's insights as their starting-point.

[60] J. Nelson, "La cour impériale de Charlemagne", *La royauté et les élites dans l'Europe carolingienne*, ed. R. Le Jan (Lille, 1998), pp. 177–191.

[61] Alcuin, *Epistolae*, ed. E. Dümmler, *MGH Epp. KA* II, Ep. 149, p. 244, with, n. 2, Dümmler's musing that the *filia* might have been Charlemagne's wife Liutgard.

[62] Dierkens, "Autour de la tombe", pp. 175–178.

eunuchs in the palace at Constantinople.[63] But they could push their own candidate. In 814 that candidate was perhaps Charlemagne's cousin Wala. Such a hypothesis would explain the Astronomer's curious remark: 'there was the greatest fear that Wala, whom [the emperor] had held in the very highest standing, might perhaps undertake some mischief . . .'[64] Apparently Louis the Pious, his father's designated heir, had foreseen problems. This may be a contributory factor in explaining why Charlemagne was buried the day he died: those in control at the palace wanted to stay in control, and therefore to forestall the entry of a successor, Louis the Pious, who would inevitably oust the kitchen-cabinet of the previous regime, *coetus qui permaximus erat femineus*, 'the very large crowd of women'.[65] A parallel that comes to mind is the similarly rapid exequies of Edward the Confessor followed by Harold's coronation on the same day, 6 January 1066 at Westminster.[66] Note that both Charlemagne and Edward died in the month of January, a time of year when the need to forestall the corpse's rapid putrefaction can hardly have been a factor.[67] Even if burial on the day of death was normal for laymen as well as ecclesiastics, exceptional circumstances could justify delay.[68] In

---

[63] S. Tougher, 'Byzantine eunuchs: an overview, with special reference to their creation and origin", in L. James ed., *Women, Men and Eunuchs. Gender in Byzantium* (London, 1997), pp. 168–184.

[64] Astronomer, *Vita Hludowici*, c. 21, p. 346.

[65] *Ibid.*

[66] Nelson, "The rites of the Conqueror", p. 395. Edward's widow Edith, who was also Harold's sister, is prominently depicted at Edward's deathbed in the Bayeux Tapestry, ed. D.M. Wilson, *The Bayeux Tapestry* (London, 1985), plate 30. For her role in January 1066, see P.A. Stafford, *Queen Emma and Queen Edith. Queenship and Women's Power in Eleventh-Century England* (Oxford, 1997), pp. 273–274.

[67] On embalming, see below. Dierkens, "Autour de la tombe", p. 164, notes that Charlemagne died on a Saturday, and says that those in charge of his burial would not have wished it to take place on a Sunday. They could, however, have waited till Monday.

[68] The Visigothic Council of Valencia (549), c. 4, J. Vivès ed., *Concilios visigóticos e hispano-romanos* (Barcelona/Madrid, 1963), p. 63, prescribed same-day burial for bishops; but there is no Frankish conciliar echo of that, though the Council of Orleans (533), c. 5, warned against delay in burying a bishop *ne cuiuslibet corpusculum diutius inhumatum neglegentia interveniente solvatur*, J. Gaudemet and B. Basdevant edd., *Les Canons des Conciles Mérovingiens*, 2 vols. (Paris, 1989), vol. 1, p. 198. D. Bullough, "Burial, community and belief in the early medieval West", *Ideal and Reality in Frankish and Anglo-Saxon Society*, ed. P. Wormald (Oxford, 1983), pp. 177–201, at 191 and n. 36, assembles other evidence for same-day burial for bishops and abbots, and p. 200, for an early ninth-century noble Bavarian layman. Pippin is not said to have been buried on the same day as his death (24 September) but perhaps this is to be inferred: cf above. Dierkens, "La mort", p. 43, notes without further comment that Charlemagne was buried 'le jour même de sa mort'.

both 814 and 1066, there were political reasons for haste: whoever controlled the dead ruler's funeral was in a strong position to control the succession.

In January 814, Louis the Pious was in Aquitaine. The fact that he had already the previous year been crowned *consors regni*, heir to the imperial title, gave him no purchase on events in Aachen.[69] Yet, according to the Astronomer, Louis had already summoned an assembly for 14 February, 'as if by some presentiment',[70] and so was in a position to march on Aachen in strength. He subsequently dated his reign-years from 2 February, evidently the day on which he had learned of Charlemagne's death and been 'recognised', in the view of himself and his entourage, as the sole heir.[71] Wala chose the better part of valour, and hastened south to acknowledge Louis, 'commending himself according to the custom of the Franks'. The date on which Louis reached Aachen is significant too: the thirtieth day after his father's death. This was the crucial day in the ritual remembering of the dead.[72] If Louis had not been able to manage the funeral itself, he could still ensure for himself a central role in Charlemagne's commemoration, making it coincide with his own *adventus* at Aachen. Charlemagne's death could thus be presented as legitimating Louis's succession, hence reinforcing the message of 813. Louis needed to arrange this so carefully because the interregnum created by Charlemagne's swift burial had in fact been so dangerous. Rituals in which Louis played no part threatened his succession: he responded with counter-rituals which assured it. At the same time he ostentatiously paid the outstanding bill for his father's funeral-expenses: in asserting that Louis 'provided for' the funeral, the Astronomer contrives to present him as having carried out correctly the heir's normal responsibility, despite the anomaly of his absence on the day.[73] Where another modern historian detects the Astronomer

---

[69] Einhard, *Vita Karoli*, c. 30, p. 34.

[70] Astronomer, *Vita Hludowici*, c. 20, p. 344: '*quasi quodam . . . praesagio . . .*'

[71] P. Depreux, "Wann begann Kaiser Ludwig zu regieren?", *Mitteilungen des Instituts für Österreichische Geschichtsforschung* 102 (1994), pp. 253–270.

[72] H. Herold, "Der Dreissigste und die rechtgeschichtliche Bedeutung des Totengedächtnisses", *Zeitschrift für Schweizerisches Recht* 57 (1937), pp. 375–420; A. Angenendt, "Theologie und Liturgie der mittelalterlichen Toten-Memoria", *Memoria. Der geschichtliche Zeugniswert des liturgischen Gedenkens im Mittelalter*, eds. K. Schmid and J. Wollasch (Munich, 1984), pp. 79–199, at 172–173, 186–7.

[73] Nithard, *Historiarum libri IV*, ed. and trans. P. Lauer, *Histoire des fils de Louis le Pieux* (Paris, 1926), I, c. 2, pp. 6–7, also records this expenditure *causa funeris* which

writing 'quite inaccurately' at this point,[74] I read a piece of tactful elision on the one hand serving to demonstrate Louis's filial piety, on the other to gloss over the real difficulty of Louis's position in the days and weeks that followed 28 January.

One further crucial detail marked Charlemagne's burial: his body was laid in an antique marble sarcophagus which had been brought to Francia from Italy and must have been carefully prepared in advance.[75] Einhard says that Charlemagne when building the church at Aachen 'saw to the bringing up from Rome and Ravenna of columns and works in marble (marmora)', adding that these could not be got elsewhere.[76] Such transalpine transporting in the second half of Charlemagne's reign seems the likeliest context for the coming of the sarcophagus to Aachen.[77] Einhard gives the whole text of the epitaph carved on the arch which was constructed above the wall-

---

Louis paid out of his late father's treasure. Perhaps Nithard was relying on the Astronomer here, as suggested by Innes, "Charlemagne's Will", p. 839. What both writers nevertheless indicate is that Louis wanted publicly to represent himself as the perfect heir, carrying out a belated settling of accounts on his father's behalf. Innes is right to say that the will as Einhard transmits it makes no provision for the use of part of the inheritance for funeral expenses. Can we infer, though, that such was usual practice?

[74] Innes, "Charlemagne's Will", p. 839.

[75] See P.E. Schramm and F. Mütherich, Denkmale der deutschen Könige und Kaiser (Munich, 1962), no. 18, p. 120; E.G. Grimme, Der Aachener Domschatz (Düsseldorf, 1972), no. 3, p. 8. For an in some ways comparable reinvention of Mediterranean tradition still further north, see I. Henderson, "The insular and continental context of the St Andrews Sarcophagus", Scotland in Dark Age Europe, ed. B. Crawford (St Andrews, 1994), pp. 71–102. The form of this impressive eighth-century shrine recalls its models' original funerary function, and its iconography has 'secular, royal connotations' (p. 92), which Henderson suggests (pp. 79–80) parallel those of the cross-shaft found in the vicinity of the Mercian royal mausoleum at Repton and ingeniously interpreted as a memorial to King Æthelbald (d. 757): see M. Biddle and B. Kjølbye-Biddle, "The Repton Stone", Anglo-Saxon England 14 (1985), pp. 233–292. See also for both these objects, L. Webster and M. Brown, The Transformation of the Roman World (London, 1997): the Stone, catalogue no. 63, p. 225 (and fig. 99); the Sarcophagus, no. 69, p. 227, (and colour plate 65 and fig. 100), with the suggestion of a possible original function as the tomb of King Oengus (d. 761).

[76] Einhard, Vita Karoli, c. 26, p. 31. Alcuin, Ep. 149, p. 244, shows that marble columns had been imported from Italy to Aachen by c. 796. Cf. a letter from Pope Hadrian to Charlemagne agreeing a request for mosaics and marbles from Ravenna, Codex Carolinus no. 81, ed. W. Gundlach, MGH Epp. III, dated by the editor '?787', and certainly not later than 791. The statue of Theodoric was brought from Ravenna in 801, Agnellus, Liber pontificalis ecclesiae Ravennatis, c. 94, ed. O. Holder-Egger, MGH SSRL (Hannover, 1878), p. 338. For Theoderic's sarcophagus, which Charlemagne presumably saw at Ravenna, see above, n. 8.

[77] Dierkens, "Autour de la tombe", p. 166, is judicious.

niche (*arcosolium*) which housed Charlemagne's tomb below ground.[78] And a remarkably antique kind of inscription it is. The only Christian allusion is the word *orthodoxus* in the phrase *magnus atque orthodoxus imperator*. Charlemagne, it says, died at 70+ (*Decessit septuagenarius*), but there is absolutely no reference to what might have been expected to happen after death. The inscription was perhaps Einhard's own work and that may be why he gives details of it.[79] He does not mention the sarcophagus. This is surely a significant silence, to which I shall return.

Charlemagne's last visit to Rome was made in 800–1, and incidentally more than one of his daughters was with him on that occasion.[80] Several motives for planning a sarcophagus-burial come to mind, and they are by no means mutually exclusive. The first is that Charlemagne's brother and one-time rival Carloman had been buried in an antique sarcophagus in 771 at St-Rémi, Rheims,[81] when Archbishop Tilpin of Rheims presumably performed the funeral-rites. Charlemagne did not forget Rheims: or rather, he remembered to punish it by virtually ignoring it until near the close of his reign.[82]

---

[78] H. Hemsgeberg, "Gab es zu Karls des Grossen Grabtitulus eine Vorlage?", *Arbor amoena comis. 25 Jahre Mittellateinisches Seminar zu Bonn*, ed. E. Könsgen (Stuttgart, 1990), pp. 75–80; M. Innes, "The Classical Tradition in the Carolingian Renaissance: Ninth-Century Encounters with Suetonius", *International Journal of the Classical Tradition* 3 (1997), pp. 265–282, at 276, n. 39. For the *arcosolium*, which seems later to have misled some authors to imagine Charlemagne buried sitting on a throne (*solium*), see J. Kollwitz, "Arcosolium", *Reallexikon für Antike und Christentum*, vol. 1 (Stuttgart, 1950), pp. 643–645, and, with two good illustrations of late-antique examples, J. Guyon, "L'inhumation privilegiée dans un cimitière roman au IVe", in Duval and Picard edd., *L'inhumation privilegiée*, pp. 173–82, with figs. 2 and 3 at p. 181. Einhard simply uses *arcus*, meaning the arched niche. For the eleventh-century (and later) myth, see Dierkens, "Autour de la tombe", pp. 169–75, and R. Morrissey, *L'empereur à la barbe fleurie. Charlemagne dans la mythologie et l'histoire de France* (Paris, 1997), pp. 17–23, with illustrations 1 and 2 (following p. 198), and a neat citation (p. 17) from M. de Certeau, *L'Écriture de l'histoire* (Paris, 1975), p. 18: 'l'actualité cst le commencement réel de toute évocation du passé'.

[79] The fact that the inscription is transmitted independently of Einhard's *Vita Karoli* does not seem to me to preclude this possibility.

[80] *Vita Leonis III*, c. 24, ed. L. Duchesne, *Le liber pontificalis*, vol. 2, revd. C. Vogel (Paris, 1955), p. 8.

[81] See above. Cf. Hincmar's letter to Louis the German, Flodoard, *Historia Remensis Ecclesiae*, II, 20, p. 513, warning him to keep his men's hands off Neuilly because Carloman had given the *villa* to Rheims to assure his salvation.

[82] There is no record of any visit by Charlemagne to Rheims except in 804 when he met Pope Leo III there, see below, nor any record of contact between him and Tilpin, save for (i) a letter purportedly sent to Tilpin by Pope Hadrian I, which mentions Charlemagne's request of the pallium for Tilpin and the restoration

The church, and its longlived bishop, are strikingly absent from the sources for Charlemagne's reign, though Tilpin, as 'Turpin', was of course later to loom so large in Charlemagne's legend. One motive for the choice of Charlemagne's sarcophagus, then, was perhaps to trump Carloman. For Carloman's sarcophagus was, it seems, to hand at Rheims, a Roman *civitas*-site with classical remains still visible on the ground in the early Middle Ages,[83] whereas Charlemagne's had been brought direct from Rome.

A second motive, surely, was the highlighting of imperial grandeur.[84] Charlemagne's decision to be buried in a sarcophagus, and the choice of sarcophagus itself, could also have resulted from an explicit piece of *imitatio imperii*. It seems to have been a tradition, recorded in the early seventh century, that immediately after his imperial coronation, and publicly, in the presence of senate and soldiery, a Byzantine emperor summoned the monumental masons with a selection of marble-samples, to order his sarcophagus: a *memento mori*.[85] Did Charlemagne know this, and in 801, now emperor, did he follow suit?

---

of many alienated lands to Tilpin's church by Charlemagne and by Carloman. E. Lesne, "La lettre interpolée d'Adrien Ier à Tilpin", *Le Moyen Age* 26 (1913), pp. 325–351, 389–413, argued that there was a genuine core to this letter, but that much of it was forged by Hincmar; Devisse, *Hincmar*, vol. 2, pp. 651–652, argued that the forging was done not by Hincmar but by Rheims partisans of the deposed archbishop Ebbo. Sot, *Un historien*, pp. 463–464, accepts Lesne's view, with Devisse's modifications. There is no doubt the archbishop of Rheims' participation was needed in arrangements concerning the see of Mainz, and Charlemagne evidently had the pope's co-operation in getting this. None of this suggests any closeness between the king and the archbishop. (ii) a series of confirmations of Carloman's grants to St-Remi, see above, n. 42, and below. (iii) a letter of Hincmar to the East Frankish king Louis the Younger, Flodoard, *Historia* III, c. 26, p. 544, which says that Tilpin had made Charlemagne a precarial grant of the *villa* of Douzy, in return for ninths and tenths and 12 lb. of silver per annum: *cui bono*, on balance?

[83] As Flodoard reveals in the tenth century, Sot, *Un historien*, pp. 357–358. For Carloman's sarcophagus, see above, n. 50.

[84] A piece of late eighth-century Byzantine silk still on display at Aachen is said to have been used to wrap Charlemagne's body: D. Bullough, *The Age of Charlemagne* (London, 1965), p. 187, plate 75, but cf. Schramm and Mütherich, *Denkmale*, no. 6, pp. 115 and 211 (plate), who say only that this was given to the church by Charlemagne. I. Wood, "Sépultures ecclésiastiques et sénatoriales dans la vallée du Rhône (400–600)", *Médiévales* 31 (1996), pp. 13–28, discusses fifth- and sixth-century burials of high-status corpses dressed in silk clothing.

[85] The story is told in the seventh-century *Life of John the Almsgiver*, by Leontius of Naples, cited by A. Cameron, *Flavius Cresconius Corippus, In laudem Iustini Augusti minoris* (London, 1976), p. 182, commentary on Book III, ll. 60–61, p. 103: '[they] laid [Justinian's] honoured limbs in the holy tomb/ which the emperor had himself earlier built from pure gold'. Cameron infers a 'custom'; P. Karlin, "L'adieu à l'empéreur", *Byzantion* 61 (1991), pp. 112–155, at pp. 122–123, suggests instead 'une mythification', while noting many examples of emperors (including Justinian) choosing their tombs in advance.

Charlemagne's sarcophagus shows the rape of Proserpina. This image packs an immensely powerful visual punch, and surely did so for Charlemagne and his contemporaries. It could no doubt be given a Christian reading, as symbolising the ascent of the soul to heaven.[86] The further connotations of romanity and majesty would evoke the shades of ancient emperors. Why then did Einhard not mention the sarcophagus? After all he was Charlemagne's director of public works, his Bezaleel, and presumably therefore very knowledgable about old marbles. I infer that this particular one was not his choice, and that he edited it out of the *Vita Karoli* because it had been chosen by others—including others, perhaps, of whom he disapproved, namely Charlemagne's daughters, chief among them that celebrated unmarried mother Bertha.[87] If the sarcophagus was deliberately chosen for its iconography, gender may have played some role. It was the daughters of Charlemagne who, remember, were involved in arranging his funeral and perhaps in planning it in advance. They, and indeed Charlemagne himself, may have seen here a representation of female power as well as vulnerability: Ceres, goddess of fertility, is the counter-force to the male figure of Pluto god of the underworld, with Proserpina herself straddling two realms.

6. *Pippin I of Aquitaine*

Pippin of Aquitaine, Louis the Pious' second son, died on 13 December 838.[88] Pippin had shown special favour during his reign to the convent of Sainte-Croix (Holy Cross) at Poitiers, founded by St Radegund. He had given it rights to hold markets and take dues, and protection for its lands and privileges.[89] It was here that Pippin, as

---

[86] Nelson, "Women at the court", pp. 223–225, 242; for the sensitivity of Charlemagne's contemporaries to classical images and allusions, see the fine study of L. Nees, *A Tainted Mantle. Hercules and the Classical Tradition at the Carolingian Court* (Philadelphia, 1991).

[87] Nelson, "La cour impériale", pp. 185–191.

[88] *Annales Bertiniani* (hereafter *AB*), ed. F. Grat et al. (Paris, 1965), p. 26, trans. Nelson, *The Annals of St-Bertin* (Manchester, 1991), p. 40. The immediately preceding event in these Annals is a lunar eclipse on 5 December, evidently regarded as a portent. It is not known if Pippin died of an illness: his last-documented location is on 25 November at Néris (dép. Allier): J. Martindale, "Charles the Bald and the Government of the Kingdom of Aquitaine", *Charles the Bald. Court and Kingdom*, eds. M.T. Gibson and J.L. Nelson, 2nd edn (London, 1990), p. 136. Néris is nearly 200 km. east of Poitiers.

[89] *Receuil des Actes de Pépin I et Pépin II, rois d'Aquitaine (814–848)*, ed. L. Levillain

the main leader of the revolt against Louis in 830, had caused his stepmother Judith to be imprisoned for some six months.[90] Clearly the management of the convent was one in which the king had confidence. It was the only women's house on Louis the Pious' list of monasteries owing services: in Sainte-Croix's case, not warriors or gifts, but prayers 'for the well-being of the emperor and his sons and for the stability of the empire'.[91] Some idea of the community's size may be gleaned from Pippin's injunction that it should never exceed 100 nuns and 30 clergy.[92] If a twelfth-century Poitevin chronicle can be believed, he chose the nuns' burial church, the church of St Radegund where the saint herself lay, as his own burial-place.[93] This was an inconspicuous location, outside the wall of the main monastic precinct. The fact that it was a women's community might have caused problems, but in this case, Pippin had taken care to establish such good relations with the nuns that his body was not refused.[94]

Pippin's choice is explicable in both political and religious terms. Poitiers had been, since Merovingian times, a key strategic place in the Frankish kingdom, and previous Carolingians, as well as Pippin himself, had stayed there, sometimes *in palatio*, sometimes at the

---

(Paris 1926), no. III, pp. 9–12; also *Capitulare de monasterio Sanctae Crucis*, ed. A. Boretius, *MGH Capit.* I (Hanover, 1883), no. 149, p. 302. See Y. Labande-Mailfert *et al.*, *Histoire de l'abbaye de Sainte-Croix de Poitiers*, Mémoires de la Société des antiquaires de l'ouest, 4th ser. 19 (1986–7), pp. 80–85. Though Pippin's extant favours do not include grants of land, R. Collins, "Pippin I and the Kingdom of Aquitaine", *Charlemagne's Heir. New Perspectives on the Reign of Louis the Pious*, eds. P. Godman and R. Collins (Oxford, 1990), pp. 363–89, at 369, n. 36, nevertheless surmises that Pippin 'must have been a generous benefactor to the abbey'. It may be, equally, that the nuns expected their acceptance of Pippin's body to result in future benefactions from his heir. Collins further notes, p. 374, that St Leodegarius (Léger) is said to have been buried at Sainte-Croix.

[90] *AB*, 830, p. 2, trans. p. 22. According to the annal for 830, tacked on to the *Annales Mettenses Priores* by (so I have suggested) the then abbess of Chelles, Heilwig, the empress's mother, Judith impressed all the nuns by her pious demeanour: *Annales Mettenses Priores*, p. 97.

[91] *Notitia de servitio monasteriorum*, ed. K. Hallinger, *Corpus Consuetudinum Monasticarum*, vol. 1 (Siegburg, 1963), p. 497.

[92] *Capitulare de monasterio Sanctae Crucis*, cc. 6 and 7, p. 302.

[93] *Chronique de Saint-Maixent*, ed. J. Verdon (Paris, 1979), p. 50. Produced in Poitou and drawing on earlier Poitevin sources, this chronicle seems exceptionally well-informed about the region. For the identification of the church of St-Radegund as the nuns' burial church, see Labande-Mailfert, *Histoire*, p. 85.

[94] Contrast the distressing episode when, on Easter Day 901, the Byzantine emperor Leo tried to have his wife Eudokia (who had just died in childbirth) buried at the monastery of St-Lazarus, recently founded by Leo himself: the *hegoumenos* (abbot) barred the gates and ordered the corpse to be taken back to the palace. Karlin, "L'adieu", p. 149, surmises 'une sérieuse bévue du côté de l'organisation' (!).

monastery of St-Hilary, or in the nearby palace of Chasseneuil.[95] As a religious centre, the convent of Sainte-Croix combined the charisma of royal foundation by the saint-queen Radegund with the uniquely potent relic of a piece of the True Cross, sent c. 560 from Constantinople to the Franks.[96] Pippin's burial close to Radegund in the convent burial-church meant that the united forces of royal rank and special holiness transcended the rigorous gender divide enshrined in the community's rule. At the same time, burial in this little church signified the king's humility: he had opted for a gesture similar to his great-grandfather Pippin's at St-Denis. If a kingdom of Aquitaine had survived, and with an established royal mausoleum, St Radegund's house would surely have been its spiritual heart. As it was, while Sainte-Croix was the only convent in Gaul south of the Loire to achieve a continuous existence from its foundation through to the twelfth, and indeed to the twentieth, century, Poitiers flourished from the later ninth century onwards as the chief place of a ducal, not royal, dynasty of Aquitaine.[97]

7. Louis the Pious

Louis too was buried in an antique sarcophagus.[98] A recent scholar talks of 'antiquarianism':[99] hardly *le mot juste* because it smacks of something rather trivial, merely derivative. Not so! Antiquity, that is, christian antiquity, was crucially important to the elite of the Frankish world. Refashioned in being reused, it provided essential legitimation for the Carolingian empire. Louis, in the footsteps of Charlemagne but with goals of his own,[100] was busily constructing a

---

[95] Martindale, "The Government", pp. 135–6. See further C.R. Brühl, *Palatium und Civitas. Studien zur Profantopographie spätantike Civitates vom 3. bis zum 13. Jhdt*, vol. 1: Gallien (Cologne and Vienna 1975); and for the period after the 830s, Nelson, *Charles the Bald* (London, 1992), pp. 101–103, 154, 172–173.

[96] I. Wood, *The Merovingian Kingdoms* (London, 1994), pp. 136–9, with the comment, 'Radegund herself had some international status'.

[97] E. Magnou-Nortier, "Formes féminines de vie consacrée dans les pays du Midi jusqu'au début du XIIᵉ siècle", *Cahiers de Fanjeaux* 23 (1988), pp. 193–5; J. Dunbabin, *France in the Making* (Oxford, 1985), pp. 60–62, 173–179.

[98] Schramm and Mütherich, *Denkmale*, no. 23, p. 122.

[99] R. Melzak, "Antiquarianism in the Time of Louis the Pious and its Influence on the Art of Metz", *Charlemagne's Heir*, pp. 629–640.

[100] K.F. Werner, "*Hludovicus Augustus*: Gouverner l'empire chrétien—idées et réalités", *Charlemagne's Heir*, pp. 3–124.

distinctive imperial identity for his regime. Antiquity had to be his quarry, not least in the case of the sarcophagus. Unlike Charlemagne, Louis chose an explicitly christian piece, whose theme had been especially popular for sarcophagi in the late fourth and fifth centuries: Pharoah and his army and chariots sink beneath the waves, after Moses and the Israelites have crossed the Red Sea safely.[101] For Louis in particular, the choice of this iconography was a good one: just as Eusebius had likened Constantine to Moses, so at Louis' court, Walahfrid Strabo, in a poem cunningly plotted to contrast Louis with Charlemagne, hailed *his* emperor as a new Moses leading his people to freedom.[102] Moses is thus depicted on this sarcophagus. The figure at the right is Miriam, Moses' sister who rejoiced in the Israelites' salvation by beating her drum, here shown inscribed with the *chi-rho*. If Moses was the type of Louis, Miriam was the type of Louis's wife Judith. This was made perfectly explicit by Walahfrid in the same poem, where Judith was said to have 'the virtues of Miriam'.[103] 'Chosen to make a programmatic statement' the sarcophagus indeed was.[104] But when? Walahfrid's poem dates from 829 and it describes iconography (the statue of Theodoric) and ritual (a great procession) at Aachen. If he was alluding to the sarcophagus as an object familiar to those at court, then it must have been prepared for Louis *at Aachen* long before his death. In the suggestion that its choice was that of Drogo of Metz 'who took charge of Louis's remains' lies a pair of *non sequiturs*. If the poem alludes to

---

[101] Melzak, "Antiquarianism", pp. 629–34, with figures 55, 56 and 57, with further references; K. Hoffmann, *Taufsymbolik im mittelterlichen Herrscherbild* (Düsseldorf, 1968), pp. 49–50.

[102] *De imagine Tetrici, MGH Poet. Lat. Aevi Carolini* II, ed. E. Dümmler (Berlin, 1884), pp. 370–378, esp. l. 100, p. 373. See further F. Thürlemann, "Die Bedeutung der Aachener Theoderich-Statue für Karl den Grossen und bei Walahfrid Strabo. Materialen zu einer Semiotik visueller Objekte im frühen Mittelalter", *Archiv für Kulturgeschichte* 59 (1977). P. Godman, *Poets and Emperors* (Oxford, 1987), pp. 133–44, and P.E. Dutton, *The Politics of Dreaming in the Carolingian Empire* (Lincoln NA and London, 1994), pp. 100, 197, none of whom, however, quite appreciates the critical force of the Theoderic theme in setting Louis off *against* his father. H. Siemes, *Beiträge zum literarischen Bild Kaiser Ludwigs des Frommen in der Karolingerzeit* (Fribourg, 1966), pp. 144–152, was the first to link sarcophagus and poem. For Constantine in earlier medieval political thought, see E. Ewig, "Das Bild Constantins des Grossen in den ersten Jahrhunderten des abendländischen Frühmittelalter", *Historisches Jahrbuch* 75 (1956), pp. 29–46.

[103] *MGH Poet.* II, l. 197, p. 376. For Judith in the 820s, see E. Ward, "Caesar's Wife: The Career of the Empress Judith, 819–829", in Godman and Collins eds, *Charlemagne's Heir*, pp. 205–227.

[104] Melzak, "Antiquarianism", p. 631.

the sarcophagus, as I think it does, then there was time-lag of over a decade between planning the tomb and actually staging the burial, and there was a relocating of the object itself from Aachen to Metz. Louis and Judith, perhaps especially Judith, surely had something to do with the choice of the sarcophagus. Drogo, Louis's half-brother, though he had been made bishop of Metz in 823, was a much less significant court figure in 829 (or earlier) than he was to become in the later 830s. It seems unlikely that the Red Sea sarcophagus would have been chosen, in or before 829, by Drogo alone. In 829, moreover, Drogo had no formal position at court (he became arch-chaplain only in 834).

Drogo wielded much influence in 'the last years' of Louis' reign.[105] A crucial event in this context was Louis's reinstallation as emperor at Metz in 835 after his temporary deposition in 833–4.[106] In 835, the reign, and Louis's regime, acquired a kind of new beginning. It looks as if Louis's burial was replanned at this time. Whereas previously the sarcophagus stood in readiness at Aachen, it was now taken to Metz. When Louis died, rather unexpectedly, on an island in the Rhine near Ingelheim, on 20 June 840,[107] a relatively short river-journey down the Rhine and then a long pull up the Mosel saw his body to port. Metz was a location long associated with the Carolingian and Frankish past,[108] contrasting with Aachen as Toledo to Madrid or Sao Paolo to Brasilia. It was at Metz that they were busily producing a full Carolingian genealogy just in the late 830s.[109] It was here too, that Louis's mother Hildegard was buried, along with two of her daughters (Louis's sisters) and two of Charlemagne's sisters who died young.[110] Metz displayed, as Aachen could not, the centrality of female members of and in the dynasty. Judith, an even more powerful figure than Drogo in the later 830s, had quite probably had a hand in, and surely at the very least assented to, the

---

[105] Melzak, "Antiquarianism", p. 632. For some reservations about the phrase 'last years', see Nelson, "The Last Years of Louis the Pious", *Charlemagne's Heir*, pp. 147–60, with comments, p. 151, on Drogo's early career.

[106] *AB*, 835, pp. 15–7, trans. p. 32.

[107] *AB*, 840, p. 36, trans. p. 49, noting a premonitory solar eclipse on 13 May.

[108] O.G. Oexle, "Die Karolinger und die Stadt des heiligen Arnulf", *Frühmittelalterliche Studien* 1 (1967), pp. 250–364; Halsall, *Settlement*, pp. 12–4, 263–270.

[109] K.U. Jäschke, "Die karolingergenealogien aus Metz", *Rheinische Vierteljahrsblätter* 34 (1970), pp. 190–218.

[110] Paul the Deacon, *Gesta Episcoporum Mettensium*, ed. G.H. Pertz, *MGH SS* II (Hanover, 1828), pp. 260–268, at 266–267.

transporting of the sarcophagus from Aachen to Metz. Further cal-
culations may have been involved. While there was little doubt that
Lothar would reign one day as emperor in Aachen, Louis and Judith
may well have hoped, especially after the project for a two-way division between their son Charles and his older half-brother Lothar
was agreed in 839, that Metz might be included in Charles' share,
hence that he might gain custody of his father's tomb, and of what
was being developed as the prime cult-site of the Carolingian dynasty.[111]
The prospective choice of Metz was an *ad hoc* response on the part
of both Louis and Judith to the paradoxical conjuncture of more
developed imperial ideology on the one hand and imminent *divisio
regni* on the other.

But, as things turned out, Judith was far away from her husband
when he became mortally ill. Three months earlier, he had been
'forced to return' to Francia in order to campaign against his rebellious son and namesake, leaving Judith and Charles in Aquitaine.[112]
With him he evidently took a set of regalia, mentioned now for the
first time in Carolingian history. The vital components, says the Astronomer, were 'crowns and weapons', more specifically, 'a/the crown
and a/the sword adorned with gold and gems'.[113] In June 840,
the dying Louis could not entrust these to Judith for handing over
to Lothar at some future date. Thus Judith was unable to perform
the role of a stake-holder moderating the transfer of power. (She
did, however, have other, royal, regalia to send to Charles from
Aquitaine in April 841.[114]) Instead, Louis ordered his half-brother
and arch-chaplain Bishop Drogo of Metz to have the chamberlains
bring out the contents of the imperial treasury, then told Drogo to

---

[111] While the *ducatus Mosellicorum* had been assigned in 839 to the 'eastern share'
chosen by Lothar, *AB*, p. 32, trans. p. 45, Metz was near enough to the projected
border (Toul was assigned explicitly, and Verdun implicitly, to Charles) to have
been subject to negotiation, as it was, in comparable circumstances, in 869–870,
AB, p. 173, trans 169.

[112] *Annales Fuldenses* (hereafter *AF*), ed. F. Kurze, *MGH SSRG* (Hanover, 1891),
p. 30, trans. T. Reuter, *The Annals of Fulda* (Manchester, 1992), p. 17.

[113] Astronomer, *Vita Hludowici*, c. 63, p. 548: '. . . *Hlothario quidem coronam, ensem
auro gemmisque redimitum . . . misit*'; cf. *AF*, p. 31, trans. p. 18: *insignia regalia, hoc est
sceptrum imperii et corona*. Since the *AF* author precedes this statement with *'ferunt'*
('they say'), whereas the Astronomer was almost certainly an eye-witness of Louis'
death, I follow the latter's account. That both writers highlight this transmission of
the insignia seems to me significant.

[114] Nithard, *Histoire*, II, 8, pp. 60–1, singles out a/the crown among the rest of
the royal *ornatus*.

send the crown and sword directly to Lothar, with a reminder of the 839 agreement.[115] According to the Astronomer, the most prominent figure at Louis' deathbed was Drogo.[116] While this author had every reason to highlight Drogo's role,[117] his account of Louis' death, despite its 'hagiographical colouring',[118] has an authentic ring.[119] The deathbed scene, like the campaign that preceded it, and like the funeral that followed, was a masculine affair, set in 'summer and campaigning quarters (*habitacula aestiva atque expeditionalia*)'.[120] There was no wife to comfort Louis through the terrors of his dying,[121] no widow to lay out, or weep over, his body. Drogo was on the spot, to arrange the transporting of the imperial corpse to Metz, where Drogo presided over Louis' funeral rites. The presence of 'many bishops, abbots, counts and royal *vassi*, and a very large crowd of

[115] Astronomer, *Vita Hludowici*, c. 63, p. 548; cf. c. 62, p. 544: Louis had shortly before sent a messenger to Lothar in Italy summoning him to a summer assembly at Worms.

[116] Astronomer, *Vita Hludowici*, c. 63, p. 546, says that Hetti of Trier and Otgar of Mainz were also present, but that Drogo, '*quem [Hludowicus] quanto sibi propinquiorem noverat, tanto ei familiarius sua omnia et semet credebat*'. Louis's habit was to summon Drogo with a special sign made with thumb and fingers (did he snap his fingers?), c. 64, p. 548. In Louis' final days, Drogo was his daily confessor, and it was he who finally persuaded Louis to declare his forgiveness of his rebellious son and namesake.

[117] He was an imperial chaplain, hence one of Drogo's subordinates, closely involved in *res palatinae* and writing within a few months of the events of June 840: E. Tremp, "Thegan und Astronomus, die beiden Geschichtsschreiber Ludwigs des Frommen", *Charlemagne's Heir*, pp. 691–700, at 695; *idem*, *Die Überlieferung der Vita Hludowici imperatoris des Astronomus* (Hannover, 1991), pp. 142–145, with a convincing argument that the Astronomer, like Drogo, supported Lothar in 840, and, like Drogo but rather earlier, would change sides from Lothar to Charles in 841. We don't know if, like Drogo, he changed back again. I gratefully signal here the unpublished argument of Hugh Doherty that Drogo was the addressee of the Astronomer's *Vita Hludowici*.

[118] Tremp, "Thegan und Astronomus", p. 696.

[119] Cf. such details as Louis's chest being 'strengthened' by a relic of the true cross, his way of summoning Drogo's attention by signalling 'with joined thumb and fingers', and, *sicut plures mihi retulerunt*, his shouting out in German, '*Huz! huz!*', c. 64, pp. 552–3; see Tremp, "Die letzten Worte des frommen Kaisers Ludwig. Von Sinn und Unsinn heutiger Textedition", *Deutsches Archiv* 48 (1992), pp. 17–36, esp. 29–36. Clearly the Astronomer was not among the eyewitnesses of Louis' death, but knew several who were.

[120] Astronomer, *Vita Hludowici*, c. 62, p. 546. While winter residences were more likely to have a large female presence, it is worth noting that Judith had sometimes accompanied her husband on summer expeditions as well, *AB*, 833, 839, p. 9, 34–35, trans. pp. 27, 47.

[121] Astronomer, *Vita Hludowici*, c. 64, pp. 550–3: one of the most vivid early-medieval accounts of a dying agony.

clergy and laity'[122] has been taken as evidence of 'an impressive ceremony'[123] and as an 'indice de funerailles imposantes?'.[124]

8. Louis II of Italy

The Carolingians made two separate attempts at converting the Lombard kingdom into their own *regnum Italiae*. The first began with Charlemagne's son Pippin I in 781, and ended with the death of Pippin's son Bernard in 818. The second effectively began and ended with Louis II, king of Italy from 844 and (co-)emperor from 850 till his death on 12 August 875 at Brescia.[125] Pippin of Italy had been buried at S. Ambrogio, Milan, in 810, and possibly Bernard's body too had been taken there after his execution in Gaul.[126] The memory of S. Ambrogio's function as a royal mausoleum was not forgotten in Milan. Andrew of Bergamo recounted, c. 880, that when it became known that Bishop Antony of Brescia had buried Louis II 'in a tomb in the church of St Mary where lies the body of St Philaster',[127] Archbishop Anspert of Milan immediately sent two bishops (of Bergamo and Cremona) with orders to secure the 'return' of the emperor's body. The corpse was duly disinterred 'on the fifth day after Louis' death' and placed on a bier. The distance to Milan, some 70 km., was covered very fast—'I was one of the bearers', added Andrew: 'on the seventh day [after Louis' death] they buried [the emperor]

---

[122] Astronomer, *Vita Hludowici*, c. 64, pp. 554–555.

[123] Melzak, "Antiquarianism", p. 629.

[124] Dierkens, "Autour de la tombe", p. 165, but note Dierkens' question-mark. See in addition to the Astronomer's account, Nithard, *Histoire*, I, c. 8, p. 34–7; *AF* 840, p. 31, trans. pp. 17–18.

[125] Both *AB*, p. 198, and *AF*, p. 84, trans. p. 77, note the event but fail to date it. See following note. For the significance of the reigns of these Italian Carolingians, see now the unpublished London Ph.D. thesis of Geoffrey West, "Studies in Representations and Perceptions of the Carolingians in Italy" (1998).

[126] Apparently Bernard was executed at Lyon, Nithard, *Histoire*, I, 2, pp. 6–7. For Pippin's epitaph at S. Ambrogio, see E. Besta, *Storia di Milano*, vol. 2 (Milan, 1954), pp. 355–357. Besta, p. 360, is doubtful about the epitaph of Bernard 'discovered' in the same church in the fifteenth century.

[127] Andrew of Bergamo, *Historia*, c. 18, ed. G. Waitz, *MGH SSRL* (Hanover, 1878), p. 229. The cult of Philaster had been vigorously promoted by Antony's predecessor, Rampert: see W. Wattenbach and W. Levison, *Deutschlands Geschichtsquellen im Mittelalter. Vorzeit und Karolinger*, vol. IV, *Die Karolinger vom Vertrag von Verdun bis zum Herrschaftsantritt der Herrscher aus dem sächsischen Hause. Italien und das Papsttum*, revd. edn by H. Löwe (Weimar, 1963), p. 405.

in the church of the blessed confessor Ambrose'. Had the body been embalmed? Was its decomposition (the month, remember, was August) the explanation for the bearers' remarkable speed? Or had Archbishop Anspert's command been peremptory?

This episode belongs within a wider context of Carolingian patronage for Milan, including the foundation of S. Ambrogio itself (784/789), and of strong Milanese reaction to any threat to its institutional *Königsnähe*. Just as the commitment of successive Carolingian rulers to S. Ambrogio reflected the major role of Milan and its richest monastery in their efforts at state-formation, so as successive archbishops worked hard to perpetuate the link, S. Ambrogio was bidding fair to become the royal mausoleum of that state.[128] Only the failure of the Carolingian-Italian dynasty in the male line ended this promising entente.

9. *Charles the Bald*

Charles clearly gave much thought to planning his own burial and commemoration, as he did to his father's and mother's commemorations, and to other sorts of royal rituals too.[129] On 19 September 862, he endowed St-Denis with a *villa* (Senlisse near Paris) 'for the remedy of the souls of our late lord and father the emperor Louis and our mother the empress Judith, and ourselves'.[130] The revenues of the estate were to go on lighting the church, on feasts—five altogether—for the community, and on caring for the poor. The feasts would take the form of meals to commemorate Charles's birthday (13 June), consecration day (6 June), and 'restoration' in 859 (15 January, after political setbacks), this last one to be eventually replaced by the day of Charles's burial; and in addition there were to be

---

[128] I am very grateful to Girolamo Arnaldi for drawing my attention to Louis II's unburying and (re-)burying.

[129] Nelson, *Charles the Bald*, pp. 17, 113–117, 154–5, 166, 182, 219–221, 242–244; *idem*, "La mort de Charles le Chauve", *Médiévales* 31 (1996), pp. 53–66. On the day of his consecration as king of Lotharingia (9 September 869), Charles made a grant for the provision of lights in the church of St-Arnulf, seeking prayers for 'ourselves, our wife and children'. The fact that Charles's father Louis the Pious was buried here is not explicitly mentioned in this charter, however: G. Tessier, *Receuil des Actes de Charles II le Chauve*, 3 vols. (Paris, 1942–1955), vol. II, no. 328, pp. 224–226. For royal anniversaries, see below.

[130] Tessier, *Recueil*, vol. II, no. 246, pp. 53–56.

commemorative meals at St-Denis for the anniversaries of the wedding of Charles and Ermintrude (13 December), and Ermintrude's birthday (27 September), this one to be replaced by her burial day. The brethren were to say five psalms daily before the altar known as the Treasure, 'where we have planned that our burial should be, if God so wills (*ubi sepulturam nostram, si ita Deus voluerit, disposuimus*)', both during Charles's lifetime and after his death; also a priest was to say mass for Charles daily, and a lamp to be kept burning before that altar 'so that by the merits of the saints and devoted prayers of the brethren, a light shall shine perpetually for us'. The absence of any provision for Charles's descendants, especially his presumptive heir(s) might seem odd. But comparable provisions in the ninth and tenth centuries are frequently exactly like Charles's in being retrospective, that is, for antecedents rather than descendents.[131]

A second set of arrangements, on 27 March 875, were more squarely concerned with the commemoration of Charles's death, but also included his offspring and others.[132] By this charter, seven lamps were to be kept burning perpetually before the altar of the Trinity 'behind which we wish to be buried when we have been released from human laws (*post quod nos humanis solutum* (sic) *legibus sepeliri obtamus*)'. The lamps were for: 1. Charles's father 2. his mother 3. himself 4. his first wife Ermintrude 5. his second (and present) wife Richildis 6. for all his offspring alive and dead 7. for Boso and Wido and 'the other members of our household whose very great fidelity has made particularly close [as it were, like kin] to us (*reliqui familiares nostri quos maxima fidelitatis devotio nobis propinquiores effecit*)'.[133] Charles further provided for fifteen lamps to light the refectory as required; a monthly feast for the monks; and an annual feast to commemorate his own death, also the deaths of Richildis and Boso (her brother); and clothing and food for any of the king's *familiares* who might

---

[131] It may be worth noting that in 862, Charles' two elder sons were in open revolt again their father. For royal anniversaries, see M. Rouche, "Les repas de fête à l'époque carolingienne", *Manger et Boire au Moyen Âge, Actes du Colloque de Nice (15–19 octobre 1982)*, vol. 1: Aliments et Sociétés, ed. D. Menjot (Nice, 1984), pp. 265–296; A. Stoclet, "*Dies unctionis*: a note on the anniversaries of royal inaugurations in the Carolingian period", *Frühmittelalterliche Studien* 20 (1986), pp. 541–548; M. McLaughlin, *Consorting with Saints* (Ithaca NY, 1994), pp. 150–151, 161–162.

[132] Tessier, *Receuil*, no. 379, pp. 347–350.

[133] The implications for Boso's achievement of a very special *Königsnähe* are explored by S. Airlie, "The political behaviour of secular magnates in Francia, 829–879", unpublished Oxford D. Phil. thesis, 1985.

choose to enter St-Denis. Charles may have provided an ancient Roman red marble bathtub, perhaps reused as a font, to serve as his sarcophagus.[134] If so, he may have acquired it in Italy, and placed it at St-Denis when he returned from his first visit to Rome in 875–6 for his imperial coronation. Perhaps he knew (he was in touch with Ravenna clergy at just this time) that the great Theoderic had been buried in a similar receptacle.[135] Perhaps he knew of the porphyry imperial sarcophagi at Constantinople.[136] He clearly intended his tomb with its permanent lighting to evoke imperial splendour.

Charles consistently planned to be buried at St-Denis *si ita Deus voluerit*. God did not so wish: Charles died near Maurienne in the French Alps *en route* home from Italy, on 6 October 877. Hincmar tells the story in the *Annals of St-Bertin*: 'Charles had been worn down by fever, and took a powder prepared for him by his doctor, a Jew called Zedekias, a man he loved and believed in too much. He had in fact drunk a poison for which there was no antidote... He sent for the queen, who came to him. He died the eleventh day after drinking the poison, in a vile hut, on 6 October. Those who were with him opened him up, took out his intestines, put in wine and aromatics so far as they could. They put him on a bier and began to carry him to St Denis where he had wished to be buried. But they could not carry him any further because of the stink, so they put him in a barrel covered in pitch inside and outside, and wrapped in skins, but this was of no use in helping them put up with the stench. They just managed to reach Nantua, and there they consigned to the earth his body with its barrel.' A few lines further on, Hincmar adds that Charles on his deathbed had confided the regalia, crown, sword and sceptre, to the queen to transmit to his heir, her stepson, Louis the Stammerer.[137]

---

[134] B. Montesquiou-Fézensac, "Le tombeau de Charles le Chauve à St-Denis", *Bulletin de la Société des Antiquaires de France*, 1963, pp. 84–88, made this intriguing suggestion, but modified it somewhat in *Le trésor de Saint-Denis* (Paris, 1977), vol. 3, p. 105 and Pl. 93 (b): 'l'hypothèse qui en fait le premier tombeau de Charles le Chauve est tentante mais n'a pu être confirmée'. Cf. A. Erlande-Brandenburg, *Le roi est mort*, p. 80. For Charles' tomb from the thirteenth century until the eighteenth, see Montesquiou-Fézensac, *Le trésor*, vol. 2, no. 160, pp. 255–257. For the eventual fate of his bones, see above, n. 1.

[135] See above, n. 8. For Charles's contacts at Ravenna, see A. Jacob, "Une lettre de Charles le Chauve au clergé de Ravenne", *Revue d'Histoire Ecclésiastique* 67 (1972), pp. 402–422.

[136] Arce, *Funus Imperatorum*, pp. 110–5, with plates 39–41.

[137] *AB*, pp. 216–9; trans. pp. 202–203.

No moral is explicitly drawn, and the explanation for the foul stench is a rational 'scientific' one. Regino of Prüm, in reporting the rumour (*fama*) about the Jewish doctor, adds that he was a fraud and deluded men's minds with magic tricks and spells.[138] Here, and in the two other more or less contemporary accounts, whose authors are no less liable to criticise Charles in other contexts, there is a notable absence of explicit criticism.[139] There is no evidence that Charles posthumously lost credit by his death. A few years later, according to Regino, his bones were translated and 'honorably buried' at St-Denis[140] perhaps in the marble tub, in the spot he had chosen, between the altars of the Treasure and the Trinity.

But we should not oversimplify contemporaries' view of the death of Charles the Bald. The apparently rational explanation for the corpse's horrifically rapid putrefaction is not the end of the matter. Another level of meaning emerges especially in the *Annals of St-Bertin* and the *Annals of Fulda*: in both cases, the phrasing evokes the grisly death of Antiochus Epiphanes as described in the Second Book of Maccabees, ix, 8–28, struck down in his pride by a horrible illness: 'he who a little before thought he could touch the stars of heaven was the man whom no-one could now bear to carry on account of unbearableness of his stench (*propter intolerantiam foetoris*)'. Here as elsewhere in the *Annals of St-Bertin*, Hincmar could count on his audience to pick up a dark symbolic cross-reference, and to hear the critical undertone of the narrative.[141] So too, less surprisingly, the author of this section of the *Annals of Fulda* codes his usual savage critique of Charles by assimilating him to a Biblical tyrant. The same writer had already likened Charles to Sennacherib.[142]

---

[138] Regino, *Chronicon*, ed. F. Kurze, *MGH SSRG* (Hanover, 1890), s.a. 877, p. 113.

[139] *AF*, p. 90, trans. p. 83; *Annales Vedastini*, ed. B. von Simson, *MGH SRG* (Hanover, 1909), p. 42. At Nantua, Charles's tomb was adorned with a flattering poetic epitaph: *MGH Poet. Lat. aevi Carolini* IV, ed. P. de Winterfeld and K. Strecker (Berlin, 1899–1923), p. 1001.

[140] Regino, *Chronicon*, p. 113. *Annales Vedastini*, p. 42, tell a similar story. For later-medieval elaborations of this happy ending, see E.A.R. Brown, "Death and the human body in the later Middle Ages: the legislation of Boniface VIII" on the division of the corpse', *Viator* 12 (1981), pp. 221–270, reprinted in Brown, *The Monarchy of Capetian France and Royal Ceremonial*, ch. VI, esp. p. 226.

[141] For Hincmar's authorship of these annals from 861–882, see Nelson, "The Annals of St-Bertin", *Charles the Bald. Court and Kingdom*, pp. 23–40; *idem*, "History-writing at the courts of Louis the Pious and Charles the Bald", *Historiographie im frühen Mittelalter*, eds. A. Scharer and G. Scheibelreiter (Vienna, 1994), pp. 435–442.

[142] *AF*, p. 89 (alluding to II Reg. 19), trans. p. 82.

Charles's funeral in 877 could not take place as planned. Contemporaries' views were equivocal, with a strong sub-text of coded criticism for a potential tyrant. Nevertheless Charles's death was nowhere recorded as farce. Even Hincmar, for all his bitterness against Charles, makes it clear that the queen was at Charles's deathbed, and the regalia symbolising the realm itself were transferred in correct form. The sources emphasise the zeal with which Charles' followers attempted to carry out his wish to be buried at St-Denis. Charles's connexion with St Denis was certainly a very personal one. The saint was his special patron; and from 867 Charles was the lay abbot, hence the special patron on earth, of the community.[143] The commemoration of anniversaries was no exclusively royal prerogative or concern in this period: abbots and bishops, and lay aristocrats too, were similarly remembered.[144] But Charles's arrangements were clearly at the same time 'official', betokening an *imitatio imperii* with which, especially in his last years, Charles's concern became a virtual obsession. The knowledge of embalming techniques, however botched in this case, seems significant in that context.[145] Was it Italian acolytes, or the queen, or even the Jewish doctor, who suggested embalming, thus opening up (though not in Charles's case) whole new possibilities for artificial prolongation of a king's political 'life'?

What seems clear is that Charles himself had long-term plans for

---

[143] *AB*, p. 134–5, trans. p. 138. For Charles' devotion, see Nelson, "La mort de Charles le Chauve", pp. 57–58, 63.

[144] See the contributions to *Memoria. Der geschichtliche Zeugniswert des Lliturgischen Gedenkens im Mittelalter*, eds. K. Schmid and J. Wollasch (Munich, 1984), and Geary, *Phantoms, passim*. For the commemoration at various West Frankish churches of Charlemagne and his successors, see B. Schneidmüller, *Karolingische Tradition und frühes französisches Königtum. Untersuchungen zur Herrschaftslegitimation der westfränkischen Monarchie im 10. Jhdt* (Frankfurt, 1979), pp. 15–22.

[145] This is the earliest medieval instance cited by D. Schäfer, "Mittelalterliche Brauch bei der Überführung von Leichen", *Sitzungsberichte der Preussischen Akademie der Wissenschaften, Berlin*, 1920, pp. 478–98. A. Erlande-Brandenburg, *Le roi est mort*, pp. 27–30. A. Gransden, "Abbo of Fleury's 'Passio sancti Eadmundi'", *Revue Bénédictine* 105 (1995), p. 61, contends that embalming was a lost art in western Europe after the seventh century. But Louis II is conceivably another ninth-century case, see above. It seems to me likely that at least the evisceration of corpses was practised in cases like those of Archbishop Angilramn of Metz who died in October 791 on campaign ('*in itinere*', *Annales Laurisshamenses*, s.a., ed. G. Pertz, *MGH SS* I (Hanover, 1826), pp. 34–35, *Catalogus Episcoporum Mettensium*, *MGH SS* II, p. 269) against the Avars, or Nithard who died in 844 in battle in Aquitaine (see Nelson, *Charles the Bald*, pp. 6, 141), and whose bodies were transported home over long distances. The reliability of western techniques is another matter.

creating a dynastic necropole church at St-Denis. There he buried the two little sons who predeceased him in the earlier 870s.[146] An ambiguity arose precisely in these years about the relationship of mausoleum to imperial *sedes*. From 869 onwards, Charles hoped to get his hands on Aachen; and when that hope had to be abandoned, in 876, he set about the construction of a West Frankish Aachen, an Aachen-substitute, at Compiègne, his *Carlopolis*.[147] Charles's successor was buried there in April 879, after sending 'the crown and the sword and the rest of the royal insignia' to his son and namesake.[148] But it is hardly credible that Charles himself ever intended that the church at Compiègne should replace St-Denis as the West Frankish mausoleum. Charles' personal devotion was too strong for that. Charles' grandsons Louis III and Carloman were both buried at St-Denis in the 880s, as was Odo in 898,[149] and although thereafter St-Remi became the mausoleum of the tenth-century West Frankish Carolingians,[150] St-Denis re-emerged in the twelfth and thirteenth centuries as *the* royal necropolis, thanks to the zeal of Abbot Suger, but also, as Suger himself recalled, thanks to the commitment of Charles the Bald.[151]

10. *Louis the German and his heirs*

In 876, Louis the Younger king of the East Franks and Saxons buried his father 'honourably' (*honorifice*) at St-Nazarius, Lorsch.[152] Louis the German's regime had been bi-focal, based at Regensburg and Frankfurt. But there is no evidence as to where he wanted his tomb to

---

[146] *AB* s.a. 875, 877, pp. 197, 211, trans. pp. 187, 199. In 875, the queen gave birth at St-Denis, in 877, at Compiègne: see below.

[147] D. Lohrmann, "Trois palais royaux de la vallée de l'Oise d'après les travaux des érudits mauristes: Compiègne, Choisy-au-Bac, et Quierzy", *Francia* 4 (1976), pp. 121–140, at 126–127; B. Schneidmüller, *Karolingische Tradition*, pp. 101–105.

[148] *AB*, pp. 234–5, trans. pp. 215–216. Note that Louis' widow Adelaide was not entrusted with the regalia: she was not the mother of the heir, and there was a question-mark over her marital status since Louis' first wife had been repudiated: Nelson, *Charles the Bald*, pp. 232, 255–256.

[149] Louis III: *Annales Vedastini*, s.a. 882, p. 52; Carloman: *ibid.*, s.a. 884, p. 56; Odo: *ibid.*, s.a. 898, p. 79.

[150] P. Depreux, "Saint Remi", pp. 250–60.

[151] Suger, *Oeuvres complètes*, pp. 353–6. See further P.E. Schramm, *Der König von Frankreich*, 2 vols., 2nd revised edn. (Weimar, 1960), vol. I, pp. 131–144.

[152] *AF*, p. 86, trans. p. 79 with n. 6.

be.[153] Perhaps that was considered a question better left unasked, given the separateness of the component *regna* of Louis's realm, and the rivalries between his sons.[154] The eldest, Karlmann king of Bavaria, might well have wanted to arrange his father's burial at St-Emmeram, Regensburg. Conceivably a bid might have been made for Reichenau by the third son, Charles the Fat, king of Alamannia. But Louis the German died at Frankfurt on 28 August 876, and so it was Louis the Younger who was on the spot to take care of the funeral arrangements. He took his father's corpse to Lorsch for burial, on 29 August. This meant a journey of 60 km., completed in record time. Perhaps, as with Louis II of Italy the year before, hot August weather impelled haste. Perhaps the Young Louis' motives were more directly political: he needed to assert his claims to the Frankish part of his father's realm, and above all to Frankfurt, the 'chief seat' of that realm, on the one hand, against his uncle Charles the Bald, and, on the other hand, against his own brothers. It was 'a programmatic act'.[155] Louis the Younger had already shown a special interest in the Frankfurt area,[156] and he was to make Franconia the centre of a realm that promised to become larger, as Karlmann and Charles the Fat had no legitimate sons. At Lorsch to this day survive two artefacts which seem to be stylistically closely linked: one is the sandstone sarcophagus

---

[153] Four grants and three privileges of Louis the German to Lorsch are extant: *MGH DD Karol., Die Urkunden Ludwigs II*, ed. P. Kehr (Berlin, 1934), nos. 14 (834), pp. 16–17; 47 (848), pp. 63–64; 63 (852), pp. 86–87; 89 (858), pp. 127–128; 117 (865), pp. 166–167; 126 (868), pp. 176–177), 156 (874), pp. 219–220. W. Wehlt, *Reichsabtei und König dargestellt am Beispiel der Abtei Lorsch* (Göttingen, 1970), pp. 34–5, sees these as making Lorsch a specially favoured cult-site, but none indicates that Louis planned Lorsch as his burial-place, nor that he felt a special bond with Lorsch or St Nazarius, since other churches, e.g. Fulda, St-Emmeram Regenburg, received as much and more. Earlier in 876, Queen Emma had been buried at St-Emmeram, *AF*, p. 85, trans. p. 78.

[154] For these fraternal rivalries, tangled with filial resentments, see *AB*, 870, 871, 873, 874, pp. 176, 181, 190, 196, trans. pp. 170 and n. 19, 174, 182, 186; *AF*, 871, 872, 873, 874, pp. 72–73, 75, 77, 81–82, trans. pp. 64, 67, 69, 73.

[155] J. Fried, "König Ludwig der Jüngere in seiner Zeit", *Geschichtsblätter für den Kreis Bergstraße* 16 (1983), pp. 1–32, at p. 13. *Pace* Fried, however, I can find no evidence that Louis the Younger showed favour to Lorsch *before* 876. His marriage to Liutgard, daughter of the Saxon magnate Liudolf, perhaps in 869, could suggest an earlier focus of interest in Saxony, M. Becher, *Rex, Dux und Gens. Untersuchungen zur Erhebung des Sächsischen Herzogtums im 9. und 10. Jhdt.* (Husum, 1996), pp. 68, 141, with n. 823. Fried is certainly right, though, to stress Louis the Younger's political need to show strength in Franconia in the immediate aftermath of his father's death. Cf. *AF*, 870, p. 70, trans. p. 61.

[156] His meeting at Seligenstadt, *apud sanctos Marcellinum et Petrum*, with 'certain of his father's counsellors', *AF*, 874, pp. 81–82, trans. p. 73.

traditionally identified as that of Louis the German;[157] and the other
is the famous 'Lorsch gateway' traditionally linked with Charlemagne.[158] It now seems clear that both gateway and sarcophagus
should be dated to the reign of Louis the Younger, and linked with
his project of constructing a new dynastic and imperial cult-centre
at Lorsch. This Louis's two charters for Lorsch (out of a total of
only 22 for the reign) convey a much stronger sense than had any
of his father's of special attachment and familial association.[159]

If the sarcophagus was not immediately ready in late August 876,
the son would have had to bury his father in temporary accommodation first, then transfer the bones later. The gateway's construction as a funerary monument presumably followed. Arches were
sometimes associated with such monuments in antiquity. *Decoration
antiquisante* on the sandstone sarcophagus[160] matched the antique asso-
ciations of the arch. This was again *imitatio imperii*. And, as at Charlemagne's Aachen, Rome was evoked to construct a distinctively *non*-
Roman imperial ideal.[161] Louis the Younger's realm, like his father's,
embraced component *regna*: Franconia and Saxony. When Louis the
Younger's son Hugh fell in battle against Northmen at Thiméon
(prov. Hainaut, modern Belgium) in 880, his body was taken to
Lorsch for burial;[162] and when Louis himself died in the palace at

---

[157] Schramm and Mütherich, *Denkmale*, no. 37, p. 128, supplying the interesting
information that when the sarcophagus was opened in 1800, Louis was found to
have been buried wearing spurs. For spurs as signs of high male status in another
ninth-century context, see elsewhere in this volume the paper of Cristina La Rocca.

[158] W. Jacobsen, "Die Lorscher Torhalle. Zum Problem ihrer Datierung und Deu-
tung", *Jahrbuch des Zentralinstituts für Kunstgeschichte* 1 (1985), pp. 9–75; M. Exner,
"Die Reste frühmittelalterlicher Wandmalerei in de Lorscher Torhalle. Bestand,
Ergebnisse, Aufgaben", *Kloster Lorsch*, ed. T. Jülich (Darmstadt, 1993), pp. 43–63.

[159] *MGH DD Karol. I. Die Urkunden Ludwigs der Jüngere*, ed. P. Kehr (Berlin, 1934),
no. 2 (4 January 877), pp. 334–5, no. 24 (18 January 882), pp. 364–365. Charter
no. 2 seeks prayers for Louis' father, wife and offspring, no. 24, for Louis himself
and his family.

[160] Dierkens, "Autour de la tombe", p. 168.

[161] As attributed to Charles the Bald but expressed (with a pejorative spin) by
the author of *AF* 869, pp. 69–70, trans. p. 61 with n. 11 where Reuter suggests
this as 'an interpretation . . . which was current in east Francia'.

[162] Regino, *Chronicon*, s.a. 879, pp. 115–6, with a highly circumstantial account
of Hugh's death and the transport of his corpse in a casket (*in loculo compositum*) to
Lorsch. Note the contrast with the attempted transport of Charles the Bald's body
in feretro, Regino, *Chronicon*, s.a. 877, p. 113. Regino gives no indication of any
attempt at embalming in Hugh's case. He adds that Louis felt 'profound grief'.
The journey from Thiméon to Lorsch would have been some 400 km.

Frankfurt on 20 January 882, still not yet 50, he too was buried at Lorsch.[163] His last charter was a grant to Lorsch.[164]

Louis' brother and immediate successor Charles the Fat of Alemannia was buried in 888 at Reichenau,[165] but he made careful arrangements for the commemoration, with eternal lights, of his brother Louis and his father at Lorsch 'where the above-named kings are buried and await the day of resurrection'.[166] Still more significantly, he was at Lorsch in 885 on the anniversary of his father's burial, 28 August, when he issued a grant to the bishop of Langres imposing the obligation 'to pray for us and for our ancestors and every year for the day of our consecration'.[167] Arnulf, the illegitimate son of Karlmann, ruled from Bavaria, and was buried in 899 at St-Emmeram Regensburg,[168] but, again, he did not fail to arrange for the commemoration of his grandfather at Lorsch, nor of his own father at Ötting (where Karlmann had died and was buried).[169] The diversity of royal burial-places would continue under the Ottonian rulers too to reflect the composite nature of this kingdom, while in later medieval Germany, dynastic shifts within an elective monarchy would produce a similar effect.[170] In France, on the other hand, St-Denis's unique status as royal, and regnal, mausoleum would be maintained, and enhanced. The Carolingian inheritance was as diverse as Carolingian history itself had been. Ninth-century royal funerals were experiments with ideologies of power that produced fairly unpredictable, even explosive, combinations of old and new.

---

[163] *AF*, p. 97, trans. p. 91. This 'disaster' was prefigured two days earlier by the appearance of a comet.

[164] Above, n. 145.

[165] *AF*, p. 116, trans. p. 114; Regino, *Chronicon*, s.a. 888, pp. 128–129.

[166] *MGH DD Karol.* II, *Die Urkunden Karls III*, ed. P. Kehr (Berlin, 1937), D. 103 (11 June 884), p. 167.

[167] *Ibid.*, D. 129, p. 206. For appreciation of the significance of this charter (ignored by P.E. Schramm, "Salbung und Kronung bei den Ostfranken", in his collected papers, *Kaiser, Könige und Päpste*, vol. II (Stuttgart, 1968), pp. 287–305, at 294), I am grateful to Simon MacLean, who will show in his forthcoming Ph.D. thesis the role of Geilo of Langres.

[168] *AF*, s.a. 900, pp. 133–134, trans. p. 140. For St-Emmeram's subsequent short-term role as a place of commemoration for the Liutpolding duke Arnulf of Bavaria, see Geary, *Phantoms*, pp. 153–156.

[169] *MGH DD Karol.* III, *Die Urkunden Arnolfs*, ed. P. Kehr (Berlin, 1940), DD. 150, p. 229, and 167, p. 256.

[170] K.-U. Jäschke, "From famous empresses to unspectacular queens: the Romano-German Empire to Margaret of Brabant", *Queens and Queenship*, pp. 75–108, at

11. *Conclusions*

We can now set the case-studies against Dierkens' check-list of Carolingian funeral-traits:

(i) 'no sophisticated ritual'. Given that Einhard clearly does not
tell the whole story, we can hardly be sure of what arrangements
were adopted in Charlemagne's case. Haste may have been incompatible with elaborate ritual. In the other cases, however, and especially those of Louis the Pious and Louis the German, elaborate
ritual actually seems likely.

(ii) 'no dynastic necropole church'. This may be true in a narrow
sense, but only in spite of the efforts of these rulers, and of those
who were in the right place at the right time. Moreover St-Denis,
St-Arnulf, Metz, Sant'Ambrogio, Milan, and St-Nazarius, Lorsch,
clearly were just such necropole churches in the making.

(iii) 'low profile tombs'. It is true that Charlemagne's sarcophagus
was no longer on display once it was, so to speak, in (re-)use. But
Walahfrid's evidence suggests Louis's sarcophagus was on display
before his death, and maybe Charlemagne's was too. There was certainly nothing 'discrete' about above-ground sarcophagi which positively shouted meanings, as did that of Charles the Bald. The visual
impact of Charlemagne's tomb after 814 is problematic. According
to the *Annals of Fulda*, raiding Northmen stabled their horses in the
church at Aachen in 881, but the *Annals* make no mention of any
damage to Charlemagne's tomb. Should we infer that there was
nothing visible above ground to indicate the burial beneath?[171] Apart
from the fact that tomb-desecration by Northmen is not attested in
ninth-century Frankish sources, it is hard to see why these particular Northmen should have paid any attention to Charlemagne's
tomb.[172] Marble was not the sort of wealth Northmen were interested in, since it was neither easily movable nor readily convertible
into other valuable items. Was Charlemagne's tomb really so 'dis-

---

81–90. Cf. the distinctive Lombard equilibrium between the maintenance of Pavia
as the *sedes* of the elective kingdom, and the founding of different burial-churches
in the city by successive dynasties: Ward-Perkins, *From Classical Antiquity*, pp. 79–80.

[171] As suggested by Dierkens, "Autour de la tombe", p. 176.

[172] It is true that one Northman inscribed graffiti, including his own name, Half-
dan, on the upper-level marble balustrade at Haghia Sophia in Constantinople: R.I.
Page, "Rune-masters and skalds", in J. Graham-Campbell, *The Viking World* (London, 1980), pp. 162–163.

crete and humble'[173] that there was not a single external sign of it? Perhaps the impact of this huge and costly object did live on only in the memories and tales of those who had seen it on or before 28 January 814. Yet art-historical conclusions about the influence of Louis's sarcophagus on the artwork produced at Metz after 840 pre-suppose that *that* sarcophagus, at any rate, was visible to the next generation.[174] The sarcophagus-tomb of Carloman, certainly visible at St-Remigius, Rheims, later in the Middle Ages, may have been so in 872, when it was visited by Charles the Bald, with Hincmar as his guide.[175] As for the alleged lack of 'attentive commemoration': it is true that, after Louis' marking of the thirtieth day after Charle-magne's death, there is little evidence of further commemorative arrangements on Louis' part. Lothar I, however, in one of his first acts after coming to Francia in 840, endowed his father's burial church of St-Arnulf Metz, while a few months before his death, he endowed his grandfather's church at Aachen *ob emolumentum animae praefati avi nostri Karoli*.[176] Charles the Bald showed still greater inter-est in such liturgical activity; so too did Charles the Fat and Arnulf.[177]

(iv) 'summary preparation of the corpse'. Einhard says Charle-magne's body was prepared *more sollemni*. Was this a specifically royal *mos* or a general one? There is no indication here of indecent haste, despite the same-day funeral, any more than at the funerals of Car-loman and Pippin. In Louis's case, Drogo must have travelled with the imperial corpse for two or three days at least to reach Metz. The Astronomer's mention of numbers of magnates suggests that Drogo had done everything in style—according to *mos*? Efforts were made to embalm Charles the Bald and perhaps also Louis II.

(v) 'no insignia'. Louis's sending of the insignia to Lothar was noted by contemporaries as an important element in the transmis-sion of imperial power from one holder to his heir. Charles the Bald's insignia were carefully transferred to his successor. Indeed it was in 877 that for the first time a medieval royal funeral ritual was

---

[173] Dierkens, 'Autour de la tombe', p. 178.

[174] Melzak, "Antiquarianism", pp. 632–640.

[175] Hincmar, *de villa Noviliaco*, ed. H. Mordek, p. 104: *'ubi ostendi ei locum sepulchri Karlomanni regis'*. Hincmar did not lose the opportunity to remind the king of his predecessor's grants to St-Remi, including, notably, Neuilly.

[176] *MGH Diplomata Karolinorum* III, *Die Urkunden Lothars I. and Lothars II.*, ed. T. Schieffer (Berlin-Zürich, 1966), D. Lothar I no. 46, pp. 136–139, and no. 136, pp. 305–307.

[177] See above, nn. 162–163, 165.

depicted, by Hincmar, as detaching the individual man from the office, emphasing the mortality of the king in order to emphasise the immortality of the realm. This theme was picked up again in the royal inauguration rites composed by Hincmar for Charles's heir, Louis the Stammerer, in November and December 877.[178] The funeral of the old king and the inauguration of the new were linked by the transmission of the regalia, especially the sword 'with which [the dowager-queen] was to invest [Charles' successor] with the realm'. There is no direct evidence for the use of replica insignia for the burials of dead Carolingians, as there is for eleventh-century Salian kings;[179] but in this respect early Carolingian burials may have been no different from the contemporary practice in Byzantium where the crown was removed from the imperial corpse at the last minute before shrouding and interment: 'the master of ceremonies says: "take the crown off your head"; and the *praepositus* removes the crown and wraps the corpse in a purple-edged cloth and lays it in the tomb'.[180]

I have framed the foregoing as a series of reflections on Dierkens' list of differences between the rulers' funerals of the Carolingian West and those of Byzantium, or rather, of Carolingian traits that emerge by contrast with Byzantium. For his list of traits, Dierkens offered a shorter list of explanations:[181]

1. the Carolingians had no Merovingian royal model 'to prepare the way'
2. the Carolingians had a strong tradition of the ruler's humility in the face of God
3. the non-royal aristocratic traditions of the Carolingian family persisted, 'perhaps because, unlike inauguration rituals, royal funerals were not indispensable to the legitimacy of the power of the Carolingian family'.

---

[178] AB, 877, pp. 218–221, trans pp. 203–206. See also R. Jackson, *Ordines Coronationis Franciae* (Philadelphia PA, 1995), nos. VIIIA and VIIIB, pp. 114–119, with commentary at pp. 110–113.

[179] See M. Schulz-Dörrlamm, *Denkmale der Königtums II, Das Reich der Salier 1024–1125.* Katalog zur Ausstellung des Landes Rheinland-Pfalz veranstaltet vom Römisch-Germanischen Zentralmuseum Mainz (Sigmaringen, 1992), pp. 288–297.

[180] Constantine Porphyrogenitos, *De Cerimoniis (The Book of Ceremonies)*, ed. I.I. Reiske, c. 60, p. 274; Karlin, "L'adieu", p. 140. On the text, but without reference to the passage on imperial funerals, see A. Cameron, "The construction of court ritual: the Byzantine *Book of Ceremonies*", *Rituals of Royalty*, pp. 106–36. For important discussion of replica insignia in later periods, and for a thirteenth-century shift towards permanent regalia, see Carpenter, "The Burial of King Henry III", pp. 444–448.

[181] Dierkens, "Autour de la tombe", pp. 179–180.

The drift of my reflections has been to play down the contrast between the funerary practice of the Carolingians and that of Byzantium. It is not surprising, then, that I have some queries about the specifically western features offered by Dierkens as explanations. I find his first point most persuasive. There probably was a Merovingian funerary *mos*: the evidence really does fail us there. But there is certainly no western equivalent for the longstanding influence of the model of Constantine's funeral—or, to be exact, Eusebius' depiction of that funeral—on Byzantine practice over centuries.[182] Nor is there anything in the Frankish kingdom to compare with the role of church of the Holy Apostles as rulers' mausoleum through the period from the fourth to the tenth century. From the latter period onwards, however, Byzantine practice changed: as dynastic affiliation became more prominent in the conception of emperorship, burial in a family monastery within the capital began to be preferred.[183] As for the idea of the ruler's humility, there is certainly no Byzantine imperial parallel in this period for Pippin's burial at St-Denis in front of the church-porch, still less for his alleged penitential burial face-down.[184] On the other hand, the church's liturgy, in East as well as West, had a certain egalitarian quality. There was no special funeral liturgy for Byzantine emperors any more than there was one for earlier-medieval kings and queens. Indeed the notion struck a Byzantine liturgist of this period as ridiculous: 'If some people have composed special funeral rites for women and for children, I am also amazed that they've not instituted special ones for eunuchs and emperors!'[185] Byzantine imperial funerals from the eighth to the tenth century did not reflect a homogenously autocratic ideology.

Two further East-West comparisons are worth making. The first relates to the *mise-en-scène*. At Constantinople, the setting of the imperial funeral was the palace and beyond that the city itself. In the

---

[182] Eusebius, *Ecclesiastical History*, ix, 9, trans, J.L. Oulton, Loeb Classical Library (London, 1938), vol. 2, pp. 360–363. On Constantine's funeral, see now G. Dagron, *Empereur et prêtre. Étude sur le 'césaropapisme' byzantin* (Paris, 1996), pp. 148–151, and also J. Arce, in this volume.

[183] R. Morris, *Monks and Laymen in Byzantium, 843–1118* (Cambridge, 1995), pp. 134–135; see further M. Whittow, *The Making of Orthodox Byzantium* (London, 1996), pp. 337–351.

[184] See above, n. 37. The only evidence that the reason for Pippin's wish for burial *prostratus non supinus* was to atone for his father's sins (!) comes from Suger, *Liber de rebus in administratione sua gestis*, c. 25, *Oeuvres*, p. 187.

[185] *Euchologion sive Rituale Graecorum*, ed. J. Goar (Venice, 1647), p. 289, quoted by Karlin, "L'adieu", p. 117 (the translation is mine).

palace in the great Triclinium of the Nineteen Beds, site of the most magnificent official occasions, there took place the lying-in-state. Here, in the centre of the hive of government, called forward by the master of ceremonies, the officials came to take their leave of the defunct emperor. Government would continue, under a new emperor. To the palace too came the people with loud cries and moans. They, or perhaps representative figures, filed past the bier. Then the funeral procession moved off from the palace via the great central street, the Mesè, to the church of the Holy Apostles, two and a half km. away. It was all very public; and this reflected the continuance within Byzantine ideology of certain republican ideals.[186] The emperor, in death as in life, came face to face with the crowd. Senators and soldiers and clergy also played their parts in the ritual. And since all were city-based, all could be mobilised for great ritual occasions. Since the emperor resided in the city, his death was likely to occur there. If it occurred elsewhere, embalming permitted the corpse to be brought to Constantinople. The emperor's funeral thus embodied and displayed the administrative nature and popular legitimation of his regime. And for all its incipient dynasticism, Byzantine emperorship was in the end a matter of official succession, not family descent. Significantly, the emperor's son and heir, if there was one, did not necessarily organise, or even participate prominently, in his father's funeral. The government machine rolled on its own.

Contrast Francia: a land of palaces without cities, hence quite different kinds of palace, and of the king's hall as patrimonial household writ large. Aachen in the reigns of Charlemagne and Louis the Pious was the nearest thing the Carolingians had to a capital. There, between palace and church ran a wooden arcade at most 150 m. long: no great processional route was available for the ruler's funeral cortège. When the ruler's corpse was laid out, whether at Aachen or elsewhere, there was no master of ceremonies to summon forward the officials, and only a limited number of officials to summon. Nor, unless the ruler's death had been expected for some time (as perhaps was Carloman's case in 771) or happened to coincide with an assembly or military campaign (as in the case of Louis the

---

[186] H.G. Beck, "Senat und Volk von Konstantinopel", *Sitzungsberichte der bayerischen Akademie der Wissenschaften*, phil.-hist. Klasse, 1966; cf. A. Kazhdan, "The Aristocracy and the Imperial Ideal", in M. Angold ed., *The Byzantine Aristocracy IX to XII Centuries* (Oxford, 1984), pp. 43–57.

Pious in 840) was there any possibility of assembling the elite of the whole realm. Though some aristocrats had houses at Aachen in the reigns of Charlemagne and Louis, the total population of normal residents of all ranks and statuses can hardly have exceeded a few thousand. Legitimate rulership depended on dynastic succession. The family, in principle the sons and heirs above all, expected to play central parts in the funeral rites. But the way of life of these rulers, their frequent journeyings, and, no less crucial, their practice of farming out their sons to subkingdoms, made it unlikely that all the sons, or any son, would be in attendance at the father's deathbed. There were no effective embalming techniques to permit delay. Royal funerals thus often had to take place in the absence of the primary heir. In such cases, other family members, sometimes women who in any case had important roles in the mourning of kin, took the lead.

The varied story of Carolingian royal funerals, with its multi-centredness and notable lack of some forms of continuity, highlights a fundamental trait of Carolingian monarchy, its partibility, which in some ways might seem to have inhibited institutional and ritual formation.[187] Yet the case-studies collectively show other traits as characteristic and as important: the setting of limits to partition, the emergence in the ninth century of coherent successor-states, in some cases with a long future, each with its own royal mausoleum in a major cult-site, and the existence of a dynastic consciousness which lasted over generations and counteracted the centrifugal force of family divisions. These latter features are symptomatic of deep continuities linking the Carolingian period with what followed in the tenth century. The point is worth stressing because much recent historiography on post-Carolingian monarchy, especially on the Ottonians, has tended to stress difference from Carolingian predecessors, not least in regard to ritual.[188] True, Carolingian royal funerals attracted a lot less attention from contemporary writers than did the Ottonian equivalents. This may say as much, though, about differences of genre (annals are not histories) and authorial ambition (Nithard, let alone Hincmar or Regino, never aspired to the grand scale

---

[187] See now the fine study of B. Kasten, *Königssöhne und Königsherrschaft. Untersuchungen zur Teilhabe am Reich in der Merowinger- und Karolingerzeit*, MGH Schriften 44 (Hannover, 1997).

[188] See above and n. 13; also G. Koziol, *Begging Pardon and Favour. Ritual and Political Order in Early Medieval France* (Cornell, 1992). But cf. for continuities, Reynolds, "The Historiography of the Medieval State".

of Widukind or Thietmar or even Richer) as about different realities. Even from thread-bare eighth- and ninth-century sources, Carolingian royal funerals emerge as something more than noble ones. They were ritual events loaded with significance for a public—the court[189]—that, while restricted, included leading political actors, ecclesiastical and lay. Royal funerals played a part in legitimising the power of successors by focusing attention on cult-sites that were regnal[190] as well as royal, and by deploying symbols of regality, of royal office to be borne in humility. Here they complemented Frankish rituals of kingmaking which in the ninth century came to incorporate a profession or oath.[191] The Carolingian's funeral thus did not only mark an end to his earthly career: it expressed the hope of his immediate family and entourage, his clergy and his faithful men that the king's fulfilment of his promise would be rewarded in the beginning of an eternal reign.[192]

BIBLIOGRAPHY

Primary Sources

Agnellus, *Liber pontificalis ecclesiae Ravennatis*, c. 94, ed. O. Holder-Egger, *MGH SSRL* (Hanover, 1878).
Alcuin, *Epistolae*, ed. E. Dümmler, *MGH Epp. KA* II (Berlin, 1895).
Annales Bertiniani, ed. F. Grat et al. (Paris, 1965), trans. J.L. Nelson, *The Annals of St-Bertin* (Manchester, 1991).
Annales Fuldenses, ed. F. Kurze, *MGH SSRG* (Hanover, 1891), trans. T. Reuter, *The Annals of Fulda* (Manchester, 1993).
Annales Laurisshamenses, ed. G. Pertz, *MGH SS* I (Hanover, 1826).
Annales Mettenses Priores, ed. B. von Simson, *MGH SSRG* (Hanover-Leipzig, 1905).
Annales regni Francorum, ed. F. Kurze, *MGH SSRG* (Hanover, 1895).
Annales Vedastini, ed. B. von Simson, *MGH SSRG* (Hanover, 1909).
Andrew of Bergamo, *Historia*, ed. G. Waitz, *MGH SSRL* (Hanover 1878).
The Anglo-Saxon Chronicle. MS. 'A', ed. J.M. Bately (Cambridge, 1986).
Astronomer, *Vita Hludowici*, c. 22, ed. E. Tremp, *MGH SSRG* (Hanover, 1995).
Chronique de Saint-Maixent, ed. J. Verdon (Paris, 1979).

---

[189] For justification of this term in the Carolingian context, see Nelson, "La cour impériale de Charlemagne"; and the contributions to C. Cubitt ed., *Court Culture in the Early Middle Ages* (forthcoming, 1999).

[190] I use the word in the sense proposed by Susan Reynolds, to denote what pertains to the realm: S. Reynolds, *Kingdoms and Communities in Western Europe 900–1300*, 2nd edn (Oxford, 1997), p. 254.

[191] Nelson, *Politics and Ritual*, ch. 7.

[192] P.E. Schramm, "Mitherrschaft in Himmel", in his collected papers, *Kaiser, Könige und Päpste*, vol. I, pp. 79–85.

Catalogus Episcoporum Mettensium, ed. G. Pertz *MGH SS* II (Berlin, 1829).

Codex Carolinus no. 81, ed. W. Gundlach, *MGH Epp.* III (Berlin, 1892).

Constantine Porphyrogenitos, *De Cerimoniis (The Book of Ceremonies)*, ed. I.I. Reiske, *Corpus Scriptorum Historicorum Byzantinorum*, 2 vols. (Bonn, 1829–30).

Les Canons des Conciles Mérovingiens, 2 vols., eds. J. Gaudemet, and B. Basdevant (Paris, 1989).

Concilios visigóticos e hispano-romanos, ed. J. Vives (Barcelona-Madrid, 1963).

Corippus, Flavius Cresconius, *In laudem Iustini Augusti minoris*, ed. A. Cameron (London, 1976).

Einhard, *Vita Karoli*, ed. O. Holder Egger, *MGH SSRG* (Hanover-Leipzig, 1911).

Euchologion sive Rituale Graecorum, ed. J. Goar (Venice, 1647).

Eusebius, *Vita Constantini*, in *Eusebius: Werke*, ed. F. Winkelmann, vol. I (Berlin, 1975).

Eusebius, *Ecclesiastical History*, trans, J.L. Oulton, Loeb Classical Library (London, 1938).

Flodoard, *Historia Remensis Ecclesiae*, ed. I. Heller and G. Waitz, *MGH SS* XIII, (Hanover, 1881).

Fredegar, *Chronicon*, ed. Wallace-Hadrill, J.M., *The Fourth Book of the Chronicle of Fredegar with its Continuations* (London, 1960).

Hincmar of Rheims, *de villa Noviliaco*, ed. H. Mordek, "Ein exemplarischer Rechtsstreit: Hinkmar von Reims und das Landgut Neuilly-Saint-Front", *Zeitschrift für Rechtsgeschichte*, kan. abt. 114 (1997), pp. 86–112.

Lampert of Hersfeld, *Annales, Lamperti Opera*, ed. O. Holder-Egger, *MGH SSRG* (Hanover-Leipzig, 1894).

Liber Historiae Francorum, c. 50, ed. B. Krusch, *MGH, SSRM* II (Hanover, 1888).

Le liber pontificalis, ed. L. Duchesne, revd. C. Vogel, 2 vols. (Paris, 1955).

MGH Capitularia, vol. I, ed. A. Boretius (Hanover, 1883).

MGH DD Karol. I, Die Urkunden Pippins, Karlmanns und Karls des Grossen, ed. A. Dopsch et al., revd. E. Mühlbacher (Hanover, 1906).

MGH DD Karol. III, Die Urkunden Lothars I. and Lothars II., ed. T. Schieffer (Berlin-Zürich, 1966).

MGH DD Karol. regum Germ. I Die Urkunden Ludwigs des Deutschen, Karlmanns und Ludwigs des Jüngeren, ed. P. Kehr (Berlin, 1934).

MGH DD Karol. regum Germ. II, Die Urkunden Karls III, ed. P. Kehr (Berlin, 1937).

MGH DD Karol. regum Germ. III, Die Urkunden Arnolfs, ed. P. Kehr (Berlin, 1940).

MGH Epp. Karolini Aevi III, ed. E. Dümmler (Berlin, 1899).

MGH Poet. Lat. Aevi Carolini II, ed. E. Dümmler (Berlin, 1884).

MGH Poet. Lat. aevi Carolini IV, ed. P. de Winterfeld and K. Strecker (Berlin, 1899–1923).

Nithard, *Historiarum libri IV*, ed. and trans. P. Lauer, *Histoire des fils de Louis le Pieux* (Paris, 1926).

Notitia de servitio monasteriorum, ed. K. Hallinger, *Corpus Consuetudinum Monasticarum*, vol. 1 (Siegburg, 1963).

Paul the Deacon, *Gesta Episcoporum Mettensium*, ed. G.H. Pertz, *MGH SS* II (Hanover, 1828).

Receuil des Actes de Charles II le Chauve, 3 vols., ed. G. Tessier (Paris, 1942–1955).

Receuil des Actes de Pépin I et Pépin II, rois d'Aquitaine (814–848), ed. L. Levillain (Paris, 1926).

Regino, *Chronicon*, ed. F. Kurze, *MGH SSRG* (Hanover, 1890).

Suger of St-Denis, *Liber de rebus in administratione sua gestis*, ed. A. Lecoy de la Marche (Paris, 1867).

Thegan, *Vita Hludowici*, ed. G. Pertz, *MGH SS* II (Berlin, 1829).

Vita Sanctae Balthildis, ed. B. Krusch, *MGH SSRM* II (Hanover, 1888), pp. 447–74.

Walahfrid Strabo, *De imagine Tetrici*, *MGH Poet. Lat. Aevi Carolini* II, ed. E. Dümmler (Berlin, 1884), pp. 370–8.

Secondary sources

Airlie, S., "The political behaviour of secular magnates in Francia, 829–879", unpublished Oxford D. Phil. thesis, 1985.

——, "Private bodies and the body politic in the divorce case of Lothar II", *Past and Present* 158 (1998). pp. 3–38.

Althoff, G., *Verwandte, Freunde und Getreue* (Darmstadt, 1990).

——, *Spielregeln der Politik im Mittelalter. Kommunikation in Frieden und Fehde* (Sigmaringen, 1997).

Angenendt, A., "Bonifatius und das *Sacramentum initiationis*. Zugleich ein Beitrag zur Geschichte der Firmung", *Römische Quartalschrift für christliche Altertumskunde und Kirchengeschichte* 72 (1977), pp. 133–83.

——, "Theologie und Liturgie der mittelalterlichen Toten-Memoria", *Memoria. Der geschichtliche Zeugniswert des liturgischen Gedenkens im Mittelalter*, eds. K. Schmid and J. Wollasch (Munich, 1984), pp. 79–199.

——, *Das Frühmittelalter, Die abendländische Christenheit von 400 bis 900* (Stuttgart, 1990).

——, "*In porticu ecclesiae sepultus*. Ein Beispiel von himmlisch-irdischer Spiegelung", *Iconologia Sacra. Mythos, Bildkunst und Dichtungin der Religions- und Sozialgeschichte Alteuropas. Festschrift für Karl Hauck*, eds. H. Keller and N. Staubach (Berlin and New York, 1994), pp. 68–80.

Arce, J., *Funus Imperatorum: Los funerales de los emperadores romanos* (Madrid, 1988), esp. pp. 159–63.

Barthélemy, D., "Diversité des ordalies médiévales", *Revue Historique* 280 (1988), pp. 3–25.

Becher, M., *Rex, Dux und Gens. Untersuchungen zur Erhebung des Sächsischen Herzogtums im 9. und 10. Jhdt.* (Husum, 1996).

Beck, H.G., 'Senat und Volk von Konstantinople', *Sitzungsberichte der bayerischen Akademie der Wissenschaften*, phil.-hist. Klasse, 1966.

Besta, E., *Storia di Milano* (Milan, 1954).

Biddle, M., and Kjølbye-Biddle, B. "The Repton Stone", *Anglo-Saxon England* 14 (1985), pp. 233–92.

Bloch, M., "Death, Women and Power", in Bloch, M. and J. Parry eds., *Death and the Regeneration of Life* (Cambridge, 1982), pp. 211–30.

Bloch, M. and Parry, J., eds., *Death and the Regeneration of Life* (Cambridge, 1982).

Bornscheuer, L., *Miseriae regum. Untersuchungen zum Krisen- und Totesgedanken in der herrschaftstheologischen Vorstellungen der ottonisch-salischen Zeit* (Berlin, 1968).

Brown, E.A.R., "Death and the human body in the later Middle Ages: the legislation of Boniface VIII on the division of the corpse", *Viator* 12 (1981), pp. 221–70, reprinted E.A.R. Brown, *The Monarchy of Capetian France and Royal Ceremonial* (London, 1991), ch. VI.

——, "Burying and Unburying the Kings of France", *Persons in Groups: Social Behaviour as Identity Formation in Medieval and Renaissance Europe*, ed. R.C. Trexler (Binghampton NY, 1985), pp. 241–266, repr. E.A.R. Brown, *The Monarchy of Capetian France and Royal Ceremonial* (London, 1991), ch. IX.

——, *The Monarchy of Capetian France and Royal Ceremonial* (London, 1991).

Brühl, C.R., *Palatium und Civitas. Studien zur Profantopographie spätantike Civitates vom 3. bis zum 13. Jhdt*, vol. 1: Gallien (Cologne and Vienna 1975).

Brulet, R., *et al.*, *Les fouilles du quartier Saint-Brice à Tournai. L'environnement funéraire de la sépulture de Childéric*, 2 vols. (Louvain-la-Neuve, 1990, 1991).

Bullough, D., *The Age of Charlemagne* (London, 1965).

——, "Burial, community and belief in the early medieval west", *Ideal and Reality in Frankish and Anglo-Saxon Society*, eds. P. Wormald *et al.* (Oxford, 1983), pp. 177–201.

Cameron, A., "The construction of court ritual: the Byzantine *Book of Ceremonies*", *Rituals of Royalty*, pp. 106–36.

Cannadine, D. and Price, S., eds., *Rituals of Royalty. Power and Ceremonial in Traditional Societies* (Cambridge, 1987).

Carpenter, D., "The Burial of King Henry III, the Regalia and Royal Ideology", in his collected papers, *The Reign of Henry III* (London, 1996), pp. 427–61.

Carver, M.O.H., "Kingship and material culture in early Anglo-Saxon East Anglia", *The Origins of Anglo-Saxon Kingdoms*, ed. S. Bassett (Leicester, 1989), pp. 141–58.

——, *The Age of Sutton Hoo: the Seventh Century in Northern Europe* (Woodbridge, 1992).

——, "The Anglo-Saxon cemetery at Sutton Hoo: an interim report", *The Age of Sutton Hoo: the Seventh Century in Northern Europe*, ed. M. Carver (Woodbridge, 1992), pp. 343–71.

Collins, R., "Pippin I and the Kingdom of Aquitaine", *Charlemagne's Heir. New Perspectives on the Reign of Louis the Pious*, eds. P. Godman and R. Collins (Oxford, 1990), pp. 363–89.

——, "Deception and misrepresentation in early eighth century Frankish historiography," *Karl Martell*, eds. J. Jarnut *et al.*, pp. 227–47.

Cubitt, C., ed., *Court Culture in the Early Middle Ages* (forthcoming, 1999).

Dagron, G., *Empereur et prêtre. Étude sur le 'césaropapisme' byzantin* (Paris, 1996).

de Certeau, M., *L'Écriture de l'histoire* (Paris, 1975).

De Jong, M., *In Samuel's Image. Child Oblation in the Early Medieval West* (Leiden, 1996).

Depreux, P., "Saint Remi et la royauté carolingienne", *Revue Historique* 285 (1991), pp. 235–60.

——, "La dévotion à saint Rémi de Reims aux IXe et Xe siècles", *Cahiers de civilisation médiévale* 35 (1992), pp. 111–29.

——, "Wann begann Kaiser Ludwig zu regieren?", *Mitteilungen des Instituts für Österreichische Geschichtsforschung* 102 (1994), pp. 253–70.

Devisse, J., *Hincmar, archevêque de Reims, 845–882*, 3 vols. (Geneva, 1976).

Dierkens, A., "Le tombeau de Charlemagne", *Byzantion* 61 (1991), pp. 156–80.

——, "La mort, les funérailles et la tombe du roi Pépin le Bref (768)", *Médiévales* 31 (1996), pp. 37–52.

Duggan, A., ed., *Queens and Queenship in Medieval Europe* (Woodbridge, 1997).

Dunbabin, J., *France in the Making* (Oxford, 1985).

Dutton, P.E., *The Politics of Dreaming in the Carolingian Empire* (Lincoln NA and London, 1994).

Duval, Y. and Picard, J.-C., eds., *L'Inhumation privilegiée du IVe au VIIIe siècle* (Paris, 1986).

Effros, B., "Beyond cemetery walls: early medieval funerary topography and Christian salvation", *Early Medieval Europe* 6 (1997), pp. 1–23.

Erlande-Brandenburg, A., *Le roi est mort: Étude sur les funérailles, les sépultures et les tombeaux des rois de France jusqu'à la fin du XIIIe siècle* (Geneva, 1975).

Ewig, "Das Bild Constantins des Grossen in den ersten Jahrhunderten des abendländischen Frühmittelalter", *Historisches Jahrbuch* 75 (1956), pp. 29–46.

Exner, M., "Die Reste frühmittelalterlicher Wandmalerei in de Lorscher Torhalle. Bestand, Ergebnisse, Aufgaben", *Kloster Lorsch*, ed. T. Jülich (Darmstadt, 1993), pp. 43–63.

Falkenstein, *Karl der Grosse und die Entstehung des Aachener Marienstiftes* (Paderborn and Munich, 1981).

Falkenstein, L., "Charlemagne et Aix-la-Chapelle", *Byzantion* 61 (1991), pp. 231–89.

Fisher, J.D.C., *Christian Initiation in the Medieval West* (London, 1965).

Fried, J., "König Ludwig der Jüngere in seiner Zeit", *Geschichtsblätter für den Kreis Bergstraße* 16 (1983), pp. 1–32.

Gaudemet, J., 'Les ordalies au moyen âge', *Receuils Jean Bodin* 17 (1965), pp. 99–135.

Geary, P., *Phantoms of Remembrance. Memory and Oblivion at the End of the First Millenium* (Princeton, 1994).

Giesey, R., *The Royal Funeral Ceremony in Renaissance France* (Geneva, 1960).

——, "Inaugural aspects of French royal ceremonials", *Coronations. Medieval and Modern Monarchioc Ritual*, ed. J.M. Bak (Berkeley CA and London, 1990), pp. 35–45.

Godman, P., *Poets and Emperors* (Oxford, 1987).

—— and Collins, R. eds., *Charlemagne's Heir. New Perspectives on the Reign of Louis the Pious* (Oxford, 1990).

Goody, J., *Succession to High Office* (Cambridge, 1966).

Gransden, A., "Abbo of Fleury's '*Passio sancti Eadmundi*'", *Revue Bénédictine* 105 (1995), pp. 20–78.

Grimme, E.G., *Der Aachener Domschatz* (Düsseldorf, 1972).

Guyon, J., "L'inhumation privilegiée dans un cimitière roman au IVe", in Y. Duval and J.-C. Picard edd., *L'inhumation privilegiée*, pp. 173–82.

Hallam, E., "Royal burial and the cult of kingship in France and England, 1060–1330", *Journal of Medieval History* 8 (1982), pp. 359–80.

Halsall, G., *Settlement and Social Organization. The Merovingian region of Metz* (Cambridge, 1995).

Hamann-MacLean, R., "Die Reimser Denkmale des französischen Königtums im 12. Jhdt. Saint-Remi als Grabkirche im frühen und hohen Mittelalter", *Beiträge zur Bildung der französischen Nation im Früh- und Hochmittelalter*, ed. H. Beumann (Sigmaringen, 1983), pp. 93–259.

Heidrich, I., "Titulatur und Urkunden der arnulfischen Hausmeier", *Archiv für Diplomatik* 11/12 (1965/66), pp. 71–279.

——, "Die Urkunden Pippins der Mittler und Karls Martells. Beobachtungen zu ihrer zeitlichen und räumlichen Streuung", *Karl Martell in seiner Zeit*, eds. J. Jarnut, U. Nonn and M. Richter (Sigmaringen, 1994), pp. 23–33.

Hemsgeberg, H., "Gab es zu Karls des Grossen Grabtitulus eine Vorlage?", *Arbor amoena comis. 25 Jahre Mittellateinisches Seminar zu Bonn*, ed. E. Könsgen (Stuttgart, 1990), pp. 75–80.

Hen, Y., *Culture and Religion in Merovingian Gaul, AD 481–751* (Leiden, 1995).

Henderson, I., "The insular and continental context of the St Andrews Sarcophagus", *Scotland in Dark Age Europe*, ed. B. Crawford (St Andrews, 1994), pp. 71–102.

Herold, H., "Der Dreissigste und die rechtgeschichtliche Bedeutung des Totengedächtnisses", *Zeitschrift für Schweizerisches Recht* 57 (1937), pp. 375–420.

Hoffmann, K., *Taufsymbolik im mittelterlichen Herrschbild* (Düsseldorf, 1968).

Humphreys, S.C. and King, H., eds., *Mortality and Immortality: the Anthropology and Archaeology of Death* (London, 1981).

Huntingdon, R. and Metcalf, P., *Celebrations of Death* (Cambridge, 1979).

Innes, M., "Charlemagne's Will: Piety, Politics and the Imperial Succession", *English Historical Review* 112 (1997), pp. 833–55.

——, "The Classical Tradition in the Carolingian Renaissance: Ninth-Century Encounters with Suetonius", *International Journal of the Classical Tradition* 3 (1997), pp. 265–82.

Jackson, R.A., *Ordines Coronationis Franciae* (Philadelphia PA, 1995).

Jacob, A., "Une lettre de Charles le Chauve au clergé de Ravenne", *Revue d'Histoire Ecclésiastique* 67 (1972), pp. 402–22.

Jacobsen, W., "Die Lorscher Torhalle. Zum Problem ihrer Datierung und Deutung", *Jahrbuch des Kentralinstituts für Kunstgeschichte* 1 (1985), pp. 9–75.

Jäschke, K.U., "Die karolingergenealogien aus Metz", *Rheinische Vierteljahrsblätter* 34 (1970), pp. 190–218.

——, "From famous empresses to unspectacular queens: the Romano-German Empire to Margaret of Brabant", *Queens and Queenship in Medieval Europe*, ed. A. Duggan (Woodbridge, 1997), pp. 75–108.

James, E., "Burial and Status in the Early Medieval West", *Transactions of the Royal Historical Society* 5th series, 39 (1989), pp. 23–40.

Jarnut, J., "Ein Bruderkampf und seine Folgen: die Krise des Frankenreiches

(768–771)," *Herrschaft, Kirche, Kultur. Beiträge zur Geschichte des Mittelalters. Festschrift für Friedrich Prinz zu seinem 65. Geburtstag*, eds G. Jenal and S. Haarländer (Stuttgart, 1993), pp. 165–76.

Kantorowicz, E.H., *Laudes regiae. A Study in Liturgical Acclamations and Medieval Ruler Worship* (Berkeley CA, 1946).

——, *The King's Two Bodies* (Princeton, 1957).

Karlin, P., "L'adieu à l'empéreur", *Byzantion* 61 (1991), pp. 112–55.

Kasten, B., *Königssöhne und Königsherrschaft. Untersuchungen zur Teilhabe am Reich in der Merowinger- und Karolingerzeit*, MGH Schriften 44 (Hanover, 1997).

Kazanski, M. and P. Périn, "Le mobilier funéraire de la tombe de Childéric", *Revue Archéologique de Picardie* 3–4 (1988), pp. 13–38.

Kazhdan, A.P., "The Aristocracy and the Imperial Ideal", in M. Angold ed., *The Byzantine Aristocracy IX to XII Centuries* (Oxford, 1984), pp. 43–57.

—— and Epstein, A.W. *Change in Byzantine Culture in the Eleventh and Twelfth Centuries* (Berkeley-London, 1985).

Keefe, S.A., "Carolingian baptismal expositions: a handlist of tracts and manuscripts", *Carolingian Essays*, ed. U. Blümenthal, (Washington, 1983), pp. 169–237.

Kollwitz, J., "Arcosolium", *Reallexikon für Antike und Christentum*, vol. 1 (Stuttgart, 1950), pp. 643–5.

Koziol, G., *Begging Pardon and Favour. Ritual and Political Order in Early Medieval France* (Cornell, 1992).

Krüger, K.H., *Königsgrabkirchen der Franken, Angelsachsen und Langobarden bis zur Mitte des 8.Jhdts* (Munich, 1971).

Labande-Mailfert, Y., *et al. Histoire de l'abbaye de Sainte-Croix de Poitiers*, Mémoires de la Société des antiquaires de l'ouest, 4th ser. 19 (1986–7).

Laporte, J., *Le trésor des saints de Chelles* (Chelles, 1988).

Le Goff, J., "Le roi dans l'Occident médiéval", *Kings and Kingship in Medieval Europe*, ed. A. Duggan (London, 1993), pp. 1–40.

Le Jan, R., *Famille et pouvoir dans le monde franc (VIIe-Xe siècle). Essai d'anthropologie sociale* (Paris, 1995).

Lesne, E., "La lettre interpolée d'Adrien Ier à Tilpin", *Le Moyen Age* 26 (1913), pp. 325–51.

Lewis, A., *Royal Succession in Capetian France: Studies on Familial Order and the State* (Cambridge MA, 1981).

Leyser, K., *Communications and Power in Medieval Europe. vol. 1, The Carolingian and Ottonian Centuries*, ed. T. Reuter (London, 1994).

Lohrmann, D., "Trois palais royaux de la vallée de l'Oise d'après les travaux des érudits mauristes: Compiègne, Choisy-au-Bac, et Quierzy", *Francia* 4 (1976), pp. 121–40.

Lynch, J., *Godparents and Kinship in Early Medieval Europe* (Princeton, 1986).

McCormick, M., "The liturgy of war in the early Middle Ages", *Viator* 15 (1984), pp. 1–23.

——, *Eternal Victory. Triumphal Rulership in Late Antiquity, Byzantium and the Early Medieval West* (Cambridge, 1986).

McLaughlin, M., *Consorting with Saints* (Ithaca NY, 1994).

Magnou-Nortier, "Formes féminines de vie consacrée dans les pays du Midi jusqu'au début du XIIe siècle", *Cahiers de Fanjeaux* 23 (1988), pp. 00–0.

Martindale, J., "Charles the Bald and the Government of the Kingdom of Aquitaine", *Charles the Bald. Court and Kingdom*, eds. M.T. Gibson and J.L. Nelson, 2nd edn (London, 1990), pp. 115–38.

Melzak, R., "Antiquarianism in the Time of Louis the Pious and its Influence on the Art of Metz", *Charlemagne's Heir*, pp. 629–40.

Montesquiou-Fézensac, B., "Le tombeau de Charles le Chauve à St-Denis", *Bulletin de la Société des Antiquaires de France*, 1963, pp. 84–8.

——, *Le trésor de Saint-Denis*, 3 vols. (Paris, 1977).

Mordek, H., "Ein exemplarischer Rechtsstreit: Hinkmar von Reims und das Landgut Neuilly-Saint-Front", *Zeitschrift für Rechtsgeschichte*, kan. abt. 114 (1997), pp. 86–112.

Morris, R., *Monks and Laymen in Byzantium, 843–1118* (Cambridge, 1995).

Morrissey, J., *L'empereur à la barbe fleurie. Charlemagne dans la mythologie et l'histoire de France* (Paris, 1997).

Müller-Wille, M., "Königsgrab und Königsgrabkirchen: Funde und Befunde im Frühmittelalterlichen und Mittelalterlichen Nordeuopa", *Bericht der Römisch-Germanischen Kommission* 63 (1982), pp. 350–411.

Nees, L., *A Tainted Mantle. Hercules and the Classical Tradition at the Carolingian Court* (Philadelphia, 1991).

Nelson, J.L., 'Royal inaugurations', *Early Medieval Kingship*, eds. P. Sawyer and I. Wood (Leeds, 1977), pp. 50–71, repr. in Nelson, *Politics and Ritual in Early Medieval Europe* (London, 1986), pp. 283–308.

——, "Symbols in context: rulers' inauguration rituals in Byzantium and the West in the earlier Middle Ages", *Studies in Church History* 13 (1976), pp. 97–119, repr. in Nelson, *Politics and Ritual*, pp. 259–82.

——, 'Carolingian royal ritual', *Rituals of Royalty*, eds. Cannadine and Price, pp. 137–80, repr. in Nelson, *The Frankish World* (London, 1996), pp. 99–132.

——, "The rites of the Conqueror", *Proceedings of the Battle Conference on Anglo-Norman Studies* 4 (1982), pp. 117–32, repr. in Nelson, *Politics and Ritual in Early Medieval Europe* (London, 1986).

——, "The Annals of St-Bertin", in M.T. Gibson and J.L. Nelson eds., *Charles the Bald. Court and Kingdom*, pp. 23–40.

——, "The Last Years of Louis the Pious", *Charlemagne's Heir*, pp. 147–60, repr. in Nelson, *The Frankish World*, pp. 37–50.

——, "Gender and genre in women historians of the earlier Middle Ages", *L'historiographie médiévale en Europe*, ed. J.-P. Genet (Paris, 1991), pp. 149–63, repr. Nelson, *The Frankish World*, pp. 183–98.

——, *Charles the Bald* (London, 1992).

——, "Women at the court of Charlemagne: a case of monstrous regiment?", *Medieval Queenship*, ed. J.C. Parsons (New York, 1993), pp. 43–61, reprinted (with a few revisions) in Nelson, *The Frankish World*, pp. 223–42.

——, "Parents, children and the Church in the earlier Middle Ages", *Studies in Church History* 31 (1994), pp. 81–114.

——, "History-writing at the courts of Louis the Pious and Charles the Bald", *Historiographie im frühen Mittelalter*, eds. A. Scharer and G. Scheibelreiter (Vienna, 1994), pp. 435–42.

——, "La mort de Charles le Chauve", *Médiévales* 31 (1996), pp. 53–66.

——, "Early medieval rites of queen-making and the shaping of medieval queenship', *Queens and Queenship in Medieval Europe*, ed. A. Duggan, pp. 301–15.

——, "Violence in the Carolingian world and the ritualization of ninth-century warfare", *Violence and Society in the Early Medieval West: Private, Public and Ritual* (Woodbridge, 1997), ed. G. Halsall, pp. 90–107.

——, "La cour impériale de Charlemagne", *La royauté et les élites dans l'Europe carolingienne*, ed. R. Le Jan (Lille, 1998), pp. 177–91.

Oexle, O.G., "Die Karolinger und die Stadt des heiligen Arnulf", *Frühmittelalterliche Studien* 1 (1967), pp. 250–364.

Page, R.I., "Rune-masters and skalds", in J. Graham-Campbell, *The Viking World* (London, 1980), pp. 154–71.

Palazzo, E., *Le moyen âge des origines au XIIIᵉ siècle (Histoire des livres liturgiques)* (Paris, 1993).

Parsons, J.C., "'Never was a body buried in England with such solemnity and honour': the Burials and Posthumous Commemorations of English Queens to 1500", *Queens and Queenship*, ed. A. Duggan, pp. 317–37.

Paxton, F., *Christianizing Death. The Creation of a Ritual Process in Early Medieval Europe* (Ithaca NY and London, 1990).

Périn, P., "Saint-Germain-des-Prés, première nécropole des rois de France", *Médiévales* 31 (1996), pp. 29–36.

Price, S., "From noble funerals to divine cult: the consecration of Roman Emperors", *Rituals of Royalty*, eds. Cannadine and Price, pp. 56–105.

Reynolds, R., "The organization, law and liturgy of the western Church, 700–900', *The New Cambridge Medieval History*, vol. II, ed. R. McKitterick (Cambridge, 1995), pp. 587–621 and 991–3 (bibliography).

Reynolds, S., *Kingdoms and Communities in Western Europe 900–1300*, 2nd edn (Oxford, 1997).

——, "The Historiography of the Medieval State", *Companion to Historiography*, ed. M. Bentley (London, 1997), pp. 117–38.

Richter, M., "Neues zu den Anfängen des Klosters Reichenau", *Zeitschrift für die Geschichte des Oberrheins* 144 (1996), pp. 1–18.

Rouche, "Les repas de fête à l'époque carolingienne", *Manger et Boire au Moyen Âge, Actes du Colloque de Nice (15–19 octobre 1982)*, vol. 1: Aliments et Sociétés, ed. D. Menjot (Nice, 1984), pp. 265–96.

Ruiz, T.F., 'Une royauté sans sacre: la monarchie castillane du bas moyen âge', *Annales ESC* 39 (1984), pp. 429–53.

Santantoni, A., *L'ordinazione episcopale* (Rome, 1976).

Schäfer, D., "Mittelalterliche Brauch bei der Überführung von Leichen", *Sitzungsberichte der Preussischen Akademie der Wissenschaften, Berlin* (1920), pp. 478–98.

Schmid, K. and Wollasch, J., eds., *Memoria. Der geschichtliche Zeugniswert des Liturgischen Gedenkens im Mittelalter*, eds. (Munich, 1984).

Schneidmüller, B., *Karolingische Tradition und frühes französisches Königtum. Untersuchungen zur Herrschaftslegitimation der westfränkischen Monarchie im 10. Jhdt* (Frankfurt, 1979).

Schramm, *Der König von Frankreich*, 2 vols., 2nd revised edn. (Weimar, 1960).

Schramm, P.E. and Mütherich, F., *Denkmale der deutschen Könige und Kaiser* (Munich, 1962).

——, "Mitherrschaft in Himmel", in Schramm, *Kaiser, Könige und Päpste*, 4 vols. (Stuttgart, 1968), vol. I, pp. 79–85.

——, "Salbung und Kronung bei den Ostfranken", in Schramm, *Kaiser, Könige und Päpste*, vol. II, pp. 287–305.

Schulz-Dörrlamm, M., *Denkmale der Königtums II, Das Reich der Salier 1024–1125*. Katalog zur Ausstellung des Landes Rheinland-Pfalz veranstaltet vom Römisch-Germanischen Zentralmuseum Mainz (Sigmaringen, 1992).

Siemes, H., *Beiträge zum literarischen Bild Kaiser Ludwigs des Frommen in der Karolingerzeit* (Fribourg, 1966).

Smith, J.M., "Religion and lay society", *The New Cambridge Medieval History*, vol. II, ed. R. McKitterick (Cambridge, 1995), pp. 654–78, 1002–6 (bibliography).

Smith, "Gender and ideology in the earlier Middle Ages", *Studies in Church History* 34 (1999, forthcoming).

Sot, M., *Un historien et son Église. Flodoard de Reims* (Paris, 1993).

Stafford, P.A., *Queen Emma and Queen Edith. Queenship and Women's Power in Eleventh-Century England* (Oxford, 1997).

Stoclet, A., "*Dies unctionis*: a note on the anniversaries of royal inaugurations in the Carolingian period", *Frühmittelalterliche Studien* 20 (1986), pp. 541–8.

Stratmann, M., "Die Königs- und Privaturkunden für die Reimser Kirche bis gegen 900", *Deutsches Archiv* 52 (1996), pp. 1–56.

Thürlemann, F., "Die Bedeutung der Aachener Theoderich-Statue für Karl den

Grossen und bei Walahfrid Strabo. Materialen zu einer Semiotik visueller Objekte im frühen Mittelalter", *Archiv für Kulturgeschichte* 59 (1977), pp. 25–65.

Tougher, S., 'Byzantine eunuchs: an overview, with special reference to their creation and origin", in L. James ed., *Women, Men and Eunuchs. Gender in Byzantium* (London, 1997), pp. 168–84.

Tremp, E., "Thegan und Astronomus, die beiden Geschichtsschreiber Ludwigs des Frommen", *Charlemagne's Heir*, eds. Godman and Collins, pp. 691–700.

——, *Die Überlieferung der Vita Hludowici imperatoris des Astronomus* (Hannover, 1991).

——, "Die letzten Worte des frommen Kaisers Ludwig. Von Sinn und Unsinn heutiger Textedition", *Deutsches Archiv* 48 (1992), pp. 17–36.

Vogel, C., "La réforme liturgique sous Charlemagne", *Das geistige Leben*, ed. B. Bischoff, vol. 2 of *Karl der Grosse*, general ed. W. Braunfels, 5 vols. (Düsseldorf, 1965), pp. 95–155.

——, "Les rites de la célébration du mariage: leur signification dans la formation du lien durant le haut Moyen age", *Settimane Spoleto* 24 (1976), pp. 397–465.

——, *Medieval Liturgy. An Introduction to the Sources*, revised and trans. W.G. Story and N. Rasmussen (Washington, 1986).

Wallace-Hadrill, J.M., "The graves of kings", *Studi Medievali* 3rd series 1 (1960), pp. 177–94, reprinted in J.M. Wallace-Hadrill, *Early Medieval History* (Oxford 1975), pp. 39–59.

Ward, E., "Caesar's Wife: The Career of the Empress Judith, 819–829", *Charlemagne's Heir*, eds. Godman and Collins, pp. 205–27.

Wattenbach, W. and Levison, W., *Deutschlands Geschichtsquellen im Mittelalter. Vorzeit und Karolinger*, vol. IV, *Die Karolinger vom Vertrag von Verdun bis zum Herrschaftsantritt der Herrscher aus dem sächsischen Hause. Italien und das Papsttum*, revd. edn by H. Löwe (Weimar, 1963).

Ward-Perkins, B., *From Classical Atiquity to the Middle Ages. Urban Public Building in Northern and Central Italy AD 300–850* (Oxford, 1984).

Webster, L. and M. Brown, *The Transformation of the Roman World* (London, 1997).

Wehlt, W., *Reichsabtei und König dargestellt am Beispiel der Abtei Lorsch* (Göttingen, 1970).

Werner, K.F., "*Hludovicus Augustus*: Gouverner l'empire chrétien—idées et réalités", *Charlemagne's Heir*, eds. Godman and Collins, pp. 3–124.

West, G., "Studies in Representations and Perceptions of the Carolingians in Italy" unpublished University of London Ph.D. thesis, 1998.

Wickham, C., *Early Medieval Italy* (London, 1981).

Wilentz, S., ed., *Rites of Power: Symbolism, Ritual and Politics since the Middle Ages* (Philadelphia, 1983).

Wilson, D., *The Bayeux Tapestry* (London, 1985).

Wood, I., *The Merovingian Kingdoms* (London, 1994).

——, "Sépultures ecclésiastiques et sénatoriales dans la vallée du Rhône (400–600)", *Médiévales* 31 (1996), pp. 13–28.

TRANSFORMATIONS OF PENANCE

Mayke de Jong

1. *Narratives of penance*

Grand Narratives cannot be made to disappear.[1] At best one can identify and analyse these persistent paradigms, locate them in the ideology in which they originated, and subsequently use them as tools to uncover significant discrepancies. But when present-day Grand Narratives correspond with those from the past, or have even emerged directly from them, it is more difficult to construct this *'inventaire des différences'*.[2] The history of Late Antique and early medieval penance is a case in point. Compared with the grandest narrative of all, the Decline and Fall of the Roman Empire, the generally current story of penance is a relatively modest tale, but it is certainly one of decline. Here is the Standard Narrative. Originally, a 'canonical' or 'public' penance was a dramatic ritual of purification performed within small Christian communities excluding grave sinners from their midst. For the duration of their penance the outcasts became part of a clearly recognisable 'order of penitents' (*ordo paenitent(i)um*). A penance of this sort could only be imposed by the bishop; more-over, it could only be performed once in a lifetime, for the cleans-ing force of reconciliation was like that of baptism, and could therefore not be repeated. In the West the decline of this penitential practice already set in by the end of the fourth century, when crippling life-long obligations were imposed upon former penitents. They could neither marry, nor hold public office or become clerics. *Paenitentia publica* fell into disuse because of these impossibly heavy obligations, which scared away the growing multitude of Christians seeking atone-ment and reconciliation. At best, penance was delayed until death

---

[1] As Chris Wickham put it: 'I would wish to see Grand Narratives as images that can be analysed historically; but I would not want to abolish them. Far from it; I would want to cut off their moralistic excrescences and use them for what they are: scientific paradigms.' C.J. Wickham, *Gossip and resistance among the medieval peas-antry* (Birmingham, 1995; inaugural lecture), p. 25.

[2] P. Veyne, *L'Inventaire des différences. Leçon inaugurale au Collège de France* (Paris, 1976).

was near and its dire consequences could no longer affect sinners. In the words of the most influential historian of penance:

> At the close of Christian antiquity canonical penance had come to a dead end in its development. The increasing rigidity of its forms had gradually conducted it to the utopian objective of obliging all the faithful sooner or later to a kind of monastic renunciation of the world. The result of such an excessive demand was that the ecclesiastical penance ceased to play any practical part in life, and was almost exclusively regarded simply as a means of preparation for death. Precisely in the years when sins importuned men most strongly there was no sacramental remedy at their disposal. No amount of pastoral care by way of preaching, personal admonition or penal measures could make up for the privation of the sacrament.[3]

Not only did public penance supposedly dwindle into a deathbed ritual, but by the days of Gregory of Tours its essentially voluntary and communal aspects had disappeared as well. Sinners who had undertaken a penance of their own volition no longer manifested themselves as a discernible *ordo paenitentum* in the episcopal churches. Instead, public penance became a mere punishment, a coercive measure imposed by bishops on those guilty of serious crimes like adultery, murder or idolatry.[4] This was the penitential wasteland confronting Columbanus when he arrived on the Continent in 590; it also provided the background for the subsequent 'triumphant migration' of private penance to the European mainland. Columbanus came upon

---

[3] B. Poschmann, *Penance and the Anointing of the* Sick (Freiburg/New York, 1964), p. 123; see more generally his chapter on canonical penance from the fourth to the sixth centuries: its development and decline, ibid., pp. 81–121, with an extensive survey of older literature; furthermore, B. Poschmann, *Die abendländische Kirchenbuße im Ausgang des christlichen Altertums*, (Münchener Studien zur historischen Theologie 7) (München, 1928); C. Vogel, *La discipline pénitentielle en Gaule des origines à la fin du VIIᵉ siècle* (Paris, 1952). Collections of sources: C. Vogel, *Le pécheur et la pénitence dans l'église Ancienne* (Paris, 1966); H. Karpp, Die Buße. Quellen zur Entstehung des altkirchlichen Busswesens, *Traditio Christiana* 1 (Zürich, 1969); P. Saint-Roch, *La pénitence dans les conciles et les letters des papes des origines à la mort de Grégoire le Grand* (Vatican City, 1991). Still useful as a survey: E. Amman, "Pénitence", *Dictionnaire de Théologie Catholique* 12 (1933) cols. 722–948; for the liturgy of penance, see J.A. Jungmann, *Die lateinischen Bußriten in ihrer geschichtlichen Entwicklung* (Innsbruck, 1932).

[4] Vogel, *La discipline pénitentielle en Gaule*, pp. 157–8: De moins en moins, donc, on voit dans les églises l'ordo des pénitents. Les contemporains de Grégoire de Tours se font de la pénitence antique une autre conception que leurs prédécesseurs gallo-romains. La penitentia devient une peine, une mesure coercitive—comme l'excommunication—qu'infligent les évêques à certains coupables justiciables, dès les origines, de la pénitence canonique: adultères, homicides, idolatres.

a scene of darkness and created light, introducing a repeatable type of penance covering grave as well as venial sins, which, moreover, could be administered by priests.[5]

To this narrative of penance present-day historians still subscribe.[6] Yet the idea that between c. 400 and c. 600 Christians in the West 'lacked' easy access to frequent sacramental penance is obviously anachronistic, for it is inspired by a norm of frequent confession and absolution that only became more general in the thirteenth century.[7] For similar reasons, the 'tariffed' penance of the Early Middle Ages has been viewed as the direct forerunner of the 'private' confession as prescribed by the Fourth Council of Lateran (1215). Hence, early medieval *paenitentia occulta* or penance performed *absconse*, which earned these names by the absence of a humiliating ritual, misleadingly came to be called *paenitentia privata*.[8] Measured against this post-Lateran yardstick, public penance has always been in a state of decline.

---

[5] Poschmann, *Penance and the Anointing of the Sick*, p. 123: In the absence of a penitential institution which was obligatory and repeatedly available to all, the great mass of men in that age of brutalised morals put off not only the *accipere paenitentiam*, but also the *agere paenitentiam*. The situation is illustrated in a brief remark of the monk Jonas in the Life of Columban (...) stating that on the arrival of the great missionary in Gaul, about 590, *paenitentiae medicamenta et mortificationis amor vix vel paucis in illis reperiebatur locis*. Cf. also C. Vogel, *Le pécheur et la pénitence au Moyen Age* (Paris, 1965), p. 23.

[6] For a recent example among many, see M. de Jong "Power and humility in Carolingian society: the penance of Louis de Pious", *Early Medieval Europe* 1 (1992), p. 43: Already in sixth-century Gaul canonical penance had dwindled into a deathbed ritual; the irrevocable consequences were simply too severe to live with. Small wonder that the Irish and Anglo-Saxon practice of secret confession in front of a priest, and private repeatable penance, rapidly won ground. For the notion of a 'penitential void' in sixth-century Gaul, see C. Vogel, 'Penitence', *Encyclopedia of the Early Church* (Cambridge, 1992), pp. 667–668.

[7] This is not to say that annual confession and penance were an unknown phenomenon in the Carolingian period; cf. R. Meens, "The Frequency and Nature of Early Medieval Penance", *Handling Sin. Confession in the Middle Ages*, eds., P. Biler and A. Minnis (Woodbridge, 1998), pp. 35–61, arguing against A. Murray, "Confession before 1215", *Transactions of the Royal Historical Society*, 6th Series, 3 (London, 1993), pp. 51–81. The issue I discuss here is the automatic projection of a supposed need for frequent and 'sacramental' penance on Late Antique and early medieval societies.

[8] Cf. M. de Jong, "'What was public about public penance?' *Paenitentia publica* and justice in the Carolingian world", *La Giustizia ne'll Alto Medioevo (secoli IX–XI)* II, (Settimane di studio 42) (Spoleto, 1997), pp. 863–902; for an excellent analysis of the rise of the notion of *paenitentia privata* from the 1160s onwards, see M.C. Mansfield, *The Humiliation of Sinners. Public Penance in Thirteenth-Century France* (Ithaca, N.Y/London, 1995), pp. 21–34.

Recently, Peter Brown sketched the outlines of a more subtle perspective on what he has called 'la "peccatisation" du monde.'[9] In Brown's view, public penance and its great drama of humiliation belonged to the authoritarian and vertical structures of the late Roman world, where divine and imperial amnesty were both capable of erasing all sins in one sudden gesture of mercy, even on the eve of death. Yet from the fourth century onwards there was also a forcible counter-current stressing the need for permanent atonement throughout life.[10] After a long gestation, it was this balance of exactly calculated sin and merit which gained the upper hand, through the introduction of a rigorous 'tariffed' penance stemming from a non-Roman and horizontally organised society: Ireland. In the course of the seventh and eighth centuries the non-Roman Christian North saw the diffusion of a penitential system requiring painstaking atonement, even for sins one had forgotten and could therefore not confess. This heralded the true 'end of Antiquity': the image of God as the almighty and merciful emperor had given way to the detailed accountability of the individual for all sins, even the most secret ones.

Brown's approach steers mercifully clear of the rhetoric of decline, yet in its insistence on the impact of insular penance it remains close to the Grand Narrative, to the extent that the disappearance of the great drama of public penance is perceived as the end of Antiquity. At the root of all these accounts of penitential change is the notion of 'early Christian' public penance as a dramatic ritual of exclusion involving the entire community.

> In the Early Church, reparation for sin had been a dramatic group experience. It was the members of the 'people of God' as a whole who excluded notorious sinners from their midst, allowed them to continue on the fringes of the Church, as a separate category of 'penitents', and then granted them the 'peace' of reconciliation, through a fully public ceremony conducted by the bishop. Penance was a collective drama, that still assumed that the 'people of God' were a minority—a pool of light surrounded by the shadows of a pagan world. It was better to endure for a time the humiliation of fully public exclu-

---

[9] P. Brown, "Vers la naissance du Purgatoire, Amnistie et pénitence dans le christianisme occidental de l'Antiquité tardive au Haut Moyen Âge", *Annales HSS* 52 (1997), pp. 1247–1261, esp. p. 1260.

[10] Brown follows E. Rebillard, *In hora mortis. Évolution de la pastorale chrétienne de la mort aux IVe et Ve siècles* (Rome, 1994), who has argued for a 'redefinition of penance' in the fifth century, with a Christian's entire life becoming marked by daily acts of atonement (cf. esp. pp. 157–67).

sion from the 'people of God' followed by an equally public ritual of reconciliation, than to fall into that outer darkness.[11]

Penitents appeared collectively in church, publicly bewailing their sins and receiving their penance from the bishop. Only after having given 'satisfaction' in an equally public manner, as part of a recognisable *ordo paenitentum* regularly present in church, would they be readmitted to the community of the faithful. This communal ritual of exclusion, it is suggested, was ubiquitous in pre-Constantinian Christendom, but proved ill suited to a world of mass Christianity.[12] Yet the clearest picture of this 'original' public penance comes from a ninth-century writer, Bishop Jonas of Orléans. His purpose was to underscore the huge decline between the Golden Age of 'early Christianity' and his own dreadful age; his sources of information concerning a canonical 'order of penitents' submitting to the proper rituals derived from the fifth- and sixth-century West. This was the very period in which the rigidity of the demands imposed on ex-penitents presumably made public penance an impossible proposition for everyday life. Are we to believe that the emergence of public penance coincided with its decline, and that this decline lasted for centuries?

Or did these rituals of exclusion only become 'canonical' precisely in this period of so-called decline, when bishops in Rome, Spain and Gaul produced a corpus of *canones* reflecting on the penitential exclusion of sinners from the community? Public penance was indeed a ritual of power: the power of bishops. To say that the emergence of an 'order of penitents' went hand in hand with the rise of a 'monarchical episcopate' is perhaps an overstatement,[13] but it is not far from the truth. Public penance was the bishops' affair *par excellence*, for they were the only ones who could legitimately perform this rite. Whenever conciliar activity was intense—first in Gaul in the fifth and sixth centuries, then in Spain in the seventh, and finally in the Carolingian kingdoms—*paenitentia publica* featured on the agenda as an integral part of strategies to strengthen episcopal authority. Carolingian bishops attempting to 'revive' public penance called for a return to the ancient *canones*.[14] To a large extent, however, this

---

[11] P. Brown, *The Rise of Western Christendom. Triumph and Diversity, AD 200–1000* (Cambridge, Ma./Oxford), p. 157.

[12] Brown, *The Rise of Western Christendom*, p. 157; see above, n. 4.

[13] Karpp, *Die Buße*, p. xvi.

[14] Council of Chalon (a. 813), c. 25, M.G.H., Conc. II/1, p. 278: *Paenitentiam agere iuxta antiquam canonum constitutionem in plerisque locis ab usu recessit, et neque excommunicandi*

authoritative 'antiquity' embodied in canonical texts had been shaped
by their predecessors living in a past that was not quite so distant
as the reformers thought or presented it. One may well wonder
whether public penance indeed needed to be 'revived' in the early
ninth century. It may have been more a matter of bishops attempting to regain control of an instrument of discipline and *correctio* that
had by then moved from the episcopal to the monastic and the royal
sphere. Modern historians of penitence have followed the Carolingian rhetoric of decline, but with an assumption of their own not
shared by ninth-century authors: that 'public' or 'canonical' penance
was something to be undertaken by or imposed indiscriminately on
all those who had committed grave sins, regardless of their social
position. The ideal of an egalitarian *Urchristentum* is central to this
image of dramatic group rituals holding Christian communities
together. However, Late Antique and early medieval *paenitentia publica* was not 'public' ritual in the sense that it applied equally to all
serious sinners. Public penance made sense when there was honour
to be lost *and* regained through public humiliation. The exclusive-
ness of public penance is one of the issues explored in this chapter;
another is the dependence of modern scholarship on Carolingian
interpretations of 'original' public penance. This is no more than a
first attempt to grapple with a problem to which I hope to do more
justice in the near future.

2. *The elusive* ordo paenitentum

The modern account of 'original' public penance as a dramatic ritual of exclusion resembles that of Jonas of Orléans (d. 840), with
some significant differences. 'Who nowadays performs a penance
according to the example of the Fathers and sanctioned by canonical authority? Which grave sinner liable to be punished by a public penance puts down his military belt and comes to church in the
presence of all the faithful to be separated from Christ's body? Who,
in sackcloth and ashes, raises the remorseful lament of the penitents

---

neque reconciliandi antiqui moris ordo servatur. Ut a domno imperatore impetretur adiutatorium,
qualiter, si qui publice peccet, publica multetur paenitentia et secundum ordinem canonum pro
merito suo et excommunicantur et reconcilietur. Cf. De Jong, "What was public about public penance?", pp. 867–869.

of yore?' Jonas sang the praises of a ritual he clearly intended for those wearing a *cingulum militiae*, the symbolic trappings of high office in the Carolingian political world.[15] He situated this public punishment in a lost world of pristine Christianity. It is clear, Jonas claimed, that 'in the early days of our faith' (*religionis nostrae priscis temporibus*) someone who had received a regular public penance from the bishop was immediately recognisable to all, so the entire Christian community would pray for the culprit.[16]

The Age of the Fathers has left only scant information on the 'order of penitents' and public rituals of exclusion in *Urchristentum*. Jerome wrote admiringly about the matron Fabiola, who had divorced her adulterous spouse to marry another man while her first husband was still alive, and voluntarily atoned for her sin by entering the Lateran basilica in sackcloth the day before Easter. 'With all Rome watching' she stood in the *ordo paenitentum* while the bishop, the priests and the people all commiserated with her totally abject appearance.[17] Her conspicuous humiliation earned her reconciliation on the very day she publicly confessed her sins in the Lateran basilica. This gesture, along with her subsequent donation of all her worldly goods to the poor, was clearly extraordinary; afterwards Fabiola became a staunch supporter of monks and an influential figure in the Roman Christian community. Fabiola's penance was certainly a 'dramatic group ritual', but also a ritual for the happy and exemplary few. Jerome's praise of this extraordinary woman says little about everyday

---

[15] About the deposition of the cingulum militiae as a gesture of penance in the ninth and tenth centuries, see K. Leyser, "Early medieval canon law and the beginnings of knighthood", *Institutionen, Kultur und Gesellschaft im Mittelalter*, eds. L. Fenske et al. (Sigmaringen, 1984), pp. 554–557; also De Jong, "Power and humility", pp. 43–47.

[16] Jonas of Orléans, *De institutione laicali*, I, c. 10, PL 106, cols. 138B/C: *Perrari namque sunt hodie in Ecclesia, qui talem agant poenitentiam, qualem antiquorum Patrum poenitentium exempla, et auctoritas canonica sancit. Quis namque criminis reus, qui utique poenitentia publica debuit mulctari, cingulum militiae deponit, et a liminibus Ecclesiae coetuque fidelium arcetur, et a Christi corpore separatur? Quis porro in cinere, et cilicio, more poenitentium antiquorum lamenta poenitudinis suscipit?(. . .) Unde colligitur quia religionis nostrae priscis temporibus, dum quis secundum constitutum sibi a sacerdote usque ad satisfactionem cilicio indutus, et cinere conspersus, habitu incultus, humique prostratus, lacrymusque profusus videbatur, statim poenitens agnoscebatur, ut ei a Domino ignosceretur, ab omnibus deprecabatur. Nunc autem in coetu Christiano idcirco vix poenitens agnoscitur, quia pene nihil horum erga poenitentes agitur. Quapropter credibile est, ut sicut alia multa in religione Christiana viluerunt, ita quoque praemissus poenitentiae modus, ab usu, quod formidolosum est, recesserit.*

[17] Jerome, *Epistolae* no. 77, c. 4, ed. I. Hilberg, CSEL 54 (Vienna/Leipzig, 1912) p. 40.

rituals of public penance, or about less conspicuous penitents constituting a separate 'order'. The same goes for the most famous public penitent of the fourth century West, the Emperor Theodosius.
His public confession and request for forgiveness earned the emperor
a fulsome eulogy—but only after his death—from Ambrose of Milan,
the formidable archbishop who had excommunicated the imperial
sinner after the massacre in Thessalonike. 'What private men blush
at, the emperor did not blush to do: to perform penance publicly.
Afterwards there was not a day when he did not deplore his sin'.[18]
This is the morally uplifting version of the story; Ambrose's biographer Paulinus has Theodosius protesting that since David committed both adultery and murder with impunity, he did not see why
he should submit to Ambrose's discipline.[19]

Only rarely does one catch a glimpse of less exalted sinners being
subjected to more public forms of atonement. A North-African collection of *canones* demands a public imposition of penance for notorious and scandalous crimes.[20] The catalogue of sins in this category
might vary over time, but murder, adultery, heresy and sacrilege
formed its hard core. In such cases an excommunication and subsequent penance would be in order, unless the sinner had voluntarily undertaken a penance. Presumably, someone could also ask
for a penance if the sins in question did not 'perturb the entire
ecclesia', thus improving his or her reputation, rather than being
defamed by this action. One of Augustine's Easter sermons gives the
impression that becoming a penitent was not such a bad thing. He
scornfully referred to the utter complacency of Hippo's many penitents. 'There is an abundance of penitents here; when they come
up for the imposition of hands, they form a vast queue (*ordo longissimus*). "Pray, penitents". And the penitents go and pray. I scrutinise

---

[18] Ambrose, *De obitu Theodosii* c. 34, Migne, PL 16, col. 1459; ed. O. Faller,
CSEL 73 (Vienna, 1955), p. 388: *Quod privati erubescent, non erubuit imperator,
publice agere poenitentiam; neque ullus postea dies fuit, quo non illum doleret
errorem.* Cf. F.E. Consilino, "Teodosio e il ruolo del principe cristiano dal De obitu
di Ambrogio alle storie ecclesiastiche", *Cristianesimo nella storia: Richerche storiche, esegetiche,
teologiche* 15 (1994), pp. 257–277.
[19] Paulinus of Milan, *Vita Ambrosii*, c. 24, PL 14, col. 35.
[20] *Breuiarium Hipponense* c. 30c, ed. C. Munier, *Conciliae Africae*, A. 345-A. 525,
CCSL 149 (Turnhout, 1974) pp. 41–2: *Cuiuscumque autem paenitentis publicum et uul-
gatissimum crimen est, quod uniuersam ecclesiam commouerit, ante absidam manus est imponan-
tur.* This collection was confirmed by the Council of Carthage of 28 August 397;
cf. Munier, Introduction, pp. xxii–xxiii.

the penitents and find people who live in sin'.[21] For the duration of their atonement they had to stand in church in a special 'place of penance' (*locus paenitentiae/paenitentium*), but nobody seemed to mind this very much. Those who had acted of their own accord went on with their lives as if nothing had happened, and those who had been forced to do penance because of an excommunication did not want to leave it, as if the *locus paenitentiae* was a choice spot. What should have been a place of humility had become a place of iniquity.[22] The impression one gets is of penitents for whom regularly receiving the episcopal imposition of hands in the *locus paenitentae* was not a particular burden. This expression is used as a spatial concept here, yet in biblical commentary it often assumed a more metaphorical meaning: the opportunity to atone accorded by God to mankind.[23]

These three stories about a pious matron, an exemplary emperor, and a group of complacent penitents who did not mind being relegated to the *locus paenitentiae*, are central building blocks in the grand narrative about the early history of an 'order of penitents'. To this Sozomen's report on penitential practices in Rome is usually added, though it should be kept in mind that this citizen of Contantinople wrote his Ecclesiastical History between 443 and 450. Sozomen painted a lively picture of Roman penitents standing in their specially assigned place in church, excluded from communion. After the celebration of Mass they prostrated themselves, sighing and moaning, while the bishop did likewise, and the entire community was in tears. After the bishop rose, he invited the prostrated penitents to get to their feet as well, and gave them his blessing. All penitents

---

[21] Augustine, Sermo 23, c. 8, ed. S. Poque, *Augustin d'Hippone, Sermons pour la Paque*, S.C. 116 (Paris, 1966), p. 276: *Abundant hic paenitentes; quando illis inponitur manus, fit ordo longissimus. "Orate paenitentes". Et eunt orate paenitentes. Discutio paenitentes et invenio male viventes.*

[22] Augustine, Sermo 23, c. 8, ed. Poque, S.C. 116, p. 276: *Aliqui ipsi sibi paenitentiae locum petierunt; aliqui excommunicati a nobis in paenitentium locum redacti sunt. Et qui sibi petierunt hoc volunt facere quod faciebant et qui a nobis excommunicati in paenitentium locum redacti sunt nolunt inde surgere, quasi electus sit locus paenitentium. Qui debet esse locus humilitatis, fit locus iniquitatis.* Poque translates '*locus paenitentium*' as 'rang des pénitents'; I would prefer 'the place for the penitents'.

[23] Job 24, 23: *. . . dedit ei Deus locum paenitentiae et ille abutitur eo in superbiam oculi autem eius sunt in viis illius . . .*; cf. Also Sap. 12, 10 and 19, and Hebr. 12, 17. *Locus paenitentiae* in the sense of 'possibility to do penance' is ubiquitous in patristic writing, as becomes clear from a search of the electronic database CETEDOC. For an influential example, see Augustine, *De civitate Dei*, I, cc. 17 and 25, ed. B. Dombart & A. Kalb, CCSL 47 (Turnhout, 1955), pp. 18 and 26.

voluntarily abstained from food, washing and other comforts, only
to regain their lawful place within the church when the bishop
decided their penance had lasted long enough. 'This is what the
Roman bishops have done from time immemorial until the present
day', said Sozomen. He was obviously impressed with the fact that
the head of the Western Church personally conducted these rituals.[24]

Sozomen's contention that such rituals had remained unchanged
since 'time immemorial' has convinced church historians that the
search for an ancient Roman ritual of penance is a viable operation. Sozomen's report should not be taken at face value, however.
It should not be taken at face value. Impressive ritual always looks
ancient and venerable, especially in the eyes of an admiring foreign
visitor. In fact it is impossible to discover how penitential ritual in
Rome actually developed. The *ordo agentibus publicam paenitentiam* of
the Vatican Gelasian Sacramentary (the socalled Old Gelasian sacramentary, Vat. Reg. 316) demands that penitents should be dressed
in a hairshirt on Ash Wednesday, to remain locked up until Maundy
Thursday, when they were to be reconciled.[25] However, this is not
the testimony to ancient Roman liturgy it was once taken for. The
manuscript was produced around 750 by Frankish nuns; it is a copy
of sacramentary that was composed in Francia in the second half of
the seventh or the early eighth century.[26] The prescription for the
ritual of penance may contain some Roman elements, but these are
difficult to identify. The text as we now know it is the result of liturgical developments in Gaul and Spain, which continued until the
time of the composition of the sacramentary, that is, not long before

---

[24] Sozomen, *Historia ecclesiastica* VII, c. 16, PG 67, cols. 1461–1462; cf. E. Amman,
"*Pénitence*", cols. 797–798. A. Labate, "Sozomen", *Encyclopedia of the Ancient Church* 2
(Cambridge, 1992), p. 790. A sixth-century monk working under Cassiodorus' super-
vision incorporated a Latin translation of the work into a compilation of three
Church histories; cf. W. Jacob and R. Hanslik, *Cassiodorii Epihanii Historia Ecclesiae
Tripartita* IX, c. 35, CSEL 71 (Vienna, 1952), pp. 553–554: *Haec ergo antiquitatus
Romani pontifices usque ad nostrum conservaverunt tempus.*

[25] *Liber sacramentarium Romanae Aecclesiae ordines anni circuli (Sacramentarium Gelasianum)*,
ed. L.C. Mohlberg, with L. Eizenhöfer & O. Siffring (Rome, 1960), I, 15–16 and
38, pp. 17–58. For a survey of the Gelasian sacramentaries, see B. Moreton, *The
Eighth-century Gelasian Sacramentary: a Study in Tradition* (Oxford, 1976), pp. 198–205.

[26] Vogel, *La discipline pénitentielle en Gaule*, pp. 182, 188–190; C. Vogel, *Medieval
Liturgy. An Introduction to the Sources* (Washington, 1986, transl.), p. 113. In favour of
Chelles: B. Bischoff, "Die Kölner Nonnenhandschriften und das Scriptorium von
Chelles", in B. Bischoff, *Mittelalterliche Studien* I (Stuttgart, 1965), pp. 17–35. Argu-
ing for Jouarre: R. McKitterick, "Nuns' scriptoria' in England and Francia in the
eighth century", *Francia* 19 (1989), pp. 1–35, esp. p. 14.

the now extant manuscript was copied. In other words, we do not owe the earliest *ordo* of public penance to some venerable and untainted Roman tradition, but to centuries of later liturgical creativity in Gaul and Spain.[27]

This provenance is significant, for it is outside Rome we have to look for references to a 'order of penitents'. The latter only surfaces—albeit rarely—in fifth-century conciliar decrees from Gaul. The council of Orange (441) decided that those who had undertaken a deathbed penance and subsequently recovered should 'stand in the order of penitents', to be readmitted to communion only after due penance and reconciliation.[28] This decree was included in a canonical collection put together between 442 and 506.[29] An unambiguously spatial separation of penitents during church services also occurs in the council of Épaon (517) chaired by Bishop Avitus of Vienne, two years after the conversion of the Burgundian King Sigismund from Arianism to orthodox Christianity. At the time the bishops in Épaon were faced with people who had converted to Arianism; they found themselves hampered in their efforts to readmit these apostates to the Church by ancient traditions requiring an impossibly lengthy penance. Hence, they decided that a penance of two years might suffice if the penitents would make an extra effort. They should fast strictly for three days each week and come to church often, observing proper humility there by standing and praying 'in the place of the penitents' (*in loco paenitentum*). If these *lapsi* obeyed all this, they would be readmitted to communion after two years; if not, they would have to submit to the much longer penance of the older canonical statutes.[30] This suggests that Avitus and his bishops

---

[27] E.g. the *cilicium* for penitents, mentioned in this ordo, was prescribed for the first time by the Council of Agde (506) and Caesarius of Arles; see below, n. 47. For a more extensive discussion of the so-called Old Gelasian Sacramentary, with references to older literature, see Y. Hen, "The liturgy of Willibrord", *Anglo-Saxon England* 26 (1997), pp. 41–61 (esp. pp. 48–50). I am grateful to Yitzhak Hen for sharing his views with me. He rightly argues against an official 'Romanisation' of Frankish liturgy, and in favour of a gradual adaptation of heterogeneous liturgical traditions to Frankish needs.

[28] Council of Orange (441), c. 3, ed. C. Munier, *Concilia Galliae*, A. 314-A.506, CCSL 148 (Turnhout, 1963), pp. 78–9.

[29] The so-called Second Council of Arles, c. 28 (27), CCSL 148, p. 120.

[30] Council of Épaon (517), c. 29, ed. C. De Clercq, *Concilia Galliae A. 511-A.695*, CVSL 148A (Turnhout, 1963), p. 114. The translation of in *loco paenitentum* as 'au rang des pénitents' is yet another instance of the influence of the 'grand narrative' of penance; cf. J. Gaudemet and B. Basdevant, *Les canons des conciles Mérovingiens*

did indeed envisage a separate group of penitents present in church, but the decree also indicates that this was not something expected of everyone: those submitting to this humiliation presumably had opted for an intensified and therefore shorter atonement.

In other words: public penitents showed up, more or less regularly, as a distinct group in church. But what else was public about their atonement? Their actual penance was performed elsewhere; for the duration thereof they stood in a separate place and received the *impositio manus*, the imposition of hands, from the bishop, which was to speed up their reconciliation. Some may have perceived this a humiliation; others, like the penitents chastised by Augustine, did not mind their separate status. Whatever the case, this is a far cry from an *ordo paenitentium* constituting an ostracised group within society. So where does this notion, so dear to church historians, actually come from? As far as I can see, this idea rests on a misinterpretation of the Council of Nicaea (325), which demanded that penitents progressed for long years through successive penitential ranks and stages.[31] Because of the tremendous authority of this oecumenical council, it has been assumed that this was a general practice in 'early Christianity', while the council actually dealt with a very specific case: Christians who had lapsed into paganism during recent persecutions.[32] On top of this, we find ourselves in a time warp, for the penitential decrees of Nicaea only became common knowledge in the West after c. 545, when Dionysius Exiguus translated them into Latin.[33]

This takes us back to the sixth century. Avitus of Vienne (d. 518) and his colleague Caesarius of Arles (d. 542), two bishops spanning

---

(V^e–VIIe siècles. Texte Latin de l'édition C. De Clercq. Introductions, traduction et notes, 1, S.C. 353 (Paris, 1989), p. 115.

[31] Council of Nicaea c. 11, ed. J. Alberigo, J.A. Dossetti, P.P. Joannou, C. Leonardi, P. Prodi, Conciliorum Oecumenicorum Decreta, (Turnhout, 1973) p. 11: *Quo quod enim veraciter paenitudinem gerunt, fideles tribus annis inter audientes habeantur et sex annis omni humilitati succumbant, duobus autem annis praeter oblationem populo in oratione communicent.*

[32] Cf. P. Galtier, "Les canons pénitentiels de Nicée", *Gregorianum* 29 (1948), pp. 288–94, who argues against the assumption that the *viaticum* (communion for the dead) originated from the same set of Nicaean canons (cc. 11–13). In his view the 'stages of penance' were a custom peculiar to Asia Minor, which never spread elsewhere. These canons did have an impact on Carolingian public penance, however; I will explore this issue elsewhere.

[33] Cf. *Ecclesiae occidentalis monumenta iuris antiquissima* I, ed. C.H. Turner (Oxford, 1939), pp. 265–267.

the divide between Late Antiquity and the Early Middle Ages, are the first to supply more precise information on how public penance may have functioned on a more regular basis. Clearly mid-life public atonement co-existed with 'emergency penance' as a last resource in the face of death. The issues Avitus and Caesarius struggled with were traditional ones: should bishops impose a deathbed penance on younger people, and what was to be done if they recovered.[34] If one discards misguided notions about the 'original' penance of pre-Constantinian Christianity, it is hard to see why penance in fear of death was a sign of the 'decline' of public penitence. Bishops tended to agree that for the majority of ordinary Christians, sackcloth and ashes were best put off until the business of living was over. Like Ambrose before him,[35] Avitus was acutely conscious of the fact that once someone had become a penitent, his sins would be counted against him with a vengeance. An ordinary person might have sexual intercourse on his dying day without committing a mortal sin, but a penitent doing so should be suspended from communion. 'It is better to stay in a state of salvation, however humble and unambitious it be, than to destroy that state by breaking the most important rules'.[36]

It should be stressed that this 'emergency penitence' (*paenitentia momentanea* or *subitanea*) was not an automatic or general death rite, comparable to a modern deathbed communion (*viaticum*).[37] Although

---

[34] In an influential letter to Bishop Rusticus of Narbonne, Pope Leo I (441–461) took a lenient stance, advising the bishops in Gaul to allow marriage to young 'emergency' penitents who had recovered and then were unable to keep their vows. They could delay their penance until their end was really near. Cf. Leo I, *Epistolae* no. 167, c. 14, PL 54, col. 1207A/B. About papal letters on penance in extremis to bishops in Gaul and Spain, see Rebillard, *In hora mortis*, pp. 209–224.

[35] Ambrose, *De paenitentia*, II, c. xi, 104, ed. R. Gryson, S.C. 179 (Paris, 1971) p. 198: *Melius est ergo tunc quiescere cum excercere non queas opera paenitentiae, ne in ipsa paenitentia fiat quod postea indigeat paenitentia.*

[36] Avitus, *Epistolae*, no. 4, ed. R. Peiper, MGH AA VI, 2, pp. 30–31: . . . *cum melius sit manere intra quantulamcumque salutem humilitate mediocrum, quam ipsam salutem ex toto destrui violatione summorum . . .*

[37] Commenting on the *viaticum* serving as the reconciliation for deathbed penitents who had not yet completed their atonement, Paxton suggests a possible conflation of penance and the last Communion in the sixth century; see F.S. Paxton, *Christianizing Death. The Creation of a Ritual Process in Early Medieval Europe* (Ithaca, N.Y/London, 1990), pp. 52–53. The evidence cited (the Council of Gerona (517), see below, n. 59) indeed points in this direction, yet the *benedictio paenitentiae* and the *viaticum* remained two different things: mortually ill penitents might receive the *benedictio paenitentiae*, the blessing enabling them to face death, but if they recovered they should resume their penance. Also distinguishing between penance and the *viaticum*:

the ritual time-span might be expected to be shorter, this was nonetheless a formal and public penance with similar obligations. If these
were not yet discharged on the eve of death, the *viaticum* served as
a rite of reconciliation. The fact that penitential obligations after
recovery were such a crucial issue suggests that a deathbed penance
was also sought in the hope it might ward off death. Above all, a
penance *in extremis* meant dying well prepared: it was a 'good death'.[38]
Predictably, this practice elicited criticism from semi-Pelagian circles,
which insisted that salvation depended largely on the way one had
lived one's life. Was an emergency penance really effective, or did
it come too late?[39] These views seem to have had some influence at
the Burgundian court, for Avitus had to furnish king Gundobad with
the following explanation:

> To say that the penance which you call 'momentary' (subitanea), that
> is to say taken on in sickness as if at the moment of death, is no use
> to anyone, is a ruling contrary to truth, and cruel. For in the eyes of
> divine mercy, even the confession of a humble person ought not to
> lack fruit'. Given that a man will be judged by the path on which he
> was found at the moment of his death, even the expression of his will-
> ingness to be punished—provided it be genuine—must be pleasing to
> God.[40]

Council of Agde (*506*), c. 15, CCSL 148, p. 201. About the *viaticum*, see now
E. Rebillard, "La naissance du viatique. Se préparer à mourir en Italie et en Gaule
au Vᵉ siècle", *Médiévales* 20 (1991), pp. 15–21.

[38] The importance of penance as a prestigious preparation for death also becomes
clear from a small corpus of sixth- en seventh-century inscriptions from Southern
Gaul and Spain; cf. *Inscriptions Chrétiennes de la Gaule antérieures au VIIIᵉ siècle*, ed.
E. Le Blant, 2 vols. (Paris, 1856/1865), nrs. 66, 623, 663, 708; *Recueil des Inscriptions Chrétiennes de la Gaule antérieures à la Renaissance carolingienne*, vol. 15, Viennoise
du Nord, ed. F. Descombes (Paris, 1986), nrs. 98a, 527, 283; *Inscripciones Cristianas
de la España Romana y Visigoda*, 2nd edition, ed. J. Vives (Barcelona, 1969), nrs. 44,
57, 142, 178, 480, 586. I am grateful to Mark Handley, who generously shared
these references with me; an in-depth analysis of this material exceeds the limits of
this chapter.

[39] For the background to this debate, see D.J. Nodes, "*De Subitanea Paenitentia* in
the Letters of Faustus of Riez and Avitus of Vienne", *Recherches de Théologie Ancienne
et Médiévale* 55 (1988), pp. 30–40.

[40] Avitus, *Epistolae*, no. 4, ed. R. Peiper, MGH AA VI, 2, pp. 30, ll. 5–11:
. . . *paenitentiam, quam proprie momentaneam nominastis, id est in aegritudine quasi sub momento
mortis acceptam nihil aut nulli prodesse adversa veritati et admodum cruda definitio est. Apud
divinam quippe misericordiam vel ipsa humilitas confitentis non debet fructu carere. Quia, cum
legimus, quod qualitate vitae anterioris abolita, qua plerumque contigit et peccare iustos et respicere
peccatores, in ea quis via iudicetur, qua obitus sui tempore fuerit deprehensus, incunctanter cre-
denda sit vel ipsa correctionis voluntas placere, si vera sit.* I am grateful to Ian Wood and
Danuta Schanzer for allowing me to use the translation of Avitus's letters they are
currently preparing. See also Avitus, *Epistolae*, no. 18, p. 50 where the bishop of

Caesarius had more reservations about emergency penance than Avitus. After all, before he became a bishop he had been a monk, so he felt more strongly about the need to work hard towards one's own salvation. The metropolitan of Arles did not want to deny emergency penance to anyone, nor would he say that it was entirely useless, especially if the penitent exerted himself in almsgiving, forgiving and asking forgiveness, and was prepared to perform a proper penance in the event of recovery. Yet Caesarius warned his audience that an emergency penance offered no guarantee of salvation. How would you like it, he asked, if your slave served your enemies while he was young and vigorous, only to return to your service once he grew old?[41] In a series of sermons Caesarius urged his flock not to delay penance until it was too late. Medical metaphors abound. Grave sins (*crimina capitalia*) needed instant treatment by penance, Caesarius said, lest the sores fester; sins are wounds, penance their dressing and ointment. Likewise, a lifetime of cumulative minor sins (*minuta peccata*) might add up to an equally heavy burden requiring a formal penance imposed by the bishop: good works and alms by themselves would not be enough to merit God's forgiveness.

In Caesarius' view a deathbed penance was only second best, and people should be aware of the risks they took, but this does not necessarily spell a decline of any sort. The comparison between the few who, not unlike the Cathar *perfecti* of a later age, opted for a mid-life penitence and stuck to it, and the many who delayed atonement until the eve of death was a traditional one, which, for obvious reasons, favoured the former. These categories had existed from the second century: Tertullian (160–220) already mentioned people putting off their penance because they could not face the consequences of this shaming ritual.[42] Caesarius' sermons reveal another and more

---

Vienne argues that Vincomalus, who had contracted a forbidden marriage, should lead a penitential life without being forced to undertake a formal penance; this he should do in old age, when he no longer had 'the opportunity to sin' (*. . . patiatur paenitentiam, cum perdat peccandi occasionem . . .*). This case is discussed by I.N. Wood, "Incest, law and the Bible in sixth-century Gaul", *Early Medieval Europe* 7 (1998), pp. 297–299.

[41] Caesarius of Arles, *Sermones*, 64, 3, ed. M.-J. Delage, *Césaire d'Arles, Sermons au Peuple*, 3, S.C. 330 (Paris, 1986), p. 100.

[42] Tertullian, *De Paenitentia*, X,1, CCSL 1 (Turnhout, 1954), p. 337: *Plerosque tamen hoc opus ut publicationem sui aut suffugere aut de die in diem differre praesumo pudoris magis memores quam salutis, velut illi, qui in partibus verecundioribus corpora contracta vexatione conscientiam medentium vitant et ita cum erubescentia sua pereunt.* Cf Karpp, *Die Buße*, pp. 178–9.

important divide in the penitential ranks. Addressing 'those asking publicly for penance', he wrote:

> Whoever receives penitence publicly might also have done this more secretly, but I believe that, considering the multitude of his sins, he realises that he cannot do enough against such serious evil by himself; for this reason, he wishes to enlist the aid of the entire people.[43]

In other words, there were two kinds of public penitents, but some were more public than others, for their penance was imposed in the course of an eminently public ritual. A collection of older African conciliar texts circulating in Gaul spoke of 'public and most widely known of crimes perturbing the entire church' that required a public imposition of penance.[44] What may have been a new development is Caesarius' assumption that sinners might resort to an equally legitimate 'more secret' version of penance. This was not a reference to deathbed penance, for the imposition of *paenitentia momentanea* could be as public as that of its more prestigious counterpart. The main difference between *publice* and *secretius* lay in the defamatory character of the public ritual. Caesarius was not the only one to make this distinction. A generation earlier, the priest Gennadius of Marseilles contrasted a public penance on the one hand, and a 'secret satisfaction' performed by withdrawing from secular life (*mutatio saecularis habitus*) on the other. There can have been little secrecy about someone suddenly declaring himself a penitent by donning religious garb. Still, the sinner was spared the humiliation of becoming a penitent in front of many witnesses, and of having to present himself (or herself) regularly in church for similar public gestures of atonement.[45] This distinction between a dramatic public humiliation on the one hand, and more discrete varieties of atonement on the other, is absent in patristic sources, but seems to have been commonplace in Gaul by c. 500. This is important for the understanding of Carolingian perceptions of authoritative 'early Christian' penance, for

---

[43] Caesarius of Arles, *Sermones*, 67,1, ed. Delage, S.C. 330, p. 126: *Et quidem ille, qui paenitentiam publice accepit, poterat eam secretius agere: sed credo considerans multitudinem peccatorum suorum videt se contra tam gravia mala solum non posse sufficere; ideo adiutorium totius populi cupit expetere.*

[44] See above, n. 20.

[45] Gennadius, *De ecclesiasticis dogmatibus* c. 22, ed. C.H. Turner, *Journal of Theological Studies* 7 (1906), p. 94. Gennadius was probably the compiler of the Statuta Ecclesiastica Antiqua; see C. Munier, *Les Statuta Ecclesiastica Antiqua* (Paris, 1960). See S. Pricoco, "Gennadius of Marseilles", *Encyclopedia of the Early Church* 1, p. 342; Gennadius was still alive at the time of Pope Gelasius I (492–496).

Jonas and his fellow reform bishops referred to the penitential practice in Caesarius' day and age when they called for the return to
canonical penance.

Caesarius' seems to have envisaged a dramatic group ritual involving 'the entire people', with the sinner publicly asking for excommunication and declaring him/herself to be unworthy of the Eucharist.
He (or she) wore the sackcloth (*cilicium*) turning the penitent into a
goat among sheep, an innovation first recorded by the Council of
Agde (506) chaired by Caesarius.[46] All this sounds remarkably similar to what Bishop Jonas of Orléans' imagined to have been good
practice in the earliest days of Christianity. Jonas could have been
inspired by Caesarius' sermons, and believed them to be Augustine's;
in the ninth century a substantial part of Caesarius' oeuvre, including his sermons on penance, circulated as Augustine's work.[47] Even
if this was not the case, Caesarius' prestige among reform-minded
Carolingian bishops was such that he represented the kind of canonical authority that by definition belonged to 'antiquity', or even to
the 'earliest days of our faith' *religionis nostrae priscis temporibus*.[48] Yet
the public penitents Caesarius had in mind may have formed a
broader and socially more heterogeneous category than the penitents
envisaged by Jonas. They stood to lose an established social position
and marital status,[49] thus requiring royal examples to be waved in
front of them by their hectoring bishop. Had royal dignity or royal
dress prevented King David, an adulterer and a murderer, from
doing penance? Had he waited until he was an old man? On the
contrary, David had acted immediately, prostrating himself in sackcloth and ashes, sighing and bewailing his sins.[50] To be *in militia*

---

[46] Council of Agde (506), c. 15, CCSL 148, p. 201: *Paenitentes, tempore quo paenitentiam petunt, impositionem manuum et cilicium super caput a sacerdotes sicut ubique constitutum est, consequantur; et si aut comas non deposuerint, aut uestimenta non mutauerint, abiiciantur
et nisi digne paenituerint, non recipiantur.*

[47] W.E. Klingshirn, *Caesarius of Arles. The Making of a Christian Community in Late
Antique Gaul* (Cambridge, 1994), p. 9. This is evident from the survey of manuscripts
containing Caesarius sermons: see G. Morin, *S. Caesarii Arelatensis sermones. Sancti
Caesarii opera omnia* I (Maredsous, 1937), pp. xxv–cxv. I am grateful to David Ganz
for reminding me of this. However, Jonas may also have referred to the rites of
public penance in contemporary sacramentaries.

[48] See above, n. 12. About Caesarius' influence: Klingshirn, *Caesarius of Arles*, pp.
273–86.

[49] Caesarius, Sermones, 65,1, ed. Delage S.C. 330, p. 110: *Sed forte est aliquis qui
dicat: Ego in militia positus sum, uxorem habeo, et ideo paenitentiam agere quomodo possum?*

[50] Caesarius, *Sermones*, 65,1, ed. Delage, S.C. 330, p. 110.

positus in the sixth century may not have had quite the same élitist connotations as possessing a *cingulum militiae* did in the ninth, but relinquishing one's social privileges still was a high ideal to aspire to. Is this the reason why the only specific example recorded in Caesarius' work is that of a bishop? Accused of scandalous sexual sins, Contumeliosus of Riez publicly proclaimed his guilt 'in a gathering of bishops and laymen', to be deposed and dispatched to a monastery to perform his penance.[51]

2. *Penance and conversion*

A lifetime of small sins might accumulate to the equivalent of a *crimen capitalis*, but according to Caesarius public penance and involvement of the faithful was above all a 'medication' for grave sins (*crimina*) murder, adultery, fornication, idolatry or apostasy. The few instances of the type of public confession envisaged by Caesarius and Jonas involve bishops, however, who like Contumeliosus had been found guilty of sexual misbehaviour. It is easy to see why bishops were especially vulnerable to such accusation, and also why the results of their trial by peers found its way into conciliar records. Canon law as it evolved over the centuries held that a bishop publicly humiliating himself did not undertake a *paenitentia publica*, for clerics should not have to suffer the double punishment of a deposition followed by a proper 'ecclesiastical penance'.[52] However, if one no longer imposes a juridical straightjacket on unruly early medieval texts, what bishops actually did (or were supposed to have done) looks very much like a public penance. They prostrated themselves and confessed their sins to a 'multitude of clerics and laymen'.[53] The main

---

[51] Council of Marseilles (533), CCSL 148A, p. 85: *Cum ad ciuitate Massiliensem propter requirenda et discutienda ea, quae de fratre nostro Contumilioso episcopo fuerant deuulgata, sacerdotes domini conuenissint, residentibus sanctis episcopis cum grandi diligentia discussis omnibus secundum quod gesta, quae nobis praesentibus facta sunt, continent, multa turpia et inhonesta supra dictus Contumiliosus conuictus ore proprio se confessus est perpetrasse, ita ut non solum reuincere testis non potuerit, sed etiam publice in conuentu episcoporum et laicorum, qui interfuerant, in terram se proiciens clamauerit se grauiter in deum et in ordine pontificali peccasse.*
  Pro qua re propter disciplinam catholicae religionis utile ac salubre omnibus uisum est, ut supra dictus Contumeliosus in Casensi monasterio ad agendam paenitentiam uel ad expianda ea, quae ammiserat, mitteritur; quam rem stodio paenitendi et ipse libenter amplexus est.

[52] Poschmann, *Penance and the Anointing of the Sick*, pp. 111–112; Amman, "La pénitence", col. 803; Vogel, "Penitence", p. 667.

[53] See n. 52 above.

difference was that they performed their penance in the seclusion of the monastic confines.

But could lay people not have done the same? What was the relation between public penance and monastic life? I shall address this problem by approaching it from a different angle, namely the surprising number of sixth- and seventh-century *canones*, both from Gaul and Spain, that link public penance with the clerical state. According to the Grand Narrative of the history of penance, life-long impediments imposed on ex-penitents speeded up the decline of 'canonical' penance, and one of the most important of these impediments was the inability of former penitents to become clerics. They were tainted for life, and therefore unsuitable for ministering to the laity.[54] Yet the evidence points in a different direction. The majority of the texts cited by modern authors to illustrate the existence of an ecclesiastical 'dogma' excluding ex-penitents from the clergy seem to refer to 'those who have accepted a penance' or, simply, 'penitents', not to those who had already completed their atonement. Moreover, the issue is so central to episcopal concerns that it seems as if the recruitment of penitents into the clergy may have been a rather common occurrence, notwithstanding the dishonouring effects of their public humiliation. The influential *Statuta Ecclesiae Antiqua*, a canonical collection compiled in Gaul around 475, decreed that no penitent should be made a cleric, even if he might be a good one; bishops who consecrated such men knowingly would be deprived of their right to ordain clergy.[55] Other conciliar *acta* from fifth and early sixth-century Gaul just briefly state that penitents should not become clerics, and equally briefly that clerics should not be denied a penance.[56] These texts refer in a general way to '*clerici*', but in 524 a synod in

---

[54] Poschmann, *Penance and the Anointing of the Sick*, p. 105; De Clercq, "Penitence"; Saint-Roch, *La pénitence dans les conciles*, p. 41.

[55] *Statuta Ecclesiae Antiqua* c. 84, CCSL 148, p. 179: *Ex paenitentibus, quamuis bonus, clericus non ordinetur; si per ignorantiam episcopi factus fuerit, deponatur a clero, quia se ordinationis tempore non prodidit fuisse paenitente; si autem sciens episcopus ordinauit, etiam ipse ab episcopatus sui ordinandi dumtaxat potestate priuetur.*

[56] Council of Agde (a. 506) c. 43, CCSL 148, p. 211: *De paenitentibus id placuit obseruari, quod sancti patres nostri synodali sententia statuerunt, ut nullus de his clericus ordinetur; et qui iam sunt per ignorantiam ordinati, ut sicut bigami aut internuptarum mariti locum teneant*; see also the Council of Épaon (517) c. 3, CCSL 148A, p. 25. Clerics not to be denied a penance: Council of Orange (441) c. 4, CCSL 148, p. 79: *Paenitencia desiderantibus etiam clericis non neganda*; repeated in the so-called Second council of Arles (a collecton of canonical law of the mid-fifth century) c. 29, CCSL 148, p. 120.

Arles chaired by Caesarius introduced a differentiation: nobody who
was penitent, had married for the second time or had married a
widow should become either a priest or a deacon. Bishops yielding
to pressure and violating this rule were forbidden to celebrate Mass
for a year.[57] In other words, it was only the '*presbyteri vel diaconatus
honor*', the 'honourable' higher orders from which penitents were
barred.[58] A contemporary gathering of Spanish bishops opted for a
different compromise: those who had undertaken a deathbed penance
but got well again could become clerics, provided they had not manifested their penitential state publicly in church or persisted in their
sins.[59] As for others aspiring to the clergy, their penance would only
be a real impediment if it had entailed a public confession to widely
known crimes (*manifesta scelera*).[60]

These texts are too haphazard and contradictory to amount to
anything like a unified 'doctrine of penance', still less do they allow
much insight into actual practice. What does become clear, however, is that it was primarily the publicity of penance and the noto-
riety of sins confessed which discredited future clerics, and that clerics
in higher orders were the ones who really needed worrying about.
But what if 'good' penitents ate only 'herbs, vegetables and little
fishes', even after having been readmitted to communion, as Cae-

---

[57] Council of Arles (524), c. 3, CCSL 148A, p. 44; one finds this concentration
on the priest and deacon already in the Council of Orléans (511) c. 9, CCSL 148A.
p. 7, where these higher orders are singled out as those deserving deposition and
excommunication if they had committed *crimina capitalia*.

[58] A remarkably explicit and early conciliar text from Spain stipulated that former penitents should not be admitted to the clergy, yet they might be admitted to
the lower orders, provided they performed no important (and public) cultic acts.
Ex-penitents were defined as follows: *Ex poenitente vero dicimus de eo, qui post babtismum
aut pro diversis criminibus gravissimusque peccatis publicam poenitentiam gerens sub cilicio divini
fuerit reconciliatus altario*. Cf. *First* Council of Toledo (397–400), c. 2, *Concilios visigóticos e hispano-romanos*, ed. J. Vives (Barcelona/Madrid, 1963), p. 20; similarly, the
Council of Braga II (572), c. 23, ed. Vives, p. 93. See De Jong, "What was public about public penance", pp. 872–875.

[59] Council of Gerona (517), c. 9, ed. Vives, p. 41: *Is vero qui aegritudinis langorem
depressus poenitentiae benedictionem, quod viaticum deputamus, per communionem acceperit, et post-
modum revalescens caput poenitentiae in ecclesia publice non subdiderit, si prohibitis vitiis non
detinetur obnoxius, admittatur ad clerum*. Similarly, *Statuta Ecclesiae Antiqua* c. 21, CCSL
148, p. 170.

[60] Council of Gerona (517), ed. Vives, c. 9b, p. 41: *Hi qui in discrimine constituti
poenitentiam accipiunt nulla manifesta scelera confitentes, sed tantum peccatores se praedicantes,
huismodi si revaluerint, possunt etiam per morum probitatem ad gradus ecclesiasticos pervenire; qui
vero ita poenitentiam accipiunt, ut aliquod mortale peccatum perpetrasse publice fateantur, ad clerum
vel honores ecclesiasticos pervenire nullatenus possunt, qui se confessione propria notaverunt.*

sarius hoped they would?[61] Bishops may have been inclined to accept penitents into their clergy as long as their reputation had not become tainted by having openly admitted to grievous sins, for the same reason they drafted monks into the clerical ranks.[62] Unlike laymen, monks and penitents had already left 'the world'; they would need no lengthy preparation or purification.

Already at an early stage the boundaries between monasticism, penance and the secular clergy had become permeable. Salvian, the undisputed Jeremiah of fifth-century Gaul, assumed that like monks, nuns and higher secular clerics, *penitentes* were a subcategory of the *sancti*, that is, those who had retired from secular life.[63] The conciliar vocabulary of penance in fifth- and early sixth-century Gaul speaks volumes. A man or woman might 'convert' to penance, make a 'profession of penance' (*professio paenitentiae*), or receive the 'blessing of penance' (*benedictio paenitentiae*). All these expressions referred to a definite farewell to the lay state. As the Council of Orléans (511) convened by Clovis had it: 'those who after undertaking a penance have relinquished the religious obligations of their profession and relapsed into a secular way of life, should be suspended from communion and banished from the company of all Catholics'.[64]

All this makes it difficult to distinguish between an 'ecclesiastical

---

[61] Caesarius, *Sermones*, 67,3, S.C. 330, p. 132: *Et ideo etiam reconciliatus paenitens, ubicumque aut in suo aut in alieno convivio olera aut legumina aut pisciculos invenire potuerit, aliam carnem non debet accipere.* A late seventh-century text, the first Passion of Praeiectus, contains a story about three penitents who were mocked because of their ascetic diet: *Passio Praeiecti* c. 8, ed. B. Krusch, MGH SSRM V, p. 230.

[62] About the early phase of this development, see D. König, *Amt und Askese. Priesteramt und Mönchtum bei den lateinischen Kirchenvätern in vorbenediktinischer Zeit*, (Regulae Benedicti Studia, Supplementa 12) (St. Ottilien, 1985), pp. 210–223. A decree against monks who had left their monastery to marry entering the secular clergy indicates that the boundary between the regular and secular clergy was easily crossed. First Council of Orléans (511) c. 21, CCSL 148A, p. 10: *Monachus si in monasterio conuersus uel pallium conprobatus fuerit accepisse, et postea uxori fuerit sociatus, tantae praeuaricationis reus numquam ecclesiastici gradus officium sortiatur.* Cf. M. de Jong, "Imitatio morum. The cloister and clerical purity in the Carolingian world", *Medieval Purity and Piety. Essays on Celibacy and Reform*, ed. M. Frassetto (New York, 1998), pp. 49–80.

[63] Salvian of Marseille, *Epistolae* XI, 11, ed. G. Lagarrigue, *Salvien de Marseille, Oeuvres*, 1, S.C. 176 (Paris, 1971), p. 126. Elsewhere Salvian complained that penance had become superficial; penitents no longer behaved like *religiosi*, as they should, but like *saeculares*; cf. Salvian, *De gubernatione Dei*, V, c. 10, pp. 50–55, ed. Lagarrigue, *Salvien de Marseille, Oeuvres*, vol. 1, S.C. 220 (Paris, 1975), pp. 350–352.

[64] First Council of Orléans (511), c. 11, CCSL 148A, p. 8: *De his, qui suscepta paenitentia religionem suae professionis obliti ad saecularia relabuntur, placuit eos et a communione suspendi et ab omnium catholicorum conuiuio separari.*

penance' proper and a *conversio*. The ensuing confusion emerges from Poschmann's rather desperate denial:

> In spite, however, of their similar character and obligations, ecclesiastical penance and *conversio* were juridically regarded as quite distinct. The former, too, still continued to be defamatory, at least in theory, the latter was regarded as a state of perfection. Whereas penance carried irregularity with it, *conversio* became a preliminary condition for admission to the clergy.[65]

This is a heroic attempt to salvage a sacramental *Kirchenbuße* in the face of texts making it impossible to identify anything of the sort. Some penitents were more dishonourable than others, probably because they had openly confessed to more flagrant and well-known sins. For all its later monastic connotations, the expression '*professio paenitentiae*' not only refers to the enduring nature of penitential obligations but also to the public nature of this declaration. The ensuing 'scandal' may have caused some penitents to be mentioned in one breath with those who were disfigured or had been publicly possessed by demons,[66] yet all of those who 'professed' or 'converted' to penance were expected effectively to leave the world. Hence, Avitus and his bishops did not wish to consecrate widows as deaconesses, but if they wished to convert, they could ask for an official penance (*benedictio penitentiae*);[67] the Council of Orléans (538) used the word *conversio* for those becoming clerics *and* penitents.[68] A return to their 'worldly dress and life' would mean a life-long excommunication.[69]

---

[65] Poschmann, *Penance and the Anointing of the Sick*, p. 114.

[66] Third Council of Orléans (538) c. 6, CCSL 148A, p. 116: *De clericorum praemittenda conuertione id omnimodis obseruetur, ne ullus ex lahicis ante annualem conuersationem uel aetatem legitimam, id est uiginta quinque annorum diaconus et trigenta presbyter, ordinetur, ita ut de ipsis quoque, qui ordinandi sunt clerici, regulare costodiatur studium, ne aut duarum uxorum uir aut renupte maritus aut paenitentiam professus aut simus corpore uel qui publice aliquando adreptus est ad supra scriptus ordines promoueatur.*

[67] Council of Épaon (517) c. 21, CCSL 148A, p. 29: *Veduarum consecrationem, quas diaconas uocitant, ab omni regione nostra paenitus abrogamus, sola paenitentiae benedictione, si conuerti ambiunt, inponenda.*

[68] The Third Council of Orléans (538) c. 27, CCSL 148A, p. 124 speaks *of 'de paenitentum conuersione'*, warning against giving the *benedictio paenitentiae* to young people, or without the consent of the spouse; conversion to the clerical state: cf. above, n. 54. Conversion to monastic life: First Council of Orléans (511) c. 21, CCSL 148A, p. 10; Second Council of Tours (567), c. 16, CCSL 148A, pp. 181–182. About penance as a *conversio*, see De Clercq, *La discipline pénitentielle en Gaule*, pp. 128–138; A. Fitzgerald, *Conversion through Penance in the Italian Church of the IVth and Vth Centuries* (Lewinston, 1988).

[69] Third Council of Orléans (538), c. 28, CCSL 148A, p. 124: *Si quis paenitentiae*

The actual atonement might lead to a readmission to communion within a definite time span, but 'converting to penance' was something one did for life.

There is nothing particularly new or revolutionary about this, for in biblical and patristic tradition the notions of *paenitentia* and *conversio* were closely linked. It is also easy to see why penance and monasticism became increasingly conflated. Bishops insisted that men doing a penance could be identified by their tonsure, women by the fact that they had 'changed their clothes', that is, now wore the habit of a penitent.[70] This did not necessarily mean an automatic entry into a monastic community; the traditional option was that of an ascetic life at home.[71] Yet as the influence of monasticism grew in the course of the sixth and seventh centuries, so did the number of penitents becoming monks and nuns. After all, before child oblation became the prevailing way of entering monastic life,[72] monasteries were penitential communities consisting largely of adults wishing to atone for past sins; hence, rituals of penance played a central role in the daily lives of monks and nuns. Interestingly, the same holds true for forms of penance specifically denoted as 'public' and bearing some resemblance to its counterpart outside the monastery, though with significant differences. When John Cassian (c. 400) spoke of a *paenitentia publica*, he had a punishment in mind that could be repeated time and again, for sins as insignificant as breaking a pot.[73] The 'public' in front of whom the culprit prostrated himself, asking

---

benedictione suscepta ad saecularem habitum militiamque reverti praesumpserit, viatico concesso usque ad exitum excommunicatione plectatur'.

[70] Council of Agde (506) c. 15, CCSL 148, p. 201 (see above, n. 47); Caesarius, Sermo 67,1, ed. Delage, S.C. 330, p. 126. For a similar insistence on tonsure for men and a religious habit for women see the Third Council of Toledo (589) c. 12, ed. Vives, pp. 128–9; cf. also the Council of Barcelona (540), c. 6, ed. Vives, p. 53.

[71] For examples of highborn Gallo-Romans of the fifth century opting for a conversion to penance while remaining in their families, see Poschmann, *Die abendländische Kirchenbuße*, pp. 131–133; E. Griffe, "Un example de pénitence publique au Vᵉ siècle", *Bulletin de la littérature ecclésiastique* (1958), pp. 170–175. Cf. also the First Council of Barcelona (540), c. 7, ed. Vives, p. 58: penitents should lead a frugal life at home.

[72] M. de Jong, *In Samuel's Image. Child Oblation in the Early Medieval West* (New York/Leiden/Cologne, 1996).

[73] John Cassian, *De institutione coenobiorum* IV, c. 16,1, ed. J.-C. Guy, *Jean Cassien, Institutions cénobitiques*, S.C. 109 (Paris, 1965), p 140; see also IV, c. 20, p. 148 where John Cassian praises the strictness of Eastern monasticism: even the loss of three lentils required a *paenitentia publica*.

forgiveness, consisted of the abbot and the community; the *paenitentia* consisted of this very act of public humiliation.[74] In a traditional
monastic context, the distinction between 'secret' and 'public' was
one of degree, not of two different types of penance. If a monk was
disobedient and arrogant, the *Regula Benedicti* prescribed that his
seniors were to admonish him secretly and repeatedly; if this did not
help, he should be 'publicly scolded in the presence of all' (*obiurgi-
tur publice coram omnibus*).[75] If this did not change his behaviour, he
should be either excommunicated or whipped. Monastic excommunication also was a graduated affair. Grave sins merited exclusion
from both the table (the community) and the oratory (the cult), and
nobody was allowed to communicate in any way with the culprit.[76]
There were lesser degrees of excommunication as well, which were
at the abbot's discretion: forcing a monk to eat apart, and denying
him any prominent role in the liturgy, although he could still enter
the oratory.[77]

Such monastic rituals of public exclusion were ubiquitous. 'If someone is excommunicated for whatever reason', wrote Caesarius in his
Rule for nuns, 'she should be removed from the community to a
place designated by the abbess, living in the company of one of her
spiritual sisters, until she receives forgiveness by humbly doing
penance'.[78] As the example of Contumeliosus and others shows, the
penitential nature of monastic life turned the cloister into an ideal
place for the higher echelons of the clergy to atone for their sins.
At this particular time, the doubtful privilege of an enforced monastic penance was still restricted to higher clerics, but soon Merovingian kings discovered the uses of this traditional tool of ecclesiastical
discipline.

---

[74] John Cassian, *De institutione coenobiorum* II, cc. 15,2 and 16, ed. Guy, pp. 86–88:
*Sane si quis pro admisso quolibet delicto fuerit ab oratione suspensus, nullus cum eo prorsus
orandi habet licentiam, antequam summissa in terram paenitentia reconciliatio eius et admissi venia
coram fratribus cunctis publice fuerit ab abbate concessa.*

[75] *Regula Benedicti* c. 23, ed. A. de Vogüé and J. Neufville, *La Règle de Saint Benoît*,
S.C. 181–182 (Paris, 1971), p. 542.

[76] *Regula Benedicti* c. 25, S.C. 182, p. 546.

[77] *Regula Benedicti* c. 24, S.C. 182, p. 544.

[78] Caesarius of Arles, *Regula ad virgines* c. 34, ed. A. de Vogüé, *Césaire, Oeuvres
monastiques* I, S.C. 345 (Paris, 1988) p. 214: *Si qua vero pro quacumque re excommunicata
fuerit, remota a congregatione, in loco quo abbatissa iusserit, cum una de spiritalibus sororibus
resideat, quousque humiliter paenitendo indulgentiam accipiat.*

3. Varieties of penance

Within the traditional Grand Narrative of penance, Gregory of Tours marks the transition from orderly Gallo-Roman practice to early medieval confusion and barbarism. This impression of change owes a lot to the specific nature of the sources and their particular rhetoric. To proceed from Caesarius' sermons or conciliar legislation to Gregory's garrulous stories inevitably means stepping into a different world, if only because of the sudden wealth of detail on offer.[79] Hence, Gregory spells the beginning of the Early Middle Ages. To others, however, he belongs to the world of late Antiquity. Peter Brown considers Gregory to be 'sub-Roman' in his attitude to penance. His world resounded with great scenes of pardon, reflecting the daily experience of élites regularly involved the drama of justice and pardon, abject humiliation and protection.[80]

It is tempting to flesh out the bare bones of conciliar texts by lively illustrations from Gregory's work, but the perspective of the bishop of Tours is no more representative of 'Merovingian practice' than the more formal pronouncements of the conciliar *acta* produced by his colleagues. Gregory's information is specific and elaborate, intended to establish the post-hoc reputation of his protagonists, including himself. His array of stories about penance is dazzling; it ranges from unofficial and short-lived acts of atonement to more formal conversions, either in mid-life or in the face of impending death.[81]

---

[79] Since the days of Poschmann and Vogel Gregory's work has been the focus of much sophisticated scholarly attention; his *Historiae* no longer offer easy proof of early medieval barbarism and decline. For some examples of new approaches to Gregory see G. de Nie, *Views from a many-windowed tower. Studies of imagination in the works of Gregory of Tours* (Amsterdam, 1987); W. Goffart, *The Narrators of Barbarian History (AD 550–800): Jordanes, Gregory of Tours, Bede, Paul the Deacon* (Princeton, 1988); R. Van Dam, *Saints and their miracles in Late Antique Gaul* (Princeton, 1993); I.N. Wood, "The secret histories of Gregory of Tours", *Revue Belge de Philologie et d'Histoire* 71 (1993), pp. 253–270; A.H.B. Breukelaar, *Historiography and episcopal authority in sixth-century Gaul. The Histories of Gregory of Tours interpreted in their historical context* (Göttingen, 1994); M. Heinzelmann, *Gregor von Tours (538–594). "Zehn Bücher Geschichte". Historiographie und Gesellschaftskonzept im 6. Jahrhundert* (Darmstadt, 1994).

[80] Brown, "Vers la naissance du Purgatoire", pp. 1254–1255.

[81] Some examples of 'unofficial' penance in Gregory's work, that is, without obvious clerical intervention: Saint Martin unleashes a rain of stones on Kings Childebert and Theudebert, who, *humo prostrati, poenitentiam agebant* (*Historiae*, III, c. 28, ed. B. Krusch, MGH SSRM I/1, p. 125); a captive rebel requests the imposition of penance from a priest (*Historiae* V, c. 31, p. 231); a penitent about to be hanged is saved (*De virtutibus sancti Martini*, III, c. 53, ed. B. Krusch, MGH SSRM I, p. 645; a blind woman performs a penance in her home and can see again (*De*

Yet it was to the public penance of his own colleagues that the
bishop of Tours devoted his most complex and extensive narratives.
Bishops performing a public penance were not simply a good story,
but also one that mattered, for their collective reputation was at
stake, including Gregory's own.

His anecdote about Bishop Urbicus of Clermont's seduction by
his own wife is set innocuously in a distant past, but reflected a
problem that had long bothered episcopal gatherings.[82] Urbicus apparently repented of his sin and temporarily retired to a monastery in
his own diocese to perform a penance, returning to his episcopal
city afterwards.[83] Urbicus' transgression and atonement conform to
a rather traditional pattern, but not so the chapter about Sagittarius and Salonius, two bishops engaging in extortion, murder, adultery and every other crime in the calendar. Here it was king Guntram
who was depicted as pulling the disciplinary strings. He convened
the council that deposed the bishops, but granted them a hearing
with Pope John III, who subsequently ordered them to be restored
to office. After committing a lurid series of further crimes, the king
called both men to court, but refused to receive them before they
had been proven innocent. The furious Sagittarius reciprocated by
spreading evil rumours about the king; Guntram, equally incensed,
deprived them of their horses, possessions and servants, and 'had
them shut up in monasteries far removed from each other, to do
penance', with only one cleric in attendance. The counts were sternly
instructed to keep them under armed guard and ban all visitors.[84]

---

virtutibus sancti Martini, III, c. 56, pp. 645–6). More formal and public types of
penance: the referendary Marcus undertakes a deathbed penance (*Historiae* VI,
c. 28, p. 295); the aristocratic lady Berthegund uses a conversion to penance to
escape from her husband (*Historiae* IX, c. 33, pp. 452–3); the full weight of canonical penance brought to bear on the rebel nuns of Poitiers, after a public confession of guilt (*Historiae* IX, c. 41 and X, c. 15, pp. 468–469, 508). Monasticism and
penance: Romanus and Lupicinus found monasteries as an act of penance (*Vitae
Patrum*, I, c. 3, p. 666); the recluse Friardus, together with abbot Sabaudus who
was once a courtier, plus a deacon, go to an island together to do penance (*Vitae
Patrum*, X, c. 2, p. 707). For the expression *agere paenitentiam* in the sense of 'being
sorry', i.e. regretting certain actions, see *Historiae* V, c. 34 and X, c. 15).

[82] De Jong, "Imitatio morum".

[83] Gregory, *Historiae* I, c. 44, p. 29: *Dehinc tardius ad se reversus et de perpetrato scelere
condolens, acturus paenitentiam, diocesis suae monasterium appetit, ibique cum gemitu ac lacrimis
quae commiserit diluens ad urbem propriam est reversus'*. From this sinful union a daughter was born who became a nun.

[84] Gregory, *Historiae*, V, c. 20, p. 228: *His auditis, rex commotus valde, tam equos quam
pueros vel quaecunque habere poterant abstulit; ipsosque in monasteriis a se longiori accessu dimo-*

But this is not the end of the saga about this two some. In 579 the old charges (*antiqua calamitas*) against Salonius and Sagittarius, adultery and homicide, were reiterated during a council in Chalon. The bishops, however, decided that the two men had cleansed themselves sufficiently from these crimes by their penitence. Hence, it took fresh accusations—offending the king and betraying the fatherland—to get the two deposed and locked up in the *basilica* of Saint Marcellus. They took flight and became wanderers on the face of the earth.[85]

Gregory's indignation is clear: these men should have been deposed forthwith. As in the case of Urbicus, there is no question of penance in a monastery being incompatible with episcopal office. On the contrary, this was the way bishops had atoned for their sins since the days of Contumeliosus. The novelty of this tale is not that penance became more 'coercive', but that it could be a king rather than bishops themselves who did the coercing. Heavy-handed royal might interfered at every stage in Gregory's 'tale of two criminal colleagues'. It was King Guntram who decided the pair should get another chance, and subsequently dispatched them to do penance in monasteries when they did not live up to it; the same king suspended the excommunication of another bishop involved in the case. By the time the council of Chalon moved in for the kill, Sagittarius and Salonius had fallen definitively from royal grace; at least, this is suggested by the eminently political charges brought against them. But according to Gregory the bishops in Chalon were not just royal stooges: they insisted that the penance of Sagittarius and Salonius had been validly performed, so they could not be deposed for the crimes they had already properly atoned for. Possibly, this detail was also intended to emphasise royal arbitrariness in a field that was traditionally the prerogative of bishops. A king trying to beat the bishops at their own game were certainly on Gregory's mind when he related the dramatic events of 577 surrounding the trial and downfall of Praetextatus of Rouen. Suspected by King Chilperic of supporting his rebellious son Merovech, Praetextatus found himself accused of theft. Gregory's record of the trial is a brilliant piece of auto-hagiography, in the shape of a battle wits between the king and

---

tis, in quibus paenitentiam agerent, includi praecepit, non amplius quam singulos eis clericos relin-quens: iudices locorum terribiliter commonens, ut ipsos cum armatis custodire debeant, ne cui ad eos visitandos ullus pateat aditus.
[85] Gregory, *Historiae* V, c. 27, p. 233.

Gregory himself, who spoke up for his colleague, but in fact asserted the bishops' superiority in matters of canon law.[86] When Chilperic saw that he was getting nowhere with his accusations, and Fredegund's bribes had been turned down, the king tricked Praetextatus into a public confession of his sins by leading him to expect royal pardon in return:

> When the argument reached a pitch, Praetextatus suddenly prostrated himself and said: 'I have sinned against Heaven and before Thee, most merciful king; I am an evil murderer; I wanted to kill you and to place your son on the throne'. As Praetextatus said this, the king prostrated himself at the bishops' feet and said: 'Most pious bishops, you hear this man confess to be guilty of an execrable crime'. As we, weeping, raised the king from the ground, he ordered Praetextatus to leave the church'.[87]

There is a curious double-entendre here, and even an element of parody. Chilperic led the hapless bishop to believe that a public humiliation in front of the king would earn him royal pardon, but then turned this essentially secular ritual into an eminently 'canonical' public confession that would justify the bishop's deposition.[88] Praetextatus had been accused of theft, but he confessed to being a murderer without actually being anything of the sort, for he merely

---

[86] The trial occupies one of Gregory's longest chapters: *Historiae* V, c. 18, pp. 216–225. I cannot do justice to the many complications of this text, which should be read and analysed in conjunction with Gregory's apologetic and equally extensive chapter about his own trial (*Historiae* V, c. 49, pp. 258–63). I arrived at conclusions roughly similar to those of Ph. Buc, who in his forthcoming book *The Dangers of Ritual* (Princeton UP) will discuss Praetextatus' trial more extensively than I can do here. I am grateful to Philippe Buc for sending me the relevant chapter.

[87] Gregory, *Historiae* V, c. 18, p. 222: *Cumque haec alterceratio altius tolleretur, Praetextatus episcopus, prostratus solo, ait: 'Peccavi in caelo et coram te [Luc. 15, 18], o rex misericorissime; ego sum homicida nefandus; ego te interficere et filio tuo in solio tuo erigere'. Haec eo dicente, prosternitur rex coram pedibus sacerdotum, dicens: 'Audite, o piissime sacerdotes, reum crimen exsecrabile confitentem'. Cumque nos flentes regem elevassemus a solo, iussit eum basilicam egredi.*

[88] About secular and ecclesiastical rituals of begging for pardon in the tenth and eleventh centuries, see G. Koziol, *Begging for Pardon and Favor. Ritual and Political Order in Early Medieval France* (Ithaca, N.Y., 1992). Praetextatus' plea for royal pardon is reminiscent of what would come to be called *harmiscara* in Carolingian sources; about *harmiscara*, see De Jong, "Humility and power", with references to other literature. Chilperic himself put pressure on the bishops by humiliating himself, borrowing a clerical gesture of humiliation and thus totally upsetting the right order according to which a king should be 'high' instead of 'low'. Similar tactics would be used extensively in the humiliation of saints, a ritual common in the eleventh and twelfth centuries. Cf. P.J. Geary, "Humiliation of saints", P.J. Geary, *Living with the Dead in the Middle Ages* (Ithaca, N.Y./London, 1994), pp. 95–115.

owned up to the intention to kill the king. Gregory' version of the events had a central message: whenever kings encroached upon the bishops' territory, they were bound to fail. This point is driven home in the sequel to Praetextatus' confession. Chilperic sent the gathering a book of *canones* with four new pages inserted stating that a bishop convicted of murder, adultery or perjury should be expelled from his bishopric.[89] The king erred on three counts. Good *canones* were ancient, not new; the text cited was not relevant to the theft Praetextatus' had been accused of, and only partly to his strange confession to intended murder; finally, a canon singling out a bishop for deposition in the case of adultery, perjury or murder was unheard of. Nevertheless, the bishops dropped their unfortunate colleague like a hot brick. The king then demanded an unorthodox penitential ritual that would suit the culprit's public confession: Praetacxtus was to have his tunic rent, or, alternatively, Psalm 108 containing the maledictions against Judas Iscariot should be read over his head.[90] This was not a penitential psalm, but an extremely vengeful one, containing the useful phrase 'let another have his bishopric'.[91] The rent tunic was double-edged as well, for it alluded not only to Old Testament gestures of penance, but also to Christs' *tunica* which was *not* rent by the soldiers at the Cross.[92] Moreover, the king violated

---

[89] Gregory, *Historiae* V, c. 18, pp. 222–223: *Ipse vero ad metatum discessit, transmittens librum canonum, in quo erat quaternio novus adnixus, habens canones quasi apostolicus, contintentes haec:"Episcopus in homicidio, adulterio et periurio depraehensus, a sacerdotio divellatur'*. Krusch (ibid., p. 223, n. 1) thought that Gregory inaccurately cited an apostolic canon from the collection of Dionysius Exiguus Cf. *Canones qui dicuntur apostolorum collectionis Dionysianae*, c. 25, *Ecclesiase occidentalis monumenta iuris antiquissima* I, ed. C.H. Turner (Oxford, 1939), p. 18: *Episcopus aut presbyter aut diaconus, qui in fornicatione aut periurio aut furto captus est, deponatur, non tamen communione privetur.* This seems unlikely, for the crucial addition '*non tamen communione privetur*' is omitted by Gregory. Futhermore, he calls the royal additions '*quasi apostolicus*'; most unusually, it only mentions a bishop losing his *sacerdotium*, not other clerics in higher orders.

[90] Gregory, *Historiae* V, c. 18: *His ita gestis, petiit rex, ut aut tonicam eius scinderetur aut centesimus octavus psalmus, qui maledictionibus Scarioticas continet, super caput eius recitaretur aut certe iudicium contra eum scriberetur, ne in perpetuo communicaret.*

[91] '*Et episcopatum eius accipiat alter*' (Ps. 108, 8). For the connection with Judas, see Acts 1, 20. The Council of Tours (c. 25, CCSL 148A, pp. 192–193) ordered this psalm to be chanted against the 'slayers of the poor'; cf. B.H. Rosenwein, *Negotiating Space. Power, Restraint and Privileges of Immunity in Early Medieval Europe* (Ithaca, N.Y, 1999), p. 43; for its use in a monastic (and later) context, see L.K. Little, *Benedictine Maledictions: Liturgical Cursing in Romanesque France* (Ithaca, N.Y., 1993), pp. 63–64. The penitential psalms: 6, 31, 37, 50, 101, 129 and 142.

[92] For the tearing of clothes as a gesture of penance, see Job. 1, 20, II Reg. 3, 31; about Christ's indivisible tunic, Joh. 19, 23–24; Ps. 19, 24. In patristic exegesis Christ's tunic often signified the unity of the Church.

canonical tradition by ordering a written verdict banning Praetextatus perpetually from communion.[93] Inserting himself into his own
narrative, Gregory protested, for Chilperic had promised him to do
nothing that was contrary to the *canones*, but all to no avail. Praetextatus ended up as an exile on the Isle of Jersey—until Chilperic
died, that is. Then the bishop returned to his see and set out to
Paris to plead his case before King Guntram, the new ruler. There
he found himself up against his old foe Queen Fredegund, who maintained that Praetextatus had been deposed by forty-five bishops and
therefore could not be restored to office. But the bishop of Paris
prevented another council from meeting and firmly told the king
that Praetextatus had been sentenced to do penance, not to be completely removed from his bishopric. So Guntram, more amenable to
episcopal advice than his predecessor, invited Praetextatus to dinner
and all was well again.[94]

Such scenes were certainly dramatic, but were they necessarily
'sub-Roman'? As in the case of Contumeliosus, the 'publicity' of confession is an important element in Gregory's tales of episcopal penance.
The council of Mâcon (583–585) excommunicated bishop Ursicinus
of Cahors for having publicly confessed his aid to the rebel Gun-
dovald and imposed a penance on him. For three years he was forbidden to cut his hair or beard, take meat and wine or perform any
liturgical actions, but otherwise he could carry on with the administration of his diocese as usual.[95] The fact the bishop performed his
penance *in situ* and in full view of his flock mirrored his public confession. Chilperic tricked Praetextatus in a public admission of guilt
and added to the effect by prostrating himself as well, loudly proclaiming the bishop's guilt. The open avowal of guilt merited a public penance according to ancient and authoritative canonical texts,
moving the ball firmly into the episcopal court—or into the king's?
This was the issue highlighted by Gregory's narrative about Praetextatus. In other respects as well, Chilperic was a king who caused
unease by moving into episcopal territory: he published a theologi-

---

[93] See above, n. 92.
[94] Gregory, *Historiae* VII, c. 16, pp. 337–338.
[95] Gregory, *Historiae* VIII, c. 20, p. 386: *Ursicinus Cadurcensis episcopus excommuni-
catur, pro eo quod Gundovaldum excepisse publice est confessus, accepto huiusmodi placito, ut,
paenitentiam tribus annis agens, neque capillum, neque barbam tonderet, vino et carnibus abstineret,
missas* celebrare, *clericos ordinare, aecclesiasque et crisma benedicere, eulogias dare paenitus non
auderet, utilitas tamen ecclesiae per eius ordinationem, sicut solita erat, omnino exerceretur.*

cal treatise, wrote bad poetry, and added four Greek letters to the Latin alphabet.[96] All this leads up to Gregory's apologetic report on what must have been one of the more traumatic events in his life: his trial for treason and calumny by the same King Chilperic.[97] As is clear from the story about Salonius and Sagittarius, kings sending bishops off to atone in a monastery did not necessarily meet with episcopal disapproval; in fact, Gregory's colleagues seem to have gone along happily with Chilperic's efforts to get Praetextatus deposed. Yet the domain of public penance was fraught with contention and uncertainty, precisely because it was an instrument of public power and *correctio*, wielded by kings and bishops alike. In the course of the seventh century the 'political' version of public penance only gained in importance, with royal opponents being exiled to royal monasteries.

During the political turbulence of the 670s, it was Luxeuil, the supposed harbinger of 'private penance', that served as a place of exile for two eminently public penitents: bishop Leudegar of Autun and the *maior domus* Ebroin. There were good reasons for this. Luxeuil was a royal monastery, and furthermore, it was a penitential community.

The reputation of its founder as a penitential innovator has been firmly established by Jonas of Bobbio. In his Life of Columbanus Jonas painted the bleak scene found by Columbanus on his arrival in'the Gauls'. Due to the devastation of foreign invasions or the negligence of ecclesiastical leadership 'there still remained some Christian faith, but the medication of penance and the love of mortification were hardly to be found there, or only in a few places'.[98] Jonas's rather evasive language in itself (*vix vel paucis ... locis*) speaks against taking these sentences at face value, and the same goes for his vague reference to the causes of penitential decline. This was a hagiographer singing the praises of his saint some forty years after the event[99]

---

[96] Gregory, *Historiae* V, c. 44, pp. 252–4.

[97] Gregory, *Historiae* V, c. 49, pp. 260–2.

[98] Jonas of Bobbio, *Vita Columbani* I, c. 5, ed. B. Krusch, MGH SSRM IV, p. 71: *A Brittannicis ergo sinibus progressi, ad Gallias tendunt, ubi tunc vel ob frequentia hostium externorum vel negligentia praesulum religionis virtus pena abolita habebatur. Fides tantum manebat christiana, nam penitentiae medicamenta et mortificationis amor vix vel paucis in ea repperiebatur locis.*

[99] The Life of Columbanus was probably written between 639 and 643; about this text, see I.N. Wood, "The Vita Columbani and Merovingian hagiography", *Peritia* 1 (1982), pp. 63–80; I.N. Wood, *The Merovingian Kingdoms* (450–751) (London, 1994), pp. 184–197.

with the aid of a string of *topoi*. Writing about 'medication of penance and the love of mortification' (*paenitentiae medicamentae et morificationis amor*) that had virtually disappeared, Jonas linked two themes that had long been the business of monks, nuns and others who had 'converted' to penance. Whenever Jonas spoke of the *medicamenta* (or, alternatively, *fomenta*) of penance, he situated these firmly within a monastic context. His famous story about the explosive growth of Luxeuil is about people flocking from everywhere to 'the medication of penance' and the monastery becoming too small to hold all these people with their different religious ways of life (*conversatio*).[100] Given that Columbanus founded a new monastery to accommodate all those seeking the *medicamenta paenitentiae*, there can be little doubt what Jonas had in mind: this medication was to be found within the monastic confines.

Those in search of a penitential revolution seem to overlook the many traditional elements in so-called 'Columbanian' hagiography and monastic rules. Jonas's one mention of daily confession[101] pales into insignificance compared with his interest in 'emergency penance' in the case of impending death. Mortally ill, the rebellious monk Roccolenus of Bobbio sought the aid of his abbot to ward off eternal damnation by 'the medication of penance'. His fellow rebels, however, 'ignoring the opportunity of penance given to them' (*datum locum paenitentiae contempserunt*) had to die without this consolation.[102] The young nun Deurechilda, who had converted to Faremoutiers together with her sinful mother, performed a more worthy deathbed penance. The entire community watched in silence while the abbess administered the *digna medicamenta paenitentia* to Deurechilda. By her exemplary life and deathbed penance, she managed to save her mother, who gained salvation after only 40 days before following her daughter into death.[103] The theme of this story is a familiar one. The 'good death' of those prepared well in advance was preferable over the penance of sinners who had left it too late,[104] but any penance, however belated, was better than none at all.

---

[100] Jonas, *Vita Columbani* I, c. 10, p. 76.

[101] Jonas, *Vita Columbani* II, c. 19, pp. 138–139.

[102] Jonas, *Vita Columbani* II, c. 1, p. 114. This is most likely the traditional expression based on Job 24, 23; see above, n. 21.

[103] Jonas, *Vita Columbani* II, c. 13, pp. 133–134.

[104] For another example of a dramatic and very public deathbed penance within a monastic context, see the Life of Amatus, abbot of Remiremont: *Vita Amati* c. 11, ed. B. Krusch, MGH SSRM IV, pp. 219–220.

In Jonas's Life of Columbanus the practice of frequent confession remains embedded in a solid fabric of more traditional forms of monastic atonement. The same holds true for the monastic rules associated with Columbanus. The rule for women ascribed to Walde-bert was equally heavily indebted, if not more, to older traditions of public confession and exclusion. The author clearly envisaged some-thing like an order of penitents within a monastic setting. A nun returning to the monastery after having fled, fearing eternal judge-ment, should be readmitted after having performed a penance; if she ran off twice or thrice, she was to remain *in extremo loco inter paenitentes*, to be examined carefully until she seemed to be on an even keel again.[105] Nuns who had sinned gravely were forbidden to attend the office with their sisters. They had to 'sing the office secretly in a different oratory'. Once finished, they had to await the others at the entrance of the main church of the convent, prostrating them-selves when the congregation filed out and asking them for their prayers, as public penitents had done for centuries. When this Rule stipulates that nuns speaking to the excommunicated should be sub-jected to a 'regular penance' (*si qua transgressa hanc regulam fuerit, reg-ulari poenitentiae subjacebit*),[106] there is no reason to assume that it necessarily refers to a 'punishment according to the penitential rules or books of penance the monastery had at its disposal'.[107] There was nothing new in such monastic rituals of public exclusion, and nei-ther is there any sign that they were disappearing as a result of a 'Columbanian' penitential revolution.[108]

Epilogue

Unsurprisingly, the Merovingian episcopate remained oblivious to the 'triumphant migration of private penance'. As one historian noted

---

[105] [Waldebert], *Regula cuiusdam patris ad virgines*, c. 21, PL 88, col. 1068.

[106] *Regula cuiusdam patris* c. 19, PL 88, col. 1067.

[107] Gisela Muschiol, *Famula Dei. Zur Liturgie im merowingischen Frauenklöstern*, (Beiträge zur Geschichte des alten Mönchtums und des Benediktinertums 42) (Münster, 1994), p. 230. Elsewhere (p. 248) Muschiol rightly observes that such monastic varieties of public exclusion followed a pattern similar to the 'canonical' penance practised in the outside world.

[108] Cf. Donatus of Besançon, *Regula ad virgines* c. 13, ed. A. de Vogüé, *Benedictina* 78 (1978), p. 258, following the Regula Benedicti; Caesarius of Arles, *Regula ad vir-gines* c. 34. ed. De Vogüé, pp. 214–6 [Waldebert], *Regula cuiusdam patris ad virgines* c. 19, PL 88, col. 1067.

early on, 'if Columbanus was doing something new and something
which undermined episcopal authority, it is strange that there is no
hint of opposition to this from the Merovingian bishops . . .'.[109] But
is the idea of monks posing a threat to episcopal authority not an
a-priori assumption, just like the idea that Columbanus was Irish, and
therefore an innovator?[110] This is not the place for a detailed discussion of the development of what has come to be called 'private'
or 'tariffed' penance and its relation to Irish and Anglo-Saxon monasticism. Research on this topic has flourished in the past decades,
challenging the traditional view that private penance was an automatic extension of monastic practice, insular and otherwise, to the
laity and secular clergy.[111] Yet for all the progress made, these sophisticated discussions continue to be dominated by the Grand Narrative of the history of penance. The crucial questions revolve around
a series of dichotomies: monastic versus lay penance, 'tariffed' penance
versus public varieties thereof, or canonical penance versus penitential practices 'without any juridical relevance'.[112] In other words, the
issue at stake is still whether penance was 'sacramental' or 'official'—
that is, administered by a bishop or a priest. In the eyes of modern scholars, internal monastic penance does not qualify as such, for
here it was the abbot or abbess or their representative who heard
the confession and imposed a penance. Things only become really
interesting—that is, 'sacramental'—if priests enter upon the scene,
regularly meting out penance to the laity. Yet the earliest hagiographical witness to something resembling frequent confession and
penance among the laity concerns an abbess: Bertila (d. 705/13)
attracted Chelles' *familia* and 'its very own neighbours' to the benefits
of communion, for which they should prepare by confession and
penance.[113]

---

[109] I.N. Wood, "The *Vita Columbani* and Merovingian hagiography", p. 73.

[110] For a critical and inspiring assessment of Columbanian myths concerning
immunity and exemption, see Rosenwein, *Negotiating Space*, pp. 59–73.

[111] For an excellent survey, see L. Körntgen, *Studien zu den Quellen der Frühmittelalterliche Bußbücher*, (Qellen und Forschungen zum Recht im Mittelalter 7) (Sigmaringen, 1993), pp. 50–86, esp. pp. 64–66. For a recent discussion of the diffusion
of penance in the lay world which is solidly based on manucript evidence, cf. Meens
"The Frequency and Nature of Early Medieval Penance", pp. 35–61.

[112] Körntgen, *Studien*, pp. 66–72; cf. ibid., p. 67, about the prayer for penitents
'ohne Kirchenrechtlichte Relevanz', with reference to Poschmann, *Die abendländische
Kirchenbuße*, pp. 237–239.

[113] *Vita Bertilae*, c. 6, ed. W. Levison, MGH SSRM VI, p. 106: *Familiam quoque
monasterii sive vicinos propinquos per sanctam communionem attrahebat, ut, datis confessionibus,*

The opposition between internal penitential practice in the monastic domain on the one hand, and 'official' penance in the world outside on the other, seems both artificial and anachronistic. Throughout Late Antiquity and the early Middle Ages, monasteries were the powerhouses of penance *par excellence*. The impact of monastic penance on the world outside did not begin with Columbanus, nor were religious communities immune to the influence of episcopal rituals of public penance. In these experimental gardens new varieties of atonement were developed, but these existed side by side with older traditions of public exclusion. Outside the monastic confines, bishops continued to legislate about public penance.[114] At the Council of Chalon-sur-Saône (647–653), they expressed their unanimous view that penance was necessary to save one's soul, and that they should be the ones to impose it. They also sent a letter to Bishop Theudorius of Arles telling him they were deeply shocked at the rumours of his indecent life, and also at the document in which he had publicised his profession of penance. Surely Theudorius had also read that such an action was incompatible with the exercise of episcopal duties?[115] They probably expected their errant colleague to retire to a monastery, as penitent bishops had done for centuries.

Instead of concentrating on the decline of an episcopal public penance and the spread of a monastic 'private' alternative, it would be worth investigating the extent to which monastic communities throughout the seventh and eighth centuries were instrumental in transmitting traditions of and knowledge about episcopal rituals of public penance. Did they help to shape the very notion of a properly 'canonical' *paenitentia publica* cherished by Carolingian reform-minded bishops?

---

paenitentiam pro peccatis suis agerent'. Cf. L. van der Essen, "Bertila", *Dictionnaire d'Histoire et de Géographie Ecclésiastique* 8 (1935), cols. 1004–1005.

[114] Council of Clichy (a. 626–627), c. 10, CCSL 148A, p. 293: *Si quis infra prescriptum canone gradum incestuoso ordine cum his personis, quibus a diuinis regulis prohibitum est, coniunx est, usquequo paenitentiam sequestratione testentur, utrique communione priuentur et neque in palatio habere militiam neque in* forum *agendarum causarum licentiam non habebunt.* By the ninth century incest had become a particularly public crime, and therefore liable to a *paenitentia publica*; cf. De Jong, "What was *public*' about public penance', pp. 898–900; eadem, 'An unsolved riddle: early medieval incest legislation', ed. I. Wood, *The Franks and Alamanni in the Merovingian period: an ethnographic perspective,* (Studies in Historical Archaeoethnology 3) (Woodbridge, 1998), pp. 107–140.

[115] Council of Chalon (647–653), CCSL 148A, p. 310: *Unde nos credimus etiam legisse necnon paenitus ignoramus, quod, qui publice penitentia profiteretur, episcopale cathedra nec tenere nec regere potest.*

After all, the earliest *ordo* of public penance, once held to be ancient
and Roman, originated in Northern Gaul and was copied around
750 by nuns from Chelles or Jouarre.[116] Not long before, the monastery
of Corbie produced a new edition of a canonical collection (the *Vetus
Gallica*), adding a systematic section with older *canones* concerning
public penance.[117] Apparently eighth-century monks and nuns remained
keenly interested in the ancient and venerable tradition of episcopal
paenitentia publica. When Jonas of Orléans looked back nostalgically
at penance in the 'earliest days of our religion', this past was less
distant than he suggested. His ideal of droves of public penitents
participating in dramatic group rituals orchestrated by bishops proves
more elusive than either Jonas or later historians imagined it to be,
at least as an 'early Christian' phenomenon. Yet monasteries, with
their long and varied tradition of penance, public and otherwise,
provided Carolingian rulers with a 'model for Empire'.[118] This rested
on the crucial notion that the sins of individuals tainted the whole
Christian community (*ecclesia*), be it a monastery or a Christian realm,
and that notorious sins which had perturbed the entire *ecclesia* should
be atoned for by an equally public satisfaction. By this time, bishops shared public penance as an instrument of discipline with secular rulers. Powerful secular opponents were exiled to royal monasteries
to do penance for their political—and therefore public—sins, joining those who had converted less spectacularly to a lifetime of penance.
As in the old days, the truly public sinners were those with a reputation that mattered. Carolingian bishops who perceived and presented themselves as recapturing a distant canonical past, battling
against a heritage of pervasive decline, are an entirely different matter altogether.[119]

---

[116] See above, n. 25.

[117] H. Mordek, *Kirchenrecht und Reform im Frankenreich. Die Collectio Vetus Gallica, die
älteste systematische Kanonnessammlung des Fränkischen Gallien*, (Beiträge zur Geschichte
und Quellenkunde des Mittelalters 1) (Berlin/New York, 1975), pp. 86–92, 214–7,
597–613. Mordek (p. 86) suggests that this revision originated in the second quarter of the eighth century.

[118] Th.F.X. Noble, "The monastic ideal as a model for empire: the case of Louis
the Pious", *Revue Bénédictine* 86 (1976), pp. 235–250.

[119] I am greatly indebted to Rosamond McKitterick and Jinty Nelson; their sup-
portive criticism of earlier drafts of this chapter. Philippe Buc, Fred Paxton and
Barbara Rosenwein kindly read the penultimate draft and offered helpful comments.
I rewrote this chapter during a sabbatical year in the autumn of 1998 in Trinity
College, Cambridge. I would like to express my gratitude to the Master and Fel-
lows of the College for providing me with an ideal environment for research.

BIBLIOGRAPHY

Primary sources

Ambrose, *De obitu Theodosii*, ed. O. Faller, CSEL 73 (Vienna, 1955), pp. 369–401.
Ambrose, *De paenitentia*, II, ed. R. Gryson, S.C. 179 (Paris, 1971).
Augustine, *De civitate Dei*, I, ed. B. Dombart and A. Kalb, CCSL 47–48 (Turnhout, 1955).
——, *Sermones*, ed. S. Poque, *Augustin d'Hippone, Sermons pour la Paque*, S.C. 116 (Paris, 1966).
Avitus of Vienne, *Epistolae*, no. 4, ed. R. Peiper, MGH A A VI/2.
Caesarius of Arles, *Sermones*, ed. M.-J. Delage, *Césaire d'Arles, Sermons au Peuple*, III, S.C. 330 (Paris, 1986).
S. Caesarii Arelatensis sermones, ed. G. Morin, *Sancti Caesarii opera omnia* I (Maredsous, 1937).
Caesarius of Arles, *Regula ad virgines*, ed. A. de Vogüé and J. Courreau, *Césaire, Oeuvres monastiques* I, S.C. 345 (Paris, 1988).
John Cassian, *De institutione coenobiorum*, ed. J.-C. Guy, *Jean Cassien, Institutions cénobitiques*, S.C. 109 (Paris, 1965).
Cassiodorii Epihanii Historia Ecclesiae Tripartita, ed. W. Jacob and R. Hanslik, CSEL 71 (Vienna, 1952).
Conciliae Africae, A. 345-A. 525, ed. C. Munier, CCSL 149 (Turnhout, 1974).
Concilia Galliae, A. 314-A. 506, ed. C. Munier, CCSL 148 (Turnhout, 1963).
Concilia Galliae A. 511-A. 695, ed. C. De Clercq, CSSL 148A (Turnhout, 1963).
Conciliorum Oecumenicorum Decreta, eds. J. Alberigo, J.A. Dossetti, P.P. Joannou, C. Leonardi, P. Prodi (Turnhout, 1973).
Concilios visigóticos e hispano-romanos, ed. J. Vives (Barcelona/Madrid, 1963).
Donatus of Besançon, *Regula ad virgines*, ed. A. de Vogüé, *Benedictina* 78 (1978), pp. 237–313.
Ecclesiae occidentalis monumenta iuris antiquissima I, ed. C.H. Turner (Oxford, 1939).
Gaudemet, J. and B. Basdevant, *Les canons des conciles Mérovingiens (V^e–VIIe siècles. Texte Latin de l'édition C. De Clercq. Introductions, traduction et notes*, vol. 1, S.C. 353 (Paris, 1989).
Gennadius, *De ecclesiasticis dogmatibus*, ed. C.H. Turner, *Journal of Theological Studies* 7 (1906), pp. 78–99.
Gregory of Tours, *Historiae*, ed. B. Krusch, MGH SSRM I/1.
Gregory of Tours, *De virtutibus sancti Martini*, ed. B. Krusch, MGH SSRM I, pp. 584–566.
Gregory of Tours, *Vitae patrum*, ed. B. Krusch, MGH SSRM I, pp. 661–774.
Inscripciones Cristianas de la España Romana y Visigoda, 2nd edition, ed. J. Vives (Barcelona, 1969).
Inscriptions Chrétiennes de la Gaule antérieures au VIIIe siècle, ed. E. Le Blant, 2 vols. (Paris, 1856/1865).
Jerome, *Epistolae*, 4 vols., ed. I. Hilberg, CSEL 54–57 (Vienna/Leipzig, 1910–1921).
Jonas of Bobbio, *Vita Columbani abbatis discipulorumque eius*, ed. B. Krusch, MGH SSRM IV, pp. 61–152.
Jonas of Orléans, *De institutione laicali*, I, c. 10, PL 106, cols. 121–278.
Leo I, *Epistolae*, PL 54, cols. 593–1218.
Liber sacramentarium Romanae Aecclesiae ordines anni circuli (Sacramentarium Gelasianum), ed. L.C. Mohlberg, with L. Eizenhöfer and O. Siffring (Rome, 1960).
Paulinus of Milan, *Vita Ambrosii*, PL 14, cols. 27–46.
Recueil des Inscriptions Chrétiennes de la Gaule antérieures á la Renaissance carolingienne, vol. 15, Viennoise du Nord, ed. F. Descombes (Paris, 1986).
Regula Benedicti, ed. A. de Vogüé and J. Neufville, *La Règle de Saint Benoit*, S.C. 181–186 (Paris, 1971–1972).

Sozomen, *Historia ecclesiastica* VII, c. 16, PG 67, cols. 1461–1462.
Salvian of Marseille, *Epistulae*, ed. G. Lagarrigue, *Salvien de Marseille, Oeuvres*, I, S.C. 176 (Paris, 1971), pp. 76–132.
Salvian of Marseille, *De gubernatione Dei*, ed. G. Lagarrigue, *Salvien de Marseille, Oeuvres*, vol. 1, S.C. 220 (Paris, 1975), pp. 96–526.
Tertullian, *De Paenitentia*, CCSL 1 (Turnhout, 1954), pp. 321–340.
Vita Bertilae, ed. W. Levison, MGH SRM VI, pp. 101–109.
[Waldebert], *Regula cuiusdam patris ad virgines*, Migne PL 88, cols. 1053–1070.

Secondary sources

Amman, E., "Pénitence", *Dictionnaire de Théologie Catholique* 12 (Paris, 1933) cols. 722–948.
Bischoff, B., "Die Kölner Nonnenhandschriften und das Scriptorium von Chelles", B. Bischoff, *Mittelalterliche Studien* I (Stuttgart, 1965), pp. 17–35.
Breukelaar, A.H.B., *Historiography and episcopal authority in sixth-century Gaul. The Histories of Gregory of Tours interpreted in their historical context* (Göttingen, 1994).
Brown, P., *The Rise of Western Christendom. Triumph and Diversity, AD 200–1000* (Cambridge, Ma./Oxford, 1996).
———, "Vers la naissance du Purgatoire, Amnistie et pénitence dans le christianisme occidental de l'Antiquité tardive au Haut Moyen Age", *Annales HSS* 52 (1997), pp. 1247–1261.
Consilino, F.E., "Teodosio e il ruolo del principe cristiano dal *De obitu* di Ambrogio alle storie ecclesiastiche", *Cristianesimo nella storia: Richerche storiche, esegetiche, teologiche* 15 (1994), pp. 257–277.
Essen, L. van der, "Bertila", *Dictionnaire d'Histoire et de Géographie Ecclésiastique* 8 (Paris, 1935), cols. 1004–1005.
Fitzgerald, A., *Conversion through Penance in the Italian Church of the IVth and Vth Centuries* (Lewinston, 1988).
Galtier, P., "Les canons pénitentiels de Nicée", *Gregorianum* 29 (1948), pp. 288–294.
Geary, P.J., "Humiliation of saints", P.J. Geary, *Living with the Dead in the Middle Ages* (Ithaca, N.Y./London, 1994), pp. 95–115.
Goffart, W., *The Narrators of Barbarian History (AD 550–800): Jordanes, Gregory of Tours, Bede, Paul the Deacon* (Princeton, 1988).
Griffe, E., "Un example de pénitence publique au Ve siècle", *Bulletin de la littérature ecclésiastique* (1958), pp. 170–175.
Heinzelmann, M., *Gregor von Tours (538–594). "Zehn Bücher Geschichte". Historiographie und Gesellschaftskonzept im 6. Jahrhundert* (Darmstadt, 1994).
Hen, Y., "The liturgy of Willibrord", *Anglo-Saxon England* 26 (1997), pp. 41–61.
Jong, M. de, "Power and humility in Carolingian society: the penance of Louis de Pious", *Early Medieval Europe* 1 (1992), pp. 29–52.
———, *In Samuel's Image. Child Oblation in the Early Medieval West* (New York/Leiden/Cologne, 1996).
———, "What was *public* about public penance? *Paenitentia publica* and justice in the Carolingian world", *La Giustizia ne'll Alto Medioevo (secoli IX–XI)* II, (Settimane di studio 42) (Spoleto, 1997), pp. 863–902.
———, "*Imitatio morum*. The cloister and clerical purity in the Carolingian world", *Medieval Purity and Piety. Essays on Celibacy and Reform*, ed M. Frassetto (New York, 1998), pp. 49–80.
———, "An unsolved riddle: early medieval incest legislation", *The Franks and Alamanni in the Merovingian period: an ethnographic perspective*, ed. I.N. Wood (Studies in Historical Archaeoethnology 3) (Woodbridge, 1998), pp. 107–140.
Jungmann, J.A., *Die lateinischen Bussriten in ihrer geschichtlichen Entwicklung* (Innsbruck, 1932).

Karpp, H., *Die Busse. Quellen zur Entstehung des altkirchlichen Busswesens*, (Traditio Christiana 1) (Zürich, 1969).

Klingshirn, W.E., *Caesarius of Arles. The Making of a Christian Community in Late Antique Gaul* (Cambridge, 1994).

König, D., *Amt und Askese. Priesteramt und Mönchtum bei den lateinischen Kirchenvätern in vorbenediktinischer Zeit*, (Regulae Benedicti Studia, Supplementa 12) (St. Ottilien, 1985).

Körntgen, L., *Studien zu den Quellen der Frühmittelalterlichen Bußbücher*. Quellen und Forschungen zum Recht im Mittelalter 7 (Sigmaringen, 1993).

Koziol, G., *Begging for Pardon and Favor. Ritual and Political Order in Early Medieval France* (Ithaca, N.Y, 1992).

Labate, A., "Sozomen", *Encyclopedia of the Ancient Church* 2 (Cambridge, 1992), p. 790.

Leyser, K., "Early medieval canon law and the beginnings of knighthood", *Institutionen, Kultur und Gesellschaft im Mittelalter*, eds. L. Fenske et al. (Sigmaringen, 1984), pp. 530–573.

Little, L.K., *Benedictine Maledictions: Liturgical Cursing in Romanesque France* (Ithaca, N.Y., 1993).

Mansfield, M.C., *The Humiliation of Sinners. Public Penance in Thirteenth-Century France* (Ithaca, N.Y/London, 1995).

McKitterick, R., "Nuns' scriptoria in England and Francia in the eighth century", *Francia* 19 (1989), pp. 1–35.

Meens, R., "The Frequency and Nature of Early Medieval Penance", *Handling Sin. Confession in the Middle Ages*, ed. P. Biler and A. Minnis (Woodbridge, 1998), pp. 35–61.

Mordek, H., *Kirchenrecht und Reform im Frankenreich. Die Collectio Vetus Gallica, die älteste systematische Kanonessammlung des Fränkischen Gallien,*. (Beiträge zur Geschichte und Quellenkunde des Mittelalters 1) (Berlin/New York, 1975).

Moreton, B., *The Eighth-Century Gelasian Sacramentary: a Study in Tradition* (Oxford, 1976).

Munier, C., *Les Statuta Ecclesiastica Antiqua* (Paris, 1960).

Murray, A., "Confession before 1215", *Transactions of the Royal Historical Society*, 6th Series, 3 (London, 1993), pp. 51–81.

Muschiol, G., *Famula Dei. Zur Liturgie im merowingischen Frauenklöstern*, Beiträge zur Geschichte des alten Mönchtums und des Benediktinertums 42 (Münster, 1994).

Nie, G. de, *Views from a many-windowed tower. Studies of imagination in the works of Gregory of Tours* (Amsterdam, 1987).

Noble, Th.F.X., "The monastic ideal as a model for empire: the case of Louis the Pious", *Revue Bénédictine* 86 (1976), pp. 235–250.

Nodes, D.J., '*De Subitanea Paenitentia* in the Letters of Faustus of Riez and Avitus of Vienne', *Recherches de Théologie Ancienne et Médiévale* 55 (1988).

Paxton, F.S., *Christianizing Death. The Creation of a Ritual Process in Early Medieval Europe* (Ithaca, N.Y/London, 1990).

Poschmann, B., *Die abendländische Kirchenbuße im Ausgang des christlichen Altertums*, Münchener Studien zur historischen Theologie 7 (München, 1928).

——, *Penance and the Anointing of the Sick* (Freiburg/New York, 1964).

Pricoco, S., "Gennadius of Marseilles", *Encyclopedia of the Early Church* 1 (Cambdridge, 1992), p. 342.

Rebillard, E., "La naissance du viatique. Se préparer á mourir en Italie et en Gaule au Vᵉ siècle", *Médiévales* 20 (1991), pp. 15–21.

——, *In hora mortis. . . . volution de la pastorale chrétienne de la mort aux IVᵉ et Vᵉ siècles* (Rome, 1994).

Rosenwein, B.H., *Negotiating Space. Power, Restraint and Privileges of Immunity in Early Medieval Europe* (Ithaca, N.Y., 1999).

Saint-Roch, P., *La pénitence dans les conciles et les letters des papes des origines á la mort de Grégoire le Grand* (Vatican City, 1991).

Van Dam, R., *Saints and their miracles in Late Antique Gaul* (Princeton, 1993).

Veyne, P., *L'Inventaire des différences. Leçon inaugurale au Collège de France* (Paris, 1976).

Vogel, C., *La discipline pénitentielle en Gaule des origines á la fin du VIIe siècle* (Paris, 1952).

———, *Le pécheur et la pénitence dans l'église Ancienne* (Paris, 1966).

———, *Le pécheur et la pénitence au Moyen Age* (Paris, 1969).

———, *Medieval Liturgy. An Introduction to the Sources* (Washington, 1986).

———, "Pénitence", *Encyclopedia of the Early Church* (Cambridge, 1992), pp. 667–668.

Wickham, C.J., *Gossip and resistance among the medieval peasantry* (Birmingham, 1995 inaugural lecture).

Wood, I.N., "The Vita Columbani and Merovingian hagiography", *Peritia* 1 (1982), pp. 63–80.

———, "The secret histories of Gregory of Tours", *Revue Belge de Philologie et d'Histoire* 71 (1993), pp. 253–270.

———, *The Merovingian Kingdoms, 450–751* (London, 1994).

———, "Incest, law and the Bible in sixth-century Gaul", *Early Medieval Europe* 7 (1998), pp. 291–304.

THE DEAD AND THEIR GIFTS. THE WILL OF EBERHARD, COUNT OF FRIULI, AND HIS WIFE GISELA, DAUGHTER OF LOUIS THE PIOUS (863–864)[§]

Christina La Rocca* and Luigi Provero**

> Heirlooms have become so, not that the future owners of them may be assured of so much wealth, but that the son or grandson or descendant may enjoy the satisfaction which is derived from saying, my father or my grandfather sat in that chair, or looked as he now looks in that picture, or was graced by wearing on his breast that very ornament which you now see lying beneath the glass.
>
> (A. Trollope, The Eustace Diamonds, p. 258).

1. *Wills and Death in the early Middle Ages*

The history of death has been very fashionable during the last twenty years. Rituals of death, wills and processes of interaction between the living and the dead have been the subject of a wide range of researches for every chronological period and topographical context: this success was so widespread as to persuade Michel Vovelle that the history of death was no longer "un jardin à la française dont les modernistes avaient le monopole",[1] but had been transformed into a general subject for the historians of every period. Interest now centred on capturing, through people's recorded thoughts and actions as they contemplated the end of their life and through the documents associated with these, valuable evidence for religious, cultural and economic behaviour directed not only to death but—and especially—to life. Many sources have been investigated from this point

---

[§] This research has developed together by both authors. CLR has been primarily responsible for sections 1, 2, 3.2; and LP for sections 3.1., 4.1, 4.3, 4.4.; while sections 4.2 and 5 have been jointly written.

* University of Padua

** University of Turin

[1] M. Vovelle, "Encore la mort: un peu plus qu'une mode?", *Annales E.S.C.* 37 (1982), pp. 276–287, with the quotation at 277: "A French-style garden monopolised by modernists."

of view: funeral-rituals of Roman emperors and aristocrats have proved significant in reassessing family power and imperial succession,[2] changes in liturgy during the Carolingian period have been studied in relation to the christianisation of death,[3] burial practices and the topographical distribution of graves have been examined as important ways in which family prestige and power were established.[4]

Wills remain, neverthless, the fundamental type of source for studying changing attitudes towards death; and late medieval and modern historians have paid particular attention to written testaments for the rich and varied information they offer. The abundance of wills surviving from the thirteenth century onwards has encouraged a variety of approaches: from a large number of quantitative studies on wealth distribution, to a series of studies aimed at understanding qualitative changes in religious attitudes coinciding with the advent of new religious institutions in the twelfth and thirteenth centuries.[5]

Only the early middle ages have been relatively excluded from this historiographically fashionable concern with death, despite the fact that the study of early medieval burial practices was the basis

---

[2] S. Price, "From noble funerals to divine cult: the consecration of Roman Emperors", *Rituals of Royalty. Power and Ceremonial in traditional Societies*, eds. D. Cannadine and S. Price (Cambridge, 1987), pp. 56–105; J. Arce, *'Funus imperatorum'. Los funerales de los emperadores romanos* (Madrid, 1988); on roman aristocratic burial practices, see also K. Hopkins, *Death and Renewal. Sociological Studies in Roman History* 2 (Cambridge, 1983).

[3] P.A. Février, "La mort chrétienne", *Segni e riti nella chiesa altomedievale occidentale* (Spoleto, 1987) (Settimane di studio del Centro Italiano di Studi sull'alto medioevo 37), pp. 881–942; F. Paxton, *Christianizing Death. The Creation of a Ritual Process in Early Medieval Europe* (Ithaca and London, 1990).

[4] I. Morris, *Burials and ancient Society. The Rise of the Greek City-State* (Cambridge, 1987); L. Headeger, *Iron-Age Societies* (Oxford and Cambridge (Mass.), 1992); *Death in Towns. Urban Responses to the Dying and the Dead* (Leicester London New York, 1992).

[5] Many examples of both tendencies can be quoted: an example of quantitative study is S. Epstein, *Wills and Wealth in Medieval Genoa (1150–1250)* (Cambridge and London, 1984); examples of a use of wills as sources for change in religious behaviour are: A. Rigon, "Orientamenti religiosi e pratica testamentaria a Padova nei secoli XII–XIV (prime ricerche)", *'Nolens intestatus decedere'. Il testamento come fonte della storia religiosa e sociale* (Perugia, 1985), pp. 40–53, V. Pasche, *"Pour le salut de mon ame". Les Lausannois face à la mort (XIV⁰ siècle)* (Lausanne, 1989); A. Rigon, "I testamenti come atti di religiosità pauperistica", *La conversione alla povertà nell'Italia dei secoli XII–XIV* (Spoleto, 1991) (Atti del XXVII Convegno storico internazionale del Centro di studi sulla spiritualità medievale), pp. 391–414. For a general review of different approaches, M. Vovelle, "Les attitudes devant la mort: problèmes de méthode, approches et lectures différentes", *Annales E.S.C.* 31 (1976), pp. 120–132; M. Bertram, "Mittelalterliche Testamente. Zur Entdeckung einer Quellengattung in Italien", *Quellen und Forschungen aus italienischen Archiven und Bibliotheken* 68 (1988), pp. 509–544.

both for the discovery of national identities at the end of the nineteenth century and for the establishment, in most European countries, of an historical sub-discipline dealing specifically with the Middle
Ages.[6] There is certainly a problem here of sources and specialisms:
while for the period between the sixth and eighth centuries death
has been studied through archaeological evidence of furnished burials,[7] the supply of such data for the eighth and ninth centuries gradually fails. At the same time the presumed lack of written records
has discouraged historians from studying attitudes towards death during the period from the eighth to the eleventh century. Which sources
are lacking? If we stick to the legal approach, the answer is obvious: in the short 'history of wills' that precedes every late medieval
study, we find everyone underlines the juridical *hiatus* separating the
twelfth- and especially thirteenth-century will from earlier analogues:
only in the twelfth century did the rediscovery of Roman law allowed
the renaissance of the will in the forms prescribed in Roman tradition. The end of the Roman Empire had brought with it the end
of wills.[8] For late medievalists early medieval wills do not exist.

The *hiatus* thus allegedly established is the result of a merely formal break, because documents intended to determine the future in
the event of someone's death are in fact quite common during the
early Middle Ages:[9] in the words of the legal historian Amelotti,

---

[6] For a general overview: C. La Rocca, "Uno specialismo mancato. Esordi e fallimento dell'archeologia medievale italiana alla fine dell'Ottocento", *Archeologia Medievale*
20 (1993), pp. 13–43; for France: P. Périn, *La datation des tombes mérovingiennes* (Paris,
1980), pp. 5–37; for England: N. Higham, *Rome, Britain and the Anglo-Saxons* (London,
1992), pp. 2–12; for Germany: G.P. Fehring, *Einfürung in die Archäologie des Mittelalters* (Darmstadt, 1987), pp. 1–5 (English translation: The Archaeology of Medieval
Germany, an introduction, London, 1991).

[7] See, for example R. Chapman, I. Kinnes, K. Randsborg (eds.), *The Archaeology
of Death* (Cambridge, 1981).

[8] For example, on the legal side, M. Amelotti, *Il testamento romano attraverso la prassi
documentale. I. Le forme classiche di testamento* (Firenze, 1966); P. Vaccari, "Donazioni.
Diritto intermedio", *Novissimo Digesto italiano* 6 (Torino, 1971), pp. 231–233; C. Giardina, "Successioni. Diritto intermedio", *Novissimo Digesto italiano* 18 (Torino, 1971),
pp. 727–748; G. Vismara, *Scritti di storia giuridica* 6 (Milano, 1988), pp. 109–146.
The formal break in the production of testaments between the sixth century and
the twelfth is fully accepted, for example, by J. Chiffoleau, *La comptabilité de l'au-
delà. Les hommes, la mort et la religion dans la région d'Avignon à la fin du Moyen Age (vers
1320–1480)* (Rome, 1980) (Collection de l'Ecole Française de Rome 47) and
C. Piacitelli, "La carità negli atti di ultima volontà milanesi del XII secolo", *La
carità a Milano nei secoli XII–XV*, eds. M.P. Alberzoni and O. Grassi (Milano, 1989),
pp. 167–186.

[9] The formal difference between Roman and early medieval wills has been underlined by G. Spreckelmeyer, "Zur rechtlichen Funktion frühmittelalterlicher Testamente",

from the sixth century "gli atti paratestamentari soverchiano, sostituendo spesso o talora inquinando con loro clausole, l'istituto testamentario (. . .). Accentrare l'indagine su questo e ricordare marginalmente quelli significa non solo coartare tale realtà, ma rinunciare a coglierne i motivi di fondo"[10]. It would certainly be wrong to assume that from the sixth century to the twelfth aristocratic concern with preserving/maintaining the integrity of landed patrimonies and movable possessions was simply manifested by observing the law: as has been said of the Roman period too, "law was not everything. People established foundations just as they drew up wills, without the benefit of lawyers".[11] If it is true that the full, formal drawing-up of the Roman will—with its *clausolae*, the presence of seven witnesses, the revocability that could be laid down in a codicil[12]—was no longer current practice after the sixth century, it is nevertheless impossible to conclude that that early Middle Ages saw only indifference towards the destiny of family properties. Although not expressed following any strictly Roman pattern, various early medieval documentary forms can be identified, the *donatio pro anima*, the *donatio post obitum*, the *charta iudicati*, the *charta dispositionis*, through which people sought to assure the destiny of their valuable goods (land, animals, movables). Often more than one charter was used to express a person's last will,[13] and the combination of these documents concerning the disposition of possessions after death can be interpreted as an early medieval will. Thus even if the Roman structure of the Roman will was lost, what was certainly not lost was the desire to determine the future.

It would clearly be useless to study early medieval testaments merely to underline how different they are from late medieval and

---

Recht und Schrift im Mittelalter, ed. P. Classen (Sigmaringen, 1977) (Vorträge und Forschungen 23), pp. 91–113.

[10] M. Amelotti, "Testamenti ed atti paratestamentari nei papiri bizantini", *Proceedings of the Twelfth International Congress of Papirology*, ed. D.H. Samuel (Toronto, 1970), pp. 15–17.

[11] Hopkins, *Death and Renewal. Sociological Studies in Roman History*, p. 252 (pp. 235–253 on the social use of wills in classical times).

[12] Amelotti, *Il testamento romano attraverso la prassi documentaria*, I. *Le forme classiche del testamento*, pp. 18–25.

[13] For explicit declarations of this attitude, examples in *Ch.La.A.*, XXX, 60–62, n. 905 (727 September 1); 67–68, n. 906 (726–729); *Ch.La.A.*, XXVIII, 61, n. 855 (777 March 8); *Ch.La.A.*, XXVI, 48, n. 806 (763); 70–72, n. 811 (783 July); *Ch.La.A.*, XXXVII, 32, n. 1078 (781 December 3). See also the charters quoted at n. 25 below.

Roman ones: that would mean examining them only to define what they are not. We need to try out different techniques of investigation and ask different questions, because the approach (whether quantitative or qualitative) of late medieval historians is unsuitable for early medieval charters, chiefly because of their formal structure. If the most relevant aspect of late medieval wills is standardisation due to notarial intervention, the characteristic of early medieval wills is local variety: over the *longue durée* between the sixth century and the eleventh we confront a process of formation and formal experimentation intimately related to the efforts of a section of society to perpetuate its status through the continuity of its landed possessions and rights. The differences between testaments, even in their formal aspects and structure, are expressions of different local traditions and differing relationships between power and local societies. True, it is important to distinguish between the relatively common *donationes pro anima* of land and movables to ecclesiastical institutions, and the charters called *charta iudicati* or *charta dispositionis*, valid only after death, which represent in formal terms the early medieval version of the will.[14] But it is no less important to stress the formal similarities between the structures of these documentary types, especially in the first part of each document (the protocol), which makes frequent use of biblical citations bearing on the relationship between the value of a gift and salvation.[15] The transmission of goods, whether within the family or to an ecclesiastical institution, during a donor's lifetime or after his/her death, is therefore conceived as a gift that has its religious counter-gift in salvation, and its practical one in the opportunity to safeguard family property and status.

---

[14] Bertram, "Mittelalterliche Testamente. Zur Entdeckung einer Quellengattung in Italien", pp. 511–515; B. Kasten, "Erbrechtliche Verfügungen des 8. und 9. Jahrhunderts", *Zeitschrift der Savigny-Stiftung für Rechtsgeschichte-Germanistische Abteilung* 108 (1990), pp. 240–246.

[15] *CDL*, I, n. 30, (722) '*nolite thesaurizare vobis super terram, ubi furis effodiunt et furantur, sed thesaurizate vobis thesaurum in caelum, ubi fur, id est diabolus, non adpropinquat. Et iterum dicens: facite vobis amicus de mamone iniquitatis, ut cum defeceritis recipiam vos in aeterna tabernacula*". *CDL*, I, 165–171, n. 50 (730, December 1): '*Quisquis in hoc seculo, dum advivere meruerit, semper de aeterna vita cogitare et peragere videatur, ut dum venerit ad exeunte sacro Dei iudicio, de gravia sua pondera leviter possit ad vitam aeternam pertingere; quoniam in hoc seculo nulla meliora esse cognoscitur quam in Deo vivere semper'*. *CDL*, I, 229–232, n. 78 (742): '*De spe eterne vitae salutis animae remedium cogitat, qui in sanctis locis de suis rebus confer terrena, ut a Christo recipiat eterna celestia. Et ut votis meis expleatur dilectio, oblatione meam munera offero, non quantum debeo, set quantum valeo'*. *CDL*, I, 238–244, n. 82 (745): '*Rottopert vir magnificus de Grate, considerans casus umane fragilitatis et repentinam mortem*

The formal influences between *donationes pro anima* and wills become clearer when we investigate the social use of written wills during the early Middle Ages: while from the thirteenth century onwards, there was an increase in the number of people who chose to have a written will, and these people varied in social level from aristocrats to merchants or even to modest landholders, in the early middle ages the number of people who made a written will was relatively small and socially restricted to members of the aristocracy, both lay (men, women, and widows in particular) and ecclesiastical.[16] We can assume that even the decision to have a written will drawn up was at the same time a significant way of underlining social difference and specificity of life style, and an expression of a particular need on the part of the élite—the need to avoid the dispersal of land and family property entailed by the observance of customary german law, which made no difference between sons and daughters, or between legitimate and illegitimate children. The risk of land dispersal was very high and that could mean the end of aristocratic status, privileges and power.[17]

Associated with landed property was the capacity to mark and maintain social relationships and boundaries through the display of material wealth: furthermore, in a society like that of Lombard Italy, where to be an aristocrat meant to possess land (as much as possible), *status* was the object of continuous discussion and re-negotiation, through the networks created by gift-exchange, and through an ostentatious life-style.[18]

An early medieval aristocrat who made a written will intended to obtain, on the practical side, at least two different results. The first

---

venturam, previdi de rebus meis dispositionem facere vel pro anima mea iudicare, ut, cum de hoc seculo vocare iussero, michi pro sua pietate peccatorum meorum veniam condonare dignetur'.

[16] It does not seem necessary to stress the ecclesiastical influence on the structure of wills as strongly as does Spreckelmeyer, "Zur rechtlichen Funktion frühmittelalterlicher Testamente", pp. 95–98.

[17] G. Tabacco, "La connessione fra potere e possesso nel regno franco e nel regno longobardo", *I problemi dell'Occidente nel secolo* 8 (Spoleto, 1973) (Settimane di studio del Centro italiano di studi sull'alto medioevo 20), pp. 133–168.

[18] On gift-exchange: J. Parry, "The gift, the Indian gift and the 'Indian gift'", *Man* n.s. 21 (1986), pp. 453–473; A. Gurevic, "Représentations et attitudes à l'égard de la propriété pendant le haut moyen âge", *Annales E.S.C.* 27 (1972), pp. 523–547; R. Michalowski, "Le don d'amitié dans la société carolingienne et les 'Translations sanctorum'", *Hagiographie, culture et sociétés. IVᵉ–XIIᵉ siècle* (Paris, 1981), pp. 399–416. The importance of gift-exchange in early medieval society as a means of negotiation of *status* has been shown by C. Wickham, *Land and Power. Studies in Italian and European Social History. 400–1200* (London, 1994), pp. 201–226.

was the opportunity to make a written list of goods, that is to select and inventorise movable items, land and people that defined the status of the family; the second was the creation of exceptions, the ensuring of a perpetual change in the future despite the law.[19] In the tenth century, Rather bishop of Verona, could imagine talking to representative figures of the different social categories of his own day, asking them to list their status symbols. When he got to the *dives*, he listed a sequence of land, serfs and animals, together with the respect shown by society, and the possession of gold and silver objects:[20] that is, the same sort of goods as were listed in the wills. In both the uses and the needs which they typically underline, early medieval written wills were an important means of 'distinction' for local élites.[21]

The use of written wills varies considerably amongst early medieval kingdoms: while in Gaul there is a continuity in their use, the written documentation starts later elsewhere, for example, at the beginning of the eighth century for Lombard Italy, and in the ninth century for Anglo-Saxon England. It is important, however, to see the adoption of written wills as a change related to the role of death rituals in perpetuating family status. Throughout Europe, one can observe, in graves of the fifth and sixth centuries, the appearence of grave-goods including weapons and precious objects (buckles, belts, rings, and so forth): this practice has its main diffusion (in quality of objects and quantity of graves) at the beginning of the seventh century, while from the eighth century it slowly disappears. Traditional analyses—focusing especially on the initial moment of change (that is, who introduced furnished burials, and why)—linked the grave goods with the impact of the barbarians and their disappearence to the impact of christianity. Thanks to recent work, archaeologists are now more deeply aware of the social relevance of funerary rituals: these are now understood in terms of efforts made by the family of the dead person to reassert its social position, transforming the

---

[19] A. Prosperi, "Premessa", *I vivi e i morti* (Bologna, 1982) (= *Quaderni Storici* 50 (1982)), pp. 391–410.

[20] Ratherius, *Praeloquiorum libri sex*, I, XVII, ed. P.L.D. Reid (Turnhout, 1984) (Corpus Christianorum, continuatio mediaevalis 46A), 34: *'Dic rogo, in quibus rebus constant divitiae tuae? "In possessionibus" inquis "praediorum, servorum, ancillarum, equorum, boum, ceterarumque pecudum; in obsecundatione obsequentium, delectatione canum, accipitrum, habundantia vestium, utensilium, frumenti, vini et olei, armorum, argenti et auri atque gemmarum'.*

[21] We use 'distinction' in the sense of P. Bourdieu, *La distinction* (Paris, 1979).

suspension potentially caused by death into a moment of active proposition. Variations in death rituals are therefore related to the society of the living: thus in Roman times aristocratic élites consigned their fame to inscriptions and to monumental family graves, addressed to the city as the principal audience for assertions of family continuity,[22] whereas in the barbarian kingdoms death rituals were addressed to a more local community, and the dynastic memory of the individual was tied to the specific memory of the rituals of burying: rituals that left no external sign of the dead and were left, instead, to immaterial memory.

But, for our purposes, the most interesting moment of change is the disappearance of grave goods. This has often been linked with christianisation: only recently has it been suggested that change came about in the first place through the determined choice of a christian aristocracy keen to underline its difference "en choisissant d'exprimer à travers la mort l'humilité" (choosing to express humility through death).[23] But the decrease of social investment in grave goods had its counterbalance in the focussing of attention, in death rituals, on the elements which preceded and followed the funeral, chiefly through leaving a permanent testimony of the dead with the aid of the written word. Wills and written epitaphs and funerary inscriptions, and the use of precious sculpted sarcophagi,[24] refer the value and status of the dead, and of their families in the future, to a wider audience, in both time and space. By means of the legitimising value of the written word, the balance of ritual and memory shifts from the moment of burial to posterity. At this point the value of the items formerly placed in the grave to show status, also became different, because they were no longer treasured up within the grave but could be used and displayed as items possessed by a particular individual: they became precious gifts to the church, above all, or to members of the family, underlying the continuity of status and function of the family itself. Some wills mention a series of personal items (*mobilia*—a special kind of movable) as integral parts of the person making the will: the willing of these objects, whether accu-

---

[22] Hopkins, *Death and Renewal. Sociological Studies in Roman History*, pp. 207–233.

[23] B.K. Young, "Exemple aristocratique et mode funéraire dans la Gaule mérovingienne", *Annales E.S.C.* 41 (1986), pp. 79–407 (the quotation is at 381).

[24] For example, the funerary inscriptions for Lombard royal graves in Pavia: F.E. Consolino, "La poesia epigrafica pavese", *Storia di Pavia* II (Milano, 1985), pp. 137–145.

rately listed or only mentioned in general terms, together with land, constitutes a definition and transmission of *status symbols*.[25]

While Merovingian, Anglo-Saxon and Carolingian testaments have received some attention from the diplomatic and structural point of view,[26] early medieval Italy has not yet been examined from this point of view, for either the Lombard or Carolingian periods.[27] As starting point for future research, the present study will deal with a very famous will dating from the second half of the ninth century, the will of Eberhard count of Friuli and his wife Gisela. As it refers to a great man of Frankish origin settled in northen Italy, this document allows comparison to be made with the well-studied Carolingian wills of Francia[28] and exemplifies their transformation in the Italian context. Further, being made by a count and his wife, this will can be seen as a key point in the definition of a family strategy of redirecting potential developments of territorial and dynastic power in response to transformations in the role and ambitions of public officers during the controversial period of the dissolution of the Carolingian empire.

---

[25] Lombard lists of movables are generally expressed by the *formula*: '*omnem schirpas meas, pannos, usitilia, lignea, vel ferrea, ramentea, auricalca, aurum, argentos*' (*Ch.La.A.*, XXXVIII, 26, n. 1102 (786 January)). Some examples of explicit exclusion of movables from the charter *post obitum* are in *Ch.La.A.*, XL, 8–10, n. 1158 (797 May 10); 29, n. 1164 (798 March 6); 36, n. 1166 (798 June 10); 78, n. 1180 (800 February); *Ch.La.A.*, XXXIX, 78–79; n. 1145 (795 March 25); *Ch.La.A.*, XXXVIII, 78, n. 1089 (783 December 29); 26, n. 1102 (786 January); 61, n. 1114 (787 December 1); *Ch.La.A.*, XXXVI, 18, n. 1045 (773 August); 46, n. 1057 (776 August); 51, n. 1059 (777 January). A list of movables given to Ghittia *Dei ancilla* and to her daughters in 768–774 included: '*tres solidi et uno tremisse, seu et uno soldu Beneventano, duo anula aurie, uno pario (. . .), uno petio de auro, unu baltio cum banda et fibila de augento inaurato, et bracile (. . .) to argento [. . .], coclari argentei, sporuni argentei*' (*Ch.La.A.*, XXVI, 56–58, n. 808).

[26] U. Nonn, "Merowingische Testamente. Studien zum Fortleben einer römischen Urkundenform im Frankenreich", *Archiv für Diplomatik* 18 (1972), pp. 1–129; P.J. Geary, *Aristocracy in Provence. The Rhône Basin at the Dawn of the carolingian Age* (Stuttgart, 1985) (Monographien zur Geschichte des Mittelalters 31); Kasten, "Erbrechtliche Verfügungen des 8. und 9. Jahrhunderts", pp. 261–388; M. Sheehan, *The Will in Medieval England: from the Conversion of the Anglo-Saxons to the End of the thirteenth Century* (Toronto, 1969).

[27] Of the legal literature, only an old study by L. Palumbo, *Testamento romano e testamento longobardo*, (1892) is helpful.

[28] Spreckelmeyer, "Zur rechtlichen Funktion frühmittelalterlicher Testamente", pp. 91–113.

2. The will of Gisela and Eberhard

2.1. The background of an unusual couple

One of the most famous ninth-century wills is certainly that of Eberhard, count of Friuli, and his wife Gisela, daughter of Louis the Pious and his second wife Judith, and sister of Charles the Bald. Datable to 863–864, this very rich and famous document has been used since the eighteenth century as a source of information on several topics: aristocratic treasures,[29] the history of the Frankish aristocracy and public officers,[30] regional history,[31] and book possession and lay literacy during the Carolingian age.[32] One approach, however, has not yet been taken, namely to look at the will as a will, that is, to consider the aim and structure of the document itself. This is precisely the way we propose to analyse it here. One particular misleading feature of earlier discussions has been their treatment of the document as if it were the will of Eberhard alone—as if his wife Gisela remained only in the background. This is the will of a couple, in which Gisela's role is, as we hope to show, very important indeed. Wills of couples are not in fact very common, though there are a few Anglo-Saxon examples. In the ninth century it was apparently quite rare for husband and wife to be close in age. Among the Saxon aristocracy, a married woman, as Leyser has pointed out, was generally a lot younger than her husband, so they

[29] P. Riché, "Trésors et collections d'aristocrates laiques carolingiens", *Cahiers Archéologiques* 22 (1972), pp. 39–46 (now in Riché, *Instruction et vie religieuse dans le Haut Moyen Age* (London, 1981), n. 9, pp. 39–46); P.E. Schramm, "Baugen-armillae: zur Geschichte der königlichen Armspangen", *Herrschaftszeichen und Staatssymbolik*, II, ed. P.E. Schramm, (Stuttgart, 1955) (*M.G.H.*, Schriften 13/2); P. Riché, "Les aristocrates carolingiens collectionneurs d'objects d'art (VIIIe–Xe siècles)", *Les Cahiers de Saint-Michel de Cuxa* 23 (1992), pp. 83–87.

[30] P. Hirsch, *Die Erhebung Berengars I von Friaul zum König im Italien* (Inaugural-Dissertation zur Erlangung der Doktorwürde der Hohen Philosophischen Fakultät der Kaiser-Wilhelms-Universität zu Strassburg) (Strassburg, 1910), exp. 44–46.

[31] F. Stefani, "I duchi e marchesi della marca del Friuli e di Verona", *Archivio Veneto* 4 (1874), pp. 19–33; P. Paschini, "Le vicende politiche e religiose dei Friuli nei secoli IX e X", *Nuovo Archivio Veneto* 21 (1911), pp. 40–46; P. Cammarosano, "L'alto medioevo", *Storia della società friulana* I, *Il Medioevo*, ed. P. Cammarosano (Udine, 1988), pp. 66–75; H. Krahwinkler, *Friaul in Frühmittelalter. Geschichte einer Region vom Ende des fünften bis zum Ende des zehnten Jahrhunderts* (Wien-Koln, 1992), pp. 245–291.

[32] P. Riché, "La bibliothèque de trois aristocrates laïcs carolingiens", *Le Moyen Age* 69 (1963), pp. 87–104; R. McKitterick, *The Carolingians and the written Word* (Cambridge, 1989), pp. 245–250.

were unlikely to need to make a will at the same time.[33] The decision to do so in the case of Eberhard and Gisela is therefore interesting because it underlines the specific aim of transmitting goods to the couple's children, perhaps referring to the bilateral origins of dynastic legitimacy. Such double legitimacy derives in this case from the wife's line of descent from the Carolingian family and from the local roots of the husband's power.

The couple we are dealing with was no ordinary one: not only because the partners were members of the higher aristocracy of the Carolingian Empire, but because of their respective kin. Let's consider Eberhard first. His father Unroch[34] was a *missus* of Charlemagne between 801–813 and a witness to Charlemagne's will (811) as transcribed by Einhard;[35] he is documented as *comes* in 839 and retired to the monastery of St-Bertin where he died probably in 853.[36] Unroch's area of interest and activity seems to have lain in the northern part of Neustria, that is, approximately in the same region where Eberhard and Gisela a generation later controlled a large amount of their landed patrimony. It is impossible to identify the extent and exact location of Unroch's holdings, however.[37] If Unroch belongs to that very restricted circle of public officers who managed to maintain their public position during the complex transition

---

[33] K.J. Leyser, *Rule and Conflict in an early medieval Society. Ottonian Saxony* (London, 1979), pp. 52–62.

[34] A different relationship between Unroch and Eberhard has been argued for, but not convincingly, on the basis of onomastic evidence: see F. Vianello, "Gli Unrochingi e la famiglia di Beggo conte di Parigi", *Bullettino dell'Istituto storico italiano per il Medioevo e Archivio Muratoriano* 91 (1984), pp. 337–369.

[35] Einhard, *Vita Karoli imperatoris*, ed. O. Holder-Hegger (Hannover, 1911) (*M.G.H., Scriptores rerum Germanicarum in usum scholarum*), c. 33.

[36] On Unroch's biography, see R. Hennebicque-Le Jan, "Prosopographica neustrica: les agents du roi en Neustrie de 639 à 840", *La Neustrie. Les Pays au nord de la Loire de 650 à 850* I, ed. H. Atsma (Sigmaringen, 1989), pp. 231–68, at 257, no. 188.

[37] A tradition collected by L.A. Muratori made Eberhard the son of Unroch who allegedly was the son of *Heiricus Dux*, who defeated the Avars in 796: Eberhard's family would thus have been entirely local and Lombard, satisfying local Friulan needs for autonomy and independence: L.A. Muratori, *Dissertatio XXII. De legibus Italicorum et statutorum origine*, in: Muratori, *Antiquitates Italicae Medii Aevi* II (Mediolani, 1739), colms. 233–235; and as a local example, G.G. Liruti, *Notizia delle cose del Friuli* 5 (Udine, 1777), pp. 235–240. This hypothesis was disproved by A. Hofmeister, "Markgrafen und Markgrafschaften im italienischen Königreich in der Zeit von Karl dem Grossen bis auf Otto den Grossen (774–962)", *Mitteilungen des Instituts für Österreichische Geschichtsforschung*, 7/2 (1906), pp. 317–318, and independently, by É. Favre, "La famille d'Évrard, marquis de Frioul, dans le royaume franc de l'ouest", *Études d'histoire du Moyen Age dédiés à Gabriel Monod* (Paris, 1896), pp. 155–162.

from Charlemagne's entourage to that of Louis the Pious,[38] Eberhard's career seems connected entirely with his fidelity to the Emperor Louis and, after Louis' death, to Lothar I and his son Louis II in the *regnum Italiae*. Although there is no certain evidence, it seems likely that Eberhard was named *comes* of a portion of the *ducatus Foroiulensis* immediately after its division into four parts following the deposition of the *dux* Baldric in 828.[39] It would be difficult to date Eberhard's Italian presence to a slightly later period, by classifying him among the Frankish aristocrats who were deprived of their lands and followed Lothar to Italy after his defeat in 834.[40] In fact the annalistic sources that noted Eberhard's appearence on the scene picked him out because of his relationship to Louis the Pious, and stressed his loyalty to the emperor. In 836 the embassy from Italy to Louis consisted of "Walach qui erat abbas, et Rihhardus perfidus et Ebarhardus fidelis:"[41] this man's outstanding quality probably made him an attractive son-in-law for Louis and his wife Judith.

Only after 834, the year of Lothar's defeat but also the date from which he made determined efforts to rule in Italy acting exclusively as *rex Italiae*,[42] Eberhard's name is regularly attested in public documents, acting both as a local *comes* and as an ambassador of Lothar and later of his son Louis II.[43] Public documents are the only ones in which Eberhard's activity is recorded, while his local activity remains obscure.[44] A similar pattern (and, for us historians, a simi-

---

[38] K.F. Werner, "'Hlodovicus Augustus'. Gouverner l'empire chrétien. Idées et réalités", *Charlemagne's Heir. New Perspectives on the Reign of Louis the Pious (814–840)*, eds. P. Godman and R. Collins (Oxford, 1990), pp. 31–54; J. Jarnut, "Ludwig der Fromme, Lothar I. und das *Regnum Italiae*", *Charlemagne's Heir. New Perspectives on the Reign of Louis the Pious (814–840)*, eds. P. Godman and R. Collins (Oxford, 1990), pp. 349–351.

[39] Astronomer, *Vita Hludowici imperatoris*, ed. R. Rau, in *Quellen zur karolingischen Reichsgeschichte* I (Berlin, 1955) (Ausgewählte Quellen zur deutschen Geschichte des Mittelalters V), 631: '*Itidemque Baldrico duci Foroiulensi dum obiceretur et probatum sit, eius ignavia et incuriam vastatam a Bulgaris regionem nostram, pulsus est ducatu, et inter quattuor comites eiusdem est potestas dissecta*'.

[40] Jarnut, "Ludwig der Fromme, Lothar I. und das *Regnum Italiae*", p. 359 seems to prefer this solution instead.

[41] Thegan, *Vita Hludowici imperatoris*, ed. R. Rau, in *Quellen zur karolingischen Reichsgeschichte* I (Berlin, 1955) (Ausgewählte Quellen zur deutschen Geschichte des Mittelalters 5), p. 250.

[42] Jarnut, "Ludwig der Fromme, Lothar I. und das *Regnum Italiae*", pp. 357–359.

[43] Details on Eberhard's career are examined with full bibliography by Krahwinkler, *Friaul in Frühmittelalter. Geschichte einer Region vom Ende des fünften bis zum Ende des zehnten Jahrhunderts*, pp. 245–266; cf. I. Feers, "Eberardo, marchese del Friuli", *Dizionario Biografico degli Italiani* 42 (Roma, 1993), pp. 252–255.

[44] In 841 Eberhard, intervening with Lothar I in favour of Duke Peter of Venice,

lar problem) is common in the case of many Frankish aristocrats, whose careers are documented only in fragmentary references in annals and royal or imperial charters.[45]

The development of Eberhard's career coincided with a marked increase in Lothar's activities, both in establishing an autonomous policy and in revealing his imperial ambitions.[46] These trends advanced still further under Lothar's son Louis II. There can be no doubt that Eberhard's fortunes in Italy were promoted by his relationship to both Louis the Pious and Lothar. It has been argued that the marriage with Gisela took place around 836,[47] two years after Lothar's exile to Italy: it was a deliberate attempt by the imperial couple to create, through their daughter's union with one of the most faithful of the emperor's *fideles*, a platform of consensus for Charles the Bald in Italy.[48] At the same time Gisela's dowry-lands, probably located in the area of the Scheldt,[49] might, it was hoped, ensure similar support for her brother in the northen territories of the empire. The

---

is called '*fidelis comes noster*': *Lotharii I diplomata*', *M.G.H., Diplomata karolinorum*, III, ed. Th. Schieffer (Berlin, 1966), pp. 170–171, n. 62 (841, September 1). In 843, with Bishop Notting of Verona, Eberhard asks Lothar to respect the will of Count Alboin in favour of the church of Aquileia: *Lotharii I Diplomata*, pp. 192–193, n. 76 (843, August 22). At a date between 834 and 850, Eberhard pleaded on behalf of Andrew, patriarch of Aquileia, *Lotharii I diplomata*, pp. 348–349, no. 186 (now lost). In 855, in a request on behalf of Teutmarus, patriarch of Aquileia (*Ludovici II diplomata*, ed. K. Wagner (Roma, 1994) (Fonti per la storia dell'Italia medievale, Antiquitates 3), pp. 98–99, no. 17), Eberhard is called '*illustrissimus comes dilectusque compater noster*' In 865 Eberhard acts as *missus* of Louis II in Como, and is called '*vassus et senescallus domni imperatoris*': *I placiti del regnum Italiae*, ed. C. Manaresi, I (Roma, 1955) (Fonti per la storia d'Italia 92), pp. 246–248, no. 68 (865, March, Como). For a possible identification with another Eberhard, of the Supponid family cf. E. Hlawitschka, *Franken, Alemannen, Bayern und Burgunder in Oberitalien (774–962)* (Freiburg im Breisgau, 1960), p. 180.

[45] Cf. for all these, D.A. Bullough, "Leo 'qui apud Hlotarium magni loci habebatur' et le gouvernement du 'regnum Italiae' à l'époque carolingienne", *Le Moyen Age* 67 (1961), pp. 237–245.

[46] Jarnut, "Ludwig der Fromme, Lothar I. und das *Regnum Italiae*", pp. 354–359.

[47] The marriage to Gisela is dated by Agnellus of Ravenna (late ninth century) before 840, when Louis the Pious died: *Liber pontificalis ecclesie Ravennatis*, ed. O. Holder Hegger, *M.G.H., Scriptores rerum langobardicarum et italicarum* (Berlin, 1878), p. 389: '*Ad Carolum vero plus fertilem et optimam [Hludovicus imperator] largivit partem, et Giselam, filiam suam, tradidit marito Curadum [sic] nomine, piissimus homo*'. *Hic et haec Iudith augusta parturit*'.

[48] See J. L. Nelson, *Charles the Bald* (London and New York, 1992), pp. 27–28. On royal control of aristocratic marriages: J. L. Nelson, "The Last Years of Louis the Pious", *Charlemagne's Heir. New Perspectives on the Reign of Louis the Pious (814–840)*, eds. P. Godman and R. Collins (Oxford, 1990), pp. 147–159, at 152–153.

[49] Cf. P. Grierson, "The Identity of the unnamed Fisc in the '*Breviarium exempla*'", *Revue Belge de Philologie et histoire* 18 (1939), pp. 437–459 (Gisela's patrimony, 442).

couple were widely different in age: while Eberhard around 836 was certainly a mature man, while Gisela, probably born around 821,[50] was a young girl of 15.

Gisela's position here was unusual: she was not acting out the traditional role of aristocratic women in securing power for her family; on the contrary, she was building for her husband's family a strong connection to the imperial lineage. It has been argued that in Frankish society, where there was no right of progeniture, the king's sisters and daughters were generally destined for monastic careers: their marriages might have entailed problems and complications for the succession,[51] because they could transmit to their husband and children a legitimate aspiration to the royal title. The marriage between Eberhard and Gisela is therefore an anomaly, understandable only in the context of a strengthening of Judith's descent-line, a policy vigorously pursued by the empress herself:[52] if her son Charles the Bald had failed to secure a kingdom, or died without heirs, Gisela's son might legitimately have claimed a right of succession to a royal title.

Eberhard and Gisela had nine children. Their names show their parents' desire to identify the new family partly by reference to its imperial connection: while the names of Eberhard, Berengar, Adalard, Unroch belong to the Unruoching name-stock (these were in fact the names of Eberhard himself, his two brothers and his father), those of Rudolph, Heilwig and Judith explicitly recalled Gisela's descent from the family of her mother the empress,[53] while the name of the last daughter, called Gisela like her mother, clearly echoed that of Charlemagne's favourite sister.[54] These choices of names taken

---

[50] E. Ward, "Caesar's Wife: the Empress Judith", *Charlemagne's Heir. New Perspectives on the Reign of Louis the Pious (814–840)*, eds. P. Godman and R. Collins (Oxford, 1990), p. 209 relates Gisela's birth to the reaffirmation of the *Ordinatio imperii* made in 821 by Louis the Pious at the assembly of Nijmegen.

[51] Women's capacity to transmit by inheritance not only patrimony but also jurisdictional power is well analysed in P. Stafford, "Sons and mothers: Family Politics in the Early Middle Ages", *Medieval Women*, ed. D. Baker (Oxford, 1978), pp. 79–100, at pp. 95–96; a traditional widespread idea denies this capacity: see F.-L. Ganshof, "Le statut de la femme dans la monarchie franque", *La femme* II (Bruxelles, 1962) (Recueil de la Société Jean Bodin pour l'histoire comparative des institutions 12), p. 54.

[52] Ward, "Caesar's Wife: the Empress Judith", pp. 212–213.

[53] Rudolf was the brother of Judith; Heilwig was Judith's mother: K.F. Werner, "Die Nachkommen Karls des Grossen", *Karl der Grosse* I (Düsseldorf, 1965), pp. 412–447.

[54] K.F. Werner, "Bedeutende Adelsfamilien im Reich Karls der Grosse: Excursus I: Die Unruochingen", *Karl der Grosse* I (Düsseldorf, 1965), pp. 133–137.

from both father's and mother's kin could reflect a choice in the political direction of the new family,[55] but Gisela also took the opportunity to assert certain claims by using an imperial name for one of her daughters.[56]

The availability of certain names was not the only advantage that marriage to Gisela offered Eberhard: in more general terms, it brought contacts with a cultural milieu involving the ecclesiastical literati active at the courts of Louis the Pious and Gisela's brother Charles the Bald. Poets were inspired to mark key events in the couple's lives: Gisela's fertility was celebrated twice, once in a lament on the death of her first-born son, Eberhard, and then in a poem of rejoicing at the birth of Unroch, and Eberhard's military exploits were praised in encomiastic form by Sedulius Scottus, an expert panegyrist of emperors and kings, who managed to offer his poetry to all the rival sons of Louis the Pious without being labelled the partisan of any one of them![57] The special role of Eberhard as Gisela's husband, and the imperial descent of their children, did not escape Sedulius, who praised Unroch as the child in whom *Ludewicus avus praecelsus Caesar in orbe emicat augusto semine.*[58]

Through the union with Gisela, Eberhard was able to rise above the aristocracy of his own time, acquiring a dynastic identity that, in its strength and literary celebratity, was modelled on the peculiar features of royal dynasties. This new branch of the Unruoching family was therefore the product of two convergent ambitions: on Eberhard's side, his descent-line was singled out by the transmission to it of his public office of *comes*,[59] while the union with Gisela added

---

[55] C.B. Bouchard, "Family structure and family consciousness among the aristocracy in the ninth to the eleventh centuries", *Francia* 14 (1986), pp. 639–658 shows that the naming structure in the ninth century is orientated towards a patrilinear choice, restricting the possibilities of naming to a small group of ancestors.

[56] Werner, "Die Nachkommen Karls des Grossen", p. 447. We can also stress that Judith's side too was connected to the monastic cults of Carolingian royal saints, expecially Balthild's at Chelles, administered successively by Charlemagne's sister Gisela and Judith's mother Heilwig: J.L. Nelson, "Queens as Jezebels: Brunhild and Balthild in merovingian History", *Politics and Ritual in Early Medieval Europe* (London, 1986), pp. 1–48, at 40–44; Ward, "Caesar's Wife: the Empress Judith", p. 209.

[57] P. Godman, *Poets and Emperors. Frankish Politics and Carolingian Poetry* (Oxford, 1987), pp. 154–160.

[58] *M.G.H., Poetae latini aevi karolini*, III/I, ed. L. Traube (Berlin, 1896), p. 202, n. XXXVIII: 'His eminent grandfather the Emperor Louis is manifested in the world in his imperial seed'. The *planctus* for the child Eberhard is at 201, no. XXXVII.

[59] On the evolution of Italian dynasties of this level, G. Tabacco, "Regno, impero

a strong tinge of 'imperial' aspiration. The will that Eberhard and Gisela had drawn up for them *in curte nostra Musiestre* thus represented a coherent attempt to define the special quality and public functions of their own new family. The decision to have a joint will, even though Gisela would have been only about 40 in 863, signified the transmission through a written document of the couple's combined qualities.

2.2. *The will: diplomatic structure*

The document does not survive in its original form. It was included in the eleventh-century cartulary of the abbey of Cysoing (near modern Lille), and there is some debate about the way in which it has come down to us. It was copied several times.[60] It seems clear, however, that the monks of Cysoing when they copied the document into their *cartolarium*, did not reproduce the text in full.[61] They probably omitted the whole protocol, with the opening *invocatio* and concluding *datatio* or dating-clause.[62]

From the formal and structural point of view, the will presents at least two peculiarities worth signalling. First, it is the will of a public officer and his wife. Parallel cases suggest that the use of a written will may have been relatively common among Carolingian *comites*: we have the text of the will of Count Eccard of Macon,[63] and there are mentions of other comital wills in charters from the early years of the ninth century.[64] The public function of these *auctores* is to some

---

e aristocrazie nell'Italia postcarolingia", *Sperimentazioni del potere nell'alto medioevo* (Torino, 1993), pp. 99–100.

[60] The principal edition of the document is *Cartulaire de l'Abbaye de Cysoing*, ed. I. De Coussemaker (Lille, 1885), pp. 1–5, n. 1; Stefani, "I duchi e marchesi della marca del Friuli e di Verona", pp. 25–29.

[61] On the transmission of the document and its authenticity O. Oppermann, *Die älteren Urkunden des Klosters Blandinium und die Anfange der Stadt Gent* I (Utrecht, Leipzig and München, 1928), pp. 440–445.

[62] See diplomatistic analysis of merovingian wills by Nonn, "Merovingische Testamente. Studien zum Fortleben einer römischen Urkundenform in Frankreich", pp. 58–93; Kasten, "Erbrechtliche Verfügungen des 8. und 9. Jahrhunderts", pp. 247–261. From the very beginning the document is different from points 4, 5, 6 and 7 of Nonn's structure for Frankish testaments (*Handlungsfähigkeit* and *Innere Begrundung*, *Testamentserklarung*, *Angaben über Schreiber*) are missing and it is not possible to say if they ever existed. Also the *codicillum* is missing.

[63] *Recueil des chartes de l'abbaye de Saint-Benoit-sur-Loire* I, ed. M. Prou and A. Vidier (Paris, 1900), pp. 59–67, no. 25 (876).

[64] Some Italian examples: in 809 the will of Count Hadumar of Verona (*CDV,*

extent reflected in the formulaic structure of their wills. Eberhard's will in particular presents a strikingly hybrid form, a mixing of public and private document: he acts as a private *testator* but does not forget his public functions as an imperial officer. The second peculiarity about this will is that, unlike other examples from the Carolingian period, it does not specify the destination of the couple's property in its entirety: the *testamentum divisionis* of Eberhard and Gisela concerns only the goods given to their children, while the goods given to ecclesiastical institutions are not included.[65]

The will's hybrid form is particularly evident at its very beginning, in the *dispositio*, which is structured as a public *arenga*, a short *narratio* and a *promulgatio*. At the outset it is declared that both Eberhard and his wife Gisela are having the document written so that, after their deaths, their children can know exactly what belongs to them *sine aliquo impedimento vel animositatis iurgio* ("without any obstacle or envious dispute"), underlining that the written division is rational *(rationabili executione)* and precise *(articulatim)*. This formula seems to stress from the very start two distinct features that can help us to understand the spirit of this document: on the one hand, a written division is necessary to avoid uncertainty and conflict between the children; on the other, it evidently legitimizes and shapes the children's (and especially the sons') future political roles. The formal cause of the division is therefore very different from those that usually appear in contemporary wills, generally inspired as they were by spiritual needs (concern with the soul's fate at the Last Judgement), or by the illness of the *testator*. What is spelled out here is the need to avoid intra-familial conflict in the next generation. It is worth stressing the similarity to the so-called "testament" of Charlemagne, reproduced by Einhard: Charles too provided for the "description and division" of his goods *ut heredes sui, omni ambiguitate remota, quid ad se pertinere deberet, liquido cognoscere et sine lite atque contentione sua inter se conpetenti partitione dividere potuissent.*[66] Another striking comparison

---

I, pp. 103–107, n. 89 (809, May 13)); in 843 the will of Count Alboin of Friuli is mentioned *(Lothari I Diplomata*, pp. 192– 193, no. 76 (843, August 22)).

[65] See, for example differences from other contemporary wills: those of Engelbertus of Erbé (province of Verona) *(CDV*, I, n. 181, pp. 264–272 (846)); the Venetian *Dux*, Giustinianus Particiacus *(Documenti relativi alla storia di Venezia anteriori al Mille*, I, ed. R. Cessi, Padova 1940, no. 53, pp. 93–99, (829)), and Eccard of Mâcon *(Recueil des chartes de l'abbaye de saint- Benoît-sur-Loire*, no. 25, (876)).

[66] Einhard, *Vita Karoli imperatoris*, c. 33: 'so that his heirs should be free from all doubt and know clearly what belongs to them and be able to share their property

may be seen in the *formulae* used in the documents laying down the imperial succession, like Charlemagne's *Divisio regnorum* (806) or Louis the Pious's *Ordinatio imperii* (806). In both of them, the reason for a written document is to avoid litigation and controversy between the children. In the 806 *Divisio*, Charlemagne explains: "That we may not leave confusion and disorder or bequeath them controversies, strife and disputes by speaking of the realm as a whole, we have rather divided the whole body of the realm into three portions and had the portion which each of them must defend and rule described and designated in such a way that each of them, content with his portion as specified by our ordinance, may with God's help strive both to defend the borders of his kingdom which march with those of foreign peoples and to maintain peace and amity with his brother."[67] The will of Eberhard and Gisela, or its immediate model, seems therefore directly inspired by documents ordering the imperial succession, and by implication presupposes a similar purpose in the nature and distribution of the inheritance, both in land and in movables.

From its opening, the text underlines the common feature of the goods to be divided, insistently using the word *nostrum*—'ours'—to refer not only to the children, but also to the land and *mobilia*, showing that the property belongs to both husband and wife. The necessity for impartiality, furthermore, means that in a long list of goods, carefully selected from among Eberhard and Gisela's possessions, every landed estate, every object, is identified as having belonged to

---

by suitable partition without litigation or strife' (quoted from the translation in P.E. Dutton, *Carolingian Civilization* (Ontario, 1993), p. 41). An analogous arrangement almost exactly contemporary with Eberhard's was King Æthelwulf's 'testamentary letter' (*hereditaria immo commendatoria epistola*) of 856/7, which divided his realm between his two eldest sons and his *propria hereditas* between his sons, daughter and other kin: Asser, *Gesta Ælfredi* c. 16, ed. W. Stevenson (Oxford, 1905), pp. 14–5. Æthelwulf had just returned via Francia from a visit to Rome.

[67] '*Non ut confuse atque inordinate vel sub totius regni denominatione iurgi vel litis controversiam eis relinquamus, sed trina portione totum regni corpus dividentes, quam quisque illorum tueri vel regere debeat porcionem describere et desiugnare fecimus; eo videlicet modo, ut sua quisque portione contentus iuxta ordinationem nostram, et fines regni sui qui ad alienigenas extenduntur cum Dei adiutorio nitatur defendere et pacem atque caritatem cum fratre custodire*', *Divisio regnorum*, 6 February 806, prologue, in *Capitularia regum Francorum*, I, ed. A. Boretius (*M.G.H.*, *Legum sectio*, II, *Capitularia regum Francorum*, I), p. 127 (trans. cited from P.D. King, *Charlemagne. Translated Sources* (Kendal, 1987), p. 251); *Ordinatio imperii*, July 817, *ibid.*, 270–271: '*... quamvis haec admonitio devote ac fideliter fieret, nequaquam nobis nec his qui sanum sapiunt visum fuit, ut amore filiorum aut gratia unitas imperii a Deo nobis conservati divisione humana scinderetur, ne forte hac occasione scandalum in sancta ecclesia oriretur*'.

them both. This is not irrelevant, for Gisela's imperial lineage and Eberhard's role as public officer could transmit to objects and land the special value associated with the legitimacy of office and family status, and, at the same time, aspirations towards a higher status and enhanced political power: it was to be the association of Gisela's imperial lineage and Eberhard's regionally-based power that legitimised Berengar's quest to become king of Italy and then emperor.[68]

Public function and private status are equally present in the document. The long *dispositio* is divided into three parts, each one with a similar structure, concerning respectively land, personal gear, and equipment and books belonging to Eberhard's and Gisela's chapel (*paramentum nostrum, paramentum capellae nostrae, libri eiusdem capellae nostrae*). Within each section the four sons are listed, then the three daughters. While in the first part of the document the daughters are simply mentioned by their names, the sons are explicitly listed by age: Unroch is termed the *primogenitus*, Berengar *secundus*, Adalard *tertius*, Rodulf *quartus*. Only in the list of the books bequeathed, where the sons' birth-order is no longer stressed, is Hengeltrud called *primogenita filia nostra*. This gender division does not correspond to the real birth-order of the children, as far we can see from the list included in the *Martirologium et Obituarium Cysoniensis ecclesie*:[69] here Hengeltrud and not Unroch appears to be the first-born child, or, at least, the first to have survived.[70] A formal *minatio* concludes the section about estates: whoever dares to usurp this land will have to pay one thousand *libras auri*. That is a formula used in public documents probably meaning the total loss of property, since 1,000 lb. of gold was an enormous amount.[71]

The central and longest part of the *dispositio* concerns, in a similar

---

[68] *Gesta Berengarii imperatoris*, in *M.G.H. Poetae latini aevi karolini*, IV/I, ed. P. de Winterfeld (Berlin, 1899), pp. 358–359 and *Annales Fuldenses*, ed. F. Kurze (Berlin, 1981) (*M.G.H. Scriptores in usum Scholarum*, VII), p. 129 say that Berengar managed to obtain political power as far as the river Adda *'quasi ereditario iure'*.

[69] *Cartulaire de l'Abbaye de Cysoing*, p. 11, no. 6: the list made by Gisela is linked with arrangements for the celebration of the anniversaries of the deaths of members of her *cognatio*, and includes: 'Hengeltrude, Unroch, Berengario, Adelardo, Rodulpho, Hellwich, Gilla, Judich'.

[70] The first male son, called Eberhard like his father, died soon after his birth. See the *planctus* written for him by Sedulius in *M.G.H., Poetae latini aevi karolini*, III, i, no. XXXVII, 201.

[71] Cf. A. Rovelli, "Circolazione monetaria e formulari notarili nell'Italia altomedievale", *Bullettino dell'Istituto Storico Italiano per il Medioevo e Archivio Muratoriano* 98 (1992), pp. 133–144.

sequence which separates sons from daughters in order of birth, the *mobilia* of Eberhard and Gisela and the precious objects of their chapel. A third section is devoted to a list of the books belonging to the chapel, and in this a fourth daughter, Gisela, is also included. To judge from parallel provisions in contemporary testaments, it is likely that after the division of the land and *mobilia*, there originally followed a section, which the monks of Cysoing did not copy, about the distribution of the animals and serfs.[72] The last part of the *dispositio* contains, on the usual pattern,[73] formal guarantees of validity, including the *caput generale*: Unroch and the *fideles* will be responsible for carrying out the division following the wishes of Eberhard and Gisela. The *rogatio* is missing and the eschatocol again lists the seven children in order of birth and sex, listing the witnesses as well, but not mentioning the name of the *scriptor* of the charter. The witnesses are all called *fideles*. They include *Adalroch nepos noster*, who can be identified as the *missus* of Charles the Fat in Turin in 880.[74] None of them seem to belong to the local context of Friuli. The final *datatio* mentions that the will had been written in Italy *in comitatu Tarvisiano* in the fiscal domain of *Musestre* (now the village of Musestre sul Sile). The original subscriptions are missing.

The structure of Eberhard's and Gisela's will, despite the omission of some sections by later transcribers, can thus be seen to have mentioned all the status symbols that normally appear in ninth-century wills (land, movables, animals and serfs); but, as this will's explicit purpose is to divide the couple's possessions between the children, leaving gifts to the church to be dealt with in other charters (for example, the foundation-charter of the monastery of Cysoing), the list of the children takes priority over the list of property: a strict relationship is then established between each child and his or her possessions, are these in turn are divided into separate categories.

---

[72] Distributions of animals and serfs are in fact common in contemporary testaments written in the Veneto region, for instance, the will of Engelberto di Erbé (*CDV*, I, p. 269, no. 181 (846 May 28)), the will of Billongus, bishop of Verona (*CDV*, I, pp. 274–278, no. 182 (846)); the will of Audo, bishop of Verona (*CDV*, I, pp. 326–328, no. 219 (860)). See also the testament of Walgarius, Eberhard's chaplain (865), listing 'pecora quam plurima' (*Cartulaire de l'abbaye de Cysoing*, no. II, p. 6).

[73] Nonn, "Merovingische Testamente. Studien zum Fortleben einer römischen Urkundenform in Frankreich", pp. 72–77.

[74] Hlawitschka, *Franken, Alamannen, Bayern und Burgunder in Oberitalien (774–962)*, p. 113; *Karoli III diplomata*, ed. P.F. Kehr (Berlin, 1937) (*M.G.H. Diplomata regum Germaniae ex stirpe Karolinorum*, II), no. 25, p. 41.

Through this listing of possessions, the social *persona* of every child is characterised, and clearly differentiated from those of the other children, underlining the specific investment, both in quantity and quality, made in him or her by the parents. The distribution of land and movables in separate lists is a way of identifying different characterisations of male and female children; it also permits the marking-out of different degrees of legal status and different possibilities for the future career of each child.

3. *The will and its gifts*

3.1. *Land*

We shall look first at the division of the landed property of Eberhard and Gisela. The analysis is problematic because many placenames are difficult to localize and the estates are very widely dispersed in the kingdoms of Italy, Germany, Middle Francia (Lotharingia) and West Francia. The historical debate of the late nineteenth and early twentieth centuries over the identification of these places been fully examined by Paul Hirsch, whose conclusions largely stand.[75] It may be useful therefore to summarize his hypotheses, first on the list of estates in the will, and then on the general principles of the land division made by the couple.

The portion attributed to the eldest son Unroch is evidently very extensive but the terms are hardly specific: *quicquid in Langobardia et in Alamannia de proprietate habere videmur*, with all these properties' dependences *preter Balguinet*, that is, except for Balingen in Württemberg, which is assigned to his sister Judith. The will gives no precise indication on the extent of the patrimony: the only Italian place mentioned is the estate *(curtis)* of Musestre, where the document was drawn up, and we can infer that that this too was to become Unroch's property. At least some traces of this patrimony can be inferred by the subsequent presence of Berengar, who later took Unroch's place on the Italian political scene; the numerous sources relating to Berengar allow us to identify in the area between Friuli and the Veneto

---

[75] Hirsch, *Die Erhebung Berengars I von Friaul zum König im Italien*, pp. 62–65; the most recent analysis is that of Krahwinkler, *Friaul in Frühmittelalter. Geschichte einer Region vom Ende des fünften bis zum Ende des zehnten Jahrhunderts*, pp. 262ff.

(that is the north-eastern part of northen Italy) the region where the family's clients and patrimony were based, but it is not possible to identify the estates or their locations.[76]

Berengar was to get the *curtis* of Annappes (to the east of modern Lille), with all its dependences apart from Gruson (given to the church of Cysoing and under Adalard's control); he was also to receive the *curtis* of *Hildinam*, in the Hesbaye, a place for which at least three different sites have been proposed in the area south of Louvain. Berengar also received all his parents' landed property in the county of Condroz, between Liège and Namur, south of the River Meuse.

The third brother Adalard received the *curtis* of Cysoing, with Camphin and Gruson (both in a small area south-east of Lille), together with the property given to the monastery of Cysoing, with the duty of safeguarding the patrimony of this church; he also received the *curtis* of Somain, a little further south.

Rudolph was to get the villages of Vitry and Maistaing (both to the south of Lille),[77] apart from the church of Vitry, a dependence of the church of Cysoing. He also received *Scelleburd*, perhaps identifiable as Schelle, a little south of Antwerp,[78] and all the landed patrimony *in comitatu Tassandrio* ("in the county of Toxandria"), north-east of Antwerp.[79]

---

[76] G. Arnaldi, "Berengario I", *Dizionario Biografico degli Italiani* 9 (Roma, 1967), pp. 2, 8 and 14; S. Gasparri, "Dall'età longobarda al secolo X", *Storia di Treviso*, II, *Il Medioevo*, eds. D. Rando and G.M. Varanini (Venezia, 1991), pp. 27–28.

[77] De Coussemaker's edition has "Vitrei vicum", that is the village of Vitry; Hofmeister instead reads "Vitrei, Vius", interpreting it as Vitry and Vis (another village further south): Hirsch, *Die Erhebung Berengars I von Friaul zum König im Italien*, p. 63.

[78] The will specifies that this is the village *'quod Mat[f]ridus dudum habuit'*: On this person cfr. I. Depoin, "Le duc Evrard du Frioul et les trois comtes Matfrid", *Annales de la Société d'archéologie de Bruxelles* 13 (1899), pp. 50–60, although remembering the negative judgement given by Hirsch, *Die Erhebung Berengars I von Friaul zum König im Italien*, p. 33 footnote.

[79] On the county of Texandria, see M. Costambeys, "An aristocratic community on the northern Frankish frontier. 690–726", *Early Medieval Europe* 3 (1994), pp. 39–62, although not specifically dealing with our problems. Generally, for territorial division of this district C. Piot, "Les pagi de la Belgique et leurs subdivisions pendant le Moyen Age", *Mémoires couronnés et mémoires des savants étrangers publiés par l'académie royale des sciences, des lettres et des beaux-arts de Belgique* 39 (Brussels, 1879), and the annexed charter. See also: F. Theuws, *De archeologie van de periferie. Studies naar de bewoning en samenleving in het Maas-Demer-Scheldegebied in de Vroege Middeleeuwen* (Amsterdam, 1988), pp. 97–159 (with all historical references to Texandrie) and F. Theuws and A.-J. Bijsterveld, "Der Maas-Demer-Schelde Raum in Ottonischer und Salischer Kaiserzeit", *Siedlungen und Landesausbau zur Salierzeit, Teil 1, In den*

To the list of estates assigned to the sons, two clauses (*clausolae*) are added, which are very important for our understanding of the principles on which Eberhard and Gisela worked out the details of their division. They ordered, "if Adalard or Rudolf should have fewer manses than Berengar, they must even up [their shares] between themselves from Annappes, together with the *mancipia* on the land there" (*si minus Adalardus aut Rodulphus de mansis habuerint, quam Berrengharius, de Anaspio adequare inter eos, cum mancipiis que supersedent, debeant*), and that redistribution must occur if *rex Langobardorum, vel Francorum vel etiam Alamannorum* should take part of his patrimony from any of the sons. It is clear that the fundamental principle here is equality between the the last three sons, although the requirement of territorial coherence to underpin political control is present as well. Unroch *primogenitus* is, however, clearly excluded from this principle of equality.[80]

As far as the daughters are concerned, Ingeltrud was granted *Ermen et Mareshem*. These two places have not been securely identified, but the likeliest hypothesis is that they were contiguous: perhaps Herent and Merchtem, north of Brussels, or Harmellen and Meersen, on the right bank of the lower Rhine, not far from Utrecht. More certain, though, is the identification of the estates given to Judith: Balingen in Württemberg, and Heliwsheim on the right bank of the Rhine. The third sister Heilwig is granted land in the most solid area of family power, to the east and south-east of Lille, on both banks of the River Scheldt: Ootegen, Luinhue and Vendegie, and one *mansus* in Angreau. A fourth daughter Gisela is not listed here: she was in fact a nun at San Salvatore/S.Giulia in Brescia, and her landed endowment would have been given to her at the moment of her entry into the convent.[81]

---

nördlichen Landschaften des Reiches, ed. H.W. Böhme (Sigmaringen, 1991), pp. 109–146, and note 15 (with wrong date (867) for the will) for a discussion of the late Carolingian and later political geography of the region.

[80] See below, for the hierarchy of the sons and the parents' different political plans for them.

[81] This imperial connection should not be forgotten, as the monastery of San Salvatore/S. Giulia was probably the morning-gift of Judith, the wife of Louis the Pious, and the centre of female imperial patronage in Italy. *Codex diplomaticus Langobardie*, ed. G. Porro Lambertenghi (Torino, 1873) (H.P.M., 13), no. CIII, cols. 103–104 (819–825): see Ward, "Caesar's Wife: the Empress Judith", pp. 207–8; S. Wemple, "S. Salvatore, S. Giulia: a case study in the endowment and patronage of a major female monastery in Northern Italy", *Women of the medieval World: essays in honour of J.H. Mundy*, eds. J. Kirschner and S. Wemple (Oxford, 1985), pp. 85–91.

The principles inspiring the various parts of the division are therefore not identical. The criterion of territorial coherence is a priority for Unroch alone: he receives the entire Italian patrimony and almost all of the German one. In the cases of the other sons, this need is subordinated to the aim of having an equal division and perhaps also (at least for Berengar and Rudolph) of distributing between them the original Frankish patrimonial base in its different areas. In this context it is significant that in the territory of Lille and Cysoing (*in Galliis*, as Gisela was to express it in a charter of 869),[82] where the West Frankish patrimony was located, land was given to the three younger sons (Berengar, Adalard and Rudolph) and to Heilwig. As regards Adalard, his role as abbot of Cysoing,[83] reinforcing the Unruochings' probably strong rights of patronage over this church (it is the *ecclesia nostra* of the will),[84] suggests that his allocation was part of a more general coordination of the family's policy for its patrimony, for other lands in this area were entrusted to Berengar, the second-born son, and the only lay son active in this region. But a similar interpretation does not apply to Rudolph's share: he was abbot of St.-Bertin and St.-Vaast, two royal monasteries lacking any strong link with the Unruochings, and he suc-

---

Founded by Lombard royal couple Ansa and Desiderius, in the second half of eighth century, San Salvatore continued to hold the function of a royal protectorate after the Frankish conquest too; it became one of the most important places of devotional continuity under the patronage of Carolingian emperors' wives, and later of the wives of the *reges Italiae*. The tradition of giving it to the ruler's wife as morning-gift was followed by the kings of Italy Lothar and Louis II. In 837 Hirmingard, Lothar's I wife, acted together with her husband in favour of the monastery; in 848 and 851 she got Lothar to grant that after her death the convent should belong to her daughter Gisela '*ut quamdiu in hac erumnali luce manserit, teneat atque possideat et ordine fructuario gubernet atque disponat*' (*Lotharii I diplomata*, pp. 113–115, no. 35 (15 December 837); pp. 241–242, no. 101 (16 March 848); pp. 262–266, no. 115 (8 September 851). Louis II confirmed his father's wishes in 856 (*Ludovici II diplomata*, pp. 105–108, nos. 21–22 (May 856)), and in 861 gave the convent to his sick daughter Gisela, stating that after her death the Empress Engelberga '*mater eius sub omni integritate succedat diebusque vitae suae possideat*' (*Ludovici II diplomata*, pp. 136–137, n. 34 (13 January 861)); in 868 Engelberga's rights over the convent were said to be transferred to Hirmengard, daughter of Engelberga and Louis II (*Ludovici II diplomata*, pp. 160–161, n. 48 (28 April 868)).

[82] *Cartulaire de l'abbaye de Cysoing*, p. 7, no. 3.

[83] See below for Adalard and his function as abbot of Cysoing.

[84] For a general evaluation of aristocratic patronage rights over monasteries during the Carolingian and post Carolingian periods, see C.H. Lawrence, *Medieval Monasticism. Forms of Religious Life in Western Europe in the Middle Ages* (Harlow, 1984), pp. 69–74, pp. 133–135; for a good example of a monastery's function as guarantee of a family's unity, see B. Ruggiero, *Principi, nobiltà e Chiesa nel Mezzogiorno longobardo. L'esempio di s. Massimo di Salerno* (Napoli, 1973).

ceeded Adalard at Cysoing only a few years later. Nor can it be relevant in the case of Heilwig, whose marriage to Count Hucbold opened the way instead to the forming of a new family, who after the Unruochings' political project in this area ended in failure would will try in vain to recover Eberhard's political and patrimonial heritage.

The hierarchy described by this part of the text is quite simple. There is a clear break between the first-born son and the other sons: Unroch is assigned not a specific series of places, but the whole patrimony owned in Italy and Germany; moreover the rules assuring equal shares in the patrimony to other three sons do not apply to Unroch. On the other hand we find here no trace of that distinction between laymen and ecclesiastics which is clear in the distribution of the movable goods. The younger sons are distinguished from one another neither by the quantity of their shares in the landed property (equal for Berengar, Adalard and Rudolph) nor by the nature of these shares: each receives whole *curtes*, and both Berengar and Rudolph obtain all the family's lands in a particular county. The distinction between sons and daughters is clearly there, however, even if in a weak form: first, daughters are excluded from the rule that guarantees equality between the sons' shares; further, in the daughters' shares there is no trace of an attempt to assign to one heir all the family's patrimony in a single county, as we find in the cases of Berengar and Adalard. Hence, despite our ignorance of the extent of the lands granted, we can be fairly sure that the daughters received smaller shares in the patrimony.

The territorial cohesion of landed property cannot be considered a differentiating feature as between sons and daughters: a principle of territorial cohesion is present, although not predominant, in the definition of the shares of both sons and daughters. While it is possible to see a strategic aim in the distribution of the sons' shares, a similar concern in assigning the daughters' shares is not totally absent, and is indeed clear in Heilwig's case. The strongest distinction made in this document is that between the older daughters and Gisela, the nun at San Salvatore/S. Giulia, whose landed endowment had already been established and thus totally escapes the will's provisions.

3.2. *Movables and books*

The second part of the *dispositio*, and the main subject of the will, is the list of movable wealth: it comprises almost three-quarters of the document. The structure of this second part corresponds to that of first concerning the landed property. The movables are divided into three categories (*paramentum nostrum, paramentum capellae nostrae, libri capellae nostrae*), but while for each son and daughter the first two categories are listed together, there is a separate list of the books. The personal items are listed in a similar order for each son. The list contains swords, belts and apparel first, then vessels, then armour. For the daughters only vessels are included (see tab. 1). It is certainly a treasure-hoard, and Pierre Riché has studied it as such in comparing it with inventories of church treasures, but this is not its main characteristic. In fact it is, as it were, a snap-shot of a treasure-hoard at the moment of its transmission to the next generation, when Eberhard and Gisela are dividing it: the items are therefore selected, assigned and listed. They obviously do not represent the couple's entire personal property, but rather, a selection of particularly significant objects embodying their owner's social identity.[85]

It could well be that his association with monastic milieux gave Eberhard the idea of making such a precise list, in other words that ecclesiastical practice provided a cultural model.[86] But ecclesiastical lists in this period were made in order to *avoid* the dispersal of goods. This is a list with a different meaning. It has often been stressed that the formation of the Carolingian aristocracy was closely associated with individual enterprise. The basis for the consolidation of aristocratic status was a man's military success: this is the aspect that Sedulius Scottus, despite his conventional style, so strongly underlines in the three poems written for Eberhard.[87] His prowess in battle against the infidels is acclaimed. He is called *domitor malorum ac pius heros* ("the man who tames evil-doers, and the hero who does his duty", *bellipotens ductor, flos, decus atque patrum, ecclesiae murus* ("commander potent in battle, flower and glory of his fathers, the bastion

---

[85] Riché, "Trésors et collections d'aristocrates laïques carolingiens", pp. 39–46. The role of *mobilia* in testaments has been examined for later periods, on the assumption that they simply were objects to be sold (to pay off the testator's debts): A. Paravicini Bagliani, *I testamenti dei cardinali del Duecento* (Roma, 1980) (Miscellanea della Società romana di storia patria, 25), pp. CXXXIII–CXXXIV.

[86] "Obsession for lists" is the expression used by M. Innes and R. McKitterick, "The Writing of History", in *Carolingian Culture. Emulation and innovation* (Cambridge, 1994), pp. 193–220, at p. 200. The relevance and importance of lists is discussed by McKitterick, *The Carolingians and the written Word*, pp. 163–165.

[87] The use of stereotypes in Sedulius's panegyrics has been examined recently by Godman, *Poets and Emperors. Frankish Politics and Carolingian Poetry*, pp. 155–165.

of the church"), *splendor Francigenum Christicolumque decus* ("splendour of the Frankish people, glory of those who worship Christ"). Eberhard could only be compared with Gideon, the judge charged by God with the defeat of Israel's enemies.[88]

It is not surprising, then, that the list of *mobilia* is so precise: all Eberhard's belongings, because they were his, carried with them the *status* and the military value of their proprietor. In transmitting and mentioning them one by one in an almost descriptive way he made each recognizable. The testament was therefore a unique opportunity to list those items and so give them a new life: what Eberhard had certainly learnt from his ecclesiastical entourage is that what is written exists and has a definite owner, whereas what remains unwritten or unlisted loses both these qualities. The selection of the items, apparently so objective, is in fact a way of defining the social *persona* of the old owner while at the same time foreseeing and planning for the status of the new. The testament is the written transcription of the *rite de passage* that envisages not only Eberhard's prospects in the next world, but also, and especially, the future of his heirs who are to possess the weapons and objects that formerly belonged to him. In writing their testament, Eberhard and Gisela were fully conscious of the relevance of the written word.[89]

The first group of objects is clearly related to Eberhard's "official dress". Unroch receives golden accoutrements, consisting of a golden decorated sword (*spatha*), a golden knife, a gold-decorated belt, two golden spurs, a gold-embroidered tunic and cloak, a golden buckle, and finally an additional sword). Berengar gets two swords adorned with silver and gold, two knifes, two belts, two spurs, and a gold-embroidered tunic. Adalhard receives two swords embellished with ivory and gold, two knifes, and three belts. Rudolph gets three swords, one hundred *mancosi*, that is Arab gold coins, and one belt. If they were not yet the symbols of their owner's public function as seems to be the case in the tenth century, these objects certainly created the visible distinction of aristocratic men.[90] "Belts heavy with golden

---

[88] Quotations respectively from Sedulius Scottus, *Carmina*, XXXIX, LIII, LXVII, in *M.G̃.H. Poetae latini Aevi Karolini*, III/1, pp. 202, 212, 220.

[89] Naming and listing were fundamental uses of the written word in the Carolingian period, as shown by J.L. Nelson, "Literacy in Carolingian government", *The uses of Literacy in Early Medieval Europe*, ed. R. McKitterick (Cambridge, 1990), pp. 294–296 (258–296).

[90] Cf. K. Leyser, *Communications and Power in Medieval Europe. The Carolingian and*

strap-fittings and gem-encrusted knives, exquisite garments and heels weighed down with spurs" (*cingula balteis aureis et gemmeis cultris onerata, exquisitaeque vestes et calcaria talos onerantia*) were the "ornaments of secular glory" (*saecularis ornamenta gloriae*) which Louis the Pious wanted churchmen to abandon.[91] These "ornaments" were the signs of the status and military function of the secular aristocracy.[92] They constituted the *cingulum militiae*, which announced the social identity of the élite layman.[93] The belt, in particular, was to be the badge of public comital duty in the tenth century. Liutprand of Cremona reports many cases in point. The marquis Boso could be identified because "he had a golden belt of amazing length and width which glittered with the gleam of many precious stones" (*mirae longitudinis et latitudinis aureum habebat balteum qui multarum et pretiosarum splendebat nitore gemmarum*).[94] Getting rid of his belt was for Adalbert, marquis of Ivrea, the way to become unrecognisable and thus to escape the Magyars.[95] King Arnulf ordered the count of Bergamo to be hanged on the city gate "with his sword, belt, arm-rings and all the rest of his most precious attire" (*cum ense, balteo, armillis ceterisque pretiosissimis indumentis*).[96]

But some of these objects, notably the spurs and the gold-embroidered garment, are peculiar to the first two of Eberhard's sons, Unroch and Berengar, the laymen. At the same time, Unroch differs from his younger brother because he gets two items that are peculiar to him: the gold-embroidered cloak and the golden buckle. Unroch's equipment has another distinctive feature: it is formed by

---

Ottonian Centuries, ed. T. Reuter (London and Rio Grande, 1994), pp. 51–71; D. Barthélemy, "Qu'est-ce que la chevalerie, en France aux Xᵉ et XIᵉ siécles?", *Revue Historique* 290(1994), pp. 15–73.

[91] Astronomer, *Vita Hludowici imperatoris*, XXVIII, 622.

[92] Cf. Nithard, *Historiarum libri III*, ed. E. Muller (Hannover, 1956) (*M.G.H., Scriptores rerum germanicarum in usum scholarum*, 8), II, 8: without their public *insigna* Charles the Bald and his men are deprived of their identity: J.L. Nelson, "Ninth-century knighthood: the evidence of Nithard", *Studies in Medieval History presented to R. Allen Brown*, eds. C. Harper-Bill, C.J. Holdsworth and J. Nelson (Woodbridge, 1989), pp. 255–266.

[93] See M. De Jong, "Power and humility in Carolingian society: the public penance of Louis the Pious", *Early Medieval Europe* 1 (1992), pp. 39–47.

[94] Liutprand, *Antapodosis*, ed. J. Becker (Hannover and Leipzig, 1915) (*M.G.H., Scriptores rerum Germanicarum in usum scholarum*), IV, 12.

[95] Liutprand, *Antapodosis*, II, 62: '*balteum armillasque aureas omnemque preciosum apparatum proiecit vilibusque se militis sui induit vestimentis, ne ab Hungariis, qui esset, dinosceretur*'.

[96] Liutprand, *Antapodosis*, I, 23. On the value of this example: G. Gandino, *Il vocabolario politico e sociale di Liutprando da Cremona* (Roma, 1995), pp. 91–94.

only one object of each type, while in his brothers' equipment there are pairs, or threes, of similar objects: two swords, two belts, two knifes for Berengar; two swords, three belts, two knifes for Adalhard; three swords for Rudolph. In receiving unique and special objects Unroch seems to acquire a special importance in comparison to the other three sons: his golden equipment appears to be the attire *par excellence* that hands on to him his father's legitimating authority. Provided with unique objects, Unroch is clearly distinguished from his brothers: the division strongly underlines the special value of the first-born son, presenting him as the son in which maternal and paternal investment is concentrated through the transmission of the family's outstanding claims to rank.

Very precisely concerned with social position is the second part of the *paramentum nostrum* section, for the objects here are associated with display in the context of feasting. To be regarded as a rich man (*dives*), the aristocrat had to be perceived as generous and and had to share his wealth with his *fideles*: The feast was a prime occasion for negotiating status and power. Large vessels to hold drink, silver spoons, and drinking-cups are equally distributed between the four sons, underlying the essential value of these items as a basic kit.[97] While daughters are excluded from the section on official dress, each gets one item for ostentatious consumption of drink: one silver cup each for Engiltrud and Iudith, one silver vessel for Heilvick.

In this perspective too, we can consider the liturgical objects in the section on "the equipment of our chapel" (*De paramento capellae nostrae*).[98] The objects listed here are essential parts of Eberhard's cultural environment, in which lay and ecclesiastical aristocrats played co-ordinated roles. These objects were therefore not just complementary but essential elements in the definition of the family's status and the ambitions. In this section, again, Unroch is clearly privileged with unique objects: first and foremost, there is the *corona cum ligno domini*, that is, the relic of the True Cross set in a votive crown,

---

[97] The *gorale*, interpreted by S. Lusuardi Siena, "Trezzo e le terre dell'Adda", *La necropoli longobarda di Trezzo sull'Adda*, ed. E. Roffia (Firenze, 1986), pp. 178–179 as a piece of armour is obviously a drinking-cup as suggested by Riché, "Trésors et collections d'aristocrates", p. 43, n. 39.

[98] It is not our intention here to examine in detail the liturgical objects given by Eberhard: in a local perspective they have recently been studied by D. Gaborit-Chopin, "Les trésors de Neustrie du VII⁰ au IX⁰ siècle d'aprés les sources écrites: orfévrerie et sculpture sur ivoire", *La Neustrie. Les Pays au Nord de la Loire de 650 à 850*, II, ed. H. Atsma (Sigmaringen, 1989), pp. 258–293.

which had formerly belonged to the Carolingian family;[99] then there were other precious gifts granted to the chapel such as the *flabellum* (liturgical fan), the *armilla* (arm-ring), the *pipa* (pitch-pipe) and the *pecten* (liturgical comb).[100] Precious religious objects, possibly including ancient ones like the *vas ad bibendum marmoreum* (marble drinking-cup) given to Adalard,[101] were evidence of the prestige gained by the chapel through the munificence of its patrons, and could at the same time be used as gifts to the church, to tighten the bonds of devotion. Interestingly, Berengar was said, in the early tenth century, to have given Bishop Elbuncus of Parma a "phylactery which my senior [i.e. father] the lord Berengar, the most pious king, gave me, adorned with gold, gems and pearls and having in the middle a beryl-stone carved with the crucifixion" (*filacterium quod senior meus domnus Berengarius piissimus rex mihi dedit cum auro et gemmis et margaritiis ornatum et in medio habens berillum cum cricifixo*): could this be the "*filacterium de auro paratum*" given by his father?[102] Following his father's example, the younger Berengar made gifts to the church of Monza to build up his chapel treasure, thus linking himself to the old seat of ecclesiastical munificence of the catholic Lombard kings.[103]

The final part of the section on *paramentum nostrum* includes the body armour. In particular, and in order of importance, *bruniae*, byrnies or mail-shirts, are given to all four sons; helmets are given, one each, to Unroch, Berengar and Adalhard; *manicae*, arm-guards, are given, one to each of those three and a pair for Rudolph; and two *bembergae*, greaves, are given to Unroch and Adalhard. Thus Unroch and Adalard each get a complete set of body armour, while the other two lack one item of the set. Unroch's uniqueness there-

---

[99] P.E. Schramm, "Der 'Talisman' Karls des Grossen mit Ausblicken auf die mittelalterlichen Brust-Kreuze und -reliquiare", *Herrschaftszeichen und Staatssymbolik*, I (Stuttgart, 1954) (*M.G.H.*, Schriften, 13/1), p. 312. The earliest example of a private relic is the Merovingian case of Erminthrude: H. Atsma and J. Vezin, "Deux testaments sur papyrus de l'époque mérovingienne: étude paléographique", *Haut Moyen-Age. Culture, éducation et société. Etudes Offertes à Pierre Riché* (Paris, 1990), pp. 157–168.

[100] Schramm, "Baugen-armillae: zur Geschichte der königlichen Armspangen", pp. 538–553.

[101] Gaborit-Chopin, "Les trésors de Neustrie du VIIe au IXe siècle d'aprés les sources écrites: orfévrerie et sculpture sur ivoire", p. 270.

[102] *Le carte degli archivi parmensi dei secoli X–XI*, ed. G. Drei (Parma, 1924), pp. 51–56, n. IX (913 april); cf. E. Falconi, "Il testamento del vescovo Elbunco", *Archivio storico per le province parmensi*, 4a s., 9 (1957), pp. 46–67. On Elbunco, see F. Bougard, "Elbungo (Elbunco)", *Dizionario Biografico degli Italiani* 43 (Roma, 1993), pp. 379–380.

[103] *Codex Diplomaticus Langobardie*, no. 340, cols. 570–571, dated 888–915.

fore is not reflected in his military equipment: instead, almost the same items go to the lay sons (Unroch and Berengar) as to the ecclesiastical ones (Adalard and Rudolph). This is not surprising, because defensive weapons denoted participation in the army and were strongly associated with the possession of a landed patrimony.[104] While the sword also indicated status, and carrying a sword was thus considered a hallmark of the elite's distinction, other weapons were supposed to be worn only in time of war and were associated with the aggressive behaviour of the *homo faidosus*: their display at inappropriate times was prohibited.[105] The possession and circulation of byrnies was a constant worry for Carolingian kings: byrnies were seen as crucial defensive weapons for the Carolingian army, and illegal trade in them, although severely restricted, was identified by Charles the Bald in the Edict of Pîtres (864) as one of the main reasons for the successes of the Northmen: whoever dared to sell a *brunia* to the enemy was called "a traitor to the fatherland and betrayer of christendom" (*proditor patrie et expositor christianitatis*) and condemned to death.[106] The *brunia* was thus a sort of "secret weapon" of the Carolingian army, and its possession and distribution was, at least theoretically, controlled by the state. Having four *bruniae* to bequeath is therefore another of Eberhard's most striking attributes: he could furnish each of his four sons with the most precious equipment for war. That *bruniae* and other items of body-armour, like the helmet,

---

[104] For ecclesiastical sons, we can recall the military activity of Rudolph against the Northmen: F.-L. Ganshof, *La Belgique carolingienne* (Bruxelles, 1958), pp. 40–44.

[105] See, for example, *Capitulare missorum in Theodonis villa datum secundum generale* (805), c. 21, in *Capitularia regum Francorum*, I, pp. 122–126, at p. 123: '*De armis non portandis. De armis infra patriam non portandis, id est scutis et lanceis et loricis, et si faidosus sit discutiatur*' (inserted also in *Ansegisi abbatis capitularium collectio*, ibid., 425), trans. P.D. King, *Charlemagne. Translated Sources*, p. 248: 'Concerning not bearing arms within the country, that is, shields and spears and coats of mail. And if he [an offender] should be engaged in a feud, let there be an inquiry. . . .'

[106] *Capitulare Haristallense* (March 799), c. 20, in *Capitularia regum Francorum*, I, p. 51 ('*De brunias ut nullus foris nostro regno vendere praesumat*'); *Capitulare missorum in Theodonis villa datum secundum generale* (805), c. 23, p. 123 (prohibition on merchants' selling *arma et brunias* to the Slavs and the Avars); *Capitulare missorum*, (803), c. 7, in *Capitularia regum Francorum*, I, p. 115 ('*Ut bauga et brunias non dentur negotiatoribus*'); *Edictum Pistense* (25 June 864), c. 25, in *Capitularia regum Francorum*, II/1, ed. A. Boretius, V. Krause (Hannoverae, 1890) (*M.G.H., Legum sectio*, II, *Capitularia regum Francorum*, II), p. 321: '*quia peccatis nostris exigentibus in nostra vicinia Nortmanni deveniunt et eis a nostris bruniae et arma atque caballi aut pro redemptione dantur aut pro pretii cupiditate venundantur*'. On this subject, cf. S. Coupland, "Carolingian arms and armour", *Viator* 21 (1990), pp. 29–50; A.A. Settia, "Le radici tecnologiche della cavalleria medioevale", *Rivista Storica Italiana* 97 (1985), pp. 268–269.

were very valuable indeed is showed by the fact that they are extremely rare in grave-goods, but instead are sometimes found in hoards.[107]

As is well known, the chapel of Eberhard and Gisela possessed many books. The will listed these and provided for their distribution. The book-list also included Gisela, the daughter sent to Italy to become a nun.[108] In this section too, Unroch got the lion's share. He received not only more books, but also special books that clearly distinguish him from his brothers: first of all, the Bible and the New Testament, but also the barbarian law-codes and Vegetius' treatise on the *Ars militaris*.[109] Unroch's *social persona* was thus defined by the bequest to him of books dealing with administration and justice and referring both to Francia, his parents' region of origin, and to Italy and Germany where Unroch's private patrimony lay and where his future public career might well develop. Continuity with his father's role was implied by his possession of the books which would aid him in carrying out public duties. Unroch's brothers were not given these "instruments of government". Yet in the case of certain texts, more than one copy was available to be bequeathed. The *Vita Martini* was given to Berengar, Adalhard and Rudolph, and Isidore's *Sinonima* to Unroch, Engeltrud and Berengar, while Unroch and his sister Iudith each received the *Lex Langobardorum*. If by their quantity and the variety of their subjects Unroch's books clearly suggest that he had special uses for literacy, still the number of books that all the heirs, sons and daughters alike, had in common indicate the value attributed by elite laypeople to the possession of certain fundamental texts as a marker of social pre-eminence.

Books were an important and special gift, and their value could be appreciated and used for different purposes. The will assigned Unroch the "civil books", but in the case of the sons in ecclesiastical life it strongly underlined their membership by birth of the Unruoching family: Adalhard, abbot of Cysoing, was given the psalter "which we have had for our personal use" (*quod ad nostrum opus habuimus*); while the youngest son Rudolph, abbot of St-Bertin and

---

[107] See H. Härke's paper in this volume.

[108] This Gisela has sometimes been confused with Eberhard's wife: McKitterick, 'The Carolingians and the written Word', p. 248; S.G. Bell, "Medieval Women Book Owners: arbiters of lay piety and ambassadors of culture", *Women and Power in the Middle Ages*, eds. M. Erler and M. Kowaleski (Athens and London, 1988), pp. 149–187, at p. 155.

[109] Eberhard and Gisela's books have been fully exhamined by McKitterick, *The Carolingians and the written word*, pp. 245–250.

St-Vaast, got the special present of the psalter of his mother (*quem Gisela ad opus suum habuit*) and the old missal used in the chapel (*quod semper in nostra capella habuimus*). The monasteries where Eberhard's sons lived would enjoy the possession of the books used by the *piissimus comes* and his royal wife, and the bequest to the abbot reinforced the whole community's link to the abbot's family, who would be commemorated as donors and patrons. By comparison with the land and movables, the books were also more impartially divided between sons and daughters: Engeltrud, Judith and Heilwich got four books each, though Gisela got only two, while the sons (except Unroch) each received eight. With the books, at least, the division seems to discriminate less against the daughters of the family, and this suggests the value of the books as a kind of investment in these women. The sets of books given to the daughters do on the whole have a devotional slant. Again in Judith's case, the books included the *Sermo de ebrietate* referring perhaps to the counter-example of sobriety transmitted by her Biblical namesake. Although fewer in quantity, the devotional and personal quality of the books given to the daughters suited the women's function as keepers of memory, praying for the family dead and transmitting their *gesta* and example.

Eberhard's and Gisela's will is therefore conceived as a set of lists, internally structured with a striking difference between the extremely detailed list of the movables, and the very general list of the landed property. After all, the *articulatio* promised by Gisela and Eberhard at the beginning of the document referred, precisely, only to movable wealth. Listing the landed property in general terms left prospects open. Eberhard did not have to defend his land and movables against the ambitions of rival powers—such a defence being the usual reason for precise listing of property—but left his children, especially Unroch, the possibility of settling in areas only vaguely identified in the will, of enlarging their possessions, and of asserting their membership of his family. That this indeterminacy is particularly clear in Unroch's case does not really contradict the pre-eminence expressed by his lion's share of the movable goods. Unroch is the first-born son, that is the one in the prime position to inherit the title and the function of his father: in mentioning large areas of political influence and official duty (*quidquid in Langobardia et in Alemannia de proprietate habere videmur*), Eberhard and Gisela were, it seems, not only thinking about their own land but also about the larger power that went with public functions—functions which Unroch had all the material attributes to be considered worth of. For the other three male children the division was meant to be equal: this very insistence on equality clearly indicated the parents' differential investmentments in Unroch and in his brothers, and pointed towards further distinctions between them so far as wealth and prospects were concerned. Equality determined the potential inheritance rights and rank for all the male members of the Unruoching family, but effectively the sons were separated into two groups, with respect to both land and movables. Eberhard and Gisela clearly knew that the only possible way to be deprived of their land was through confiscation: they hid the difference between the land Eberhard administered as public officer and the land that constituted their private patrimony, for they presented their fiscal property as if it were personal, as *nostra*—"ours". Thus the place where the will was drawn up was termed *curtis nostra Musiestris*,[110] when in fact it was fiscal property. *Nostrum* was used in a very ambiguous way: while for the movables and books it meant the possessions of the couple, in the case of the land it conflated the fiscal estates used by Eberhard as public officer with the *allodia* of the family. The written testament was therefore part of the wider process by which public titles were dynasticised, that is, made hereditary, and the *comitatus* was transformed into a bundle of seigneurial powers.

Eberhard's and Gisela's offspring are therefore divided into two gender groups, and listed with their inheritances, in a perspective of descending privilege, simply in terms of the quantity of lands and objects granted to them, from the eldest to the youngest. If we compare the children listed in the will to the list of Gisela's *cognatio* in 874,[111] we can see that in the will the birth-order is respected only for the sons. Among the daughters Judith seems from the 874 evidence to have been younger than Heilwig, and not, as the will suggests, the other way round. Could it be that the will's inversion of the true order here is due to the fact that Heilwig was the only daughter to be destined for marriage and therefore got a smaller

---

[110] Gasparri, "Dall'età longobarda al secolo X", p. 27, pp. 30–32. The *curtis 'iuris regni nostri que dicitur Musestre'* was in fact granted by Berengar, king of Italy, to his client, the cleric Ino: *I diplomi di Berengario I*, ed. L. Schiaparelli (Roma, 1903) (Fonti per la storia d'Italia, 35), n. 138 (28 July 922, Verona), pp. 354–356; Krahwinkler, *Friaul in Frühmittelalter. Geschichte einer Region vom Ende des fünften bis zum Ende des zehnten Jahrhunderts*, pp. 262–263, f. 84, 87, 90.

[111] *Cartulaire de l'abbaye de Cysoing*, 11, no. 6.

share of the inheritance than her sisters, but that this had to be justified by presenting her as the youngest girl?

4. *A project for the future*

4.1. *Political project and political consciousness in the will*

The will shows us several principles of classification and hierarchization of Eberhard's and Gisela's sons and daughters. A complete picture of the internal relationships of the family can be obtained only by a separate analysis of different parts of the text, and a subsequent integration of the data. An integrated view allows us to perceive political patterns involving the different sons, and distinct areas of action in which these patterns emerge fully. If we think in geographical terms, we can discern the presence, simultaneously, of family involvement in two territorial areas, Italy and northern France. In undertaking the following analysis of the will's internal elements, we shall not let hindsight skew our interpretation. We certainly do not regard the will as an expression of a perfect foreknowledge of the family's political future, especially of the imperial future of Berengar: we are well aware of the risks of historical teleology. We do think, however, that the will reveals consciousness of dynastic interest and the outlines of a possible political project.[112]

The strongest hints of such a political project in the text, concerned Unroch: he was given a very substantial endowment of patrimonial lands; to him were delegated the dynasty's entire interests across large areas; and he was assigned certain symbols that associate him with power of a royal kind (his gold-embroidered cloak, his special equipment, his law-books, and peculiarly precious relics). Unroch thus stood out quite distinctly among the group of Eberhard's sons. This throws light on the Unruochings' political prospects in the mid-860s: Unroch was the central figure, but success remained uncertain and risks were clearly seen in the assimilation of Eberhard's official and patrimonial powers and their concentration on

---

[112] An interpretation of the will as a perfect prediction of the political future seems to be found in Krahwinkler, *Friaul in Frühmittelalter. Geschichte einer Region vom Ende des fünften bis zum Ende des zehnten Jahrhunderts*, pp. 261–264.

the eldest son, given the absence as yet of any undisputed right of primogeniture. The dynasty's interests focused not on Francia, where the family presence was sustained by rich fiscal lands[113] and a private monastery which could function as a centre of dynastic identification and organization,[114] but on Italy, where the power-base consisted of a rich patrimony, probably of fiscal origins,[115] a large clientele or following[116] and above all the control of a key public function.[117] In the northern area is well known a quite relevant patrimony and it's possible to suppose the presence of local clienteles (not expressely known probably because of the scarcity of sources[118]), it's important to stress as the clear distinction between the two areas come from a larger dimension of dinastic presence, perhaps from wider opportunities in the unstable italian kingdom, but surely from the availability of legitimacy sources and of an articulated network of

---

[113] For the fiscal character of many places owned by the Unruochings in this region, see *Cartulaire de Cysoing*, 7–9, no. 3 (*'fiscum nomine Summinium [ ] actum Vitreiaco villa publica [ ] actum fisco Cisonio'*); Grierson, "The Identity of the unnamed Fisc in the 'Breviarium exempla'", pp. 437–461; Ganshof, La Belgique Carolingienne, pp. 76–78.

[114] The convent of San Salvatore/S. Giulia in Brescia cannot be regarded as such: the Unruoching presence there was surely important, but it was not simply a centre of Unroching dynastic identification (they were not, after all, the founders), nor did the Unrochings exercise patronage rights there such as we see at Cysoing. The description of San Salvatore/S. Giulia as "appannaggio degli Unruochingi", Vianello, "Gli Unrochingi e la famiglia di Beggo conte di Parigi", p. 351 footnote, is rather surprising.

[115] Eberhard's Italian patrimony is not known in detail, but we can suppose that he had a goodly share of fiscal property, given the way he inserted himself into the region: for Eberhard in Friuli, see Krahwinkler, *Friaul in Frühmittelalter. Geschichte einer Region vom Ende des fünften bis zum Ende des zehnten Jahrhunderts*, pp. 245–266; the only Italian place mentioned in the will, Musestre, is a fiscal *curtis*.

[116] The importance of clienteles can be deduced only in the following period, from the action of Berengar: Arnaldi, "Berengario". In Eberhard's will, written at the fiscal *curtis* of Musestre, in the county of Treviso, we find a group of witnesses defined as *fideles* of the count: all their names are Frankish, but an area of origin or of patrimonial presence cannot be identified for any one of them. This list shows Eberhard with a clientele, but does not allow us to understand how it was actually used on the ground.

[117] For the function of monasteries and public offices as instruments of dynastic identification and as organizational centres for the political projects of magnate families, see G. Sergi, "Anscarici, Arduinici, Aleramici: elementi per una comparazione fra dinastie marchionali", *Formazione e strutture dei ceti dominanti nel medioevo: marchesi, conti e visconti nel regno italico (secc. IX–XII)* (Roma, 1988) (Nuovi Studi Storici, 1), pp. 11–28.

[118] Unruoching sources for this region correspond to few documents in the cartulary of Cysoing. We lack the rich sources concerning Berengar's royal power in Italy which constitute our main evidence for Unruoching use of clienteles.

social ties, connected of the undiscussed control of the public office.

The dynasty's plans in the area around Cysoing are harder to discern.[119] One crucial preliminary question is that of Adalard's status: lay or ecclesiastical? While in Rudolph's case, there is no doubt,[120] in Adalard's case the sources are simply insufficient for certainty. Nevertheless, it does seem likely that he too was established in an ecclesiastical career. The will itself offers some interesting hints. The movables bequeathed to Adalard resemble those to Rudolph and are clearly different from Unroch's and Berengar's: Adalard does not receive objects symbolizing secular power.[121] Moreover the *clausolae* on Adalard's landed endowment assign him the *curtis* of Cysoing, Camphin and Gruson, "with everything pertaining to that church", and the task of protect the abbey's patrimony. This second *formula* suggests that Adalard was an ecclesiastical (rather than a lay-) abbot of Cysoing. Other charters of this period preserved in the Cysoing cartulary confirm this impression. In 865, when Eberhard was still alive, the priest Walgar give to the monastery of Cysoing some lands in the county of Tournai "on the orders of my lord (*dominus*) Eberhard", and this charter was subscribed by Adalard, "lord (*senior*) of that place".[122] This power over Cysoing, though still undefined, presupposes Adalard's control of the abbey itself. The will records no previous grants to the sons, yet it does say that control of the village of Cysoing had been given to the local church: control of the church (as its abbot) could thus explain Adalard's right to call himself lord of Cysoing before Eberhard's death. A later gift by Gisela to Adalard, in 869, shows that Adalard's patrimony and that of the abbey were legally distinct: Adalard obtained the *curtis* of Somain, "except for the *mansi* given to the monastery" which had to remain at the monks' disposition; but at the same time the charter, preserved in the Cysoing cartulary, shows that, after Adalard's death, Somain passed under the abbey's control, and it was clearly stated

---

[119] Property in the regions of Liège, Brussels and Antwerp does not seem to have been central to the political project.

[120] See Favre, "La famille d'Évrard, marquis de Frioul, dans le royaume franc de l'ouest", pp. 158–160; M. Sot, *Un historien et son église au Xe siècle: Flodoard de Reims* (Paris, 1993), pp. 134f. and p. 159; Rudolph's election as abbot of Cysoing must be dated after Adalard's death. For St.-Bertin, see *Le polyptique de l'abbaye de Saint-Bertin (844–859)*, eds. F.-L. Ganshof, F. Godding-Ganshof and A. de Smet (Paris, 1975).

[121] See below.

[122] *Cartulaire de Cysoing*, pp. 5–7, no. 2.

that none of Adalard's brothers should have any right to it.[123] Adalard's patrimony and that of the abbey were thus closely linked (by the common control of the court of Somain), but it's equally clear that Adalard had no sons and that no sons were foreseen: further evidence for his ecclesiastical status. Finally, in 870, Adalard subscribe the confirmation of Gisela and Rudolph for Cysoing, without any specification of the fonction accomplished by him in this place and in this charter.[124]

No one of these data is conclusive, but altogether they shape a coherent image, and they allow us to think quite surely that Adalard was an ecclesiastic, and that he had the control on the Cysoing abbey.

Adalard's patrimony has to be seen in the context of the strong link between the Unrochings and the church of Cysoing; and while Rudolph's land could not provide a base for a parallel development, the dynasty's interests in this area could be managed as a whole. Berengar was able to dispose of a probably considerable patrimony, concentrated in a relatively small area, sustained by such powerful forms of legitimisation as the tie with the imperial family, a dynastic tradition of high office, and the foundation of a private monastery. There were significant differences between two political projects entrusted to Unroch on the one hand, and Berengar on the other. The different parts of the will show different hierarchies of relationships involving the sons: while the land division shows a clear distinction between Unroch and Berengar, the symbolic objects assigned to these two make them look quite similar. At the moment the will was made, both Francia and northern Italy offered the family similar prospects of power built up from similar combinations of resources. Eberhard is hardly likely to have contemplated, at this point, any future prospects for his dynasty of kingship in Italy.

Eberhard's project for his two elder sons seems analogous, with the integration of different power bases, enriched in Italy by the dynastic control of public office, with the aim to obtain a patrimonial

---

[123] *Cartulaire de Cysoing*, pp. 7f., no. 3.

[124] *Cartulaire de Cysoing*, pp. 8f., no. 4; in this charter it is especially interesting to see that Gisela and Rudolph act apparently with full autonomy, as the family's representatives, while Adalard is not involved in the document as a member of the family. The subscription (*'signum Adalardi'*) does not reveal his function; we have to remember that the charter is preserved in Cysoing's medieval cartulary, where the text was perhaps incompletely transcribed.

control of public powers in both the regions. But to verify the importance of the title of duke of Friuli, and differences between the dynasty's Italian and Frankish projects, we have to analyse the Unruochings' action towards ecclesiastical and monastical institutions, for that is a vital clue to their political projects.

4.2. *Local monasteries and the role of the Gisela's*

The will provides indirect yet telling evidence for the Unrochings' dynastic ambitions in what it reveals of the family's investment in its women. Thanks to women's more general function of transmitting memory, and their particular role in funerary rituals, it is in fact from sources concerned with death that we learn most about this family's consciousness of its identity. In the will, Eberhard's daughter Gisela appears only in the list of books bequeathed. As noted above, she was the namesake of her mother and of Charlemagne's beloved sister, and had been given as a nun to the most famous royal convent in northern Italy, San Salvatore/S. Giulia at Brescia. A tradition of patronage established by the last Lombard queen had been taken up, after a generation or so, by the Carolingians. In the ninth century, queenly protection enhanced San Salvatore's prestige and enriched it by generous gifts: at the same time, from the queen's standpoint, San Salvatore was a most useful place for building up a personal network of relationships with the local aristocracy. The Empress Judith's ambitions for her own offspring led to the establishment of another tradition, which survived for some time in the context of the *regnum italicum*, of bestowing the name of "Gisela" on one daughter in each generation, and then giving that daughter to the convent at Brescia.

The inaugurator of this tradition was Judith's daughter and Eberhard's wife: Gisela herself. A study of successive Gisela's at San Salvatore indicates that two families competed "by Gisela's" for control of San Salvatore in the second half of the ninth century: these were the Unruochings and the Carolingians. It was as if the royal/imperial family had seen a danger implicit in the action of Eberhard's wife: the placing of an Unroching Gisela at San Salvatore might legitimate Unruoching royal ambitions. Subsequent Gisela's, Carolingian and Unruoching, became the instruments and symbols of their families' competition for the Italian kingdom. The Obituary List of San Salvatore/S. Giulia which preserves the memory of Carolingian patronage by commemorating a series of Giselas, also records Eberhard's daughter and other members of the Unruoching family: Brescia's nuns prayed for the Unruochings just as they prayed for the Carolingians.[125]

The link with San Salvatore, through the gift of a daughter whose name strongly recalled the Carolingians, provided Eberhard with both a means of affirming his own familial identity, and a way of forming relationships with the local society of northern Italy. We must set this link, therefore, in the larger context of Eberhard's dealings with Italian churches. Here the evidence of royal charters (unfortunately no relevant private documents survive) shows us Eberhard more than once exercising a well-defined function as an intermediary between the empire and the churches of north-east Italy. In Lothar's diploma of 841 to the duke of Venice, for instance, the duke's request is said to have been presented "by our faithful count Eberhard and by his [the duke's] *missus* named Patrick" (per Heverardum fidelem comitem nostrum ac per missum suum Patritium nomine).[126] In specifying these two intermediaries, the diploma insists on Eberhard's character as an imperial representative and a figure of local power, with whom the duke's envoy could co-operate in introducing the duke's request and obtaining imperial intervention.

Eberhard is entitled in new ways in the diplomas of Lothar's son Louis II: "our most illustrious count and beloved co-father" (illustrissimus comes dilectusque compater noster) in 855, "our most beloved duke and our personal servant" (dilectissimus dux et familiaris noster) in 856.[127] But if these *formulae* illustrate an evolution in the relationship between Eberhard and the imperial family, his function of intermediary remains unchanged: this is significant, for it

---

[125] *Codice necrologico liturgico del monastero di San Salvatore o S. Giulia in Brescia*, ed. A. Valentini (Brescia, 1887), p. 78, p. 80: '*Domnus imperator Lotharius tradidit filiam suam dominam Gislam secundum ordinem sancte regule omnus Hludovicus imperator tradidit filiam suam Gislam*', '*Dominus Eberardus dux tradidit filiam suam Gislam*'. The Unruoching group for commemoration is listed at p. 9 (f. 8r.) and includes, in order: '*Eberardus, Gisla, Unroc Ava, Beringeri, Adelard, Engiltrude, Rodulfus, Iudid, Ellvic*'. See: H. Becher, "Das Königliche Frauenkloster San Salvatore/Santa Giulia im Brescia im Spiegel seiner Memorialüberlieferung, *Frümittelalterliche Studien* 17 (1983), pp. 299–392; M. De Jong, *In Samuel's Image. Child Oblation in the Early Medieval West* (Leiden 1996). The daughters of Unroch and Berengar were later to be given to the convent in their turn: *Annales Fuldenses*, p. 105. See further, above n. 81.

[126] *M.G.H.*, *Diplomata Karolinorum*, III, p. 171, no. 62.

[127] *Ludovici II diplomata*, ed. K. Wagner (Roma, 1994) (Fonti per la storia dell'Italia medievale, Antiquitates, 3), p. 98, no. 17, and p. 103, no. 19.

identifies Eberhard as a strong and reliable interlocutor on behalf of local churches, even if scarcity of evidence leaves obscure the full extent and shape of Eberhard's interventions. But in Lothar's diploma of 843 for the patriarch of Aquileia, acting alongside Eberhard as interemediary between local church and empire is Notting, bishop of Verona.[128] A series of diplomatic missions conducted by the two men allowed Eberhard to create a strong tie with this influential prelate, who was, in succession, bishop of Vercelli, then of Verona and finally of Brescia.[129] Through the Brescia connexion and the exercise of public authority, involving a bishop who acted in concert with Eberhard and served as part of the diplomatic machine of Louis II,[130] the Unruochings were able to respond to the administrative needs of local churches. Within the framework of Unruoching patronage of San Salvatore/S. Giulia, Gisela was assigned the task of consolidating the royal aspect of this bond. Notting's function was not limited to inserting Eberhard into the Brescian context. According to the *Translatio sancti Callixti Cisonium*, it was Notting who helped Eberhard in furnishing prestigious relics for the family monastery of Cysoing.[131]

If in Italy we can speak of Unruoching ecclesiastical patronage functioning in support of family prestige, in Francia the Unruochings' investment in Cysoing produced a similar outcome in rather different ways. Eberhard's will was not the only document he made in anticipation of his own death: like several other members of the aristocracy, he spelled out his last wishes in a number of endowments across several documents. It is often forgotten that Cysoing's very foundation was an integral part of a series of acts of this kind. A substantial part of the Unruochings' landed expansion in Francia took place around Cysoing and through the abbey founded there by Eberhard. Here too, it was Gisela's task to promote the monastery's function as a seat of family prestige and cult: here Eberard's body was buried, and here Gisela saw to the provision of graves for herself

---

[128] *M.G.H., Diplomata Karolinorum*, III, p. 192, no. 76.

[129] See K. Schmid, *Kloster Hirsau und seine Stifter* (Freiburg, 1959), a study almost completely devoted to Notting's family.

[130] The great importance of Notting in the kingdom of Louis II is underlined in P. Delogu, "Strutture politiche e ideologia nel regno di Ludovico II", *Bullettino dell'Istituto storico italiano del Medioevo* 80 (1968), pp. 151–152.

[131] *Translatio sancti Calixti Cisonium*, ed. O. Holder-Egger, in *M.G.H., Scriptores*, XV/I (Hannover, 1887), pp. 418–422.

and for her eldest daughter Engeltrud. Gisela's aim clearly was that Cysoing, as the dynastic church, should be supplied with relics that attracted more gifts and should help construct the image of the founder as *püssimus*. Gisela's role in carrying out the rituals of death and in caring for her husband's body was characteristically that of an aristocratic woman. In establishing an annual commemoration of her close relatives, Gisela enunciated the following list: "I have decreed that there should be an annual meal for the Emperor Louis my father, and the Empress Judith my mother, and for the glorious King Charles my—if I dare say so—full brother, and for my off-spring . . ., and also for all my kindred" (*anniversariam refectionem decrevi fieri pro Ludovico imperatore, patre meo, et pro Judith imperatrice, matre mea, et pro glorioso rege Karolo, si fari audeam, germano, et pro prole mea (. . .) nec non et pro omni cognatione mea*).[132] Here Gisela was perpetuating the imperial aspirations of her sons, asserting her own crucial role in transmitting the legitimacy of their Carolingian succession, and, last but not least, specifying the monastery of Cysoing as the place where its founders' souls would receive particular care.

Both main areas of Unruoching power were therefore marked by family activity focused on ecclesiastical and monastic institutions. But what the family did in each area was quite different. In Francia we see the typical attitude of a great dynasty consolidating its local lord-ship, operating by the foundation and endowment of a monastery, and the establishing of strong bonds of patronage over it. In Italy the Unruochings' bond with San Salvatore/S. Giulia meant above all an evocation of Carolingian legitimacy, even if they also various other moves to strengthen their local position by cultivating monas-tic and secular churches. Co-operation with bishops was in fact one of Eberhard's most the most significant fields of activity: here he was most conspicuously the royal officer, functioning as intermediary between local powers and the monarchy. What were involved in the two regions were different levels and different instruments of inter-vention: in Italy, the taking of monastic vows by a daughter and the family's strong ideological representation in the Obituary List of San Salvatore/S. Giulia; in Francia, the foundation and patrimonial endowment of a monastery identified with the family through rights of patronage, burials and gifts of highly symbolic books.

---

[132] *Cartulaire de Cysoing*, p. 11, no. 6.

In these distinct forms of action directed towards churches and monasteries, the hybrid character of Eberhard's power, as public officer and as representative of a growing dynasty, is clearly displayed. In Italy, the public aspect predominates, in Francia, the dynastic. Both aspects played their parts in defining Eberhard's activities in both regions. But it is precisely the differences that reveal the two elements of this hybrid power as still clearly distinct in the minds of Eberhard and his kin. The existence of patrimonial lands in Italy did not make Eberhard forget that he had more ancient resources of patrimony, patronage, and political support in Francia. Thus it was in Francia that the dynasty could take most comprehensive action towards the building up of a lordship. In Italy, the Unruochings' presence was essentially that of public officers who, even if they had taken initial steps towards the patrimonialisation of their office, acted above all as intermediaries between province and empire.

4.3. *The careers of the sons of Eberhard and Gisela*

In the Unruochings' history during the last decades of the ninth century, the distinction between northern Italy and Francia remained important. Dynastic destinies in Italy were entrusted, as we have seen, to Unroch. But the sources for his comparatively brief Italian career[133] fail to show how he moved to strengthen his local position or how he managed his dynastic patrimony. Nearly all the sparse evidence concerns his participation in Louis II's expedition to southern Italy in 872.[134] It is only with Berengar, who succeeded Unroch in the the Italian patrimony, that the sources become rich and various enough to show how this man's personal power grew through his exploitation of patrimonial lands and a loyal *clientela*, until he obtained first the royal crown of Italy and then the imperial crown as well. This is not the place for details on Berengar's long career.[135] We would like simply to draw attention to the still-live debate among

---

[133] He probably died in 874 or thereabouts: Hlawitschka, *Franken, Alamannen, Bayern und Burgunder in Oberitalien (774–962)*, p. 277; Arnaldi, "Berengario I", p. 1.

[134] Hlawitschka, *Franken, Alamannen, Bayern und Burgunder in Oberitalien (774–962)*, p. 276.

[135] The best analysis of Berengar's career is still Arnaldi, "Berengario I", pp. 1–26; but see also *idem*, "Da Berengario agli Ottoni", *Storia di Brescia*, I, ed. G. Treccani degli Alfieri (Brescia, 1961), pp. 485–517; cf. V. Fumagalli, *Il regno italico* (Torino, 1978), pp. 171–193.

historians on the question of how much his power-base in Friuli contributed to Berengar's success. How important, in other words, was
the Unruoching inheritance in north-east Italy? Some scholars think
that Berengar's power was always closely linked to his regional base;
others see the Friulan region as simply supplying some institutional
support for a career which actually lacked any solid territorial base.[136]
Our analysis of the will offers no clear answer to the problem. It
does suggest, however, that the relevant political investment in Italy
had already been made for Unroch, at a time when the chances of
an Italian crown for the Unruochings were fairly remote. That local
investment is probably what the Unruochings bet on in 863–864,
but did Eberhard lay a similar bet in the 870s? We can only say
that that seems possible, even likely.

The transfer of Berengar to Italy in 870, and his succession to
Unroch in 874 or soon after, produced a deep change in family
plans for the region around Lille. It almost certainly brought about
the failure of the person probably seen at the time, and visible to
us now, through the documents of Cysoing,[137] as the principal man-
ager of the dynasty's local strength: Gisela. In the years immediately
following Eberhard's death, Gisela's determined character played a
central role in the family's local fortunes. She pursued three consistent lines of action: the recovery from her brother, Charles the Bald,
of dynastic lands lost by Eberhard; the distribution of these to her
sons, probably with the aim, above all, of guaranteeing the equity
of the division, as laid down in the will;[138] and the protection of the
monastery of Cysoing both by her patrimonial endowment, and by
a forging a stronger identification between church and dynasty.

This last point needs a little more attention, because it suggests
certain respects in which the family's arrangements had remained
incomplete at the time of Eberhard's death. Gisela acted with deter-

---

[136] The first interpretation is, for example, offered by Stefano Gasparri, who says
that 'anche quando, a partire dall'888, Berengario ottenne il trono, il suo potere
restò sempre concentrato nella marca, intesa però nel senso largo espresso negli
Annali di Fulda, estesa cioè a tutta l'area veneta": Gasparri, "Dall'età longobarda
al secolo X', p. 28; the second interpretation can be found in Cammarosano, "L'alto
medioevo", p. 61 and p. 67.

[137] *Cartulaire de Cysoing*, pp. 7–11, nos. 3–6, from 869 and 874.

[138] These two aims seem to be shown in *Cartulaire de Cysoing*, p. 7, no. 3; Gisela
recalls the restitution made by Charles the Bald, and goes on to declare that she
has decided to give part of this property to the monastery of Cysoing, and '*ceteras
res a me in Galliis habitas, inter tres infantes meos, Rodulfum videlicet, et Berengarium, nec non
et te, dulcissime fili, Adelarde, per singulas portiones dividere*'.

mination, together with her son Unroch, to secure the bringing back of Eberhard's body from Italy to Cysoing, and his burial near the altar of the oratory; at the same time Gisela arranged for her own burial in the monastery, and prepared for this by additional gifts. But the bond between the family and the church was expressed above all by the election of Adalard and then Rudolph as abbots of Cysoing. It is particularly interesting that Rudolph, already abbot of St.-Bertin and St.-Vaast, took Adalard's place as abbot of Cysoing after his death. It is Rudolph, with his well-known role in dealing with the Vikings, who shows how, in the deep crisis of imperial power in this region, a family of this kind and level could seize its chances, if it was represented by a strong man. If that man was a layman, an enduring local dynasty could be created. But Rudolph, for all his capabilities in co-ordinating military forces, and for all his potential for extending his political activity to a regional scale, was not a layman. His kinds of strength would be the basis for the achievement of the counts of Flanders: their success in some sense reflects what might have been, had Italy not beckoned, the outcome of the political project entrusted to Berengar in Eberhard's and Gisela's will.[139]

4.4. *Eberhard after the Unruochings*

The Unruochings' plans in Francia proved a dead end. Unroch's death, Berengar's move to Italy and consequent total separation from Francia, and the fact that the two ecclesiastical sons who remained there could have no heirs: these factors together ended every possibility. The end of the Frankish branch of the Unruochings signified the death not only of a dynasty, but also of a political project. It created an empty space in the network of social bonds and forms of legitimation that Eberhard and Gisela had constructed. Into this political and territorial space, other powers tried to insert themselves. Various seigneurial dynasties secured control of countships in the region. There is no clear evidence of their trying to recover any of the old Unruoching patrimony, though vestiges of continuity of this sort may well have remained. Some of these seigneurial families may

---

[139] For Rudolph's role in co-ordinating defence against the Northmen, and for a short discussion of the chances offered in this region to local powers because of the crisis in the kingdom, see Ganshof, *La Belgique carolingienne*, pp. 40–46.

have been descended from one of Heilwig's successive marriages, in which the old Unruoching names were reused.[140] There is evidence of a truly remarkable bid for a symbolic retrieval of something of the Unruochings' position, on the part of Count Hucbald, husband of Eberhard's daughter Heilwig: thanks to Flodoard, we know that after the death of Rudolph, who had bequeathed Cysoing to the church of Rheims, Hucbald tried to prevent both the legal transfer of the monastery, and the literal transfer of its relics of St. Calixtus which he gained temporary possession of while they were being taken to St Quentin on the orders of the archbishop of Rheims.[141] Hucbald was interested not only in the monastery, but in the relics that Eberhard had obtained for Cysoing. Hucbald was attempting to recover some symbols of the succession to Unruoching power. As for the counts of Flanders, their first moves to expand into this region led them into some places with Unruoching connexions, and they also established control of the abbeys of S. Bertin and S. Vaast, which had formerly been within the Unruochings' orbit.[142]

The Unruoching inheritance continued to exert an influence on levels other than the political, seigneurial and dynastic: the figure of Eberhard was remembered, embellished and used in local monastic culture by his so-called canonization. As noted above, Eberhard's body was brought "home" to Cysoing by Gisela and Unroch. Two centuries later, the body of St. Eberhard was twice recalled in dedication charters of two churches of the region.[143] The identification with our count seems clear, for some twelfth-century documents record a cult of St. Eberhard in the church of Cysoing. During the twelfth century, and under the impetus of the archbishop of Rheims, Cysoing was completely restored thanks to the arrival there of Augustinian canons who made successful efforts to recover some of the monastic lands.[144] Alongside this revival of the church of Cysoing,

---

[140] For Heilwig, her two marriages (to Hucbald count of Ostrevant and to Roger of Laon) and for her descendents, see P. Grierson, "La maison d'Évrard de Frioul et les origines du comté de Flandre", *Revue du nord* 24 (1938), pp. 258–264; Sot, *Un historien et son église au Xe siècle: Flodoard de Reims*, p. 220.

[141] These vicissitudes are studied in Favre, "La famille d'Évrard, marquis de Frioul, dans le royaume franc de l'ouest", pp. 160f., who was the first to link Hucbald to the Unruoching family.

[142] See F.-L. Ganshof, *La Flandre sous les premiers comtes* (Bruxelles, 1944), pp. 19–23; F.-L. Ganshof, "Les origines du comté de Flandre. A propos d'un ouvrage récent", *Revue belge de Philologie et d'Histoire* 16 (1937), pp. 367–385.

[143] J. Bataille, *Cysoing. Les seigneurs, l'abbaye, la ville, la paroisse* (Lille, 1934), p. 30.

[144] *Cartulaire de Cysoing*, pp. 12–17, nos. 8–11, p. 30, no. 25, p. 43; no. 34.

the canons sponsored a recovery of the memory of Eberhard, now revered as a saint.[145] Nor was this simply the canons' invention, for some traces of a sponaneous beatification of Eberhard can already be found, as just noted, in the previous century. Such a cult is most likely to be successful if based on a local tradition. Moreover, the recover of the memory of Eberhard as Cysoing's founder was accompanied by a diffusion of the name "Eberhard" in the region, perhaps based on the toponym, well-attested in the twelfth century and still in use today, of a "St. Eberhard's ditch" at Cysoing.[146] The traditions about Eberhard were confused: in local sources he was called "St. Eberhard the confessor", and only in the late Middle Ages did new learned discoveries permit the reassertion of the historical personage's military character.[147] In the last centuries of the Middle Ages, attention to this saint increased with the exhumation of his body, and the appearance of a liturgy and some hagiographical sources for him.[148] But all these developments show quite clearly that Eberhard's canonization had no connexion with the Unruoching political project, any more than had the original translation of Eberhard's body to Cysoing. The canonization was a purely ecclesiastical move made by Cysoing's canons who, probably on the basis of a confused local memory, found in Eberhard a suitable founding figure to attract a cult.

5. *Conclusions*

Many clues help us to grasp that a basic functions of the will of Eberhard and Gisela was to shape the characteristics and political ambitions of the new family produced by the couple. For one thing, there is the way Gisela and Eberhard refer to themselves: Gisela is

---

[145] *Cartulaire de Cysoing*, p. 77, no. 57.

[146] For the ditch: *Cartulaire de Cysoing*, p. 24, no. 20; p. 161, no. 129; p. 176, no. 132; for some other men called Eberhard in the twelfth century in this region: *Cartulaire de Cysoing*, p. 27, no. 21; p. 36, no. 28; p. 41, no. 32; p. 45, no. 35; pp. 58f., no. 43 f.; pp. 84, no. 63.

[147] For the different qualities attributed to St. Eberhard in this period, see the charters listed in the following note. We should stress that in the early Middle Ages 14 saints or *beati* called Eberhard are known (mostly unrecognized by the Church): *Bibliotheca sanctorum*, V (Roma, 1964), cols. 378–389.

[148] *Cartulaire de Cysoing*, p. 216, no. 169; p. 218, no. 171; pp. 361–363, no. 265; pp. 364f., no. 267; pp. 509–512, nos. 316–318, pp. 764–788; pp. 898–905, no. 20.

never said to be Louis's daughter, but instead Eberhard's *coniux*, nor is Eberhard identified as Unroch's son. So we have no evident link with the past, such as an explicit dynastic reference. Instead a strong investment in the family's future is founded on Eberhard's role, prestige and function, and on Gisela's role as legitimate representative of the Carolingian line, in the present. The project is therefore to create a totally new family whose potentially imperial characteristics, transmitted by Gisela to her sons, are clearly expressed by the vocabulary used in the will: Eberhard's and Gisela's *formulae*, words, land, weapons, books, and liturgical vestments and vessels were the clearest evidence of their status. The division between sons and daughters by birth-order and gender tends therefore to identify a single descent-line with special claims to legitimate authority. These claims are expressed in the implicit difference between the *primogenitus* Unroch and the other children, and in the quality and quantity of his inheritance: the difference emerges less from formal assertion than directly through the list itself. The family's investment in Unroch was not intended to substain stable but limited aspirations to local power in Francia: it was a bet laid on public office as a source of prestige and, potentially, of still more valuable prizes.

At the same time the list of *mobilia* distinguishes the lay sons (Unroch and Berengar) from the ecclesiastical (Adalard and Rudolph): only the former have political futures. In such dynastic terms, the daughters are relatively insignificant, although the absence of a hierarchy between them, the inversion of the birth-order of Judith and Heilwig and the equality of the gifts made to them, limit the dispersion of the Unruochings' landed property to potential new families without denying these women's capacity to share in the founding of new dynasties through their marriages. Gisela's special task is to affirm the Carolingian connection.

The will attempted, as it were, to "predestine" the family. In the short run, it apparently succeeded. Unroch was the first son of a count of Friuli to be named count himself, that is, to retain his father's title; and when Unroch died, his brother Berengar managed to obtain the title in his place. The family was committed to establishing a territorial power in Friuli not only as a political base from which to pursue royal aspirations, but also as the core of a territorial princedom. Friuli began, with Eberhard's family, to function as a platform for individual and family success, and it did so in terms both of the office of countship (or dukedom) and of the territorial district with which the office was linked. Continuity was achieved in both respects.[149]

The will also conveys the life-style of this couple, whose ambitions were shown in their imitation of an "imperial" attitude towards the patronage of scholars. The relationship between Eberhard and these learned churchmen was founded on a shared interest in the elaboration of a new culture: the hospitality Eberhard gave to Gottschalk and Anastasius the Librarian was symptomatic of the lay elite's cultural liveliness during the reign of Louis the Pious,[150] but also denoted the special prestige of Eberhard's entourage.[151] Perhaps it was precisely at Eberhard's court that Gottschalk developed his theory of double predestination, developing ideas already present in the patriarchate of Aquileia at least in the 840's.[152] By comparing Eberhard with Gideon, Sedulius Scottus presents Eberhard as the intellectual layman who devoted himself to defending his *patria* from the infidels, and showed the kingly virtue of piety.[153]

Eberhard and Gisela, in making their will, made a number of thoughtful choices which reflected the options of both public and private power available to the Carolingian elite. The care they took is particularly clear in their distribution of precious objects—the material evidence of public prestige and private virtues. These objects were heirlooms: they legitimised the future owners' social power while buttressing the concept of a dynastic patrimony that had to be passed from one generation to the next. Taking this long perspective, Eberhard and Gisela foresaw their own commemoration after death as part of the family's future. The written document embodying their dynastic arrangements, while formally descended from Roman models and practices of will-making, acquired different functions in a mid-ninth-century context. Dhuoda, Bernard of Septimania's wife,

---

[149] See the conceptual distinctions suggested by Sergi, "Anscarici, Arduinici, Aleramici: elementi per una comparazione fra dinastie marchionali", pp. 11–15.

[150] As pointed out by Werner, "'Hlodovicus Augustus'. Gouverner l'empire chrétien. Idées et réalités", pp. 71–72.

[151] D. Ganz, "The debate on predestination", *Charles the Bald: court and kingdom*, pp. 283–302; G. Arnaldi, "Anastasio Bibliotecario", *Dizionario biografico degli Italiani*, III (Roma, 1961), pp. 25–27.

[152] Cf. C.G. Mor, "La cultura aquileiese nei secoli IX–XII", *Storia della cultura veneta dalle origini al Trecento* (Vicenza, 1976), pp. 294–295; C. La Rocca, *Pacifico di Verona* (Roma, 1995). The case against Gotteschalk made by Hrabanus Maurus to Eberhard belongs to the years 846–847 (*M.G.H.*, *Epistolae*, V, ed. E. Dümmler (Berlin, 1899), pp. 481–487, no. 42).

[153] Sedulius Scottus, *Carmina*, LXVII, p. 221.

had recommended her son William to pray for his father's ancestors "who left him their property in legitimate inheritance . . . And although Scripture says: 'Another rejoices in alien goods', it is not, as I said, others who enjoy these inheritances of the ancestors, but rather they are the possession of Bernard, your lord and father" (*qui illi res suas in legitima dimiserunt hereditate (. . .) Et licet Scriptura dicat: In bonis alienis gaudet alter, tamen eorum, ut praedixi, haereditates non extranei sed tuus possidet dominus et pater Bernardus*).[154] Gisela and Eberhard were not only "keeping while giving": they were resolutely planning the future of their family, using an ancient form for purposes that were new.

BIBLIOGRAPHY

Primary sources

Annales Fuldenses, ed. F. Kurze (Berlin, 1981) (*M.G.H., Scriptores in usum Scholarum* 7).
Astronomi *Vita Hludowici imperatoris*, ed. R. Rau, *Quellen zur karolingischen Reichsgeschichte* 1 (Berlin, 1955) (Ausgewählte Quellen zur deutschen Geschichte des Mittelalters 5)).
Capitularia regum Francorum, I, ed. A. Boretius (*M.G.H., Legum sectio* 2, *Capitularia regum Francorum* 1).
Capitularia regum Francorum, II/1, a cura di A. Boretius, V. Krause (Hannoverae, 1890) (*M.G.H., Legum sectio* 2, *Capitularia regum Francorum* 2).
Le carte degli archivi parmensi dei secoli X–XI, ed. G. Drei (Parma, 1924).
Cartulaire de l'Abbaye de Cysoing, ed. I. De Coussemaker (Lille, 1885).
CDL, I: *Codice Diplomatico Longobardo* 1, ed. L. Schiaparelli (Roma. 1929) (Fonti per la storia d'Italia, 62).
CDL, III/1: *Codice Diplomatico Longobardo* 3–1, ed. C. Brühl (Roma, 1973).
CDV, I: *Codice diplomatico veronese. Dalla caduta dell'impero romano alla fine del periodo carolingio*, ed. V. Fainelli (Venezia, 1940).
Ch.La.A., XXVI, *Chartae Latinae antiquiores* 26 (Italy 8), ed. J. Tjader (Zürich, 1987).
Ch.La.A., XXVIII: *Chartae Latinae antiquiores* 28 (Italy 9), ed. R. Marichal J. Tjader, G. Cavallo and F. Magistrale (Zürich, 1988).
Ch.La.A., XXX: *Chartae Latinae antiquiores* 30 (Italy 11), ed. P. Supino Martini (Zürich, 1988).
Ch.La.A., XXXVI: *Chartae latinae antiquiores* 36 (Italy 17), ed. G. Nicolaj (Zürich, 1990).
Ch.La.A., XXXVII: *Chartae Latinae antiquiores* 37 (Italy 18), ed. P. Supino Martini (Zürich, 1990).
Ch.La.A., XXXVIII: *Chartae Latinae antiquiores* 38 (Italy 19), ed. M. Palma (Zürich, 1990).
Ch.La.A., XXXIX: *Chartae Latinae antiquiores* 39 (Italy 20), ed. F. Magistrale (Zürich, 1991).

---

[154] Dhuoda, *Manuel pour mon fils*, ed. P. Riché (Paris, 1975), p. XIV, pp. 318–320. On this passage, see C.B. Bouchard, "Family structure and family consciousness among the aristocracy in the ninth to the eleventh centuries", *Francia* 14 (1986), pp. 639–658, at p. 642.

Ch.La.A., XL: *Chartae Latinae antiquiores* 40 (Italy 21), ed. M. Palma (Zürich, 1994).

Codex diplomaticus Langobardie, ed. G. Porro Lambertenghi (Torino, 1873) (H.P.M., 13).

Codice necrologico liturgico del monastero di San Salvatore o S.Giulia in Brescia, ed. A. Valentini (Brescia, 1887).

I diplomi di Berengario I, ed. L. Schiaparelli (Roma, 1903) (Fonti per la storia d'Italia, 35).

Documenti relativi alla storia di Venezia anteriori al Mille 1, ed. R. Cessi (Padova, 1940).

Einhardi *Vita Karoli imperatoris*, ed. O. Holder-Hegger (Hannoverae, 1911) (*M.G.H.*, *Scriptores rerum Germanicarum in usum scholarum* 25).

Gesta Berengarii imperatoris, ed. P. de Winterfeld, *M.G.H.* *Poetae latini aevi karolini* 4–1, (Berlin, 1899).

Karoli III diplomata, ed. P.F. Kehr (Berlin, 1937) (*M.G.H.* *Diplomata regum Germaniae ex stirpe Karolinorum* 2).

Liber pontificalis ecclesie Ravennatis, ed. O. Holder Hegger, *M.G.H.*, *Scriptores rerum langobardicarum et italicarum* (Berlin, 1878).

Liutprandi *Antapodosis*, ed. J. Becker (Hannover and Leipzig, 1915) (*M.G.H.*, *Scriptores rerum Germanicarum in usum scholarum*, 41, pp. 1–158.

Lotharii I diplomata, ed. Th. Schieffer, *M.G.H.*, *Diplomata karolinorum* 3 (Berlin, 1966).

Ludovici II diplomata, ed. K. Wagner (Roma, 1994) (Fonti per la storia dell'Italia medievale, Antiquitates, 3).

M.G.H., *Poetae latini aevi karolini*, III/1, ed. L. Traube (Berlin, 1896).

M.G.H. *Poetae latini aevi karolini*, IV/1, ed. P. de Winterfeld (Berlin, 1899).

Nithardi *Historiarum libri III*, ed. E. Muller (Hannover, 1956) (*M.G.H.*, Scriptores rerum germanicarum in usum scholarum, 8).

I placiti del regnum Italiae 1, ed. C. Manaresi (Roma, 1955) (Fonti per la storia d'Italia, 92).

Ratherii *Praeloquiorum libri sex* 1 and 17, ed. P.L.D. Reid (Turnhout, 1984) (Corpus Christianorum, continuatio mediaevalis, 46A).

Recueil des chartes de l'abbaye de Saint-Benoit-sur-Loire 1, ed. M. Prou and A. Vidier (Paris, 1900).

Thegani *Vita Hludowici imperatoris*, ed. R. Rau, *Quellen zur karolingischen Reichsgeschichte* 1 (Berlin, 1955) (Ausgewählte Quellen zur deutschen Geschichte des Mittelalters 5).

Secondary sources

Amelotti, M., *Il testamento romano attraverso la prassi documentaria, 1. Le forme classiche del testamento* (Firenze, 1966).

——, "Testamenti ed atti paratestamentari nei papiri bizantini", *Proceedings of the twelfth international Congress of Papirology*, ed. D.H. Samuel (Toronto, 1970), pp. 15–17.

Arce, J., '*Funus imperatorum*'. *Los funerales de los emperadores romanos*, (Madrid, 1988).

Arnaldi, G., "Berengario I", *Dizionario Biografico degli Italiani* 9, (Roma, 1967), pp. 1–26.

——, "Da Berengario agli Ottoni", *Storia di Brescia* 1, ed. G. Treccani degli Alfieri (Brescia, 1961), pp. 485–517.

——, "Anastasio Bibliotecario", *Dizionario biografico degli Italiani* 3 (Roma, 1961), pp. 25–27.

Atsma, H. and J. Vezin, "Deux testaments sur papyrus de l'époque mérovingienne: étude paléographique", *Haut Moyen-Age. Culture, éducation et société. Etudes Offertes à Pierre Riché* (Paris, 1990), pp. 157–168.

Barthélemy, D., "Qu'est-ce que la chevalerie, en France aux Xe et XIe siécles?", *Revue Historique*, 290 (1994), pp. 15–73.

Bataille, J., *Cysoing. Les seigneurs, l'abbaye, la ville, la paroisse* (Lille, 1934).

Becher, H., "Das Königliche Frauenkloster San Salvatore/Santa Giulia im Brescia im Spiegel seiner Memorialüberlieferung", *Frühmittelalterliche Studien* 17 (1983), pp. 299–392.
Bertram, M., "Mittelalterliche Testamente. Zur Entdeckung einer Quellengattung in Italien", *Quellen und Forschungen aus italienischen Archiven und Bibliotheken* 68 (1988), pp. 509–544.
Bouchard, C.B., "Family Structure and family Consciousness among the Aristocracy in the ninth to the eleventh Centuries", *Francia* 14 (1986), pp 639–658.
Bougard, F., "Elbungo (Elbunco)", *Dizionario Biografico degli Italiani* 43 (Roma, 1993), pp. 379–380.
Bourdieu, P., *La distinction* (Paris, 1979).
Bullough, D.A., "Leo 'qui apud Hlotarium magni loci habebatur' et le gouvernement du 'regnum Italiae' à l'époque carolingienne", *Le Moyen Age* 67 (1961), pp. 237–245.
Cammarosano, P., "L'alto medioevo", *Storia della società friulana*, ed. P. Cammarosano 1, *Il Medioevo* (Udine, 1988), pp. 9–155.
Chapman, R., Kinnes I., Randsborg K. (eds.), *The Archaeology of Death* (Cambridge, 1981).
Charles the Bald: court and kingdom, eds. M.T. Gibson and J.L. Nelson (Oxford, 1990).
Chiffoleau, J., *La comptabilité de l'au-delà. Les hommes, la mort et la religion dans la région d'Avignon à la fin du Moyen Age (vers 1320–1480)* (Rome, 1980) (Collection de l'Ecole Française de Rome 47).
Consolino, F.E., "La poesia epigrafica pavese", *Storia di Pavia* 2 (Milano, 1985), pp. 137–145.
Coopland, G.W., *The Abbey of St. Bertin and his Neighbourhood* (Oxford, 1914).
Coupland, S., "Carolingian arms and armory", *Viator* 21 (1990), pp. 29–50.
Costambeys, M., "An aristocratic community on the northern Frankish frontier 690–726", *Early Medieval Europe* 3 (1994), pp. 39–62.
Death in Towns. Urban Responses to the Dying and the Dead (Leicester London and New York, 1992).
Delogu, P., "Strutture politiche e ideologia nel regno di Ludovico II", *Bullettino dell'Istituto storico italiano del Medioevo* 80 (1968), pp. 137–189.
Depoin, I., "Le duc Evrard du Frioul et les trois comtes Mafrid", *Annales de la Société d'archéologie de Bruxelles* 13 (1899), pp. 45–60.
De Jong, M., "Power and humility in Carolingian society: the public penance of Louis the Pious", *Early Medieval Europe* 1 (1992), pp. 29–52.
——, *In Samuel's Image. Child Oblation in the Early Medieval West* (Leiden, 1996).
Dutton, P.E., *Carolingian Civilization* (Ontario, 1993)
Epstein, S., *Wills and Wealth in medieval Genoa (1150–1250)* (Cambridge and London, 1984).
Falconi, E., "Il testamento del vescovo Elbunco", *Archivio storico per le province parmensi* 4a s., 9 (1957), pp. 46–67.
Fattori, M.T., "I santi antenati carolingi fra mito e storia: agiografie e genealogie come strumento di potere dinastico", *Studi medievali* s. III, 34 (1993), pp. 487–561.
Favre, É., "La famille d'Évrard, marquis de Frioul, dans le royaume franc de l'ouest", *Études d'histoire du Moyen Age dédiés à Gabriel Monod* (Paris, 1896), pp. 155–162.
Feers, I., "Eberardo, marchese del Friuli", *Dizionario Biografico degli Italiani* 42 (Roma, 1993), pp. 252–255.
Fehring, G.P., *Einfürung in die Archäologie des Mittelalters* (Darmstadt, 1987).
Février, P.A., "La mort chrétienne", *Segni e riti nella chiesa altomedievale occidentale* (Spoleto, 1987) (Settimane di studio del Centro Italiano di Studi sull'alto medioevo, 37), pp. 881–942.
Fumagalli, V., *Il regno italico* (Torino, 1978).
Gaborit-Chopin, D., "Les trésors de Neustrie du VIIe au IXe siècle d'après les

sources écrites: orfévrerie et sculpture sur ivoire", *La Neustrie. Les Pays au Nord de la Loire de 650 à 850*, II, ed. H. Atsma (Sigmaringen, 1989), pp. 258–293.

Gandino, G., *Il vocabolario politico e sociale di Liutprando da Cremona* (Roma, 1995), pp. 91–94.

Ganshof, F.-L., "Les origines du comté de Flandre. A propos d'un ouvrage récent", *Revue belge de Philologie et d'Histoire* 16 (1937), pp. 367–385.

——, *La Flandre sous les premiers comtes* (Bruxelles, 1944).

——, *La Belgique carolingienne* (Bruxelles, 1958).

——, "Le statut de la femme dans la monarchie franque", *La femme* 2 (Bruxelles, 1962) (Recueil de la Société Jean Bodin pour l'histoire comparative des institutions 12).

Ganz, D., "The debate on predestination", *Charles the Bald: court and kingdom*, eds. M.T. Gibson and J.L. Nelson (Oxford, 1990), pp. 283–302.

Gasparri, S., "Dall'età longobarda al secolo X", *Storia di Treviso, 2 Il Medioevo*, eds. D. Rando and G.M. Varanini (Venezia, 1991), pp. 3–39.

Geary, P.J., *Aristocracy in Provence. The Rhône basin at the dawn of the carolingian age* (Stuttgart, 1985) (Monographien zur Geschichte des Mittelalters 31).

Giardina, C., "Successioni. Diritto intermedio", *Novissimo Digesto italiano* 18 (Torino, 1971), pp. 727–748.

Godman, P., *Poets and Emperors. Frankish Politics and Carolingian Poetry* (Oxford, 1987).

Grierson, Ph., "La maison d'Évrard de Frioul et les origines du comté de Flandre", *Revue du nord* 24 (1938), pp. 241–266.

——, "The Identity of the unnamed Fisc in the 'Breviarium exempla'", *Revue Belge de Philologie et histoire* 18 (1939), pp. 437–459.

Groag Bell, S., "Medieval Women Book Owners: arbiters of lay piety and ambassadors of culture", *Women and Power in the Middle Ages*, eds. M. Erler and M. Kowaleski (Athens and London, 1988), pp. 149–187.

Gurevic, A., "Représentations et attitudes à l'égard de la propriété pendant le haut moyen age", *Annales E.S.C.* 27 (1972), pp. 523–547.

Headeger, L., *Iron-Age Societies* (Oxford and Cambridge Mass., 1992).

Hennebicque-Le Jan, R., "Prosopographica neustrica: les agents du roi en Neustrie de 639 à 840", *La Neustrie. Les Pays au nord de la Loire de 650 à 850* 1, ed. H. Atsma (Sigmaringen, 1989), pp. 231–286.

Hirsch, P., *Die Erhebung Berengars I von Friaul zum König im Italien* (Inaugural-Dissertation zur Erlangung der Doktorwürde der Hohen Philosophischen Fakultät der Kaiser-Wilhelms-Universität zu Strassburg) (Strassburg, 1910).

Higham, N., *Rome, Britain and the Anglo-Saxons* (London, 1992).

Hlawitschka, E., *Franken, Alamannen, Bayern und Burgunder in Oberitalien (774–962)* (Freiburg im Breisgau, 1960).

Hofmeister, A., "Markgrafen und Markgrafschaften im italienischen Königreich in der Zeit von Karl dem Grossen bis auf Otto den Grossen (774–962)", *Mitteilungen des Instituts für Österreichische Geschichtsforschung* Ergänzungsband 7 (1906), pp. 215–428.

Hopkins, K., *Death and Renewal. Sociological Studies in Roman History* 2 (Cambridge, 1983).

Innes, M. and Mc Kitterick R., "The Writing of History", *Carolingian Culture. Emulation and innovation* (Cambridge, 1994), pp. 193–220.

Jarnut, J., "Ludwig der Fromme, Lothar I. und das *Regnum Italiae*", *Charlemagne's Heir. New Perspectives on the Reign of Louis the Pious (814–840)*, eds. P. Godman, R. Collins (Oxford, 1990), pp. 349–362.

Kasten, B., "Erbrechtliche Verfügungen des 8. und 9. Jahrhunderts", *Zeitschrift der Savigny-Stiftung für Rechtsgeschichte – Germanistische Abteilung* 108 (1990), pp. 236–338.

King, P.D., *Charlemagne. Translated Sources* (Kendal, 1987).

Krahwinkler, H., *Friaul in Frühmittelalter. Geschichte einer Region vom Ende des fünften bis zum Ende des zehnten Jahrhunderts* (Wien and Köln, 1992).

La Rocca, C., "Uno specialismo mancato. Esordi e fallimento dell'archeologia medievale italiana alla fine dell'Ottocento", *Archeologia Medievale* 20 (1993), pp. 13–43.

——, *Pacifico di Verona* (Roma, 1995).

Lawrence, C.H., *Medieval Monasticism. Forms of Religious Life in Western Europe in the Middle Ages* (Harlow, 1984).

Leyser, K., *Rule and Conflict in an early medieval Society. Ottonian Saxony* (London, 1979).

——, *Communications and Power in Medieval Europe. The Carolingian and Ottonian Centuries*, ed. T. Reuter (London and Rio Grande, 1994).

Lusuardi Siena, S., "Trezzo e le terre dell'Adda", *La necropoli longobarda di Trezzo sull'Adda*, ed. E. Roffia (Firenze, 1986), pp. 178–179.

Liruti, G.G, *Notizia delle cose del Friuli* 5 (Udine, 1777).

Mc Kitterick, R., *The Carolingians and the written Word* (Cambridge, 1989).

Michalowski, R., "Le don d'amitié dans la société carolingienne et les 'Translationes sanctorum'", *Hagiographie, culture et sociétés. IVe–XIIe siècle* (Paris, 1981), pp. 399–416.

Mor, C.G., "La cultura aquileiese nei secoli IX–XII", *Storia della cultura veneta dalle origini al Trecento* (Vicenza, 1976).

Morris, I., *Burials and ancient Society. The Rise of the Greek City-State* (Cambridge, 1987).

Muratori, L.A., *Dissertatio XXII. De legibus Italicorum et statutorum origine*, Muratori L.A., *Antiquitates Italicae Medii Aevi* 2 (Mediolani 1739), colms. 233–235.

Nelson, J.L., "Queens as Jezebels: Brunhild and Balthild in merovingian History", *Politics and Ritual in Early Medieval Europe* (London, 1986), pp. 1–48.

——, "The Last Years of Louis the Pious", *Charlemagne's Heir. New Perspectives on the Reign of Louis the Pious (814–840)*, eds. P. Godman and R. Collins (Oxford, 1990), pp. 147–159.

——, "Ninth century Knighthood: the evidence of Nithard", *Studies in Medieval History presented to R. Allen Brown*, eds. C. Harper-Bill, C.J. Holdsworth and J. Nelson (Woodbridge, 1989), pp. 255–266.

——, "Literacy in Carolingian government", *The uses of Literacy in Early Medieval Europe*, ed. R. Mc Kitterick (Cambridge, 1990), pp. 258–296.

——, *Charles the Bald* (London New York, 1992).

La Neustrie. Les pays au nord de la Loire de 650 à 850, ed. H. Atsma (Sigmaringen, 1989).

Nonn, U., "Merovingische Testamente. Studien zum Fortleben einer römischen Urkundenform in Frankreich", *Archiv für Diplomatik* 18 (1972), pp. 1–129.

Oppermann, O., *Die älteren Urkunden des Klosters Blandinium und die Anfänge der Stadt Gent* 1 (Utrecht, Leipzig and München, 1928).

Palumbo, L., *Testamento romano e testamento longobardo* (1892).

Paravicini Bagliani, A., *I testamenti dei cardinali del Duecento* (Roma, 1980) (Miscellanea della Società romana di storia patria 25).

Parry, J., "The gift, the indian gift and the 'indian gift'", *Man* n.s. 21, (1986), pp. 453–473.

Pasche, V., *"Pour le salut de mon ame" Les Lausannois face à la mort (XIVe siècle)* (Lausanne, 1989).

Paschini, P., *Storia del Friuli* (Udine, 1934–1936).

——, "Le vicende politiche e religiose dei Friuli nei secoli IX e X", *Nuovo Archivio Veneto* 20 (1910), pp. 229–244; 21 (1911), pp. 38–100.

Paxton, F., *Christianizing Death. The Creation of a Ritual Process in Early Medieval Europe* (Ithaca and London, 1990).

Périn, P., *La datation des tombes mérovingiennes* (Paris, 1980).

Piacitelli, P., "La carità negli atti di ultima volontà milanesi del XII secolo", *La carità a Milano nei secoli XII–XV*, eds. M.P. Alberzoni and O. Grassi (Milano, 1989), pp. 167–186.

Piot, Ch., "Les pagi de la Belgique et leurs subdivisions pendant le Moyen Age",

Mémoires couronnés et mémoires des savants étrangers publiés par l'académie royale des sciences, des lettres et des beaux-arts de Belgique 39 (Brussels, 1879).

Le polyptique de l'abbaye de Saint-Bertin (844–859), eds. F.-L. Ganshof, F. Godding-Ganshof and A. de Smet (Paris, 1975).

Price, S., "From noble funerals to divine cult: the consecration of Roman Emperors", *Rituals of Royalty. Power and Ceremonial in traditional Societies*, eds. D. Cannadine and S. Price (Cambridge, 1987), pp. 56–105.

Prosperi, A., "Premessa", *I vivi e i morti* (Bologna, 1982 (= *Quaderni Storici*, 50 (1982)), pp. 391–410.

Riché, P., "La bibliothèque de trois aristocrates laïcs carolingiens", *Le Moyen Age* 69 (1963), pp. 87–104.

———, "Trésors et collections d'aristocrates laiques carolingiens", *Cahiers Archéologiques* 22 (1972), pp. 39–46 (now in Riché P., *Instruction et vie religeuse dans le Haut Moyen Age* (London, 1981), pp. 39–46).

———, "Les aristocrates carolingiens collectionneurs d'objects d'art (VIIIᵉ–Xᵉ siècles)", *Les Cahiers de Saint-Michel de Cuxa* 23 (1992), pp. 83–87.

Rigon, A., "Orientamenti religiosi e pratica testamentaria a Padova nei secoli XII–XIV (prime ricerche)", *'Nolens intestatus decedere'. Il testamento come fonte della storia religiosa e sociale* (Perugia, 1985), pp. 40–53.

———, "I testamenti come atti di religiosità pauperistica", *La conversione alla povertà nell'Italia dei secoli XII–XIV* (Spoleto, 1991) (Atti del XXVII Convegno storico internazionale del Centro di studi sulla spiritualità medievale), pp. 391–414.

Rousseau, F., *La Meuse et le pays mosan en Belgique. Leur importance historique avant le XIIIᵉ siècle* (Namur, 1930).

Rovelli, A., "Circolazione monetaria e formulari notarili nell'Italia altomedievale", *Bullettino dell'Istituto Storico Italiano per il Medioevo e Archivio Muratoriano* 98 (1992), pp. 133–144.

Ruggiero, B., *Principi, nobiltà e Chiesa nel Mezzogiorno longobardo. L'esempio di s. Massimo di Salerno* (Napoli, 1973).

Schmid, K., *Kloster Hirsau und seine Stifter* (Freiburg, 1959).

Schramm, P.E., "Der 'Talisman' Karls des Grossen mit Ausblicken auf die mittelalterlichen Brust-Kreuze und -reliquiare", *Herrschaftszeichen und Staatssymbolik* 1 (Stuttgart, 1954) (*M.G.H.*, Schriften, 13/1), pp. 309–315.

———, "Baugen-armillae: zur Geschichte der königlichen Armspangen", *Herrschaftszeichen und Staatssymbolik* 2 (Stuttgart, 1955) (*M.G.H.*, Schriften, 13/2), pp. 538–553.

——— and Müterich F., *Denkmale des deutschen Könige und Kaiser* (München, 1981).

Sergi, G., "Anscarici, Arduinici, Aleramici: elementi per una comparazione fra dinastie marchionali", *Formazione e strutture dei ceti dominanti nel medioevo: marchesi, conti e visconti nel regno italico (secc. IX–XII)* (Roma, 1988) (Nuovi Studi Storici 1), pp. 11–28.

———, "Le corti e il mecenatismo", *Lo spazio letterario del Medioevo 1 Il medioevo latino*, eds. G. Cavallo, C. Leonardi and E. Menestò, II, *La circolazione del testo* (Roma, 1994), pp. 299–329.

Settia, A.A., "Le radici tecnologiche della cavalleria medioevale", *Rivista Storica Italiana* 97 (1985), pp. 268–269.

Sheenan, M., *The Will in Medieval England: from the Conversion of the Anglo-Saxons to the End of the thirteenth Century* (Toronto, 1969).

Sot, M., *Un historien et son église au Xᵉ siècle: Flodoard de Reims* (Paris, 1993).

Spreckelmeyer, G., "Zur rechtlichen Funktion frühmittelalterlicher Testamente", *Recht und Schrift im Mittelalter*, ed. P. Classen (Sigmaringen, 1977) (Vorträge und Forschungen, 23), pp. 91–113.

Sproemberg, H., *Die Entstehung der Grafschaft Flandern* (Berlin, 1935).

Stafford, P., "Sons and mothers: Family Politics in the Early Middle Ages", *Medieval Women*, ed. D. Baker (Oxford, 1978), pp. 79–100.

Stefani, F., "I duchi e marchesi della marca del Friuli e di Verona", *Archivio Veneto* 4 (1874), pp. 19–33.

Studien und Vorarbeiten zur Geschichte des größfränkischen und frühdeutschen Adels, ed. G. Tellenbach (Freiburg im Br., 1957) (Forschungen zur Oberrheinische Landesgeschichte, IV).

Tabacco, G., "La connessione fra potere e possesso nel regno franco e nel regno longobardo", *I problemi dell'Occidente nel secolo 8* (Spoleto, 1973) (Settimane di studio del Centro italiano di studi sull'alto medioevo 20), pp. 133–168.

——, "Regno, impero e aristocrazie nell'Italia postcarolingia", Tabacco G., *Sperimentazioni del potere nell'alto medioevo* (Torino, 1993), pp. 95–118.

Theuws, F., *De archeologie van de periferie. Studies naar de bewoning en samenleving in het Maas-Demer-Scheldegebied in de Vroege Middeleeuwen* (Amsterdam, 1988).

—— and A.-J. Bijsterveld, "Der Maas-Demer-Schelde Raum in Ottonischer und Salischer Kaiserzeit", *Siedlungen und Landesausbau zur Salierzeit, Teil 1, den nördlichen Landschaften des Reiches*, ed. H.W. Böhme (Sigmaringen, 1991), pp. 109–146.

Vaccari, P., "Donazioni. Diritto intermedio", *Novissimo Digesto italiano* 6 (Torino, 1971), pp. 231–233.

Vianello, F., "Gli Unrochingi e la famiglia di Beggo conte di Parigi", *Bullettino dell'Istituto storico italiano per il Medioevo e Archivio Muratoriano* 91 (1984), pp. 337–369.

Violante, C., "La chiesa bresciana nel medioevo", *Storia di Brescia* 1, ed. G. Treccani degli Alfieri (Brescia, 1961), pp. 999–1124.

Wemple, S., "S. Salvatore, S. Giulia: a case study in the Endowment and Patronage of a Major female monastery in Northen Italy", *Women of the medieval World: essays in honour of J.H. Mundy*, eds. J. Kirschner and S. Wemple (Oxford, 1985), pp. 85–91.

Werner, K.F., "Die Nachkommen Karls des Grossen", *Karl der Grosse* 1 (Düsseldorf, 1965), pp. 412–447.

——, "Bedeutende Adelsfamilien im Reich Karls der Grosse: Excursus I: Die Unruochingen", *Karl der Grosse* 1 (Düsseldorf, 1965), pp. 133–137.

——, "Missus, marchio, comes. Entre l'administration centrale et l'administration locale de l'Empire carolingien", *Histoire comparée de l'administration (IVe–XVIIIe siècles)* (Zürich-München, 1980).

——, "'Hlodovicus Augustus'. Gouverner l'empire chrétien. Idées et réalités", *Charlemagne's Heir. New Perspectives on the Reign of Louis the Pious (814–840)*, eds. P. Godman and R. Collins (Oxford, 1990), pp. 3–123.

Wickham, C., *Land and Power. Studies in Italian and European Social History. 400–1200* (London, 1994), pp. 201–226.

Young, B.K., "Exemple aristocratique et mode funéraire dans la Gaule mérovingienne", *Annales E.S.C.* 41 (1986), pp. 379–407.

FRANKISH GIVING OF ARMS AND RITUALS OF POWER: CONTINUITY AND CHANGE IN THE CAROLINGIAN PERIOD*

Régine Le Jan

In the picture showing the count and lay-abbot Vivian offering Charles the Bald the Bible which he had had made for him in his abbey of St Martin, Tours, the king is seated on a throne under a baldaquin. He wears a crown and ceremonial cloak, and holds a sceptre in his hand. The hand of God appears above the baldaquin and, together with two angels on either side of the arch-openings, assures the king of divine protection. Two helmeted warriors placed on the same level as the king carry spear, shield and sword.[1] This theme is exactly like the one found also in a scene depicted in the *Codex Aureus* of St Emmeram, Regensburg, where King Charles the Bald is enthroned beneath a baldaquin, crowned and clad in royal robes, without weapons, while in the lateral arcades two men carry sword, spear and shield. The warriors hold the sword in both their hands in a gesture which indicates that it does not belong to them. Captions written above the two warriors in fact make it clear that these weapons enable Christ to vanquish his enemies.[2] A third scene in the Bible of San Paolo, made c. 870 for Charles the Bald's wife, depicts King Solomon enthroned beneath a baldaquin, crowned like a Carolingian king, clad in a ceremonial cloak and flanked by two men, one of whom carries a sword, the other a spear and a shield.[3]

What we clearly have here is a classic representation of a Carolingian king. The weapons carried by the warriors belong to Christ,

* I like to thank Janet Nelson for translating this paper, and for helpful comments.

[1] First Bible of Charles the Bald, c. 846, Paris, Bibl. nat., MS, lat. 1, fol. 423, reproduced in P.E. Dutton and H.L. Kessler, *The Poetry and Paintings of the First Bible of Charles the Bald* (Ann Arbor MI, 1997), colour plate IV, facing p. 51, and black and white plate 17.

[2] *Codex Aureus* of St Emmeram, Regensburg, court school of Charles the Bald, 870, Munich, Bayerische Staatsbibliothek, Clm 14000, fol. 5v, reproduced by F. Mütherich and J.E. Gaehde, *Carolingian Painting* (London, 1977), pp. 37–38.

[3] Bible of San Paolo fuori le Mure, Rheims?, c. 870, fol. 188, reproduced in Mütherich and Gaehde, *Carolingian Painting*, p. 44.

and are handed over to the king so that he can ensure in this world
the order and peace willed by God, in other words, fulfil the *ministerium regale* (royal office). Yet there was no sense in this period that
the bearing of weapons, or their use, was reserved to the king: on
the contrary, all those men who had sufficient means had to have
'horses, weapons, shield, spear and sword' in order to serve the king
as cavalry soldiers.[4] An inquiry into formal investiture with weapons
in Frankish society thus necessarily entails an investigation of the
ideological bases of power and the way power worked, and also of
changes that occurred during the Carolingian period.

1. *Warrior culture: a culture of self-representation*

The Frankish aristocracy did not have to wait until the eleventh century to define itself as a warrior aristocracy: that was what it had
always been, just as war had been the motor of Carolingian success.
It is no exaggeration to describe Frankish aristocratic culture as a
warrior culture, and in this respect, I think, there was no break
between the fifth century and the eleventh.

Young Frankish nobles, like those of other Germanic peoples,
received an education that was essentially military. Ragnobert, a
noble of the Merovingian period, was *armis doctus*, 'trained in arms',[5]
while Count Gerald of Aurillac (d. 909) 'had been fitted from boy-
hood for secular [i.e. military] pursuits, as is customary for noble
youths'.[6] In addition to the wielding of weapons, youths were taught
how to ride on horseback. From the Merovingian period onwards,
the possession of a horse tended to isolate the nobles among the
mass of warriors.[7] At the end of the fifth century, horse-sacrifices as
part of princely burials, particularly in northern Gaul, appeared as

---

[4] *Capitulare missorum* (786 or 792), ed. A. Boretius, *MGH Capit.* I (Hannover, 1883),
no. 25, p. 67: '. . . qui . . . vel bassallitico honorati sunt cum domini sui et caballos, arma et
scuto et lancea, spata . . . habere possunt: omnes iutent.'

[5] *Passio Ragneberti martyris Bebronensis* c. 2, ed. B. Krusch, *MGH SSRM* V (Hannover, 1910), p. 205.

[6] Odo of Cluny, *Vita Geraldi Auriliacensis comitis* I, c. 4, PL 133, col. 645: '*mox
saecularibus exercitiis, sicut nobilibus pueris mos est*'. On the significance of this text, see
S. Airlie, "The anxiety of sanctity: St Gerald of Aurillac and his maker", *Journal of
Ecclesiastical History* 43 (1992), pp. 372–395.

[7] R. Le Jan, *Famille et pouvoir dans le monde franc (VIIe–Xe siècle). Essai d'anthropologie sociale* (Paris, 1995), pp. 64–66.

a kind of ritualised offering which associated the horse very closely with the exercise of power.[8] Later, the presence of spurs in certain graves played the same role. Thus, from the earliest Merovingian period, and probably long before that, the horse occupied a specific place in the system whereby power was represented: the noble owed it to himself to be a special type of horseman, and Gerald of Aurillac gave the impression of flying through the countryside, his horse went at such a gallop.[9]

Military apprenticeship began early,[10] and weapons were handed to little boys at a very young age, perhaps earlier than six.[11] Louis the Pious bore arms at the age of three when he became king of Aquitaine[12] and by seven he had grown to be a fine horseman.[13] Ermold the Black tells how during a royal hunt the young Charles the Bald, then aged hardly more than three, demanded a bow and arrows, and wielded these miniature weapons to kill a young doe which had been brought before him.[14] Even if these examples are exaggerated somewhat in order to exalt royal superiority, they show military apprenticeship beginning young.

It was not just that this military eductaion had value in itself. It was bound up in the wielding of power. It therefore had to be complemented by moral training:[15] the young noble had to acquire *prudentia*, the practical wisdom that leaders needed.[16] In the Carolingian period this aspect of education was further stressed. Mirrors for Princes highlighted it. The adolescent boy finished his education

[8] For the tomb of Childeric, see R. Brulet, "La sépulture du roi Childéric à Tournai et le site funéraire", *La noblesse romaine et les chefs barbares au IIIe au VIIe siècle*, F. Vallet and M. Kanaski, eds, (Association française d'Archéologie mérovingienne 9) (Paris, 1995), pp. 309–26. Horse-burials associated with chieftains' graves are also attested in other cemeteries of the upper Scheldt, for instance at Neuville-sur-Escaut. Cf. G. Hantute, *La cimetière mérovingien de Neuville-sur Escaut* (Denain, 1989).

[9] *Vita Geraldi* 1, c. 5, col. 645.

[10] R. Le Jan, "Apprentissages militaires, rites de passage, et remises d'armes au haut Moyen Age", *Education, apprentissages, initiation au Moyen Age, Actes du premier colloque international de Montpellier*, Cahiers du C.R.I.S.I.M.A. no. 1 (1993), pp. 214–222.

[11] *Ibid.*, pp. 217–219.

[12] Astronomer, *Vita Hludowici imperatoris* c. 4, ed. E. Tremp, *MGH SSRG* 44 (Hannover, 1995), p. 294.

[13] *Ibid.* p. 296.

[14] Ermold le Noir, *In Honorem Hludowici Pii*, ed. E. Faral, *Poème sur Louis le Pieux* (Paris, 1964), p. 183, English translation P. Godman, *Poetry of the Carolingian Renaissance* (London, 1985), pp. 256–257.

[15] Le Jan, "Apprentissages", pp. 217–218.

[16] *Ibid.*, pp. 217–219.

among other youths who had been 'commended', like him, to a *nutritor*, a 'nurturing father-figure'.[17] This practice of commendation, widespread among the Germans in the age of Tacitus,[18] was linked to warrior-comradeship and to the exercise of power. It persisted right into the central medieval period in France.[19]

In Carolingian times, adolescent noble boys belonged to groups of young *commilitones* (fellow-warriors) who together learned the functions their status entailed.[20] They participated in the ritual of the hunt (*ritus venandi*).[21] This seems indeed to have been not only a training for battle but also a ritualised exercise in swordsmanship which young nobles worked at under their lord's direction.[22] In this way the youth prepared himself to protect his own dependants by the use of arms, for such was his function in society.[23] That, at all events, is what is implied by the presence of weapon-deposits, and of the sword in particular, in the graves of young boys. One thinks of course of the little prince buried in the sixth century under the cathedral of Cologne,[24] but Heinrich Härke's work on Anglo-Saxon burials between the fifth century and the seventh shows that depositions of weapons, especially spears, in the graves of little boys or youths were not at all uncommon.[25] These weapons had a value that was symbolic in a general sense:[26] they were symbols of social supe-

---

[17] *Ibid.*, pp. 220–221.

[18] Tacitus, *Germania* c. 13, trans. H. Mattingly, revd. S.A. Handford, Penguin Classics (Harmondsworth 1970), p. 112.

[19] G. Duby, "Les 'jeunes' dans la société aristocratique de la France du Nord-Ouest au XIIe siècle", *Annales E.S.C.* septembre-octobre 1964, pp. 835–846, reprinted in Duby, *Hommes et structures du Moyen Age* (Paris, 1973), pp. 213–225, and translated in Duby, *The Chivalrous Society*, trans. C. Postan (London, 1977), pp. 112–122.

[20] Le Jan, "Apprentissages", p. 221.

[21] *Vita Trudonis confessoris Hasbanensis auctore Donati* c. 4, eds. B. Krusch and W. Levison, *MGH SSRM* VI (Hannover, 1913), p. 278.

[22] For the hunt, see J. Jarnut, "Die frühmittelalterliche Jagd unter Rechts- und sozialgeschichtlichen Aspekten", *L'Uomo di fronte al mondo animale nell'alto medeovo*, (XXXI Settimana) (Spoleto, 1985), pp. 765–798; J.L. Nelson, "Carolingian royal ritual", *Rituals of Royalty. Power and Ceremonial in Traditional Societies* , eds. D. Cannadine and S. Price (Cambridge, 1987), pp. 137–180; also H.E. Davidson, "The training of warriors", *Weapons and Warfare in Anglo-Saxon England*, ed. S.C. Hawkes (Oxford, 1989), pp. 11–23, at 11–13.

[23] Le Jan, *Famille et pouvoir*, pp. 111–113.

[24] O. Doppelfeld, "Das fränkische Knabengrab unter dem Chor des kölner Domes", *Germania* 12 (1964), pp. 156–188, and O. Doppelfeld and R. Pirling, *Fränkische Fürsten im Rheinland. Die Gräber aus dem Kölner Dom* (Düsseldorf, 1966).

[25] H. Härke, "Angelsächische Waffengräber des 5. bis 7. Jahrhunderts", *Zeitschrift für Archäologie des Mittelalters* 6, Beihefte 1 (Cologne, 1992), pp. 182–190.

[26] H. Härke, "Tombes à armes anglo-saxonnes: sépultures de guerriers ou sym-

riority, and, at least for certain individuals, of the power with which the noble man was invested or would one day be invested.

The *iuvenis* usually received his weapons when he reached adolescence.[27] Charlemagne waited for his son Louis the reach the age of puberty (he was thirteen at that point) to gird him with his sword in a solemn ceremony.[28] Louis the Pious in his turn invested his son Charles the Bald with the weapons of manhood, and specifically a sword, when Charles was fifteen.[29] Before the eighth century, a youth's investiture with weapons did not constitute a rite of passage from childhood to young-manhood: in that earlier period, there were other rituals, like the first shaving of the beard, or the hair-cutting, which sanctioned the passage from minority to majority.[30] The disappearance of those rituals seems to indicate that from the Carolingian period onwards, investiturewith weapons became the rite of passage which allowed the young noble to pass from childhood to young-manhood.

The handing over of the weapons of manhood, like marriage, became possible once the youth had come of age:[31] the adolescent became part of adult society when he received his noble's 'equipment' which would allow him to fulfil his protective function. At that period, the ritual of investiture with weapons was not connected, *pace* Jean Flori, with any magical character imputed to the weapons themselves.[32] Rather, it was already a dubbing in the true sense. The word 'dubbing' derives from the notion of equipping, and so means an investiture, because the young noble in receiving his weapons was

---

bolisme rituel", *L'armée romaine et les barbares du IIIe au VIIe siècle*, eds. F. Vallet and M. Kazanski (Mémoires publiés par l'Association francaise de l'Archéologie Mérovingienne 5) (Paris, 1993), p. 425: 9% of adolescents and boys were interred with weapons.

[27] Le Jan, "Apprentissages", pp. 222–223; Le Jan, *Famille et pouvoir*, pp. 87–89.
[28] Astronomer, *Vita Hludowici* c. 6, p. 300.
[29] *Ibid.*, c. 59, p. 526.
[30] Le Jan, "Apprentissages", p. 223.
[31] K. Leyser, "Early Medieval Canon Law and the Beginnings of Knighthood", *Institutionen, Kultur und Gesellschaft im Mittelalter. Festschrift J. Fleckenstein*, eds. L. Fenske, W. Rösener and T. Zotz (Sigmaringen, 1984), pp. 556–560, and J.L. Nelson, "Ninth-century knighthood: the evidence of Nithard", *Studies in Medieval History presented to R. Allen Brown*, eds. C. Harper-Bill, C. Holdsworth and J.L. Nelson (Woodbridge, 1989), pp. 255–266, reprinted Nelson, *The Frankish World* (London, 1996), pp. 75–88, at 84–85. J. Flori, "Les origines de l'adoubement chevaleresque", *Traditio* 35 (1979), p. 215, observes that investiture with weapons in the central Middle Ages was no longer a ritual marking the transition to adulthood.
[32] J. Flori, *L'essor de la chevalerie, XIe–XIIe siècle* (Paris, 1986), p. 53.

invested with a power—the capacity to protect and to dominate—
which came to him from his ancestors. The dubbing-ritual was thus
enmeshed in a system of social representation which assigned the
nobility its protective calling.

The weapons conferred under such circumstances could not be
ordinary ones: rather, they were swords which had been handed
down and inherited, and which carried within them the virtues of
the ancestors.[33] They thus at the same time expressed an autoge-
nous power which essentially derived from the private sphere even
though in the Carolingian period the nobility's transformation into
a *militia* allowed this power of theirs to be more closely integrated
into a general conception of the order of the world. Investiture with
weapons was thus first and foremost the ritualised expression of the
handing-over of the *mundium*, that is, of protective capacity and familial superiority, in a society which remained largely segmentary.[34]

Once equipped, the noble would never again be separated from
his sword or belt. There is plenty of evidence for this in the case
of kings: Einhard says that Charlemagne 'always had a sword at his
side',[35] and Notker tells how, on the day before that of the Lord's
resurrection, Louis the Pious would make his personal servants a gift
of everything he had taken off before bathing, except his sword and
belt.[36] It was the same for nobles. In the eighth century a Frankish
noble was depicted in the frescoes of the church of St Benedict at
Mals, in the southern Tyrol, carrying his sword in his hands.[37] The
symbolic character of weapons, especially the sword and belt, is
absolutely clear.[38] The *cingulum militiae*, the military belt, was the
expression of the social superiority conferred by the noble's bearing
of arms and of the right to wield power which was evidently associated with that. There is nothing specifically Germanic here. The

---

[33] Le Jan, "Apprentissages", p. 227. Here is a characteristic feature that recurs
in Scandinavian and Anglo-Saxon contexts: see H.E. Davidson, *The Sword in Anglo-
Saxon England* (Oxford, 1962), pp. 118–121, and *eadem*, "The training of warriors",
p. 20.

[34] Le Jan, *Famille et pouvoir*, pp. 99–116.

[35] Einhard, *Vita Karoli Magni* c. 23, ed. O. Holder-Egger, *MGH SSRG* (Hannover,
1911), p. 28. Cf. Notker, *Gesta Karoli* I, 34, ed. H.F. Haefele, *MGH SSRG*, new
series 12 (Berlin, 1962), p. 46.

[36] Notker, *Gesta Karoli* II, 22, pp. 91–92: '. . . *in illa die qua Christus, mortali tunica
exutus, incorruptibilem resumere parebat . . .*'

[37] J. Garber, "Die karolingische St. Benediktskirche in Mals", *Zeitschrift des Ferdinandeums für Tirol und Vorarlberg* 3F.59 (1915), 3, pp. 3–61.

[38] Leyser, "Early Medieval Canon Law", p. 553.

roots clearly go back deep into the use made of the ceremonial belt in Late Antiquity.[39] Intimately linked to a form of social representation associating power with protection, the *cingulum* was the distinctive badge of all those whose vocation it was to assure by their weapons the group's protection and survival and who thus exercised domination. In other words, it was the badge of nobility.

The right to a *Gefolgschaft*, an armed following, assigned to Frankish nobles so long as they met the demands and conditions set by the king,[40] was intimately bound up with the nobility's protective function. The little rural communities of the sixth and seventh centuries really did need to be organised and protected: some depended directly on royal agents, others lived under the authority and protection of a lord, a *dominus*,[41] who had himself been recognised, and perhaps sent, by the king. For if domination depended on a structure of control whose origins lay in *Hausherrschaft*, that is, in power over the household which had come to include lordship over property, power over a *familia* that had been expanded to cover dependants and companions, that power also played a part in the maintenance of the public peace to the extent that nobles served the king at local level on their own domains.[42] For the duty of protection, the *mundeburdium*, had as its corollory the exercise of a number of rights that went with social power and helped constitute its legitimacy.[43]

Nobles thus had their own armed followings by means of which they could maintain their protective function.[44] The noun *druhtin*, which in Old High German denoted the leader of a *druht*, an armed following, was generally translated by *dominus*,[45] and *Druht* appeared in the Malberg glosses to *Lex Salica* in the context of *contubernia*, a term that denoted the bands of armed companions sharing the same

---

[39] On the *cingulum*, see J.M. Van Winter, *"Cingulum militiae"*, *Revue d'histoire du droit* 44 (1976), pp. 1–92; J. Flori, *L'essor*, p. 216; Leyser, "Early Medieval Canon Law", pp. 549–566; S. Krüger, *"Character militaris* und *character indelibilis"*, in Fenske *et al.* eds., *Institutionen*, pp. 580–581.

[40] Le Jan, *Famille et pouvoir*, pp. 111–113, 127–130.

[41] *Ibid.*, pp. 102–103.

[42] *Ibid.*, pp. 101, 121–122.

[43] *Ibid.*, pp. 116–122.

[44] R. Le Jan, "Satellites et bandes armées dans le monde franc (VII⁰–X⁰ siècle)", *Le combattant au moyen âge*, Société des historiens médiévistes de l'Enseignement supérieur (Paris, 1991), pp. 98–102.

[45] R. Schmidt-Wiegand, "Fränkische *Druht* und *Druhtin*. Zur historischen Terminologie im Bereich der Sozialgeschichte", *Historische Forschungen für W. Schlesinger*, ed. H. Beumann (Cologne and Vienna, 1974), pp. 524–535.

life (originally the same tent[46]). In *Lex Salica*, the numbers involved in these armed followings seem to range between three and nine men.[47] It is worth noting too that in the Laws of King Ine of Wessex (688–726), armed followings comprising betweeen eight and thirty-five men were deemed bands of criminals. If there were more than thirty-five, the group was considered 'an army'.[48] Small numbers of able-bodied men were doubtless enough to maintain control over the small groups who in the sixth century gathered around a leader, his family and his companions. It is this sort of hierrarchical structure at any rate which is evident in Merovingian cemeteries at Neuville-sur-Scheldt (Nord),[49] Giberville (Calvados),[50] or Bâle-Bernerring in Switzerland.[51] In all three cases, the graves of the leader and his family, surrounded by other graves of men who carried swords and axes, were quite distinctive because of their location and also because of the richness of their grave-goods: swords for men, jewellery for women.

From the eighth century on, the disappearance of chieftains' graves and the increasing rarity of weapons and especially of long swords, henceforth reserved for rich burials, no doubt reflect the growing stratification of society and the growth of bonds of dependence. Literary sources clearly show that the great magnates of this period could mobilise warrior-bands considerably larger than a few dozen. The importance of military followings now depended only on the wealth and power of the *domini*, the lords, and those *domini* now recruited their trusty warriors on their own domains among their own dependents, as well as outside them, among the *pauperes*.[52] Landed power had become the basis for real military power, at the same time as bonds of fidelity were developing. In a collection of legal *formulae* from Tours is one in which a free man, driven by necessity and maybe also by ambition commends himself to a powerful man. This text dates, significantly, to the beginning of the eighth century.[53]

---

[46] Le Jan, *Famille et pouvoir*, p. 112.

[47] *Pactus legis salicae* XLII. 3, ed. K.E. Eckhardt, *MGH LL in quarto* IV, 1 (Hannover, 1962), p. 163.

[48] *Laws of Ine* c. 13.1, trans. D. Whitelock, *English Historical Documents* vol. I, revd. edn. (London 1979), p. 400.

[49] Hantute, *Le cimitière mérovingien de Neuville-sur-Escaut*, p. 105.

[50] C. Pilet *et al.*, "Les nécropoles de Giberville (Calvados), fin du Ve-fin du VIIᵉ siècle après J.C.", *Archéologie médiévale* 20 (1990), p. 53.

[51] M. Martin, *Das fränkische Graberfeld von Basel-Bernerring* (Mainz, 1976).

[52] Le Jan, "Satellites", p. 99.

[53] Le Jan, *Famille et pouvoir*, pp. 124–125.

The Carolingians made no attempt to stamp out the right of nobles to recruit trusty warriors—the *vassi, vassalli,* or *caballarii* who were soon to be termed *milites.* But they did try to control the use of these small armies by requiring that vassals be *casati,* 'housed', that is, given lands and households of their own which reduced their dependence on their lords.[54] Without abolishing the protective calling of the nobility, the Carolingians tried to integrate them more tightly into a pyramid of responsibilities, and this entailed a stricter control of the use of weapons. Charlemagne in 779 forbade the forming of *trustes,* that is, bands of household warriors entirely subject to their masters' call. Charlemagne required lords to house the vassals from whom they demanded military service.[55] This measure, subsequently repeated several times, simply accorded with developments already under way. It did not produce the effects intended, but it certainly contributed to the raising of vassals' social status, to distinguishing the *belligerantes* (wagers of war) from the rest of the population, and to integrating all those who bore arms into the edifice of the *imperium christianum.*

The Carolingian noble thus remained first and foremost a warleader, wearing the sword and belt which over the centuries had become the symbol of protective power. Aristocratic equipment, however,—and it might be better to call it aristocratic, and *a fortiore* royal, adornment—also had a quality of ostentation reflecting both social rank and a hierarchy of protection. In other words, it was also part of a culture of display. The Franks loved gold, silver, precious stones, sumptuous clothes, furs: all that belonged to the culture of ostentation and to aristocratic self-representation. Among items of aristocratic costume, the cloak and the richly adorned weapons held a special place that was in some sense ideological. Charlemagne's everyday wear included 'a long blue cloak', and 'he always wore at his side a sword whose hilt and baldric were adorned with gold and silver', but on feast-days, 'he girded on a sword adorned with precious stones [and] he wore a gold-embroidered garment, shoes adorned with precious stones, a gold brooch to keep his cloak in place, and a gold diadem also adorned with precious stones'.[56] After the baptism of the Danish king Harold, Louis the Pious proceeded to the banquet 'resplendent in gold and glittering with precious

---

[54] Le Jan, "Satellites", pp. 103–4; *eadem, Famille et pouvoir,* pp. 129–130.
[55] *MGH Capit.* I, no. 20, c. 14, p. 50; no. 24, c. 15, p. 66.
[56] Einhard, *Vita Karoli* c. 23, p. 28.

stones', while his little son Charles was 'shining with gold' and the queen had 'a gold crown on her head and wore robes sparkling with gold'.[57] Louis' sword was decorated with gold,[58] his baldric adorned with gold and precious stones.[59] The monk of St-Gall emphasises the ceremonial cloak, the white or blue mantle as worn by the Franks of old;[60] and Eberhard of Friuli distributed among his various sons his cloaks decorated with gold and silver.[61] There can be no doubt that among the Franks as for the Romans, the ceremonial cloak played a part in marking out leading men, and was a key element in denoting social rank.[62]

Glittering and richly decorated weapons were another important element,[63] as proved by their presence in the graves of leading men.[64] *Lex Ripuaria*, drawn up for the Austrasian Franks in Dagobert's reign (629–42), punished the theft of one such sword with its sheath (*spatha cum scogilo*) by a fine of seven solidi instead of the three demanded for the theft of an ordinary sword.[65] In the Carolingian period, the sword encrusted with gold and precious stones was part of the regalia, yet precious weapons never became a prerogative of kings alone. Eberhard of Friuli owned nine long swords of which four were decorated with gold and silver, six daggers (*facila*) adorned with gold, four coats of mail, three helmets, and one hauberk, greaves, four golden spurs decorated with precious stones, four gauntlets, and seven baldrics of which six had gold and precious stones on them.[66] Count Eccard of Autun for his part bequeathed to his kinsmen substantial pieces of weaponry including a richly decorated sword and a gold adorned baldric.[67]

---

[57] Ermold, *Poème*, p. 177.

[58] *Ibid.*, p. 173.

[59] Astronomer, *Vita Hludowici* c. 28, p. 378; cf. Thegan, *Gesta Hludowici imperatoris* c. 33, ed. E. Tremp, *MGH SSRG* 54 (Hannover, 1995), p. 202.

[60] Notker, *Gesta Karoli* I, 34, p. 46.

[61] *Cartulaire de l'abbaye de Cysoing et de ses dépendances*, ed. I. de Coussemaker (Lille, 1886), pp. 1–5. See further Cristina La Rocca and Luigi Provero in this volume.

[62] Le Jan, *Famille et pouvoir*, pp. 62–63.

[63] Le Jan, "Apprentissages", pp. 226–227.

[64] H. Vierck, "Ein westphalisches 'Adelsgrab' des 8. Jahrhundert n. Chr. Zum archäologischen Nachweis der spätsächsischen und frühkarolingischen Oberschichten", *Studien zur Sachsenforschung* 2 ed. H.J. Hässler (Hildesheim, 1980), pp. 458–488.

[65] *Lex Ribuaria* 40. 11, ed. K.E. Eckhardt, *MGH LL in quarto* III, 2 (Hannover, 1954), p. 94.

[66] *Cartulaire de Cysoing*, pp. 1–5.

[67] *Receuil de chartes de l'abbaye de Saint-Benoît-sur-Loire*, eds. M. Prou and A. Vidier, 2 vols. (Orleans and Paris, 1900–1924), vol. 1, p. 64.

Clearly such weapons were not used for fighting: their splendour displayed a status and calling, they marked out the *domini* from others who carried swords. Such parade-weapons were thus carefully preserved in family treasure-hoards, among the precious objects which enabled nobles to gain recognition as such from their own kind while assuring their domination over the less powerful.[68] Investigation of wills, especially that of Eberhard, shows that precious weapons were distributed between sons,[69] because they were the symbols of family superiority.[70]

2. *The circulation of weapons and the hierarchy of exchange*

The symbolic force of richly adorned weapons—sword, belt, and also spurs—was such that rituals of integration involving the kin-group, real or fictive, depended on the conferring of arms. Among the inhabitants of Tacitus's *Germania*, the youth received his weapons from a chief, from his father, or from one of his kinsmen.[71] In the eighth and ninth centuries, the young man was usually armed by his father: Charlemagne armed his son Louis, and Louis in turn handed over weapons to his son Charles. The father of Gamalbert girded his son with the arms of the *militia* (military service).[72] The importance of the paternal relationship in the ritual of dubbing does not arise only from the fact that this was a ritual investiture of power transmitted from father to son. There was something else too. The gift of weapons was at the same time the symbolic act whereby other forms of relationship were created: it was to be found at the very heart of the system of filiation.

Adoption by weapons, as practised by the barbarians,[73] created a bond of artificial fatherhood between two individuals of different age but equal power. King Guntramn (564–89) in adopting his nephew

---

[68] Cf. the paper of Heinrich Härke in this volume.

[69] Cf. the paper of Jos Baselmans in this volume.

[70] Cf. Härke, in this volume.

[71] Tacitus, *Germania* c. 13, p. 112.

[72] *Vita Gamalberti presbyteri Michaelbuchensis* c. 2, eds. B. Krusch and W. Levison, *MGH SSRM* VII (Hannover and Leipzig, 1920), p. 187: '*Pater autem cum eum ut heredem et filium nutrire cuperet et, ut moris est, ad usum militiae institueret, armigerum sibimet aliquoties fecit arma que militaria aur suspendit puero aut praecinxit . . .*'. This *Vita* dates from the end of the tenth century or the beginning of the eleventh.

[73] Le Jan, "Apprentissages", pp. 223–224.

Childebert handed him a spear.[74] In the Bayeux Tapestry, the scene in which Duke William invests Harold with arms surely belongs within this same tradition of adoption by weapons: since it followed the marriage-project just arranged between Harold and William's daughter, and also the victory over Conan of Brittany just won by William with Harold's help, the ceremony consummated a double process of entry into sonship and entry into membership of the duke's military following, the whole thing being finally completed by the oath sworn by Harold to William, now his adoptive father, before he returned to England.[75]

The lay ceremonies that followed princely baptism in the Carolingian period also took the form of adoption by weapons: in 826, after his godson, the Danish king Harold, emerged from the baptismal font and was clothed in the white robe of the newly-baptised, Louis the Pious gave him precious clothes, a baldric adorned with precious stones, and his own decorated sword and golden spurs. The ceremony was then completed by the oath of fidelity sworn by Harold to the emperor.[76] The same form of adoption by arms followed the submission of Scandinavian warlords in 873.[77]

Entry into sonship in one form or another thus evidently created a bond of fidelity and and *amicitia* (friendship), both expressed in the gift of weapons.[78] The son who received his arms from his father bound himself to love and respect him, to pray for him, to be loyal to him always, in life as in death—for the fidelity thus created was not broken by death: the *memoria*, the offering of prayers for the dead, was a commanding necessity that weighed on a son after his father's passing.[79] This was exactly what Dhuoda told her son.[80] The father and the adult son entered into a new relationship, still a hierarchical one, but now founded on a freely-agreed fidelity which in

---

[74] Gregory of Tours, *Historiarum Libri Decem* VII, 33, ed. B. Krusch and W. Levison, *MGH SSRM* I, revd. edn. (Hannover, 1951), p. 353. For other instances, see Le Jan, "Apprentissages", pp. 223–224.

[75] D.M. Wilson, *The Bayeux Tapestry* (London, 1985), plates 18–24.

[76] Ermold, *Poème*, p. 173.

[77] Notker, *Gesta Karoli* II, 19, p. 90: '*Qui a primoribus palacii quasi in adoptionem filiorum suscepti de camera quidem Caesaris candidatum a patrinis vero suis habitum Francorum in vestibus preciosis et armis caeterisque ornatibus acceperunt.*'

[78] Heinrich Härke, in this volume, observes that for the Anglo-Saxons too the gift of weapons created obligations. I would put this in terms of the creation of a bond of fidelity.

[79] Le Jan, *Famille et pouvoir*, pp. 78–79.

[80] Dhuoda, *Liber Manualis*, ed. P. Riché (Paris, 1975), VIII, 7, pp. 310–311.

its turn determined an *amicitia*. All this makes it easier to see why tensions in the heart of the Carolingian family, the revolts of sons against their father, especially in the case of the sons of Louis the Pious, seemed to contemporaries a scandal that sapped the very foundations of the social order.

Other forms of entry into filiation, adoption by arms, or godparenthood, created a similar duty of fidelity often expressed by the giving of an oath. This must lead us to look more closely at what entry into vassalage meant. Certainly adoption by arms, godparenthood, and vassalage should not be seen as identical. Nevertheless, there were inextricable links between these types of bonding: things were by no means as distinct in contemporaries' eyes as they have sometimes looked to twentieth-century historians. Entry into membership of the military houshold, like entry into vassalage, was an entry into a fidelity sanctioned by oath.[81] Someone less powerful commended himself to someone more powerful, binding himself to serve and be faithful to him. The lord undertook to protect his vassal. Entry into vassalage, moreover, was sanctioned since time immemorial by a gift which took the form of an investiture with weapons. Tacitus reports that the noble youth would demand that his chief give him a war-horse and a spear;[82] and when the Danish king Harold became Louis the Pious's vassal in 814, Louis made him a ceremonial gift of a horse and weapons 'as is the custom'.[83]

We know nothing about which weapons were given to vassals, whether they were of a standard type, or specially decorated. Probably the latter were reserved for the most powerful. Nevertheless, the development of bonds of vassalage in the eighth and ninth centuries and the swift rise in the social standing of vassals led to the growth of vertical relationships within and outside blood-ties, and the proliferation of bonds of artificial kinship. While entry into filiation created a tie of fidelity, entry into vassalage also created a bond of artificial filiation. True, the terms of the exchange were reversed, for in vassalage fidelity came first and it led, in a sense, to the artificial filiation. Still, the difference was not so great, and

---

[81] In the twelfth century, Scandinavian warriors entering the king's *comitatus* swore an oath: Saxo Grammaticus, *Gesta Danorum*, eds. J. Olrik and H. Ræder (Copenhagen, 1931).

[82] Tacitus, *Germania* c. 14, p. 113.

[83] Ermold, *Poème*, line 2493: '*Mox quoque Caesar ovans francisco more veterno/ Dat sibi equum nec non, ut solet, arma simul . . .*'

all things considered, the gift of weapons always expressed a fidelity
which was both hierarchical and reciprocal, and which took its place
within the broader framework of relationships of filiation.

3. Militia saecularis

In the Carolingian period, relationships of filiation and fidelity were
integrated into the system whereby society was represented. They
became the pivot around which were organised all forms of power-
relations whose function was to ensure the harmony of the world.
When Charlemagne addressed his son Louis whom he had just
crowned emperor at Aachen in 813, he told him 'to honour the
priests like fathers, to love the people like children, . . . to be a father
of the powerless (*pauperum pater*)'.[84] In the hierarchy of protection
which sustained the construction of power put in place by the Carolingians, the emperor governing the Christian empire[85] was the
supreme father, the guarantor of order and peace. Society as a whole
was organised around a ladder of fidelity with the emperor at the
top. All free men were asked to choose a lord for themselves, an
artificial father who stood in place of the supreme father, the emperor.

Notker invoked this kind of hierarchical ordering of society when
he described the ritual in which Louis the Pious gave presents to all
who served him in the palace, each according to his rank: 'sword-
belts, arms and very rich clothes for the most noble, and for those
lower down the scale, Frisian cloaks of various colours'.[86] The exchange
of gifts between the lord and his faithful men, in this case the king
and his household servants, was not specifically Frankish. It can be
found, for instance, in Anglo-Saxon England.[87] What I think is very
Carolingian, however, and quite new, is the fact that the gift took

---

[84] Thegan, *Gesta Hludowici* c. 6, p. 182.
[85] K.F. Werner, "*Hludowicus Augustus*: Gouverner l'empire chrétien—idées et réalités", *Charlemagne's Heir. New Perspectives on the Reign of Louis the Pious*, eds. P. Godman and R. Collins (Oxford, 1990), pp. 3–124, at 56–65.
[86] Notker, *Gesta Karoli* II, 21, p. 92: '*In qua etiam cunctis in palatio ministrantibus et
in curte regia servientibus iuxta singulorum personas donativa largitus est, ita ut nobilioribus
quibuscumque aut balteos aut fascilones preciosissimaque vestimenta a latissimo imperio perlata
distribui iuberet; inferioribus vero saga Fresonica omnimodi coloris darentur; porro custodibus equorum pistoribusque et cocis indumenta linea cum laneis semispatiisque, prout opus habebant, proicer-
entur.*'
[87] See Härke in this volume.

the form of a rank-order. The ritual reproduced the the representation of the 'ordered society' in the Carolingian sense of the term: the king gave to each man objects that symbolised his status— weapons and precious clothes for the more noble, more ordinary clothing for the rest. This ceremony thus complements the scenes in the *Codex Aureus* and the Vivian Bible: the weapons of Christ were given in trust to the king so that he might fulfil his *ministerium*, his office, just as the most noble of the Franks received from the king the tokens of their social superiority.

This kind of ritual reinforced social hierarchy: the king, supreme protector and dispenser of riches, was placed at the summit of the body social: next beneath him, the magnates, invested with the symbols of the *militia saecularis*, helped him in his protective mission, while the less powerful served in their own fashion under the protection of the great. All this belongs quite clearly in the sphere of ideology, but it's worth recalling how heavily ideology weighed in the thinking of Carolnigian rulers, of the churchmen who surrounded them, and no doubt of the lay *proceres* as well.[88]

The transformation of the Frankish nobility into a *militia* which served divinely-instituted order by its weapons was intimately linked to the definition of the royal office and the bringing into being of the *imperium christianum*. The aristocracy's acquisition of increased power in the eighth century was followed by a reappraisal of the place assigned to the nobility in the construction of the *imperium christianum*. The Carolingians' accession to kingship entailed the promotion of the high aristocracy, closely linked as it was to the exercise of royal power.[89] Or rather, the aristocracy shared in royalty's mission. According to the Clausula de unctione Pippini, probably a work of Louis the Pious' reign, when the pope consecrated Charles and Carloman in 754 on the occasion of Pipin's second anointing, this time at St-Denis, Queen Bertrada was blessed along with them and the pope re-established the dynastic principle which the coup d'état of 751 had shaken to its foundations.[90] The pope also blessed the leading aristocrats and thereby confirmed royal superiority, based on the anointing, while at the same time sanctifying the protective

---

[88] Cf. Nelson, "Ninth-century knighthood", pp. 84–85.

[89] Le Jan, *Famille et pouvoir*, pp. 130–135.

[90] *Clausula de unctione Pippini regis*, ed. G. Waitz, *MGH SS* XV, 1 (Hannover, 1887), p. 1. For the dating issue, see A. Stoclet, "La '*Clausula de unctione Pippini regis*': mises au point et nouvelles hypothèses", *Francia* 8 (1980), pp. 1–42.

mission with which the magnates were invested. In 816, Pope Stephen
IV who had come to Rheims to crown Louis the Pious, on the same
occasion blessed and crowned the Empress Ermengard and also
honoured the emperor, the empress and all the magnates by giving
them gifts.[91]

The place of the aristocracy in the Christian empire, and that of
all the *ministri*, was legitimised by papal benediction, but in the ideological context in which sanctification was defined, the aristocracy's
power could not be dissociated from the royal power from which it
derived. In other words, the aristocracy were associated in the royal
mission, in a *ministerium regale* increasingly clearly defined by the Frankish bishops. '[The king] must be the defender of the Church and
of the servants of God ... He must guard by his weapons and by
his protection the Church of Christ, and defend from wretchedness
widows, orphans, the weak and all who are needy.'[92] To associate
them more firmly in this mission, the emperor gave the aristocracy
the weapons which symbolised it.

If Louis the Pious was depicted as *miles Christi* in the *De laudibus
sanctae crucis* of Hrabanus Maurus,[93] this was because, in the hierarchy of powers that sustained the *imperium christianum*, the emperor
was placed at the top and held his power directly from God. The
scenes in the *Codex Aureus* and the Vivian Bible indicated that the
ruler's weapons were Christ's weapons and that he used them on
Christ's behalf, and this is what justified the blessing of the royal
arms in the ninth century.[94] Beneath the ruler were the aristocracy,
or rather, all those who based their power to command and to protect on the virtues of their ancestors, and all those who bore arms
and who possessed arms as their inheritance, as symbols of their
families' charisma.

The Church took no part in the ceremonies whereby young nobles
were invested with weapons. Was this because of a kind of reserve
with regard to a ritual that the Church did not control, as Dominique

---

[91] Thegan, *Gesta Hludowici* c. 17, p. 198.

[92] Jonas of Orleans and the Council of Paris, 829: *MGH Capit.* II, ed. A. Boretius
(Hannover, 1897), no. 196, c. 56, p. 47.

[93] E. Sears, "Louis the Pious as *Miles Christi*. The Dedicatory Image in Hrabanus
Maurus's *De laudibus sanctae crucis*", *Charlemagne's Heir*, eds. P. Godman and R. Collins,
pp. 605–628. Cf. J. Nelson, "Kingship and Royal Government", *The New Cambridge
Medieval History* vol. II, ed. R. McKitterick (Cambridge, 1995), pp. 383–430, at
427–428.

[94] Cf. Flori, *L'essor*, pp. 110–111.

Barthélemy has suggested for the eleventh century?[95] My own view is that in the Carolingian period the Church did not see any need to involve itself. There were two reasons, one relating to power structures, the other to ideology. In the first place, Frankish society was in broad terms segmentary, in the sense that at local level protection was exercised primarily through the structure of landed estates.[96] Investing with weapons was thus the ritualised expression of a power to command that was transmitted directly from father (biological or fictive) to son, within a decentralised structure, and this remained unquestioned because the Carolingians constructed the *imperium christianum* by starting with what already existed. They tried to derive some benefit from developments already under way, particularly from the tendency towards a more clearly-defined social hierarchy, so that they could organise that society behind the king. In the second place, the scenes in the Vivian Bible and the *Codex Aureus*, and others too, belonged to the sphere of ideology. They imposed the image of a king who was God's strong right arm, the necessary intermediary between God and the nobility. By the chain of paternity and through the medium of hierarchical fidelity, the king became the supreme father of all nobles. Thus the nobility found itself invested with a mission which derived directly from that of the king. There was no need for any royal giving of weapons, nor of any blessing of weapons: it was enough that the *ministerium regale* was defined as a ministry in religious terms, and that the ruler's own weapons were blessed. The nobiliy were thus invited to put their arms at the service of the Carolingian order, protecting the Church and the weak: this is what Stephen II's blessing of the magnates had already implied.

The new funerary practices which appeared in the eighth century were certainly linked in part with the transformation of the Frankish nobility into a *militia saecularis* associated with the royal office. Until the seventh century in Gaul, and until the eighth century in Germany, weapons, including the long sword, had been deposited in graves.[97] Although this practice was rare in what is now modern

---

[95] D. Barthélemy, "Qu'est-ce que la chevalerie en France aux Xᵉ et XIᵉ siècles?", *Revue Historique* 290/1 (1994), p. 54, reprinted in D. Barthélemy, *La mutation de l'an mil a-t-elle eu lieu?* (Paris, 1997).

[96] Le Jan, *Famille et pouvoir*, pp. 108–111, 128.

[97] H. Steuer, "Zur Bewaffnung und Sozialstruktur der Merowingerzeit", *Nachrichten aus Niedersachsens Urgeschichte* 37 (1968), pp. 18–87, and *idem*, "Helm und Ringschwert: Prunkbewaffnung und Rangabzeichen germanischer Krieger im 1. Jahrtausend. Eine Übersicht", *Studien zur Sachsenforschung* 6 (1987), pp. 189–236.

Belgium and western Germany, it seems to have been quite frequent in some central areas of Gaul, in Champagne and the Paris region, for instance, in burials of the late sixth- and seventh-centuries, even when the total assemblage of grave goods was small. In the late sixth and seventh centuries, however, such weapon-depositions are found only in rich graves.[98] The practice had come to symbolise the power to command. What was the deep meaning of these depositions?[99] They were not linked to the age of the deceased, for weapons are found in the graves of men who had lived to a relatively advanced age and were thus no longer capable of fighting,[100] but they certainly expressed the idea that the deceased would retain his rank in the next world and that it was therefore right to furnish him with the ornaments that symbolised that rank. Such practices were linked with a conception of death viewed as a simple passage to a world beyond where the hierarchy of the living, that is, a hierarchy of powers, would be maintained.

Weapon-deposition in graves was clearly a ritual of power too. Since the giving of arms to the young adolescent was a kind of investiture, the placing of those arms in the grave could represent a new kind of investiture, or, more precisely, it could effect a new investiture with power, this time in the hereafter. Obviously, deepening adherence to the doctrines of the Last Judgement and the resurrection of the body would deprive these funeral practices of any religious significance. For Christians, death signified total dispossession. It re-established an original equality, for every Christian had to show humility at the moment of his or her leaving of this world. Entry into a monastery entailed a similar dispossession. The earliest evidence for the placing of weapons on the altar seems to date from the end of the eighth century—unsurprisingly, for it was in the second half of the eighth century that ideological reflection on the meaning of office (*ministerium*) took firm shape. Around 785, when the

---

[98] P. Périn, "Les caractères généraux des nécropoles mérovingiennes de la Champagne du Nord et de Paris", *Septentrion* 3 (1973), pp. 23–36; B. Young, *Quatre cimitières mérovingiens de l'est de la France: Lavoye, Dieue-sur-Meuse, Mézières, et Mazerny. Étude quantitative des pratiques funéraires*, (BAR International Series 208) (Oxford, 1984).

[99] For the symbolism of weapon-depositions, and for northern Gaul, see the paper of Frans Theuws and Monica Alkemade in this volume.

[100] H. Härke, "'Warrior graves'? The background of the Anglo-Saxon weapon burial rite", *Past and Present* 126 (1990), pp. 22–43, and H. Härke, "Tombes à armes anglo-saxonnes", pp. 425–436, shows that the presence of weapons in graves is to be explained by Germanic origin, by wealth, and also by the family's social standing.

young Wulfhard was offered by his parents to St-Martin, Tours, he placed on the altar his weapons and his shorn hair, 'as had become customary for nobles'.[101] Though there were earlier cases, it was really in the ninth century that the placing of arms on the altar was integrated into the ritual of monastic profession. In his Commentary on the Rule of St Benedict, Hildemar declared that the weapons-deposition should be performed after two months' stay in the community, and that this rite should henceforth bind the novice to monastic life, though full profession would follow a year later.[102] This was the ritual procedure followed at Corbie in Adalard's time, and, over a century later, when Leubald entered Cluny in 951, he laid his weapons on the altar, and cut his hair and beard.[103]

In placing his weapons on the altar, the noble not only abandoned his lay status (the tonsure was enough for that) but, as Barthélemy has observed, he also stripped himself of his noble clothing.[104] In other words, he abandoned the *militia saecularis*, and 'divested' himself of the power involved in arms-bearing.[105] A similar gesture was made in 938 by Thankmar, rebellious son of Henry I of Germany: he placed his weapons and his golden neck-ring on the altar of the church of St-Peter, Heresburg, where he had taken refuge to escape the pursuit of his father's warriors.[106]

In the ninth century, the custom of laying weapons on the altar seems to have become well established in the case of noble who quitted the world of their own free will to vow themselves to Christ's service. The same custom was observed by those on whom bishops had imposed public penance, for the Church assumed the right to deny the bearing of arms to those who violated their commitments. The most famous of such penitents was Louis the Pious himself.[107]

---

[101] E. Mabille, "La pancarte noire de Saint-Martin de Tours", *Mémoires de la Société archéologique de Touraine* 17 (1865), no. 37.

[102] Hildemar, *Expositio regulae S. Benedicti* c. 58, ed. R. Mittermüller (Regensburg, 1880), pp. 537–538. See M. de Jong, "Power and humility in Carolingian society: the public penance of Louis the Pious", *Early Medieval Europe* 1 (1992), pp. 44–45, and M. de Jong, *In Samuel's Image. Child Oblation in the Early Medieval West* (Leiden, New York and London, 1996), pp. 71–72.

[103] A. Bernard and A. Bruel eds, *Receuil des chartes de l'abbaye de Cluny*, 5 vols. (Paris 1876–1903), I, no. 802, p. 756.

[104] Barthélemy, "Qu'est-ce que la chevalerie . . .?", p. 55, n. 214.

[105] de Jong, "Power and humility", pp. 45, 50.

[106] Widukind, *Rerum gestarum saxonicarum libri III*, ed. P. Hirsch and H.E. Lohmann, *MGH SSRG* 60 (Hannover, 1935), II, 11, p. 77.

[107] de Jong, "Power and humility", pp. 29–52.

In 833 he was accused of having caused 'scandal' in the Church
and endangered the stability of the empire by his derelictions and
crimes. He was made to send his wife away, and he was adjudged
unworthy to exercise the *militia saecularis*. He had to confess his crimes
publicly, and then laid his weapons on the altar (*cingulum militiae deposuit et super altare collocavit*). He donned the garb of a penitent, and
the bishops imposed penitential conditions on him. Finally he declared
his life-long renunciation of the *militia saecularis* (*ut post tantam talemque
poenitentiam nemo ultra ad militiam saecularem redeat*),[108] in other words,
of royal power itself.[109] Murderers of bishops,[110] and parricides,[111]
were also condemned to renounce their functions in the world, that
is, warfare and marriage, by giving up their weapons and putting
aside their wives.

Make no mistake about it, these measures were not directed at
the *pagenses*, harshly subject as they were to the 'justice' of *potentes*.[112]
No, these measures were aimed at men who wore the *cingulum militiae*, the emperor first and foremost, and then the aristocracy. Was
the target still more specific? Was the *cingulum militiae* reserved, as
Jean Flori has suggested, to those who bore the highest public office?[113]
Or was it the badge of all who bore arms, that is, the whole *regni
militia*, in a word: the nobility?

A closer look at the crimes of which the Emperor Louis was
accused shows the public and private domains inextricably mixed.
He was condemned for having failed in his office by violating the
oaths he had sworn to his father (he had promised to protect his
brothers, his close kin and his nephew Bernard), also to his sons, his

---

[108] *Episcoporum de poenitentia, quam Hlodowicus imperator professus est, relatio compendien-
sis*, October 833, *MGH Capit.* II, no. 197, pp. 51–55. In Agobard's *Cartula*, the
emperor is said to have laid his weapons on the altar (*deposita arma manu propria et
ad crepidinem altaris proiecta*), *MGH Capit.* II, no. 198, p. 57. Cf. *Annales Fuldenses* s.a.
834, ed. F. Kurze, *MGH SSRG* 7 (Hannover, 1891), p. 27: 'Post haec iudicio episcoporum arma deposuit et ad agendam poenitentiam inclusus est, uxor in Italiam ducta.'

[109] As rightly observed by Flori, *L'essor*, p. 46.

[110] *Concilium et capitulare de clericorum percussoribus* c. 4, *MGH Capit.* I, no. 176,
p. 361.

[111] Council of Mainz, 847, cc. 20 and 24, ed. W. Hartmann, *MGH Conc. aevi
Karolini* III, 843–859 (Hannover, 1984), pp. 171–172.

[112] See J. Nelson, "Dispute settlement in Carolingian West Francia", in J. Nelson,
The Frankish World, p. 58, and R. Le Jan, "Justice royale et pratiques sociales dans
le regnum franc au IXe siècle", *La Giustizzia nell'alto medioevo (secoli IX–XI)*. (Settimane di studio del centro italiano di studi sull'alto medioevo XLIX) (Spoleto 1997),
pp. 79–80.

[113] Flori, *L'essor*, pp. 46–47.

faithful men, and his whole people; for having caused the people's ruin by embarking on campaigns that were futile, and damaging to the public peace; for having provoked conflict between his sons by going back on the plans for the empire's future division which he himself had made in 817, and for failing to use his paternal authority to impose a peaceful settlement; and, finally, for having ignored the advice of churchmen and hence put at risk the salvation of the Christian people. Louis had clearly failed in all his paternal responsibilities—towards his son, his kin, his faithful men, his people. The lack of any clear distinction between public and private is very obvious here: royal power was a matter of public *defensio* and private *mundeburdium* combined.[114]

A man's laying-down of his weapons, and of the *cingulum militiae* in particular, clearly implied a renunciation of any kind of public function whatsoever. The Council of Pavia set this out explicitly in 850.[115] In my view, however, the *militia regni* should not be understood as restricted only to the *proceres*, the magnates. On the contrary, I think that in the context of the controlled decentralisation of power that characterised the period,[116] it covered all adult males in the nobility, that is, all who bore noble arms. This is what's implied by a canon of the Council of Tribur (895), which lays down that homicide is punishable by forty days' penance, consisting of fasting, sexual abstinence and the laying down of secular arms.[117] The powerful man had to humble himself, and hence had to strip himself of the attributes of power. Mayke de Jong has definitively shown just how far Carolingian clergy went in their insistence on the saving virtue of humility, especially for those whose social responsibilities entailed the bearing of arms.[118] Eleventh-century *milites* committed themselves to exactly this kind of renunciation when they swore to observe the Truce of God.

Laying-down of arms, or, as Dominique Barthélemy has called it, 'un-dubbing'[119] or 'dis-investiture', thus represented a change of status, voluntary for some, involuntary for others. In the ninth century,

---

[114] Le Jan, *Famille et pouvoir*, p. 100.
[115] Council of Pavia, 850, c. 12, *MGH Capit.* II, no. 120, p. 120: '*nullo militiae secularis uti cingulo nullamque reipublicae debent administrare dignitatem*'.
[116] Le Jan, *Famille et pouvoir*, ch. IV.
[117] Council of Tribur (895), c. 55, *MGH Capit.* II, no. 252, p. 242.
[118] de Jong, "Power and humility", pp. 31–35.
[119] Barthélemy, "Qu'est-ce que la chevalerie", p. 54.

the Church claimed a monopoly on requiring *belligerantes* to renounce their function if and when they breached the most sacred obligations of their status: in laying his arms on the altar, a man gave up the protective vocation that belonged to him as a noble. In requiring such renunciations, the Church was not putting itself in the king's place. The Church put its spiritual arms at the service of the *imperium christianum*, for the king's mission was to govern the Christian empire[120] and the bishops, as his *adiutores*,[121] had to help him in that task. In the idealised organisation of Carolingian society, the king was the supreme bearer of responsibility for order and peace, and the *militia saecularis* shared in that mission and that office (*ministerium*).

The defining of a *militia* in the service of the *imperium christianum* was the christianised and idealised version of that hierarchy of protection and service on which the Carolingian social order rested. At first glance, this might look as if it contradicted the representation of a lay society ordered from top to bottom beneath the king. Earlier medieval churchmen long remained attached to model of social organisation in which the laity constituted a single *ordo*, characterised by the married state,[122] and hence marked off from the other two *ordines*. But in fact there was no contradiction, because the Carolingian version of the three orders was not a functional one. It was intended to impose on the entire population, ecclesiastical and lay alike, a rule related to each of three ways of life: the Rule of St Benedict for monks, the clerical rule and celibacy for secular clergy, and Christian marriage and subjection to the duties of fidelity for lay people. Marriage was indeed the only point on which the obligations of all lay people coincided, and it did not correspond to a social function for there was none that could apply to the laity as a whole. Lay status was thus defined by reference not to any particular function, but to the married state.

The laying-down of arms as a requirement imposed by ninth-century bishops meant that the nobility's protective function was now firmly embedded in the ideological construct of the *imperium christianum*. In November 858, Hincmar of Rheims, in the letter written from Quierzy on behalf of himself and his episcopal colleagues to Louis the German, could thus assign to the *regni militia* the mission

[120] Werner, "*Hludowicus Augustus*", p. 63.
[121] de Jong, "Power and humility", pp. 39–43.
[122] J. Chelini, *L'aube du Moyen Âge. Naissance de la Chétienté occidentale* (Paris, 1991).

of assuring the peace and defence of the Church.[123] The nobility, organised and conceived as a *militia*, was given the task, along with the king, of defending a divinely-established order. In a privilege addressed to Odo of Beauvais on 28 April 863, Pope Nicholas I mentioned a royal grant to the church of Beauvais in which compensation was given for property which had been lost and which the king was unable to recover without doing harm to the *militia* of his realm.[124] The royal *fideles* thus formed a *regia militia* whose function was to fight for the realm.

Beyond any differences of social rank reflected in how men looked, all nobles, from *proceres regni* to simple *vassi*, were thus bound in a common identity which distinguished them from other free men. What defined that identity was arms-bearing and the social role that went with it. When Heiric of Auxerre around the year 875 offered a new way of thinking about the orders of society, he put clergy and monks in a single *ordo*, and split the laity into two *ordines*, that of the *belligerantes* and that of the *agricolantes*.[125] Here we really do have a trifunctional classification. Heiric himself was a monk, and perhaps more aware of social realities than were Carolingian bishops. In reviving the ancient Indo-European ideology of the three orders, which had probably reached him via the writings of Isidore of Seville,[126] Heiric took account of changes that were under way in his own times. The Carolingian political structure had rested on the active participation of free men in the defence of the realm. The use of weapons was not reserved to the nobility, but open to all free men who had sufficient means. To be sure, a distinction was made between bearing arms and using them. The *pagenses*, the free men of the *pagus* who were summoned to the army under their count's command, had to lay down their weapons within forty days after their return from campaign.[127] This was why Carolingian rulers did

---

[123] *MGH Conc. aevi Karolini* III, no. 41, c. 7, p. 414.

[124] Nicholas I, *Privilegium pro ecclesia Bellovacensi Nicolai papae I*, PL 119, col. 813: '... *non restituere se posse dixit ne suae reipublicae militiam defraudare videretur*'.

[125] Heiric of Auxerre, *De miraculis sancti Germani episcopi Autissiodorensis* II, 18, PL 124, col. 1254. See D. Iogna-Prat, "Le 'baptême' du schéma des trois ordres fonctionnels. L'apport de l'école d'Auxerre dans la seconde moitié du IXᵉ siècle", *Annales E.S.C.* janvier-février 1986, pp. 101–126.

[126] *Etymologiae* IX, 4, 7, ed. J. Orozreta, 2 vols. (Madrid 1982), I, p. 776. Cf. Iogna-Prat, "Le 'baptême'", pp. 108–110.

[127] *Capitulare missorum Wormatiense*, August 829, c. 13, *MGH Capit.* II, no. 192, p. 16; *Edictum Pistense*, June 864, c. 33, *MGH Capit.* II, no. 273, p. 325: '*Postquam*

not regard the *pagenses*, who most of the time were protected by public officer-holders, as needing to be permanent arms-bearers. For as
soon as a *pagensis* had returned from the host, he had to put down
his bow and arrows, and his sword if he had one, and make do
with the knife or the stout stick which he would seldom be without.
Of course, neither great men nor *vassi* had to lay down their arms
in this way: like the noble depicted in the church at Mals, they were
by definition arms-bearers, in virtue of their protective function.

In the second half of the ninth century, though, the *pagenses* went
less and less often to join the army, while the use of arms increasingly became the strict preserve of members of the *militia*. Gradually, defence became the business of the *belligerantes*, as distinct from
the *agricolantes*. The former had to undergo the hardships of military
service (the *militia*), while the latter endured the hardships of man-
ual labour. In the early tenth century, Odo of Cluny, another monk,
offered his own definition of the *armata militia* as an *ordo pugnatorum*,[128]
and while he denounced the exactions of the *potentes* just as strongly
as his predecessors had done, he offered in the example of Gerald
of Aurillac a way of using the *ius armatae militiae*—one which the ideology of the nobility would seize and develop. It was the task of the
members of the *ordo pugnatorum* to guarantee the defence of the *iner-
mes*, and at the same time these fighters had to submit to apostolic
commands by fighting against the enemies of God, and by repressing violence: in short, by putting their swords at God's service.[129]

Thus the monks projected onto the *militia* the royal ideology developed by ninth-century bishops. This projection was not the result of
any wish to devalue royal power nor of any displacement of royal
ideology in the direction of the *militia*. The monks did however take
note of the weakening of royal power; and they registered the ideological changes that had occurred since the end of the ninth century. The mission of the *militia* remained the same, but now it no
longer seemed to derive from the royal *ministerium* Instead it was
justified, just as the royal office was, in terms of a direct commis-
sion from God.[130]

---

*comes et pagenses de qualibet expeditione hostili reversi fuerit, ex eo die super quadranginta noctes
sit bannus resisus, quod in lingua theodisca scaftlegi, id est armorum depositio, vocatur'.*

[128] *Vita Geraldi* I, c. 8, PL 133, col. 647.
[129] *Ibid.*, cols. 646–647.
[130] Other symptoms of these changes include new kinds of princely titles: see
R. Le Jan, "*Domnus, illuster, nobilis*: les mutations du pouvoir au Xe siècle", *Haut*

Perhaps this new conception, and this new arrangement, should be linked with a new funeral practice reserved for the nobility. The author of the *Vita Gangulfi*, writing in the tenth century, described how the saint's weapons—his helmet, his mail-shirt, his sword and his arm-guards—were displayed in the church built in his honour.[131] These were all elements of the noble's equipment, and the practice of displaying them in this way foreshadows later 'chivalric' funerals.[132] It treats death as a point of rupture, when the weapons that served the noble in the Church's defence now have to be returned to it. The deposition of arms thus looks like a sort of symbolic restitution, or counter-gift.

The Carolingian period saw changes of fundamental importance. As they contemplated their political environment, churchmen were led to define royal power as a *ministerium*, in which the king wielded God-given arms to govern and defend the people of God. The sword and the sword-belt therefore became the symbols of the *militia saecularis*. That is why bishops required those who, voluntarily or otherwise, ceased to serve the *imperium christianum*, in other words the Church, to lay down their arms. In this conception of an ordered society, the nobility had no *ministerium* of its own, because it shared in that of the ruler. The definition of an *ordo pugnatorum* towards the end of the ninth century assigned a more autonomous function to the *belligerantes*. That function was, I think, the product of monks' reflecting on the political and ideological changes of the world they lived in.

In Frankish society, the circulation of weapons had always had tremendous symbolic significance, especially where the weapons in question were valuable, highly ornamented, and handed down from the past. Investiture with weapons had roots that went deep into ancient warrior traditions linking the right to bear arms, the exercise of power, and the armed protection of the group. This custom, and its associated ritual, were ensconsed in a system of social relations which guaranteed social equilibrium by blending filiation and

---

Moyen Age: culture, éducation et société, études offertes à Pierre Riché, ed. M. Sot (Paris, 1990), pp. 442–447; Le Jan, *Famille et pouvoir*, pp. 138–141.

[131] *Vita Gangulfi martyris Varennensis* c. 3, ed. W. Levison, *MGH SSRM* VII, p. 159: 'Cuius rei [i.e. Gangulf's military skill] *indicium facit insignis eius armatura, quae hodieque conservatur in ecclesia eius in honore et nomine dedicata, quam sacratissima eius inlustrat praesentia; ubi habentur reposita galea, lorica, gladius eius et brachialia'*.

[132] A. Erlande-Brandenbourg, *Le roi est mort. Étude sur les funérailles, les sépultures et les tombeaux des rois de France jusqu'à la fin du XIIIᵉ siècle* (Geneva 1975).

fidelity. The circulation of weapons, drawn into an ellipse by hierarchical exchange, was thus an essential element of social regulation and adjustment, while at the same time it maintained social hierarchy.

BIBLIOGRAPHY

Primary sources

Annales Fuldenses, ed. F. Kurze, *MGH SSRG* 7 (Hannover, 1891).
Astronomer, *Vita Hludowici imperatoris*, ed. E. Tremp, *MGH SSRG* 44 (Hannover, 1995).
Cartulaire de l'abbaye de Cysoing et de ses dépendences, ed. I. de Coussemaker (Lille, 1886).
Clausula de unctione Pippini regis, ed. G. Waitz, *MGH SS* XV, 1 (Hannover, 1887).
Dhuoda, *Liber Manualis*, ed. P. Riché (Paris, 1975).
Einhard, *Vita Karoli Magni*, ed. O. Holder-Egger, *MGH SSRG* (Hannover, 1911).
Ermold le Noir, *In Honorem Hludowici Pii*, ed. E. Faral, *Poème sur Louis le Pieux* (Paris, 1964). English translation P. Godman, *Poetry of the Carolingian Renaissance* (London, 1985), pp. 256–257.
Gregory of Tours, *Historiarum Libri Decem*, ed. B. Krusch and W. Levison, *MGH SSRM* I, revd. edn. (Hannover, 1951).
Heiric of Auxerre, *De miraculis sancti Germani episcopi Autissiodorensis*, PL 124.
Hildemar, *Expositio regulae S. Benedicti*, ed. R. Mittermüller (Regensburg, 1880), pp. 537–538.
Isidore of Sevilla, *Etymologiae*, ed. J. Orozreta (Madrid 1982).
Laws of Ine, trans. D. Whitelock, *English Historical Documents* vol. I, revd. edn. (London 1979).
Lex Ribuaria, ed. K.E. Eckhardt, *MGH LL in quarto* III, 2 (Hannover, 1954).
MGH Capitularia Regum Francorum I, ed. A. Boretius (Hannover, 1883) and II, ed. A. Boretius and V. Krause (Hannover, 1897).
MGH Conc. aevi Karolini III, 843–859, ed. W. Hartmann (Hannover, 1984).
Nicholas I, *Privilegium pro ecclesia Bellovacensi Nicolai papae I*, PL 119.
Notker, *Gesta Karoli*, ed. H.F. Haefele, *MGH SSRG*, new series 12 (Berlin, 1962).
Pactus legis salicae, ed. K.E. Eckhardt, *MGH LL in quarto* IV, 1 (Hannover, 1962).
Passio Ragneberti martyris Bebronensis, ed. B. Krusch, *MGH SSRM* V (Hannover, 1910).
Odo of Cluny, *Vita Geraldi Auriliacensis comitis* I, PL 133.
Receuil de chartes de l'abbaye de Saint-Benoît-sur-Loire, eds. M. Prou and A. Vidier (Orleans and Paris, 1900–1924).
Receuil des chartes de l'abbaye de Cluny, eds. Bernard A. and A. Bruel (Paris 1876–1903).
Saxo Grammaticus, *Gesta Danorum*, eds. J. Olrik and H. Ræder (Copenhagen, 1931).
Tacitus, *Germania*, trans. H. Mattingly, revd. S.A. Handford (Harmondsworth 1970).
Thegan, *Gesta Hludowici imperatoris*, ed. E. Tremp, *MGH SSRG* 54 (Hannover, 1995).
Vita Gamalberti presbyteri Michaelbuchensis, eds. B. Krusch and W. Levison, *MGH SSRM* VII (Hannover and Leipzig, 1920).
Vita Gangulfi martyris Varennensis, ed. W. Levison, *MGH SSRM* VII.
Vita Trudonis confessoris Hasbanensis auctore Donati, eds. B. Krusch and W. Levison, *MGH SSRM* VI (Hannover, 1913).
Widukind, *Rerum gestarum saxonicarum libri III*, ed. P. Hirsch and H.E. Lohmann, *MGH SSRG* 60 (Hannover, 1935).

Secondary sources

Airlie, S., "The anxiety of sanctity: St Gerald of Aurillac and his maker", *Journal of Ecclesiastical History* 43 (1992), pp. 372–395.

Barthélemy, D., "Qu'est-ce que la chevalerie en France aux Xe et XIe siècles?", *Revue Historique* 290/1 (1994), pp. 15–74. Reprinted in D. Barthélemy, *La mutation de l'an mil a-t-elle eu lieu?* (Paris, 1997).

Brulet, R., "La sépulture du roi Childéric à Tournai et le site funéraire", *La noblesse romaine et les chefs barbares au IIIe au VIIe siècle*, eds. F. Vallet and M. Kazanski (Memoires de l' Association française d'Archéologie mérovingienne 9) (Paris, 1995), pp. 309–326.

Chelini, J., *L'aube du Moyen Age. Naissance de la Chrétienté occidentale* (Paris, 1991).

Davidson, H.E., *The Sword in Anglo-Saxon England* (Oxford, 1962).

——, "The training of warriors", *Weapons and Warfare in Anglo-Saxon England*, ed. S.C. Hawkes (Oxford, 1989), pp. 11–23.

Doppelfeld O. and R. Pirling, *Fränkische Fürsten im Rheinland. Die Gräber aus dem Kölner Dom* (Düsseldorf, 1966).

Doppelfeld, O., "Das fränkische Knabengrab unter dem Chor des Kölner Domes", *Germania* 12 (1964), pp. 156–188.

Duby, G., "Les 'jeunes' dans la société aristocratique de la France du Nord-Ouest au XIIe siècle", *Annales E.S.C.* septembre-octobre 1964, pp. 835–846, reprinted in G. Duby, *Hommes et structures du Moyen Age* (Paris, 1973), pp. 213–25, and translated in G. Duby, *The Chivalrous Society*, trans. C. Postan (London, 1977), pp. 112–122.

Dutton P.E. and H.L. Kessler, *The Poetry and Paintings of the First Bible of Charles the Bald* (Ann Arbor MI, 1997).

Erlande-Brandenbourg, A., *Le roi est mort. Étude sur les funérailles, les sépultures et les tombeaux des rois de France jusqu'à la fin du XIIIe siècle* (Geneva 1975).

Flori, J., "Les origines de l'adoubement chevaleresque. Etude des remises d'armes dans les chroniques et annales latines du Ixe au XIIIe siècle", *Traditio* 35 (1979), pp. 209–272.

——, *L'essor de la chevalerie, XIe–XIIe siècle* (Paris, 1986).

Garber, J., "Die karolingische St. Benediktskirche in Mals", *Zeitschrift des Ferdinandeums für Tirol und Vorarlberg* 3F.59 (1915), 3, pp. 3–61.

Hantute, G., *La cimetière mérovingien de Neuville-sur-Escaut* (Denain 1989).

Härke, H., "'Warrior graves'? The background of the Anglo-Saxon weapon burial rite", *Past and Present* 126 (1990), pp. 22–43.

——, "Angelsächsische Waffengräber des 5. bis 7. Jahrhunderts", *Zeitschrift für Archäologie des Mittelalters* 6, Beihefte 1 (Cologne, 1992).

——, "Tombes à armes anglo-saxonnes: sépultures de guerriers ou symbolisme rituel", *L'armée romaine et les barbares du IIIe au VIIe siècle*, eds. F. Vallet and M. Kazanski (Mémoires publiés par l'Association française de l'Archéologie Mérovingienne 5) (Paris, 1993), pp. 425–436.

Iogna-Prat, D., "Le 'baptême' du schéma des trois ordres fonctionnels. L'apport de l'école d'Auxerre dans la seconde moitié du IXe siècle", *Annales Economies, Sociétés, Cultures*, janvier-février 1986, pp. 101–126.

Jarnut, J., "Die frühmittelalterliche Jagd unter Rechts- und sozialgeschichtlichen Aspekten", *L'Uomo di fronte al mondo animale nell'alto medoevo*, (Settimane di studio del centro italiano di studi sull'alto medioevo XXXI) (Spoleto, 1985), pp. 765–798.

Jong, M. de, "Power and humility in Carolingian society: the public penance of Louis the Pious", *Early Medieval Europe* 1 (1992), pp. 44–45.

——, *In Samuel's Image. Child Oblation in the Early Medieval West* (Leiden, New York and London, 1996).

Krüger, S., "Character *militaris* und character *indelibilis*. Ein Beitrag zum Verhältnis von *Miles* und *Clericus* im Mittelalter", *Institutionen, Kultur und Gesellschaft im Mittelalter. Festschrift für Josef Fleckenstein zu seiner 65. Geburtstag*, eds. Fenske *et al.* (Sigmaringen, 1984), pp. 567–580.

Le Jan, R., "Apprentissages militaires, rites de passage, et remises d'armes au haut Moyen Age", *Education, apprentissages, initiation au Moyen Age, Actes du premier colloque international de Montpellier*, (Cahiers du C.R.I.S.I.M.A. no. 1) (1993), pp. 214–222.

——, "*Domnus, illuster, nobilis*: les mutations du pouvoir au Xe siècle", *Haut Moyen Age: culture, éducation et société, études offertes à Pierre Riché*, ed. M. Sot (Paris, 1990), pp. 442–447.

——, "Justice royale et pratiques sociales dans le regnum franc au IXe siècle", *La Giustizzia nell'alto medioevo (secoli IX–XI)*. (Settimane di studio del centro italiano di studi sull'alto medioevo XLIX) (Spoleto 1997), pp. 79–80.

——, "Satellites et bandes armées dans le monde franc (VIIe–Xe siècle)", *Le combattant au moyen âge*, (Société des historiens médiévistes de l'Enseignement supérieur) (Paris, 1991), pp. 98–102.

——, *Famille et pouvoir dans le monde franc (VIIe–Xe siècle). Essai d'anthropologie sociale* (Paris, 1995).

Leyser, K., "Early Medieval Canon Law and the Beginnings of Knighthood", *Institutionen, Kultur und Gesellschaft im Mittelalter. Festschrift J. Fleckenstein*, eds. L. Fenske, W. Rösener and T. Zotz (Sigmaringen, 1984), pp. 556–560.

Mabille, E., "La pancarte noire de Saint-Martin de Tours", *Mémoires de la Société archéologique de Touraine* 17 (1865), no. 37.

Martin, M., *Das fränkische Graberfeld von Basel-Bernerring* (Mainz, 1976).

Mütherich F. and J.E. Gaehde, *Carolingian Painting* (London, 1977).

Nelson, J., "Dispute settlement in Carolingian West Francia", J. Nelson, *The Frankish World* (London, 1996), pp. 00.

——, "Kingship and Royal Government", *The New Cambridge Medieval History* vol. II, ed. R. McKitterick (Cambridge, 1995), pp. 383–430.

Nelson, J.L., "Carolingian royal ritual", *Rituals of Royalty. Power and Ceremonial in Traditional Societies*, eds. D. Cannadine and S. Price (Cambridge, 1987), pp. 137–180.

——, "Ninth-century knighthood: the evidence of Nithard", *Studies in Medieval History presented to R. Allen Brown*, eds. C. Harper-Bill, C. Holdsworth and J.L. Nelson (Woodbridge, 1989), pp. 255–66, reprinted in J. Nelson, *The Frankish World* (London, 1996), pp. 75–88.

Périn, P., "Les caractères généraux des nécropoles mérovingiennes de la Champagne du Nord et de Paris", *Septentrion* 3 (1973), pp. 23–36.

Pilet *et al.*, C., "Les nécropoles de Giberville (Calvados), fin du Ve-fin du VIIe siècle après J.C.", *Archéologie médiévale* 20 (1990), pp. 3–140.

Schmidt-Wiegand, R., "Fränkische *Druht* und *Druhtin*. Zur historischen Terminologie im Bereich der Sozialgeschichte", *Historische Forschungen für W. Schlesinger*, ed. H. Beumann (Cologne and Vienna, 1974), pp. 524–535.

Sears, E., "Louis the Pious as *Miles Christi*. The Dedicatory Image in Hrabanus Maurus's *De laudibus sanctae crucis*", *Charlemagne's Heir. New Perspectives on the Reign of Louis the Pious*, eds. P. Godman and R. Collins (Oxford, 1990), pp. 605–628.

Steuer, H., "Helm und Ringschwert: Prunkbewaffnung und Rangabzeichen germanischer Krieger im 1. Jahrtausend. Eine Übersicht", *Studien zur Sachsenforschung* 6 (1987), pp. 189–236.

——, "Zur Bewaffnung und Sozialstruktur der Merowingerzeit", *Nachrichten aus Niedersachsens Urgeschichte* 37 (1968), pp. 18–87.

Stoclet, A., "La '*Clausula de unctione Pippini regis*': mises au point et nouvelles hypothèses", *Francia* 8 (1980), pp. 1–42.

Vierck, H., "Ein westphalisches 'Adelsgrab' des 8. Jahrhundert n. Chr. Zum archäologischen Nachweis der spätsächsischen und frühkarolingischen Oberschichten", *Studien zur Sachsenforschung* 2 ed. H.J. Hässler (Hildesheim, 1980), pp. 458–488.

Werner, K.F., "*Hludowicus Augustus*: Gouverner l'empire chrétien—idées et réalités", *Charlemagne's Heir. New Perspectives on the Reign of Louis the Pious*, eds. P. Godman and R. Collins (Oxford, 1990), pp. 3–124.

Wilson, D.M., *The Bayeux Tapestry* (London, 1985).

Winter, J.M. van, "*Cingulum militiae*", *Revue d'histoire du droit* 44 (1976), pp. 1–92.

Young, B., *Quatre cimitières mérovingiens de l'est de la France: Lavoye, Dieue-sur-Meuse, Mézières, et Mazerny. Étude quantitative des pratiques funéraires*, (BAR International Series 208) (Oxford, 1984).

BEYOND POWER. CEREMONIAL EXCHANGES
IN *BEOWULF*

Jos Bazelmans

1. *Warriors and Lords in the late Pre- and Protohistory of transalpine Europe*

In the study of long-term developments in the organisation of societies in the late pre- and protohistory of transalpine Europe, the relationship between a lord or king and the warriors in his closest retinue is held to be a phenomenon of special importance.[1] In German language literature the concept of *Gefolgschaft* is generally used to designate this relationship. In his famous definition of the concept Walter Schlesinger expressed the character of *Gefolgschaft* as follows: *a relationship [. . .] which is freely entered into, based on trust, obliges the man to [give] counsel and (military) help, and the lord to [give] protection and 'kindness'.*[2] This definition of *Gefolgschaft* has attracted much criticism. The critique was largely a reaction to Schlesinger's belief that the warrior's oath of allegiance had a specific Germanic and sacred character.[3] It has, however, been generally accepted, following Schlesinger, that *Gefolgschaft* should be described as a *'formalised and*

---

[1] For instance: H. Steuer, *Frühgeschichtliche Sozialstrukturen im Mitteleuropa. Eine Analyse der Auswertungsmethoden des archäologischen Quellenmaterials* (Göttingen, 1982) and H. Steuer, "Archaeology and history: proposals on the social structure of the Merovingian kingdom", *The birth of Europe: archaeology and social developments in the first millennium AD*, ed. K. Randsborg (Rome, 1989); N. Roymans, *Tribal societies in northern Gaul. An anthropological perspective* (Amsterdam, 1990), pp. 38–43, and R. Wenskus, "Die neuere Diskussion um Gefolgschaft und Herrschaft in Tacitus' *Germania*", *Beiträge zum Verständnis der* Germania des Tacitus 2. *Bericht über die Kolloquien der Kommission für die Altertumskunde Nord- und Mitteleuropas im Jahre 1986 und 1987*, eds. G. Neumann and H. Seemann (Göttingen, 1992).

[2] *'[Gefolgschaft ist] ein Verhältnis [. . .] das freiwillig eingegangen wird, auf Treue gegründet ist und den Mann zu Rat and (kriegerischer) Hilfe, den Herrn zu Schutz und 'Milde' verpflichtet'.* W. Schlesinger, "Herrschaft und Gefolgschaft in der germanisch-deutschen Verfassungsgeschichte", *Historische Zeitschrift* 176 (1953), p. 235.

[3] Some even doubted the existence of an early Germanic, Tacitean oath of allegiance. F. Graus, "Über die sogenannte germanische Treue", *Historica* 1 (1959) and K. Kroeschell, "Die Treue in der deutschen Rechtsgeschichte", *Studi Medievali Serie terza* 10 (1969), pp. 465–498; cf. W. Kienast, "Germanische Treue und 'Königsheil'", *Historische Zeitschrift* 227 (1977), pp. 265–324; and Wenskus, "Die neuere Diskussion um Gefolgschaft und Herrschaft in Tacitus' *Germania*".

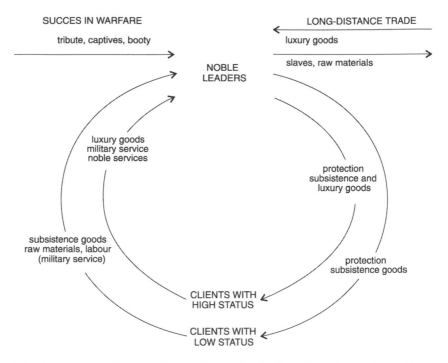

Fig. 1. Diagram of patron-client relationships in Late Iron Age societies (from Roymans, *Tribal societies in northern Gaul. An anthropological perspective*, fig. 3.4)

long-lasting relationship of reciprocity'.[4] Without paying much attention to aspects of legal history, as Schlesinger did, several researchers have since tried to model the 'economics' of *Gefolgschaft*. Other relationships which a lord or king had with subordinates and with other lords or kings are often drawn into the picture. As an example I reproduce here Nico Roymans' depiction of the system of exchange relations characteristic of late prehistoric Germano-Celtic clientship in Northern Gaul and the Lower Rhine delta (fig. 1[5]).

The retinue of a leader is, as we can ascertain from Roymans' diagram, both the result of the application of sources of power and

---

[4] Wenskus, "Die neuere Diskussion um Gefolgschaft und Herrschaft in Tacitus' *Germania*", pp. 314–315.

[5] Roymans, *Tribal societies in northern Gaul. An anthropological perspective*, fig. 3.4. Cf. fig. 10.1 in C. Haselgrove, "Culture process on the periphery: Belgic Gaul and Rome during the late Republic and early Empire", *Centre and periphery in the ancient world*, eds M. Rowlands, M. Larsen and K. Kristiansen (Cambridge, 1987), pp. 104–124.

itself a source of power. On the one hand the lord or king recruits followers by presenting them with valuables; on the other hand as leader of a retinue he acquires valuables because to others he is an interesting political, marriage or trading partner, or because he can seize valuables by force either as booty or tribute. In view of this politico-economic interpretation, it is understandable that Reinhard Wenskus defines the sociological significance of *Gefolgschaft* as follows: *'the particular importance of the concept of* Gefolgschaft *for constitutional history lies in its importance for the origins of lordship and hence for the constitutional forms that gave rise to the state'.*[6] As the members of the *Gefolgschaft* could be recruited from outside 'natural' groups based on kinship or ethnicity, the *Gefolgschaft* was a revolutionary form of organisation markedly different from the old, prehistoric order of so-called *Kleinstämme* (small tribes). The *Gefolgschaft* formed an important step on the road to state formation.[7]

In this paper I want to take up the discussion of *Gefolgschaft* on the basis of an anthropological analysis of the exchange of gifts in the Old English poem *Beowulf*.[8] The aim of this analysis is to go beyond the politico-economic perspective on *Gefolgschaft* as described above. Without following Schlesinger, I will argue for an interpretation of *Gefolgschaft* in ritual-cosmological terms. Before presenting my analysis of exchange in *Beowulf*, I will discuss the structuralistic perspective which guides my research and which was developed by the French sociologist Louis Dumont and his French and Dutch pupils. They can be regarded as the direct heirs of Marcel Mauss, the founder of the anthropology of the gift. They offer in fact an elaboration of the most important idea that Mauss expressed in his famous *Essai sur le don*,[9] namely that the participants in exchange and the objects of exchange are commensurable.

---

[6] *'die besondere Bedeutung des Begriffs der Gefolgschaft für die Verfassungsgeschichte [liegt] in seiner Wichtigkeit für die Entstehung von Herrschaft und damit für staatliche Verfassungsformen'.* Wenskus, "Die neuere Diskussion um Gefolgschaft und Herrschaft in Tacitus' *Germania*", p. 311.

[7] Cf. J. Bazelmans, "Conceptualising Early Germanic political structure. A review of the concept of Gefolgschaft", *Images of the past. Studies on ancient societies in North-western Europe*, eds. N. Roymans and F. Theuws (Amsterdam, 1991), pp. 91–130.

[8] I presume the poem to be of late 7th, 8th or early 9th century date (J. Bazelmans, *Eén voor allen, allen voor één. Tacitus' Germania, de Oudengelse Beowulf en het ritueel-kosmologische karakter van de relatie tussen heer en krijger-volgeling in Germaanse samenlevingen* (Amsterdam, 1996), pp. 114–139). On the dating of *Beowulf*, see especially R.D. Fulk, *A history of Old English meter* (Philadelphia, 1992).

[9] M. Mauss, "Essai sur le don. Forme et raison de l'échange dans les sociétés archaïques", *L'Année sociologique* 1 (1923–1924), pp. 30–186.

2. *L'esprit de la chose donnée*

In his essay on the gift Mauss sets out to gain insight into the form
and reason for exchange in so-called 'archaic' societies. He is brief
about the mode of exchange: what he calls 'the gift system' (*régime
du don*). On the face of it the primitive gift is disinterested but in
reality there is an obligation to give, receive and reciprocate. The
main purpose of Mauss' inquiry is not so much the ethnographic
description of various forms of primitive exchange, but the formulation of a general theory about the collective, symbolic representations of the relationships between the gift, the giver and the recipient
that warrant the giving, receiving and reciprocating of gifts.

Explaining the obligation to give and receive presents no problem for Mauss: nót to give and nót to receive means the avoiding
or rejecting of a social bond.[10] Mauss has more difficulty explaining
that a gift should be reciprocated. In archaic societies there is after
all no legal, i.e. state-enforced, guarantee that the parties will honour the agreed exchange. The representation of the object of exchange
in the society of the New Zealand Maori is to Mauss the key to a
general theory of obligation.[11] In the conceptual universe of the Maori
the gift is *animated*: it carries something in it of the giver or something that originates from where it belongs. The gift leads its own
life, has its own personality and if it forms part of an exchange it
will seek a return to the place of origin or make sure that the originator will receive an equivalent. Because of its animated nature the
gift has a magical and religious influence on the recipient that can
be dangerous or lethal if the recipient hangs on to the gift.[12]

In an influential commentary on the essay, Claude Lévi-Strauss
distanced himself from Mauss because Mauss took the beliefs of the
Maori for his own theory.[13] According to Lévi-Strauss we should not
be content with the disciplining effect of this native theory about the
gift and the obligation to reciprocate. On the contrary, the exchange

---

[10] Mauss, "Essai sur le don. Forme et raison de l'échange dans les sociétés
archaïque", p. 50ff.
[11] Mauss, "Essai sur le don. Forme et raison de l'échange dans les sociétés
archaïques", p. 45ff. In this connection he speaks of *la jurisprudence mythique des Maori*,
p. 74).
[12] Cf. J. Parry, "The gift, the Indian gift and the 'Indian gift'", *Man* N.S. 21
(1986), pp. 465–466.
[13] C. Lévi-Strauss, "Introduction à l'oeuvre de Marcel Mauss, *Sociologie et anthropologie*, Marcel Mauss (Paris, 1950), pp. ix–lii.

of gifts should be regarded as a realisation of a generally human *principle of reciprocity*. And this principle is founded on the bipolar structuring which is applied in social interaction by human thought. Reciprocity connects *ego* and *alter* in such a way that *ego*, as knowing subject, can feel part of the whole, thus transcending the contradictions of the natural world to assert his humanity.[14]

In their turn, followers of Dumont have criticised Lévi-Strauss' reinterpretation of Mauss and rehabilitated Mauss' views.[15] For various reasons they have adopted a critical attitude towards Lévi-Strauss' well-known and pioneering analysis of the elementary structures of kinship which in his eyes represent different manifestations of the universal principle of reciprocity.[16] Thus Cécile Barraud and her associates reject the naming in advance of exchange in terms of reciprocity but they prefer to operate with the understanding that the people themselves have of their exchange.[17] However, for the present argument this is not the most important point of their critique. They note that in Lévi-Strauss' analysis of structures underlying preferential marriage, the participants in exchange (men) are strictly separated from the objects of exchange (women),[18] whereas, as Mauss had emphasized, a relationship is more than the rearrangement of objects between subjects: '(. . .) it is (. . .) by doing violence to the frontier between subjects and objects [that] he [Mauss] reflects a profound reality of numerous exchange systems, that the objects convey something of the persons who set them in motion. For Mauss, exchanges cease to be inexplicable "if we realise that there exists, above all, an intertwining of spiritual ties between things which are to some degree soul, and individuals and groups that treat each other to some degree as things"'.[19] This important issue of the commensurability of subject and object in gift exchange (as opposed to the incommensurability of subject and object in commodity exchange)

---

[14] Cf. J. van Baal, *Man's quest for partnership. The anthropological foundation of ethics and religion* (Assen, 1981), pp. 92–93.

[15] C. Barraud, D. de Coppet, A. Iteanu and R. Jamous, *Of relations and the dead. Four societies viewed from the angle of their exchanges* (Oxford and Providence, 1994).

[16] C. Lévi-Strauss, *Les structures élémentaires de la parenté* (Paris, 1949). Elementary structures are those systems which prescribe marriage with a certain type of relative.

[17] Barraud *et al.*, *Of relations and the dead. Four societies viewed from the angle of their exchanges*, pp. 2–3 and 105–107.

[18] Cf. T. Ingold, *Evolution and social life* (Cambridge, 1986), pp. 270–271.

[19] Barraud *et al.*, *Of relations and the dead. Four societies viewed from the angle of their exchanges*, pp. 3–4. The quotation within this quotation is from the French Mauss anthology *Sociologie et anthropologie* (Paris, 1950), p. 163 (translation Barraud et al.).

has attracted the attention recently of researchers who while not
indebted to Dumont's research have reached conclusions that are to
a certain extent similar.

In *The gender of the gift*, for instance, Marilyn Strathern does not
aim her arrows at Lévi-Strauss' work but at studies of exchange that
attach special importance to labour and see alienation as the appropriation of value based on labour.[20] According to Strathern the importance attached to labour is based on an understanding of the individual
which is characteristic of modern thought. In the modern point of
view the person is a self-contained entity, i.e. a 'natural' owner of
what he has, does or produces.[21] Strathern argues that this view is
at odds with that of tribal societies where a person is depicted as
something composite and divisible, that is, as something created in
transactions. The 'tribal' person is not so much an author of objects
of exchange and exchange itself, but a product of a cycle of exchanges.
When studying tribal systems we should not focus our attention on
the discrepancy in the sphere of exchange between the 'real' relations of production and the 'distorted' representations of things but
on the merging of on the one hand the production of objects and
on the other hand the production of social relations by the circulation of what is produced. Work always refers here to the social relationships in which it came about and therefore does not acquire the
abstract, commodity-like character of modern labour. Work, i.e. the
production of objects, is in fact an objectification of social relations.
The produced object can only be understood as an artefact of the
relationship between persons and in that sense there is no question
of a simple and serial authorship but a multiple and combined one.[22]
It is therefore not possible to speak of property: '[persons] can only
dispose of items by enchaining themselves in relations with others.'[23]
Because there is no property, there can also be no alienation. Dominance is not based on the appropriation of surplus, as in a system
of commodity exchange: '[i]n a gift economy, we might argue that

---

[20] M. Strathern, *The gender of the gift. Problems with women and problems with society
in Melanesia* (Berkeley, Los Angeles and London, 1988), pp. 133–167.

[21] Strathern, *The gender of the gift. Problems with women and problems with society in
Melanesia*, p. 157.

[22] Cf. N. Thomas, *Entangled objects. Exchange, material culture, and colonialism in the
Pacific* (Cambridge (Mass.) and London, 1991), pp. 53–4 and M. MacKenzie, *Androgynous objects. String bags and gender in central New Guinea* (Chur, 1991), pp. 159–60.

[23] Strathern, *The gender of the gift. Problems with women and problems with society in
Melanesia*, p. 161.

those who dominate are those who determine the connections and
disconnections created by the circulation of objects'.[24] Not the means
of production but (the relationships between) people form the relevant 'capital' here.[25]

Although his sources of inspiration do not have an ethnographic
nature, as with Strathern, but a theoretical one, we can find in Tim
Ingold a similar formulation of the relationship between subject and
object of exchange.[26] According to Ingold, we should take seriously
Mauss' suggestion that the gift is inextricably linked with the person
of the giver. On the face of it, Ingold states, Mauss seems to assume
that reciprocity in exchange is anchored in something outside a person; the obligation to reciprocate is after all part of the collective,
that is supra-individual, representations of society. Yet upon closer
inspection, Ingold thinks, Mauss seems to emphasize in particular
the fact that in exhange a person gives himself, and he does this
because he owes his own person and his possessions to others. Acts
of exchange are therefore not successive moments in the life of society but events in the irreversible enfolding of the social life of persons. In other words, the exchange of gifts is not the realization of
roles outlined by society but is the way in which the participants in
the exchange mutually constitute each other and become part of
each other. The keyword here is 'intersubjectivity'.

In Ingold's view on gift exchange the time-factor plays an important role.[27] The construction, reproduction and transformation of
intersubjectivity, which takes shape in exchange, is a process that
can only be understood when it is related to the advance of *real time*:
'[a]s the material embodiment of a constitutive process the gift is
(. . .) imbued with duration, carrying with it a history of relations
among those through whose hands it has passed, and by bearing the
intent of the giver, projecting these relations into the future'.[28] The
exchange of gifts is therefore, according to Ingold, a directed process
and the spirit of the gift, that is its living quality, corresponds exactly
with the time that passes between the receiving and passing on of

---

[24] Strathern, *The gender of the gift. Problems with women and problems with society in Melanesia*, p. 167.

[25] Cf. A. Appadurai, "Introduction: commodities and the politics of value", *The social life of things*, ed. A. Appadurai (Cambridge, 1986), p. 19.

[26] Ingold, *Evolution and social life*, p. 263ff.

[27] Ingold, *Evolution and social life*, pp. 269–277.

[28] Ingold, *Evolution and social life*, p. 269.

the gift. The longer the delay, the greater the gift is valued for the history that it acquires in the hands of the temporary owner.[29]

These perceptions of how participants in exchange become part of each other through the exchange of objects are for Ingold the basis for the development of what he calls a *constitutive* approach in the study of human societies. This approach assumes that what a person wants or does is not determined by human nature or by cultural prescription but is shaped, together with what he is, in his relations with others. That which occurs at a certain moment as independent of the human will, is nothing less than the past that has made the person into what he is; a past of mutual involvement with others, on the basis of which the future is necessarily a projection. Evocatively phrased, this means an *enfolding* of consciousness in social process and an *unfolding* of consciousness in social process.[30]

Ingold adopts here a critical attitude towards approaches, including the Durkheimian, that see society as a supra-individual essence; approaches that reify what is at best a useful abstraction. Cultural rules do not determine the actions of man in a mechanistic manner but rather provide a means to act. Justly, his critique can also be declared applicable to the perspective employed by Dumont and his pupils. In an elaboration of Dumont's idea that ideology is constitutive, Jos Platenkamp for instance speaks of the shared representations of the East Indonesian Tobelo that *precede* and *determine* the institutions of Tobelo society.[31] And Cécile Barraud *et al.* state that the totality of exchanges '[reveal] a *pre-existing* configuration of values which orders all the society's relations, its various exchanges, and its specific construction of the world'.[32] A better formulation would be that in exchange, relations and values are reproduced beyond the life of discrete persons but that the reproduction of those ideas and values is encased in the movement of the whole that can be discerned in the analysis of exchange. Theoretically that movement is repetitive but in reality it is a movement in historical time. Anticipating my discussion of the approach propagated by Dumont *cum*

---

[29] Cf. A.B. Weiner, *Inalienable possessions: the paradox of keeping-while-giving* (Berkeley, Los Angeles and Oxford, 1992).

[30] Ingold, *Evolution and social life*, p. 248.

[31] J.D.M. Platenkamp, *Tobelo. Ideas and values of a North Moluccan society* (Leiden, 1988), p. 7.

[32] Barraud *et al.*, *Of relations and the dead. Four societies viewed from the angle of their exchanges*, p. 107, emphasis JB.

suis I would like to give in its defence a few short critical comments on Ingold's argument. In his analysis of the exchange of gifts, Ingold in fact only takes the dyadic social relation between two persons as his point of departure and he regards that which defines each of them as a person, his consciousness, as the product of their mutual involvement. It is, however, questionable—and Dumont's and his associates' research draw our attention to this—whether in the study of exchange we can limit ourselves to the sphere of the interpersonal human and whether it is possible to define the essence of the person in universal terms. In most societies it is not only relationships between humans that are relevant but also those between these persons and other supernatural entities. The person takes shape in this culture-specific totality of relationships. As we will see in the next paragraph, the birth, life, and death of a person are often regarded as a process in which different constituents, varying from society to society, are joined together, developed, and broken up again, and these constituents, which come together in a human being through exchange, in the end do not have a social but a supernatural origin. In that sense the spirit of the gift can also not (only) be equated with the unique history of the relations between human participants in exchange. The value of an object of exchange (also) originates in different categories of supernatural partners in the exchange identified by the human participants themselves. In the overall configuration of relations, social as well as supernatural, we discern 'society as a whole'. We herewith reach the root of the approach employed by Dumont and his associates.

3. *Objects of exchange and the constitution of the person*

Dumont, a pupil of Marcel Mauss, achieved an international reputation with his research on India and the Indian caste system.[33] His Indian research was a first step in a project to compare modern and nonmodern societies and modern and nonmodern ideologies. After the completion of his influential study on the caste system *Homo hierarchicus*, he therefore turned away from the sociology of India and concentrated on a study of the origin and development of modern

---

[33] L. Dumont, *Homo hierarchicus. The caste system and its implications* (Chicago and London, 1980 (1966)).

ideology.[34] Louis Dumont's work has been influential in both France and the Netherlands.[35] Work done in Dumont's footsteps is not, however, concerned with modern and nonmodern civilizations but with tribal societies, mostly those of Papua New Guinea and Eastern Indonesia.

Central in Dumont's work is the concept of *structure*. A definition of this concept is to be found *Homo hierarchicus*. Dumont distinguishes between two languages with which the human and non-human world can be described.[36] In one language, the emphasis lies on the various elements that are autonomous and interact with each other on the basis of their own individuality. This language corresponds well with our modern, individualistic world view. In the other language elements are regarded as the product of a network of relationships: an element is only 'other' in relation to others from which it derives the possibility of meaning something. For a system of relationships, whose elements disappear when we make an inventory of the relationships, Dumont reserves the concept of *structure*. According to him, the latter language corresponds well with the traditional, holistic world-view of nonmodern societies.

The linguistic foundation of the concept of structure reflects the Dumontians' concentration in the first place on the ideology of a society. By *ideology* Dumont means the whole or system of ideas ánd values.[37] Dumont's emphasis on the indissoluble connection of the cognitive-existential and the normative makes us aware of the role often played in modern anthropology by a division between the two concepts. When comparing societies, anthropologists usually select elements *a priori* (such as lineages, kingship, women as object of exchange, economy, etc.),[38] whereas the definition, interrelation ánd appreciation of distinct meaningful elements differ from society to society. A comparison of societies should therefore be in the first place *a comparison of ideologies*.[39]

---

[34] L. Dumont, *From Mandeville to Marx. The genesis and triumph of economic ideology* (Chicago, 1977) and L. Dumont, *German ideology. From France to Germany and back* (Chicago and London, 1991).

[35] Cf. Platenkamp 1991.

[36] Dumont, *Homo hierarchicus. The caste system and its implications*, pp. 39–42.

[37] Dumont, *Homo hierarchicus. The caste system and its implications*, pp. 36–39 and note 1a.

[38] Cf. Barraud *et al.*, *Of relations and the dead. Four societies viewed from the angle of their exchanges*, p. 3.

[39] Cf. C. Barraud and J. Platenkamp, "Rituals and the comparison of societies", *Bijdragen van het Instituut voor Taal-, Land- en Volkenkunde* 146 (1990), p. 104.

In a system of ideas and values the different *relationships* meaningful to that society are named and interrelated. In addition, these relationships are evaluated in such a system in terms of a *hierarchy* of values.[40] And finally, an ideology offers the different *contexts* in which these relationships are expressed and the rules for proper behaviour for these different contexts. Contrary to what we might expect at first sight, the configuration of relationships is not seen purely as a mental phenomenon determining societal relations in practice; these researchers are concerned with reality as lived by the participants. It is in this context that exchange enjoys special interest. Exchange shows which relationships are relevant, which values are at stake in them and how they are hierachically linked.

In the Dumontian study of exchange, attention does not focus on the interaction between discrete individuals or groups but on *society as a whole*. Characteristic for nonmodern societies is the holistic ideology mentioned above. Such an ideology specifies not only the relationships between the living, society in a strict sense, but also those between the living and ancestors, spirits and gods, society in a broad sense, or society as a socio-cosmic whole.[41] In modern society a strict distinction is made between the living and the dead:[42] the living participate in exchange in a politico-economic field that is located in the here and now and totally stripped of reference to entities outside that field, while the dead have only been allocated a place in private religious beliefs. The modern distinction between the living and the dead is clearest in judicial and medical representations. Here the difference is depicted as something unbridgeable: after death a living person becomes an object, a body. In nonmodern societies, however, the barrier between the living and the dead is not unbridgeable but on the contrary a place of contact and exchange. Here, at this highest level of value for tribal societies, occurs the transformation of qualities essential for the continued existence of human life. The living person in these nonmodern societies is therefore totally dependent on relationships between society and the encompassing

---

[40] For the concept of hierarchy, see Dumont, *Homo hierarchicus. The caste system and its implications, passim*, but in particular pp. 239–245.

[41] The universe of exchange is thus much larger than the socio-political arena to which many studies of exchange (for instance Weiner, *Inalienable possessions: the paradox of keeping-while giving* and Appadurai, "Introduction: commodities and the politics of value") restrict themselves.

[42] For this and the following, see Barraud *et al.*, *Of relations and the dead. Four societies viewed from the angle of their exchanges*, pp. 112–113.

supernatural order, and he occupies the right place in this order to safeguard its reproduction.

Central in the Dumontian study of exchange is the commensurability of subject and object as discussed in the previous paragraph. However, we are not dealing here only with the point to which Ingold draws attention, that is the mutual involvement of social persons in constituting each other, but with the specific way in which every nonmodern society offers, through exchange, a realization of the whole universe of which both supernatural entities and people are part. In other words, discrete persons or groups come into being in a variety of relationships with social and supernatural entities, which run through them and move them into action. It is in this complex field of relations, according to the Dumontians, that the person comes into being as a human, develops into a complete and mature human being, and, after death, becomes an ancestor in the supernatural world. These successive transformations of the person can be regarded as the joining, the articulation and the breaking up again of different *cultural-specific* constituents. The exchange of gifts plays a decisive role here. The successive transformations of the person in fact do not form a natural-biological, autonomous, or automatic process, as perceived in modern society; they demand the activation of different relations within society as a whole and are effected by the exchange of gifts. A study of exchange that takes this into account, shows, in the spirit of Mauss' statements on the commensurability of subject and object in exchange, '. . . *how the constituent parts of the person are conceived of as valorized parts of exchange objects*'.[43] The constituent parts of the person circulate in various rituals in which the transformation of man is realized and these rituals form one encompassing totality of exchanges. Within this whole, all relations are characterised and arranged hierarchically and thus society, in a wider sense of the word, is formed as a whole and renewed time and again.[44]

---

[43] Platenkamp, *Tobelo. Ideas and values of a North Moluccan society*, p. 8 (emphasis JB).

[44] In a comparative study of exchange systems an object can therefore never be disentangled from the cultural-specific system of relations and values. There is therefore no point at which the exchange of a certain object or a group of objects can be extricated from the whole of exchanges characteristic for a certain society. The same (kinds of) objects can be the same in a material sense but the value attached to them differs from society to society. Furthermore, the value of an object within a society is not always the same, because it is determined by the relationship in

In the next paragraph I will offer a concrete illustration of the Dumontian perspective on exchange and by means of the ethnography of the 'Are'are of the Solomon Islands I will show how subject and object are commensurable in exchange, that is, how the constituents of the person are depicted as the valued parts of objects of exchange; how discrete persons and groups come into being in ritual exchanges associated with the life-cycle and are transformed into ancestors and how the totality of exchanges, in which the transformation of man is realized, forms a single whole.

4. *Exchange among the 'Are'are of the Solomon Islands*

In 'Are'are thinking, the person is seen as a temporary merging of three constituents: 'body', 'breath' and ancestral 'image'.[45] To a greater or lesser degree, other living organisms share these constituents: cultivated plants are only 'body'; domesticated pigs 'body' and 'breath'; and ancestors are only 'image'. In accordance with this hierarchy the three elements 'body', 'breath' and 'image' are thought to circulate in the shape of taro tubers, pigs and shell money respectively. Marriage plays an important pioneering role in the bringing together of these constituents in a discrete person. For a better understanding of the circulation it is, however, necessary to look first at the funeral ritual in which the breaking-up of the different constituents of the deceased person is realized (see fig. 2).

At every 'funeral feast', persons who have been the deceased's longtime partners in exchange offer shell money to the 'grave-digger' who, along with his group, plays a central role in the performance of the ritual by supplying pigs and taro tubers to be distributed among the participants. The shell money brought to the 'grave-digger' is counted and announced publicly: it represents the 'image' of the deceased, that is the deceased in his greatest glory. With this

---

which it is exchanged, and therefore by the value level to which this relation is related (examples of both to be found in Barraud *et al.*, *Of relations and the dead. Four societies viewed from the angle of their exchanges*, p. 21 and pp. 72–73).

[45] The ethnography of the 'Are'are decribed below can be found in De Coppet's contribution to Barraud *et al.*, *Of relations and the dead. Four societies viewed from the angle of their exchanges*, pp. 9–12 and 40–65, and in D. de Coppet, "The life-giving death", *Mortality and immortality. The anthropology and archaeology of death*, eds. S.C. Humphreys and H. King (London, 1981), pp. 175–204.

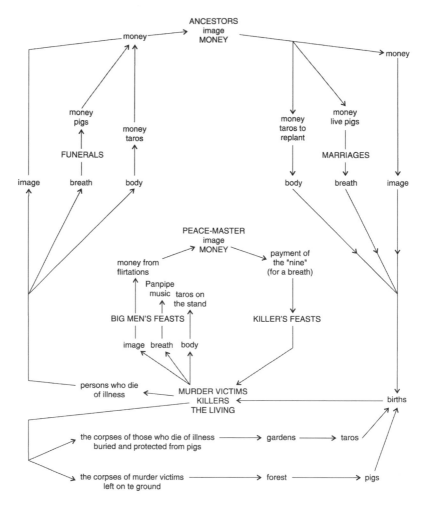

Fig. 2. The circulation of 'body' (taros), 'breath' (pigs) and 'image' (shell money) with the 'Are'are of the Solomon Islands (adapted from Barraud et al., *Of relations and the dead. Four societies viewed from the angle of their exchanges*, chart 3).

collecting of shell money, the deceased is transformed into an ancestor. The 'grave-digger' in his turn gives the shell money to the people who helped him assemble the pigs and taro tubers. After two or three years the family of the deceased gives a so-called 'return funeral feast' where all the participants who gave shell money are refunded an equal quantity. In the collection and distribution of shell money at 'funeral feasts' and 'return funeral feasts', we discern a continuous merging and fragmentation of the ancestor image.

At the 'funeral feast', however, not only the transformation of the 'image' is important. The 'feast' is meant to resolve the person into his three constituents. The group of the 'grave-digger' and the group of surviving relatives each in fact supply half of the quantity of taro tubers and pigs that are divided between the participants. The 'breath' and the 'body' of pigs and taro tubers respectively 'cover' the 'breath' and the 'body' of the deceased. It is important to note that in exchange for these contributions *shell money* is collected by the exchange partners of the group of relatives. The group of relatives in turn gives shell money to the 'grave-digger' and his group. Both gifts mark the end of an exchange relationship because the shell money constitutes a paying-off of debts. All elements united in the ritual, in the shape of taro tubers, pigs and shell money, are therefore translated into shell money (fig. 2, left half). From this it follows that the most important part of man is the 'image' represented by shell money and that this element also represents a more encompassing whole. The 'image' in fact holds for the discrete person the promise of one's dissolution in the circulation of the 'image' of the ancestors, that is of *all* ancestors, made anonymous in the undifferentiated shell money.

With a marriage an exchange takes place that is in many aspects the reverse of that occurring at a funeral. From the man's group a sum of shell money is given to the woman's group. Part of the sum is meant in exchange for the woman and need not be returned. The remainder of the sum, however, is a loan that has to be given back at a 'return feast'. The return does not take place in shell money only, but in taro tubers and pigs, as well as shell money. In other words, a transformation from ancestral 'image' is effected through the marriage of 'body', 'breath', and 'image', ready to be united again in a newly born child (fig. 2, right half).

As the man's group often acts as the group of the 'grave-digger', both groups, related by marriage, have double and opposite tasks in which ancestral shell money plays a central role. Marriage is a funeral in reverse: it makes future births possible on account of the fact that the woman's group realizes the transformation of shell money into the three constituents which are important for the person; a funeral on the other hand effects the breaking-up of a person into these three constituents and translates them into one of these, namely shell money.

This analysis of 'Are'are exchange makes it possible to illustrate in a more concrete way the difference emphasized by Dumont and his associates between modern and nonmodern notions of life and death and of the relationship between the living and the dead. Where in modern ideology marriage and funeral are two separate rituals, of which marriage is situated *in* life and funeral *after* the termination of life, in 'Are'are society the two are linked by the encompassing circulation of ancestral image/shell money. The ritual tasks at marriage and funeral ceremonies are situated respectively *before* life and *after* death. Both rituals link up death, caused by the ancestors, with the synthesis effected by man of what is human in conception and birth.

In summary, we can argue that for the 'Are'are, funerals are more important than marriages because in the first the three constituents are translated into shell money[46] and ancestors take shape, whereas in the second, shell money is broken up into the three constituents and thereby the conditions are established for the creation of man. In view of this analysis we should regard the society of the 'Are'are in a wider sense, that is the totality composed of the living and the dominant ancestors, as the whole universe of exchange. Such societies are therefore called 'cosmomorphic' by the Dumontians. There are, however, societies in which relations of the highest level of value transcend this society of men and ancestors. Here, for instance, there are relationships with a god or gods that are important for more than one society. Where such transcendent subjects play a role, for instance the christian God, the universe is not described exhaustively when we concentrate only on the (exchange) relations between the living and the dead. Such societies are to a greater or lesser extent 'universalistic'.[47]

To conclude this paragraph I would like to dwell briefly on the basis of 'Are'are ethnography of the place of the individual in cosmomorphic societies, a subject I will return to in my analysis of *Beowulf*. In *Homo hierarchicus* Dumont pointed out that in studying a society one should not limit oneself to the ideological. Although the view of the participants deserves first attention, the anthropologist

---

[46] Ancestral image/shell money is therefore at the same time part and whole, it is one of the constituents ànd it includes both other constituents.

[47] Where it is possible to generalize on the most important relations, that is the relations between on the one hand the living and on the other the ancestors and spirits in cosmomorphic societies, and on relations that transcend this level, for instance between the living and the gods/a god in more universalistic societies, it is impossible to generalize about which relations in a society play a more subordinate role and in which contexts these relations are expressed.

should expose by intercultural comparison the elements that are not part of indigenous consciousness.[48] Outside the ideology in non-modern societies, we will, for instance, find what in our eyes are socio-political and economic phenomena or the entity that we call the individual: 'those data which we can recover thanks to the notions we have of them in our own ideology may be called the (comparative) concomitants of the ideological system'.[49] We should not, however, give an independent place to these *non-ideological phenomena*, as often happens in analysis, because we will then fail to notice the devaluation of these phenomena in the ideology of nonmodern societies. They should be placed in and related to the ideology that accompanies them: '. . . it is only in relation to the totality thus reconstructed that the ideology takes on its true sociological significance'.[50] The 'Are'are are a good example of this. From the above, it is clear how in the society of the 'Are'are the discrete person takes shape as a human and after death is transformed into an ancestor in a coherent sequence of ceremonial acts of exchange in which all members of the community are involved. Thus every act of exchange is not an expression of a personal motivation of an individual subject but part of a grand ritual project, the parts of which are ordered according to a necessary sequence. Every 'Are'are participates in the circulation in which the society of the living is absorbed into the encompassing universe of the living and the dead and with which the continuous renewal of life is realised. Noteworthy within the encompassing whole is, however, the complementary relation between the so-called 'peace-master' and the 'killer' who together make up bigmanship in 'Are'are society. The former realizes a position of 'greatness' during a feast where unmarried men bring together shell money and he thereby develops into a 'big man'. The greatness of the 'big man' seems comparable to the image of the newly-created ancestor which is expressed during the 'funeral feast' described above. It can be argued, however, that the realisation of the 'greatness' associated with a discrete person is subordinate to the higher task of

---

[48] Dumont, *Homo hierarchicus. The caste system and its implications*, p. 37.

[49] Dumont, *Homo hierarchicus. The caste system and its implications*, p. 38.

[50] Dumont, *Homo hierarchicus. The caste system and its implications*, p. 38. Dumont's approach therefore does not imply that the economic is a secondary phenomenon: '[t]o say this is to deeply misunderstand the notion of hierarchy; the inferior, the subordinate, certainly exists and at the same time is ideologically incapable of moving out of its limitations' (p. xxxvii).

reproducing the socio-cosmic universe. This is implied, for instance, in the fact that the money collected for the 'big man' is not ancestral shell money but shell money that represents the 'image' of murder victims, a category of deceased that will never have funerals and therefore never will be ancestors. Furthermore, we are dealing here only with a temporary personification of 'greatness', since the participants, who behave as ancestors, destroy the gardens and plantations of the 'big man' and because the 'big man' must return the money after the feast. Only in the length of the interval between episodes of exchange do the participants seem to have a certain freedom of initiative.[51] The 'killer' on the other hand does seem to have the character of an individual standing apart from the encompassing socio-cosmic universe by assuming for himself the ancestors' privilege of killing people. These murdered people are moreover important within society as they contribute to the shaping of the 'image' of the 'big man': after all 'blood money', expressed in shell money, is offered by the 'peace-master' to whoever succeeds in killing one of the people of the killer's group in order thus to 'cover' the 'breath' of the victim. Within 'Are'are ideology there seems explicitly to be room here for the individual subject, albeit at a subordinate level of value. In addition, it should be noted, however, that the 'killer' alienates himself from society and from the ancestors.

5. *Beowulf: heathen ancestors in a Christian perspective*

In the literature on the Old English *Beowulf*, the question as to what extent Christian teachings determined the poem's contents is much discussed. Examining this question gives insight into the poem's perspective on wealth in general and exchange of valuables in particular. Are secular or Christian values normative in *Beowulf*? Should we judge the actions of the principal characters in terms of generosity and meanness or charity and greed? I will briefly indicate the importance of these questions by considering Jonathan Parry's paper "The gift, the Indian gift and the 'Indian gift'".[52] Here Parry identified two key traits of societies which have the idea of the pure gift, that is, the gift which need not be reciprocated. First, these are

---

[51] Cf. Barraud *et al.*, *Of relations and the dead. Four societies viewed from the angle of their exchanges*, p. 9. Compare Ingold's remarks above on the factor time in exchange.

[52] Parry, "The gift, the Indian gift and 'the Indian gift'".

state societies with a developed division of labour and a relatively large commercial sector. In these societies the ideology of the pure gift has come into being because a distinction is made between a domain in which one is considered to act altruisticly and one in which one puts one's own interests first. Second, and even more important, within these societies most people are followers of one of the world religions. These religions, Parry argues, are characterized by the idea of redemption. People who have acted justly in life are admitted to a hereafter from which all suffering has been eliminated. Within such a perspective on the world beyond, the pure gift can play an important role in the relations between people and religious specialists. As the aims of the givers are located in a future existence, they should not expect or even avoid the religious intermediary's reciprocation of the gift. The gift for which nothing is returned in the here and now offers a possibility to extricate oneself from the profane, that is from sin, and is thereby a means to attain redemption.

In Parry's characterization of societies with the pure gift, we recognize much of the early medieval Christian views on man and the hereafter, and of the exchange relations in early medieval Christianity between laymen, religious persons, church institutions, and God. Bede gives us a good example of how the new Christian notions contrasted with the traditional Anglo-Saxon perspective on exchange. In *The Ecclesiastical History of the English People*, Bede describes the recriminations between King Oswine of Deira (644–651) and Bishop Aidan after the latter had given to a beggar, out of charity, a valuable gift he had just received from the king, namely a beautiful horse.[53] Where in traditional notions of exchange the gift was inextricably linked to the social status of both giver and recipient, in a Christian perspective the gift should ideally be free of such considerations. In the church's views, what was normative was not the secular interaction between social partners of noble birth but the procurement of God's blessing by renouncing worldly pleasures and goods. The influential suggestion of some scholars is that this Christian perspective on valuables is the key in an interpretation of *Beowulf*. I will show that we need not take this suggestion seriously. This does not imply, however, that *Beowulf* provides us with an image of a pre-Christian exchange system, nor that it offers us an exclusively secular

---

[53] *HE* 14.3. B. Colgrave and R.A.B. Mynors, *Bede's Ecclesiastical history of the English people*, (Oxford, 1991 (1969)), pp. 258–259.

perspective on exchange. The Christian poet was obliged, as we shall see later, to take the relationships that his principal characters had with the world beyond from biblical or patristic models. This insight is very important because a study of exchange must cover, as we have seen above, relationships between the human and the super-natural world.

The debate over the role of the Christian faith in *Beowulf* can be attributed largely to the poem's ambiguous character. At first sight it seems as if the poet paints a portrait of the past in which he allows heathen customs to go hand in hand with statements by the principal characters with a Christian slant. The descriptions of hea-then rituals are not very detailed and we learn nothing of heathen notions of the world of the gods, the cosmos or the end of time; the principal characters thank and honour *one* god. Although they know god/God exists, they never address God directly nor pray to him for help. Furthermore, they do know a story of Creation but there is no reference in it to God as the creator of man or heaven.[54] On the whole we do not get the impression that they are familiar with Christian cosmology or eschatology. The problem is that as regards religious outlook the poet hardly seems to distinguish him-self from the principal characters. He does mention Cain and the Flood and he points to God as the one who reigned in all times but he refrains from specific Christian statements. It is perhaps not surprising that in a sketch of a far, heathen past he does not refer to priests, church services, saints, relics, or church obligations, such as the giving of alms,[55] but it is strange that when he uses a chris-tian-historical and -eschatological perspective he does not mention the fall of the angels, the fall of man, the redemption, the end-times, the resurrection of the dead, the Last Judgement and heaven. When we add to that that he does not unequivocally translate the virtu-ous and unvirtuous behaviour of his principal characters into Chris-tian virtues and sins, and that he seems to write without disapproval, and sometimes with (much) admiration, about the seizing of trea-sure, the reaping of glory and the perpetrating of blood feud, then it raises the question of how much the poet distinguishes himself from his principal characters. This question has been answered in

---

[54] Fr. Klaeber, "Die christliche Elemente im *Beowulf*", *Anglia. Zeitschrift für englische Philologie* 35 (N.F. 23) (1911), p. 114.

[55] Cf. Klaeber, "Die christliche Elemente im *Beowulf*", p. 481.

many different ways in the course of time but it is generally argued nowadays that there is an important difference in religious knowledge between the principal characters and the poet as narrator and commentator. Building on the work of J.R.R. Tolkien, Marijane Osborn and Fred Robinson have shown how the poet on the one hand makes a distinction between the pre-Christian, heroic perspective of the principal characters who lived in days long past and the superior, and, for the principal characters inaccessible, Christian perspective of the poet and his public,[56] but on the other hand reproduces the heathen and Christian points of view in such a way that the differences are not made all that clear.[57] The reprehensible and hopeless character of the heathen perspective is thereby not put too obviously and possibilities are created of arousing a certain admiration for the thoughts and deeds of the heathen, and thus damned, principal characters.

Since Frederick Klaeber's work it has generally been accepted that *Beowulf* is a more or less original poem created in Christian times.[58] It is therefore not the case, as many 19th century researchers thought, that an essentially heathen poem was committed to paper by a churchman and completed with Christian additions and changes.[59] The poet, however, had a keen interest in the heathen past. References to Heremod, Ingeld, Sigemund etc. indicate that he used tales from the oral tradition which was strongly rooted in the pre-Christian period. And we can interpret *Beowulf* as a story about the Scandinavian ancestors of Anglo-Saxon royal families.[60] The question is, however, to what extent *Beowulf*, as a relatively new composition, shows the influence of Christian doctrine. Does the Christian element only relate to a 'varnish', which made it possible to keep telling old tales from oral tradition about the life of the ancestors, or was ancestral history retold from a Christian perspective as a result of

---

[56] M. Osborn, "The Great Feud: scriptural history and strife in *Beowulf*", *Publications of the Modern Language Association of America* 93 (1978) and F.C. Robinson, Beowulf *and the apposite style*, (Knoxville, 1985).

[57] Important here is the poet's use of appositions or juxtaposed elements (Robinson, Beowulf *and the appositive style*).

[58] Klaeber, "Die christliche Elemente im *Beowulf*", (1911 and 1912).

[59] As for instance F. Blackburn, "The Christian coloring in the *Beowulf*", *Publications of the Modern Language Association of America* 12 (1897), pp. 205–225 and L. Ettmüller, Beowulf. *Heldengedicht des achten Jahrhunderts* (Zurich, 1840).

[60] See K. Sisam, "Anglo-Saxon genealogies", *Proceedings of the British Academy* 39 (1953), pp. 287–348, for Scandinavian ancestors in Anglo-Saxon, royal genealogies.

which it acquired a totally new meaning? In the former case this meant that all references to pre-Christian religious representations were indeed banned from the story but also that the poet could freely describe the social relations and profane ethics rooted in the pre-Christian past.[61] Supporters of this profane interpretation of *Beowulf* either think the poet's Christianity was limited,[62] or that Christianity, apart from the poet's religious affiliations, is irrelevant for the interpretation of the poem.[63] In the latter case, of a retelling of the ancestral history in Christian terms, the poet had to find a place for the ancestors in Christian eschatology. Which place did heathen man occupy in world history from Genesis and the Apocalypse?

The former, wordly interpretation of *Beowulf* is endorsed by few scholars. It is clear that the depth of the poet's Christian belief need not be questioned.[64] As was shown by Dorothy Whitelock, in his vocabulary, expressions and metaphors, the poet owed much to the Latin and Old English Christian homiletic and literary tradition. The supremacy of God over all time which the poet explicitly mentioned, the descent of Grendel and Grendel's mother from Cain, and the association, unmentioned in the poem but generally accepted in the Early Middle Ages, of the dragon with the devil make it clear that the poet employs a christian-historical perspective. This does not mean though that ancestral social relations and their moral basis do not come up for discussion. But how does their Christian-inspired re-evaluation take shape in the poem. In other words: are the perceptions and the actions of the principal characters interpreted in a christian-positive or -negative sense? Are Hroðgar and Beowulf examples of people that, without knowing God's revelation, act according to the highest principles attainable for heathens, or are they as heirs to Adam unable by definition to offer defence against the temp-

---

[61] M.D. Cherniss, *Ingeld and Christ. Heroic concepts and values in Old English Christian poetry* (The Hague and Paris, 1972) and M.A. Parker, *Beowulf and Christianity* (New York, 1987).

[62] H. Chadwick, *The heroic age* (Cambridge, 1912), pp. 47–56; J. Halverson, "*Beowulf* and the pitfalls of piety", *University of Toronto Quarterly* 35 (1966), pp. 260–278. and W. Whallon, *Formula, character, and context: studies in Homeric, Old English, and Old Testament poetry* (Washington, 1969).

[63] Parker, *Beowulf and Christianity* and K. Sisam, *The structure of Beowulf* (Oxford, 1965), pp. 17–28 and 72–79.

[64] Klaeber, "Die christliche Elemente im *Beowulf*" (1911 and 1912), J.R.R. Tolkien, "*Beowulf*. The monsters and the critics", *An anthology of Beowulf criticsm*, ed. L.E. Nicholson (Notre Dame, 1963 (1936)), and D. Whitelock, *The audience of Beowulf* (Oxford, 1951).

tations of life which corrupt man and incite man to sin? Are the principal characters part of the false paradise of the *civitas terrena* and are they all victims of the inescapable delusion of wordly prosperity and purportedly admirable heroic behaviour, or do they belong to the city of men who through their unfamiliarity with the suffering and dying of Christ have no prospect of redemption but nonetheless, with changing success, fight against evil? The first option[65] can be properly rejected because it does not do justice to the appreciation the poet has for the wisdom and the actions of the principal characters nor to the differences created by the poet between people that do and do not worship idols and are and are not bloodthirsty and niggardly.[66] The second option leaves room for very different interpretations of the thoughts and deeds of the principal characters.

When we concentrate on the *Werdegang* of Beowulf we can distinguish three interpretations. Firstly, some scholars think that he undergoes a development in his beliefs that in the end results in a kind of altruistic behaviour that we would not expect of a heathen, and in this he is a *figura* of Christ.[67] Secondly, other scholars think that initially Beowulf manages to arm himself against pride and greed but that in the end he succumbs to earthly temptations and sins because he is spiritually weakened by success and wealth, and in this he is a new Adam.[68] And finally, other scholars again suggest that he, without knowing it, fights on God's side against eternal evil and wages a heroic struggle against the primordial enemies of God, but that his battle cannot possibly be decisive as he is a heathen.[69] Since each position implies a different perspective with respect to (the exchange of) valuables in *Beowulf*, I will briefly elaborate on these.

According to Charles Donahue, Beowulf's fight is about an altruistic seizing of a treasure. By distributing the treasure to his people

---

[65] For instance B.F. Huppé, *The hero and the earthly city. A reading of* Beowulf (Binghampton, 1984).

[66] Cf. J.D. Niles, Beowulf. *The poem and its tradition* (Cambridge, 1983), p. 85.

[67] C. Donahue, "*Beowulf*, Ireland and the natural good", *Traditio. Studies in ancient and medieval history, thought and religion* 7 (1949–1951), pp. 263–277, and C. Donahue, "*Beowulf* and the Christian tradition: a reconsideration from a Celtic stance", *Traditio. Studies in ancient and medieval history, thought and religion* 21 (1965), pp. 55–116.

[68] M.E. Goldsmith, *The mode and meaning of* Beowulf (London, 1970).

[69] Tolkien, "*Beowulf*. The monsters and the critics". Osborn, "The Great Feud: scriptural history and strife in *Beowulf*"; and Robinson, Beowulf *and the appositive style*.

he performs a truly Christian act of charity, not equalled among heathens. Donahue's typological interpretation of *Beowulf* has for various reasons not found acceptance. For example, a typological interpretation outside Holy Scripture is considered to be out of the question.[70] We could add to this that Donahue's interpretation of Beowulf's deeds in terms of Christian charity, is rather far-fetched where the seizing of treasure is seen as producing fame for the conqueror which will live on long after death (therefore Beowulf is not that altruistic); where the generosity of a king is generally accepted and positively valued; and where the inheritance of a sizeable *thesaurus* from king to successor means some guarantee for the continued existence of both the royal family and the people.

According to Margaret Goldsmith the patristic discourse on pride and greed are normative for an interpretation of Beowulf's doings: '*Beowulf* is a Christian allegory of the life of man'.[71] The life of man, and especially of heathen man, is characterized by continuous diabolical temptations to sin, and a life devoted to God should therefore be a life of continuous struggle against them. However, the heathen marked by Adam's sin is originally a weak partner in the struggle and Beowulf is an example of this. In his youth and prime Beowulf manages indeed to ban pride and greed but this is different at the end of his life. The corrupting influence of wealth, power, and success has done its work and Beowulf has become susceptible to earthly temptations. In the last phase of his life we see in Beowulf an arrogant trust in his own ability, when he turns away from God, and a selfish pursuit of personal wealth and glory. Whereas people that know themselves to be pervaded by God's message offer wordly treasure in exchange for a heavenly life, Beowulf, spiritually limited as he is, sets his heart on seizing the dragon's treasure. Goldsmith's interpretation of *Beowulf* is also controversial. Criticism has focussed on her interpretation of *Beowulf* as allegory—early medieval authors were expected to write clearly and not to imitate the obscurities in the Bible;[72] on her interpretation of Hroðgar's speech as a discourse on sin; and, in that context, on her condemnation of the deeds of

---

[70] Goldsmith, *The mode and meaning of* Beowulf, pp. 72–73.

[71] Goldsmith, *The mode and meaning of* Beowulf, p. 4.

[72] Donahue in P. Clemoes and S. Greenfield, "Allegorical, typological or neither? Three short papers on the allegorical approach to *Beowulf* and a discussion", *Anglo-Saxon England* 2 (1973), p. 293.

the old Beowulf. I would like to go briefly into the last two points of critique.[73]

In her interpretation in religious terms of the values articulated in Hroðgar's speech, Goldsmith takes up an isolated position. She herself indicates that the speech leaves much to be desired in doctrinal clarity, perhaps because the poet wanted to suggest that Hroðgar lived in a time when God's revelations were as yet unknown. Her interpretation rests on a small number of passages that are in fact too meagre to assume that Hroðgar employs a complex and coherent ethics anchored in Christian eschatology.[74] Nobody denies that Hroðgar warns against pride and arrogance but few doubt that we are dealing here with nothing more than secular, everyday wisdom that is of great, practical and political importance. Beowulf is urged to be generous and mild towards his relatives, followers and people and not to listen to thoughts that suggest that he can manage without good relations with his fellows. We are here less concerned with pride and greed than with complacency, cruelty, and above all niggardliness.[75] Niggardliness is not so much denounced because it is motivated by an excessive individual desire for earthly goods but because it means a serious breach of the exchange of gifts essential for the constitution of person and society. In the next paragraph I will show what I mean by the latter. Beowulf, during his whole life, as explained in the words of Hroðgar, Wiglaf, his followers or the poet himself, is an example of the attitude advocated by Hroðgar. And to the very end! He takes action against a monster that is after the total destruction of his people; he does not seize the treasure for himself but for his people; before the fight he subjects himself to an examination of his conscience that turns out positively (and the poet

---

[73] For various critiques of the allegoric interpretation of *Beowulf*, see Cherniss, *Ingeld and Christ. Heroic concepts and values in Old English Christian poetry*, p. 130; Donahue in Clemoes and Greenfield, "Allegorical, typological or neither? Three short papers on the allegorical approach to *Beowulf* and a discussion", p. 293; Parker, *Beowulf and Christianity*, p. 90; P. Wormald, "Bede, *Beowulf* and the conversion of the Anglo-Saxon aristocracy", *Bede and Anglo-Saxon England*, ed. R.T. Farrell (Oxford, 1978), p. 93, and J.D.A. Ogilvy and D.C. Baker, *Reading* Beowulf. *An introduction to the poem, its background and its style* (Norman, 1983), p. 170.

[74] Her argument turns on the expression *ece rædas* ('everlasting, eternal gains') and on the passage in which a unnamed king is struck by the arrows of a murderer or evil spirit and becomes greedy.

[75] Wormald, "Bede, *Beowulf* and the conversion of the Anglo-Saxon aristocracy", pp. 92–93.

does not say that he thinks otherwise); and at the close of the poem the praises of his followers are bestowed on him without the poet making explicit negative comments. Paradoxically, Goldsmith's exclusive attention to the evaluation of Beowulf's motivation and actions distracts from those that are guilty: it is not Beowulf but the thief that stole the cup from the dragon's treasure and it is Beowulf's best men who abandon him in the struggle against the dragon!

After rejection of both a christian-typological and an -allegoric interpretation of *Beowulf* we arrive at an interpretation that does view the life of the principal characters in christian-historical terms but that does not take Christian virtues and sins as the point of departure for an evaluation of their thoughts and deeds. The undertaking of the poet to write about his ancestors was one full of pitfalls.[76] Heathen ancestors were not a common subject of reflection for churchmen. For one reason or other, however, there was a churchman, or somebody close to the clergy,[77] who was interested in the ancestors of Anglo-Saxon royalty, which is not surprising in view of the direct links between the clergy and aristocracy,[78] and who expressed this in an unusual manner. That the poet wanted to take pains to find a respectable place for his ancestors in Christian world history is a convincing suggestion. He had to proceed there very carefully, however, as accepted ecclesiastical opinion on heathens was almost exclusively negative[79] and actually stood in the way of an appreciative description. In order not to alienate his public nor to fall victim to church denunciation the poet ad to avoid all references to pre-Christian religious conceptions, insofar he still knew them, for these were regarded as blasphemous.[80] However, he also could not ascribe a Christian faith to his characters as it was clear to everybody that the poem concerned people who lived in an age before the conversion to Christianity.[81] The poet was unable to get round

---

[76] Cf. Wormald, "Bede, *Beowulf* and the conversion of the Anglo-Saxon aristocracy" and "Anglo-Saxon society and literature", *The Cambridge companion to Old English literature*, eds. M. Godden and M. Lapidge (Cambridge, 1991), pp. 1–22 and Robinson, Beowulf *and the appositive style*.

[77] For writing as a church monopoly, see C.P. Wormald, "The uses of literacy in Anglo-Saxon England and its neighbours", *Transactions of the Royal Historical Society, fifth series* 27 (1977), pp. 15–114 and Wormald, "Bede, *Beowulf* and the conversion of the Anglo Saxon aristocracy", pp. 38–39.

[78] Cf. Wormald, "Bede, *Beowulf* and the conversion of the Anglo-Saxon aristocracy".

[79] Cf. Robinson, Beowulf *and the appositive style*, pp. 7–8.

[80] Robinson, Beowulf *and the appositive style*, p. 11 note 28.

[81] Robinson, Beowulf *and the appositive style*, pp. 9–10.

the fact that these men were excluded from the redemption realized by Christ's death on the cross, although in some passages the poet seems to suggest for some of his leading characters more than in principle should have been possible. Various scholars have pointed out that biblical descriptions of the pre-Mosaic era could have served as a model for a description of a pre-Christian age in which Anglo-Saxon ancestors could be described as pre-Christians and not necessarily as heathens.[82] People from the era of the law of nature, the direct descendants of Noah, were able to fathom the creation and on that basis to know God.[83] However, it was therefore not possible for them to direct themselves to God as He had not yet revealed himself. This has one very important implication for the poem, in the light of my study of exchange in *Beowulf*: God can 'only' be considered the creator and donor of the aristocratic riches and wealth which is so characteristic of the world evoked in the poem. The people were not able, however, to acquire his benevolence or a heavenly future, for instance by acts of charity towards the poor or by gifts to God's representatives on earth. Life according to the law of nature translates itself into hope not for resurrection but for the accepted reward of earthly life: to achieve wealth, honour and fame and to establish a name that will live on amongst the people until long after death. The description in *Beowulf* of the patterns of exchange between man and other-worldly beings is therefore based on nothing more than 'literary' imagination. Nevertheless in the poet's descriptions of the rituals surrounding death, there are elements that point to what in pre-Christian times had been a special involvement with the ancestors.

---

[82] Tolkien, "*Beowulf*. The monsters and the critics"; Donahue, "*Beowulf*, Ireland and the natural good" and "*Beowulf* and the Christian tradition: a reconsideration from a Celtic stance"; Osborn, "The Great Feud: scriptural history and strife in *Beowulf*", pp. 978–979. Cf. Wormald, "Bede, *Beowulf* and the conversion of the Anglo-Saxon aristocracy", p. 64, and P. Wormald, "Anglo-Saxon society and literature".

[83] See the book of *Job* for the God-fearingness and justice of somebody who was neither Jew nor Christian; and the letter from Paul to the Christians of Rome (*Romans* 1, 14–15 and 19–21) for the abilities of heathens to fathom the creation and to know God and his law.

6. Beowulf: *ceremonial exchanges and the constitution of person and society*

An outline was given above of the Dumontian perspective on exchange. A point by point summary may serve as guideline for my discussion of the exchange of gifts in *Beowulf*.

A Dumontian analysis considers:

1. which relationships are specified within a system of ideas and values. We are dealing here with relations both between people themselves, society in a strict sense, and between people and beings in the supernatural world, society in a wide sense.
2. how a society thinks about the constitution of the person. Which constituents play a role, which relationships are involved in the various constituents, and how are these valued, and in what way are the constituents of the person related to objects of exchange?
3. how, in the totality of relationships, the discrete person comes into being in exchange, develops into a fully-fledged person, and, after death, becomes an ancestor. These successive transformations of the person will thus be regarded as the bringing together, developing and breaking up of his constituents. In the sum of ritual exchanges in which the transformation of man is realized, 'society as a whole' can be recognized.

6.1. *A universe of relationships*

A careful reading of *Beowulf* makes clear that words, phrases and descriptions used by the poet serve as a good illustration of the language discerned by Dumont in which structure is expressed; here we have an example of a language in which a person is not a separate entity, but an other in relation to others.

In the first place, in particular when characterizing kings, queens and prominent noblemen, the poet uses compounds that express a relationship. In words such as for instance *þeodcyning* (king of a people), *mandryhten* (lord of a man), *leodfruma* (prince of a people), *folccwen* (queen of a people) or *dryhtguma* (man of a retinue, that is follower) a relationship is made explicit.

In the second place, and of greater importance, the poet uses phrases and short descriptions to introduce new persons and name already known ones or to have persons address each other in direct speech or speak about others. Hardly anybody in *Beowulf* is not presented without a relationship being laid down between this person and another or others. In considering how this is done, it is well to distinguish between people that belong to a royal family, and those how do not, and between men and women.

An example may clarify how the kings and sons of kings are introduced, characterized in passing, or addressed. In line 12 of the poem the poet says the Danish king Scyld begot a son without informing us immediately of the child's name; this name, Beow, follows six lines later (18a), immediately followed in the next half line (19a) by the statement that he is Scyld's son (*Scyldes eafera*). And finally Beow is called *Scyldinga* (descendant of Scyld) in line 53. This example is typical for almost every man that becomes, is, or could be a king. Concerning such a man, we are always told in a short phrase or statement whose son he is, and in all cases the father is then mentioned, but hardly ever the mother. In the same vein, when we already know somebody, the poet or a character using direct speech commonly does not cite the person's proper name but he choses a phrase that indicates his descent.

The high value attached to descent in the male line is expressed in another way too. In *Beowulf* we find in fact a number of examples of the phenomenon of alliterating names. The male descendants of the Danish king Healfdene are a case in point (fig. 3). In this series we see regularly recurring the name element *hroð* or *hreð*, glory or victory.[84]

In introducing and naming warrior-followers or specific groups of followers, the poet and persons using direct speech give phrases and descriptions from which it is made clear who his/their lord is. At times a lord using direct speech addresses his follower as friend (*wine*), or followers address each other with this phrase. In many cases the poet also indicates, apart from a relationship to a lord, a bond of kinship. When we examine these it appears that the relational embedding of these warrior-followers differs from that of men of royal descent: sometimes in those cases other kin than the father are mentioned. Probably these are kin-related men who are also followers of the same lord. Sometimes, however, the father is mentioned but there are indications that this happens not only to mark male descent

---

[84] Fr. Klaeber, Beowulf *and the* Fight at Finnsburg, (Lexington (Mass.) 1950³ (1922)), xxxii, note 3.

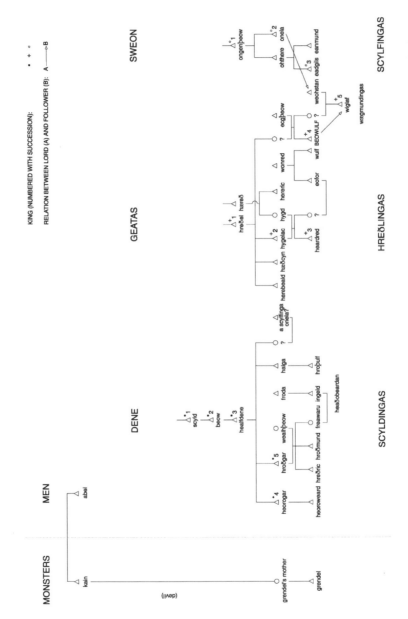

Fig. 3. The genealogy of monsters and of man and the royal genealogies of the *Scyldingas, Hreðlingas* and *Scylfingas*.

but to indicate a continuation by the son of an already existing relationship between his father as a warrior-follower and the king or royal line.[85]

Women in *Beowulf* are an entirely different matter. Except for the mourning maiden at Beowulf's funeral pyre, of whom we only know that she belongs to the Geats, every women is the daughter and/or (future) wife of a king and she is thus named by the poet. These assignings of women point to the role of the king as bridegiver and -taker. It is, however, remarkable that, with a single exception, in the case of all women married to kings of the three most important royal families, we are not told who was her father (Hygd is an exception, she is *Hæreðes dohtor*), and that all the women whose fathers' names are mentioned are women given in marriage by the three most important royal families to subordinate kings or other groups. This usage indicates the status implications of the relationship between bridegiver and bridetaker: who after all can be the bridegiver to a king with such great power as Hroðgar or Ongenþeow?

The relational perspective employed by the poet and his principal characters enables us to draw up a diagram of three interconnected genealogies in which nearly 40 of the 75 persons figuring in the poem can be accommodated (see fig. 3).

Hitherto our main concern has been with relationships between two specific persons who are usually mentioned by name. As we have seen, these bonds were determined by kinship, friendship or lordship. But in addition, in short phrases or descriptions the poet specifies relationships between specific persons, almost exclusively kings and prominent warrior-followers, and *categories* of people: either royal families and named ethnic groups or unnamed tribes, warriors and groups of warriors. Although distinctions are not clear-cut, we can distinguish four sorts of relationships; those of friendship (for instance Hroðgar as *wine Scyldinga*, friend of the Scyldingas); exchange (for instance Beowulf as *wilgeofa Wedra leoda* (a joy-giver (or lord) of the Weders people); lordship (Hroðgar as *brego Beorth-Dena*, the lord of bright-Danes); and protection (Hroðgar as *helm Scyldinga*).[86] Here,

---

[85] Bazelmans, *Eén voor allen, allen voor één*, pp. 186–187.

[86] In this summary of relations the role of the king as a wager of war is not dealt with. This role is twofold. On the one hand he has to actively protect his followers and people against violence coming from outside and on the other hand he has to take the initiative for military expeditions. In the latter he should, however, show restraint.

my sole concern is with the role of the king as a distributor of treasure.

Does the king's generosity apply only to his direct followers or to all his people as well, the latter is not clearly attested. Important in this context is the fact that one of the closest warrior-followers of the Danish king Hroðgar, Æschere, is himself a distributor of gold (*sincgyfa, Bw.* 1342a). Furthermore, we can discern from various other passages that warrior-followers of the king have their own halls, retinues and lordship over people. So, it is conceivable that the warrior-followers provide their own followers with gifts. In other words, the relation between king and people is multi-staged.

Above I have indicated how in both compound words and short phrases used by the poet and by persons in direct speech, a structural or relational perspective is expressed. Further relationships, their genesis and development are also a focus of attention in the poet's narrative and in the dialogues. They allow us a deeper understanding of the bonds of kinship and lordship, protection, and exchange. Moreover, we also get an impression of relationships of revenge and compensatory wergild payments, of relationships arising from shared engagement in warfare against both human and monstrous opponents, as well as relationships with God. I will not go into this further in this context as the narrative will be dealt with in paragraph 6.3.

The way in which the poet speaks about people both in his own words and in the direct speech of his personages, offers us a first orientation to the person and his embedding in relations with others. Although some persons, such as Hroðgar and Beowulf, have a pronounced self-consciousness and distinguish themselves by special thoughts and deeds, nobody, and no group either, can be detached from another or others. From the systematic and explicit way in which relations are laid out, it emerges that the compounds and phrases that indicate relationships, are not a peculiarity of the poet or of his poetic language, nor that they are solely answers to the requirements of alliteration and metre. In the world of *Beowulf* one is son or daughter of a father; one is brother, *nefa* or relative of a male relation; one is wife, follower or friend of a lord or king; one is the son of a father who was already a protégé of one's king or one is descendant of a male ancestor or the subordinate or protégé of a lord or king.

Up to now we have spoken exclusively about relationships within the world of the people. But the earthly *middangeard*, the sea-surrounded centre of the universe between heaven and hell, offers also a place for monsters, and people have to deal with these creatures of a different nature. We get to know three of them as the successive opponents of Beowulf. Beowulf's first trial is a fight with Grendel, a creature quite the opposite of relationship-dominated man. Grendel is a fatherless (!), solitary, therefore relationless!,[87] male giant who only ventures out at night. As a regular visitor of marshes and waste lands, he walks the paths where exiles (also relationless) go. He is a supernaturally strong, savage, cheerless and greedy man-eater and drinker of human blood. Together with (also man-eating) giants and elves, he belongs to the damned descendants of Cain. Grendel and his relatives who are characterized by sin and crime, carry, as Cain did, God's wrath and are embroiled in a feud (a relationship of a negative kind) with God. Grendel is therefore described as a *feond on helle* and as *helle hæfton* (a prisoner of hell). At his death he lays down his heathen soul and is admitted to hell.

Beowulf's second opponent is Grendel's mother and she has, though smaller and weaker, much in common with her son. During Beowulf's visit to the cave of Grendel's mother it emerges that the world of monsters shows both important similarities to and differences from that of the humans. Grendel's mother too lives in a hall and has a treasure at her disposal. The hall, however, is dark and located under a deep water populated by monsters, and from the treasure she neither uses the weapons (or only in dire need) nor distributes valuables to enter into social relationships. Grendel's mother's abode is not the hall of a king (a man) who exerts peaceful control *over* people but that of a monster (a woman) who exerts a control of violence *against* people.

It is important to establish that Grendel and his relatives represent the world of the damned of which man can only become part by his own doing. Thus people who kill relatives (i.e. destroy relationships) or direct themselves to heathen idols (i.e. destroy their relation with God), and kings who are greedy (i.e. do not enter into relationships), place themselves outside the human world where God's mercy applies. Like monsters, they live alone, and therefore without joy, and are seriously tormented. Ultimately they will, like the mortal monsters, be admitted to hell.

---

[87] Grendel is a solitary one (*agenga*).

Of a totally different nature is Beowulf's third opponent, the old, and frighteningly multicoloured dragon that lives in a (burial?)mound on the moors. No clear picture is sketched of the dragon either, but it is clear that he spits fire, flies, and only leaves his lair at night and is much feared by the people in the land. With the dragon we touch upon the most important controversies over the poem's interpretation. This 50 feet long nameless creature, distinguishes himself from Grendel and his mother because his origin remains unnamed and because he is not, at least not in the poem, explicitly assigned a diabolical character. For some scholars the dragon is nothing more than a special, 'natural' creature and a worthy opponent of the warlike Beowulf, for others the dragon is a symbol of the devil and evil, and early medieval sources seem to confirm this. It is made clear in the poem that he is by nature a protector of 'dead' (i.e. unused) treasure. If one disturbs his abode or his treasure, he will revenge that in an excessive manner.

We have spoken above of people and monsters that populate the world: kings rule over their people and the ancestral lands, while monsters reign over the areas that are by preference avoided by people. God (*god*), however, is, both in the words of the poet and the principal characters, the real ruler. This shows well in the qualifications attributed to him (*se ælmihtiga, alwalda, ece drihten, fæder alwalda* etc.). The controversies over the place of the Christian God in the poem have already been looked at. Now, my discussion concentrates on the interpretation of the concept *wyrd*.[88] Some think that with this concept, both the poet and the principal characters express a pre-Christian power independent of, and superior to God and that in many cases words for God are in fact to be regarded as synonyms for *wyrd*. Most Old English specialists, however, do not subscribe to this interpretation. God in *Beowulf*, for both the poet and the principal characters, is to be regarded as the ultimate power. We should, however, make a distinction between what God commands, and therefore should happen, and what God only knows, and therefore can, but need not happen. When we are dealing with matters of life and death, this means that the doomed will die (God

---

[88] On *wyrd*, see B.J. Timmer, "*Wyrd* in Anglo-Saxon prose and poetry", *Neophilologus* 26 (1941), pp. 24–33; E.G. Stanley, *The search for Anglo-Saxon paganism* (Totowa (New York), 1975), pp. 92–94 and B. Mitchell, *An invitation to Old English and Anglo-Saxon England* (Oxford en Cambridge (Mass.), 1995.

determines destiny), whereas the non-doomed can, but need not die. For this last category of people, events are determined by destiny with the power to take or save life, but also by man himself. He is, with God's help, but also by resolute and vigorous action, to a certain extent able to influence destiny and to delay death.

As regards man's relation with God, the principal characters in *Beowulf* are monotheists, not in a Christian but in a pre-Mosaic sense: they know God and thank him for his benevolence but they cannot address him directly. Biblical and patristic models of this representation suggest that such men know God because they are created in his image and because they know how to fathom the creation but that they cannot communicate with him because God has not revealed himself yet. Further, and very important in the present context, is the point that God, in the imagination of the principal characters, is the originator of royal power and of what distinguishes noblemen from others (cf. *Bw.* 1724a–1734). God gives kings to the people; kings in their turn receive their lordship, the land, the people, the stronghold, the throne, and the treasures, from God. They are, and this certainly comes up in the words of Hroðgar and Beowulf, dependent on him for wisdom, physical strength, victories and glory. The relation between God and the people is of the highest level of value.

6.2. *The human person and objects of exchange*

As we have seen above, in the aristocratic system of ideas and values expressed in *Beowulf*, the most important relationships are specified between the various social categories (that is between kings, queens, king's sons, king's daughters, warrior-followers and members of the people), defined in correlation with, and in reference to categories of supernatural creatures (where we might make a distinction between the this-worldly monsters and the other-worldly God). Here, following the Dumontian approach, I suggest that these relationships constituting the total universe form the basis of the circulation of beings and things as realized in rituals. In which way does this circulation provide the context for the characterisation and hierarchical arrangement of relationships within this universe; for the coming into being of man as a discrete person and for the repeated renewal of society? In this context it is important to remember that the circulation of beings and things is not, as we are inclined to think on the basis of our own modern views on subject and object, to be conceived as a re-arrangement of objects between subjects. Taking up the argument that in nonmodern societies subject and object are commensurable in exchange, I will now claim its relevance to our understanding of the involvement of Anglo-Saxon man with objects of exchange.

Anglo-Saxon views on the constitution of the person are an uncultivated field of research. However, an important impetus has been given by Malcolm Godden in *Anglo-Saxons on the Mind*.[89] Godden's distinctions of *mod* (mind), *sawol* (soul) and *ic* ('a subject or an agent of thinking') have great value for an analysis of the person in *Beowulf*. With a view to the *total* constitution of the person—the person is also 'physical substance' with an 'image'—Godden's account may be expanded as follows:

1. the human person is not only a combination of *mod*, *sawol*, and *ic* but in the first place 'physical substance': the body (*lic* or *lichoma*) or the merging of blood (*blod*), flesh (*flæsc*), and bones (*ban*). We know that the body perishes after death or is burnt by human agency. Yet we learn nothing in *Beowulf* about the materialization of the body as substance in conception, pregnancy, or birth we learn nothing in *Beowulf*.

2. people have souls (*sawl* or *sawol*). As Godden has indicated, and this is confirmed in *Beowulf*:
   - mind and soul are not identical as some early medieval Anglo-Saxon churchmen asserted
   - attention only goes to the soul with the approach of death, at the moment of death, or after death.[90]

As in accepted Christian discourse, so in *Beowulf* the destination of the soul after death is dependent on behaviour during life. It is remarkable that monsters also have souls. This is to be interpreted as a hallmark of the human origin of the descendants of Cain. The soul of a monster disappears after death into hell, of course. We learn nothing in *Beowulf* about the origin of the soul and how the soul is brought together with body at conception or birth. Godden has remarked that there was disagreement among prominent church-

---

[89] M.R. Godden, "The Anglo-Saxons on the mind", *Learning and literature in Anglo-Saxon England*, eds. M. Lapidge and H. Gneuss (Cambridge, 1985), pp. 271–298.

[90] We can add that it is clear from *Beowulf* that the soul houses in the heart (2819b–2820a; cf. Hroðgar's speech).

men over this question.[91] Some were of the opinion that the soul derives from God, has been in existence from the beginning of time and therefore may reach the child via the parents; others thought the soul did not exist in advance but that God implanted it into the foetus 'in an individual act of creation'.[92] We may assume in both cases that the uniting of soul and body depends on exchange between men and God. As we know, this interaction is absent in *Beowulf*.

3. a constituent that Godden does not include in his account of indigenous, Anglo-Saxon concepts of the person, is 'life' (*lif, ealdor* or *feorh*). Life-force in *Beowulf* is probably associated with soul and spirit: 'life' (or life-force, or also physical force) seems to be a constituent that penetrates the whole body and encompasses *ic* and *mod*. Contrary to our ignorance on the time of origin of the soul we know of life that it has its origin in God's creation. In the (pre-Mosaic) story of the creation told by the *scop* of Hroðgar, we read: *lif eac gesceop // cynna gehwylcum / þara ðe cwice hwyrfaþ:* life (he) also created // for race (or species) each / which alive moves (*Bw.* 97b–98).[93] From this we can infer that where the soul is exclusively reserved for man and for men that are placed outside society by God or by their unrighteous behaviour (i.e. exiles and monsters), animals as well as men have life. How life and body are united is not clear but marriage will have been conceived as playing an important role here. Yet in *Beowulf* is no direct association between bridegivers and the bringing of life, in the form of descendants. Women bring peace between royal families that were previously on a war footing. In that sense it is women who as 'peace-weavers' of a relationship, provide a situation in which life can *continue to exist*. The share of women in conception, pregnancy, and birth remains unmentioned. When there are new royal offspring *kings* are said to have brought forth (*cennan, Bw.* 12b) children, or children are said to have arisen (*wæcnan, Bw.*

---

[91] Godden, "The Anglo-Saxons on the mind", pp. 283–285.

[92] Godden, "The Anglo-Saxons on the mind", p. 284.

[93] For this and all following quotations of *Beowulf* I base myself on the Old English text as reproduced in G. Jack, Beowulf. *A student edition* (Oxford, 1994). As translation I have opted for the very literal translation by J. Porter, Beowulf. *Text and translation* (Middlesex, 1991). Porter has, however, an inclination to translate words and compounds too literally and he thereby usually chooses the archaic meaning of a word. In many places I have therefore chosen the translation of individual words, compounds, phrases and difficult passages suggested by M. Alexander, Beowulf (Harmondsworth, 1995), Jack, Beowulf. *A student edition*, and Klaeber, Beowulf *and the Fight at Finnsburg*.

60a en 1960b) from *kings*. There is something similar in the phrase
Beowulf uses in lamenting his lack of descendants: he has no heir
lice gelenge, belonging to the body (*Bw.* 2732a). On the basis of *Beowulf*
it is difficult to address the problem of how in exchange, for instance
in rituals around marriage and birth, the conditions are created for
a potential, and actual, merging of body and life.[94]

If it is a matter of what happens to life after death, there is a big
difference between soul and life. The former has, as we have seen
earlier, an existence after death, in hell or under the protection of
God, whereas life ends with death, either by the head's been cleaved
in half, or the heart's being pierced.

4. Godden's reproduction of the character of *mod* (or *hige*, *modsefa*,
or *sefa*) corresponds well with the image that *Beowulf* offers of the
mind; it is the seat and the origin of positive (happiness, affection,
kindness, courage, and resolution) and negative (sorrow, pain, and
'darkening') states of mind and thoughts. But *mod* can also produce
dispositions with disastrous effect on social intercourse. Rage and
uncontrolled desire can lead to the unbridled use of power, to the
killing of relatives and followers, and to the ceasing of the distribution of treasure. According to Godden, the *ic* should restrain the
mind in these later possibilities. The question is, however, whether
the *ic* occupies such an independent position in *Beowulf.* This merits further research; from different passages we can in fact infer the
contrary: wisdom resides in the heart or the mind and wise words
stem from the heart or the mind.[95] It is this wisdom that makes a
measured use of force possible, prevents one from thinking that one
can do without other people and makes it possible to anticipate in
the right way the weakening of power through illness or old age, or
to death.

5. Totally outside Godden's consideration remains the constituent
that I would like to call 'worth', a translation of Old English *weorð*,
or 'image', in referring to the external recognizability of this constituent. As self-consciousness in nonmodern societies is inextricably

---

[94] For the relationship, as yet never systematically researched, between valuables
and 'life', see P. Taylor, "The traditional language of treasure in *Beowulf*", *Journal
of English and Germanic philology* 85 (1986), pp. 191–205.

[95] According to Hroðgar, Beowulf is *on mode frod*, wise in the heart (*Bw.* 1844b)
and that is clear in the words that '*witig drihten // on sefan sende*'; 'wise God // sent
in heart/mind' (*Bw.* 1841b–1842a).

linked to appearance, we should in considering the total constitution of a person have an eye not only for the internal but also for the external. A quotation from *Beowulf* might clarify this. When Hroðgar's coastguard sees Beowulf and his men come ashore in the land of the Danes, he says:

> *'Næfre ic maran geseah*
> *eorla ofer eorþan / ðonne is eower sum,*
> *secg on searwum. / Nis þæt seldguma*
> *wæpnum geweorðad /—næfre him his wlite leoge,*
> *ænlic ansyn!'*

> 'Never I bigger saw
> warrior on earth / than is one of you
> man in arms. / Not is this a mere retainer
> by weapons made worthy /—may his looks never belie',
> his matchless appearance!' (247b–251a)

Also Wulgar, who speaks to them outside Hroðgar's royal hall, is impressed, not only by Beowulf but by his whole group: *'Ne seah ic elþeodige // þus manige men / modiglicran'*; 'Not saw I foreign // thus any man / braver in appearance' (336b–337). He therefore advises Hroðgar not to refuse to speak to Beowulf:

> *'Hy on wiggetawum / wyrðe þinceað*
> *eorla geæhtlan; / huru se aldor deah,*
> *se þæm heaðorincum / hider wisede.'*

> 'They by war-equipment / worthy appear
> of warrior's esteem / indeed the leader is strong (*or* good),
> who the warriors /hither led' (368–369a).

In these three passages are linked together on the one hand the *appearance* of Beowulf as warrior and on the other hand expectations about his strength and courage and the honour to be bestowed on him. It is as regards this outward constituent that *Beowulf* gives a good impression of the connection between a constituent of the person and objects of exchange. The key here is the verb *weorðian* encountered in the first passage.

In 1953 Ernst Leisi was the first to make the point that valuables in *Beowulf* are identified with honour and fame.[96] According to Leisi, Germanic societies before and after the migration period are characterized by an ethical-politico-economic system which we can typify

---

[96] E. Leisi, "Gold and Manneswert im *Beowulf*", *Anglia* 71 (1953), pp. 259–273.

as an *Ehrensold-Ordnung*.[97] In this social order wealth is not a commodity but something which can only be obtained through the relationship between lord and follower. Wealth forms the symbolisation of the most important aristocratic values and expresses successful participation in aristocratic society. A wealthy man, in the Anglo-Saxon sense of the word, therefore does not only have many material goods but is in particular also virtuous and happy:[98] a 'rich' lord or king is generous, and a 'rich' follower is loyal and brave and both take part in feasts where drink provides a *rauschhaft gesteigertes Lebensgefühl*, an atmosphere wrested from everyday life of *Ehrgeiz, Männerstolz und Prahlerei*. As Leisi states, the significance of wealth in a Germanic society therefore does not lie in its aesthetic enjoyment or the life comforts that it yields—after all valuable gifts should be passed on[99]—but *in the raising of the personal worth* of the giver or recipient of it.[100] The lord or king who is generous, as he is expected to be,[101] or the follower who carries out the obligation of passing on a gift, enlarges his worth or fame. And by the lord's gift of horses, land, weapons, jewelry or rings, the potentially present, male capacities, *Manneswert* in Leisi's terms (for him, it involves bravery above all), will burgeon, or the *Manneswert* shown in battle by the follower will be made visible. In this context the interpretation of the verb *weorðian* is of the utmost importance. This means both 'to give' and 'to embellish' but also 'to honour'.

A more penetrating formulation of Leisi's idea that valuables are a *Wert- und Tugendanzeiger* (a signifier of value or virtue) is offered by Michael Cherniss.[102] He observes, following Leisi, that valuable gifts

---

[97] Leisi, "Gold und Manneswert im *Beowulf*", p. 267. This concept is directly grafted onto Mauss' *monnaie de renommé* (ibid. 271, note 1).

[98] Several Old English words for 'rich' therefore can mean 'happy', 'proud' or 'powerful'; and words for 'wealth' also 'fame', 'benefaction', 'honour', 'success', or 'virtue' (Leisi, "Gold und Manneswert im *Beowulf*", pp. 259–260).

[99] For the obligation of passing on the gift, see Leisi, "Gold und Manneswert im *Beowulf*", pp. 265–266. In this context Leisi points out that *mað(ð)um* does indeed stand for 'valuable' but that, also where there is no question of exchange, it always means 'gift' as well.

[100] Leisi, "Gold und Manneswert im *Beowulf*", p. 262.

[101] Cf. *Maxims II*, 28b–29a: 'The king belongs in his hall, sharing out rings' (translation S.A.J. Bradley, *Anglo-Saxon Poetry. An antology of Old English poems in prose translation with introduction and headnotes* (London and Melbourne, 1982), p. 514). More general is *Maxims I*, 155a: 'gold is meant for giving' (translation Bradley, *Anglo-Saxon Poetry*, p. 350).

[102] Cherniss, *Ingeld and Christ*, in particular chapter 4. For the merit of Cherniss' description and analysis, see Niles, Beowulf. *The poem and its tradition*, pp. 213–214.

are the material manifestation of the honour that is due to a warrior on the basis of manly virtues which in principle are characteristic of him, or of the admirable deeds he has done: valuables are the visible signs of the inherent or proven worth of those that own them. Although Cherniss often speaks of the one as the symbol of the other, that is the valuables as a token, manifestation or indication of a person's inherent or proven physical and moral worth, he states in a much more careful way that valuables and worth are in fact interchangeable.[103] On the basis of his virtues and deeds a warrior is entitled to valuables that confer honour but the valuables he owns make him into an honoured man who will certainly be of worth, even though this is not immediately clear to the onlooker on the basis of his words and deeds. In other words, a man is wealthy because he is a successful warrior but he is also a successful warrior because he is wealthy. It is therefore not the case that the owner determines the value of valuables or the reverse, in fact both are true: 'the process of giving and receiving honor will become completely circular; from owners to treasure to owner to treasure again'.[104]

Cherniss illustrates the reciprocal nature of human worth and the value of treasures by the great importance that is attached to an object's genealogy.[105] The value of an object is made clear by giving a review of the people who have had it in the past and the special worth of those that now possess it is thereby made clear at the same time. Without the poet's telling anything about the descent and the actions of a person, the possession of an ancient treasure makes the owner into a worthy warrior. His life will be an example of heroic actions by which something substantial will be added to the value of the treasure.

After this review of the constitution of the person and of the identification of valuable objects of exchange with constituents of the person, we are able to name and value the relationships in which the different constituents play a role. *Beowulf* provides relatively little when we are dealing with the merging of 'body' and 'life' realized in ceremonial exchanges.[106] The way in which the producing of children is conveyed, seems to suggest that 'life', and in particular the qualities

---

[103] Cherniss, *Ingeld and Christ*, pp. 94–97.
[104] Cherniss, *Ingeld and Christ*, p. 97.
[105] Cf. Leisi, "Gold und Manneswert im *Beowulf*", pp. 261–262.
[106] The constituent 'life' in relation to exchange, however, is implicitly present in the whole poem. Where exchange is absent, death reigns.

of 'strength' and 'courage' associated with it, is passed on in a line
of male descendants, without much attention to the bridegivers and
the exchange of valuables realized in marriage. We could name this
highly appreciated relationship of descent in terms of the value of
'continuity'. The situation is different when we are dealing with the
royal family as bridegiver. Where the king's daughter is given in
marriage to a non-royal family the latter seems to participate in the
qualities of the royal family: the royal family is in this case a giver
of 'life' (or of the qualities 'strength' and 'courage'). Here the key is
what I would like to call the value of 'fertility'. The matter is much
clearer when we speak of the constituent 'worth'. The perspective
on 'worth' and valuables developed by Leisi and Cherniss has been
crucial to the construction of the model I shall present in the following pages. Cherniss does indeed give a lucid analysis of the connection between honour and fame and valuables but in the final
analysis, however, he returns to a value that has always dominated
the discussion on *Gefolgschaft*: loyalty (or *Treue*), in Cherniss' eyes the
basis of Germanic, heroic society:[107] '[t]he gifts from lord to thanes
and from thanes to lord *reflect* the loyalty and veneration between
the members of the *comitatus*'.[108] The problem with the concept of
loyalty is that, although it has an Old English equivalent (*treow*), it
has such strong idealistic connotations. I prefer to give a different
name to the most important value in the relationship between king
or lord and follower. This is because I look upon 'worth' in the context of the life cycle of the warrior-follower. In the relationship
between king or lord and follower there is a step-by-step articulation of the 'worth' of both warrior-follower and king. The visualization and enlargement of 'worth' is realized for the warrior-follower
on the one hand by the efforts of the lord who provides him with
famous weapons and later with valuables and land, and by the efforts
of the warrior-follower himself who achieves fame in his warlike
enterprises, and on the other hand for the king by the efforts of the
warrior-follower who offers him the booty of his glorious enterprises.
The value that is at stake in this relationship I would therefore like
to call 'reputation'. We are dealing here not with a psychological
disposition, loyalty, expressed in the exchanges between and the
behaviour of king and warrior-follower, but with the development

---

[107] Cherniss, *Ingeld and Christ*, pp. 30–59.
[108] Cherniss, *Ingeld and Christ*, p. 98 (emphasis JB).

of a quality indispensable for the aristocratic warrior-follower. In this development the king is essential: he mediates between the ancestral 'worth' on the one hand, built up by himself and his predecessors, and embodied in the valuables of the royal family, and the warrior-follower on the other hand. The king in his turn is dependent on the ceremonial participation of his adult warrior-followers in order to realize his transition from king to ancestor.

What remains is to name the most encompassing relationship, that between the people and God. The possible, contrasting destinies of the 'soul' after death (to hell or to God's protection) suggest that in the relation between God and the people there is a key value that we can name 'righteousness', that is in the law of nature, in the pre-Mosaic sense. About the way in which men work for the merging and breaking up of 'body' and 'soul' and for the salvation of the soul after death we learn nothing, because the principal characters cannot communicate with God.

6.3. *The life-cycle of Beowulf and the constitution of person and society through ceremonial exchange*

In this section I develop a model for the social structure as described in *Beowulf*. I will include three elements discussed above:

1. the most important relationships between discrete social categories
2. the constituents relevant to the development of a fully-fledged, mature aristocratic person
3. the values determinant for the relations in which man is constituted. On the basis of Beowulf's course of life I shall unite the different elements into one model (see fig. 4) by giving attention to three additional elements:
4. the socio-morphological topography of the world
5. the various rituals that are bound up with the life cycle of the warrior-follower and the king
6. the ceremonial exchanges in the rituals just mentioned: in marriage and funerary rituals and festive-ceremonial occasions in which the king shows his generosity.

The full circle in fig. 4, starting on the far left and to be read anti-clockwise, represents the full life cycle of a person such as Beowulf: that is to say of a son of a prominent warrior-follower and also a king's daughter's- or sister's son, who ultimately becomes king himself.

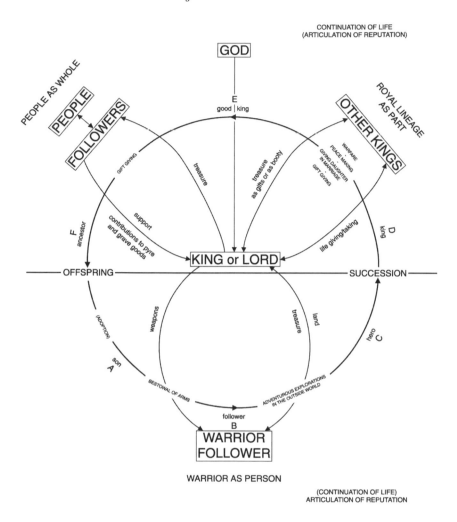

Fig. 4. A ritual-cosmological model of the relationship between lord and warrior-follower in *Beowulf*.

The model has, however, wider validity, even though it is inspired by the exceptional life history of Beowulf. The lower half of the model need not only apply to a child who is a relative of the king but can apply also to children not related to the king, or to children of the king himself who stay with their father because they have rights to the throne. And the upper half need not necessarily only apply to a king but can apply also to a non-royal lord of an area within a kingdom. The model thus applies to the three most important, male life cycles, namely of:

a. a king's son (who becomes a king)
b. a king's daughter-/sister's son who comes to the king's court and develops into a mature follower with his own lordship within the kingdom, or in an exceptional case becomes king himself (like Beowulf)
c. a child not related to the royal family who is accepted in the king's hall and there develops into a mature follower with his own lordship within the kingdom, and in exceptional cases is given a daughter in marriage by the king (like Eofor; the son arising from such a marriage falls into category b).

Beowulf tells the life-story of its eponymous hero. In the first part of the poem we are introduced to the young Geat Beowulf who as warrior-follower of the Geatish king Hygelac sets off for the land of the Danes in order to fight the monster Grendel. Although his achievements are of an exceptional nature, we should see them as an example of the behaviour expected of a young warrior-follower close to a king.

For a good understanding of the life of Beowulf it is necessary briefly to dwell on his father Ecgþeow. Ecgþeow was not a member of a royal family but was a prominent person, married to a daughter of the Geatish king Hreðel. From this we may infer that Ecgþeow belonged to the close warrior-followers of Hreðel and for one reason or another enjoyed his special benevolence. Remarkable, in the light of this special relation between Ecgþeow and the Geatish king, is a fact mentioned by the Danish king Hroðgar. For he tells that when Ecgþeow caused a great feud by killing the Wylfing Heaþolaf, his relatives, and we may count his lord and kinsman Hreðel also among them, did not dare to grant him protection. *De facto* kinless, he was therefore forced to seek shelter abroad and he found that with the Danish king Hroðgar.[109] The latter defused the feud by paying *wergild* to the Wylfingas. In exchange for this Ecgþeow swore an oath to Hroðgar by which a relationship of dependence was created between the two men (and their respective families). Yet the lack of support from Hreðel's side and the new tie with Hroðgar

---

[109] The lack of relatives is also something that occupies Beowulf.

do not seem to imply a breach with Ecgþeow's Geatish lord and king, because his son Beowulf accomplishes the most important steps in his life-cycle in relation to a succession of Geatish kings.

The first memorable fact in Beowulf's life is his acceptance at the age of seven into the community in the king's hall of the Geatish king Hreðel: a transition from the group of children (*umbor*) to that of the boys (*cnythas*). A first transfer of glorious treasures from Hreðel's ancestral hoard to the young child meant the first visualization of Beowulf's 'worth': they made visible for the first time the aristocratic qualities that Beowulf possessed potentially. The admittance of the still quite young Beowulf into the community of Hreðel's hall we take as the first point on the life cycle represented in fig. 4 (see fig. 4, under A). With Beowulf we are dealing here to a certain extent with a special case, as he is admitted into the king's hall also because he is the daughter's son of the king. To the group of young children in the hall also belong, however, the sons of the king, the (fatherless) sons of the (dead) king's brothers and the sons of warrior-followers who do not have a tie by marriage with the royal family. Point a in fig. 4 is thereby also the point of departure for many other children who will later develop into young warrior-followers.

An important next step in the articulation of Beowulf's 'worth' is the granting of weapons to the youth Beowulf by his lord and king Hreðel and his father. From the former he receives a very special coat of mail that is considered to be the work of the smith Weland, and therefore to be of very good, supernatural quality; from the latter he very probably receives a sword, an old heirloom. With the granting of weapons he is admitted into the group of young warrior-followers or maguþegnas of the king that live in his hall (fig. 4, under B). By the granting of weapons the other categories of children also join the so-called *geogoð*. It is unclear, however, whether we are dealing here with an individual ceremony or a collective one, involving the other boys in the group.

The result of the granting of weapons is clearly described in the words of Hroðgar's coastguard.[110] Hroðgar's close warrior-follower Wulgar, too, associates the weapons and the appearance of Beowulf and his partners with their strength and courage and their worthiness of respect.

Beowulf's period as a young warrior-follower is marked by shock-

---

[110] See above.

ing events within the Geatish royal family of the *Hreðlingas*. Beowulf survives three successive kings, yet these changes have no consequences for Beowulf's position. The successors of Hreðel also acknowledge the kin-tie between the house of the Geatish kings and Beowulf's family, and show confidence in Beowulf. It is not necessary, for example, for king Hygelac, Beowulf's third king and lord, 'to buy' a foreign warrior who could lead his troops into battle because Beowulf is very satisfactory as leader of the warrior flock.[111]

With the granting of weapons the moment has come for the young warrior-follower himself to make a contribution to the articulation of his 'worth'. The wars of the king offer possibilities here; but a prominent young warrior-follower will also, and without the king's involvement, have to start adventurous enterprises outside the kingdom to show his strength and courage (see fig. 4, between B and C). During his period as *geogoð* Beowulf first 'proves' himself impressively by slaying many monsters during a memorable sea voyage with king Breca. This is an overture to the enterprise in the land of the Danes which is described in the first part of the poem.

This first part is mainly devoted to Beowulf's greatest undertaking as a young warrior-follower: his battle against the monster Grendel who has been threatening the Danes already for twelve years without their being able to accomplish anything against him, and later against his vengeful mother. The fight with Grendel in Hroðgar's royal hall offers Beowulf the chance of increasing the glorious reputation which he established already in the adventure with Breca. But Beowulf's enterprise in the land of the Danes has other reasons too. The achievements of Beowulf are in the first place part of the links between the royal families of the *Dene* and the *Geatas*. In the past these families were hostile towards each other, but there was no longer open hostility between king Hroðgar and king Hygelac, and there may even have been friendship, rendered permanent by the exchange of gifts. King Hroðgar acknowledges that Beowulf has

---

[111] *Bw.* 2494–2498a. Notable in this passage is the contrast between the continuation of an existing bond of trust with warrior-followers who have long-standing connections with the royal family, and the 'buying' (*ceapian*, 2496) of a foreign warrior. We may assume that *ceapian*, that is derived from the sphere of exchange of alienable goods, points here to a negative judgement on the engaging of a random, unrelated, warrior. The negative connotation of the word *ceapian* also shows in the passage that states that Beowulf *bought* the treasure of the dragon with his life (*Bw.* 3012b).

come out of kindness but also because, as noted above, Hroðgar had rendered his father an important service in the past. Hroðgar consents to Beowulf's request to allow him to kill the monster, and for the first time in his life Hroðgar will entrust his hall to another. If Beowulf succeeds in killing the monster, says Hroðgar: '*Ne bið þe wilna gad // gif þu þæt ellenweorc / aldre gedigest*'; 'Not will you good things lack // if you this courageous deed / with life survive.' (*Bw.* 658–661). Hroðgar's wife Wealhþeow can also put her trust in a warrior who seems able to defeat Grendel. She has Beowulf share in the mead that she gives to her husband and his followers.

Before Beowulf can intervene that night in Hroðgar's royal hall Grendel kills one of Beowulf's followers, Hondscio. Grendel manages to escape from the fight that the monster then starts with Beowulf but Beowulf has managed to wound him mortally. With Grendel's death Beowulf has freed the Danes from all anxieties and fears; and with that Hroðgar's and Wealhþeow's most important wish has come true and Beowulf has kept his promise. The result of this achievement goes further still. Hroðgar's men who have followed the trail of the fleeing Grendel, think in fact that there is nobody in the world of humans deserving more than Beowulf of rule over a kingdom (*Bw.* 857b–861).

After Hroðgar too has learned of Beowulf's achievements, he addresses himself to him with thanks and makes it clear that henceforth he will regard him as his son:[112] '*Ne bið þe [n]ænigre gad // worolde wilna / þe ic geweald hæbbe*'; 'Not will be for you any lack // of world's wishes / if I power have' (*Bw.* 946b–950). We can see here developing a notable contrast between Beowulf and his father. Where Hroðgar by paying *wergild* behaved *de facto* as a kinsman in relation to the exiled Ecgþeow, Hroðgar creates a *de jure* bond of kinship with Beowulf, with all its mutual rights and obligations, by adopting him as a son.

Hroðgar adds:

> '*Ful oft ic for læssan / lean teohhode,*
> *hordweorþunge / hnahran rince,*
> *sæmran æt sæcce. / þu þe self hafast*
> *dædum gefremed / þæt þin [dom] lyfað*
> *awa to aldre. / Alwalda þec*
> *gode folgylde, / swa he nu gyt dyde!*'

---

[112] Later Beowulf will take a seat between the two sons of Hroðgar and Wealhþeow.

'Very often I for less / rewards bestowed
honouring with treasure / more lowly man,
weaker at battle. / You yourself have
by deeds brought about / that your fame lives
for ever and ever. / Ruler of all you
with good reward, / as he now just did!' (951–956)

This is an important passage when dealing with the character of the constituent 'worth'. As we have seen with regard to the temporality of human constituents, we can make a distinction between 'body' and 'life' on the one hand and 'soul' on the other. The temporality of the first two is limited: after death the 'body' finds its last resting-place and there is an end to life. The 'soul' on the other hand is consigned until the end of time to hell fire or admitted to God's protection. 'Worth', as we can gather from the above passage, takes up an *intermediate* position in the row of constituents: it will 'always' continue to exist, that is as long as there is a human community that keeps the recollection of the warrior-follower alive in stories and uses the gifts conquered or received by the warrior-follower. The this-worldly universality of 'worth' is expressed in a temporal sense in the above quotation: 'that your fame will live for ever and ever' and in a spatial sense in a quotation in which it is said of Beowulf that people *feor ond neah* (*Bw.* 1221a, 'far and near') will praise him.

After the restoration of the king's hall which has suffered in the fight, a feast is provided where Hroðgar, as promised, gives a number of very special, gold-decorated gifts: Healfdene's sword (a famous sword from the treasure of Hroðgar's father), a gold standard (also described as a decorated war banner), a helmet and a coat of mail. After having drunk from a cup Beowulf accepts the gifts. Beowulf need not, as the poet says, be ashamed of these: he had never seen anybody receive four such special gifts in a more friendly manner. In the end Hroðgar has eight horses with gold bridles brought in as well. One of these horses carries the decorated war saddle, embellished with valuable ornaments, with which Hroðgar has achieved his many successes. Hroðgar hands over the horses and the weapons to Beowulf and expresses the wish that he will use them well (*het hine wel brucan*, *Bw.* 1045b). Nobody who spoke the truth, so the poet says, could find fault with the way in which the king rewarded Beowulf. To Beowulf's companions Hroðgar gives valuable heirlooms as well, and orders that the death of Hondscio be compensated for with gold.

Wealhþeow too plays an important role in these ceremonies. In the first place she urges her husband to receive the Geats with kind words and to show them gratitude, mindful of the gifts that come from far and wide and are in Hroðgar's possession. In the second place, she also gives Beowulf, after she has let him share in the drinking of mead, gifts from the great treasure hoard. These items consist of a coat of mail and different kinds of gold turned into rings: two bracelets, rings, and the largest and most beautiful among neck rings. She gives these treasures not only because Beowulf has ful-filled her wish but also because she wants to be assured in the future, after Hroðgar's death, of Beowulf's advice and support when her sons assert their rights to the throne. Wealhþeow endorses Hroðgar's opinion that Beowulf has gathered fame everywhere and for ever.

The first night that the Danish followers of Hroðgar again guard the hall, Grendel's mother takes revenge by killing Æschere, the king's closest follower, and carrying him off to her lair. Hroðgar thinks that only Beowulf can continue the feud and asks him to go and seek the monster at her home. If he succeeds in coming back alive, he will again reward him with ancient treasures. Beowulf is resolute in his answer, declaring that it is better to take revenge than to mourn:

> 'Ure æghwylc sceal / ende gebidan
> worolde lifes; / wryce se þe mote
> domes ær deaþe; / þæt bið drihtguman
> unlifgendum / æfter selest.'

> 'Of us each must / end experience
> in world's life; / achieve he who may
> glory before death; / that is for warrior
> lifeless / afterwards best' (*Bw.* 1384–1389).

Before commencing the battle with Grendel's mother, Beowulf briefly dwells upon the new bond that he has with Hroðgar, and he asks Hroðgar to take over the protection of his men, should he die, and to send the treasures he has gained to his king and lord Hygelac. Already before the fight with Grendel, Beowulf had insisted to Hroðgar that if he were to die, his coat of mail, an heirloom from his first Geatish lord and king Hreðel, should be returned to Hygelac. Beowulf's desire that both his weapons and the treasures obtained by him should be returned to Hygelac makes clear that his enterprise in the land of the Danes cannot be seen as separate from his relationship with his own lord and king.

In the fight with Grendel's mother in her lair, Beowulf manages to kill the monster with the giant sword he finds there. After the fight he returns with his men to the hall of the Danish king: *Ða com in gan / ealdor ðegna, // dædcene mon / dome gewurþad, // hæle hildedeor, / Hroðgar gretan*; Then came in walking / leader of thegns, // man valiant in deeds / by renown exalted (!) // warrior brave in battle, / Hroðgar to greet (*Bw.* 1644–1646). Beowulf hands over the booty—the hilt of the giant sword and Grendel's head—to Hroðgar and he tells him his story of the fight. Hroðgar accepts the hilt with thanks and again says that Beowulf's fame will reach all corners of the world. He adds, however, that Beowulf will have to administer his great strength with wisdom of heart. If he does that, then he will develop into a blessing for his people, this in contrast to the Danish king Heremod who also had exceptional strength but who from bloodthirstyness and in a rage killed friends and table-companions and refrained from giving rings. In a long monologue Hroðgar then talks about the transitoriness of strength and the dangers of pride. He promises that the next morning he will again distribute treasures to Beowulf.

The next morning Beowulf, revered by the Danes, receives from Hroðgar twelve treasures which are not described. Beowulf promises Hroðgar that, in accordance with their new close relationship, he will give him protection in the future against hostile nations with Hygelac's help. He assures Hroðgar's son that he is welcome at the court of Hygelac.[113] Hroðgar recognizes God's hand in these words and for him they are proof that strength and wisdom come together in Beowulf. He therefore says that, when Hygelac dies, the Geats could not choose a better king than Beowulf. Now that Beowulf has brought about peace between the Geats and the Danes, Hroðgar says, treasures will be exchanged between the kings.[114]

Beowulf's adventures in the land of the Danes have been detailed

---

[113] Important at this point is Beowulf's addition: *'feorcyþðe beoð // selran gesohte / þaem þe him selfa deah'*; 'far countries are // better visited / by one who himself is of worth' (*Bw.* 1838b–1839). This statement refers to the obligation discussed above for prominent, young warrior-followers to prove themselves in enterprises initiated by themselves in the world outside the lord's kingdom.

[114] After the farewell words of Hroðgar, Beowulf and his men leave for the coast where they meet Hroðgar's coastguard who has guarded their ship. Before Beowulf and his men embark on their sea voyage, he gives a sword to the coastguard: *þæt he syðþan wæs // on meodubence / maþm[e] þy weorþr[a], // yrfelafe*; so that he after was // on mead-bench / by treasure the more honoured // by heirloom (*BW.* 1901b–1903a). Note the use of *weorðian* in this passage.

because they are exemplary for the course a young warrior-follower has to complete after the granting of weapons by king and father. Where potential aristocratic qualities are literally made visible with the ancestral weapons, it is a requirement for the youth further to expand his 'worth' by undertaking glorious activities. If he succeeds then that will be expressed in the treasures he seizes as booty or receives as thanks.

Beowulf's enterprise goes beyond the exemplary, however; he manages to seize a number of valuables that can be counted as regalia, royal treasures that in principle cannot be given away as they should be passed on from father to son within the royal family.[115] In fact they can only be purloined as booty in battle. The valuables given by Hroðgar and Wealhþeow, however, are of the right calibre for the very special achievements of Beowulf and they are an indication of Beowulf's explicitly endorsed qualifications to become king. Their giving away, however, also means a considerable loss for the Danish royal family. It is then rather tempting to connect the future conflicts between Hroðgar and Ingeld, to which the poet and Beowulf allude, with this loss of the most important regalia.[116]

---

[115] Cf. Weiner, *Inalienable possessions: the paradox of keeping-while-giving.*

[116] Beowulf's fight with Grendel and his mother cannot only be interpreted in a social sense. In other words, the significance of Beowulf's actions is not only inherent in his development as a young warrior-follower and in the history of the entanglements of different royal lines. His actions also have meaning in a more encompassing cosmological sense. As the portrayal of the poet is modelled to fit the pre-Mosaic era of the law of nature, however, it is difficult to get a complete picture of the relationships between man and the supernatural world, and I refer here in particular to the relationships between men and the monsters that populate the poem. In an attempt to get some insight into this relationships, it is necessary to dwell again upon the character of monsters in general and Grendel and his mother in particular. Facts connected with the dragon, and with Beowulf's fight with him, can thereby be included in the discussion in support. As we know, the world of the monsters shows superficial resemblances to that of man, thus Grendel and his mother, and the dragon, have treasures (!), but in almost anything else it is the opposite of the human universe. The most important difference is that monsters live *alone*. From the perspective of human society this could also be phrased as follows: because monsters live alone, valuables are useless and the monsters live alone because they hang on to valuables. In view of the analysis presented in this article, it is important that the actions of the monsters form a violation of the circulation realized in rituals of constituents which are relevant for man. Monsters kill people, that means: they tear up 'body'; bring 'life' prematurely and definitely to an end; as protagonists of the devil they destroy 'soul'; and they let perish the 'worth' of valuables. Valuables 'de-value' or rather 'de-image' because they do not circulate among people: expressively described by the poet for the treasure of the dragon in the loss of lustre and the beginning of rust. In this light, we could regard

Having noted the exemplary and the exceptional in Beowulf's achievements, we resume the thread of the story. On his return Beowulf goes to the king's hall of his lord and king Hygelac. Beowulf reports at length on his Danish adventures. He tells Hygelac that he got even with Grendel for all his evil deeds and *that he thereby honoured Hygelac's people by his actions* (*Bw.* 2095–2096a). This statement forms an important indication that Beowulf's enterprise, as we have seen already, can only be understood in the light of the relation he has with Hygelac. Following his report of the fight with Grendel, Beowulf acquaints Hygelac with the reward that fell to him, but also tells of the revenge taken by Grendel's mother and his fight with the monster in the lair deep under water. Again Hroðgar gave him treasures that Beowulf could choose for himself. Now Beowulf would like to give these gifts to Hygelac with the greatest pleasure. Beowulf adds here that he is dependent on Hygelac's affection, because he has few other kin. Apparently Hroðgar too knew this was the usual way to act because he had urged Beowulf to inform Hygelac of the way in which Hroðgar's predecessor Heorogar had treated the weapons he obtained. While adding the wish '*Bruc ealles well!*' (*Bw.* 2162b) Beowulf hands over, as behoves a kinsman, all the weapons and four horses to Hygelac. Beowulf also gives gifts to Hygelac's wife, queen Hygd, Beowulf gives gifts: three horses and a neck ring. According to the poet, Beowulf's transfer of the gifts to Hygelac and Hygd is meant to win honour. By not holding on to the gifts he also shows that he is a paragon of self-control. Never will Beowulf misuse his godgiven strength!

To conclude the ceremony Hygelac orders the richest sword of

Beowulf's actions against Grendel and his mother, and later also against the dragon, as a victory over that which is incompatible with the recursive constitution of the human person and society: *he kills the killing*; he introduces into society the valuables secured from the monsters and he acquires eternal and universal fame. The socio-genetic character of his actions gains extra relief if we realize that he: (1) enables Hroðgar at last to use the incomparable king's hall Heorot for the purpose for which it is meant: to distribute, and (2) has gained a hilt, 'on which was engraved the origin of the ancient strife, when the flood, the rushing ocean, destroyed the race of giants' (1688b–1690). It is interesting that the actions of an individual, Beowulf, are at the centre, without his, as stated explicitly, asking for or getting help from others. We can discern here a discrepancy between an exchange (singular) brought about by an individual with the supernatural world that is constituent for society, and the exchanges (plural) where it is a matter of the constitution of the human person in exchange and of the successive contributions of that person to the encompassing circulation of the constituents which are important for the human person.

the Geats, Hreðel's heirloom, to be brought in. He gives this sword to Beowulf by placing it in Beowulf's lap. Apart from the sword, Beowulf also receives seven thousand units (probably *hides*) of land, a hall, and a throne. This wellnigh royal position forms a discrete unit within the kingdom of Hygelac: in principle, it in no way diminishes the position of Beowulf's king and lord.

With the successful conclusion of his glorious enterprise in the land of the Danes, Beowulf has qualified as a fully-fledged mature warrior-follower and in view of his exceptional achievement, as a potential king too (see fig. 4, under C). The transfer of the valuables obtained by him to Hygelac and Hygd shows that the enterprise was not an individual affair. The possibility of manifesting himself as a discrete person, whose 'worth' possibly will continue to exist after his death, is offered to him by the Geatish king who has made his potential aristocratic qualities visible and has granted him glorious weapons in order to engage in battle with a certain guarantee of success. To conclude his warriorship in continuous and direct proximity to the king, Beowulf is 'loaned' his own hall, throne, and land. It is possible that we are dealing here partly with new land: the largest part will, however, consist of ancestral lands to which Beowulf's family has had rights from time immemorial. In other words, the inheritance of ancestral land from father to son depends on the son's going through various *rites de passage* as warrior, and in these rites the king has a decisive ceremonial role.

Not only Beowulf's youth and adolescence but also his life as an adult warrior-follower is marked by the violent entanglements of the Geatish royal family. His lord and king Hygelac is killed in a battle, initiated by himself, with the Frisians and Franks. After Hygelac's death, queen Hygd offers him *hord ond rice // beagas ond bregostol* (*Bw.* 2369b–2370a) as she has no faith in her son Heardred to be able to defend the Geats against other nations. Against the wishes of Hygd and the Geats, Beowulf refuses to accept the kingdom and he emphasizes that he will always support Heardred.

But Heardred's rule too is an unhappy one. He inherits from his predecessors Hæðcyn and Hygelac the enmity of the Swedish *Scylfingas*. When he offers hospitality to the two Swedish pretenders to the throne Eadgils and Eanmund, he is killed by the Swedish king Onela. It is remarkable that Onela now allows Beowulf to occupy the royal throne and to rule the Geats (see fig. 4, under D).

Beowulf's kingship is merely sketched in the poem in rather vague terms. We know that he takes revenge on king Onela because Onela was responsible for the death of Beowulf's last lord and king Heardred. We do not learn anything about other concrete involvements, whether violent or peaceful, of Beowulf with other kings. In the preamble to the fight with the dragon, the poet only says that Beowulf ruled the large Geatish kingdom for fifty years in a proper manner (see fig. 4, between D and E). Beowulf has apparently been a king who uses in a restrained though decisive manner his capacities for violence, develops into a good and valued ruler who acquires 'worth' in his generosity and warlike enterprises and takes care of the protection of his people and thereby of the continuation of life (see fig. 4, under E).

From the many words of Wiglaf we can gather how Beowulf conducted himself towards his warrior-followers. Wiglaf describes Beowulf in the ceremonial role of king as described above (see fig. 4, between E and F). Beowulf in the first place appeared as the one who gave his warrior-followers weapons and treasure. The words that Wiglaf directs at the ten warriors who accompany Beowulf but flee after battle with the dragon begins (*Bw.* 2633–2642a), show that with the treasure given to the warrior-followers the imputed warlike qualities were made visible and that the warrior-followers were obliged to repay with brave acts the king's generosity in granting the weapons. On this last point, however, Beowulf's warrior-followers renege on their obligation. According to Wiglaf, Beowulf's behaviour towards his warrior-followers had always been such that their leaving him now alone in battle was wholly undeserved. Only by killing the dragon and defending the life of their lord could Beowulf's companions, so Wiglaf declares, 'bring their shields home in a proper manner' (*Bw.* 2653–2654a). After Beowulf's death, Wiglaf therefore correctly directs reproaches against these cowards: the man who had given them most valuable weapons had found out that he had wasted his treasure on them!

In the second place Beowulf not only is the king who grants weapons to young men, but also fulfills the role of the one who loans a warrior-follower land if the latter has proved himself and can claim adulthood. A couple of passages from the story of Beowulf's fight with the dragon illustrate this point. In the first passage we are told that Wiglaf: *[g]emunde ða ða are // þe he* (that is Beowulf) *him ær forgeaf, // wicstede weligne / Wægmundinga // folcrihta gehwylc, / swa his fæder ahte*; [r]ecalled then the property (*or* honour, *or* benefit) / that he

(Beowulf) him formerly bestowed // dwelling-place rich / of Wæg-
mundings // common rights (in lands?) each, / as his father had pos-
sesssed (*Bw.* 2606–2608). In other words, at a certain moment Beowulf
has loaned Wiglaf his ancestral home (and land) and confirmed the
rights that his father Weohstan had. Exactly what these rights referred
to is difficult to say. Perhaps we are dealing with the loan of a discrete lordship over land and people within Beowulf's kingdom. Such
a lordship might originally have been an independent kingdom.[117]

In the second passage Wiglaf describes for the warrior-followers
who fled the shameful situation that has emerged after Beowulf's
death (*Bw.* 2884–2890a). New rulers who will take possession of the
kingdom of the Geats will certainly not confirm the ancestral rights
to lands of Beowulf's men—not because those men are enemies but
because they are cowards and dishonourable.[118] It is better for them
to die, so Wiglaf says.

To conclude this section, I would like to draw attention to the
role that his followers play at Beowulf's cremation and funeral. It
has often been said that the descriptions in *Beowulf* of the rites of
death are not very informative. This opinion is based in particular
on the fact that the poet (with reason) does not discuss in words the
heathen rationale for these rites: it appears for instance that the dead
will make a journey and that they should be provided with all kinds
of goods, but it is not stated where to this journey goes or what
purpose the grave gifts serve. Interestingly, however, Beowulf's ritual role in the multi-staged reaching of adulthood of his warrior-
followers, seems to find a complement in a ritual role attributed to
his warrior-followers in the last part of the poem. In the light of the
model presented in this paper, a certain act performed at Beowulf's
funeral pyre which at first sight seems an ethnographic curiosity
acquires a special meaning that was probably rooted deep in the
past. Wiglaf orders that:

> *hæleða monegum,*
> *boldagendra, / þæt hie bælwudu*
> *feorran feredon, / folcagende,*
> *godum togenes*

[117] Interesting in the case of Wiglaf and his father is that the latter was originally a warrior-follower of the Swedish king Onela.

[118] Compare, however, Beowulf who, after Heardred's death, was allowed by the
Swedish king Onela to take on the Geatish kingship, and Weohstan who exercised
his ancestral rights both under a Swedish and a Geatish king.

> warriors many,
> men who own a hall (i.e. all men who gained their adulthood in
>   relation to Beowulf), / that they wood for pyre
> from far off bring, / leaders of a people,
> to good man's side (*Bw.* 3111b–3114a).

Where during the king's life youths of aristocratic descent complete
the various *rites de passage* in relation to their king, by which they
develop into adult warrior-followers with their own hall and lordship, at the king's death the different warrior-followers each have to
make a contribution to the king's last *rite de passage* by collecting the
wood for the pyre (see fig. 4, under F). Unlike Fred Robinson, who
emphasizes the exceptional character of Beowulf's grave monument
and funeral ritual, and who therefore thinks that we are dealing here
with a rite in which Beowulf is elevated to a god,[119] I see the rite
as the way in which Beowulf is transformed into an ancestor and
by which his successor is free to take on the kingship. This transformation, in fact a partial destruction of the dead man's armour
and valuables in order thus to extricate 'body' and 'worth', is realized by the bringing together of grave gifts[120] along with the wood
for the pyre and all adult warrior-followers of the deceased lord have
a share in this task.

I suggested earlier that the relationship between a lord and his
people was in all probability a multi-staged one, that took shape via
his adult warrior-followers who had their own areas within the encompassing lordship of the king. In the contributions of the adult warrior-
followers we therefore recognize what is called within the Dumontian
perspective 'society as a whole'. Where every man who is an aristocrat as regards 'worth' emerges step-by-step in the interaction
between king and warrior-follower, the king is transformed after death
into an ancestor by the contributions of all who have become adult
in relation to him, that is by the contributions of the people as a
whole. In the society described in *Beowulf* there is in other words no
question of individuals who interact with each other on the basis of

---

[119] '. . ., a purpose which the poet intimates through muted hints, as is his wont
in alluding to his characters' paganism. An overt statement that the Geats proclaimed the dead Beowulf a god would have alienated a Christian Anglo-Saxon
audience, . . .' (F.C. Robinson, The tomb of Beowulf, in F.C. Robinson, *The tomb
of Beowulf and other essays on Old English* (Cambridge (Mass.) and Oxford), 1993,
p. 18).

[120] Compare the treasures that *of feorwegum*, from distant parts (*Bw.* 37a) are
brought together to fill the funerary ship of Scyld.

ideals and objectives prescribed by culture or nature, but of persons constituted by exchanges at different life-cycle rituals. The king plays an indispensable ritual role in these exchanges and at the death of every king, society as a whole has to realise, in exchange with other-worldly entities (those are unnamed in *Beowulf*), the transformation of the king into an ancestor before a new king can fulfil anew his ceremonial role in the constitution of aristocratic persons.

7. *Beyond power*

In the foregoing I have formulated a model for the structure of the socio-cosmic universe as described in *Beowulf*. The point of departure for the formulation of the model was the idea that the complete human person is composed of a number of constituents: 'body', 'life', 'mind', 'worth', and 'soul'. The model is focused on the constituent that I have called 'worth', and it is clear how this is exchangeable with valuable *objects* of exchange. In the different rituals related to the male life-cycle the constituents 'body' and 'worth' are successively brought together, developed and broken up again. These transformations of the person are not natural but require the activating of different relationships within the human community and also of relationships between this community and the supernatural world. The transformations are realized by the exchange of valuables. In the totality of relationships we can discern what 'society as a whole' is. The model describes in fact not only how male youths become adult in relation to a king, but also how the king at his death in relation to the constituent parts of his people, as represented by his adult warrior-followers with lordships of their own, is elevated to an ancestor.

My model has certain implications for the dominant perspective on *Gefolgschaft* as indicated in the introduction. Modern definitions and models of *Gefolgschaft* are politico-economically oriented and therefore do not satisfy the rather different requirements highlighted in the formulation of the model offered here. In the first place, accepted models only describe relationships between the living. Yet I have emphasised how relationships in the human world are embedded in a more encompassing pre-Christian or Christian socio-cosmic universe of relations. Relationships within the socio-political arena thus cannot be understood separately from the relationships that transcend them in value, that is the relationships between people and supernatural entities. As indicated, *Beowulf* poses problems if we want to chart these relationships. On the one hand a universalistic, Christian God plays a leading role, but to the pre-Mosaic principal characters He is inaccessible through exchange; on the other hand entities are recognizable, ancestors and half-human/half-animal monsters,[121] that played a key role in exchange in what before Christianization had been a cosmomorphic society.

In the second place, we tend to assume as a matter of course a modern distinction between subject and object in exchange. They are individuals of a certain social category who exchange objects and these objects are valued because they are useful, rare, or valuable. Various indications can be found in *Beowulf* that Anglo-Saxon man had a much more intensive involvement with what was exchanged. The strong identification of the Anglo-Saxons with valuables is not only the result of a preoccupation with status, power or public display. It is something that we should take rather literally. As we have seen in *Beowulf*, valuables and the constituents 'worth' and probably also 'life', both of which were essential for the development of the Anglo-Saxon aristocratic person, were equivalent. This insight forms the basis of my model of the social structure sketched out in *Beowulf*.

Thirdly and finally, the link between *Gefolgschaft* on the one hand and the life-cycle rituals of the warrior-followers and the king on the other hand is made only occasionally.[122] Analysis of *Beowulf* shows these successive rituals were an important temporal dimension of *Gefolgschaft*, and makes clear that warrior-followers, lords and kings were involved in a grand ritual project in which the king and his group of adult warrior-followers fulfilled complementary ritual roles: the warrior-followers developed from children to adults, and the deceased lord or king was transformed into an ancestor. The sociopolitical entanglements between warrior-followers themselves, between warrior-followers and kings, and between kings themselves which claim most attention in modern research, cannot be understood apart from this more *encompassing* ritual-cosmological context.

Where the concept of power is seen as central, a concept of the individual is often implied that is synonymous with our modern one:

---

[121] For the monsters, see note 116.
[122] See, however, Y. Hen, *Culture and religion in Merovingian Gaul AD 481–751* (Leiden, New York and Cologne, 1995), especially pp. 137–143.

a non-reducible entity that takes up a key position in society. Personal acts, even acts that to the participants are religiously motivated, are alleged to derive their rationale from increases of economic, socio-political or symbolic capital and enhanced authority for the actor or his group. Following Dumont, I have argued instead, that the place and valuation of the individual are ethnographic matters. One can thus point to both differences and similarities between the place and valuation of the individual among the 'Are'are and in *Beowulf*. We recognize in *Beowulf*, at the highest level of value, where the constituent 'soul' and the value 'righteousness' are central, something that is absent among the 'Are'are: what Dumont has called in a general sense 'the individual-outside-the-world', to distinguish it from the 'the individual-in-the-world' as in modern individualism, and for Christianity in particular 'the individual-in-relation-to-God'. In Christian teaching, Dumont writes: '[t]he individual soul receives eternal value from its filial relationship to God, in which relationship is also grounded human fellowship: Christians meet in Christ, whose members they are. This tremendous affirmation takes place on a level that transcends the world of man and of social institutions, although these are also from God. The infinite worth of the individual is at the same time the disparagement, the negation in terms of value, of the world as it is [. . .]'.[123]

Furthermore we see, at the level where the constituent 'image' (for the 'Are'are) or 'worth' (for *Beowulf*) and the value of 'reputation' (for both) are central, both similarities and differences between the 'Are'are and society as described in *Beowulf*.[124] It is these differences that make *Beowulf* interesting from a comparative perspective. Here the principal characters voice a pronounced self-consciousness, as expressed in the 'worth' of a person. Perhaps this self-consciousness is comparable to that of the 'peace-master' and the 'killer' among the 'Are'are. An important difference, however, is that each principal character in *Beowulf* also shows a strong ambition to remain as a namebearing entity *after* his death. People should remember him for a long time and over a vast area. This memory is anchored in

---

[123] L. Dumont, "The Christian beginnings: From the outworldly individual to the individual-in-the-world", *Essays on individualism. Modern ideology in anthropological perspective*, ed. L. Dumont (Chicago and London, 1986 (1983)), p. 30.

[124] I pass over the difference that with the cosmomorphic 'Are'are it concerns the highest level and with *Beowulf* a subordinate level (subordinate to the universalistic level of value of 'soul' and 'righteousness', see above).

the objects of exchange used by him and in objects from the built environment associated with them, such as halls and burial mounds. The individual is here not an 'individual-outside-the-world' *pur sang* but at the same time an 'individual-in-the-world', as a remembered *social* person, and 'outside-the-world', as a specific ancestor. There is no question of a complete anonymising of the 'worth' brought together in life, as in the dissolving directly after death of 'image' in the circulation of 'Are'are shell money. Two final remarks put this interpretation into perspective. *Beowulf* is no ethnography but a narrative about persons of mythical proportions, in particular Beowulf himself who in his actions lays the foundations for society.[125] What is therefore striking as regards the various objects of exchange that play a role in *Beowulf* is that we learn little about their history since it does not go back further than two generations. Yet it is worth noting that these objects are frequently only indicated as old heirlooms, something which does show a certain anonymity. A second remark concerns the role of the small gold rings, and minted and unminted gold and silver. In contrast to all other categories of gifts, these objects play a role in all relations of exchange: in the relationship between lord and warrior-follower, in the transition both from child to young warrior and from young warrior to adult; in the relationship between bridegivers and -takers; and in the relationship between royal families. From this we may carefully draw the conclusion that the different categories of gifts, and ultimately therefore also the 'worth' associated with a specific person, are convertible into these objects, or into the anonymous gold and silver that underlies these and from which new objects can be made.[126] Taking these two remarks together, we can conclude that an anonymising of 'worth', as with the 'Are'are, also plays a role in the world of *Beowulf*.

---

[125] Cf. note 116

[126] They even make the change-over possible between a 'sphere of long-term exchange' aimed at the reproduction of the socio-cosmic universe and a 'sphere of short-term exchange' where buying and selling and calculation are dominant (see for both concepts M. Bloch and J. Parry, "Introduction: money and the morality of exchange", *Money and the morality of exchange*, eds J. Parry and M. Bloch (Cambridge, 1989).

ACKNOWLEDGEMENTS

This paper is based on my dissertation (J. Bazelmans, *Één voor allen, allen voor één. Tacitus'* Germania, *de Oudengelse* Beowulf *en het ritueel-kosmologische karakter van de relatie tussen heer en krijger-volgeling in Germaanse samenlevingen* (Amsterdam, 1996) which has been published in English as *By weapons made worthy. Lords, retainers and their relationship in* Beowulf. (Amsterdam University Press, 1999). My dissertation supervisors Anthonie Heidinga (Amsterdam) and Jos Platenkamp (Münster), Rolf Bremmer (Leiden) and my colleagues at the Amsterdam Pionierproject 'Power and elite' owe many thanks. I wrote this paper as a fellow of the national research school ARCHON and I would like to thank the applicants of my grant, Wil Roebroeks, Nico Roymans and Frans Theuws, the ARCHON-board and its director prof.dr. L.P. Louwe Kooijmans (Leiden) for supporting interdisciplinary research in archaeology. Lotte Hedeager, Yitzhak Hen, Harry Fokkens and the members of the section 'Metaaltijden' of the Leiden Faculty of Archaeology read an earlier version of this paper and they are to be thanked for their constructive criticism. The Dutch text was translated by Kelly Fennema and she did a wonderful and swift job. Last but not least, Frans Theuws' and Jinty Nelson's editorial support was of immense value.

BIBLIOGRAPHY

Alexander, M., *Beowulf* (Harmondsworth, 1995).
Appadurai, A., "Introduction: commodities and the politics of value", *The social life of things*, ed. A. Appadurai (Cambridge, 1986), pp. 3–63.
Baal, J. van, *Man's quest for partnership. The anthropological foundations of ethics and religion* (Assen, 1981).
Barraud, C., D. de Coppet, A. Iteanu and R. Jamous, *Of relations and the dead. Four societies viewed from the angle of their exchanges* (Oxford and Providence, 1994 (1984)) (translation of: Des relations et des morts. Quatre sociétés vues sous l'angle des échanges, *Différences, valeurs, hiérachie. Textes offerts à Louis Dumont*, ed. J-C. Galey (Éditions de l'École des Hautes Études and Sciences Sociales, Paris).
Barraud, C., and J. Platenkamp, "Rituals and the comparison of societies", *Bijdragen van het Instituut voor Taal-, Land- en Volkenkunde* 146 (1990), pp. 103–122.
Bazelmans, J., "Conceptualising Early Germanic political structure. A review of the concept of Gefolgschaf", *Images of the past. Studies on ancient societies in Northwestern Europe*, eds. N. Roymans and F. Theuws (Amsterdam, 1991) (Studies in Pre- en Protohistorie 7), pp. 91–130.
———, *Één voor allen, allen voor één. Tacitus'* Germania, *de Oudengelse* Beowulf *en het ritueel-kosmologische karakter van de relatie tussen heer en krijger-volgeling in Germaanse samenlevingen* (Amsterdam, 1996) (Ph.D. dissertation).

Blackburn, F., "The Christian coloring in the *Beowulf*", *Publications of the Modern Language Association of America* 12 (1897), pp. 205–225.

Bloch, M., and J. Parry, "Introduction: money and the morality of exchange", *Money and the morality of exchange*, eds. J. Parry and M. Bloch (Cambridge, 1989), pp. 1–32.

Bradley, S.A.J., *Anglo-Saxon Poetry. An anthology of Old English poems in prose translation with introduction and headnotes* (London and Melbourne, 1982).

Chadwick, H., *The heroic age* (Cambridge, 1912).

Cherniss, M.D., *Ingeld and Christ. Heroic concepts and values in Old English Christian poetry* (The Hague and Paris, 1972).

Clemoes, P., and S. Greenfield, "Allegorical, typological or neither? Three short papers on the allegorical approach to *Beowulf* and a discussion", *Anglo-Saxon England* 2 (1973), pp. 285–302.

Colgrave, B, and R.A.B. Mynors, *Bede's Ecclesiastical history of the English people* (Oxford, 1991 (1969)) (Oxford Medieval Texts).

Coppet, D. de, 1981: "The life-giving death", *Mortality and immortality. The anthropology and archaeology of death*, eds. S.C. Humphreys and H. King (London, 1981) (Proceedings of a meeting of the research seminar in archaeology and related subjects held at the Institute of Archaeology, London University, in June 1980), pp. 175–204.

Donahue, C., "*Beowulf*, Ireland and the natural good", *Traditio. Studies in ancient and medieval history, thought and religion* 7 (1949–1951), pp. 263–277.

——, "*Beowulf* and the Christian tradition: a reconsideration from a Celtic stance", *Traditio. Studies in ancient and medieval history, thought and religion* 21 (1965), pp. 55–116.

Dumont, L., *Homo hierarchicus. The caste system and its implications* (Chicago and London, 1980 (1966)).

——, "The Christian beginnings: From the outworldly individual to the individual-in-the-world", *Essays on individualism. Modern ideology in anthropological perspective*, L. Dumont (Chicago and London, 1986 (1983)), pp. 23–59.

——, *From Mandeville to Marx. The genesis and triumph of economic ideology* (Chicago, 1977).

——, *German ideology. From France to Germany and back* (Chicago and London, 1991).

Ettmüller, L., Beowulf. *Heldengedicht des achten Jahrhunderts* (Zurich, 1840).

Fulk, R.D., *A history of Old English meter* (Philadelphia, 1992) (Middle Ages Series).

Godden, M.R., "The Anglo-Saxons on the mind", *Learning and literature in Anglo-Saxon England. Studies presented to Peter Clemoes on the occassion of his sixty-fifth birthday*, eds. M. Lapidge and H. Gneuss (Cambridge, 1985), pp. 271–298.

Goldsmith, M.E., *The mode and meaning of* Beowulf (London, 1970).

Graus, F., "Über die sogenannte germanische Treue", *Historica* 1 (1959), pp. 71–121.

Halverson, J., "*Beowulf* and the pitfalls of piety", *University of Toronto Quarterly* 35 (1966), pp. 260–278.

Haselgrove, C., "Culture process on the periphery: Belgic Gaul and Rome during the late Republic and early Empire", *Centre and periphery in the ancient world*, eds. M. Rowlands, M. Larsen and K. Kristiansen (Cambridge, 1987), pp. 104–124.

Hen, Y., *Culture and religion in Merovingian Gaul AD 481–751* (Leiden, New York and Cologne, 1995).

Huppé, B.F., *The hero and the earthly city. A reading of* Beowulf (Binghampton, 1984) (Medieval and Renaissance texts and studies 33).

Ingold, T., *Evolution and social life* (Cambridge, 1986).

Jack, G., Beowulf. *A student edition* (Oxford, 1994).

Kienast, W., "Germanische Treue und 'Königsheil'", *Historische Zeitschrift* 227 (1977), pp. 265–324.

Klaeber, Fr., "Die christlichen Elemente im *Beowulf*", *Anglia. Zeitschrift für englische Philologie* 35 (N.F. 23) (1911), pp. 111–136, 249–270, 453–482.

———, "Die christlichen Elemente im *Beowulf*, *Anglia*", *Zeitschrift für englische Philologie* 36 (N.F. 24) (1912), pp. 169–199.

———, *Beowulf and the Fight at Finnsburg* (Lexington, 1950³ (1922)).

Kroeschell, K., "Die Treue in der deutschen Rechtsgeschichte", *Studi Medievali*, Serie terza 10 (1969), pp. 465–498.

Leisi, E., "Gold und Manneswert im *Beowulf*", *Anglia* 71 (1953), pp. 259–273.

Lévi-Strauss, C., *Les structures élémentaires de la parenté* (Paris, 1949).

———, "Introduction à l'oeuvre de Marcel Mauss", *Sociologie et anthropologie*, Marcel Mauss (Paris, 1950), pp. ix–lii.

MacKenzie, M., *Androgynous objects. String bags and gender in central New Guinea* (Chur, 1991).

Mauss, M., "Essai sur le don. Forme et raison de l' échange dans les sociétés archaïques", *L'Année sociologique* 1 (1923–1924), pp. 30–186.

Mitchell, B., *An invitation to Old English and Anglo-Saxon England* (Oxford and Cambridge, 1995).

Niles, J.D., *Beowulf. The poem and its tradition* (Cambridge, 1983).

Ogilvy, J.D.A., and D.C. Baker, *Reading* Beowulf. *An introduction to the poem, its background and its style* (Norman, 1983).

Osborn, M., "The Great Feud: scriptural history and strife in *Beowulf*", *Publications of the Modern Language Association of America* 93 (1978), pp. 973–981.

Parker, M.A., Beowulf *and Christianity* (New York, 1987) (American University Series, Series 4, English Language and Literature 51).

Parry, J., "The gift, the Indian gift and the 'Indian gift'. The Maliowski memorial lecture 1985", *Man* N.S. 21 (1986), pp. 453–473.

Platenkamp, J.D.M., *Tobelo. Ideas and values of a North Moluccan society* (Leiden, 1988) (Ph.D. dissertation).

———, "Het samenwerkingsverband CASA-ERASME en de relatie Parijs-Leiden", *Recente ontwikkelingen in de Leidse antropologie*, ed. H.F. Vermeulen (Leiden, 1991) (ICA-publikatie 91), pp. 41–48.

Porter, J., Beowulf. *Text and translation* (Middlesex, 1991) (Anglo-Saxon Books).

Robinson, F.C., Beowulf *and the appositive style* (Knoxville, 1985).

———, "The tomb of Beowulf", *The tomb of Beowulf and other essays on Old English*, F.C. Robinson (Cambridge (Mass.) and Oxford, 1993), pp. 3–19.

Roymans, N., *Tribal societies in northern Gaul. An anthropological perspective* (Amsterdam, 1990) (Cingula 12).

Schlesinger, W., "Herrschaft und Gefolgschaft in der germanisch-deutschen Verfassungsgeschichte", *Historische Zeitschrift* 176 (1953), pp. 225–275.

Sisam, K., "Anglo-Saxon royal genealogies", *Proceedings of the British Academy* 39 (1953), pp. 287–348.

———, *The structure of* Beowulf (Oxford, 1965).

Stanley, E.G., *The search for Anglo-Saxon paganism* (Totowa, 1975).

Steuer, H., *Frühgeschichtliche Sozialstrukturen im Mitteleuropa. Eine Analyse der Auswertungsmethoden des archäologischen Quellenmaterials* (Göttingen, 1982) (Abhandlungen der Akademie der Wissenschaften in Göttingen, Philologisch-Historische Klasse, Folge 3, 128).

———, "Archaeology and history: proposals on the social structure of the Merovingian kingdom", *The birth of Europe: archaeology and social developments in the first millennium AD*, ed. K. Randsborg (Rome, 1989), pp. 100–122.

Strathern, M., *The gender of the gift. Problems with women and problems with society in Melanesia* (Berkely, Los Angeles and London, 1988), pp. 133–167.

Taylor, P., "The traditional language of treasure in *Beowulf*", *Journal of English and Germanic philology* 85 (1986), pp. 191–205.

Thomas, N., *Entangled objects. Exchange, material culture, and colonialism in the Pacific* (Cambridge (Mass.) and London, 1991).

Timmer, B.J., "*Wyrd* in Anglo-Saxon prose and poetry", *Neophilologus* 26 (1941), pp. 24–33, 213–228.

Tolkien, J.R.R., "*Beowulf*. The monsters and the critics", *An anthology of* Beowulf *criticism*, ed. L.E. Nicholson (Notre Dame, 1963), pp. 51–103 (originally published as *Proceedings of the British Academy* 22 (1936), 245–295, the Sir Israel Gollancz Memorial Lecture 1936).

Weiner, A.B., *Inalienable possessions: the paradox of keeping-while-giving*, Berkely (Los Angeles and Oxford, 1992).

Wenskus, R., "Die neuere Diskussion um Gefolgschaft und Herrschaft in Tacitus' *Germania*", *Beiträge zum Verständnis der* Germania *des Tacitus 2. Bericht über die Kolloquien der Kommission für die Altertumskunde Nord- und Mitteleuropas im Jahre 1986 und 1987*, eds. G. Neumann and H. Seemann (Göttingen, 1992) (Abhandlungen der Akademie der Wissenschaften in Göttingen. Philologisch-historische Klasse. Dritte Folge, 195), pp. 311–331.

Whallon, W., *Formula, character, and context: studies in Homeric, Old English, and Old Testament poetry* (Washington, 1969).

Whitelock, D., *The audience of* Beowulf (Oxford, 1951).

Wormald, C.P., "The uses of literacy in Anglo-Saxon England and its neighbours", *Transactions of The Royal Historical Society, fifth series* 27 (1977), pp. 95–114.

Wormald, P., "Bede, *Beowulf* and the conversion of the Anglo-Saxon aristocracy", *Bede and Anglo-Saxon England. Papers in honour of the 1300th anniversary of the birth of Bede, given at Cornell University in 1973 and 1974*, ed. R.T. Farrell (Oxford, 1978) (British Archaeological Reports 46), pp. 32–95.

——, "Anglo-Saxon society and literature", *The Cambridge companion to Old English literature*, eds. M. Godden and M. Lapidge (Cambridge, 1991), pp. 1–22.

THE CIRCULATION OF WEAPONS
IN ANGLO-SAXON SOCIETY

Heinrich Härke

Power in society is represented and continually reaffirmed by a variety of symbols and rituals which are, by their very purpose, not isolated, but interrelated. This interconnectedness makes it necessary to study them together, but this requires the analysis of several types of evidence. The traditional boundaries and specialised nature of academic disciplines all too often militate against the adoption of such a wider perspective. The discussions in the ESF Working Group 'Power and Society' have, in particular, highlighted the need for a joint treatment of historical and archaeological evidence. This paper is an attempt to provide such a treatment for one particular category of material symbols of power, and for one aspect of their use in one early medieval society.

Patterns in the archaeological evidence, and specific or incidental references in the texts suggest several mechanisms by which weapons could regularly and repeatedly change their owners, thus establishing and maintaining cycles of giving, receiving and deposition. These mechanisms and procedures operated within a framework of social relations and rituals. They are:

(1) the gift from lord to retainer (and between peers);
(2) the gift from retainer to lord (including the heriot);
(3) the heirloom;
(4) ritual deposition in graves and rivers.

These mechanisms, and the respective evidence for each of them, will be discussed below. However, before launching into the discussion and attempting to draw conclusions, it is necessary to address the problem of origin and dating of the various types of evidence marshalled below.

The evidence comprises weapon burials, river deposition, heroic poetry, law codes, wills and letters. Together, they span the entire Anglo-Saxon Period, from the fifth to the eleventh centuries: the weapon burial rite dates to the fifth to seventh/eighth centuries; the

Beowulf poem has been assigned variously to the eighth or the tenth
century, although it includes fifth century material; the laws on heriot,
and the wills date to the ninth to eleventh centuries. But it is arguable
that the various dates result primarily from the nature of the sources
themselves, and cannot be taken as proving tight dating limits for
the practices they describe or reflect.

For example, even though the custom of weapon burial ends
around AD 700, this is part of the general decline of the deposition
of grave-goods; the ritual deposition of weapons, however, seems to
continue in the form of river offerings. It is also obvious that heroic
poetry could not have been written down before the re-introduction
of literacy into England from the seventh century onwards, and
nobody would deny the existence and oral tradition of poetry before
that date, nor the existence of gift-giving, looting and other practices described in the later, written versions of the poems. And while
the earliest extant wills date from the early ninth century,[1] there can
be no doubt that the concept of inheritance was known in earlier
Anglo-Saxon society. Heirloom is referred to as an existing practice
in the earliest extant laws dating from the beginning of the seventh
century (Ethelbert of Kent, AD 602–603?), and appears to be implied
by inconsistencies in the grave-goods custom (cf. below). And for earlier Germanic society, Tacitus attests to the parallel existence of
inheritance and selective grave-goods custom.[2]

In spite of all the profound changes in Anglo-Saxon society, it
seems justified, therefore, to accept the various practices and mechanisms mentioned above as broadly contemporary, or overlapping
in time, between the seventh and ninth centuries AD. While individual practices originate earlier or continue beyond that time span,
the only context where they all appear together is the Beowulf poem.
Also, continuity of practice does not necessarily imply continuity of
meaning, and given the changing social context of the practices and
the various nature of our evidence, this is a caveat that needs to be
borne in mind throughout.

---

[1] M. Sheehan, *The will in medieval England: from the conversion of the Anglo-Saxons to the end of the thirteenth century* (Toronto, 1963), p. 23.

[2] Tacitus, *Germania*, c. 20; 27. The translation by Much has been used: R. Much (transl.), *Die Germania des Tacitus*, eds. H. Jankuhn and W. Lange (Heidelberg, 1967).

The Gift from Lord to Retainer

The function of the gift in the social order described in heroic poetry
of the post-Roman period is too well known to require further comment and analysis here.[3] The king is called 'ring-giver', 'giver of treasure', 'gold-friend of warriors', and 'provider of gold'.[4] The old king
Hrothgar advises the hero and future king Beowulf to 'study open-
handedness'.[5] The hall in which the scenes of gift-giving are played
out, becomes the 'gift-hall' or 'gold-giving hall'.[6] In return for gifts,
hospitality and protection, the king, 'sustainer of the warriors',[7] expects
and receives from his warriors pledges of loyalty and service—they
are to 'earn their mead' over which they have boastfully declared
their readiness to fight and, if necessary, die for their lord.[8]

Weapons, too, were handed out in hall to create an obligation.
This is most powerfully expressed in Wiglaf's speech as he addresses
the cowards who, by their refusal to help their lord Beowulf against
the dragon, shirk their duties:

> I remember the time, as we were taking mead
> in the banqueting hall, when we bound ourselves
> to the gracious lord who granted us arms,
> that we would make return for these trappings of war,
> these helms and hard swords . . .[9]

Like other gifts, weapons were also presented as reward for services
rendered, such as the slaying of the monster Grendel and his mother
for which the visiting hero Beowulf is rewarded by the Danish king
Hrothgar with sword, helmet, armour, eight war-horses, and other
treasures.[10]

It is not easy to differentiate and quantify the types of gifts mentioned for specific occasions, and given the formulaic nature of much

---

[3] Cf. paper by Bazelmans, this volume.

[4] Beowulf lines 1012, 1169–1171, 1476, 2070. The translation by Swanton has
been used: M. Swanton (transl.), Beowulf (Manchester, 1978).

[5] Beowulf line 1723.

[6] Beowulf lines 838, 1253, 1639.

[7] Beowulf line 3115.

[8] Beowulf lines 480–483; Finnesburh, The translation by Dobbie has been used:
E.V.K. Dobbie (transl.), The Anglo-Saxon poetic records, vol. VI: The Anglo-Saxon minor
poems (New York, 1958); Maldon lines 181–183, the translation of Whitelock has
been used: D. Whitelock (transl.), English historical documents c. 500–1042 (London
and New York, 1979²), pp. 319–324.

[9] Beowulf lines 2633–2637.

[10] Beowulf lines 1020–1045.

of heroic poetry, detailed quantification may be misleading, anyway. Gifts in the Beowulf poem include weapons, horses, unspecified treasures and gold, torques, collars, rings, arm-bands, a boar's head standard, robes, and land; the chief's stool and hall given to Beowulf apparently come with the estate given to him by Hygelac.[11] Weapons appear in more than half of all cases of gift-giving with named recipients. The only weapon types listed as gifts are swords, mail coats, and helmets (in roughly equal numbers). This limited range is of importance because other weapon types, such as shield, spear, knife (seax) and bow, are mentioned frequently throughout the poem as weapons in the hands of noble warriors.[12] If this is an attempt by the poet to heighten the impression of valuable gifts, it gives us, at the very least, an idea of the relative appreciation of certain types of weapons.

Comparison with archaeological evidence is almost impossible because the latter does not allow to distinguish clearly between gifts and other artefacts. But it has been suggested that the rings attached to some Early Saxon swords were given to retainers by the king as a mark of high esteem.[13] However, this need not imply that the sword itself had been a gift because sword and ring did not always belong together: there is evidence of rings attached, or removed, later.[14] The weapon types referred to as gifts in Beowulf are associated in Early Saxon burials with above-average wealth.[15] The complete absence in the poem of the axe (another weapon associated with wealth) may be due to chronological factors: it disappeared from graves by the early seventh century, and did not reappear as a weapon until the Late Saxon Period.

Gifts among peers are conspicuously rare in heroic poetry. In Beowulf, there is only one clear case involving a weapon.[16] On leaving the shores of Denmark, Beowulf gives a 'gold-cleated sword' to the coast guard, himself a thegn,[17] who had guarded the boat. This rarity is peculiar, and may have something to do with the nature

---

[11] *Beowulf* lines 2194–2195.

[12] H. Härke, *Angelsächsische Waffengräber des 5. bis 7. Jahrhunderts* (Köln and Bonn, 1992a), p. 46 table 1.

[13] H.R.E. Davidson, *The sword in Anglo-Saxon England* (Oxford, 1962).

[14] V.I. Evison, V.I., "The Dover ring-sword and other sword-rings and beads", *Archaeologia* 101 (1967), pp. 63–118. V.I. Evison, Sword-rings and beads, *Archaeologia* 105 (1976), pp. 303–315.

[15] Härke, *Angelsächsische Waffengräber des 5. bis 7. Jahrhunderts*, p. 160, fig. 26.

[16] *Beowulf* lines 1901–1903.

[17] Cf. *Beowulf* line 234.

and purpose of heroic poetry. Exchange of gifts between lords is attested to in other texts. In a letter from Charlemagne to King Offa of Mercia (dated AD 796), the former states that he has sent Offa 'for joy' the gift of 'a belt, a Hunnish [prob. Avar] sword and two silk palls'.[18]

The Gift from Retainer to Lord

Whilst the traditional model of the relationship between lord and retainer has gifts going in one direction, from lord to retainer, reciprocated by the latter with loyalty and service, it seems that some gifts, including weapons, were also passing in the opposite direction (fig. 1). Beowulf, on his return home, presents to king Hygelac the

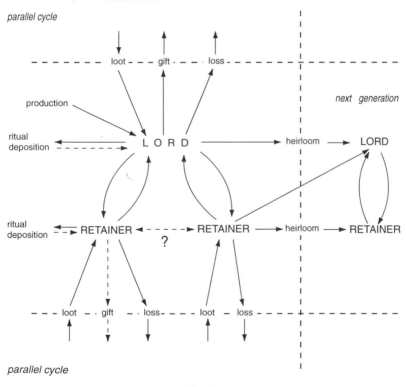

Fig. 1

---

[18] D. Whitelock, *English historical documents c. 500–1042* (London and New York, 1979²), p. 849.

gifts he has received from king Hrothgar for the slaying of Grendel, among them weapons, horses and gold.[19] The helmet, mail shirt and sword he gives to Hygelac are quite clearly not a gift from Hrothgar to Hygelac, but Beowulf's property—the poem says so. It also says that the mail shirt had belonged 'for a long while' to Hrothgar's brother and predecessor. And a Late Saxon will of the early 11th century lists a sword which the retainer Æthelwine had given to his lord Athelstan, and which was being returned to the former.[20]

Between the ninth and the eleventh centuries, the gift (or return) of weapons from follower to lord became formalised as heriot, and enshrined in law. The secular laws of King Cnut (issued probably between AD 1020 and 1023) stipulated that any nobleman of the rank of thegn or above had to provide for weapons and money to be given on the occasion of his own death to the king. This heriot was graded by rank, and differentiated by region (table 1).

rank	horses coats	helmets	mail	swords	spears	shields	money
WESSEX, MERCIA AND EAST ANGLIA:							
earl	8	4	4	4	8	8	200 mancuses
king's thegn	4	1	1	2	4	4	50 mancuses
lesser thegn	1	"a n d	?1	h i s	?1	w e a p o n s" ?1	2 pounds (Mercia+ E. Anglia only)
DANELAW							·
king's thegn	2	–	–	1	2	2	50 mancuses
king's thegn with right of jurisdiction	–	–	–	–	–	–	4 pounds
lesser thegn	–	–	–	–	–	–	2 pounds

Table 1: Heriots in the laws of Cnut

[19] *Beowulf* lines 2148–2162.
[20] *Whitelock, English historical documents c. 500–1042*, p. 596.

The emphasis on war equipment is conspicuous; money became a substitute only in the Danelaw (and in Wessex for lesser thegns who, instead of their weapons, may give their healsfang, the part of the wergild which went to the closest relatives).

This law ensured that the king had enough weapons and gold at his disposal to attract warriors into his service. Brooks has suggested that the origin of the heriot had been the return of some of the weapons with which the lord had equipped each of his followers.[21] The end of the grave-goods custom, early in the eighth century, may have led to an extension, and codification in law, of the heriot.

We may catch a glimpse of the early origins of the heriot in heroic poetry. When Beowulf announces his intention to confront Grendel, he asks his host Hrothgar:

> But if the fight should take me, you would forward to Hygelac
> this best of battle-shirts, that my breast now wears.
> The queen of warcoats, it is the bequest of Hrethel
> and from the forge of Wayland.[22]

It is interesting to note that the mail coat which is to be forwarded to Beowulf's lord, Hygelac, had originally been handed out by Hygelac's father. A close parallel is provided by the tenth century will of Ælfgar who gives to his royal lord the sword which the previous king Edmund had given him.[23] These two cases illustrate not just the return of weapons, but also the time depth involved in the circulation of certain weapons of high quality: the weapons are returned across the generations, to the successors of the lords from whom they had been received.

The Heirloom

The rules of inheritance in the Early and Middle Saxon Periods are virtually unknown.[24] Law codes refer to them only in passing, or imply their existence without specifying details.[25] This makes it impossible

---

[21] N.P. Brooks, "Arms, status and warfare in Late-Saxon England", *Ethelred the Unready*, ed. D. Hill (Oxford, 1978), pp. 91–92.

[22] *Beowulf* lines 452–455.

[23] D. Whitelock, *Anglo-Saxon wills* (Cambridge, 1930), pp. 7 and 104.

[24] Sheehan, *The will in medieval England: from the conversion of the Anglo-Saxons to the end of the thirteenth century*, p. 5.

[25] For example Ethelbert, 78; Hlothere and Eadric, 6; Ine, 23.

to establish to what degree weapons were passed on by this means
to the next generation. Incomplete weapon sets in Early Saxon graves
may provide indirect evidence of weapons not deposited with the
deceased.[26] In heroic poetry, swords are often called 'heirloom', and
in two cases at least, direct inheritance is referred to by Beowulf:

> Let Unferth have the blade that I inherited
> – he is a widely known man—this wave-patterned sword
> of rare hardness.[27]

Two aspects may be of importance here: the bequeathed sword is
clearly a very valuable, pattern-welded blade; and Beowulf appears
entitled to make provisions for the disposal of a weapon he had
acquired by way of inheritance. The second case, towards the end
of Beowulf's life when he is fatally wounded by the dragon, begins
with a statement of unfulfilled desire:

> I would now wish to give my garments in battle
> to my own son, if any such
> after-inheritor, an heir of my body,
> had been granted to me.[28]

But when he dies, he passes his helmet and armour, together with
golden collar and arm-ring, to Wiglaf, 'the last man left of our kindred, the house of the Waymundings'.[29]

Further direct evidence is provided by Late Saxon wills of the
ninth to eleventh centuries which occasionally list weapons among
the inheritable items.[30] Of the 39 wills and bequests compiled in
Whitelock's collection of Anglo-Saxon wills, 14 refer explicitly to
weapons.[31] All these cases include the transfer, or return, of military
equipment as heriot to the respective lord; four of these wills also
specify the disposal of weapons (swords and a coat of mail) to other
individuals.

The best-known, and most informative, of these is the will of

---

[26] H. Härke, "Early Saxon weapon burials: frequencies, distributions and weapon combinations", *Weapons and warfare in Anglo-Saxon England*, ed. S.C. Hawkes (Oxford, 1989); Härke, *Angelsächsische Waffengräber des 5. bis 7. Jahrhunderts*.

[27] *Beowulf* lines 1488–1490.

[28] *Beowulf* lines 2729–2732.

[29] *Beowulf* lines 2813–2814.

[30] Sheehan, *The will in medieval England: from the conversion of the Anglo-Saxons to the end of the thirteenth century*, p. 100; cf. paper by La Rocca, this volume, for a Frankish case.

[31] Whitelock, *Anglo-Saxon wills*.

Athelstan, the eldest son of king Ethelred, dating to between AD 1013 and 1015.[32] The items in the will include estates and other pieces of land, seven horses, valuable artefacts (a gold belt and arm-let, a drinking horn, a silver-coated trumpet, and a gold crucifix), and weapons. The latter comprise eleven swords and one blade, a coat of mail, and two shields. These weapons are individually described (swords by their hilt decoration or other characteristic features, shields by their shape) and assigned to their respective recipients (table 2).

social context of heirs	number of named heirs assigned to them	number of weapons	types of weapons
family	3	6	swords, mail coat
magnat	2	3	swords, shield
retainers	3	4	swords, shield
church	2	2	swords

Table 2: Weapons in the will of Athelstan

There appears to be some correlation between the social context of the heirs and the number of weapons given to them, as well as be-tween their social standing and the value of their weapons. The most valuable weapons stay within the family, left to the father and two brothers: the coat of mail, two silver-hilted swords, and the sword which had 'belonged to King Offa', apart from two other swords. The shields which may or may not be the most ordinary weapons in this will, are given to a magnate and a retainer. The swords assigned to Athelstan's mass priest (who was no allowed to wear weapons)[33] and to the church where Athelstan is to be buried, are quite valuable: an inlaid sword and a silver-hilted sword, respectively.

Some comments in the will are of relevance to the question of circulation. The coat of mail is mentioned as being presently in the possession (but obviously not ownership) of Morcar, a northern mag-nate, highlighting the possibility of lending even of high-status items. Two swords are listed as having belonged to others (King Offa and

---

[32] *Whitelock, Anglo-Saxon wills*, pp. 56–63; Whitelock, *English historical documents c. 500–1042*, pp. 593–596.
[33] *Whitelock, Anglo-Saxon wills*, p. 172.

Ulfketel, respectively), marking them out as items which have been in circulation for some time. And the retainer Æthelwine is given the sword 'he has given me'—in other words: the retainer's gift to his lord is returned on the occasion of the lord's death, an inversion of the heriot principle.

Ritual deposition

While weapons were circulating by the mechanisms identified and discussed above, some weapons were continually taken out of circulation and deposited in graves or rivers. There may even have existed a conceptual link between the gifts a person had received in life (or at the beginning of his active life), and the offerings accompanying him into his grave. This is suggested by a comment on the goods deposited in Scyld's funeral ship:

> This hoard was not less great than the gifts he had had from those who at the outset had adventured him over seas, alone, a small child.[34]

Scyld's funeral is one of three described in the *Beowulf* poem: they are the funerals of Scyld, Hnæf, and Beowulf himself.[35] All three are high-status affairs, involving two kings (Scyld and Beowulf) and one prince (Hnæf); and all three include the deposition of weapons as part of the ritual proceedings (table 3).[36]

In the case of Scyld, 'the weapons of a warrior', and more specifically swords and body-armour, were put into a boat, together with unspecified treasures (some of them said to be from far countries), and the boat was then pushed out to sea. Hnæf's pyre carried his body, together with gold, his 'bloody mail-shirt' and boar-decorated helmets, alongside the body of his nephew who had died in the same battle. When Beowulf's pyre was raised, mail-coats, shields and helmets were hung upon it 'as he had desired'; and when a barrow was raised for the remains of the hero, 'torques and jewels' from the dragon's hoard were placed in his tomb.

The impression of depositions of great 'wealth in the earth's keep-

---

[34] *Beowulf* lines 43–45.
[35] *Beowulf* lines 26–52, 1107–1124, 3137–3182.
[36] For a Lombard case of similarity between kingship rituals and burial ritual, cf. the paper by Gasparri, this volume.

funeral type	Scyld ship cast into the sea	Hnæf collective cremation	Beowulf cremation + barrow
weapons	x		
swords	x		
body armour	x	x	x
helmets		x	x
shields			x
other offerings and grave-goods:			
treasures	x		•
gold		x	x
torques and jewels			x

Table 3: Funerals in Beowulf

ing, the gold in the dirt'[37] appears to be deliberately heightened by describing multiple depositions of each weapon type, even the most precious ones (i.e. helmets, mail-coats etc.). This is in stark contrast to the burial evidence where weapon types, with the exception of the ubiquitous spear, are virtually never found in multiple sets.[38]

Archaeological evidence provides comparative data on the ritual deposition of weapons in Anglo-Saxon England. Between the early fifth and the late seventh/early eighth centuries, some 18% of all inhumation burials, and about 1 to 2% of cremations, were accompanied by weapons.[39] This practice shows marked regional and chronological variations, and its frequency varied with the age at death: relatively few subadults were accompanied by weapons, but 47% of male adult burials were. Whilst this is a high proportion, it still marks out this practice as a selective custom. Detailed analysis of the archaeological and skeletal data has led to the suggestion that in the fifth/sixth century, the deposition of weapons was used as an ethnic marker, whereas in the seventh century it became less frequent and turned increasingly into a status symbol of the social elite.[40]

---

[37] *Beowulf* lines 3166–3167.
[38] Härke, "Early Saxon weapon burials: frequencies, distributions and weapon combinations"; Härke, *Angelsächsische Waffengräber des 5. bis 7. Jahrhunderts.*
[39] H. Härke, "Warrior graves"? The background of the Anglo-Saxon weapon burial rite", *Past & Present* 126 (1990), pp. 22–43.
[40] H. Härke, "Changing symbols in a changing society: the Anglo-Saxon weapon

The full range of weapon types had been deposited in Anglo-Saxon inhumation graves (table 4).

	5th/6th cent.	7th cent.
spear	83.9	80.7
shield	55.0	33.0
sword	10.5	11.0
seax	1.6	15.6
axe	3.3	–
arrow	0.7	–
sample size	429	109

Table 4: Frequencies of weapon types in 538 datable Anglo-Saxon weapon burials; % of weapon burials with the respective type of weapon

Weapons not represented in this sample, primarily helmets and mail-coats, are not totally absent from graves, but they are rare and limited to a small number of high-status graves, such as Benty Grange and Sutton Hoo.[41] This underlines the observation that the rarest weapon types in archaeological contexts are the most frequent ones mentioned in texts as gifts, heriot, heirloom and funeral deposits. Chronological factors cannot have contributed to this discrepancy: seventh-century deposits in graves are as different from the weapon types in eighth to eleventh-century texts as are the fifth/sixth-century weapon graves.

The explanation, therefore, has to be looked for in social factors. Clearly then, the archaeological evidence from burials covers a broad social spectrum, whereas the funerals described in *Beowulf* are identified as belonging to the highest social stratum, that of kings and their kin. In other words: the swords, helmets, mail-coats and decorated shields circulating in society are almost exclusively high-status items. The fact that lower-status weapons, too, were buried may indicate that weapons were also circulating among the lower strata of

---

burial rite in the seventh century", *The age of Sutton Hoo*, ed. M. Carver (Woodbridge, 1992b), pp. 149–165.

[41] R.L.S. Bruce-Mitford, *Aspects of Anglo-Saxon archaeology: Sutton Hoo and other discoveries* (London, 1974). R.L.S. Bruce-Mitford, *The Sutton Hoo ship burial. Vol. 2: Arms, armour and regalia* (London, 1978).

society (i.e. among those men whose families participated in the weapon burial rite), but this cannot be proven.

The evidence for river deposition of weapons in Anglo-Saxon England is less abundant, but there appears to be relatively widespread evidence for this custom from the Late Saxon/Viking Period.[42] Hines has suggested that the ritual deposition of weapons seems to become more common as weapons disappear from the graves, and may be an alternative to that practice.[43] This would conform to a pattern observed for ritual deposition in prehistoric Britain and early medieval Western Europe: when weapons and valuables were deposited in graves, their deposition in rivers and bogs was rare, and vice versa.[44] In the Continental homelands of the Anglo-Saxons, weapons had been deposited in bogs in large numbers while weapon graves had been comparatively rare.[45] In the Early Saxon Period in England, the weapon burial rite became ubiquitous while river deposition declined (although it did not disappear completely if the spear types from rivers are anything to go by).[46] By the Late Saxon Period, weapon deposition had been phased out in Saxon cemeteries (though not in Viking graves) while river deposition was making a comeback.

The pattern appears to imply that there was always a mechanism by which weapons could be, and were, taken out of circulation, but the problems of the evidence suggest some caution. The clearest, and most closely datable evidence for both variants of ritual deposition comes from the Early Saxon Period. In the Late Saxon Period, it is virtually impossible to distinguish between Anglo-Saxon and Viking river deposits.[47] If it could be demonstrated that there was a continuous Anglo-Saxon tradition of ritual deposition, there is still

---

[42] R. Watson, *Viking Age river offerings in the British Isles* (York, 1995).

[43] J. Hines, "Religion", *The Anglo-Saxons: towards an ethnography*, ed. J. Hines (Woodbridge, in press).

[44] R. Bradley, "The destruction of wealth in later prehistory", *Man* 17 (1982), pp. 108–122. R. Bradley, *The passage of arms: an archaeological analysis of prehistoric hoards and votive deposits* (Cambridge, 1990).

[45] L. Hedeager, *Iron Age societies: From tribe to state in Northern Europe, 500 BC to AD 700* (Oxford and Cambridge (Mass.), 1992); J. Hines, "The military context of the adventus Saxonum some Continental evidence", *Weapons and warfare in Anglo-Saxon England*, ed. S.C. Hawkes (Oxford, 1989), pp. 25–48; M. Todd, *The northern barbarians 100 BC–AD 300*, Rev. ed. (Oxford, 1987).

[46] M.J. Swanton, *A corpus of Pagan Anglo-Saxon spear-types* (Oxford, 1974); Hines, "Religion".

[47] R. Watson, pers. comm.

the possibility that the meaning of the rituals changed over time, as Bradley has suggested for ritual deposition in prehistoric Britain.[48]

Maintaining the circulation

Deposited weapons, as well as damaged and broken ones, needed to be replaced in order to keep the circulation going. The three main methods of replacement appear to have been:

(a) production of new weapons
(b) loot
(c) grave robbery.

Most of the weapon types referred to in texts would be produced in royal or aristocratic contexts. The expertise and manpower required to make patternwelded blades, helmets and chain mail was probably beyond the capabilities of the ordinary village blacksmith; and the precious metals and materials used for the decoration of sword hilts, scabbards, helmets and mail coats (as well as some shields) required patronage which must have been beyond the means of most freemen. Close inspection of a sample of Early Saxon weapons suggests the existence of, at least, two levels of weapon production: an upper (regional?) level where sword blades and shield bosses were made, and a lower (local) level where shield bosses were fitted to boards, spearheads put on shafts, and repairs carried out.[49] The existence of an intermediate level for the production of spearheads (and similar items) is possible, unless this was carried out locally. The Early Saxon settlement evidence, and in particular the dispersed character of royal sites, does not allow the direct confirmation of workshops at high-status settlement sites in England although such a link has been found in areas with similar social structures, but a clearer settlement hierarchy including fortified élite habitation sites.[50]

---

[48] Bradley, *The passage of arms: an archaeologicalanalysis of prehistoric hoards and votive deposits*.

[49] Härke, *Angelsächsische Waffengräber des 5. bis 7. Jahrhunderts*, p. 140.

[50] For example Celtic Britain and Alamannic Southwest Germany; L. Alcock, *Economy, society and warfare among the Britons and Saxons* (Cardiff, 1987). L. Alcock, "The activities of potentates in Celtic Britain, AD 500–800: a positivist approach", *Power and politics in Early Medieval Britain and Ireland*, eds. S.T. Driscoll and M.R. Nieke (Edinburgh, 1988), pp. 22–46; V. Milojcic, "Der Runde Berg bei Urach", *Ausgrabungen in Deutschland gefördert von der Deutschen Forschungsgemeinschaft 1950–1975* (Mainz, 1975), pp. 181–198; U. Koch, *Der Runde Berg bei Urach, VIII: Frühgeschichtliche*

Looting of weapons is related in *Beowulf* in two cases, and both follow a very similar pattern:

> One sturdy warrior [Eofor] then stripped the other,
> took from Ongentheow his iron war-shirt,
> his hilted sword and his helmet also,
> the old man's accoutrement, and carried it to Hygelac.
> He accepted the harness with a handsome promise
> of rewards among the people; a promise he kept.[51]

Here, as in the case of Weoxstan killing Eanmund,[52] the valuable weapons (invariably sword, helmet and mail coat) are taken from the dead opponent and brought back to the lord of the victorious warrior. The lord, in turn, promises rewards, or immediately awards the looted weapons to his retainer who had brought them in.[53] Loot, then, was given to the lord for redistribution; this contributed to the circulation of weapons (and other goods) and oiled the wheels of the lord-follower relationship. Thus, loot was one of the basic requirements of heroic society because it brought in the goods needed to attract and maintain a warband. At the same time, loot supported the ideology of heroic society, presupposing as it did military action and success.

Grave robbery, whilst widespread in Merovingian cemeteries,[54] was much less frequent in Early Anglo-Saxon England, and mostly limited to Kent (table 5).[55]

Kentish cemeteries outside this sample have similar, or higher, incidences of robbed graves. Outside Kent, grave robbery appears to have been exceedingly rare.

It is interesting to note that the proportion of robbed weapon burials is higher at all sites than the proportion of robbed inhumations overall, suggesting that graves with weapons were targeted by the robbers who must have had knowledge of locations and contents of graves. A story related by Gregory of Tours demonstrates that in Francia, relatives occasionally recovered precious grave-goods from

---

Funde aus Bein, Geräte aus Ton und Stein aus den Plangrabungen 1967–1984 (Sigmaringen, 1994).

[51] *Beowulf* lines 2985–2990.
[52] *Beowulf* lines 2612–2618.
[53] *Beowulf* lines 2616–1618.
[54] H. Roth, "Archäologische Beobachtungen zum Grabfrevel im Merowingerreich, *Zum Grabfrevel in vor- und frühgeschichtlicher Zeit*, eds. H. Jankuhn, H. Nehlsen and H. Roth (Göttingen, 1978), pp. 53–84.
[55] Härke, *Angelsächsische Waffengräber des 5. bis 7. Jahrhunderts*, p. 65.

cemetery	number of inhumations	% robbed	number of weapon burials	% robbed
Bekesbourne II	38	2.6	4	–
Broadstairs I	113	1.8	24	8.3
Finglesham	256	3.5	28	7.1
Lyminge II	64	14.1	6	?
Polhill	130	0.8	17	5.9
Sarre	293	14.7	70	17.1

Table 5: Grave robbery in Kent

burials of family members.[56] In such cases, grave robbery may have been a means of, literally, 're-cycling' weapons, bringing them back into circulation. This could easily have created a separate sub-cycle of deposition, robbery, and re-deposition.

The circulation of weapons may have been affected by other actions and procedures, lending being one of them. For the fight against Grendel's mother, Beowulf borrows from Unferth the sword Hrunting, and returns it to him afterwards, thanking him 'for the lending of it'.[57] And it has already been noted that Athelstan's mail shirt which he included in his will was at that time with Morcar, a magnate and (one would imagine) friend of Athelstan's although he is not a beneficiary of the will.[58] Such temporary deposition of weapons with friends may not at all have been unusual. In some cases, it was necessary: the laws of Alfred (issued c. AD 885–899) stipulate that a man who breaks his oath should 'give his weapons and his possessions into his friends' keeping' while he is kept prisoner at a king's estate.[59] Short-term lending of weapons, and culpability arising from their misuse, is mentioned several times in the laws.[60] Theft must

---

[56] Gregory of Tours, *Libri Historiarum* VIII, 21. The translation used is: L. Thorpe (transl.), *Gregory of Tours: The History of the Franks*, (Harmondsworth, 1974); G. Halsall, "Female power and status in early Merovingian central Austrasia: the burial evidence", *Early Medieval Europe* 5 (1996), pp. 1–2.

[57] *Beowulf* lines 1488–1491 and 1707–1712.

[58] Cf. note 32.

[59] Laws of Alfred, 1. 2; see: D. Whitelock, *English historical documents c. 500–1042* (London and New York, 1979²), pp. 407–416.

[60] For example Alfred, 19–19. 2; see D. Whitelock, *English historical documents c. 500–1042* (London and New York, 1979²), pp. 407–416. Laws of Ethelbert, 18–20; see D. Whitelock, *English historical documents c. 500–1042* (London and New York, 1979²), pp. 391–394.

have been another means of changing ownership of weapons, but it does not require discussion in this context.

Discussion and conclusions

The mechanisms discussed above had the overall result that the same weapons could, and did, circulate in society (or sections thereof) for a considerable time, and that old weapons must have been around all the time alongside new ones. In the *Beowulf* poem, virtually every valuable sword is called 'ancient', 'ancestral' or 'heirloom'.[61] However, some caution is probably called for since the formula is applied with such regularity that it may well have been a literary convention. Even so, it may have expressed a perception or an ideal. But there is some support from other evidence for these epithets of age. Late Saxon wills suggest that swords, in particular, were handed down over several generations. The will of Athelstan lists a sword 'which belonged to King Offa'.[62] Whilst this assertion was taken at face value by Whitelock who accepted the implied age of over 200 years,[63] the statement may not be literally true; but it is safe to assume that the sword was very old and of Mercian origin.[64]

Archaeological evidence confirms that even while the deposition of weapons in graves was practised, some weapons had been around for a long time before they were deposited. The sword from Brighthampton grave 31 had fittings of various dates between the early fifth and the early sixth century,[65] suggesting that it was about 100 years old when buried. Other Early Saxon swords (e.g. from Petersfinger grave 21 and Pewsey graves 22 and 47) may not have been quite as old as that, but traces of wear and tear on, and replacement of, some of their scabbard fittings indicate a considerable period of circulation and use.[66] The York helmet, deposited in a disused well, provides similar evidence for the period after the end of the grave-goods custom. The decorative elements on the helmet suggest

---

[61] For example *Beowulf* lines 796, 1158, 1458, 1663–1664, 1903, 2563–2564, 2577, 2610, 2979.

[62] Cf. note 32.

[63] Whitelock, *Anglo-Saxon wills*, p. 171.

[64] Pers. comm. J. Nelson.

[65] T. Dickinson, *The Anglo-Saxon burial sites of the Upper Thames region, and their bearing on the history of Wessex, circa AD 400–700* (Oxford, 1976), pp. 257–263.

[66] Härke, *Angelsächsische Waffengräber des 5. bis 7. Jahrhunderts*, p. 88, footnote 106.

a date of manufacture between AD 750 and 775; the context in which it was found has been dated to the first half of the ninth century; and the extensive evidence for wear and tear (including abrasions from frequent polishing, a dent from a projectile point, and repairs of the mail curtain) confirms that the helmet had been in use for two or more generations.[67]

Wills and archaeological evidence lend some credence to the *Beowulf* formula of ancient weapons in the hands of noble warriors, and allow us to have another look at the pathways and time depth of circulation described in the poem. Some of the best information is provided on mail coats. Beowulf's own mail coat had belonged to Hrethel, his uncle and father of Hygelac, the present king.[68] In addition, Beowulf is given by Hrothgar a mail coat the successive transfers of which we can reconstruct:[69]

Heorogar (Danish king)
|
Hrothgar (Heorogar's brother and successor)
|
Beowulf (Hrothgar's guest, for his services)
|
Hygelac (Beowulf's lord and uncle, king of the Geats).

There can be little doubt that in due course, Hygelac will again hand out this mail coat to some retainer or visiting hero. But the above movements of the mail coat need not imply a time depth of more than a generation. A different pathway, and a time depth of at least two generations emerge for the weapons (helmet, mail coat and sword) which Weoxstan takes off Eanmund after killing him:[70]

Eanmund (Swedish prince in exile)
|
Weoxstan (killed Eanmund and looted his weapons)
|
Onela (Weoxstan's lord, Swedish king)
|
Weoxstan (received weapons as gift)
|
Wiglaf (son of Weoxstan).

The poem's author put it in a nut-shell: 'This mail-shirt travelled far . . .'.[71] This, indeed, seems to apply to many high-status weapons,

---

[67] Tweddle, D., *The Anglian helmet from 16–22 Coppergate* (London, 1992).
[68] *Beowulf* lines 452–455.
[69] *Beowulf* lines 2155–2162.
[70] *Beowulf* lines 2610–2624.
[71] *Beowulf*, line 2261.

and it may be one explanation for their extreme rarity in the archae-ological record. And while they were circulating and passed on from one generation to the next, their perceived value increased with age, in the process turning some of them into 'inalienable possessions' which had to be kept in the family because of their age and value.[72]

Many questions remain. Can we, or do we need to, identify an underlying idea or principle which links all these mechanisms? Can we explain it all in terms of gift-giving,[73] perhaps with the additional distinction of 'gifts to men' and 'gifts to gods'?[74] Or does Weiner's notion of 'inalienable possessions' offer a more powerful explanation for grave-goods and heirloom?[75] And in this context, what is the merit of the *hergewaete* (and *gerade*) argument which provides a link between Germanic property notions, rules of inheritance, grave-goods and (later) donations to the Church?[76]

There are also some wider questions raised by the identification of weapons circulating in the upper strata of Anglo-Saxon society. What other goods were circulating at the same time? Beowulf receives from Hrothgar and his consort not just weapons, but also other gifts of which he presents four horses and a gold standard to King Hygelac, and three horses and a golden collar to Queen Hygd.[77] Weapons, according to the testimony of graves and wills, belong to the male sphere. What, if anything, was circulating in the female sphere? Wills and laws highlight that Anglo-Saxon women did have some prop-erty rights, and their wills show a particular concern for jewellery, tapestries, precious vessels, bed furnishings and gowns, whereas men's wills dwell on war gear, horses and their trappings.[78]

Another question is: what kinds of goods, if any, were circulating

---

[72] A. Weiner, *Inalienable possessions* (Los Angeles and Oxford, 1992).

[73] M. Mauss, *The gift* (London, 1966). Cf. J. Parry, "The gift, the Indian gift and the 'Indian gift'", *Man* (N.S.) 21 (1986), pp. 453–473.

[74] C.A. Gregory, "Gifts to men and gifts to gods: gift exchange and capital accu-mulation in contemporary Papua", *Man* 15 (1980), pp. 626–652. C.A. Gregory, *Gifts and commodities* (London, 1982).

[75] Weiner, *Inalienable possessions*; J. Bazelmans, *De representatie van het geschenk in het Oud-Engelse epos 'Beowulf': het 'cultuurlijke' van het prestigegoed* (Leiden, 1992) (Conference paper).; cf. Bazelmans, this volume.

[76] P. Reinecke, "Reihengräber und Friedhöfe der Kirchen", *Germania* 9 (1925), pp. 103–107; C. Redlich, "Erbrecht und Grabbeigaben bei den Germanen", *For-schungen und Fortschritte* 24 (1948), pp. 177–180; A.J. Genrich, "Grabbeigaben und germanisches Recht", *Die Kunde* N.F. 22 (1971), pp. 189–226.

[77] *Beowulf* lines 2152–2176.

[78] Sheehan, *The will in medieval England: from the conversion of the Anglo-Saxons to the end of the thirteenth century*, p. 103.

in different sections of society, and were weapons among them? Certainly, the men of Beowulf's warband, too, carried 'ancestral swords',[79] and there is a large number of Anglo-Saxon weapon burials with the more ordinary shields and spears which may, or may not, have had their own cycles of movement and deposition. Sacred relics had separate mechanisms and spheres of circulation which did not include deposition in graves.[80] Then there is the question of transformation, of change over time. What did this circulation of goods look like in Late Roman times? Is the emphasis on weapons as gifts a post-Roman phenomenon, a consequence of social changes and the ideology of 'Heroic Society' which transformed the nature of gifts and of rituals?[81] Did Christianity when it entered the scene transform this circulation yet again, or was it affected and transformed itself by established patterns of gift-giving?

Finally, for the archaeologist it is a sobering thought that the artefactual evidence can illuminate only the tail end of this circulation of artefacts: their final deposition. At the very least, this realisation should induce some caution in the typological dating of high-status items. Beyond this, it should lead to more reflection on the context and purpose of the artefacts which are now our archaeological evidence.

ACKNOWLEDGEMENTS

I am indebted to all members of the ESF Working Group 'Power and Society' for providing the stimulating group atmosphere which encouraged me to elaborate the ideas presented in a short ad hoc presentation at our meeting in Strasbourg in 1994. I cannot claim special expertise in the evaluation of textual evidence, and whilst I have drawn on the help and advice of experts in the field, I would want to emphasize that any errors and oversights are entirely my own. In particular, I am grateful to Janet Nelson for critical as well as encouraging comments, and Cristina La Rocca for providing questions and references on wills. I also wish to thank Richard Watson

---

[79] *Beowulf* line 796.

[80] P. Geary, "Sacred commodities: the circulation of medieval relics", *The social life of things*, ed. A. Appadurai (Cambridge, 1986), pp. 169–194.

[81] Cf. Le Jan, this volume.

(York) and Guy Halsall (London) for information on river deposits and written sources on Merovingian grave robbery, respectively, and Richard Bradley (Reading) for his comments on an earlier draft of this paper.

BIBLIOGRAPHY

Primary Sources

Alfred, Laws of: D. Whitelock, *English historical documents c. 500–1042* (London and New York, 1979²), pp. 407–416.
Athelstan, Will of: D. Whitelock, *English historical documents c. 500–1042* (London and New York, 1979²), pp. 593–596.
Beowulf: M. Swanton, (transl.), *Beowulf* (Manchester, 1978) (Manchester Medieval Classics Series).
Charlemagne's letter to Offa: D. Whitelock, *English historical documents c. 500–1042* (London and New York, 1979²), pp. 848–849.
Ethelbert, Laws of: D. Whitelock, *English historical documents c. 500–1042* (London and New York, 1979²), pp. 391–394.
Finnesburh, The Fight at: E.V.K. Dobbie, (transl.), *The Anglo-Saxon poetic records, vol. VI: The Anglo-Saxon minor poems* (New York, 1958).
Gregory of Tours *Libri Historiarum decem*: L. Thorpe (transl.), *Gregory of Tours: The History of the Franks* (Harmondsworth, 1974) (Penguin Classics).
Maldon, The Battle of: D. Whitelock, (transl.), *English historical documents c. 500–1042* (London and New York, 1979²), pp. 319–324.
Tacitus, *Germania*: R. Much, (transl.), *Die Germania des Tacitus*, eds. H. Jankuhn and W. Lange (Heidelberg, 1967).

Secondary Sources

Alcock, L., *Economy, society and warfare among the Britons and Saxons* (Cardiff, 1987).
——, "The activities of potentates in Celtic Britain, AD 500–800: a positivist approach", *Power and politics in Early Medieval Britain and Ireland*, eds. S. T. Driscoll and M.R. Nieke (Edinburgh, 1988), pp. 22–46.
Bazelmans, J., *De representatie van het geschenk in het Oud-Engelse epos 'Beowulf': het 'cultuurlijke' van het prestigegoed* (Leiden, 1992) (Conference paper).
Bradley, R., "The destruction of wealth in later prehistory", *Man* 17 (1982), pp. 108–122.
——, *The passage of arms: an archaeological analysis of prehistoric hoards and votive deposits* (Cambridge, 1990).
Brooks, N.P., "Arms, status and warfare in Late-Saxon England", *Ethelred the Unready*, ed. D. Hill (Oxford, 1978) (British Archaeological Reports 59), pp. 81–103.
Bruce-Mitford, R.L.S., *Aspects of Anglo-Saxon archaeology: Sutton Hoo and other discoveries* (London, 1974).
——, *The Sutton Hoo ship burial. Vol. 2: Arms, armour and regalia* (London, 1978).
Davidson, H.R.E., *The sword in Anglo-Saxon England* (Oxford, 1962).
Dickinson, T., *The Anglo-Saxon burial sites of the Upper Thames region, and their bearing on the history of Wessex, circa AD 400–700* (Oxford, 1976) (Unpubl. D. Phil. thesis).
Evison, V.I., "The Dover ring-sword and other sword-rings and beads", *Archaeologia* 101 (1967), pp. 63–118.
——, Sword rings and beads, *Archaeologia* 105 (1976), pp. 303–315.

Geary, P., "Sacred commodities: the circulation of medieval relics", *The social life of things*, ed. A. Appadurai (Cambridge, 1986), pp. 169–194.

Genrich, A.J., "Grabbeigaben und germanisches Recht", *Die Kunde* N.F. 22 (1971), pp. 189–226.

Gregory, C.A., "Gifts to men and gifts to gods: gift exchange and capital accumulation in contemporary Papua", *Man* 15 (1980), pp. 626–652.

——, *Gifts and commodities* (London, 1982).

Härke, H., "Early Saxon weapon burials: frequencies, distributions and weapon combinations", *Weapons and warfare in Anglo-Saxon England*, ed. S.C. Hawkes (Oxford, 1989) (Oxford University Committee for Archaeology Monograph 21), pp. 49–61.

——, "Warrior graves"? The background of the Anglo-Saxon weapon burial rite", *Past & Present* 126 (1990), pp. 22–43.

——, *Angelsächsische Waffengräber des 5. bis 7. Jahrhunderts* (Köln and Bonn, 1992a) (Zeitschrift für Archäologie des Mittelalters, Beiheft 6).

——, "Changing symbols in a changing society: the Anglo-Saxon weapon burial rite in the seventh century", *The age of Sutton Hoo*, ed. M. Carver (Woodbridge, 1992b), pp. 149–165.

Halsall, G., "Female power and status in early Merovingian central Austrasia: the burial evidence", *Early Medieval Europe* 5 (1996), pp. 1–24.

Hedeager, L., *Iron Age societies: From tribe to state in Northern Europe, 500 BC to AD 700* (Oxford and Cambridge (Mass.), 1992).

Hines, J., "The military context of the adventus Saxonum some continental evidence", *Weapons and warfare in Anglo-Saxon England*, ed. S.C. Hawkes (Oxford, 1989) (Oxford University Committee for Archaeology Monograph 21), pp. 25–48.

——, "Religion", *The Anglo-Saxons: towards an ethnography*, ed. J. Hines (Woodbridge, in press).

Koch, U., *Der Runde Berg bei Urach, VIII: Frühgeschichtliche Funde aus Bein, Geräte aus Ton und Stein aus den Plangrabungen 1967–1984* (Sigmaringen, 1994) (Heidelberger Akademie der Wissenschaften, Kommission für Alamannische Altertumskunde, Schriften Bd. 14).

Mauss, M., *The gift* (London, 1966) (translation of the original French edition of 1923–1924).

Milojcic, V., "Der Runde Berg bei Urach", *Ausgrabungen in Deutschland gefördert von der Deutschen Forschungsgemeinschaft 1950–1975* (Mainz, 1975) (Römisch-Germanisches Zentral-Museum, Monographien Bd. 1.2), pp. 181–198.

Parry, J., "The gift, the Indian gift and the 'Indian gift'", *Man* (N.S.) 21 (1986), pp. 453–473.

Redlich, C., "Erbrecht und Grabbeigaben bei den Germanen", *Forschungen und Fortschritte* 24 (1948), pp. 177–180.

Reinecke, P., "Reihengräber und Friedhöfe der Kirchen", *Germania* 9 (1925), pp. 103–107.

Roth, H., "Archäologische Beobachtungen zum Grabfrevel im Merowingerreich, *Zum Grabfrevel in vor- und frühgeschichtlicher Zeit*, eds. H. Jankuhn, H. Nehlsen and H. Roth (Göttingen, 1978) (Abhandlungen der Akademie der Wissenschaften in Göttingen, Phil.-Hist. Klasse, 3rd ser., vol. 113), pp. 53–84.

Sheehan, M., *The will in medieval England: from the conversion of the Anglo-Saxons to the end of the thirteenth century* (Toronto, 1963) (Pontifical Institute of Mediaeval Studies, Studies and Texts, 6).

Swanton, M.J., *A corpus of Pagan Anglo-Saxon spear-types* (Oxford, 1974) (British Archaeological Reports 7).

Todd, M., *The northern barbarians 100 BC–AD 300*. Rev. ed. (Oxford, 1987).

Tweddle, D., *The Anglian helmet from 16–22 Coppergate* (London, 1992) (The Archaeology of York vol. 17 fasc. 8).

Watson, R., *Viking Age river offerings in the British Isles* (York, 1995) (Unpubl. M.A. thesis University of York).

Weiner, A., *Inalienable possessions. The paradox of keeping while giving* (Los Angeles and Oxford, 1992).

Whitelock, D., *Anglo-Saxon wills* (Cambridge, 1930) (Cambridge Studies in English Legal History).

——, *English historical documents c. 500–1042* (London and New York, 1979²).

A KIND OF MIRROR FOR MEN: SWORD DEPOSITIONS IN LATE ANTIQUE NORTHERN GAUL[1]

Frans Theuws and Monica Alkemade

> Along with sable furs, and slave-boys who shine with the fair colour of barbarians, your fraternity has sent me swords, so sharp that they can even cut through armour, more costly than gold for their steel. Polished splendour glows from them, and reflects in complete clarity the faces of their admirers; their edges converge on the point with such equality that you would think they were cast in the furnace, rather than shaped by files. The centre of the blade is hollowed into a beautiful groove wrinkled by serpentine patterns: there such a variety of shadows plays together that you would suppose the gleaming metal to be a tapestry of various tints. All this your grindstone has diligently sharpened, your shining sand has carefully scoured, to make the steely light into a kind of mirror for men. (. . .) For their beauty the swords might be thought the work of Vulcan, he who fashioned implements of such grace that men believed the work of his hands to be not mortal, but divine.
>
> (Cassiodorus, *Variae* V:1)[2]

1. *Introduction*

Since the nineteenth century, descriptions like these have stirred the imagination of many. The Romantic nostalgia for a world long-gone has created an image of early medieval society which in every respect contradicts the rationalism and efficiency of modern life. This modern appreciation is however ambiguous. The valuation of medieval life seems to oscillate between images of on the one hand a Paradise Lost where brave heroes' deeds smoothed the path to civilization,

[1] The topic is part of the research on late Roman and Merovingian elite-groups in Northern Gaul, which the authors since 1990 have carried out within the 'Pionier-project Power & Elite' (Instituut voor Pre- en Protohistorische Archeologie, University of Amsterdam)—financed by the Netherlands Organization for Scientific Research (N.W.O.).

[2] The translation is taken from *The* Variae *of Magnus Aurelius Cassiodorus Senator*, trans. S.J.B. Barnish (Liverpool, 1992), p. 83. The swords mentioned were received as a present by Theoderic, king of the Ostrogoths, from the king of the Warni.

and on the other a Dark Age where men's lives and actions were governed by unpredictable and exotic forces.[3] In intellectual and academic discourse the two perspectives have become almost inextricably intertwined.

The goal of this study is to analyse processes of structural transformation in Late Antique and Frankish society from an archaeological perspective. We will try to achieve this by describing and interpreting chronological and geographical patterns in sword-depositions in northern Gaul. The changing patterns in archaeological depositions are interpreted in terms of changing conceptions of social positions and changing world-views and ideologies by Late Antique and early medieval aristocrats in northern Gaul and the northern Frankish kingdom.

In modern research, the qualities of the early medieval sword are generally attributed to the field of magic, as some underdeveloped understanding of cause and effect. This modern, *etic* description is however heavily influenced by popular stereotypes of non-modern behaviour and tends to distort a proper understanding of past behaviour and thought. We will therefore work from an *emic* or participants' perspective which does more justice to contemporaneous human experience, and try to analyse the meaning of the sword in terms that are meaningful to contemporary actors.

Two types of depositions are dominant in the archaeological record from the fifth to the tenth centuries: those in graves and those in rivers. Other depositions may occur, such as those in treasures of kings and aristocrats or in churches, but these are archaeologically 'invisible' and only occasionally mentioned in written sources. In this paper, the deposition of swords will be studied as a ritual of power', i.e. one of the 'very different kinds of rituals at various levels of society which may contribute towards an understanding of the socio-cosmological order in all its aspects'.

In applying some recent thoughts and ideas on the role of objects in rituals, our focus on the deposition of swords is determined by at least two strategic considerations. First, where archaeological inven-

---

[3] Up to the present day, the centuries between the fall of the Roman Empire and the christianization of Europe (Migration Period or *Völkerwanderungszeit*) are invariably described as the 'crucial episode' in which the outlines of European history were established. Cf. also note 8.

tories and analyses of comparable prestigious find-categories remain incomplete, the position of swords as a special category of objects in late Roman and early medieval society can safely be assumed on the basis of textual and iconographic sources.[4] Second, the activities of generations of archaeologists have provided us with a relatively broad set of data for an archaeological contribution to the debate on the integration of interpretations of both material culture and texts as we consider the transformation of the Roman world.

In section two we will question some basic assumptions on the nature of archaeological sources. We do this in order to be able to formulate some alternative perspectives on the meaning of material culture deposited in late Roman and early medieval graves. In section three we proceed to delineate the special significance of the sword in establishing meaningful relationships in early medieval society. In section four we will present an analysis of late Roman and early Merovingian sword-depositions, which reveal interesting aspects of the ritual use of swords. In section five we will comment on the use of the sword in the burial ritual.

This article is a first attempt to formulate ideas on the basis of a dataset which is complex, and difficult to grasp in all its aspects.[5] Several times we will be confronted with the limitation of our present analysis. However, by making certain problems explicit and by insisting on the need to question many interpretations hitherto assumed to rest on solid ground we hope to contribute to a growing debate on the meaning of material culture in late antique and medieval society.

---

[4] Cf. O. Bouzy, "Les armes symboles d'un pouvoir politique: l'épée du sacre, la sainte lance, l'oriflamme aux VIIIe–XIIe siècles", *Francia* 22 (1995), pp. 45–47.

[5] A modern archaeological synthesis of sword-finds is lacking. There are some monographs (E. Behmer, *Das zweischneidige Schwert der germanischen Völkerwanderungszeit* (Stockholm, 1939). W. Menghin, *Das Schwert im frühen Mittelalter. Chronologisch-typologische Untersuchungen zu Langschwertern aus germanischen Gräbern des 5. bis 7. Jahrhunderts* (Stuttgart, 1983). A. Geibig, *Beiträge zur morphologischen entwicklung des Schwertes im Mittelalter. Eine Analyse des Fundmaterials vom ausgehenden 8. bis zum 12. Jahrhundert aus Sammlungen der Bundesrepublik Deutschland* (Neumünster, 1991)) but their focus is mainly on typochronological questions, which means that only a part (mostly the most prestigious items) of the finds are selected in order to reconstruct a general development (on this, see also our remarks in section 4 below). It was therefore necessary to make a new catalogue of sword finds and of sword-belt finds. Our analysis of sword-depositions forms part of the authors' research-project (cf. note 1) and spans the period AD 300 to AD 1000. This paper deals with the swords from the fifth and early sixth centuries.

2. The tradition of archaeological research

2.1. The background

In the late Roman period, a remarkable change occurs in the nature of the archaeological record from northern Gaul, the region between the rivers Rhine and Seine. From the middle of the fourth century onwards, archaeologists are confronted with a huge increase in the number of inhumation graves containing sets of weapons,[6] accessories (belts, buckles, *fibulae*, etc) and tableware (pots, saucers, goblets, buckets, etc). In the archaeology of late Roman and early medieval northern Gaul, it has become customary to refer to these graves as *Germanic*, on the basis of an assumed 'un-Roman' appearance and use of material culture.[7] The occurrence of such graves within the borders of the Roman empire has been linked with the migration of Germanic tribes from over the Rhine. In this way, archaeological evidence has been thought to fill the gap in our knowledge on the sequence of events leading up to what came to be called The Fall of the Roman Empire in the West.

The contours of a massive and dramatic *Völkerwanderung*, something that almost took on the character of a European origin myth, were established in the course of the nineteenth century in the modern historiography of the emerging European nation-states, notably France and Germany.[8] This has had far-reaching implications for

---

[6] Against prevailing opinion, A. Van Doorselaer ("Le problème des mobiliers funéraires avec armes en Gaule septentrionale a l'époque du Haut Empire romain", *Helinium* 5 (1965), pp. 118–129) maintained that the practice of burying weapons in late Roman Northern Gaul was not an entirely new phenomenon. He argued that during Roman times, weapon-burials werer never wholly absent. The spectacular increase of weapon-burial in late Roman Gaul may thus be only relative, but to our view it is not less significant. For a new discussion on Roman (first century) weapon burials and depositions at cult places see: N. Roymans, "The sword or the plough. Regional dynamics in the romanisation of Belgic Gaul and the Rhineland area", *From the sword to the plough. Three studies on the earliest romanisation of northern Gaul*, ed. N. Roymans (Amsterdam, 1996), pp. 9–126.

[7] Apart from graves, the same objects are to a lesser extent also known from watery contexts (rivers and bogs) and hoards.

[8] L. Hedeager, "The creation of a Germanic identity. A European origin-myth", *Frontières d'empire. Nature et signification des frontières romaines*, eds. P. Brun, S. Van der Leeuw and Ch.R. Whittaker (Nemours, 1993) pp. 121–131 labels the *Völkerwanderungszeit* as the 'origin myth' of many a European nation, where the peoples of prehistoric Europe are seen to have set foot on the path of history and civilization. Cf. also note 3, and Hedeager below in this volume.

the development of late Roman and early medieval archaeology in northern Gaul. A fixation on supposed Germanic characteristics led researchers to separate the finds from their find-contexts, and the finds themselves were subsequently reified into the 'material culture' of a biologically defined homogeneous, ethnic community. Since then, this material culture came to be considered as the physical reflection of 'culture', that is as the externalized version of a set of characteristics inherent in a people (*Volk*), group or nation. From that time on archaeological research was going to make a substantial contribution towards the construction of a German(ic) identity, which is a characteristic feature of the development of *Germanenforschung* in this period.[9] We would agree that in this way, early medieval grave-field research became a *pièce de résistance* in thinking on the origin and genesis of European culture, a tendency we see up to the present day reflected in different national research traditions.[10]

For the period to the end of the eighth century, late Roman and early medieval objects, and especially those from graves, constitute the major part of archaeologists' data on the processes of transformation in this northern periphery[11] of the Roman world. The object's

---

[9] For a critical review of the *Germanenforschung* see J. Bazelmans, "Conceptualising early Germanic political structure: a review of the use of the concept of Gefolgschaft", *Images of the Past. Studies on ancient societies in northwestern Europe*, eds. N. Roymans and F. Theuws (Amsterdam, 1991), pp. 91–129.

[10] It is interesting to observe that the national identity of a scholar even today can be identified on de basis of his/her approach of the subject of research. In Germany the analysis of cemeteries has been a central theme since the nineteenth century: the research had its context in the unification of the German state and the creation of a national identity. In France the analysis of early medieval cemeteries has until recently been an almost peripheral topic. Archaeological research there has been more directed towards the Roman and Celtic pre- and protohistory. Until recently the Franks were sometimes seen as a people that violated the French nation and brought down the perfect Roman civilisation. This perspective on the fall of the Roman empire can be explained against the background of the deteriorating relations between Germany and France since 1870, but was also embedded in the humanistic world-view that has lingerd on in French research since the sixteenth century. The influence of these contexts is not to be underestimated when considering the unequal state of research and publication that form one of the factors which complicate our present work. See also: B. Effros, *From Grave Goods to Christian Epitaphs: Evolution in Burial Tradition and the Expression of Social Status in Merovingian Society* (Los Angeles, 1994) (unpublished dissertation University of California).

[11] *Peripheral* both in its distance from the Roman centre(s), and in terms of degree of Romanization. Our designation 'Northern Gaul' is thus to be understood as a *frontier* zone, but not in its traditional *military* sense as the far-away and militarized border of Roman civilization. In our view the area between Rhine and Seine should be studied from the perspective of a specific long-term cultural and historical identity which from prehistory on marks its position in the interplay between north-,

ethnic identification is based essentially on three criteria: a) a *legal* one, in which the weapons deposited in graves are identified as the *Hergewede* known from later texts. On this assumption, weapon-burial is seen as the evident by-product of specific Germanic property-rights[12] and as such it has come to be seen as a '*nationales Indiz*';[13] b) a *stylistic* one, in which the shape and design of artefacts are considered both 'unRoman' and characteristic for an assumed Germanic or barbarian taste, which includes a preference for chiaroscuro (*clair-obscure*), polychromy, and abstract decoration (often put on a par with a lack of 'technical' knowledge of naturalistic representation);[14] and c) a *religious* one, in which the deposition of valuables in the grave is thought to reflect pagan conceptions on the afterlife and 'primitive' fear of the dead.[15]

central- and south-European spheres of interaction. Cf E. Wightman, "North eastern Gaul in Late Antiquity: the testimony of settlement patterns in an age of transition", *Berichten Rijksdienst Oudheidkundig Bodemonderzoek* 28 (1978), pp. 241–250. F. Theuws, "De vele lagen van de vroeg-middeleeuwse geschiedenis", *Madoc* 9 (1995), pp. 133–149. F. Theuws and H. Hiddink, "Der Kontakt zu Rom", *Die Franken, Wegbereiter Europas. Vor 1500 Jahren. König Chlodwig und seine Erben* (Mainz, 1996), pp. 754–768.

[12] At the basis of this explanation is C. Redlich, "Erbrecht und Grabbeigaben bei den Germanen", *Forschungen und Fortschritte* 24 (1948), pp. 177–180. According to her, in Germanic law everything except a man's weapon(s) was the property of the *Sippe* and not of the individual. For critical comments see for instance H. Härke, "Warrior graves? The background of the Anglo-Saxon weapon burial rite", *Past & Present* 126 (1990), pp. 22–43.

[13] J. Werner, "Zur Entstehung der Reihengräberzivilisation. Ein Beitrag zur Methode der frühgeschichtlichen Archäologie", *Archaeologia Geographica* 1 (1950), p. 25.

[14] All this can ultimately be traced back to some assumed primitive or barbarian predilection for pomp and splendour in art-historical approaches to Germanic/barbarian material culture. See, for example, the art historian E. Kitzinger, *Early Medieval Art* (London, 1983), p. 46: 'This northern art was the opposite of mediterranean art in almost every respect. (. . .) Their aim was not the representation of a particular subject (. . .) but abstract ornament. (. . .) in any case the barbarians of the north held aloof from the naturalistic art brought to perfection by the Greeks and Romans and inherited by the Christians in the mediterranean countries'. For comparable points of view in archaeology see for instance H. Steuer, "L'industrie d'art à l'époque mérovingienne", *Childéric-Clovis. 1500e anniversaire, 482–1982* (Tournai, 1982), pp. 181–200: 'l'inclination des Germains pour le pompeux' (p. 184) and: 'il suffit de comparer les bijoux francs et romains pour comprendre que les femmes germaniques concevaient le style et la beauté d'une manière très différente. Les bijoux devaient être les plus grands possible et contenir un maximum de métal précieux' (p. 186). See also: W.A. van Es, "Friezen, Franken en Vikingen, in *Romeinen, Friezen en Franken in het hart van Nederland. Van Traiectum tot Dorestat 50 v. C.–900 n. C.*, eds W.A. van Es and W. Hessing (Utrecht/Amertfoort, 1994), p. 87: 'hun praalzieke grafgebruiken . . .'

[15] Effros, *From Grave Goods to Christian Epitaphs*, pp. 68–72; and Y. Hen, *Culture and Religion in Merovingian Gaul AD 481–751* (Leiden, 1995), pp. 144–145.

It can be concluded that until the present day a tacitly accepted consensus has existed on the cultural and historical interpretation of the fourth- and fifth-century warrior graves and the Merovingian cemeteries. Their study has been conducted mainly from the perspective of a history of events (*histoire évènementielle*): that of the collapse of the Roman empire under the pressure of barbarian raids, the formation of the Germanic successor states culminating in the development of the Merovingian kingdom under Clovis (481–511), and the expansion by and downfall of his heirs. The central question has always been: how does the archaeological dataset reflect these developments?

2.2. *Some inherent problems*

The time has come to question some implicit notions underlying archaeological interpretations of material culture from late Roman and early medieval graves in northern Gaul.

The first objection considers the archaeological *concept of history*.[16] Archaeological research has suffered from an excessive readiness to assume correlations between archaeological phenomena and historical events. The bulk of the archaeological work in France and Germany on late Roman and "Frankish" burials has been directed at creating detailed typo-chronologies of material culture. The historical context related to these still remains rather old fashioned: a chronology of events or an autonomous process from primitive to modern with the evolution from tribe to state as the automatic outcome.[17] In fact the sociao-political evenemential history, the history of "everyday life" and religion still remain the fields in which the results of the burial analysis are placed.[18] The burial ritual has hardly

---

[16] See also P. Geary, " The uses of archaeological sources for Religious and Cultural History" P. Geary, Living with the dead in the Middle Ages (Ithaca and London, 1994), pp. 30–45.

[17] See for a discussion of the last process: Bazelmans, "conceptualising early Germanic political structure", pp. 106–119.

[18] To name but a few examples: H.W. Böhme, *Germanische Grabfunde des 4. bis 5. Jahrhunderts zwischen unterer Elbe und Loire. Studien zur Chronologie und Bevölkerungsgeschichte* (München, 1974). H.W. Böhme, "Der Frankenkönig Childerich zwischen Attila und Aëtius. Zu den Goldgriffspathen der Merowingerzeit", *Festschrift für Otto-Hermann Frey zum 65.Geburtstag* (Marburg, 1994) (Marburger Studien zur Vor- und Frühgeschichte 16), pp. 69–110. P. Périn, "Les tombes de «chefs» du début de l'epoque mérovingienne. Datation et interprétation historique", *La noblesse romaine et les chefs barbares du IIIᵉ au VIIᵉ siècle*, eds. F. Vallet and M. Kazanski (Paris, 1995), pp. 247–301.

been analysed in relation to histories of ideas and mentalities, although under the influence of new historical research and the perception of anthropological concepts and theories a shift in emphasis takes place. In an earlier phase of research this comparison history and material culture perhaps proved an adequate and productive way of ordering the huge amount of archaeological data (and to date it), but nowadays it is too simple. Describing archaeological phenomenona with labels like Germanic or Roman and connecting them to general narrative accounts traditionally alluded to as The Fall of the Roman Empire, The Birth of Europe or The Coming of Christianity is a reduction of what is at stake in this period: a transformation of ideological, social and economic structures and their articulation in relation to the modelling, use and meaning of space, material culture, language and text.

The second objection considers the underlying *concept of value*. In traditional archaeological research the presence of objects in graves has been reduced to a mere side-effect of their more general circulation and use in socio-economic praxis (they are cultural rubbish, '*Kulturschutt*'). Thus, different categories of objectshave been made mutually convertible by reducing them to some common denominator for indicating wealth. This has led to the development of complex statistical methods for establishing social stratification on the basis of modern conceptions of scarcity, like the input of energy (money, time, labour) or number of artifacts, on the assumption that the composition of sets of objects and/or the quality of their execution directly reflect the position and richness of the owner, his[19] position in life.

A. Wieczorek, "Die Ausbreitung der fränkischen Herrschaft in den Rheinlanden vor und seit Chlodwig I", *Die Franken, Wegbereiter Europas. Vor 1500 Jahren. König Chlodwig und seine Erben* (Mainz, 1996), pp. 241–260. Many contributions in the catalogue of the Franken exhibition in Mannheim in which the last mentioned article can be found illustrate this too with chapter titles as: Von der Vielfalt zur Einheit: Das Frankenreich entsteht; and: Vom Kleinkönigtum zum Grossreich.

[19] Here we deliberately restrict ourselves to 'his' because of the strong male bias in the *Reihengräberforschung*. Although there are vast amounts of female graves from early-medieval grave-fields, archaeological analysis has been primarily concerned with male burials in order to reconstruct social structure. Whereas sumptuous male burials are interpreted as those of rich and/or powerful males, female burials are usually seen as reflecting the position of the woman's husband or father. Inspired by theoretical developments especially in the field of social anthropology, on women's roles in the reproduction of society, a re-evaluation of the conceptual framework for the analysis of late Roman and early medieval female burials is rewarding. See G. Halsall, "Female status and power in early merovingian central Austrasia: the burial evidence", *Early Medieval Europe* 5 (1996), pp 1–24.

The third objection considers the underlying *concept of ritual* and its understanding by modern man. The deposition of objects in (to modern minds) negative contexts such as a bog or a grave is ultimately reduced to some irrational, primitive habit which the Germanic tribes only gave up under the civilizing forces of Christianity and state-formation. The question of why specific objects were used in this context, for which purpose, and in what way, is either neglected or rejected as not testable by scientific standards.[20] At best ritual seems to involve some instrumental act of manipulation or legitimation of existing power relations: the late Roman and early medieval burial-ritual is thus seen as reflecting the emergence of Germanic elites monopolizing access to prestige-goods. As such, 'ritual' tends to be thought of as limited to ideal images and ideology that mystify 'real' societal relations for the purpose of the exercise of power. The effect of this is that the *meaning* of the objects, and with that their value, remains restricted to some ready-made 'symbolism'. As such, grave-field research has been exclusively focused on a supposed passive, representational character of the burial-ritual instead of on the active and creative role of the ritual itself.

Archaeological analyses of late Roman and early medieval graves have thus been largely restricted to typo-chronological studies or studies aimed at understanding the evolution of 'autonomous' elements of Germanic culture (*Herrschaft, Gefolgschaft* [lordship, the retinue], trade, religion, technology, and so forth) or at the reconstruction of ethnic maps. As such, late Roman and early medieval archaeology remains restricted to the investigation of '*Germanic* culture' instead of processes of cultural and historical change. Since the outlines of a historical narrative were established, grave-field research took a firm 'historical' baseline: graves and objects were thought 'to speak for themselves'. When, after the Second World War, the interpretation of material culture patterns as a result of Germanic *Wanderbewegungen* (migrations) for obvious reasons became a burden, the focus shifted to 'technical' issues, like the sophistication of typo-chronology, distribution maps, technological and quantitative research. Archaeologists were apparently convinced that the problem of continuity

---

[20] See however H. Härke, *Angelsächsische Waffengräber des 5. bis 7. Jahrhunderts* (Köln, 1992) (Zeitschrift für Archäologie des Mittelalters, Beiheft 6), p. 218. Some attempts to explain the ritual refer to the deliberate destruction of wealth. This too seems to be an interpretation starting from modern conceptions of value. In the burial ritual wealth is not *destroyed* but *used*, destruction is a wrong word for taking valuables out of circulation in the socio-political sphere (cfr. Härke, this volume).

and change in late Roman and early medieval society is essentially an empirical one[21] to which chronological knowledge of stylistic, morphological or technological developments of graves and grave-goods provide the vital clues. The ultimate goal of such research might be summed up in the German dictum '*getrennt marschieren, vereint schlagen*',[22] that is a strict disciplinary division of the work was expected to provide the basis for a future decisive solution of the problem by a definitive interpretation of the empirical data.[23]

In one sense archaeological methodology has been emancipated as a result. Much effort has been spent on developing standardised ways of describing, presenting and interpreting archeological finds.[24] Yet, even after fifty years of intensive research and an ever-increasing corpus of data and publications, the 'decisive moment' does not seem to have come much closer. Despite an increasingly critical awareness of the problems of the traditional framework of historical explanation, archaeologists too often analyse the archaeological finds from the Roman and early medieval transition period in terms of a confrontation between cultures using categories like Roman versus Germanic, civilized versus primitive, pagan versus Christian. One of the reasons for this stagnation is that archaeologists have been reluctant to reflect on the specific nature of their data. The core of the problem is that in the research-tradition *evaluation* has taken the place of *analysis*. The supposed Germanic nature of graves and material culture is still taken as the *point of departure* rather than as the *object*

---

[21] Cf. A. Demandt, *Der Fall Roms. Die Auflösung des römischen Reiches im Urteil der Nachwelt* (München, 1984), p. 233: 'Die Forschung ist geneigt die Kontinuitätsfrage für ein empirisches, durch Quellenbelege lösbares Problem zu halten'.

[22] For critical remarks from a historian's view, see R. Wenskus, "Randbemerkungen zum Verhältnis von Historie und Archäologie, insbesondere mittelalterlicher Geschichte und Mittelalterarchäologie", *Geschichtswissenschaft und Archäologie. Untersuchungen zur Siedlungs-, Wirtschafts- und Kirchengeschichte*, eds. H. Jankuhn and R. Wenskus (Sigmaringen, 1979), pp. 637–657. On the history and background of the research strategy, see U. Veit, "Ethnic concepts in German prehistory: a case study on the relationship between cultural identity and archaeological objectivity", *Archaeological Approaches to Cultural Identity*, ed. S. Shennan (London, 1989), pp. 35–56.

[23] This view is still encountered for instance: Theune-Vogt in her review of Härke's *Angelsächsicshe Waffengräber des 5. bis 7. Jahrhunderts* (in *Germania* 74, 1996, pp. 645–649) where she states that dealing with historical evidence befor the archaeological analysis is dangerous because it influences the archaeological analysis.

[24] Publications of this sort are characterised by a uniform structure, in which a distinction is made between the presentation of archaeological data as such (site, landscape, catalogue of finds, distribution maps, etc.) and a *historische Auswertung* in which the archaeological data are confronted with 'the' historical context often seen as a series of events.

of study. Archaeological data do not play any role other than that of objective, neutral facts: they are indicators of ethnic affiliation, migration, or diffusion, of level of technology, of economic activities (trade), and they refer to wealth, possession and status.

From this perspective, material culture tends to be reduced to something which exists 'outside' or 'above' society itself. It is doubtful however, whether these modernist conceptualisations of material culture can yield insights into the interplay of action and thought on the part of people in non-modern societies like that of pre-industrial Europe. The modern separation and isolation of the mental and the material dimensions of life is the product of a long process of demystification of the surrounding world that went parallel to the development of a mercantile and later capitalist world-view. In our opinion, if we really want to penetrate the world of the past through the study of material culture, we will have to focus on the contexts of production, use, and exchange of objects. Material culture is a medium which human beings actively use to explore and shape their social, natural and supernatural surroundings and (consciously or unconsciously), to construct meaningful identities. This starting-point implies that we take the obviously *ritual* context of the archaeological data as a central concern, instead of brushing it away as negligible or irrelevant. The deposition of material wealth in graves, rivers, hoards or churches can obviously be considered a form of *appropriate use*. Instead of limiting this to the peculiarities of a specific ethnic group, we shall leave the traditional Roman-German dichotomy behind us and try to get insight into the *meaning* of these forms of use and their changing patterns through time and space.

2.3. *Grave-goods and an elite lifestyle*

The composition of any set of grave goods in late-Roman and early medieval graves in northern Gaul is by no means random. Here the concept of an *elite lifestyle* helps describe and order the sheer variety and quantity of data. The objects in late Roman and early medieval graves refer to a lifestyle in which three aspects seem to be of central importance: a/ martial values; b/ feasting; and c/ body-display.

In men's graves, the *martial prowess* of the deceased is underlined by one or more weapons (sword, shield, spear, throwing-axe, arrowheads). In both men's and women's graves, the importance of *feasting* is expressed by the deposition of vessels and food in various forms and materials, suggesting various specialized functions in eating, drinking and serving: ceramics, glasses, drinking-horns, buckets, metal dishes, spoons, knives, etc. The aspect of what we have called *body-display* is articulated by items which in one or another way are associated with the body. In men's graves, the eye is caught by the belt with its decorated fittings and attached weapon(s), purse, or toiletries like tweezers. To women, dress-pins (*fibulae*) are central: we have these in all kinds of forms, material and quality. There are also earrings and necklaces, composed of beads, coins, pendants of precious metal, pieces of amber. Finger-rings appear in both men's and women's graves.

Especially in the older literature, body-ornaments with their glittering and/or polychrome appearance are often connected with some 'barbarian predilection' for pomp and splendour. A similar interpretation is given for drinking and fighting, which in general are put on a par with anarchy and violence as assumed characteristic ingredients of some primitive state of mind, that is an underdeveloped control over passions and impulses.

Instead, we stress that these objects point first and foremost to a set of interconnected, contemporary *ideas* on actively taking part in society's meaningful relationships. Objects like these are the focus of transactions and events in which diverse relations are created, reproduced or terminated. Here the *sine qua non* is a shared experience of membership of the elite, and of using these objects in an *appropriate way*, that is, in actions where meaningful relations between man (persons/groups) and his surrounding social and supernatural world are activated, expressed and defined. In anthropological terms we could classify such events as *tournaments of value*, a term which Appadurai used to label complex periodic events in which people meet and compete in order to establish their position in a network of relations.[25] Participation in these is likely to be both a privilege of those in power and a way of gaining status in competetion between them. In events like these the use and exchange of the central tokens of value in the society in question must have played a key role.

Appadurai's term is useful in comparing the use of special categories of objects in such events as the burial, the battle, the feast, the military assembly (*campus martius*) and the hunt in our period. In

---

[25] A. Appadurai, *The Social Life of Things. Commodities in Cultural Perspective* (Cambridge, 1986), p. 21.

our opinion however, where Appadurai tends to restrict the importance of these events largely to the *social* arena, their *cosmological* importance is neglected too much. Bazelmans' interesting model of Anglo-Saxon social structure as depichted in *Beowulf* points to the vital importance of such culturally-significant events. If we accept Bazelmans' point that in non-modern societies the human person is made up of various constituents which are brought together, developed and separated in the course of different life-cycle-rituals or *rites de passage*,[26] we can assume that events like the ones listed above offer more than just opportunities for the display of wealth and power. They can be understood as strongly ritualized moments in which various relations within human society and between human beings and the supernatural are activated, that is, *where the person gets shape and in the combined effort of kings and lords and warrior-followers society as well*. As such, these events are essential to both person and society. At this point, we must explore some basic aspects of the function and meaning of ritual.

2.4. *Ritual*

In continental archaeological research traditions dealing with "Frankish" graves, 'ritual' more often than not tends to be limited to some passive reflection of contemporary ideal images ('ideology') which function relatively independent of 'reality'.[27] This view is however one-sided. The domain of rituals is the privileged arena in which the outlines of countless relationships are shaped; these relationships include those with the supernatural (ancestors, spirits, gods, demons, saints). Society is thus not to be reduced to the 'real', physical/visible world of the living; it comprises the supernatural as an active, constituent part of human life.[28]

---

[26] Based on an analysis of the Anglo Saxon poem *Beowulf* Bazelmans states that in Anglo-Saxon culture these constituents can be labelled as 'body', 'life', 'image' (or 'worth') and 'soul'. Cf. J. Bazelmans, *Eén voor allen, allen voor één. Tacitus'* Germania, *de Oudengelse* Beowulf, *en het ritueel-kosmologische karakter van de relatie tussen heer en krijger-volgeling in Germaanse samenlevingen* (unpublished Ph.D. dissertation, University of Amsterdam, 1996) now published in an English translation as: *By weapons made worthy. Lords, retainers and their relationship in* Beowulf (Amsterdam University Press, 1999); and Bazelmans below in this volume.

[27] In Anglo-phone archaeology (including Scandinavia) this stance has been altered radically in the last decennium. See also Geary, "The uses of Archaeological sources for Religious and Cultural History, pp. 30–45.

[28] This aspect is frequently met in the work of historians like Peter Brown notably

These considerations are of importance for the analysis of material culture as presented in the graves of late Roman and early medieval northern Gaul. The sets of objects deposited in these contexts are first and foremost part of undoubtedly complex funerary rituals of which the actual interment may have been only a small part. In view of the formalized appearance of at least part of the burial, the objects involved, and the long traditions surrounding many important graves or grave-fields, we may characterize the inhumation ritual with Maurice Godelier as one of the acts which *(. . .)* '*expriment et condensent en eux une multitude d'aspects matériels et idéels des rapports des hommes tant entre eux qu'avec la nature. Ces sont des actes et des moments de la vie sociale chargés, voir surchargés, et par là, en rapport 'symbolique' avec l'ensemble de l'organisation sociale.*'[29] In other words: the totality of the *socio-cosmological order* is involved. The burial ritual does not exclusively *reflect* situations of socio-economic practice, it is one of the moments in which man can actively *intervene* in the totality of social, natural and supernatural relationships.

Thus, contrary to what continental archaeological traditions seem to postulate, the burial ritual is not just a passive reflection of social praxis or of a static societal structure or hierarchy, it is simultaneously a *statement* (an expression of ideas) *and* an *act which affects society itself.*[30] From this it follows that society is constantly redefined and renewed by the actions and thoughts of people. Instead of regarding a given society as a self-contained, static entity, we should accept it to be a rather multi-dimensional and dynamic network which, instead of a collection of separate groups, can best be described in terms of *overlapping* relationships.[31]

In the case of burial one cannot suppose *a priori* that all important relationships are touched upon or affected in just one ritual. The relations involved in this ritual might be different from those

---

in his *The Cult of the Saints. Its Rise and Function in Latin Christianity* (Chicago-London, 1981), and Patrick Geary, *Living with the dead in the Early Middle Ages* (Ithaca-London, 1994).

[29] M. Godelier, *L'idéel et le matériel. Pensée, economies, sociétés* (Paris, 1984), p. 66. The author continues: 'Ce sont, pour reprendre l'expression de Mauss pour désigner cette classe de faits sociaux, des faits sociaux 'totaux' en ce sens qu'ils résument et expriment, donc totalisent en un moment exceptionnel, et une configuration particulière de la vie sociale, les principes de l'organisation qui sous-tend ce mode de vie'.

[30] D. de Coppet, "Introduction", *Understanding Rituals*, ed. D. de Coppet (London-New York, 1992), p. 9.

[31] M. Mann, The sources of social Power. Vol. I. From the beginning to AD 1760 (Cambridge, 1986), pp. 1–3.

in others. It *can* however be accepted that many of these rituals or ritualised social events are related to and even dependent on each other. During each of them, *aspects* of the socio-cosmological order may be involved. This means that ritual activities are not isolated events, but form part of *chains of rituals* that in the case of burials are best described as life-cycle- or life-giving rituals (at birth, marriage, maturity, etc.) that are related. Therefore, particular ritual activities cannot be studied in isolation. This implies that a tournament of value like the burial ritual must be understood in relation to the comparable ritualized events mentioned above; they can even be analyzed in terms of each other. It is with this in mind that our concept of elite lifestyle can acquire deeper significance. Up to now, we have used it only as a descriptive tool in ordering the sheer variety and quantity of data. By doing this we have established a connecting link between phenomena that, due to the perseverance of the traditional division between Roman and medieval archaeology, more often than not are studied as more or less separate collections of data.

2.5. *Again: an elite lifestyle*

At an *analytical* level we can now reformulate the elite lifestyle as *a body of specialized knowledge about the person and its constituents and society.* From this it follows that in late Roman and early medieval society in northern Gaul, knowledge of the elite lifestyle was a prerequisite for being a full (aristocratic) person within society, and for passing through the different stages of becoming this. Within the elite lifestyle, meaningful behaviour and events were specified and valued, and accordingly articulated in a hierarchy of objects. From this perspective, the elite lifestyle was not just a symbolic representation, a normative set of rules or an ideal image of society, but an essential *substantive* quality: to contemporary man it offered both source and instrument to analyse situations and behaviour, and to reflect on and respond to them in an appropriate way and with appropriate means.[32]

---

[32] We have to emphasize that we do not intend to restrict the concept of an elite lifestyle to the world-view of a class or group in society. Knowledge of the elite lifestyle and access to the necessary goods form an instrument or source of knowledge for the participants in their analysis, perception of and reaction to situations and actions within society. In our sense, the concept centres on knowledge rather than on a fixed set of norms. The elite lifestyle offers different alternatives

This implies that the various object-categories which form the contents of late Roman and early medieval graves were not just passive symbols of rank or scarce goods to be competed for; they had a *metaphorical significance* which was essential to the proper fulfilment of the ritual, and which can be outlined as follows. The objects used in rituals and events connected with the display of martial values, feasting, and body-display were an intrinsic part of the position a person inhabited in his/her network, at a specific point in time and place. Therefore, these objects were not reflections, but rather *constituents* of his/her *being*. They were the valorized parts of the different stages in life during which the person developed him/herself as a full member of society. We may call this 'identity', but we must be aware not to use that term in its modern sense, as if it were something fixed and tied to the individual. The notion of the human being as a unique and indivisible entity proves to be a modern western notion whose applicability to non-modern or non-western societies is highly questionable.

At this point in our description of lifestyle and identity in the late Roman and early medieval world it is worth stressing the role of the human body. In this highly fluid world of shifting relationships and overlapping 'identities', it was the body which was the natural point of reference in human experience and reflections on the encompassing socio-cosmological order and its constituents. In this sense we can attribute to the body a *liminal* position which is to be explained by the human condition itself: the body is the site where the union of several dimensions of Life, broadly speaking concerning the mental and the material, is most directly and most obviously sensed and experienced. Everything the body does, *when* and *where* and *how* it dresses up, fights, feasts etc, is guided by a shared image of Life itself.

This 'mental' perspective on the body can throw some light on the question of why we see the elite lifestyle so strongly represented in late Roman and early medieval grave-ritual. We could characterize the body as an active and substantive metaphor, used in every context which refers to the existence, continuation and renewal of

---

for acting, which means that this source of knowledge can be 'used' in different ways by different groups and even in different ways by a single person. R. Muchembled, *L'invention de l'homme moderne: sensibilités, moeurs et comportements collectifs sous l'Ancien Régime* (Paris, 1988).

Life. Therefore, the elite lifestyle is not just a normative image of idealized behaviour but an articulation of central concepts and values in late Roman and early medieval northern Gaul. Starting from the above definitions of society and the person, death implies the disappearance of a specific junction in this fluid network of relationships. This temporary break-down (of society) causes the need to perpetuate and renew society and its constituents by accompanying the deceased person in his/her transition from the world of the living to the community of the ancestors. Thus, grave-field and burial ritual fulfil a dual, essential role in the cycle of life and death of both the person and society. The burial ritual is the final step in a chain of rituals and ritualised events which guide the person through the different, culturally defined stages of social life. At the same time, the burial ritual is essential in the transition of the level of the person to that of the collectivity, i.e. the reproduction of society in the long term.

It is clear that in thinking along these lines we perceive the cemetery (as an archaeological phenomenon) in a different way: it is not the passive reflection of a community's social and economic hierarchy, but a place where a community is actively constituted by way of ritual performances. The grave-field as a centre of ritual activities is of vital importance to both person and society: it is one of the places where a community materialises through the persons that acknowledge their membership. It offers persons the opportunity to define themselves in time and place, that is in the cosmological order; and at the same time the reproduction and continuity of the community is warranted because here in the burial ground rest persons who are transformed into ancestors.[33]

2.6. *Resuming*

From the previous discussion of the interpretation of late-Roman and early medieval burials it can be deduced that the modern concept of 'reality' as a 'true', 'impartial' starting point for the analysis

---

[33] The transformation of the dead into ancestors is a process that is more complex than we heve sketched here. The rituals involved will differ according to context (time and place), the local interpretation of the relations between the living, the dead and the ancestors, the extent to which a local or regional network is embedded in a larger whole, and the position a dead person or the group(s) he/she belonged to had, or want to assume, in that larger network.

of ritual acts in non-western or non-modern societies is non-productive. Today we incline to separate the physical and supernatural world in a very strict way. The latter is extremely abstract, exists in the heads of people, exists independent of time and place. This perceived opposition is the parallel for the division that has been made since Descartes between Ideal and Reality (ideology and praxis), between thinking and acting (*Denken* vs *Handeln*).[34] This dichotomy, however, seems less relevant if one realises that by doing, people actually experience and shape 'reality'. By saying this, we plead for an *emic* definition of 'reality', instead of an *etic* one in which the modern western notion of what is real is elevated to the status of a universal, objective standard.[35] It does not imply that we advocate a post-modern, relativist approach in which every hope for the reconstruction of historical reality is given up; it is our conviction that instead of imposing our modern notions on the material found in archaeological contexts, we have to delineate an *inside* or *actor's view* which does not degrade non-modern people to primitive or not-yet-civilized beings or prototypes of western man. In fact we have to seek for their rationale in their own terms. Thus we also avoid giving modern ideology a time depth and universality which it does not have.

To sum up, what seems to pass for an archaeological consensus that ritual is 'empty form' which relates to ideal representations needs to be discarded, for it greatly hampers any understanding of the archaeological data-set which in the case of late Roman and early medieval northern Gaul almost exclusively consists of ritual deposits. If archaeologists aim to develop an interpretative approach to material culture from ritual contexts, it is not acceptable to separate the different spheres that make up human existence (for instance the social and the supernatural), for they make up an interwoven whole that is understood as such by participants of non-modern societies.[36] Therefore we cannot leave out of the discussion the *substance* of the

---

[34] See H. Härke, "Intentionale und funktionale Daten. Ein Beitrag zur Theorie und Methodik der Gräberarchäologie", *Archäologisches Korrespondenzblatt* 23 (1993), pp. 141–146, for examples of the way in which this analytical division in interpretation and archaeological data is employed.

[35] Cf. De Coppet, "Introduction", p. 3.

[36] It is often stated that taking a subject apart for analytical reasons is acceptable. We have to realise that taking apart a society or a person is always ideologically informed and does not need to coincide with the categories of the groups or societies under study.

ideas underlying the material culture used in rituals; these ideas give human behaviour meaning and direction through the values that are related to it. Seen from this angle of human cognition, it may be clear that the use ofobjects in ritual activities is of more fundamental significance than just the evident side-effect of their more general use and circulation in social and economic practice.

These considerations are of consequence for the central theme of this paper. The deposition of swords in graves cannot be studied in isolation. In section three we will therefore first concentrate on ideas underlying the use and circulation of swords in late Roman and early medieval society by situating their meaning and value in the broader context of production, use and exchange.

3. *The Ideology of the sword*

3.1. *The sword in early medieval life and thought*

In the previous section we pointed out the broader material and cultural context of the objects deposited in late Roman and early medieval graves. Here we will proceed by focusing on one class of objects which has long stirred the imagination of researchers, the *spatha* or double-edged long-sword.

As appears from countless written, iconographic and archaeological sources, the meaning of the sword was widely shared in the early medieval kingdoms in north-western Europe. The sword was anything but a neutral object whose function was limited to fighting. Swords were described as living beings, inhibited with personal characteristics; they carried fierce names, their deeds were commemorated, their appearance was praised and they were worn and exchanged on special occasions.[37] A few examples will suffice to illustrate this.

A Frankish example is provided by Gregory of Tours' description of the sons of Waddo, who vainly hoped to bribe King Gunthram for their and their father's unfaithful behaviour by presenting him a sword: *'(They) handed over a huge baldric decorated with gold and precious stones, and a marvellous sword the pommel of which was made of gold and*

---

[37] Cf. Bouzy "Les armes symboles d'un pouvoir politique: l'épée du sacre, la sainte lance, l'oriflamme aux VIIIe–XIIe siècles".

Spanish jewels.[38] Another example from the Frankish world is Ein-hard's description of Charlemagne: '*He wrapped himself in a blue cloak and always had a sword strapped to his side, with a hilt and belt of gold and silver. Sometimes he would use a jewelled sword, but this was only on great feast days or when ambassadors came from foreign peoples*'.[39] A famous sword from the Anglo-Saxon world bears the name of Hrunting. It is the sword that young Beowulf receives of one of Hrothgar's men in order to fight Grendel, the monster which terrifies his kingdom. '*Hrunting was its name; unique and ancient, its edge was iron, annealed in venom and tempered in blood; in battle it never failed any hero whose hand took it up at his setting out on a stern adventure for the house of foes. This was not the first time that it had to do heroic work*'.[40] In the same poem, another sword is described as follows: '*He saw among the armour there the sword to bring him victory, a Giant sword from former days: formidable were its edges, a warrior's admiration. This wonder of its kind was yet so enormous that no other man would be equal to bearing it in battle-play -it was a Giant's forge that had fashioned it so well*'.[41]

Despite the impression that the early medieval sword was a mag-ical weapon to fight supernatural forces, a superficial comparison of these texts does however suggest that swords were only given and employed in very specific contexts: if the continuation of a people or royal lineage was threatened, as in the first passage cited from *Beowulf*, or when relations of subordination or equality were estab-lished, as in the passage from Gregory, or as when Offa, King of Mercia, received from Charlemagne a sword of 'Avar workmanship'.[42]

On the basis of these examples we can characterize the sword represented in texts as a medium of intervention in situations where the continuation or renewal of the encompassing order was involved. By this situations are meant in which relations are defined that con-

---

[38] *Historia Francorum* X, 21. The translation is taken from *Gregory of Tours: The His-tory of the Franks*, translated by. L. Thorpe (Harmondsworth, 1974), p. 580.

[39] Einhard, *Vita Caroli Magni*, c. 24. The translation is taken from *Einhard and Notker the Stammerer. Two Lives of Charlemagne*, translated with an introduction by L. Thorpe (London, 1969).

[40] *Beowulf*, 1456f. The translation is taken from *Beowulf. A verse translation* by M. Alexander (Harmontdsworth, 1973), p. 97.

[41] *Beowulf*, 1557f., The translation is taken from *Beowulf. A verse translation* by M. Alexander

[42] H.E. Davidson, *The Sword in Anglo-Saxon England* (Oxford, 1962), p. 109 and p. 175. For examples of exchange of swords between lord and follower in socio-political practice, see Härke and Bazelmans in this volume.

cern a group or society, for instance the succesful reproduction of a royal lineage or position within an elite network. Thus we arrive at a level that surpasses that of the individual person: that of the cosmological order. Through the sword the owner/user stands in a direct relation to the reproductive forces of life. It is for this reason that the sword takes on a special position in the interaction between the social and supernatural world.

In this constellation the special role of elite groups in the reproduction of the encompassing order is emphasized. Because of his descent and training the young warrior is gifted with the necessary capabilities for the use of the sword and with the knowledge of the proper contexts of use. This makes the sword a special prerogative for elite groups and a symbol of their obvious dominant position.[43] The sword is thus related to contemporary ideas on what society *is* and how it is perpetually redefined and renewed by the actions of heroic people.

There is no 'magic' involved in this.[44] Although in the sword the power of intervention is sealed it does not seem to be obvious that intervention will happen. Success is not something that can be planned or forced, but one can make *strategies* in order to arrive at wished-for results. It depends on *who* handels the sword, *how* and with *what purpose*.

This brings us to the just or proper use of the sword (see also section 2). A number of texts record what can happen if the sword is not respected or is used in an unjust manner. The person who damages Tyrfing, the wondersword mentioned in the Hervararsaga, will not live the other day.[45] Kormakssaga tells how the sword Skovnung is to be used: his unjust user will be punished because luck will be no longer his.[46]

However, we can also put forward (in an analysis of the meaning(s) of the sword) that it is through the sword that the complexity of human existence is veiled. As is the case with most symbols

---

[43] Up to the present day, the sword is used as a metaphor of society-as-a-whole in modern discourse. Its early medieval significance as a medium for intervention in the socio-cosmological order is easily translated into christian terms: the sword is an instrument for recreating a divine order, cf. W. Ullmann, *Medieval Political Thought* (Harmondsworth, 1975), pp. 75–80 and p. 110.

[44] Cf M. Douglas, *Purity and Danger: an Analysis of Concepts of ollution and Taboo* (London, 1966), p. 59.

[45] Behmer, *Das zweischneidige Schwert der germanischen Völkerwanderungszeit*, p. 13.

[46] Davidson, *The Sword in Anglo-Saxon England*, p. 166.

the sword has its opposite meanings: it brings fame and glory, but also death and destruction. Probably because of this, all participants attribute an important role to the sword in the proces of continuation of the social and encompassing order, to such an extent that an intrinsic force is ascribed to the object itself. This represents a response to some fundamental human questions and problems on the nature and origin of Life itself: the inconsistencies and inscrutabilities of daily life in the face of the (constructed) image of an enduring social and cosmic order.

This same uneasiness is reflected in the *origin* or *production* of valued swords and objects comparable to those presented in the written sources: they are not made by human hand, they are there or they come into being. Origin and production are veiled or are ascribed to exceptional creatures that exist outside the human community, like the mythical smith Weland in the Nibelungensaga, or dwarfs, or giants; or in a christian context, bishops, saints, angels, ancestors or God.[47]

Now that we have outlined the broader contexts of production, use and exchange which in our view are significant for clarifying the meaning of the sword in early medieval society, we will focus on the *value* of the sword.

Every now and then, in archaeological publications swords are mentioned which seem to be rather worn-out or repaired. More often than not, the choice of, so it seems to modern eyes, a worthless, old-fashioned or second-rate weapon is interpreted as a cheap solution to the assumed heavy burden of providing the dead with grave goods. It should be clear that these modern concepts of value inhibit any real understanding of the deposition of valued items. In section 2 we have seen that objects used in rituals are meaningful and ideologically dominant objects, a fact that we substantiated with the sword as our example. The question is: how does an object, in this case a sword, obtain its value? The most obvious solution seems to point to examples of swords executed with precious stones and

---

[47] The most famous example is St. Eligius or Eloi (588–660), bishop of Noyon and patron saint of smiths and all kinds of metalworkers. As an artisan he produced numerous works of art, especially reliquaries, for the Merovingian kings Clothar II and Dagobert I. A later example of a sword received from God is discussed by P. Geary "Germanic tradition and Royal Ideology in the ninth century: The visio Karoli Magni", P. Geary, *Living with the Dead in the Early Middle Ages* (Ithaca-London, 1994), pp. 49–76.

materials (gold, silver, garnets) and complicated techniques (cloisonné, filigrain, incrustation). We should however reject an exclusively modern material perspective and be careful not to equate the value of these swords with their material costliness. First and foremost, the value of the sword is a *cultural construct* which is due to the special meaning of the sword as outlined above. As such, it is not the precious appearance and execution alone which renders the object valuable, in fact they seem to be the *logical consequence* of its meaning! Form and meaning cannot be separated but are inextricably bound up in a coherent whole. It is for this reason that in prestige goods materials are employed that relate to contemporary ideas on origin, purity and continuity of life, like precious stones, precious metals (gold, silver), bone, ivory, horn and amber.[48]

In the approach to non-modern concepts of value the concept of 'cultural biography' can provide interesting insights into the deposition of seemingly 'useless' swords in graves. It was introduced in social anthropology by Kopytoff to describe the trajectory of an individual object through the different spheres of production, consumption and exchange.[49] Along this trajectory the value of the object accumulates as a result of an association with special persons, groups or events. This is all the more interesting when we consider those puzzling examples of swords which seem to be built up from parts of different date and origin, like the Köyliö-sword (Kjuloholm Isle, Finland), which was found in a grave from the Merovingian period, but provided with a Migration period (V-A) pommel;[50] the Brighthampton sword with fittings from the early-fifth up to the early-sixth century;[51] and possibly the swords from the Swedish boat-graves Valsgärde 7 and Vendel I.[52]

---

[48] It is interesting to compare these materials, that cannot be reduced to something else, with the *prima materia* in alchemy and hermetic philosophy. Here too it is not possible to separate form from content or meaning.

[49] I. Kopytoff, "The cultural biography of things: commoditisation as a process", *The Social Life of Things. Commodities in Cultural Perspective*, ed. A. Appadurai (Cambridge, 1986), pp. 64–91.

[50] A. Erä-Esko, "Ein Schwert der Merowingerzeit mit völkerwanderungszeitlichem Knauf aus Grab A 5 von der Insel Kjuloholm, Gemeinde Köyliö, Südwestfinnland", *Archäologische Beiträge zur Chronologie der Völkerwanderungszeit* eds. G. Kossack and J. Reichstein (Bonn, 1977) (Antiquitas Reihe 3, Band 20), pp. 79–85.

[51] Härke, *Angelsächsische Waffengräber des 5. bis 7.Jahrhunderts*, p. 88 (for other examples from Anglo-Saxon England see his note 106).

[52] G. Arwidsson, *Valsgärde 7* (Uppsala, 1977), a.o. p. 128. The same observation, that the object is composed of parts of different date and origin, has been sug-

3.2. Swords' lives. Some examples of cultural biographies from various regions and periods

The above examples show that first and foremost, the sword is a *composite artefact*, which means that it is composed of different parts that, from a technical point of view, can be combined without problem. This aspect may throw some light on the above-mentioned circumstance that in many texts, the origin and production of famous swords is often left open or veiled. The production of a sword is much more than just the one-time-transformation of raw materials into a functional weapon. The creative act is in fact a process which never ceases as long as the object continues to be used and exchanged by persons or groups. As such, the deposition of a sword implies that the object was deliberately taken out of the human circuit of production, use and exchange in which it could acquire value. From this perspective we can interpret these swords as items which had long been in circulation, like the treasured heirlooms mentioned in written sources, before they were deposited.[53]

The importance of the cultural biography of swords can be illustrated by the history of several specimens in the archaeological record. To do so, we again stress the composite character of swords and scabbards as outlined above.[54]

Swords and scabbards may have been altered in three ways during their 'life'. First, alterations may have occurred to the sword by adding or taking away individual elements of the hilt or by replacing one hilt by another. Second, alterations to the scabbard may have occurred by adding or taking away individual elements. Third, the existing combination of sword and scabbard may be split up by putting the sword in another scabbard.[55]

---

gested for the helmets deposited in the boat-graves from the Swedish Mälaren-region by M. Alkemade, "A history of Vendel Period archaeology. Observations on the relationship between written sources and archaeological interpretations", *Images of the past. Studies on ancient societies in Northwestern Europe*, ed. N. Roymans and F. Theuws (Amsterdam, 1991) (Studies in Pre- en Protohistorie 7), pp. 267–297.

[53] See Härke, *Angelsächsische Waffengräber des 5. bis 7. Jahrhunderts*, p. 54, and Härke below in this volume.

[54] The archaeological practice of the splitting up of swords into a number of individual elements that have distribution patterns of their own may in itself be proof of the composite character of swords and scabbards. This point will be further elaborated in our section 4 below, by discussing the works of Menghin, *Das Schwert im frühen Mittelalter* and Geibig, *Beiträge zur morphologischen Entwicklung des Schwertes im Mittelalter* on sword-finds.

[55] See also Härke, *Angelsächsische Waffengräber des 5. bis 7. Jahrhunderts*, p. 221, and

Examples of the first are some of the so-called ring-swords from the sixth century, of which it is noted that the attachment of the ring-ornament was not foreseen in the original design of the hilt, and others where an existing ornament has been removed.[56] These swords also seem to have had different appearances in different contexts or lifecycle-stages. A more recent example of a sword whose hilt has undergone alterations is the sword from the *Domschatzkammer* in Essen (Germany) from ca AD 1000, that was turned into a relic.[57] For that purpose it was ornamented with gold foil and precious stones in a way that made it impossible to use as a fighting-weapon any more. These changes mark both the change over from one context to another (its deposition in the church treasure), and the different stages in the life of the sword.

An example of the alteration of the existing combination of sword and scabbard is provided by the famous royal sword of the German Empire (the *Reichsschwert*), now in the *Kunsthistorisches Museum* in Vienna.[58] The sword can be dated to the late 12th century; the scabbard, with the figures of the Frankish and German kings from Charlemagne to Henry III to the late 11th century. The original scabbard of the sword is lost, or should one rather say the original sword

---

our section 4 below. Quast, *Die merowingerzeitlichen Grabfunde aus Gültlingen (Stadt Wildberg, Kreis Calw)*, p. 49 indicates that swords and scabbards are not necessarily products of the same workshop. However, he sees the swords of the Krefelder type (= Samson-Oberlörick-Abingdon-type) as a proof that swords and scabbards in those cases were acquired together ('Die aus dem fränkischen Raum stammenden Spathen vom Typ Samson-Oberlörick-Abingdon lassen zwar erkennen daß Schwert und Scheide geschlossen bezogen wurden, doch muß dies keine Herstellung beider Teile in einer Werkstatt implizieren'). Quast obviously accepts the possible production in different workshops for swords and scabbards but sticks to the idea that once combined, sword and scabbard remain a fixed and static combination. As we will show in section 4, this seems to us the wrong conclusion.

[56] H. Steuer, "Helm und Ringschwert. Prunkbewaffnung und Rangabzeichen germanischer Krieger", *Studien zur Sachsenforschung* 6 (1987), note 62 mentions some interesting examples listed in V.I. Evison, "The Dover ring-sword and other sword-rings and beads", *Archaeologia* 101 (1967), pp. 63–118: the Vallstenarum-sword whose hilt dates from the first half of the sixth century which was provided only c. 600 with a ring-ornament that spoilt part of the existing *cloisonné*-work; the swords from Dover and Sarre where ring-ornaments were attached to older hilts; and the Faversham-sword where an old ring-ornament was attached to a younger hilt. The hilt of the ring-sword from Coombe seems to have been built up from different parts, to which the ring-ornament was only later attached.

[57] *Bernward von Hildesheim und das Zeitalter der Ottonen. Katalog der Ausstellung Hildesheim*, Band 2 (Hildesheim/Mainz, 1993), pp. 388–389.

[58] M. Schulze-Dörlamm, *Das Reichsschwert. Ein Herrschaftszeichen des Saliers Heinrich IV. und des Welfen Otto IV.* (Sigmaringen, 1995).

belonging to this important scabbard is lost? What is clear is that what is generally called the *Reichsschwert* is in fact a crucial combination of a sword and a scabbard. From the evidence presented below it can also be deduced that the deposition of a combination of sword *and* scabbard may not have been a regular phenomenon. It could well be the case that often only a sword was deposited and that the scabbard was kept in circulation.

These examples demonstrate that swords and scabbards probably at least since the fifth century have histories of their own, cultural biographies that include their (mythical) production, use and circulation (its inheritance included), and deposition, be it in a grave, a treasure, a church, or in a river.[59] The deposition itself implies that the object was deliberately extracted from further circulation and exchange in the social sphere and 'converted' to another, supernatural or long-term sphere. Although that sword may have lived on as a myth, its biography came to an end, and as such its deposition can be seen as a decisive step in a chain of rituals, both in the life of the sword and of the person or group to which it was important.

These observations illustrate our criticism of modern archaeological practice of ever-refining typologies and chronologies of archaeological data in order to arrive at deeper historical insights. In fact, levelling out and brushing away some essential characteristics of the data-set severely hampers a properly historical analysis of the changing use of material culture. Thanks to its dominant role in early-medieval reflections on the socio-cosmic order, the sword offers an interesting source for describing and analysing (changing) society from within.[60]

From the evidence gathered up to now in Belgium, the Netherlands and Germany north of the Main and west of the Elbe, it can

---

[59] The many objects that are found in rivers or lakes are more often than not considered to have been accidentally lost during a fight along the river or a crossing by boat. A recent example is Geibig's study on swords *(Beiträge zur morphologischen Entwicklung des Schwertes im Mittelalter. Eine analyse des Fundmaterials vom ausgehenden 8. bis zum 12. Jahrhundert aus Sammlungen der Bundesrepublik Deutschland)* which for this reason seems to miss an important conclusion (on the basis of his distribution maps it becomes clear that the deposition pattern of swords in his research-area varies through time and space). We are convinced that some of the river-finds were the result of deliberate ritual deposition. This topic, difficult to 'prove' as it is, is nowadays very slowly getting some attention in medieval archaeology.

[60] In a sense, this research is complementary to the one-sided fixation on written sources that describe and analyse late-Roman and early medieval northern Gaul mainly from a Roman and ecclesiastical or Byzantine perspective.

be deduced that sword (and/or *Langsax*) depositions occur only in c. 16% of the known cemeteries. Furthermore, of these cemeteries 79% contain not more than one or two examples. It can therefore be concluded that most men who owned or used a sword were not buried with it. This implies that it must have been only special circumstances in the life of a person or a group which caused a man to be buried with a sword. The deposition of a sword in a grave thus must have had a meaning which surpasses the traditional explanation that it was merely a mark of power and rank that at the burial of any sword bearer could have taken place. Apart from northern Gaul, the practice of sword-deposition in graves is only known in specific areas (Anglo-Saxon England, the Alamannic area, Lombard Italy, certain parts of Scandinavia and parts of the Slav territories). Therefore, despite comparable attitudes towards the sword throughout early medieval Europe, there are divergences in ritual use which point to diachronic and synchronic variation in contemporary notions of its 'appropriate use'. In the sections that follow we will illustrate this by describing some patterns in the ritual deposition of swords in the fifth and early sixth centuries.

4. *Sword depositions in Late Antique and early Merovingian Gaul*

Of all the swords and sword depositions of early medieval northwestern Europe those of the fifth century have been most thoroughly studied.[61] The reasons are obvious: they are the most exquisite ones;

---

[61] Basic literature is: K. Böhner, "Das Langschwert des Frankenkönigs Childerich", *Bonner Jahrbücher* 148 (1948), pp. 218–248. Werner, "Zur Entstehung der Reihengräberzivilisation. Ein Beitrag zur Methode der frühgeschichtlichen Archäologie". J. Werner, "Zu frankischen Schwertern des 5. Jahrhunderts (Oberlörick-Samson-Abingdon)", *Germania* 31 (1953), pp. 38–44. Böhme, *Germanische Grabfunde des 4. bis 5. Jahrhunderts zwischen unterer Elbe und Loire. Studien zur Chronologie und Bevölkerungsgeschichte.* F. Vallet, "A propos des tombes à épées d'apparat de la Rue Saint-Pierre (Oise) et d'Arcy-Sainte-Restitue (Aisne)", *Revue archéologique de Picardie* 3/4 (1988), pp. 45–55. Menghin, *Das Schwert im frühen Mittelalter. Chronologisch-typologische Untersuchungen zu Langschwertern aus germanischen Gräbern des 5. bis 7.Jahrhunderts.* K. Böhner, "Germanische Schwerter des 5. and 6. Jahrhunderts", *Jahrbuch des Römisch-Germanischen Zentralmuseums Mainz* 34 (1987), pp. 411–490. M. Martin, "Bemerkungen zur chronologischen Gliederung der frühen Merowingerzeit", *Germania* 67 (1989), pp. 121–141. D. Quast, *Die merowingerzeitlichen Grabfunde aus Gültlingen (Stadt Wildberg, Kreis Calw)* (Stuttgart, 1993). Böhme, "Der Frankenkönig Childerich zwischen Attila und Aëtius. Zu den Goldgriffspathen der Merowingerzeit", *Festschrift für Otto-Hermann Frey zum 65.Geburtstag*, pp. 69–110.

the one sword that can be attributed to a king (the Merovingian Childeric I) is included in this group;[62] the sword burials of this period are part of the early history of the Frankish kingdom. Interpretations of the presence of different sword types and the distribution patterns of their deposition are mostly given in ethnic terms. The distribution patterns of the depositions are often interpreted as the result of the expansion of various ethnic groups over ever-increasing geographical areas. In this section we will question the traditional interpretations of the sword types and sword depositions in terms of ethnic dichotomies (Germanic-Roman, Franks-Romans, Franks-Alamans) and provide an alternative interpretation for their deposition based on the ideas voiced in the previous sections.

4.1. Swords of the fifth century

What kind of swords are present in the archeological record of the fifth century? A number of well-known graves provide the anchorpoints in the analysis of the material culture of the period. Most famous is the grave of Childeric (died 481/2) found in Tournai in 1653.[63] The grave goods included a sword of which the hilt and scabbard mouthpiece are decorated with gold-foil and with garnets in a so-called cloisonné technique.[64] Other swords with this type of decoration are found elsewhere in northern Gaul. This is the first group of swords and scabbards (fig. 2).

Another important grave is nr. 43 from the large cemetery at Krefeld-Gellep on the Rhine (fig. 1).[65] In this grave a relatively simple sword with an ivory hilt was found in a scabbard onto which bronze fittings at the mouth, edges and lower point are attached.

---

[62] Böhner "Das Langschwert des Frankenkönigs Childerich". J. Werner, "Childeric. Histoire et Archéologie", *Histoire et Archeologie* 56 (1981), pp. 20–29.

[63] J. Werner, "Données nouvelles sur la sépulture royale de Childéric", *Les fouilles du quartier Saint Brice à Tournai 2. L'environnement funéraire de la sépulture de Childéric*, ed. R. Brulet (Tournai, 1991), pp. 14–22.

[64] Colour illustrations of the sword can be found in: H. Pirenne/B. Lyon/ A. Guillou/F. Gabrieli/H. Steuer, *Mahomet et Charlemagne. Bysance, Islam et Occident dans le haut moyen age* (Milan, 1986), p. 299 fig. 177; Werner, "Childeric. Histoire et Archeologie", p. 25. *Gallien in der Spätantike. Von Kaiser Constantin zu Frankenkönig Childerik* (Mainz, 1980), p. 239.

[65] Pirling, R., *Das römisch-fränkische Gräberfeld von Krefeld-Gellep* I–II (Berlin, 1966), I, pp. 184–185; II, pp. 19–20 and Tafel 10, 121 and 130. Colour illustration: *Die Franken. Wegbereiter Europas. Vor 1500 Jahren König Chlodwig und seine Erben* (Mainz, 1996), p. 97, Abb. 71.

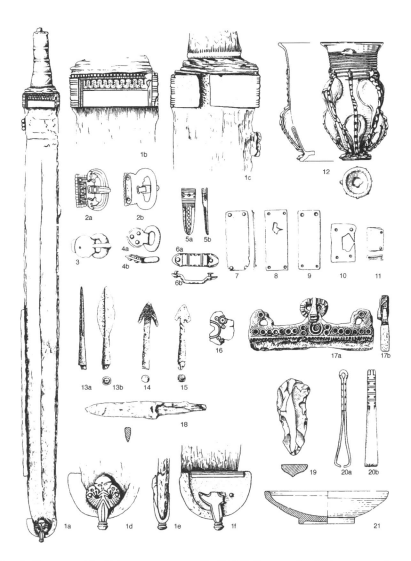

Fig. 1. In grave 43 of the cemetery at Krefeld-Gellep on the Rhine a sword was found in a scabbard ornamented with bronze fittings (1b and 1d). Among the other items are the remains of the baldric (2), a glass beaker (12), remains of a purse (17), a pair of tweezers (20), a shallow bowl (21) and the heads of arrows (13–15). Various scales. (After Pirling, *Das römisch-fränkische Gräberfeld von Krefeld-Gellep*, II, *Tafel* 10).

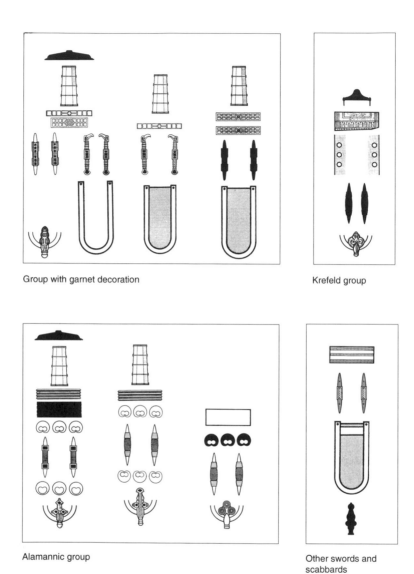

Group with garnet decoration

Krefeld group

Alamannic group

Other swords and scabbards

Fig. 2. The metal fittings of sword and scabbard of four groups of swords/scabbards according to Menghin (*Das Schwert im frühen Mittelalter*). In each rectangle it concerns from top to bottom: the hilt (not in the two groups on the right), scabbard mouth piece, fittings to attach the baldrick, fittings to reinforce the lower end of the scabbard.

The bronze fittings attached to reinforce the lower point of the scabbard, show a decoration of a human face *en face* between two birds' heads (the German term is *Maskenortband* (fig. 1, 1D)). Other examples are known. Böhme recently analysed the dating of these 'Krefeld swords' anew and came to the conclusion that they belong to the second half or even the last third of the fifth century rather than to the second third of that century.[66] The dating of the swords is still a matter of debate. Some of them may have been buried as early as the middle of the fifth century. Many burials with swords in Krefelder scabbards will date from the second half of the fifth century. The Krefelder scabbards form our second group (fig. 2).

The swords in the scabbards do not necessarily belong exclusively to this group. Similar swords are known from southwestern Germany (Alamannia), although they are often found in scabbards with different metal fittings, among which the rivets with a 'pelta-like' knob are a distinctive element.[67] These scabbards form the third group (fig. 2).

Next to these three groups of swords and scabbards there is a fourth group of scabbards characterised by simple bronze or silver fittings of some variety.

Menghin studied the swords and scabbards of these groups in great detail and defined several types based on combinations of metal fittings (fig. 2). He calls these types sword types although this characterisation is misleading.[68] The consequences of defining fixed types for the interpretation of the sword depositions are more drastic than can be perceived at first sight because his sword types are in fact a combination of swords and scabbards that may have had a more

---

[66] Böhme, "Der Frankenkönig Childerich zwischen Attila und Aëtius", pp. 82–98. This is a reaction to Martin's attempt to date the swords to the second third of the fifth century. Böhme's designation 'Krefeld swords' parallels the group which is also known as Samson-Oberlörick-Abingdon (Werner, "Zu fränkischen Schwertern des 5. Jahrhunderts (Oberlörick-Samson-Abingdon)") or *Schwerter mit maskenverzierten Ortbänden* (Böhner, "Germanische Schwerter des 5. and 6. Jahrhunderts"). They are Menghin's type IIa.

[67] It is Böhners, "Germanische Schwerter des 5. and 6. Jahrhunderts", *Gruppe C*. For colour plates see R. Christlein, *Die Alamannen. Archäologie eines lebendigen Volkes* (Stuttgart and Aalen, 1991³), Tafel 42, 44 (the Pleidelsheim sword) and Quast, *Die merowingerzeitlichen Grabfunde aus Gültlingen (Stadt Wildberg, Kreis Calw)*, Tafel 21 and 24 (the Gültlingen swords).

[68] Härke, *Angelsächsische Waffengräber des 5. bis 7.Jahrhunderts*, p. 88 is aware of this problem when he remarks that the current *Schwerttypen* are in fact *Beschlagkombinationstypen*.

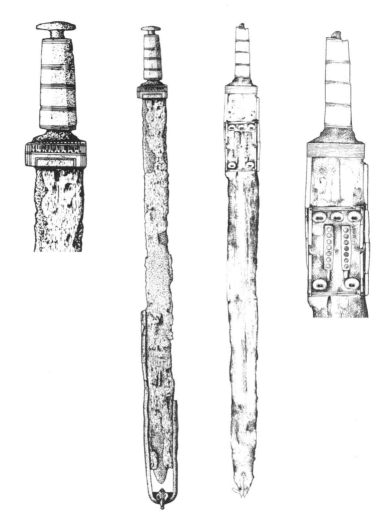

Fig. 3. Swords and scabbards from the grave of 1901 from Gültlingen (right) and
grave 21 from Hemmingen (left) (various scales) (see note 70).

dynamic 'life' than is suggested by the definition of a limited number of types. To explain this, it is helpful to recall the illustration of
two swords from Alamannia in Christlein's well-known book on the
Alamans.[69] The swords belong to two different types: the Hemmingen sword is of the Samson-Oberlörick type (type IIa, which is the

---

[69] See note 67. They are the sword from grave 21 from the cemetery at Hemmingen and the sword of grave 71 from Pleidelsheim.

same as Böhme's Krefelder type), the Pleidelsheim sword is of the Basel-Gotterbarmweg-Entringen type (type IIIa) in the typology of Menghin. In fig. 3 a similar combination is presented.[70] On closer inspection it turns out that the swords are (almost) identical, but that the scabbards have different combinations of metal fittings. Obviously identical swords could be put in different scabbards. Other examples could be added.[71] This suggests that there may have been no fixed combinations of a sword and scabbard. The typologies in current use do not fit our needs because they are based on the presupposition that a sword and scabbard combination was an indivisible whole from the moment of their production or combination.[72] Our point should be clear: the current typologies do not allow a grasp of the essence of the use of the sword during its existence (see paragraph 3). The combinations brought together under single types only form the tail end of the respective biographies of swords and scabbards: they are the 'frozen' combinations at the time of their deposition.

The same goes for the individual scabbards and swords. Christlein's illustration shows that the front of the hilt of the Pleidelsheim sword is decorated with a thin gold foil, as is the sword from Gültlingen in our fig. 3. Swords with gold foils like these are brought together by archaeologists under the category of 'gold-hilted swords' (*Goldgriffspathen*). These gold foils could however easily be taken off or put on again.[73] Gold-hilted swords thus do not constitute a type. They represent a specific state in which a sword might be, at a certain point in its biography. Some swords were buried in this state and the combination was 'frozen', other swords that show no gold-foil

---

[70] The swords are those of the grave of 1901 from Gültlingen (Quast, *Die merowingerzeitlichen Grabfunde aus Gültlingen (Stadt Wildberg, Kreis Calw)*, Taf. 5 and 6) and of grave 21 from Hemmingen (H.F. Müller, *Das Alamannische Gräberfeld von Hemmingen (Kreis Ludwigsburg)* (Stuttgart, 1976), Taf. 7). The iron knob that must once have been present at the top of the Gültlingen sword has disappeared. The hilt of the Gültlingen sword is covered with a thin gold foil on the front side.

[71] A fine example in this context is the sword in grave 21 at Petersfinger: Menghin, *Das Schwert im frühen Mittelalter*, nr. 18 with the wrong dating of the combination, see Härke, *Angelsächsische Waffengräber des 5. bis 7. Jahrhunderts*, p. 88. A sixth-century ringsword is put in a fifth-century scabbard of the Krefeld type.

[72] The sword and scabbard of a single combination could each have been produced in different workshops (see note 55).

[73] Vallet, "A propos des tombes à épées d'apparat de la Rue Saint-Pierre (Oise) et d'Arcy-Sainte-Restitue (Aisne)", p. 52) supposes that the gold foils were attached to the sword at the moment of deposition. See also Quast, *Die merowingerzeitlichen Grabfunde aus Gültlingen (Stadt Wildberg, Kreis Calw)*, p. 21.

on the hilt may have been 'gold-hilted swords' at an earlier stage in their existence.[74] Swords may have witnessed other alterations as well, as indicated in section 3: new hilts could be attached to older blades and vice-versa; new elements could be attached to existing hilts. That this was possible is proven by the repaired sword in Flonheim grave 5. Such a repair was only possible by taking the hilt apart.[75] An example of a complete change of the hilt cannot be given because precise dating of blades of the fifth and early sixth century, which would anable different dates for hilt and blade to be established, is almost impossible. One can however imagine that blades were produced in one place and that the ornaments of hilt and scabbard were added later. Maybe this was the case with the swordblades that Theoderic received from the king of the Warni (see the citation at the beginning of this paper). Finally, scabbards too may have undergone alterations such as are exemplified by the scabbard in grave 9 from Maastricht Saint Servatius church and the scabbard from Düsseldorf-Oberlörick that combine elements from the Krefeld and 'Alamannic' scabbards.[76]

A conclusion that can be drawn is that modern typochronological studies are based on the presupposition that swords and scabbards are static objects from the moment they are produced and that combinations of swords and scabbards are indivisible once they come into existence. However, the concept of the cultural biography of objects draws our attention to the fact that swords and scabbards are composite artifacts that may be altered and combined during their 'life'. That this is the case already in the fifth and sixth cen-

---

[74] The combination of a gold-foil on the hilt of a sword and a Krefeld-type scabbard has not been found yet. The database is small, however, so that it may be too early to conclude that this combination did not occur and that gold-foils and Krefeld scabbards are mutually exclusive elements.

[75] H. Ament, *Fränkische Adelsgräber von Flonheim in Rheinhessen* (Berlin, 1970), p. 54.

[76] The metal fitting of the lower end of the Maastricht scabbard is the *Maskenortband*; the mouthpiece of the scabbard cannot be brought under a specific type, since on the scabbard at least one pelta-like rivet was attached (J. Ypey, "Enkele 5deeeuwse vondsten uit Zuid- en Noord-Nederland", *Westerheem* 34 (1985), p. 7; Böhme, "Der Frankenkönig Childerich zwischen Attila und Aëtius. Zu den Goldgriffspathen der Merowingerzeit", pp. 95–96). Only remains of a scabbard were found, and no remains of a sword are mentioned, which is important. The scabbard from Düsseldorf-Oberlörick combines a scabbard mouthpiece of the Krefeld type and fittings to attach the sword belt to the scabbard (*Riemendurchzüge*) similar to those of 'Alamannic' scabbards (Menghin, *Das Schwert im frühen Mittelalter. Chronologisch-typologische Untersuchungen zu Langschwertern aus germanischen Gräbern des 5. bis 7.Jahrhunderts*, p. 194).

turies is supported by the evidence. This is also the very reason why Menghin could include only a few specimens under each type he defined. The major drawback of the currently used typologies is that they emphasise the moment of production (which is a modern pre-occupation) and do not allow us to grasp the dynamics in the social, ceremonial or ideological *use* of the sword or the meaning(s) given to it. It is however, exactly because of their ceremonial use in ritual that we have this collection of swords. Swords of the exquisite quality of those of the fifth and early sixth centuries were circulating among the highest ranking persons in northern Gaul. They were used as gifts or in ceremonial exchange and given meaning in the way set out in the previous sections.[77] The physical appearance of the swords and scabbards was not static and depended on their use and exchange in aristocratic networks. This conclusion stands in contrast to the present interpretations of the swords which stress the dependance of the physical appearance of the swords on ethnic entities, based on the presupposition that they were produced according to an ethnic norm. To strengthen our case we will now turn to an analysis of the distribution patterns of the sword depositions.

4.2. *Sword depositions and their distribution over northern Gaul*

In this section we will discuss the distribution of the four groups of swords and scabbards described: the Krefeld scabbards, the garnet-decorated swords and scabbards, the 'Alamannic' scabbards, and the scabbards decorated with bronze and silver fittings that differ from the other three groups.

Garnet-decorated swords and scabbards
This is the only group in which both swords and scabbards are relevant.[78] In several cases the swords are decorated with garnets too, although there are only five known cases of such combinations in

---

[77] See also Bazelmans in this volume.

[78] Although the sword graves of the four groups discussed here are divided into two chronological horizons contemporary with Childeric and Clovis by several archaeologists, we treat them here as one group. The division into two groups is often based on individual elements of the scabbard which is to our opinion an unsatisfactory method. Moreover there is often a confusion of arguments on the dating of the swords and the dating of the graves. Sometimes swords are dated by relating them to metal fittings that are found on other dated swords, dates that then turn out to be dates of burials. The disentangling of the arguments on the

which both swords and scabbards are decorated with garnets.[79] In the other ten cases only garnet-decorated scabbards are found. All finds are grave finds and thus buried during a ritual. This will certainly determine the distribution pattern. The garnet-decorated swords and scabbards are found along the Rhine and in the area between the Seine and the Aisne (fig. 4). The find of Childeric's sword at Tournai is in an outlying position, as is the find in Cologne.[80] Two garnet-decorated scabbards are found east of the Rhine, one in the Wetterau, one in the Alamannic area. Both scabbard mouthpieces

---

dating of the swords is a task far beyond the scope of this contribution. One way out is a seriation of all metal fittings on swords and scabbards that provides possible criteria for grouping these. In Menghin's grouping not only sword and scabbard fittings are included but also other objects from the graves. One wonders what is actually grouped: swords or combinations of objects? His group B is characterised by cloisonné ornamented belt-buckles, not by the fittings of the sword or of scabbards. Group A is characterised by a mixture of pommels and grave finds. From his tabulation of elements that constitute the basis of his grouping of swords or swordgraves it is difficult to grasp whether it is justified to distinguish between swords of groups A and B. Finally a seriation of swords and swordgraves provides us with a grouping of sword graves, but no more than that. It shows which graves are more or less identical in relation to a selected number of variables and which are different from each other. Further conclusions drawn from that grouping are a matter of interpretation. A grouping of swords is often too readily accepted as reflecting chronology. Other explanations are often not considered. See also the grouping by Martin ("Bemerkungen zur chronologischen Gliederung der frühen Merowingerzeit") and the comments by Périn, ("Les tombes de «chefs» du début de l'epoque mérovingienne. Datation et interprétation historique") on this and Böhme's dating of the Krefelder scabbards. The grouping might relate to the existence of certain aristocratic networks with their respective ritual repertoires (burial customs). For these reasons we prefer to treat the groups of swords mentioned above as a whole until a proper disentangling of datings of swords and graves has been carried out.

[79] Tournai, Arcy-Sainte-Restitue, Lavoye, Planig, Flonheim grave 5 (for these swords see Menghin, *Das Schwert im frühen Mittelalter. Chronologisch-typologische Untersuchungen zu Langschwertern aus germanischen Gräbern des 5. bis 7. Jahrhunderts*). Pouan has not been included in this group for the garnet-decoration on top of the pommel is of an entirely different character from that of the other five examples mentioned. If it is to be included there are of course six combinations. In the graves of Tournai and Pouan there are also long saxes in scabbards both of which are decorated with garnets.

[80] The dating of the sword and grave (Saint Severin's church grave 205) is a matter of debate. Menghin (*Das Schwert im frühen Mittelalter*, p. 173 and 241) places the grave in his *Zeitstufe* III, that is after c. 530. Päffgen (B. Päffgen, *Die Ausgrabungen in St. Severin zu Köln* (Mainz, 1992), I, pp. 453–456) dates the sword to the second half of the fifth century. Again the date of the (production of the) sword and the date of its burial may differ considerably, and both Päffgen and Menghin may be right. As we are interested in the burial ritual it may be wrong to put this find on the map, for it might date from the period following that under study here. On the other hand this burial may be another example of one in which an 'old' highly valued sword with an interesting cultural biography was employed.

Fig. 4. The distribution of finds (mainly burials) in the north of swords and scab-bards decorated with garnets. 1. combination of garnet-decorated sword and garnet-decorated scabbard; 2. garnet-decorated scabbard, 3. borders of provinces.

resemble mouth pieces found in Gaul. One scabbard with a similar mouthpiece has been found at Nocera Umbra in north Italy, but this fifth-century scabbard was combined with a ring-sword from the sixth century.

Krefeld scabbards

Krefeld scabbards hardly exist as a type. Only five scabbards are found with the combination of a mouthpiece and, at the lower end, a bronze fitting with the motif of a human mask between two birds.[81] In thirteen other instances only one of the two fittings has been

---

[81] Krefeld Gellep grave 43; Hemmingen grave 21; Abingdon grave 42; Samson graves 11 and 12 (see for these combinations of fittings Menghin, *Das Schwert im frühen Mittelalter. Chronologisch-typologische Untersuchungen zu Langschwertern aus germanischen Gräbern des 5. bis 7. Jahrhunderts*).

Fig. 5. The distribution of finds (mainly burials) of Krefeld scabbards. 1. Full combination of metal fittings; 2. scabbard with either a Krefeld mouthpiece or Krefeld end-fitting; 3. stray finds of metal fittings of Krefeld scabbards.

found. Krefeld scabbards are mainly found in graves in the northern Meuse valley (fig. 5). Some stray finds of individual fittings found in the central Netherlands and in the Frisian area are difficult to interpret.[82] They may have got there as scrap metal in later times or Krefelder swords may have circulated there but not been deposited in graves during a burial ritual. Krefeld scabbards are also found on the Rhine, in the Alamannic area, in England (that is the upper Thames valley)[83] and north of the Seine: all these scabbards were found in graves.

---

[82] Recently a mouthpiece with runic inscription was found at Tiel (prov. of Gelderland, Netherlands) as a stray find: A. Bosman and T. Looijenga, "A runic inscription from Bergakker (Gelderland), The Netherlands", *Amsterdamer Beiträge zur älteren Germanistik* 46 (1996), pp. 9–16.

[83] Härke indicated to me the different distribution patterns for the different sword/scabbard combinations in England.

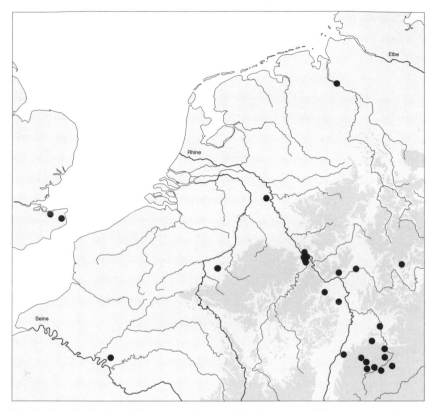

Fig. 6. The distribution of finds (mainly burials) in the north of 'Alamannic' scabbards.

'Alamannic' scabbards

'Alamannic' scabbards are found in the Alamannic area, in Rhein-hessen and around Wiesbaden, in England (that is in Kent) and in the valleys of the Meuse, Seine and Elbe (fig. 6). If one does not count Rhine-Hessen and the Wiesbaden area as Alamannic terri-tory,[84] then it turns out that almost as many 'Alamannic' scabbards are found outside the Alamannic area as within it.[85]

---

[84] To include them in the Alamannic territory on the basis of sword finds is to create a circular argument as will be clear later. See also Wieczorek, "Die Ausbreitung der fränkischen Herrschaft in den Rheinlanden vor und seit Chlodwig I", pp. 241–260.

[85] The two scabbards found in Basel are just outside the bottom edge of the map. The second gold hilted sword of Entringen (G. Schmitt, "Ein frühmerowingisches Einzelgrab bei Entringen, Gem. Ammerbuch, Kreis Tübingen", *Fundberichte aus Baden-Württemberg* 11 (1986), pp. 359–380) is not mapped for it is not possible to determine what the scabbard looked like since no metal fittings were preserved. The wooden remains of the scabbard and the woodcarving on it resemble the 'Alamannic' scabbard of Basel-Kleinhüningen grave 63.

Fig. 7. The distribution of finds (mainly burials) of swords in scabbards with 'other
forms' of metal fittings.

Other swords and scabbards

In this group swords and scabbards are taken together that cannot
be placed among any of the previously mentioned groups.[86] The
metal fittings of these scabbards are either of bronze or of silver. They
are found in the Meuse, Rhine, Weser and Elbe valleys, in the Wetterau and the lower Main valley, the Alamannic area, in northern
France, and in England (that is in Middle-/East Anglia) (fig. 7).

---

[86] Included on this map are scabbards with the fittings of the Haillot-Mezières
type, the scabbards with the Eberfingen-Haillot type mouthpiece, the scabbard end
fittings of the Langen type and Wageningen-Wenigumstadt type. All types according to Menghin, *Das Schwert im frühen Mittelalter. Chronologisch-typologische Untersuchungen
zu Langschwertern aus germanischen Gräbern des 5. bis 7.Jahrhunderts.* Next there are three
swords from the cemetery at Liebenau and one sword/scabbard from Nebel, hill 1;
Bremen-Mahndorf and Guldenstein, the river finds from Stade-Lühesand and scabbard end fittings from Krefeld-Gellep grave 205, Ockstadt, Mülhofen, Ditzingen
and Churchover.

4.3. *First comments on traditional interpretations of the distribution patterns*

The distribution pattern as described above has invited archaeologists to put ethnic labels on the various sword types. The 'Alamannic' swords have been labelled as such because there is a concentration of findplaces in the Alamannic area. Garnet-decorated swords and scabbards have been considered 'Frankish' because their distribution is restricted to Frankish territories.[87] By assuming that the swords were made in the areas where they were found, the argument was taken further and conclusions were drawn that included an evaluation of the artistic capacities of various tribes.[88] Werner suggested that the Krefeld swords were produced at some place in the Meuse valley, possibly Namur, because there is a concentration of graves containing Krefeld swords in that region.[89] He also suggested that the swords were made in a Late Antique, that is a non-'Germanic' tradition. Once these interpretations were put forward, the various types of swords were reified and started a life of their own with their ethnic labels and became Frankish, Alamannic, Germanic or Roman swords.[90] Such identifications should be the object of research instead of being considered given facts (see section 2). They lead to circular arguments like the one drawn by Schulze-Dörlamm from the presence of 'Alamannic' swords and other 'Alamannic' finds in the Neuwieder Bekken in the lower Moselle valley. She concluded that the Alamans had extended their territory to the north in the second

---

[87] Böhner, "Das Langschwert des Frankenkönigs Childerich", p. 243: 'Ihre (that is the type III swords) Verbreitung verdichtet sich nun so auffällig (zwölf Stück) in dem verhältnismässig engen Gebiet, das nach der allgemeinen Annahme den Alamannen nach der 496 von den Franken erlittenen Niederlage verblieb, dass sie wohl als ein alamannischer Schwerttyp bezeichnet werden dürfen' and: 'In der Verbreitung der Schwerter des Types II (they are swords related to the one in Childeric's grave) and Types III spiegelt sich also im Grossen und Ganzen das Siedlungsverhältnis der Franken und Alamannen nach 496 wieder'.

[88] Böhner, "Das Langschwert des Frankenkönigs Childerich", pp. 243–244: 'Aus ihrer (the sword distribution patterns) Betrachtung geht hervor dass die Alamannen in der Folgezeit (that is after 496, see note 79) durchaus noch eine eigene Goldschmiedekunst besassen, die sich aber an Pracht und Reichtum der Ausstattung mit jenen hervorragenden fränkischen Werkstätten nicht messen konnte. Zweifellos ist dieser Unterschied durch die überlegene politische Macht des Frankenreiches bedingt'.

[89] Werner, "Zu fränkischen Schwertern des 5. Jahrhunderts (Oberlörick-Samson-Abingdon)", p. 42.

[90] Böhme ("Der Frankenkönig Childerich zwischen Attila und Aëtius. Zu den Goldgriffspathen der Merowingerzeit") recently suggested that another northern Gaulish provenance of some of the swords may be considered.

half of the fifth century before they were driven back by Clovis shortly after 496.[91] Her view is based on the supposition that it is possible to distinguish a '*typisch alamannischer Spatha*'.[92] In this way the geographical expansion of tribal entities as homogeneous totalities is reconstructed as if they were like the expanding nations of the nineteenth century.

In what follows we will question this line of reasoning by pointing to the context of the depositions, the specific content of the concept of ethnicity as used by archaeologists and the overall distribution pattern of the swords.

The context of the sword depositions
Almost all sword and scabbard depositions discussed above are grave finds. That means that their deposition is part of a specific ritual and that the distribution patterns of the depositions is determined by the presence or absence of the performance of this ritual at the death of a person (see section 2.4). By interpreting sword types in ethnic terms like Frankish or Alamannic on the basis of concentrations of depositions in their respective 'territories', two related, but different spheres of actions, each with different archaeological correlates, are not clearly distinguished in explaining the distribution pattern. The first sphere has to do with the production, distribution and circulation of swords in northern Gaul in socio-political practice, that is the exchange of swords between kings and aristocrats, fathers and sons, lords and followers. However, the geographical extent of the exchange networks may not be identical to the area where the ritual of depositing a sword in a grave is practised. The second sphere has to do with the use of swords in the burial ritual in certain areas. The uses of the sword in the 'social' sphere and in the 'ritual' sphere will certainly be related.

We have already noted that only a small proportion of those men who carried a sword or possessed several swords are buried with

---

[91] M. Schulze-Dörlamm, *Die spätrömischen und frühmittelalterlichen Gräberfelder von Gondorf, Gem. Kobern-Gondorf, Kr. Mayen-Koblenz* (Stuttgart, 1990), pp. 382–383. On the uncertainties of the chronological reconstruction of the military encounters of the Franks and the Alamans in this region: E. Ewig, *Frühes Mittelalter* (Düsseldorf, 1980), pp. 15–16; Wieczorek, "Die Ausbreitung der fränkischen Herrschaft in den Rheinlanden vor und seit Chlodwig I".

[92] Schulze-Dörlamm, *Die spätrömischen und frühmittelalterlichen Gräberfelder von Gondorf, Gem. Kobern-Gondorf, Kr. Mayen-Koblenz* p. 382.

one.[93] The burial of a sword seems to be exeptional, practised in specific circumstances (we will come back to this later).

The conceptualisation of ethnicity and value
The concept of ethnicity used in archeological interpretations that leads to the identification of Roman, Frankish or Alamannic swords has been criticised in recent years.[94] Traditionally in archaeology ethnic identity has been seen as a static status, an inherent disposition that was externally reflected with the help of signs (*fibulae*, belt types etc.). Historians using anthropological insights related to this topic have questioned this static view on ethnic identity and pointed to the dynamic character and subjective aspects in the process of identifying oneself and others and to the political character and political use of ethnic identifications of other groups.[95] Archaeologists of the early Frankish world on the continent, have however up to now hardly picked up this discussion and still work with a concept of ethnic identity as a preconceived, historically given condition to which individual members of a group have to adhere wherever they are, whatever positions they assume. This 'belonging to' is thought to be represented by being clothed in the prescribed way and wearing the prescribed signs in death. As a consequence homogeneous cultures are believed to have existed and are reconstructed, and then put in opposition to each other. This concept of culture (with homogeneity in thoughts and behaviour as its core element) has a long tradition in archaeology. An alternative conceptualisation of culture is that which values a person's or a group's capacity to reflect on their cultural context and cultural sources, to interpret them in discourse with

---

[93] See section 3.2.
[94] A review of the ideas on ethnicity in vogue in historiography and archeology started with Wenskus' (R. Wenskus, *Stammesbildung und Verfassung. Das Werden der frühmittelalterlichen Gentes* (Köln/Graz, 1961)) analysis of northwestern European tribes. The amount of literature on this topic is rapidly growing: of importance to our subject are: P. Geary, "Ethnic identity as a situational construct in the early middle ages", *Mitteilungen der Anthropologischen Gesellschaft in Wien* 113 (1983), pp. 15–26. W. Pohl, "Conceptions of ethnicity in Early Medieval studies", *Archaeologia Polona* 29 (1991), pp. 39–49. W. Pohl, "Tradition, Ethnogenese und literarische Gestaltung: eine Zwischenbalanz", *Ethnogenese und Überlieferung. Angewandte Methoden der Frühmittelalterforschung*, eds. K. Brunner and B. Mesta (Wenen/München, 1994), pp. 9–26. H. Wolfram, "*Origo et Religio*. Ethnic traditions and literature in early medieval texts", *Early Medieval Europe* 3 (1994), pp. 19–38.
[95] See the literature mentioned in note 94 above.

others and to define and represent their or its position in society.[96] When archaeologists detach themselves from the traditional views on ethnic identity and combine new ones with new ideas on the value of objects (see sections 2.2 and 3.1), other possible interpretations of the spatial distribution of sword burials can be given. Recent studies on the value of objects in non-western societies indicate that 'value' is composed of different elements that are symbolically linked.[97] Material value is associated with 'values' attributed to an object, during its'life', that is its circulation or non-circulation. As regards the swords studied here, it is important to note that their value may also be constituted by their linking to important values in society (the elite life style discussed above) or specific constituents of the person (like body, soul and spirit) that are brought together or separated in rituals so that persons (in our case the person as aristocrat) are constituted or dissolved. In anthropological terms: object and subject are commensurable and it is exactly this that determines the objects value. New conceptions on ethnic identity and 'value' thus allow us to develop a deeper understanding of the use of the sword in the burial ritual.

The overall distribution pattern of sword depositions in northern Gaul
We have shown that the ethnic interpretation of sword types is mainly based on supposed concentrations of depositions of different types in different regions. In the modern research on the swords it is suggested that different types have almost mutually exclusive distribution patterns. We have already seen that 'types' hardly exist as such and that the bringing together of various swords under a type is in fact a denial of the individual appearance of each object and of the biographies of swords, scabbards and combinations of them. There are only four Krefeld scabbards that can be brought under the model type description. Can the other scabbards with only one metal fitting be attributed to this group? To what extent can we neglect elements of the type description? Asking these questions means undermining the ethnic meaning attached by archaeologists to the regional con-

---

[96] F. Barth, "Towards greater naturalism in conceptualizing societies", *Conceptualizing Society*, ed. A. Kuper (London and New York, 1992), pp. 17–33. Theuws, "De vele lagen van de vroeg-middeleeuwse geschiedenis".

[97] Bazelmans, *Eén voor allen, allen voor één. Tacitus' Germania, de oudengelse Beowulf en het ritueel-cosmologische karakter van de relatie tussen heer en volgeling in Germaanse samenlevingen*, chapter 3 and Bazelmans, below in this volume, for a discussion of recent in anthropological research on this topic.

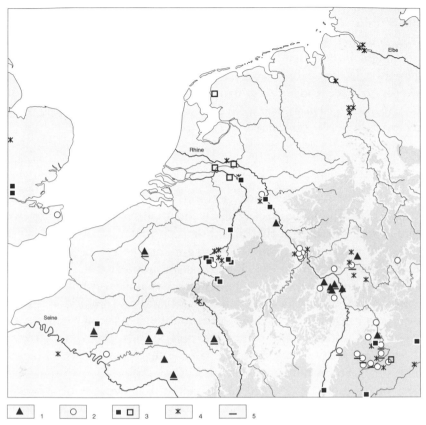

Fig. 8. The distribution of finds (mainly burials) of all forms of swords and scabbards from the second half of the fifth and beginning of the sixth centuries. 1. garnet-ornamented swords and scabbards; 2. 'Alamannic' scabbards; 3. Krefeld scabbards; 4. 'other' forms; 5. swords with hilt with gold foil (*Goldgriffspatha*).

centrations of sword depositions. There are no regional concentrations other than those created by archaeologists who bring together a number of elements under a type and leave out others.[98] The ethnic interpretation can be further questioned by looking at the overall distribution pattern of sword depositions (fig. 8). It appears that the distribution patterns of the different groups are hardly mutually exclusive. The intermingling of the distribution patterns makes clear that there is no 'norm' that prevents men in a given region being buried with 'strange' swords. In fact the overall distribution pattern

---

[98] That is why Menghin had to give so many distribution maps of individual elements of swords and scabbards of which the distribution patterns often match only superficially.

shows that swords of all forms and shapes circulated in northern Gaul and the regions east of the Rhine. The only possible exception might be the area between the Aisne and the Seine where only garnet-decorated swords and scabbards are buried, although other swords may have circulated there. This may be the result of our present state of knowledge for relatively few fifth- and sixth-century swords have been discovered in that region up to now.

4.4. *First conclusions regarding the distribution pattern of sword depositions*

On the basis of the evidence discussed above and an examination of the presuppositions in vogue in the modern historiography we came to the conclusion that an ethnic interpretation of sword types and an ethnic background to the distribution patterns of sword depositions must be questioned. The great variation in the appearance of swords and scabbards points to their dynamic use not as a sign with a fixed relation between object and what is signified, but as a symbol surrounded by a cloud of meanings depending on the context of use and the observer of the object. As Cohen pointed out: the sharing of a symbol need not mean the sharing of meanings.[99] This observation stands in contrast to the ethnic interpretation that rests on the idea that swords and scabbards have a static physical appearance during their lifetime and accordingly are used in a static sense as signs.

The overall distribution pattern shows that all kinds of forms of swords and scabbards were deposited (and circulated) in northern Gaul and adjacent regions. It is because of this that we conclude that the distribution pattern of sword depositions is first of all determined by the exchange and circulation of swords in aristocratic networks that may have kings as their central nodes. It is, of course, also determined by the swords' use in the burial ritual, and we will deal with this part of the interpretation in the next section.

The written evidence clearly demonstrates that swords and other objects were important gifts that circulated within these networks. The composition of the networks (in terms of persons and groups)

---

[99] On signs and symbols see: E. Leach, *Culture and Communication. The Logic by which Symbols are Connected. An Introduction to the Use of Structuralist Analysis in Social Anthropology* (Cambridge, 1976). A. Cohen, *The Symbolic Construction of Community* (Chichester, 1985).

might alter over time in relation to the political needs of the moment. Many, if not all of these networks seem to have been centred on kings or important lords that are indicated in the written sources in various ways. Bazelmans provides an important model for under-standing the nature of the relations in such groups of kings and aris-tocrats, or lords and followers by analysing on the basis of the *Beowulf* how the ceremonial exchange of precious objects is related to a series of lifecycle rituals in which a man is contituted as a warrior/aristo-crat/king.[100] The king plays a central role in this series of rituals for he is the mediator between the warrior/follower and the ancestors or God who are/is vital in obtaining the essential constituents of a man as warrior/aristocrat. The network centred on the king thus becomes a ritual-cosmological entity that is essential in the warriors' representation of identity. Although categories of objects (like swords) may be brought in relation to important constituents of the warrior as a person and to values in general (see chapters 2 and 3) it remains an open question to what extent the specific physical appearance of individual swords in the possession of a warrior identifies him as a member of a specific network, for the written sources indicate that objects are not only exchanged within but also between networks. The individual objects may have been known first and foremost by the (hi)stories attached to them. It must be recalled that Beowulf, when he landed in the land of the Danes, was received by a watch-man, a high-ranking man who identified Beowulf by his gear as a great warrior, but could not identify him as a Geat. He did identify them as important men. The watchman therefor is first and fore-most interested in the 'antecedents' of Beowulf who identifies him-self first by telling that he is one of king Hygelacs hearth-companions and then by telling the name of his father.[101]

This perspective on the relation between material culture and the warrior as person complicates our conceptualisation of ethnic iden-tity and ethnicity. Above we stated that an ethnic interpretation of sword types and the distribution pattern of sword depositions must be questioned: we can now be more precise. The idea that archae-ologically defined sword types were 'signs' for designating member-ship of a specific ethnic group defined as a homogeneous whole (the

---

[100] See note 97.
[101] *Beowulf*, 229–257. The translation is taken from: *Beowulf. A Verse Translation* by M. Alexander.

traditional view) has to be discarded. We might accept that swords circulated in king-aristocrat networks as ritual-cosmological entities but we do not know whether all swords of a single type or category identified by archaeologists can be ascribed to a single network. This being said we also have to conclude that membership of such a network did not automatically lead at death to a burial rite in which a sword deposition was practised. Why was it that members of a certain network were buried in different ways? To answer that question we will now turn to the use of the sword in the burial ritual and then return to the use of the sword in the networks.

5. *The deposition of the sword in a grave during the funerary ritual*

The question that we now again have to deal with is simple to ask but difficult to answer: why should a high-ranking man be buried with a sword in the fifth and sixth centuries? The answer is almost impossible to give in individual cases because the contexts in which the men in sword graves were buried differ considerably. Some men are interred in isolated spots,[102] some in existing cemeteries,[103] others are the first buried on the site and attract burials from later generations (the so-called *Gründergräber* or founders' graves).[104] In some cemeteries more than one grave with a costly sword is found,[105] although as a rule there is only one such sword-burial in a cemetery. Some sword burials are found in christian cultplaces[106] or under

---

[102] Entringen, the grave of 1904 (Schmitt, "Ein frühmerowingisches Einzelgrab bei Entringen, Gem. Ammerbuch, Kreis Tübingen").

[103] Krefeld-Gellep grave 43 (Pirling, *Das römisch-fränkische Gräberfeld von Krefeld-Gellep* I–II, I, 184–185; II 19–20, and Tafel 10, 120, 121, 130).

[104] Lavoye grave 319 (R. Joffroy, *Le cimetière de Lavoye (Meuse). Nécropole mérovingienne* (Paris, 1974)). Childeric's grave may be considered as such although it is not the first at the site (R. Brulet, *Les fouilles du quartier Saint-Brice à Tournai. 2 L'environnement funéraire de la sépulture de Childéric* (Louvain, 1991), pp. 184–192. R. Brulet, "Tournai und der Bestattungsplatz um Saint Brice", *Die Franken, Wegbereiter Europas. Vor 1500 Jahren. König Chlodwig und seine Erben* (Mainz, 1996), pp. 166–167).

[105] Hemmingen grave 2 and 21 (Müller, *Das Alamannische Gräberfeld von Hemmingen (Kreis Ludwigsburg)*. Gültlingen graves from 1889 and 1901 (Quast, *Die merowingerzeitlichen Grabfunde aus Gültlingen (Stadt Wildberg, Kreis Calw)*).

[106] Cologne, Saint Severin church, grave 205 (Menhin, *Das Schwert im frühen Mittelalter. Chronologisch-typologische Untersuchungen zu Langschwertern aus germanischen Gräbern des 5. bis 7. Jahrhunderts*, p. 241 note 85 and p. 335 note 10; Päffgen, *Die Ausgrabungen in St. Severin zu Köln*, pp. 317–324); Maastricht, Saint Servatius church, grave 9 (Ypey, "Enkele 5de-eeuwse vondsten uit Zuid- en Noord-Nederland", pp. 6–10).

a tumulus[107] and many of them are located near a Roman town,[108] fortress[109] or a hillfort.[110] However, burials in a rural context are present as well. The archaeologist searching for a regularly recurring topographical context for the sword graves will be disappointed for there seems to be no norm regarding their location in the natural, cultural and monumental landscape and the form and layout of the sepulchres whose occupants were, we can assume important men. In what follows we will try to give an outline of an answer to the question put forward above in accordance with the concepts presented in sections one to three. In answering the question we suggest a distinction here too between two spheres of interpretation.[111] The first sphere concerns a changing discourse on power and related to that changes in aristocratic values in Late Antique northern Gaul. Here we touch on the world of ideas and values that are part of and give form to an elite life style and its repertoire of rituals. However, if wecan hypothesise why weapons were deposited in graves in general we are still unable to explain why this only happened in certain cases, for it is clear that most men whocarried exquisite swords when living were not buried with them. The second sphere of interpretation thus relates to the specific socio-political circumstances in which the deposition of a sword during a burial is a relevant ritual.

5.1. *The deposition of swords and aristocratic values*

An interpretation of the meaning of the deposition of swords in graves in the second half of the fifth century can only be given if we include in the anlysisthe development of the ritual of sword depo-

---

[107] Childeric's grave at Tournai (Brulet, *Les fouilles du quartier Saint-Brice à Tournai. 2 L'environnement funéraire de la sépulture de Childéric*, pp. 184–192).

[108] See notes 61 and 63.

[109] Krefeld-Gellep: see note 65; Maastricht: see note 76.

[110] Probably Samson graves 11 and 12 (A. Dasnoy, "La necropole de Samson (IVe–VIe siècles)", *Annales de la Société archeologique de Namur* 54 (1968), pp. 277–333); Vieuxville (J. Alenus-Lecerf, "Le cimetière de Vieuxville: quelques considerations préliminaires", *La civilisation mérovingienne dans le bassin Mosan*, eds. M. Otte and J. Willems (Liège, 1986), pp. 181–193. R. Brulet, *La Gaule septentrionale aus Bas-Empire. Occupation du sol et défense du territoire dans l'arrière-pays du limes au IVe et Ve siècle* (Trier, 1990), p. 324).

[111] This is not to say that these two spheres were perceived as separate in Late Antiquity.

sition and that of weapon burials in the preceding period.[112] The weapon burials of the fourth century have recently become the subject of a renewed scholarly debate, since their identification as graves of Germanic warriors serving the Roman army has been criticised.[113] An analysis of these burials goes far beyond the scope of this article. We will confine us here to offering a number of ideas and suggestions on the character of 'Germanic' weapon burials in northern Gaul. We have to distinguish three phases in the development of the weapon burial rite. The first phase comprises almost the entire fourth century, the second phase the late fourth century and the first half of the fifth, and the third phase the second half of the fifth century and the beginning of the sixth.[114]

Sword burials dating from before the middle of the fifth century in northern Gaul (that is from the first and second phase) are rare. Twenty to thirty examples are known, including some in northern Germany. They are found along the Rhine, in the Meuse valley and

---

[112] Werner ("Zur Entstehung der Reihengräberzivilisation. Ein Beitrag zur Methode der frühgeschichtlichen Archäologie") regarded the weapon burials of the fourth and early fifth centuries as the origin of the later Frankish burial custom of depositing large quantities of objects in graves. Périn also stressed that it was the Franks, who settled in northern Gaul in the fifth century, that took over the funerary habits of the Germanic settlers already there. He labelled their culture as 'Romano-franque' (P. Périn, "L'assimilation ethnique vue par l'archéologie", *Histoire et Archéologie* 56 (1981), p. 42. P. Périn, "A propos de publications récentes concernant le peuplement en Gaule à l'epoque mérovingienne: la <question franque>", *Archéologie Médiévale* 11 (1981), pp. 125–145).

[113] The standard work on this is still: Böhme, *Germanische Grabfunde des 4. bis 5. Jahrhunderts zwischen unterer Elbe und Loire. Studien zur Chronologie und Bevölkerungsgeschichte*, see also: H. W. Böhme, "Tombes germaniques des IVe et Ve siècles en Gaule du nord. Chronologie—Distribution—Interprétation", *Problèmes de chronologie relative et absolue concernant les cimetières mérovingiens d'entre Loire et Rhin*, eds. M. Fleury and P. Périn (Paris, 1978), pp. 21–38. More recent are: Perin, "A propos de publications récentes concernant le peuplement en Gaule à l'époque mérovingienne: la <question franque>". P. Périn and L.-Ch. Feffer, *Les Francs. 1 A la conquête de la Gaule; 2 A l'origine de la France* (Paris, 1987). E. James, *The Franks* (Oxford, 1988), pp. 44–51. C. Seiller, "Les Germains dans l'armée romaine tardive en Gaule septentrionale, le témoignage de l'archéologie", *L'armée romaine et les barbares du IIIe au VIIe siècles*, eds. F. Vallet and M. Kazanski (Paris, 1993), pp. 187–193, and other contributions in: F. Vallet and M. Kazanski, eds., *L'armée romaine et les barbares du IIIe au VIIe siècles* (Paris, 1993). For a critique of the interpretation of the weapon burials as those of Germanic soldiers see: G. Halsall, "The origins of the *Reihengräberzivilization*: forty years on", *Fifth-Century Gaul: a Crisis of Identity?* eds. J. Drinkwater and H. Elton (Cambridge, 1992), pp. 196–207, and C.R. Whittaker, *Frontiers of the Roman Empire. A Social and Economic Study* (Baltimore, 1994).

[114] On distribution maps of Late Antique weapon burials, the first two phases are often taken together. This obliterates an important development taking place at the end of the fourth century.

in the eastern part of Picardy. It is important to note that most of them date from the late fourth century and the first half of the fifth.[115] Thus there are hardly sword burials in the first phase. The small number of known sword graves indicates that the deposition of a sword in a grave must have been a rare occasion in these days, even if we accept that many graves containing swords still await discovery. The late-Roman sword graves are, in comparison to other graves of the period lavishly furnished with grave goods that are almost without exception of (northern) Gallic or Roman provenance. Some of these men were buried in sarcophagi like the person found in Bonn-Jakobstrasse[116] or the 'chef militaire' from Vermand.[117]

In modern historiography, these and similar graves are usually interpreted as those of Germanic chiefs who had served in the Roman army.[118] In relation to this interpretation, certain questions arise: why is it that only a few Germanic militairy chiefs are buried in this way?[119] why should it be important to show a Germanic ethnic background or identity at death after a career in the Roman army? does the deposition of a weapon in the grave relate to ethnic identity? if ethnic identity is an important element in the burial ritual, who is giving form to the ritual practice? and finally: are the objects in graves that we classify as weapons to be seen exclusively as weapons?[120]

---

[115] Böhme, *Germanische Grabfunde des 4. bis 5. Jahrhunderts zwischen unterer Elbe und Loire. Studien zur Chronologie und Bevölkerungsgeschichte*, pp. 97–100. Recently it has been suggested that some of the Krefeld swords may date from before the middle of the fifth century. We are inclined to follow Böhme's dating of the swords to the second half of the fifth century, see note 66.

[116] D. Haupt, "Spätrömisches Grab mit Waffenbeigabe aus Bonn", *Archeologie en Historie. Opgedragen aan H. Brunsting bij zijn zeventigste verjaardag*, eds. W.A. van Es et alii (Bussum, 1973), pp. 315–326.

[117] Böhme, *Germanische Grabfunde des 4. bis 5. Jahrhunderts zwischen unterer Elbe und Loire. Studien zur Chronologie und Bevölkerungsgeschichte*, pp. 331–332, Tafel 137.

[118] See for instance the many contributions on this topic in Vallet/Kazanski, *L'armée romaine et les barbares du IIIe au VIIe siècles*. There are doubts voiced by Périn, "A propos de publications récentes concernant le peuplement en Gaule a l'epoque mérovingienne: la <question franque>"; Périn/Feffer, *Les Francs. 1 A la conquete de la Gaule; 2 A l'origine de la France*, pp. 64–69 and B. Young, "Que sait-on des Germains et des Francs?" *Histoire et Archeologie* 56 (1981), pp. 12–19.

[119] And why is this ritual not practised by the Burgundians and the Visigoths in Gaul? See for an explanation regarding the Wisigoths which is difficult to accept: P. Périn, "L'armée de Vidimer et la question des dépots funéraires chez les Wisigoths en Gaule et en Espagne (V^e–VIe siècles)", *L'armée romaine et les barbares du IIIe au VIIe siècles*, eds. F. Vallet and M. Kazanski (Paris, 1995), pp. 411–423, and note 142 below for comments on his interpretations.

[120] The question has been asked before: Härke, *Angelsächsische Waffengräber des 5. bis 7.Jahrhunderts*, pp. 220 and 224; H. Härke, "Tombes à armes anglo-saxonnes:

The identification of the sword and weapon graves as those of Germanic soldiers depends to some extent on a strictly functional interpretation of the objects deposited in the graves as weapons. It also depends on the location of sword graves near walled towns, fortresses and hillforts, which has invited archaeologists to relate the weapons to the military architecture of these places. Thus the men buried with swords are seen as local military commanders or the military complement of a hillfort.[121] A critique of this interpretation of the sword graves (and the older weapon graves to which we will turn presently) has recently been formulated by Halsall.[122] He suggests that the weapon graves should be interpreted as those of local aristocrats 'displaying their power in the community more overtly in their funerals than had hitherto been usual'.[123] This occurred, according to Halsall, in a situation where competition for local control became stronger after the dissolution of effective imperial authority. Whittaker came to the same conclusion on the basis of evidence from a much larger region: he observed that the weapon graves have a strong military idiom, and often appear to belong only to families of high status.[124] It is therefore difficult, he says, to 'make a cultural separation between Germans and Romans in this period'.[125] The

---

sépultures des guerriers ou symbolysme rituel?", *L'armée romaine et les barbares du III*
au VII *siècles*, eds. F. Vallet and M. Kazanski, (Paris, 1993), pp. 425–436.

[121] Brulet, *La Gaule septentrionale aus Bas-Empire. Occupation du sol et défense du terri-*
toire dans l'arriere-pays du limes au IV *et V* *siècles*, p. 324; Böhme, *Germanische Grab-*
funde des 4. bis 5. Jahrhunderts zwischen unterer Elbe und Loire. Studien zur Chronologie und
Bevölkerungsgeschichte, pp. 182–186. In one case the find of the remains of a sword, mailcoat and saddle made the author search for the cavalry unit in which the mounted man in question was thought to have served (H. Chew, "Une sépulture militaire de l'époque romaine tardive à Sarry (Marne)", *L'armée romaine et les bar-*
bares du III *au VII* *siècles*, eds. F. Vallet and M. Kazanski (Paris, 1993), pp. 313–321).
[122] Halsall, "The origins of the *Reihengräberzivilization*: forty years on".
[123] Halsall, "The origins of the *Reihengräberzivilization*: forty years on", p. 207. This interpretation however does not explain why *weapons* were introduced in the ritual and why the need for a more lavish ritual expression of power did not lead for instance to an increase in the deposition of food (in pottery and glass vessels) and other objects in the grave.
[124] Whittaker, *Frontiers of the Roman Empire. A Social and Economic Study*, p. 235. He refers to the presence of children's graves among the weapon burials. To this obser-vation the presence of lavishly furnished women's graves in the burial grounds con-cerned and the occurrence of burials in sarcophagi (Bonn, Vermand) can be added.
[125] Böhme qualified the late Roman civilisation of northern Gaul which produced the weapon graves as a *Mischzivilisation* (Böhme, *Germanische Grabfunde des 4. bis 5.*
Jahrhunderts zwischen unterer Elbe und Loire. Studien zur Chronologie und Bevölkerungsgeschichte
pp. 205–206). However, it was obviously not mixed to the extent that Romans and Germanic people could no longer be identified on the basis of their respective mate-

recent debate brings to the surface alternative interpretations for the presence of the weapon graves of the late-Roman period, that is of the fourth-early fifth centuries. We have to take these into account if we want to arrive at an interpretation of the sword graves of the second half of the fifth century. The interpretationoffered here is a further elaboration of those given by Halsall and Whittaker. Their interpretations have in common the idea that the presence of the weapon burials and the form of the ritual are related to the sphere of socio-political *practice*.[126] We will put forward the suggestion that the presence of weapon burials and the form of the ritual are related to changes in the world of ideas and values of aristocratic groups.[127]

The sword depositions of the late fourth and fifth centuries (phase 2) occured in a situation where the power positions of local and regional aristocratic groups were changing drastically as a consequence of the gradual elimination of Roman state control. Now that protection by state institutions has become less effective the *domini* of northern Gaul to an increasing extent turned to the deployment of force themselves in order to protect their clientèles and property. In the words of Whittaker, the developments led to a situation in which landlords became warlords and warlords turned into landlords.[128] Whatever label we apply to the *domini* of the late fourth and

---

rial cultures, because, according to Böhme, Germanic graves can be clearly distinguished from Roman graves.

[126] Halsall sees the weapon burials as a means of 'displaying their (that is the families concerned) power in the community more overtly in relation to competition for power at the local level' (Halsall, "The origins of the *Reihengräberzivilization*: forty years on", p. 207). Whittaker interprets the weapon graves as those of the powerful that rose to prominence as a consequence of the development of a 'border culture' in which the militarisation and nucleation of the population were important elements (Whittaker, *Frontiers of the Roman Empire. A Social and Economic Study*, pp. 232–240). This development turned warlords into landlords and landlords into warlords (Whittaker, *Frontiers of the Roman Empire. A social and economic study*, pp. 257–278).

[127] See also L. Hedeager, "The creation of a Germanic identity. A European origin-myth", *Frontières d'empire. Nature et signification des frontières romaines*, eds. P. Brun, S. van der Leeuw and Chr. R. Whittaker (Nemours, 1993) (Actes de la Table Ronde de Nemours 1992), pp. 121–131, for related interpretations. We however do not think that a '*Germanic*' ideology is necessarily involved in the development of the late Roman burial ritual.

[128] See note 126 for a development that is mainly situated in the fifth century. It is however doubtful whether this development can belinked with the bulk of the weapon graves in northern Gaul. The development described by Whittaker relates to the highest echelons in the aristocracy, or at least the examples given are from these echelons. The weapon graves seem to relate to lower-ranking aristocrats with local or regional power bases. To what extent these *domini* were involved in warring

fifth century, this aristocratic group with interests that were to some extent common will have been very diverse in terms of regions of origin and ideas and values. After one or two generations following the late-Roman period, this diversity may have been blurred and simultaneously reinforced by new arrivals. However, we think it is doubtful that the weapon graves are there as a direct result of the newly developed situation in terms of the *practice* of the excercise of power. In other words: their presence is not a mere reflection of the presence of *domini* with new power bases.[129] It is our suggestion that the sword graves relate to the development of a new *discourse* on the excercise of power: in other words, they relate to the development of new ideas concerning the elite lifestyle of a heterogeneous group of aristocrats such as characterised northern Gaul in Late Antiquity. Martial values will have formed an important new element in the elite lifestyle in northern Gaul as we explained in section 2. These values emerged in relation to the idea that a *dominus* must be able to give protection by force if necessary. Rituals will have played an important role in the creation, formulation and implementation of these new ideas and values and a new discourse on aristocratic power. The burial ritual, as one in a chain of life cycle rituals, will have been important in this as well. Depositing weapons in a grave of a man who was turned into an ancestor at the funerary ritual, was thus an act that gave form to newly developing martial aristocratic values relating to the new practices in the excercise of power.

Still the question remains why only a few aristocrats were interred in this way. Was it not important for all aristocratic groups to participate in this ritual formation of new ideas? Was it not necessary for all aristocrats that the constituents of the warrior as person were dissociated in ritual? In any way we can observe as archaeologists that the answer in each case is: obviously not. A burial ritual that include the deposition of precious objects was probably practised in special circumstances. The occasion might have been the one in which a person was turned into an 'important' (maybe founding) an-

---

on a regular basis is difficult to establish. Whittaker's phrasing 'landlords turning to militarism' may not be the most accurate one. One would rather phrase the process in terms proposed here (with protection as the central concept) which means that their use of force is an extension of their traditional position of *patronus*.

[129] Cfr. H.W. Böhme, "Adelsgräber im Frankenreich. Archäologische Zeugnisse zur Herausbildung einer Herrenschicht unter den merowingischen Königen", *Jahrbuch des Römisch-Germanischen Zentralmuseums Mainz* 40 (1993), pp. 397–534.

cestor, which implies that not all the dead were transformed into 'important' ancestors. The ritual might have been aimed at exchanging a person with the supernatural world or the world of the ancestors, for particular reasons which meant that the objects deposited related to the specific values involved. These were not necessarily all the important aristocratic values, they might have been those related to the capacities an 'important' ancestor was expected to have. The deposition of weapons in the grave might have indicated that the (founding) ancestor was especially expected to protect the burial community.

What was essential was that the performance of these rituals contributed to the increased sharing of new values by aristocrats whose origins and cultural backgrounds were very different. The ritual thus contributed to the integration of different aristocrats in a newly perceived "class" of local and regional leaders. In our opinion then the weapon graves of the late fourth and fifth centuries did not signify the 'Germanic' ethnic identity of a part of the aristocracy, neither did they relate to the 'military' functions (in the strict or formal sense) of the men in question. In fact, in the traditional interpretation, the weapon burials referred to positions of the past, but in our interpretation the ritual refers to positions and values of the future.

Although there may have developed new shared values, the variety in the deposition modes of swords in graves and in burial locations shows that there was enough room for "individual" perception and interpretation of these values (see section 2.5) and thus enough room for an "individual" elaboration of the ritual, for instance in respect of the choice of location. As we noted above: many sword burials are found near 'defensible' sites. Burying the dead next to these sites was apparently an important symbolic act in the creation of ancestors that had the task of protecting their group. Archaeologists have been puzzled about the small size of a number of groups that buried their dead near the hillforts of the Meuse region.[130] The

---

[130] These cemeteries date from the end of the fourth and first half of the fifth centuries (Brulet, *La Gaule septentrionale aus Bas-Empire. Occupation du sol et défense du territoire dans l'arriere-pays du limes au IVe et Ve siecle*, p. 324; Périn/Feffer, *Les Francs. 1 A la conquete de la Gaule; 2 A l'origine de la France*, pp. 67–68; H.W. Böhme, "Söldner und Siedler im spätantiken Nordgallien", *Die Franken, Wegbereiter Europas. Vor 1500 Jahren. König Chlodwig und seine Erben* (Mainz, 1996), pp. 96–97; H.W. Böhme, "Les découvertes dus Bas-empire à Vireux-Molhain. Considérations générales", *Le cimetiere et la fortification du Bas-empire de Vireux-Molhain, Dep. Ardennes*, ed. J.-P. Lemant (Mainz, 1985), p. 76). Some of them continued to be used into the (early) Merovin-

groups are often regarded as the military complement of the fortresses. In view of what we suggested earlier we interpret the small groups of graves as those of the leading families in the region, who gave form to their position by choosing exceptional sepulchre locations which referred to their ancestors and their capacity to give protection. Men, women[131] and children were buried there with all the material culture that point ed to an elite lifestyle, but not necessarily to their 'Germanic' origin or status as soldiers.[132]

If this interpretation of late fourth- and fifth-century sword graves is correct, what about the fourth-century weapon graves of the first phase? Are they the graves of Germanic soldiers or *foederati*? It is generally accepted that the late-Roman sword graves are a further elaboration of the fourth century ritual of weapon burial. What is characteristic of fourth- century weapon graves? An inspection of the range of weapon types deposited in fourth-century graves reveals that it is very restricted. Axes, lances and arrowheads form the bulk of the weapons found. Not all authors consider arrowheads as weapons, for bows and arrows may refer to the hunt rather than to armed combat.[133] Böhme could list 129 weapon graves (including those of the late fourth and fifth centuries) of which 73% contained an axe.[134] This means that almost all fourth-century male 'weapon' graves con-

gian period. Brulet explains the non-continuity of others (Furfooz, Vireux-Molhain) by pointing to the small amount of space available on the site, which, after some time, prohibited a further extension of the cemetery.

[131] It is a significant fact that in the women's graves of the Meuse valley relatively few typical 'Germanic' brooches are found (see distribution maps in Böhme, *Germanische Grabfunde des 4. bis 5. Jahrhunderts zwischen unterer Elbe und Loire. Studien zur Chronologie und Bevölkerungsgeschichte*).

[132] The hillfortresses had been in use in a previous period (c. AD 300) after which they fell into disuse in the middle of the fourth century. No burials are found that can be attributed to this first phase in the use of the fortresses. In the course of the second half of the fourth century many fortresses were used again. It is only in the late fourth century that lavishly furnished graves were dug in their vicinity. Small 'Germanic' cemeteries are also found in the countryside. Böhme interpreted these as the cemeteries of small Germanic groups that were ceded *villa* lands tilled by native Gallo-Roman labourers (Böhme, "Tombes germaniques des IVe et Ve siècles en Gaule du nord. Chronologie—Distribution—Interprétation", pp. 32–35).

[133] Böhme, *Germanische Grabfunde des 4. bis 5. Jahrhunderts zwischen unterer Elbe und Loire. Studien zur Chronologie und Bevölkerungsgeschichte*, p. 110, p. 163 (note 817).

[134] Many new weapon graves have been discovered since. Most of the newly discovered fourth-century weapon graves contain axes and lances, see for example Seillier "Les Germains dans l'armée romaine tardive en Gaule septentrionale, le témoignage de l'archéologie"; R. Pirling, "Römische Gräber mit barbarischem Einschlag auf den Gräberfeldern von Krefeld-Gellep:, *L'armée romaine et les barbares du IIIe au VIIe siècles* eds. F. Vallet and M. Kazanski (Paris, 1993), pp. 109–123.

tain an axe.[135] In a major part of these, the axe was the *only* weapon, though others also contained a lance. In a small number of graves, only a lance was deposited.[136] Why should it have been that out of a set of possible weapons the axe was chosen as the main weapon for deposition in the grave of a soldier of Germanic origin who had served in the Roman army? In the modern historiography of these graves hardly any attention has been paid to the meaning of the choice of the deposition of an axe or a lance in a funerary ritual.[137] In order to establish the meaning of the choice it is important to analyse the full range of uses and meanings attributed to the objects in question. It is not very helpful to give just one (functional) interpretation of the object and leave out others. It is exactly the presence of a range of uses and meanings referring to various aspects of an elite life style that determines the use of the objects as symbols in a burial ritual. The use of a single object could thus be interpreted and given meaning in different ways. The lance can be considered an important symbol because it referred to different fields of meaning. Authority was involved, as is illustrated in the late-Roman iconography of coins and silver plates among others.[138] The iconography of silver plates and glass bowls shows that the lance was important in hunting as well.[139] Its deposition in a grave at a funerary ritual may have referred to the position of authority of the man

---

[135] The remaining weapon graves are mainly the more lavishly furnished (sword) graves of the late fourth and fifth centuries.

[136] Böhme, *Germanische Grabfunde des 4. bis 5. Jahrhunderts zwischen unterer Elbe und Loire. Studien zur Chronologie und Bevölkerungsgeschichte*, pp. 163–165.

[137] One interpretation is that the axe is a typically Frankish weapon: E. Zöllner, *Geschichte der Franken bis zur Mitte des sechsten Jahrhunderts* (München, 1970); H. Ament, "Franken und Romanen im Merowingerreich als archäologisches Forschungsproblem", *Bonner Jahrbücher* 178 (1978), pp. 377–394. If that is the case do we have to conclude that all axe graves are those of Frankish men? Because in later periods axes and lances form part of the grave inventories with weapons found in Frankish and Alamannic burials it has been uncritically accepted that these objects were deposited as weapons too in the fourth century. As indicated above this assumption is the result of a functional interpretation of the objects concerned as weapons (see also Härke, *Angelsächsische Waffengräber des 5. bis 7. Jahrhunderts*, pp. 222–224 and note 112). Here, our starting point is a symbolic interpretation of the deposition of the axes and lances.

[138] On the later seal-ring found in Childeric's grave at Tournai a lance is depicted (see also the contribution by Gasparri in this volume). A well-known dish from Kertch (Crimea) shows the scene of the triumph of Constantius II. He is depicted seated on horseback holding a spear or lance (J.P.C. Kent and K.S. Painter, eds., *Wealth of the Roman World AD 300–700* (London, 1977), p. 25.

[139] *Gallien in der Spätantike* (Mainz, 1980), pp. 220–221.

involved and to an aristocratic activity par excellence, the hunt, at
the same time, instead of referring to his supposed military position.
What about the axe: was this object deposited as a weapon, or could
the deposition also have had other meanings? The problem of finding answers to such questions is that an object like an axe may have
had different functions and a variety of symbolic meanings that were
brought together in the act of deposition.[140] A functional interpretation of an axe as a weapon leads to a diminishing of the range of
possible interpretations of the deposition and raises the question why
it is that from a range of weapons the axe was chosen for deposition in a grave. The deposition of an axe in children's graves,[141] and
the small size of the axes indicate that such a functional interpretation of the axe as a weapon is not the only possible on. Moreover,
some axe types are difficult to classify as throwing axes.[142] Of some
interest in relation to this problem is the find of a hair-pin in a
woman's grave near Samson on the Meuse river.[143] It has the form

---

[140] See section 3 below.

[141] Important observations in this respect have been made in graves III-64 and
III-65 of the cemetery of Saint Severin's church in Cologne, both the graves of
young boys, buried in sarcophagi. In each of them an axe was found next to pottery,
glass vessels and belts. The graves are, however, of a younger date: the middle or
the third quarter of the fifth century (B. Päffgen, *Die Ausgrabungen in St. Severin zu
Köln* (Mainz, 1992), II, pp. 227–230 and Taf 49, 50 and 124. Bierbrauer (V. Bierbrauer, "Romanen im fränkischen Siedelgebiet", *Die Franken, Wegbereiter Europas. Vor
1500 Jahren. König Chlodwig und seine Erben* (Mainz, 1996), pp. 110–120) points to
the fact that in this cemetery (following traditional criteria with the help of which
Germanic and Roman graves are distinguished) Frankish people were buried only
after c. 500. The two boy's graves that date from the fifth century are in his opinion an exception to this rule, for they are *germanisch-fränkische Knaben* because they
have weapons, that is axes, in their sarcophagi. The rest of the grave goods, food
and drink in vessels, relate to a burial rite in vogue since Roman times. Bierbrauer
overlooks another surprising find in this cemetery: grave I-69, which contains seven
jugs, two whetstones, a razor blade, a pair of scissors, two rings, four coins(two of
Hadrian, one of Antoninus Pius, one of Caracalla) and an axe. The grave is dated
to the first half of the third century! We will argue that these might as well be
Roman burials, or, better; that the presence of axes in graves like these can be no
argument to support an ethnic identification of the boys as Roman or Germanic.
Similar (fifth-century) boys-graves with axes have been found at Utrecht (H.L. De
Groot, *Een levensteken uit de vijfde eeuw. Het grafveld aan het Pieterskerkhof*, (Utrecht, 1991),
pp. 10–13.

[142] Böhme, *Germanische Grabfunde des 4. bis 5. Jahrhunderts zwischen unterer Elbe und
Loire. Studien zur Chronologie und Bevölkerungsgeschichte*, pp. 104–110: the *Bartäxte* and
the *Breitäxte* mit *Schaftröhre*.

[143] Dasnoy, "La necropole de Samson (IVᵉ–VIᵉ siècles)", pp. 326–327. A comparable
object, however of a different axe type and later in date was found in the late-
Roman/Merovingian cemetery of Saint Servatius church in Maastricht (P. Glazema
and J. Ypey, *Merovingische ambachtskunst* (Baarn, 1956), fig. 55.

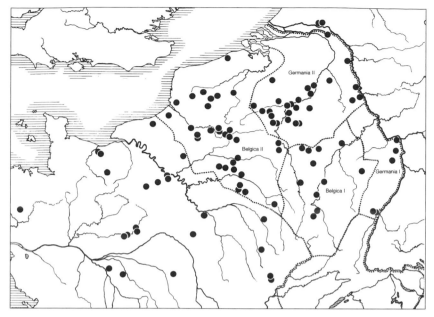

Fig. 9. The distribution of weapon burials in northern Gaul from the fourth century and the first half of the fifth century (after Böhme, "Les découvertes du Bas-empire à Vireux-Molhain. Considérations générales", Fig. 75)

of an axe with a long shaft. The form of the shaft is of course also determined by the function of the object as a hairpin. Axes may have been weapons (throwing or battle axes) but the possiblity cannot be excluded that in the act of the axe-deposition reference was also made to its use as a tool. The axe may well have been a symbol with a multitude of meanings and may have referred to authority like the lance and the (bows and) arrows. A suggestion that we would like to put forward, but that needs further elaboration, is that the deposition of the axe referred both to a warrior idiom and to the reoccupation and claiming of lands (an agrarian idiom) that had been left deserted after the gradual depopulation of parts of northern Gaul from the beginning of the third century onwards (fig. 9).[144] The essential point of the choice of the axe as an object to be

---

[144] That may be the reason for a larger concentration of axe, lance or arrow graves to the north of the river Seine, a distribution pattern that fades away in a southerly direction where a smaller amount of *villae* will have been deserted and left 'unattended'. A fact that needs further explanation is that the distribution pattern of these graves differs of that of the late fourth- and fifth-century sword graves in that they also regularly occur in Picardy and the Moselle valley. This does not seem to be in accordance with the hypothesis that it was the Franks who took over and continued the ritual of weapon burials. It is also significant that axe, lance and

deposited in the grave is that it referred to different aspects (values) of aristocratic leadership in Late Antique northern Gaul. Thus the symbolic language of the burial rite might be more complex than has hitherto been suggested. The deposition of an axe, lance or (bow and) arrows formed in our view, part of a ritual which gave form to new types of (local) claims on land and people that were not based on previous (ancestral) occupation of the land, and new ideas on the exercise of power.[145] In this context the reference to the hunt is interesting. The hunt was an aristocratic activity, but it was not just a exclusively leisure occupation. The hunt is an occasion at which social positions were defined, leadership and courage could be demonstrated,[146] and important in this context, during which claims on the land could be represented. Thus, although the deposition of an axe, a lance and (bow and) arrows did not often coincide in a single grave, they were parts of a coherent set of symbolic acts related to new conceptions of aristocratic power in certain situations. The families that practised the deposition of one or more of these objects in the grave of a man or a child, may have come from 'barbarian' regions across the Rhine, others may have originated from other parts of the Roman empire, some might be of local origin, but it was not their origin that they were representing in ritual. Again, the ritual did not refer to positions of the past, but to positions and values of the future. In our interpretation, the idea

---

arrow burials are not so common in the Rhine area (see next section). See Böhme's distribution map of weapon burials in: J.-P. Lemant, *Le cimetière et la fortification du Bas-empire de Vireux-Molhain, Dep. Ardennes* (Mainz, 1985), p. 85 (our fig. 9). A point that needs further elaboration but will not be dealt with here is that the use of the axe in the burial ritual in the fourth century may have been the reason for its special meaning as a weapon in later times.

[145] Böhme suggested that some of the 'Germanic' burials were the graves of new Germanic owners of *villae* tilled by Roman labourers (see also note 123). Our interpretation differs from this one in that we do not think that the burials necessarily refer either to a Germanic origin of the deceased or to their military status.

[146] J. Jarnut, "Die frühmittelalterliche Jagd unter rechts- und sozialgeschichtlichen Aspekten", *L'uomo di Fronte al mondo animale nell'alto medievo* (Spoleto, 1985) (Settimane di studio del centro Italiano di studi sull'alto medievo 31), pp. 765–808; J. Verdon, "Recherches sur la chasse en occident durant le haut moyen âge", *Revue Belge de Philologie et d'histoire* 56 (1978), pp. 805–829. A. Demandt, *Die Spätantike. Römische Geschichte von Diocletian bis Justitian 284–565 n. Chr.* (München, 1989) (Handbuch der Altertumswissenschaft III,6), pp. 326–327 and J. Nelson, "The Lord's anointed and the People's choice: Carolingian Royal Ritual", *Rituals of Royalty. Power and ceremonial in Traditional Societies*, eds. D. Cannadine and S. Price (Cambridge, 1987), pp. 137–180.

that the sepulchres with axes, lances and arrows were weapon graves has been questioned.[147] This is in accordance with the interpretation given above for the late fourth- and fifth-century weapon (and sword) graves. In the fourth century, local *domini* could still count to some degree on protection by institutions of the Roman state. The idea that *domini* had to be able to protect their clientèles, by force, the elaboration of a new elite life style including martial ideas, and the development of a new ritual repertoire that came with it, seem to be developments mainly of the late fourth century.

Still, we are puzzled by the problem of the small numbers of male aristocratic graves with axes, lances and bows and arrows in the fourth century, and of graves with swords in the second half of the fifth and beginning of the sixth century. The new burial rituals were important in giving form to a new aristocratic lifestyle but obviously not every death of an aristocrat triggered off this ritual. It is suggested that the burials we know of were those of men who for specific reasons were given exeptional burials in which they were 'exchanged' with the ancestral world. They were turned into ancestors in a burial ritual in which the objects that figured were associated with the most important aristocratic value for the burial community: the capacity to give protection. We cannot therefore follow Whittaker in qualifying the idiom of the ritual as 'military'.[148]

   With this conclusion we leave the first sphere of interpretation for the fifth century sword burials, that relating to the changing discourse on power, and to the changes in norms and values of aristocratic groups, that is, the sphere of the elite life style, We now turn to the second sphere of interpretation, that of the socio-political context of the sword-burials.

5.2. *The ritual deposition of swords and socio-political practice*

At the end of section 4.2, we concluded that the distribution pattern of sword burials was determined by a/ the production, distribution

---

[147] In fact this interpretation is in accordance with the idea that late-Roman soldiers as a rule were not interred with their weapons. The *locus classicus* in archaeology to illustrate this point is the cemetery of the fortress at Oudenburg where no 'real' weapon graves are found. They are relatively rare in the cemetery of the fortress at Krefeld-Gellep as well.

[148] Whittaker, *Frontiers of the Roman Empire. A Social and Economic Study*, p. 235.

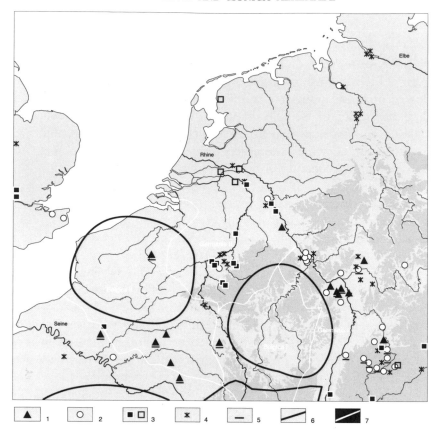

Fig. 10. The distribution of sword finds (mainly burials) from the second half of
the fifth and beginning of the sixth centuries in northern Gaul is uneven. Four
(inhabited) regions that lack sword burials are indicated on the map. 1. garnet-
ornamented swords and scabbards; 2. 'Alamannic' scabbards; 3. Krefeld scabbards;
4. 'other' forms; 5. swords with hilt with gold foil (*Goldgriffspatha*), 6. areas with no
sword finds, 7. borders of provinces.

and circulation of swords and scabbards in aristocratic networks and
b/ the use of the sword in the burial ritual. We also concluded that
the distribution pattern most probably does not reflect the total geographical scope of the exchange networks in which the swords circulated because only a small fraction of the men that possessed or
used one or more were buried with them.

A closer look at the distribution of sword burials over northern
Gaul reveals an interesting pattern. There are large regions where
no sword burials have been found up to now (fig. 10). They are:
northwestern France (Picardy) and western Belgium (with the notable
exeption of Childeric's grave at Tournai); the Moselle valley and
adjoining regions; Burgundy and finally the region south of the Seine.

It is unlikely that in the 'empty' regions, no high-ranking aristocrats were active in the second half of the fifth century. It is also unlikely that no exquisite swords circulated in these regions. On the contrary, contemporary texts explicitly mention kings and aristocratic groups in these areas. It is in Picardy and in western Belgium that the Salian Francs are thought to have been present.[149] In the Moselle valley comparable supra-regional 'Roman' power structures might to some degree have been intact as is indicated by the references to Arbogast in the texts.[150] To the south of the Seine, the Gallo-Roman senatorial aristocracy was well established as were the Burgundian kings and aristocracy to the south-east.[151] It is a remarkable fact that in those areas where sizable groups of Germanic origin (Salian Francs, Burgundians, and outside our study area the Western Goths[152]) are

---

[149] James, *The Franks*, pp. 51–77; Wood, *The Merovingian Kingdoms 450–751*, pp. 38–41. The geographical extent of Childeric's power is a matter of debate: is it the Roman province of Belgica II (the graves with garnet-decorated swords in the Marne-Aisne region are more or less situated on the southern border of this province!) or just the northern part of it because Syagrius allegedly controlled the region around Soissons? However posing the question in this way may be false for polities like the one controlled by Childeric may have been characterised by aristocratic networks rather than by territorial control. The extent of the networks does not necessarily imply a full coverage of the areas concerned.

[150] James, *The Francs*, pp. 73–75; Wood, *The Merovingian Kingdoms 450–751*, p. 36; Demandt, *Die Spätantike. Römische Geschichte von Diocletian bis Justitian 284–565 n. Chr.*, pp. 180, 373.

[151] R.W. Mathisen, R.W., *Roman Aristocrats in Barbarian Gaul. Strategies for Survival in an Age of Transition* (Austin, 1993). Wood, *The Merovingian Kingdoms 450–751*, pp. 8–10, pp. 51–54. H. Gaillard de Sémainville, "Burgondes et Francs", *Histoire et Archéologie* 56 (1981), pp. 56–63.

[152] E. James, "Cemeteries and the problem of frankish settlement in Gaul", *Names, Words and Graves: Early Medieval Settlement*, ed. P.H. Saywer (Leeds, 1979), pp. 55–89.; P. Périn, "L'armé de Vidimer et la question des dépôts funéraires chez les Wisigoths en Gaule et en Espagne (V^e–VIe siècles)", *L'armée romaine et les barbares du IIIe au VIIe siècles*, eds. F. Vallet and M. Kazanski (Paris, 1993), pp. 411–423. Périn's interpretation of the absence of 'Germanic'-style burials in Gothia is not very convincing. He states that the western Goths no longer possessed any 'Germanic' objects from their homelands when they arrived in southern France. They might have obtained new objects en route in the Roman empire, but these no longer identified them as western Goths. Conceptualising the relationship between material culture and people in this way, so that objects become objectified as they are in modern western society is to misunderstand the meaning of material culture such as that used in the early medieval burial ritual. Could not the Goths have had the objects produced if they had wanted to use them in the burial ritual? The deposition of objects in graves has thus been interpreted as an act of secondary importance, meaningless, being no more than a reflection of the goods available, because availability was outside people's control (grave goods = cultural garbage). The later 'Gothic' burials in Spain were in Périn's view the result of the arrival of an army lead by Vidimer of which the members and their families still wore the 'national costume'. This would have given the western Goths a new chance to take up the

thought to have been in power, no sword burials are found. This is quite problematic. More then one explanation is possible. In view of the interpretations for a sword burial given above, we have to conclude that in these areas (core areas of king-aristocrat networks) it was not necessary to create ancestors that could give protection. Was the king as protector so near (in both physical and mental senses) that it was not necessary to perform this ritual? We must infer that in those areas where we would expect the burial ritual to have played an important role in establishing new aristocratic values, these rituals were absent. Why? We also have to conclude that if local competition provided the main incentive for the burial ritual, as Halsall states, it did not do so in those areas where we might have expected that such competition would have been most intense. Were there no sword burials in these areas because elite positions and values at the upper level of the aristocracy were relatively well defined?[153] Were swords kept in circulation whether through inheritance or through a restitution of the swords received from a lord or king?[154] In view of the small number of sword burials in general in the early middle ages, the transmission of swords to the next generation must have been the normal practice already in the period under consideration. An explanation for the non-presence of sword burials in the regions mentioned should be compatible with an explanation for their presence in other regions.

The sword depositions are found in 'peripheral regions' where a decentralised power structure prevailed and where positions of author-

---

clothing styles and burial customs of the Goths. This interpretation ignores the meanings of the deposition of objects at funerary rituals and clings to a static conceptualisation of ethnic identity. The Germanic burials are seen as a direct reflection of the world of the living and their clothing habits and are thought to be there as a result of historic events like the arrival of a group of warriors. Interpretations like these include all the presuppositions of the (nation based) historiography of burials since the nineteenth century. We will return to this problem later.

[153] Sword burials are found in Picardy and the Moselle valley in the sixth century. The less costly ornamentation of the swords found in the graves *might* indicate that a lower-ranking stratum of aristocrats was involved which sought to define its position *vis-à-vis* higherranking groups. A study of all sword depositions from the fifth to the tenth centuries in northern Gaul (by Theuws) indicates that the practice of sword deposition in a funerary ritual was taken up in each new period by a lower-ranking stratum of aristocrats in relation to the higher stratum of the preceding period. At the same time the practice of sword deposition in the grave disappeared in a northerly direction. In the fifth century the first aristocrats to define new positions were the highest ranking ones.

[154] See Härke, below in this volume.

ity at a local or regional level were not fixed and had to be constantly defined and renewed.[155] These regions are the Meuse valley, the Rhine valley, the Seine-Marne-Oise region, and the Alamannic territory (fig. 10). It is generally thought that in the Rhineland the Rhenish Francs established a polity headed by kings residing in Cologne as the Salian Francs did in north-western France.[156] However, belief in the existence of this polity could be the result of modern historiographical reconstruction on the basis of evidence that is chronologically and geographically very diverse and difficult to interpret, rather than representing historical reality.[157] The distribution pattern of the sword graves indicates that the power structures of the Salian and the Rhenish Francs polities were different in character.

An interesting conclusion can also be drawn in relation to the Seine-Marne-Oise valleys. The presence of sword burials there supports James' idea that there was no such thing as a supra-regional kingdom of Syagrius.[158] The sword depositions point instead to a decentralised power structure in the Seine-Marne-Oise region. The area seems to have assumed a peripheral position between the Salian Francs, a Moselle-based power-group, the Burgundians and the Roman world to the south.[159] In the Alamannic area there was no

---

[155] That sword burials like the ones discussed are mainly found in peripheral regions has been suggested before by Hedeager ("Kingdoms, ethnicity and material culture: Denmark in a European perspective") although on a much larger European scale. However, it has been difficult to establish up to now which regions are peripheral (the result seems to be determined by the geographical scale of the analysis).

[156] Ewig, *Frühes Mittelalter*, pp. 9–17. The opinion presented here contrasts with that of James, *The Franks*, p. 74. See also Wieczorek "Die Ausbreitung der fränkischen Herrschaft in den Rheinlannden vor und seit Chlodwig I".

[157] In fact there is no contemporary evidence for kings at Cologne from the days of Childeric. Their hypothetical presence is based on the supposition that the Cologne kings contemporary with Clovis had ancestors with the same position. If there were kings at Cologne before Clovis' time (which cannot be excluded) it is difficult to establish the territory they controlled, or, more correctly, to establish the extent of the network in which they formed nodal points. It could have been only a small area along the Rhine north and south of Cologne and need not have covered the entire territory of Germania II. Wieczorek supposes that Belgica I was brought under the control of the Salian Franks by Clovis and was not under the control of the Rhenish Franks (Wieczorek, "Die Ausbreitung der fränkischen Herrschaft in den Rheinlanden vor und seit Chlodwig I", pp. 256–257 and Abb. 176).

[158] James, *The Franks*, pp. 67–71. See also the comments by Périn (P. Périn, "Les tombes de «chefs» du début de l'epoque mérovingienne. Datation et interprétation historique", *La noblesse romaine et les chefs barbares du IIIe au VIIe siècle* eds. F. Vallet and M. Kazanski (Paris, 1995), pp. 253–256) and R. le Jan, *Histoire de la France: origines et premier essor 480–1180* (Paris, 1996), pp. 17–18.

[159] It is probably no coincidence that the later *sedes regnorum* of the Frankish sub-

supraregional power structure either. The texts seem to indicate that a variety of petty kings and aristocrats formed a patchwork of local and regional dominions that was open to manipulation from different sides.[160]

As we have said, the distribution pattern of sword burials reflect neither the total geographical extension of the circulation of costly swords or of the networks in which they circulated, nor the geographical extent of ethnic units. On the other hand what it does suggest is that the position of the man buried with a sword depended in the first place on membership of an open-ended aristocratic network that had as its core a king associated with one of the supraregional power groups already mentioned or on membership of a network based on the Roman aristocracy to the south or even in the Mediterranean. In the case of the Burgundians and the Salian Francs one could think of networks of which some warriors were constituted as persons in a way described by Bazelmans in this volume. However, it is difficult to establish to what extent a ritual-cosmological entity as described by him is identical to a socio-political network of a king. The man buried with a sword could either be one of local origin who had entered into relations with a ruler and received a sword and other gifts as the relationships' material counterpart.[161] The sword made the other king 'present'. It remains possible however, that the men buried with swords were members of (ritually constituted) groups who settled in peripheral areas for various reasons. In the latter case they might have brought with them the objects found in their graves, or got them later. The deposition of a sword in a grave was thus a multilayered symbolic act. First, the burial group might seek protection from a 'founding' ancestor. Second, the burial group was defining the aristocratic values thought to be important in this context. Third, the ritual marked the capacity of the burial group involved to give protection in the sphere of socio-political practice. Finally, the deposition of the sword made

---

kingdoms are found in this (in the fifth century peripheral) area, in which later after Clovis the main landed resources of the Merovingian dynasty were. It might also have been 'neutral ground', a region that originally belonged to neither (one of) the Frankish kings, nor the Burgundians.

[160] W. Hartung, *Süddeutschland in der frühen Merowingerzeit. Studien zur Gesellschaft, Herrschaft, Stammesbildung bei Alamannen und Bajuwaren* (Wiesbaden, 1983), pp. 80–90.

[161] They might have been men who had been educated (as young boys) at the court of another king. Is there a link with boy's graves like those discussed in note 132?

explicit that this ancestor and the burial group could rely on the protection of a higher-ranking order, one of royal nature, the source of well-being for an entire group.[162] This ritual creation of protective ancestors and associated values would continue to take place during the entire Merovingian period at various social levels.[163]

Again we have to stress that the distribution pattern of sword burials does not reflect the circulation of swords in socio-political practice or the geographical extent of the aristocratic networks. What we can establish is that the ceremonial exchange of swords was an important element of these aristocratic networks. The confused overall distribution pattern of sword and scabbard types suggests this.

These conclusions force us to reflect on the ethnic connotations of sword burials. In the ethnic discussion we have to distinguish between a number of elements. First, there are the textual constructions of (ethnic) identity by late antique and early-medieval authors that may relate to specific socio-political practices, however the way in which they relate to these practices may vary from case to case. Second, there is the older interpretation of these as social groups existing as homogeneous totalities.[164] Thirth, there is the modern interpretation of the "subjective" character of these textual constructions, in which (ethnic) identity is seen as a "situational construct" by individuals as well as groups.[165] Fourth, there is the interpretation of ethnic groups as ritual-cosmologically constituted entities, as proposed by Bazelmans in this volume. The ritual participation in these entities is related to the formation of collective identities. This is especially important for young warriors for they operate outside the group. Fifth, there are the material constructions of identities in the past. Sixth, there are the archaeological typologies of objects, in

---

[162] We have not developed this point further here, but sword depositions in this period and in the Merovingian period might indicate royal links of some kind, although we have not gone through the material yet in enough detail to establish this with certainty.

[163] In fact, the ritual played an important role in establishing different layers (down the scale) in the Merovingian aristocracy.

[164] See for a discussion of the different interpretations of textual constructions of ethnic identities: Wenskus, *Stammesbildung und Verfassung. Das Werden der frühmittelalterlichen Gentes* ; P.J. Heather, *Goths and Romans 332–489* (Oxford, 1991), pp. 34–67; Pohl, "Conceptions of ethnicity in Early Medieval studies". P. Heather, *The Goths* (Oxford, 1996), pp. 3–7; P. Amory, *People and Identity in Ostrogothic Italy 489–554* (Cambridge, 1997), pp. 13–42.

[165] Geary, "Ethnic identity as a situational construct in the early middle ages", pp. 15–26.

this case swords, of which we do not know whether they fit ancient classifications. Seventh there are the correlations made by archaeologists of two and six.

From this enumeration it will be clear that there is a complex relation between material culture and ethnic identity. What seems to be clear to us is that there are no simple relations between textual and material constructions of identity. We might even question the possibility whether the modern archaeological ordering of material culture allows us to grasp the essence of material constructions of identity.

This is not to say that swords played no role in material constructions of identity. On the contrary. In Bazelmans model objects play an important role in creating these identities. What we question is whether the archaeologically defined groups of swords as we have them now, reflect specific ethnic entities of which we now know that they are textual constructions. These groups of swords are not "national" products. Following our line of reasoning the swords and scabbards (or parts of them) need not have been and most likely were not produced in the areas where they are found. It is more likely that they were produced in the areas where no sword depositions are present, that is in Picardy, the Moselle valley, Burgundy and the Roman south or the Mediterranean. Böhme recently suggested that the swords and scabbards with garnet-decoration were Mediterranean products.[166] This would imply that they got to the north through Roman aristocratic networks, which is the most plausible explanation for the presence of such a sword in the grave of Childeric I.[167] In view of what has been stated above on aristocratic

---

[166] Böhme, "Der Frankenkönig Childerich zwischen Attila und Aëtius. Zu den Goldgriffspathen der Merowingerzeit", p. 82. He also indicated that some of the other swords could have been Late Antique products, that is products from former Roman territory. In a footnote he adds: 'Bisher geht die Forschung im allgemeinen davon aus, dass einige der Prunkschwerter fränkischer, andere alamannischer Herkunft seien.' The thought that the swords cannot be attributed to certain ethnic territorial units is maybe so heretical in German archaeological circles that it can be presented only *sotto voce*.

[167] Werner, "Childeric. Histoire et Archéologie". James, *The Franks*, pp. 58–67. Böhme, "Der Frankenkönig Childerich zwischen Attila und Aëtius. Zu den Goldgriffspathen der Merowingerzeit". P. Périn, and M. Kazanski, "Das Grab Childerics I", *Die Franken, Wegbereiter Europas. Vor 1500 Jahren. König Chlodwig und seine Erben* (Mainz, 1996), pp. 173–182. In a reaction to Böhme's study Périn and Kazanski propose a third model for the contacts between Childeric and the southern world (alongside the existing ones pointing to the Danube region and the Byzantine court).

networks, gift- and/or ceremonial exchange, the circulation of swords and the meaning of the burial ritual, we have to conclude that the Krefelder swords were most probably not produced in the middle Meuse valley, but in regions to the west or south of it. The same goes for the so-called Alamannic swords and scabbards. It is unlikely that they originated from Alamannic workshops: instead they were products of workshops in Late Antique Gaul. Where exactly they have their origin is difficult to establish, for their appearance is not necessarily the result of a single moment of production.[168] The 'Alamannic swords' may have originated from northern Gaul, the Burgundian area or the regions where a Roman senatorial aristocracy remained in control or the Mediterraenean too. This interpretation also implies that objects like the swords and scabbards cannot be used to identify a Frankish as distinct from an Alamannic territory in the fifth and early sixth century.

Texts, for instance the *Beowulf*, clearly imply that swords were classified in a different way than we archaeologists do (which is a production-biased ordering). Individual swords circulated in ritual-cosmological entities. These swords were known by their names, stories

---

They suggest that the contacts were with the western Mediterranean, more precisely Italy, and that Childeric adapted to an aristocratic fashion for a barbarian aristocracy in the west. They point to similar finds in northern Italy to strengthen their case. Two comments can be made. First, the modern concept of 'fashion' (to indicate the preference for certain types of objects in a certain period of time) unless further elaborated seems inappropriate to qualify the presence of a set of objects (or rather a specific burial ritual) with a highly symbolic content. They were not put in the grave because is was 'fashionable' to do so. Saying that something is 'fashion' is describing what is done regularly, not explaining the acts. 'Fashion' is thus a concept like 'chronology', they are used to describe something not to explain it. Second, it is not really a third model, for Böhme clearly indicates that the Byzantine connection might have gone through Odovacer's court in Italy. There might only have been an indirect contact between Childeric and the emperor's court, but the Byzantine background seems to be essential (some of the objects in Childeric's grave actually came from workshops in Constantinople). It would be a mistake to point to northern Italy exclusively on the basis of similar finds there, just as it has been a mistake to point exclusively to the lower Danube region on the basis of comparable finds there. Rather, the finds in northern Gaul, those in Italy as well as those in the Danube area encircle the Byzantine empire to the north and the west, which is an indication that it is through networks centred on the Byzantine court that these objects circulated in barbarian tribes and kingdoms.

[168] The problem of the location of the workshop may not really be relevant, for the distribution of the swords will not have been determined by them and will not have been the result of market principles according to which workshops sell their products and have an outlet region that can be established with the help of distribution maps of identical swords (types) thouhgt for that reason to have originated from the same workshop, which of course need not necessarily have been the case.

and fame. In each entity a certain set of swords will have been present that consists of a whole range of archaeological types, a set that nevertheless is perceived as a coherent whole, for the mere fact that they were originating from the king who had received these swords, which after a process of appropriation,[169] were handed over to lords or warrior-followers. Archaeologists, however, have taken apart such sets of swords with their own classification based on identical forms. It is unlikely that the ritual cosmological entities correlate with modern archaeological groups of identical swords. This forces archaeologists to rethink the archaeological strategies to analyse their material in order to arrive at insights or models of the material constructions of identities in the past. It also forces them to think over again the relation between textual and material constructions of identities.

ACKNOWLEDGEMENTS

We would like to thank the following persons and institutions for their contribution and help in writing this article. They are the members of the *Pionier* project group "Power and Elite" at the University of Amsterdam and the members of group five of the ESF programme "The Transformation of the Roman world" for the discussions of the theme over the last years, The *Nederlandse Organisatie voor Wetenschappelijk Onderzoek* (The Dutch National Science Foundation) for financially supporting the reserach, Jos Bazelmans, Heinrich Härke, Lotte Hedeager and Jinty Nelson for critically reading previous versions of the text and Jinty Nelson for correcting the English.

BIBLIOGRAPHY

Primary sources

The Variae *of Magnus Aurelius Cassiodorus Senator*, translated by S.J.B. Barnish (Translated Texts for Historians 12) (Liverpool, 1992).
Beowulf. A verse translation by M. Alexander (Harmondsworth, 1973).
Gregory of Tours: The History of the Franks, translated by L. Thorpe (Harmondsworth, 1974).

---

[169] This element was suggested to us by Jos Bazelmans. What we cannot establish is whether this process of appropriation goes with physical alterations of the sword, such as those which we described in an earlier section of this article.

Einhard and Notker the Stammerer. Two lives of Charlemagne, translated with an introduction by L. Thorpe (London, 1969).

Secondary sources

Alenus-Lecerf, J., "Le cimetiere de Vieuxville: quelques considerations préliminaires", *La civilisation mérovingienne dans le bassin Mosan*, eds. M. Otte and J. Willems (Liège, 1986), pp. 181–193.

Alkemade, M., "A history of Vendel Period archaeology. Observations on the relationship between written sources and archaeological interpretations", *Images of the past. Studies on ancient societies in Northwestern Europe*, eds. N. Roymans and F. Theuws (Amsterdam, 1991) (Studies in Pre- en Protohistorie 7), pp. 267–297.

Ament, H., *Fränkische Adelsgräber von Flonheim in Rheinhessen* (Berlin, 1970).

———, "Franken und Romanen im Merowingerreich als archäologisches Forschungsproblem", *Bonner Jahrbücher* 178 (1978), pp. 377–394.

Amory, P. *People and Identity in Ostrogothic Italy 489–554* (Cambridge, 1997).

Appadurai, A., *The Social Life of Things. Commodities in Cultural Perspective* (Cambridge, 1986).

Arwidsson, G., *Valsgärde 7* (Uppsala, 1977).

Barth, F., "Towards greater naturalism in conceptualizing societies", *Conceptualizing society*, ed. A. Kuper (London and New York, 1992), pp. 17–33.

Bazelmans, J., "Conceptualising early Germanic political structure: a review of the use of the concept of Gefolgschaft", *Images of the past. Studies on ancient societies in Northwestern Europe*, eds. N. Roymans and F. Theuws (Amsterdam, 1991) (Studies in Pre- en Protohistorie 7), pp. 91–129.

———, *Eén voor allen, allen voor één. Tacitus' Germania, de oudengelse Beowulf en het ritueelcosmologische karakter van de relatie tussen heer en volgeling in Germaanse samenlevingen* (Amsterdam, 1996) (Typescript Dissertation in limited edition) (to be published in an English translation as: *By weapons made worthy. Lords, retainers and their relationship in Beowulf* (Amsterdam University Press, 1999).

Behmer, E., *Das zweischneidige Schwert der germanischen Völkerwanderungszeit* (Stockholm, 1939).

Bierbrauer, V., "Romanen im fränkischen Siedelgebiet", *Die Franken, Wegbereiter Europas. Vor 1500 Jahren. König Chlodwig und seine Erben* (Mainz, 1996), pp. 110–120.

Böhme, H.W., *Germanische Grabfunde des 4. bis 5. Jahrhunderts zwischen unterer Elbe und Loire. Studien zur Chronologie und Bevölkerungsgeschichte* (München, 1974).

———, "Tombes germaniques des IVᵉ et Vᵉ siècles en Gaule du nord. Chronologie—Distribution—Interprétation", *Problèmes de chronologie relative et absolue concernant les cimetières mérovingiens d'entre Loire et Rhin*, eds. M. Fleury and P. Périn (Paris, 1978), pp. 21–38.

———, "Les découvertes dus Bas-empire à Vireux-Molhain. Considérations générales", *Le cimetiere et la fortification du Bas-empire de Vireux Molhain, Dep. Ardennes*, ed. J.-P. Lemant (Mainz, 1985), pp. 76–88.

———, "Adelsgräber im Frankenreich. Archäologische Zeugnisse zur Herausbildung einer Herrenschicht unter den merowingischen Königen", *Jahrbuch des Römisch-Germanischen Zentralmuseums Mainz* 40 (1993), pp. 397–534.

———, "Der Frankenkönig Childerich zwischen Attila und Aëtius. Zu den Goldgriffspathen der Merowingerzeit", *Festschrift für Otto-Hermann Frey zum 65.Geburtstag*, (Marburg, 1994) (Marburger Studien zur Vor- und Frühgeschichte 16), pp. 69–110.

———, "Söldner und Siedler im spätantiken Nordgallien", *Die Franken, Wegbereiter Europas. Vor 1500 Jahren. König Chlodwig und seine Erben* (Mainz, 1996), pp. 91–101.

Böhner, K., "Das Langschwert des Frankenkönigs Childerich", *Bonner Jahrbücher* 148 (1948), pp. 218–248.

———, "Germanische Schwerter des 5. and 6. Jahrhunderts", *Jahrbuch des Römisch-Germanischen Zentralmuseums Mainz* 34 (1987), pp. 411–490.

Bosman, A. and T. Looijenga, "A runic inscription from Bergakker (Gelderland), The Netherlands", *Amsterdamer Beiträge zur älteren Germanistik* 46 (1996), pp. 9–16.

Bouzy, O., "Les armes symboles d'un pouvoir politique: l'épée du sacre, la sainte lance, l'oriflamme aux VIIIᵉ–XIIᵉ siècles", *Francia* 22 (1995), pp. 45–47.

Bradley, S.A.J., ed., *Anglo-Saxon Poetry* (London-Vermont, 1995 (1982).

Brown, P., *The Cult of the Saints. Its Rise and Function in Latin Christianity* (Chicago-London, 1981) (The Haskell Lectures on History of Religions, New Series 2).

Brulet, R., *La Gaule septentrionale aus Bas-Empire. Occupation du sol et défense du territoire dans l'arriere-pays du limes au IVᵉ et Vᵉ siècle* (Trier, 1990).

——, *Les fouilles du quartier Saint-Brice à Tournai. 2 L'environnement funéraire de la sépulture de Childéric* (Louvain, 1991).

——, "Tournai und der Bestattungsplatz um Saint Brice", *Die Franken, Wegbereiter Europas. Vor 1500 Jahren. König Chlodwig und seine Erben* (Mainz, 1996), pp. 163–170.

Cameron, A., *Christianity and the Rhetoric of Empire* (Berkeley-Los Angeles-Oxford, 1991).

Chew, H., "Une sépulture militaire de l'époque romaine tardive à Sarry (Marne)", *L'armée romaine et les barbares du IIIᵉ au VIIᵉ siècles*, eds. F. Vallet and M. Kazanski, (Paris, 1993), pp. 313–321.

Christlein, R., *Die Alamannen. Archäologie eines lebendigen Volkes* (Stuttgart and Aalen, 1991³).

Cohen, A., *The Symbolic Construction of Community* (Chichester, 1985).

Dasnoy, A., "La necropole de Samson (IVᵉ–VIᵉ siècles)", *Annales de la Société archeologique de Namur* 54 (1968), pp. 277–333.

Davidson, H.E., *The Sword in Anglo Saxon England* (Oxford, 1962).

De Coppet, D., "Introduction", *Understanding rituals*, ed. D. de Coppet (London-New York, 1992), pp. 1–10.

Demandt, A., *Der Fall Roms. Die Auflösung des römischen Reiches im Urteil der Nachwelt* (München, 1984).

——, *Die Spätantike. Römische Geschichte von Diocletian bis Justinian 284–565 n. Chr.* (München, 1989) (Handbuch der Altertumswissenschaft III,6).

Die Franken, Wegbereiter Europas. Vor 1500 Jahren: König Chlodwig und seine Erben (Mainz, 1996).

Doorselaer, A. van, "Le problème des mobiliers funéraires avec armes en Gaule septentrionale a l'époque du Haut Empire romain", *Helinium* 5 (1965), pp. 118–129.

Douglas, M. *Purity and Danger: an Analysis of Concepts of Pollution and Taboo* (London, 1966).

Drinkwater, J. and H. Elton eds., *Fifth-century Gaul: a Crises of Identity?* (Cambridge, 1992).

Effros, B., *From Grave Goods to Christian Epitaphs: Evolution in Burial Tradition and the Expression of Social Status in Merovingian Society* (Los Angeles, 1994) (Unpublished dissertation, University of California).

Erä-Esko, A., "Ein Schwert der Merowingerzeit mit völkerwanderungszeitlichem Knauf aus Grab A 5 von der Insel Kjuloholm, Gemeinde Köyliö, Südwestfinnland", *Archäologische Beiträge zur Chronologie der Völkerwanderungszeit*, eds. G. Kossack and J. Reichstein (Bonn, 1977) (Antiquitas Reihe 3, Band 20), pp. 79–85.

Es, W.A. van, "Friezen, Franken en Vikingen, *Romeinen, Friezen en Franken in het hart van Nederland. Van Traiectum tot Dorestat 50 v. C.- 900 n. C.*, eds W.A. van Es en W. Hessing (Utrecht/Amertfoort, 1994), pp. 82–119.

Evison, V.I., "The Dover ring-sword and other sword-rings and beads", *Archaeologia* 101 (1967), pp. 63–118.

Ewig, E., *Frühes Mittelalter* (Düsseldorf, 1980) (Rheinische Geschichte 1,2).

Gaillard de Sémainville, H., "Burgondes et Francs", *Histoire et Archéologie* 56 (1981), pp. 56–63.

Gallien in der Spätantike. Von Kaiser Constantin zu Frankenkönig Childerich (Mainz, 1980).

Geary, P., "Ethnic identity as a situational construct in the early middle ages", *Mitteilungen der Anthropologischen Gesellschaft in Wien* 113 (1983), pp. 15–26.

——, *Living with the Dead in the Middle Ages* (Ithaca-London, 1994).

——, "Germanic tradition and Royal Ideology in the ninth century: The visio Karoli Magni", P. Geary, *Living with the Dead in the Middle Ages* (Ithaca-London, 1994), pp. 49–76.

Geibig, A., *Beiträge zur morphologischen Entwicklung des Schwertes im Mittelalter. Eine Analyse des Fundmaterials vom ausgehenden 8. bis zum 12. Jahrhundert aus Sammlungen der Bundesrepublik Deutschland* (Neumünster, 1991).

Glazema, P. and J. Ypey, *Merovingische ambachtskunst* (Baarn, 1956).

Godelier, M., *L'idéel et le matériel. Pensée, economies, sociétés* (Paris, 1984).

Groot, H.L. de, *Traces at Traiectum. An archaeological survey* (Utrecht, 1992).

Halsall, G., "The origins of the Reihengräberzivilization: forty years on", *Fifth-century Gaul: a crises of Identity?* eds. J Drinkwater and H. Elton (Cambridge, 1992), pp. 196–207.

——, Female status and power in early merovingian central Austrasia: the burial evidence, *Early Medieval Europe* 5 (1996), pp 1–24.

Härke, H., "Warrior graves? The background of the Anglo-Saxon weapon burial rite", *Past & Present* 126 (1990), pp. 22–43.

——, *Angelsächsische Waffengräber des 5. bis 7. Jahrhunderts* (Köln, 1992) (Zeitschrift für Archäologie des Mittelalters, Beiheft 6).

——, "Intentionale und funktionale Daten. Ein Beitrag zur Theorie und Methodik der Gräberarchäologie", *Archäologisches Korrespondenzblatt* 23 (1993), pp. 141–146.

——, Tombes à armes anglo-saxonnes: sépultures des guerriers ou symbolysme rituel?, *L'armée romaine et les barbares du IIIe au VIIe siècles*, eds. F. Vallet and M. Kazanski, (Paris, 1993), pp. 425–436.

Hartung, W., *Süddeutschland in der frühen Merowingerzeit. Studien zur Gesellschaft, Herrschaft, Stammesbildung bei Alamannen und Bajuwaren* (Wiesbaden, 1983) (Vierteljahrschrift für Sozial- und Wirtschaftgeschichte, Beihefte 73).

Haupt, D., "Spätrömisches Grab mit Waffenbeigabe aus Bonn", *Archeologie en Historie. Opgedragen aan H. Brunsting bij zijn zeventigste verjaardag*, eds. W.A. van Es, et alii (Bussum, 1973), pp. 315–326.

Heather, P., *Goths and Romans 332–489* (Oxford, 1991).

——, *The Goths* (Oxford, 1996).

Hedeager, L., "The creation of Germanic identity. A European origin-myth", *Frontières d'empire. Nature et signification des frontières romaines*, eds. P. Brun, S. van der Leeuw and Chr. R. Whittaker (Nemours, 1993) (Actes de la Table Ronde de Nemours 1992), pp. 121–131.

——, "Kingdoms, ethnicity and material culture: Denmark in a European perspective", *The age of Sutton Hoo. The seventh century in North-western Europe*, ed. M.O.H. Carver (Woodbridge, 1992), pp. 279–300.

Hen, Y., *Culture and Religion in Merovingian Gaul AD 481–751* (Leiden, 1995).

James, E., "Cemeteries and the problem of frankisch settlement in Gaul", *Names, words and graves: Early medieval settlement*, ed. P.H. Saywer (Leeds, 1979), pp. 55–89.

——, *The Franks* (Oxford, 1988).

Jan, R. le, *Histoire de la France: origines et premier essor 480–1180* (Paris, 1996).

Jarnut, J., "Die frühmittelalterliche Jagd unter rechts-und sozialgeschichtlichen Aspekten", *L'uomo di Fronte al mondo animale nell'alto medievo* (Spoleto, 1985) (Settimane di studio del centro Italiano di studi sull'alto medievo 31), pp. 765–808.

Joffroy, R., *Le cimetière de Lavoye (Meuse). Nécropole mérevingienne* (Paris, 1974).

Kent J.P.C. and K.S. Painter, eds., *Wealth of the Roman world AD 300–700* (London, 1977).

Kitzinger, E., *Early medieval art* (London, 1983 [1940]).

Kopytoff, I., "The cultural biography of things: commoditisation as a process", *The social life of things. Commodities in cultural perspective*, ed. A. Appadurai (Cambridge, 1986), pp. 64–91.

Leach, E., *Culture and Communication. The Logic by which Symbols are connected. An Introduction to the Use of Structuralist Analysis in Social Anthropology* (Cambridge, 1976).

Lemant, J.-P., *Le cimetiere et la fortification du Bas-empire de Vireux-Molhain, Dep. Ardennes* (Mainz, 1985).

Mann, M., *The Sources of Social Power. 1 A History of Power from the Beginning to AD 1760* (Cambridge, 19872).

Martin, M., "Bemerkungen zur chronologischen Gliederung der frühen Merowingerzeit", *Germania* 67 (1989), pp. 121–141.

Mathisen, R.W., *Roman Aristocrats in Barbarian Gaul. Strategies for Survival in an Age of Transition* (Austin, 1993).

Menghin, W., *Das Schwert im frühen Mittelalter. Chronologisch-typologische Untersuchungen zu Langschwertern aus germanischen Gräbern des 5. bis 7.Jahrhunderts n. Chr.* (Stuttgart, 1983).

Muchembled, R., *L'invention de l'homme moderne: sensibilités, moeurs et comportements collectifs sous l'Ancien Régime* (Paris, 1988).

Müller, H.F., *Das alamannische Gräberfeld von Hemmingen (Kreis Ludwigsburg)* (Stuttgart, 1976).

Nelson, J., "The Lord's anointed and the People's choice: Carolingian Royal Ritual" *Rituals of Royalty. Power and ceremonial in Traditional Societies*, eds. D. Cannadine and S. Price (Cambridge, 1987), pp. 137–180.

Päffgen, B., *Die Ausgrabungen in St. Severin zu Köln* (Mainz, 1992).

Périn, P., "L'assimilation ethnique vue par l'archéologie", *Histoire et Archéologie* 56 (1981), pp. 38–47.

——, "A propos de publications récentes concernant le peuplement en Gaule a l'epoque mérovingienne: la <question franque>", *Archéologie Médiévale* 11 (1981), pp. 125–145.

——, "Les tombes de «chefs» du début de l'epoque mérovingienne. Datation et interprétation historique", *La noblesse romaine et les chefs barbares du IIIᵉ au VIIᵉ siècle*, eds. F. Vallet and M. Kazanski (Paris, 1995), pp. 247–301.

——, "L'armé de Vidimer et la question des dépots funéraires chez les Wisigoths en Gaule et en Espagne (Vᶜ–VIᶜ siècles)", *L'armée romaine et les barbares du IIIᵉ au VIIᵉ siècles*, eds. F. Vallet and M. Kazanski (Paris, 1993), pp. 411–423.

Périn, P. and L.-Ch. Feffer, *Les Francs. 1 A la conquete de la Gaule; 2 A l'origine de la France* (Paris, 1987).

Périn, P. and M. Kazanski, "Das Grab Childerichs I", *Die Franken, Wegbereiter Europas. Vor 1500 Jahren. König Chlodwig und seine Erben* (Mainz, 1996), pp. 173–182.

Pirenne, H., B. Lyon, A. Guillou, F. Gabrieli and H. Steuer, *Mahomet et Charlemagne. Bysance, Islam et Occident dans le haut moyen age* (Milan, 1986).

Pirling, R., *Das römisch-fränkische Gräberfeld von Krefeld-Gellep* I–II (Berlin, 1966).

——, "Römische Gräber mit barbarischem Einschlag auf den Gräberfeldern von Krefeld-Gellep:, *L'armée romaine et les barbares du IIIᵉ au VIIᵉ siècles* eds. F. Vallet and M. Kazanski (Paris, 1993), pp. 109–123.

Pohl, W., "Conceptions of ethnicity in Early Medieval studies", *Archaeologia Polona* 29 (1991), pp. 39–49.

——, "Tradition, Ethnogenese und literarische Gestaltung: eine Zwischenbalanz", *Ethnogenese und Überlieferung. Angewandte Methoden der Frühmittelalterforschung*, eds. K. Brunner and B. Mesta (Wenen/München, 1994), pp. 9–26.

Quast, D., *Die merowingerzeitlichen Grabfunde aus Gültlingen (Stadt Wildberg, Kreis Calw)* (Stuttgart, 1993).

Redlich, C. "Erbrecht und Grabbeigaben bei den Germanen", *Forschungen und Fortschritte* 24 (1948), pp. 177–180.

Roymans, N., "The sword or the plough. Regional dynamics in the romanisation of Belgic Gaul and the Rhineland area", *From the sword to the plough. Three studies on the earliest romanisation of northern Gaul*, ed. N. Roymans (Amsterdam, 1996), pp. 9–126.

Schmitt, G., "Ein frühmerowingisches Einzelgrab bei Entringen, Gem. Ammerbuch, Kreis Tübingen", *Fundberichte aus Baden-Württemberg* 11 (1986), pp. 359–380.

Schulze-Dörlamm, M., *Die spätrömischen und frühmittelalterlichen Gräberfelder von Gondorf, Gem. Kobern-Gondorf, Kr. Mayen-Koblenz* (Stuttgart, 1990) (Germanische Denkmäler der Völkerwanderungszeit serie B 14).

——, *Das Reichsschwert. Ein Herrschaftszeichen des Saliers Heinrich IV. und des Welfen Otto IV.* (Sigmaringen, 1995) (Römisch-Germanisches Zentralmuseum, Monographien 32).

Seiller, C., "Les Germains dans l'armée romaine tardive en Gaule septentrionale, le temoignage de l'archéologie", *L'armée romaine et les barbares du IIIᵉ au VIIᵉ siècles*, eds. F. Vallet and M. Kazanski (Paris, 1993), pp. 187–193.

Steuer, H., "L'industrie d'art à l'epoque mérovingienne", *Childéric-Clovis. 1500e anniversaire, 482–1982* (Tournai, 1982), pp. 181–200.

——, "Helm und Ringschwert: Prunkbewaffnung und Rangabzeichen germanischer Krieger. Eine Übersicht", *Studien zur Sachsenforschung* 6 (1987), pp. 189–236.

Theuws, F., "De vele lagen van de vroeg-middeleeuwse geschiedenis", *Madoc* 9 (1995), pp. 133–149.

Theuws, F. and H. Hiddink, "Der Kontakt zu Rom", *Die Franken, Wegbereiter Europas. Vor 1500 Jahren. König Chlodwig und seine Erben* (Mainz, 1996), pp. 754–768.

Ullmann, W., *Medieval Political Thought* (Harmondsworth, 1975).

Vallet, F., "A propos des tombes à épées d'apparat de la Rue Saint-Pierre (Oise) et d'Arcy-Sainte-Restitue (Aisne)", *Revue archéologieque de Picardie* 3/4 (1988), pp. 45–55.

Vallet, F. and M. Kazanski, eds., *L'armée romaine et les barbares du IIIᵉ au VIIᵉ siècles* (Paris, 1993).

Veit, U., "Ethnic concepts in German prehistory: a case study on the relationship between cultural identity and archaeological objectivity", *Archaeological approaches to cultural identity*, ed. S. Shennan (London, 1989), pp. 35–56.

Verdon, J., "Recherches sur la chasse en occident durant le haut moyen âge", *Revue Belge de Philologie et d'histoire* 56 (1978), pp. 805–829.

Wenskus, R., *Stammesbildung und Verfassung. Das Werden der frühmittelalterlichen Gentes* (Köln/Graz, 1961).

Wenskus, R., "Randbemerkungen zum Verhältnis von Historie und Archäologie, insbesondere mittelalterlicher Geschichte und Mittelalterarchäologie", *Geschichtswissenschaft und Archäologie. Untersuchungen zur Siedlungs-, Wirtschafts- und Kirchengeschichte*, eds. H. Jankuhn and R. Wenskus, (Sigmaringen, 1979) (Vorträge und Forschungen Band 22), pp. 637–657.

Werner, J., "Zur Entstehung der Reihengräberzivilisation. Ein Beitrag zur Methode der frühgeschichtlichen Archäologie", *Archaeologia Geographica* 1 (1950), pp. 23–32.

——, "Zu fränkischen Schwertern des 5. Jahrhunderts (Oberlörick-Samson-Abingdon)", *Germania* 31 (1953), pp. 38–44.

——, "Childeric. Histoire et Archéologie", *Histoire et Archeologie* 56 (1981), pp. 20–29.

——, "Données nouvelles sur la sépulture royale de Childéric", *Les fouilles du quartier Saint Brice à Tournai 2. L'environnement funéraire de la sépulture de Childéric*, ed. R. Brulet (Tournai, 1991) pp. 14–22.

Whittaker, C.R., *Frontiers of the Roman Empire. A Social and Economic Study*, (Baltimore, 1994).

Wieczorek, A., "Die Ausbreitung der fränkischen Herrschaft in den Rheinlanden vor und seit Chlodwig I", *Die Franken, Wegbereiter Europas. Vor 1500 Jahren. König Chlodwig und seine Erben* (Mainz, 1996), pp. 241–260.

Wightman, E., "North eastern Gaul in Late Antiquity: the testimony of settlement patterns in an age of transition", *Berichten Rijksdienst Oudheidkundig Bodemonderzoek* 28 (1978), pp. 241–250.

Wolfram, H., "*Origo et Religio*. Ethnic traditions and literature in early medieval texts", *Early medieval Europe* 3 (1994), pp. 19–38.

Wood, I., *Gregory of Tours* (Bangor, 1994).

——, *The Merovingian Kingdoms 450–751* (London and New York, 1994).

Ypey, J., "Enkele 5de-eeuwse vondsten uit Zuid- en Noord-Nederland", *Westerheem* 34 (1985), pp. 2–10.

Young, B., "Que sait-on des Germains et des Francs?" *Histoire et Archeologie* 56 (1981), pp. 12–19.

Zöllner, E., *Geschichte der Franken bis zur Mitte des sechsten Jahrhunderts* (München, 1970).

RITUALS OF POWER: BY WAY OF CONCLUSION

Janet L. Nelson

"If historians eschew theory of how societies operate, they imprison themselves in the commonsense notions of their own society.... Comte was right in his claim that sociology is the queen of the social and human sciences. But no queen ever worked as hard as the sociologist with pretensions needs to!"[1]

The contributors to this book would not dispute Michael Mann's claims for sociology. Nor would the historians among us wish to endorse the *annalistes'* counterclaim (and riposte to Comte) that history is queen and mistress of the social sciences. Though some of us might want to take up the cudgels for early medieval queens, who worked extremely hard *ex officio*; our collective interests, in queens, mistresses, social theory, and much else, have nothing to do with disciplinary machismo. We are committed interdisciplinarians: archaeologists and historians alike have borrowed insights from each other, and from various social and human sciences. All of us, more or less willingly, have used some theory (Mann also talks about "theoretical hunches" which may be as far as our pretensions go) to interpret our material, to help in generalising from it, and in comparing our findings, and to point to priorities.

Seeing "societies" as "constituted of multiple overlapping and intersecting [sociospatial] networks of power", Mann explains how the intersections work by bringing in Max Weber's notion of ideas which can function as switchmen or pointsmen, that is, the men who change the points on railway lines and so determine on which track the train will run thereafter.[2] In our discussions, and in preparing our

---

[1] M. Mann, *The Structures of Social Power* (London, 1986), preface, pp. vii–viii.

[2] Mann, *Structures*, pp. 22–8, though Mann suggests amending the metaphor to sources of social power as "tracklaying vehicles", which at "the 'moments' of tracklaying" produce "an autonomy of social concentration, organization, and direction that is lacking in more institutionalised times". The particular relevance of Mann's insight to the collective project of the present book is that the phases, even the centuries-long process, of the Roman World's transformation can be understood as such tracklaying moments.

contributions for this book, we contributors, whether or not invoking theoretical ancestors, have all, individually and collectively, thought
hard about ideas, and about their formation and promotion in the
particular social and political contexts we have studied. We have
been especially concerned with the cultural construction of status
and class. We have tried to identify the materials from which such
constructs are made, and the historical processes behind such *bricolage*.[3]

While we might agree with Mann that social power need not be
a zero-sum game (if A gets more, B gets less) but can be collective,
or at any rate shared,[4] we have tended to focus on the ways and
means, the times and places, by and in which, between the fifth and
ninth centuries, new power and new forms of differential access to
it were constituted and maintained. Many of us, and some quite
explicitly, would argue that these (re)-constructions of hierarchy entailed the mystification of more or less violent seizures of military
and political control, and would see this as an explanation for the
continuities underlined by Goffart and Durliat.[5] Though we have
not ignored economic dimensions and preconditions—indeed a blessing of our group's interdisciplinarity has been attentiveness to material evidence—our prime concern has been with the imaging, and
imagining, or power. For here, precisely, is where ritual comes in.
We understand [it as a mode of social power, without which such
power was, and is, quite literally, inconceivable.[6]]We have debated
the extent to which legitimation means the masking of coercion:
none of us would think that the whole story.[7] Above all, and unsur-

---

[3] C. Levi-Strauss, *The Savage Mind* (Chicago, 1970), pp. 16–33.

[4] Mann, *Structures*, pp. 6–7.

[5] W. Goffart, *Barbarians and Romans, AD 418–584: The Techniques of Accommodation*
(Princeton, 1983), and idem, *Rome's Fall and After* (London, 1989); J. Durliat, *Les
finances publiques. De Dioclétien aux Carolingiens (284–888)* (Sigmaringen, 1990). See the
important critique of C. Wickham, "La chute de Rome n'aura pas lieu", *Le Moyen
Age* 99 (1993), pp. 107–26, now reprinted in English translation in L.K. Little and
B.H. Rosenwein, *Debating the Middle Ages* (Oxford 1998), pp. 45–57.

[6] D. Cannadine, "Introduction", to D. Cannadine and S. Price edd., *Rituals of
Royalty. Power and Ceremonial in Traditional Societies* (Cambridge 1987), p. 19: "no
approach which defines power narrowly and ignores spectacle and pageantry can
possibly claim to be comprehensive... Ritual is not the mask of force but is itself
a type of power". Cf. Maurice Bloch, *Ritual, History and Power* (London, 1989), pp.
43–5, 64–70, and 78–88, invoking Weber's notion of "putting power in the bank
of ritual"; and also P. Buc, "Martyre et ritualité dans l'Antiquité tardive. Horizons
de l'écriture médiévale des rituels", *Annales ESC*, janvier-février 1997, pp. 63–92.

[7] Cf. G. Halsall ed., *Violence and Society in the Early Medieval West* (Woodbridge
1997).

prisingly, since our overriding aim is to understand transformation, we have tried to determine the balance between cultural continuity and change—a balance which itself varied greatly in space and changed much over time, between the fifth century and the ninth. To label this "the post-Roman period" may beg the very question we start from; and *pace* our ESF sponsors and leaders, even to talk of "transformation" may seem evasive. We use "the early Middle Ages" for convenience, not to foreclose on answers. Our group's basic assumption, and *raison d'être*, is that only multiple approaches, as taken here, can do justice to the multiplicity and instability of a period which we would nevertheless argue was formative in the history of Europe. We have never toed a single line, hence never expected to agree a single story. A "conclusion" in truth is a misnomer for what is only a temporary halt in an ongoing quest. Yet an epilogue at the end of a book which is but the first of a series, and among parallel series, is just such a halt, hence a good place to attempt a provisional assessment of how far our group has come, and of what has grabbed out attention *en route*.

In the historiography of power in the earlier Middle Ages, rituals of the court and of royal inaugurations loom large. Two of our chapters (3 and 4) deal with just these issues in particular early medieval kingdoms. Others approached royal ritual via its rootedness in, and persisting links with, non-royal analogues. Chapter 9 shows this connexion clearly in the case of Frankish arming rituals: it helps to explain both how these rituals were so strikingly stable over time, and how they came to affect the representation of monarchy in the Carolingian period. Chapters 10 and 11 provide complementary accounts of the symbolic uses of weapons in Anglo-Saxon England that can be reconstructed from material and textual evidence. This is ground on which archaeologists and historians can meet. They meet, too, if not quite at the death-bed then at the grave-side. A concern with rituals associated with death, and with the transmission of power over time, is shared by the authors of at least half our chapters (5 and 6, 8 and 12, as well as 10 and 11). Bringing together written and artefactual evidence has helped us perceive how ritual reproduces power. Indeed, only by such a combined approach have we become aware of how the transmission of power in life, from lord to man, from parents to children, is mirrored and modelled in the symbolism of death-bed, funeral and grave. We have come to understand death rituals in terms of power relations between the living: witness our discussions of the changing structure of the aristocratic family and the construction of a new and specifically medieval type of power in the shape of kingship.

The risks of anachronism in applying modern notions of property to the early Middle Ages have become very clear.[8] Many of the theoretical debates underlying this book have centred on gift.[9] Testaments and death-bed bequests and, perhaps more surprisingly, the deposition of goods in graves, are among the forms of gift-giving the evidence allows us to analyse. In examining what goods were given, whether weapons, drinking-vessels, liturgical equipment, clothes or books, what symbolised and transferred value, and in what ritual contexts, we show how in important ways power was signified, conserved, circulated, and transmitted across time; how social relationshiops were maintained, interrupted, or broken; and also how supernatural authority was not only invoked and implicated in these transactions, but believed to participate as an active force. Our interpretatuons of the rituals we consider in detail depend in every case on situating them in a political and ideological context. I think we have avoided what have been seen as Geertzian pitfalls (while acknowledging Geertzian inspiration): we do not see rituals as essentially self-referential, and nor do we think they offer a uniquely translucent window onto our subjects' experiences.[10] Whether we have always avoided the trap of functionalism, on the other hand, is for our reviewers to say.

Three themes have emerged from our collaborative efforts. First, we have become more keenly aware than ever before of the limitations of our evidence, whether that be textual of artefactual, and less inclinded to seek refuge in colleagues' disciplines as if the Other could supply the certainties denied by our own. Laws, wills and poems will not explain why graves are as they are, any more than the gravegoods we can examine fill the gaps in our documentation. Nevertheless, bifocal lenses properly used do let us see more, and

---

[8] Cf. the contributions to W. Davies and P. Fouracre edd., *Property and Power in the Early Middle Ages* (Cambridge, 1995).

[9] For the relevant work of Mauss, Parry, Weiner, Strathern and others, see the bibliography to chapter 1.

[10] C. Geertz, Negara: *The Theatre State in Nineteenth-Century Bali* (Princeton, 1980). Cf. also idem, *The Interpretation of Cultures: Selected Essays* (New York, 1973), especially "Thick description", pp. 3–30, and "Person, time and conduct in Bali", pp. 360–411. For criticisms, see Bloch, *Ritual, History and Power*, pp. 9–13, 208–10.

more clearly.] The archaeologists' close reading of late Roman historians (chapter 5), and of *Beowulf* (chapter 10), illuminate their finds
as much as the historians' visualising of swords or liturgical objects
do their texts (chapters 3, 4, 8 and 9). The dating, provenancing,
and localising of our material are problems we often share. We
looked at change over a huge expanse of space and time. Again and
again, we have been struck by the particularity of what we found.
If generalisation has often eluded us, so be it. Pergaps sheer diversity, and unevenness, are crucial features of the transformed world
that, by the ninth cnetury, clearly was *not* the Roman world.[11] Comparison of late Roman (and Byzantine) imperial funerals with early
medieval royal funerals (Chatpers 5 and 6) highlights the point.

Yet, paradoxically, the second effect of our shared work has been
to sharpen our definition of just how, and how much, Romanity survived into the earlier Middle Ages. We have approached the problem through iconographic and artefacual evidence of adaptation of
styles and objects, through the textual evidence of reused genres and
topoi, and, across the evidential range, through the incorporation of
Roman resources and institutions in the forms and formations of
early medieval power. Inside the frontiers of the old Europe, but
also beyond them, what has confronted us are varieties within this
overarching continuity. The self-representation of elites offers recur-
rent examples, as do early medieval kingdoms, and kingship. Some
of our group have still found it helpful to operate with contrasting
Germanic and Roman models. Others, while appreciating that models are what these are, with all the abstraction, and heuristic potential, that that implies, and while respecting colleagues' preparedness
to spurn the merely modish, would put more stress on shared traits,
parallels and continuities between, for instance, the use of written
documents in Roman provincial and barbarian regimes. It depends
of course on where you stand—by a distant northern sea or on the
shores of the Adriatic or the banks of the Tagus—and what you are
viewing: a marble sarcophagus, whoever its occupant, is an inescapably
Roman object, whereas a bracteate may strike even a viewer with
prior knowledge of its Roman archetypes as a fairly barbaric one.
But we expect even a cursory reading of our book to reinforce the

---

[11] We are well aware that the Roman world itself was neither uniform nor static. Still, we would claim that the world we have studied was yet more obviously
diverse and in a state of flux, and that its rituals displayed these differences.

sense that many kinds of power and many types of ritual (which is to say, *inter alia*, of the representation of power) in early medieval Europe can with justification be termed sub-Roman, or post-Roman, or simply, Roman, survivals.

They also attest Rome transformed—and the third, most problematic, of our collective impressions is one of transformation as change. It was a twentieth-century Italian aristocrat-novelist, writing of Italian aristocrats of a still-recent ancien régime, who had one of his characters observe, in terms an ancient Roman might have relished: "If we want things to stay as they are, things will have to change."[12] Perhaps those of us who have insisted most strongly on change have been the historians rather than the archaeologists: and perhaps, again, that's because most of the historians, as it happens, are specialists in the later rather than the earlier centuries covered by the ESF project. For Carolingianists, still more, even, than for other early medievalists, the vast sprawling performance of christianisation, whatever its sometimes near-imperceptible varieties of tempi, rhythm, instrumentation, or artistes (and it has always taken two to tango), is likely to present itself as the single most impressive cultural fact of these post-Roman centuries. This will be so, whether the emphasis is placed on power or on ritual. Christianisation is, and fundamentally, about both. Here, above all, Christianity professed to make a difference—a transformation, making all things new.

That not all contributors to this book have paid equal attention to difference of this kind is symptomatic of the surprising slowness, and patchiness, of the Church's impact, and hence its very varied reflection in the evidence. There have been scholarly misperceptions in the past, as when the abandonment of the practice of burying grave-goods with the dead was attributed to ecclesiastical hostility. In fact, as chapters 11 and 12 show, the practice was never proscribed by any church council, and its ending came about apparently endogenously, in the old Roman world and among the lately-converted Anglo-Saxons alike. Elsewhere, the tardiness of the Church's impact has simply not been perceived as a problem at all. Yet it is a striking fact that in their inaugurations, Lombard kings stuck with their spears (cf. Chapter 4), just as Anglo-Saxons kings stuck with their helmets, for centuries after conversion to Christianity. Why was

---

[12] G. Lampedusa, *The Leopard*, translated A. Colquhoun (London, 1988), p. 41.

the Church so slow to move into these areas, to intrude, to take over? And again (cf. Chapter 9), why did arming rituals remain out-with its purview almost right through the period we're concerned with? Didn't churchmen care? Did they feel they had already taken enough commanding heights? An alternative hypothesis might be that the new switchmen had not got their hands—could not get their hands dirty—on these points, that arming rituals were and remained a location of inveterate, particularly deep-rooted, profane, lay power.[13] To trace the frontiers between 'old' and 'new', but actually concur-rent, forms of power and its symbolic representation, and between different (rival?) forms of sacredness, is the trickiest of methodologi-cal acts to pull off. It is not just a matter of weighing with special care what evidence lies before us, but 'weighing' what is imponder-able because existing elsewhere, if not definitively absent. In their testament, Eberhard and Gisela said nothing of their noble/royal ancestry: they were establishing what they hoped would be the new power of their own descent-line; yet their confidence assumed famil-ial power and prestige which were old on both sides, hence differ-ently engendered, in ways decoded in Chapter 8, and which though only implicit are an ubiquitous sub-text here. Declaring their dynas-tic will in the surroundings of their own prime residence, they made no bequests to the Church. But one of the pair, at least, did that in another place, namely a family monastery, and using other doc-uments, namely charters recording that monastery's endowment, and in their testament, the couple at least referred to 'our chapel' and the holy objects its personnel required.

Putting a firm finger on the pulse of penance offers another way to check, as in chapter 7, the impact of christianisation. The very weakness of that pulse, that is, not just the scarcity of evidence but its limited, specific contexts, could indicate that penance remained in the seventh century what it had been in Late Antiquity, the badge of would-be religious *virtuosi*. Even Carolingian reformers can still be found lamenting that real penance was to be found 'hardly anywhere'. Yet from the fifth century onwards, perhaps that was the point: death-bed penitents (presumably a category quite distinct from repen-tant criminials) who survived were an exclusive group indeed, and for that very reason eminently suitable for holy orders. Did penance

---

[13] Cf. D. Barthélemy, *La mutation de l'an mil a-t-elle eu lieu?* (Paris, 1997), esp. pp. 222–286.

work as a clerical recruitment mechanism? In the ninth century, the history of penance fulfils its heuristic promise: lay persons, and not exclusively persons of the highest rank, are to be found undergoing it, and their cases are given maximum publicity at councils and assemblies.[14] Here—it's tempting to add, at least—the clergy succeeded in imposing new standards of conductr on laymen whom penance hit where it hurt, namely, in the zone of military and sexual activity. Here was mutation indeed, and of secular *habitus* in the canonical sense—also in Bourdieu's sense of a "system of durable tranposable dispositions".[15] And this surely, is what christianisation had to mean if it was to affect the fundamentals of social power? To contemplate withdrawal from the world was all very well as the voluntary decision of a man of retirement age, Charlemagne over sixty, for instance. But what Carolingian churchmen were claiming was to exclude noblemen in the prime of life from the worldly activities that were the hallmark of their sex and rank. This was for the Church to wield power through ritual in a new way. Its ritual themselves were old, attested in old books of canon law: what was new was their performance in areas of social life the clergy had not hitherto reached, the palpable extension of clerical surveillance, the visible effectiveness of peculiarly ecclesiastical sanctions. Of course politics were involved in these cases. That doesn't alter the fact that the rituals of politics had changed and in a remarkable way. To some extent, churchmen were borrowing form a pre-existing profane repertoire of shaming through demilitarisation.[16] But with the denial of sexual activity, they added something distinctively their own, and with a long currency in christian tradition. Churchmen thus made themselves indispensable to the secular powers that were, and gave a telling demonstration of their own new authority.Citing Gelasius was a recondite icing on a cake for mass-consumption.

In this book, we have concentrated on our own specialisms. The editorial hand has been light: group-members have offered what they chose, and within the broad framework of a very broad theme, no

---

[14] K. Leyser, "Early medieval canon law and the beginnings of knighthood", in his collected papers, *Communications and Power in Medieval Europe*, vol. 1: *The Carolingian and Ottonian Centuries*, ed. T. Reuter (London, 1994), pp. 51–71.

[15] P. Bourdieu, *The Logic of Practice*, trans. R. Nice (Oxford, 1990), pp. 52–79, at p. 53.

[16] J.L. Nelson, "Monks, secular men and masculinity c. 900", in D.M. Hadley ed., *Masculinity in Medieval Europe* (London, 1998), pp. 121–142.

editorial attempt has been made to direct their attention to pre-determined desideranda. The patchy coverage of the combined result has its own advantages: we have played to our strengths, as even a cursory glance as the chapter-bibliographies will show. And random pools of light in surrounding darkness may be considered an apt reflection of the distribution of the evidence. Nevertheless, and inevitably, there are some gaps to regret. Gender is one important theme underplayed in, if not absent from, our book (are the switchmen ever switchwomen? and if not, what might that reveal about the role of gender in the construction of ideology?) The power associated with place is another. Yet another, because our original group included no Central European specialist, is geographical scope which would have enhanced our findings' comparative force. We intend to make good these shortcomings, as best we can, in a companion volume. Meanwhile, we believe this one demonstrates and exemplifies some key advantages of collaborative work. We have cross-referred and connected, not only within our own group but with other groups in the larger project, especially Groups 1 and 4. Archaeologists and historians have criticised each other constructively. We have suggested to each other a number of "works most necessary for all to know".[17] Our aim in the context of our group-discussions was to stimulate shared reflection on theory that could be applied in interdisciplinary ways. Above all, the sustained effort to speak to each other across the boundaries of discipline, national traditions, and language, has produced in all of us greater clarity of expression and openness of thinking, and a widening of sympathies and horizons that could not fail to bring personal as well as intellectual benefits: benefits which each single one of us has experienced as unprecedented, and which we confidently hope will extend to our readers too. Whatever our historical subjects played, ours has been and remains the very opposite of a zero-sum game!

---

[17] I echo King Alfred, whose own prescribed authors—Augustine, Orosius, Boethius, Gregory, Bede—together with his favoured *carmina saxonica* could be recommended for anyone keen to understand the transformation of the Roman world.

BIBLIOGRAPHY

Bloch, M., *Ritual, History and Power* (London, 1989).

Bourdieu, P., *The Logic of Practice*, trans. R. Nice (Oxford, 1990).

Buc, P., "Martyre et ritualité dans l'Antiquité tardive. Horizons de l'écriture médiévale des rituels", *Annales ESC*, janvier-février 1997, pp. 63–92.

Cannadine D., and S. Price eds., *Rituals of Royalty. Power and Ceremonial in Traditional Societies* (Cambridge, 1987).

Davies W., and P. Fouracre eds., *Property and Power in the Early Middle Ages* (Cambridge, 1995).

Durliat, J., *Les finances publiques. De Dioclétien aux Carolingiens (284–888)* (Sigmaringen, 1990).

Geertz, C., Negara: *The Theatre State in Nineteenth-Century Bali* (Princeton, 1980).

——, *The Interpretation of Cultures: Selected Essays* (New York, 1973).

Goffart, W., *Barbarians and Romans, AD 418–584: The Techniques of Accommodation* (Princeton, 1983).

Goffart, W., *Rome's Fall and After* (London, 1989).

Halsall, G., ed., *Violence and Society in the Early Medieval West* (Woodbridge, 1997).

Lampedusa, G., *The Leopard*, translated A. Colquhoun (London, 1988).

Levi-Strauss, C., *The Savage Mind* (Chicago, 1970).

Leyser, K., "Early medieval canon law and the beginnings of knighthood", in his collected papers, *Communications and Power in Medieval Europe*, vol. 1: *The Carolingian and Ottonian Centuries*, ed. T. Reuter (London, 1994), pp. 51–71.

Mann, M., *The Structures of Social Power* (London, 1986).

Nelson, J.L., "Monks, secular men and masculinity c. 900, *Masculinity in Medieval Europe*, ed. D.M. Hadley (London, 1998).

Wickham, C., "La chute de Rome n'aura pas lieu", *Le Moyen Age* 99 (1993), pp. 107–26, now reprinted in English translation in L.K. Little and B.H. Rosenwein, *Debating the Middle Ages* (Oxford, 1998), pp. 45–57.

INDEX

THE TRANSFORMATION OF
THE ROMAN WORLD

A SCIENTIFIC PROGRAMME OF THE EUROPEAN SCIENCE FOUNDATION

Series Editor

IAN WOOD

ISSN 1386-4165